CORRECTIONS

third edition

Leanne F. Alarid

University of Texas at El Paso

Philip L. Reichel

University of Northern Colorado

330 Hudson Street, NY, NY 10013

Vice President, Portfolio Management: Andrew Gilfillan
Portfolio Manager: Gary Bauer
Editorial Assistant: Lynda Cramer
Senior Vice President, Marketing: David Gesell
Field Marketing Manager: Thomas Hayward
Product Marketing Manager: Kaylee Carlson
Senior Marketing Coordinator: Les Roberts
Director, Digital Studio and Content Production: Brian Hyland
Managing Producer: Cynthia Zonneveld
Manager, Rights Management: Johanna Burke
Creative Digital Lead: Mary Siener
Managing Producer, Digital Studio: Autumn Benson
Content Producer, Digital Studio: Maura Barclay
Project Management Support: Susan Hannahs, SPi Global
Manufacturing Buyer: Deidra Smith, Higher Ed, RR Donnelley
Cover Designer: Melissa Welch, StudioMontage
Cover Art: Getty Images, © Noam Galai/noamgalai.com
Full-Service Management and Composition: iEnergizer Aptara®, Ltd.
Full-Service Project Managers: Tom Benfatti and Garima Khosla, iEnergizer Aptara®, Ltd.
Printer/Bindery: LSC Communications
Cover Printer: LSC Communications
Text Font: Times LT Pro, 10/12

Library of Congress Cataloging in Publication Data

Alarid, Leanne Fiftal,
  Corrections / Leanne F. Alarid and Philip L. Reichel.—Third edition.
   pages cm
  Includes index.
  ISBN 978-0-13-454867-8 -- ISBN 0-13-454867-1
  1. Corrections—Study and teaching.   2. Punishment.   3. Criminal
justice, Administration of—Study and teaching.   I. Reichel, Philip L.
II. Title.
  HV8754.A43 2016
  365—dc23
                                    2014035222

6 2019

ISBN-10:   0-13-454867-1
ISBN-13: 978-0-13-454867-8

SVE ISBN-10:   0-13-454903-1
ISBN-13: 978-0-13-454903-3

 Pearson

Dedication

*Dedicated to Crazyhorse,
my mentor and best friend.*
L.F.A.

Dedication

*Dedicated to my grandchildren,
Estella Josephine and
Andrew Joseph.*
P.L.R.

Brief Contents

Contents

PART 2   Sentencing and Sanctions   53

Preface

Introducing the Justice Series

When best-selling authors and instructional designers come together, focused on one goal—improve student performance across the criminal justice (CJ) curriculum—you come away with a groundbreaking new series of print and digital content: the *Justice Series*.

Several years ago, we embarked on a journey to create affordable texts that engage students without sacrificing academic rigor. We tested this new format with Fagin's *CJ 2010* and Schmalleger's *Criminology* and received overwhelming support from students and instructors.

The Justice Series expands this format and philosophy to more core CJ and criminology courses, providing affordable, engaging instructor and student resources across the curriculum. As you flip through the pages, you'll notice this book doesn't rely on distracting, overly used photos to add visual appeal. Every piece of art serves a purpose—to help students learn. Our authors and instructional designers worked tirelessly to build engaging info-graphics, flowcharts, pull-out statistics, and other visuals that flow with the body of the text, provide context and engagement, and promote recall and understanding.

We organized our content around key learning objectives for each chapter, and tied everything together in a new objective-driven end-of-chapter layout. Not only is the content engaging to the student, it's easy to follow and focuses the student on the key learning objectives.

Although brief, affordable, and visually engaging, the Justice Series is a series of texts and support tools that are instructionally sound and student approved.

Additional Highlights to the Authors' Approach

- Evidence-based practices in all areas of corrections are given close attention and become a key aspect of the book's content.

- Theories of punishment are introduced early and connected to correctional policies and best practices.

- Contemporary correctional policy initiatives are discussed, which include reducing the use of administrative segregation, decreasing prison violence, improving prisoner reentry, prisoner rights, and narrowing death penalty discretion.

- Information about women offenders and female correctional staff is incorporated throughout the book rather than in one specific chapter. This integration of gender emphasizes the similarities and differences of the correctional supervision of men and women.

- Student learning is enhanced through a very clear writing style with interesting contemporary examples and remarkably up-to-date information.

Groundbreaking Instructor and Student Support

Just as the format of the Justice Series breaks new ground in publishing, so does the instructor support that accompanies the series.

Each chapter opener lists the chapter objectives to pique interest and focus students' attention on the topics to be discussed.

The book exhibits a balance among text, photos, and figures to present the information in both a text format and a visual format.

Each chapter Introduction presents a current event or story related to chapter content followed by a discussion question. This sparks interest and promotes critical thinking about chapter concepts.

Each objective has an associated icon that also appears in the related chapter section and in the end-of-chapter material. The icon is a navigational tool, making it easy to locate explanations of or find review material for a particular topic, and is also a visual key to aid memory and retention of information related to the topic.

"Think About It" features pose questions related to chapter content, promoting critical thinking, discussion, and application.

A box at the end of each chapter directs students to chapter-specific resources and additional links to extend learning and investigation.

At the end of each chapter, a real-life case example poses analytical discussion questions related to chapter content, promoting critical thinking and application of chapter concepts.

The chapter summary displays the chapter's key information as a chart with images and critical-thinking review questions embedded throughout. This visual format is designed to be a helpful study and review tool.

New to This Edition

- A new feature entitled "Voices in Corrections" provides a unique viewpoint about different correctional issues. Seven original essays were written by different authors who were either correctional practitioners or offenders.

- *How has GPS tracking of probationers affected the way probation officers do their job?*—Chapter 2

- *What was segregation like?*—Chapter 3

- *What was it like to work in a day reporting center?*—Chapter 5

- *Oftentimes, when students tour a facility using the podular direct approach, they are surprised to find a single correctional officer in the pod with supervising responsibility for the many inmates also in the pod. Can such a setup really be safe for both officer and inmates?*—Chapter 6

- *Research and media portrayals of prisons often concentrate on how prison changes prisoners—more often for the worse rather than the better. Does prison change correctional officers? How and in what manner?*—Chapter 7

- *What did you learn from your experiences in prison?*—Chapter 9

- *What did your first moments of reentry feel like?*— Chapter 10

- Over 20 figures and tables are either new or have the most updated information available throughout the text, including Figure 1–4; Figure 2–5; Figures 4–3 and 4–11; Table 6–1; Figure 6–4; Table 7–1; Figure 7–4; Figure 8–1; Table 9–1; Figures 9–5, 9–6, and 9–7; Tables 10–1 and 10–2; Table 11–4; Figures 13–1 and 13–5; and Figures 14–1 and 14–2.

- New chapter-opening vignettes have been replaced in Chapter 1 (California's attempt to reduce prison populations through realignment and Proposition 47); Chapter 5 (Ethan Couch, affluenza teen who violated probation); Chapter 8 (Inmate escapes aided by correctional officer Joyce Mitchell in New York and a volunteer teacher at the Orange County jail); and Chapter 9 (Owen Labrie, a student from a private prep school who was convicted of a sex offense).

- Chapter 1 begins with a new introduction stating how recent changes in decriminalization and closing of prisons are reducing prison population numbers; "Preadjudication Diversion" was added as a separate section to better differentiate diversion from postsentencing outcomes.

- The "Corrections in the Twenty-First Century" section in Chapter 3 has been revised and updated to include new public opinion data and updated state reforms.

- Already one of the best reviewed chapters, we believe Chapter 4 has been strengthened with a new introduction on futuristic technology, an expansion of the section on determinate and indeterminate sentencing to include the concept of structured sentences (and a new figure showing each system by state), and the addition of a section (including a new timeline) on trends in state and federal sentencing—including thousands of federal prisoners being released in 2015.

- Chapter 5 has a new introduction that explains the overarching goals of community corrections and the benefits of community supervision over incarceration. The "Problem-Solving Courts" section has been expanded to include drug courts and veterans' courts.

- Statistics and information relevant to jail population characteristics, "Jails in Indian Country," and "Jailing the Mentally Ill" have been updated in Chapter 6. Material on women involved in the criminal justice system has been expanded and a new figure describes "ten things we know about women in jails."

- A brand new section in Chapter 7 entitled "Segregation and Solitary Confinement" allows for extended discussion of special housing units and explains why this type of confinement is so controversial today. The chapter includes a new figure depicting who spends time in segregation.

- Chapter 8 has a new section highlighting misconduct behaviors while incarcerated, updated information on the way that security threat groups are structured, an updated table on prison gangs, and a more detailed explanation of the importation model.

- A new introduction paragraph reaffirming the rehabilitation goal of corrections as it relates to special needs offenders can be found in Chapter 9, along with updated material on prison visitation.

- Reentry programs and the use of education and vocational programs in prison have been completely updated in Chapter 10, along with the latest research on community reparation boards.

- To reflect important changes occurring across the country to minimize the collateral impact of a felony conviction, new material has been added in Chapter 11, to include the "Invisible Punishment" section and "Restoring Civil Rights Following a Conviction." New subsections on individual restoration methods and systemic relief methods have been added. State compliance with the federal Sex Offender Registration and Notification Act as well as state felon voting laws have been updated.

- Chapter 12 includes expanded discussion of how the *Atkins* v. *Virginia* decision has been implemented by states and whether mentally ill persons have been executed. A new "Think About It" feature has been added to bring attention to how executions may affect prison employees.

- Chapter 13 reviews research findings on the effects of applying criminal sanctions on juvenile offenders with a new Figure. Figure 13–1 has been updated to include Illinois, Massachusetts, and New Hampshire among the states with an upper age of 17. The teen courts section has been considerably expanded and updated. Information has been added on changes to state juvenile transfer laws. The 2016 USSC decision in *Montgomery* v. *Louisiana* has been added to "The Case" at the end of the chapter.

- To conclude the text with where we think the corrections system is headed in the future, we updated what works in corrections in Chapter 14. A new "Smart on Crime" initiative section has been added, and we expanded the performance-based measures and justice reinvestment initiatives. We also replaced the case study at the end of the chapter with details about the justice reinvestment initiative in Kansas.

Instructor's Manual with Test Bank

Includes content outlines for classroom discussion, teaching suggestions, and answers to selected end-of-chapter questions from the text. This also contains a Word document version of the test bank.

TestGen

This computerized test generation system gives you maximum flexibility in creating and administering tests on paper, electronically, or online. It provides state-of-the-art features for viewing and editing test bank questions, dragging a selected question into a test you are creating, and printing sleek, formatted tests in a variety of layouts. Select test items from test banks included with TestGen for quick test creation, or write your own questions from scratch. TestGen's random generator provides the option to display different text or calculated number values each time questions are used.

PowerPoint Presentations

Our presentations offer clear, straightforward outlines and notes to use for class lectures or study materials. Photos, illustrations, charts, and tables from the book are included in the presentations when applicable.

To access supplementary materials online, instructors need to request an instructor access code. Go to **www.pearsonhighered. com/irc**, where you can register for an instructor access code. Within 48 hours after registering, you will receive a confirming e-mail, including an instructor access code. Once you have received your code, go to the site and log on for full instructions on downloading the materials you wish to use.

Alternate Versions

eBooks This text is also available in multiple eBook formats. These are an exciting new choice for students looking to save money. As an alternative to purchasing the printed textbook, students can purchase an electronic version of the same content. With an eTextbook, students can search the text, make notes online, print out reading assignments that incorporate lecture notes, and bookmark important passages for later review. For more information, visit your favorite online eBook reseller or visit **www.mypearsonstore.com**.

REVEL™ is Pearson's newest way of delivering our respected content. Fully digital and highly engaging, REVEL replaces the textbook and gives students everything they need for the course. Seamlessly blending text narrative, media, and assessment, REVEL enables students to read, practice, and study in one continuous experience—for less than the cost of a traditional textbook. Learn more at **pearsonhighered.com/revel**.

▶ REVEL *for Corrections, 3e by Alarid and Reichel*

Designed for the way today's Criminal Justice students read, think and learn

REVEL offers an immersive learning experience that engages students deeply, while giving them the flexibility to learn their way. Media interactives and assessments integrated directly within the narrative enable students to delve into key concepts and reflect on their learning without breaking stride.

REVEL seamlessly combines the full content of Pearson's bestselling criminal justice titles with multimedia learning tools. You assign the topics your students cover. Author Explanatory Videos, application exercises, and short quizzes engage students and enhance their understanding of core topics as they progress through the content.

Instead of simply reading about criminal justice topics, REVEL empowers students to think critically about important concepts by completing application exercises, watching Point/CounterPoint videos, and participating in shared writing (discussion board) assignments.

Track time-on-task throughout the course

The Performance Dashboard allows you to see how much time the class or individual students have spent reading a section or doing an assignment, as well as points earned per assignment. This data helps correlate study time with performance and provides a window into where students may be having difficulty with the material.

NEW! Ever-growing Accessibility

Learning Management System Integration

REVEL offers a full integration to the Blackboard Learning Management System (LMS). Access assignments, rosters and resources, and synchronize REVEL grades with the LMS gradebook. New direct, single sign-on provides access to all the immersive REVEL content that fosters student engagement.

The REVEL App

The REVEL App further empowers students to access their course materials wherever and whenever they want. With the REVEL App, students can access REVEL directly from their iPhone or Android device and receive push notifications on assignments all while not being tethered to an Internet connection. Work done on the REVEL app syncs up to the browser version, ensuring that no one misses a beat.

Visit **www.pearsonhighered.com/revel/**

▶ Acknowledgments

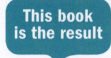 **This book is the result** of an opportunity provided to us to be part of a cutting-edge series. We would like to thank Gary Bauer and Tara Horton, for keeping us on task and providing practical suggestions for improving the book. Thanks to Leslie Lahr at Aptara for bringing this edition together. Finally, we thank the reviewers of the third edition for their innovative and important suggestions that we incorporated into this series: Peter Curcio, Briarcliffe College, Tyler Gayan, Georgia Northwestern Technical College, Melanie Norwood, University of Illinois-Chicago, Ruth Welters-Smith, Northwestern Oklahoma State University. Reviewers from previous editions include: Nancy Alleyne, Keiser University; Tyler Gayan, Georgia Northwestern Technical College; Frank Leonard, Tallahassee Community College; Eugene Matthews, Lincoln University of Missouri; Gary Neumeyer, Arizona Western College; Melissa Stacer, University of Southern Indiana; and Arkil Starke, Keiser University.

Leanne F. Alarid is Professor and Chair of the Department of Criminal Justice at The University of Texas at El Paso. Over the last 20 years, Dr. Alarid has taught undergraduate and graduate classes, and published over 50 journal articles and book chapters. She is the author of *Community-Based Corrections* (Cengage) and has edited four books, including *Behind a Convict's Eyes: Doing Time in a Modern Day Prison* (2004) and *In Her Own Words: Women Offenders' Views on Crime and Victimization* (2006). Dr. Alarid received the Founder's Award by the Academy of Criminal Justice Sciences in 2011 for her contribution to criminal justice education and service. She was recognized in the *Journal of Criminal Justice Education* as one of the top 20 female scholars in the country out of female Ph.D. graduates in criminal justice between 1996 and 2006. Dr. Alarid has worked as a counselor for a girls' group home and as a correctional case manager at an adult halfway house in Denver, Colorado.

Philip L. Reichel is Emeritus Professor at the University of Northern Colorado and Adjunct Professor at the University of New Hampshire Law School. Prior to beginning his career in academia, he worked as a counselor for the Nebraska Department of Correctional Services. During his more than 40 years in academia, he has received awards for teaching, advising, service, and scholarship. He is the author of *Comparative Criminal Justice Systems: A Topical Approach*, coeditor of the *Handbook of Transnational Crime and Justice*, and has authored or co-authored more than 40 articles and book chapters. His areas of expertise include corrections, comparative justice systems, and transnational crime. He has lectured at colleges and universities in Austria, China, Costa Rica, Germany, and Poland and has presented papers at side-events during the United Nations Congress on Crime Prevention and Criminal Justice (Brazil) and the United Nations Commission on Crime Prevention and Criminal Justice (Vienna). He currently serves as the Academy of Criminal Justice Sciences' NGO Alternate Representative to the United Nations.

1

An Evidence-Based Approach to Corrections

1 Describe how corrections is part of the criminal justice system that is dependent on decisions made earlier in the process by the police and the courts.

2 Compare and contrast institutional and community-based corrections.

3 Explain the effect that rising incarceration rates between 1970 and 2010 had on racial and economic disparity.

4 Analyze the relationships among mass media, public opinion, and the making of correctional policy.

5 Characterize the meaning of evidence-based practice and explain how it can improve the correctional system.

Visions of America, LLC/Alamy Stock Photo

WILL CALIFORNIA BE ABLE TO REDUCE ITS PRISON POPULATION?

James Rabenberg, age 36, has no history of violence and has never sold drugs. Rabenberg, an avid drug user since the 1990s, became addicted to methamphetamine, eventually lost his house, and became homeless in San Diego, California (Saslow, 2015). He tried to quit using drugs on several occasions without success. Since the homeless shelter will not accept active drug users, Rabenberg panhandles and uses his money to buy drugs on the streets. He continues to get rearrested for the possession of small amounts of meth or drug paraphernalia. Interestingly, he has declined drug treatment, preferring to plead guilty to the charges. In the past, Rabenberg would have been taken to jail with each arrest, but under a recent change in California's law, he is now issued a citation or a fine in lieu of a jail booking (Saslow, 2015). What caused this sudden change?

Back in 2007, California officials had been federally court ordered to reduce the severely overcrowded prison population by 2014. Then, with the economic crisis in 2008, the state of California made deep budget cuts in all areas of government services and could no longer afford to support the current prison population. To achieve this laudable goal, California assessed current property and drug offenders deemed *not* to be a public safety risk, and released them from jails and prisons to parole or probation supervision, a process known as "realignment." These releases were still not enough to relieve the new arrests. In 2014, California voters passed Proposition 47 to reduce drug possession and property crimes (shoplifting, fraud, theft, bad checks) worth less than $950 from a felony to a misdemeanor; the exception is if a defendant has previous convictions for murder, child molestation, or rape. The money saved from having fewer prisoners would be applied to community-based mental health and drug treatment programs, primary/secondary education, and crime victim funds.

Between January and September 2015, Mr. Rabenberg was arrested 13 times for the possession of small amounts of drugs, including one arrest when he pulled a knife on a customer outside a Starbucks when he was panhandling and became agitated (Saslow, 2015). Mr. Rabenberg's story is certainly characteristic of concerns that low-level offenders reoffend or recidivate at fairly high rates (Gerlinger & Turner, 2015), but the nature of most of those charges is no longer considered serious. Since Proposition 47 went into effect in 2015, fewer people were in jail, but it has seemingly created a different problem: Homeless population encampments (those who would have been in jail) have grown, along with more emergency room visits for overdoses and more assaults on police officers by the homeless (Saslow, 2015). On the other hand, there are concerns with using jail as a response to drug addiction and homelessness.

Ann Johansson/Corbis Historical/Getty Images

Discuss Has jail been overused for indigent drug users? How should communities respond to the problems of homelessness and drug use? Will decriminalizing drug possession and/or property offenses increase the crime rate? Is there a better way to solving California's problem without bankrupting the state?

▶ Corrections: An Integral Part of the Criminal Justice System

We live in interesting times. Since 2011, prison populations in the United States have *declined* after having consistently increased for 40 years—from 600 prison facilities in 1970 to over 1,000 prisons by 2000 (Lawrence & Travis, 2004). Did the declines have anything to do with the stock market crash of 2008 and subsequent economic downturn? What about the changes in federal sentencing guidelines? Or, was it the government's admission that the war on drugs had failed, combined with changing public attitudes toward marijuana use? Or, is it something entirely different? In any case, incarceration has shown to be a very high-cost response with very low positive returns on investment (Clement, Schwarzfeld, & Thompson, 2011). We explore the history behind how our corrections system started, reasons why prisons are so expensive, and various alternatives to incarceration.

This text is an introduction to the **corrections** system in the United States, which is considered the third component of criminal justice (CJ) that follows an alleged crime handled by the police and the court processing of that case. The corrections system is thus a phase that carries out or implements the court-ordered supervision or treatment conditions that the defendant must complete. As we discuss later in this chapter, court-ordered conditions can be implemented in a diversionary manner in lieu of sentencing or after sentencing following a guilty plea. A flowchart is depicted in Figure 1–1 to provide a broad overview of the entire CJ system. This section very briefly explains this flowchart and how criminal cases are passed from the police to the courts before some of them progress into the corrections system.

Police

When a crime is committed, a victim or witness reports the situation to the **police**. In serious cases, the police take the report in person and may collect evidence or testimony. In less serious cases, the victim reports by phone or the Internet. Other than traffic enforcement, it is clear that the police rely on *citizens* to bring most crimes to their attention. Then, based on the quality of this information, the police can investigate further and then decide whether there is enough evidence to act. In less serious cases, such as exceeding the speed limit, the police can decide to issue a warning or a **citation**. In more serious cases, such as domestic violence, an officer must arrest one or both defendants if there are visible injuries. When an arrest is made, the police drive the suspect to a city or county jail to be **booked**. In the most serious felony cases, such as homicide and robbery, the reporting officer relies on detectives to spend the time collecting evidence.

The police enforce the law, keep social order, and preserve public safety for their particular **jurisdiction**. For example, local police have boundaries within a city or county, whereas state police focus on highways and interstates within the state. A federal law enforcement agency enforces laws in places that are considered federal areas (such as national parks and post offices) or enforces violations of federal law (such as drug trafficking, counterfeiting, or terrorism) anywhere in the United States. In using their discretion, the police truly are the gatekeepers of the CJ system. Following an arrest or a citation, the case moves to the courts, which is the next social control agency.

Pretrial/Courts

The courts depend on the police's ability to identify the right suspect and to collect enough quality evidence, if needed, to corroborate the case. Corroborating evidence may include a victim who agrees to participate, credible witness statements, and physical evidence that can be collected and tested if necessary. There are four main decisions that prosecutors make: initial case screening, charging, plea offers, and case disposition. At the initial case screening, prosecutors examine the quality of the corroborating evidence to determine whether or not to charge a suspect. A prosecutor will likely **dismiss** cases if the evidence is weak or inadequately linked to that defendant for a particular offense. Depending on the

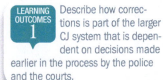

LEARNING OUTCOMES **1** Describe how corrections is part of the larger CJ system that is dependent on decisions made earlier in the process by the police and the courts.

jurisdiction and the severity of the offense, between one-third and one-half of all cases are dismissed.

Prosecutors will go forward with charging cases in which they believe there is enough evidence to hold the defendant accountable for that specific crime. The court has a considerable backlog of cases that vary between 6 and 12 months between the arrest and the time when the case is resolved by the courts. While most defendants will eventually plead guilty, a small percentage (between 1 and 5%) request a criminal trial and enter a plea of "not guilty," in which case the decision lies in the hands of a judge or jury. Although the average criminal trial lasts less than one week, a trial court's dockets are typically filled 12 to 18 months out, so a trial may not be decided until 18 months after the initial arrest. During this time, defendants with pending court appearances are out in the community on a bond that secures their reappearance, or they are on some form of **pretrial supervision** in the community.

The pretrial release decision is made following arrest so that defendants who qualify can be quickly released and supervised in the community until their next court date. This allows defendants to return to work or school and to prepare for their defense, and it keeps local jails from becoming too crowded while a criminal case is pending. Risk assessments have been developed to predict who would likely pose a threat to the public safety or likely not return for a later court appearance (Lowenkamp & Whetzel, 2009). Defendants who live in the area, are employed or go to school, and have a cell phone are qualified for immediate release. Defendants who have active warrants or pending charges, have previously failed to appear, or are already on correctional supervision may be released later with higher bail amounts or may be denied release altogether (Pretrial Justice Institute, 2009).

Preadjudication Diversion

Early on in the court process, the judge may offer **diversion** or deferred adjudication to misdemeanor or first-time felony defendants who have not yet been formally sentenced. Diversion allows the defendant to be supervised in the community *before* pleading guilty. If the defendant successfully completes diversion, the offender's charges are dropped and, because the defendant was never sentenced, the individual does not have a formal record of conviction. However, if the offender on diversion supervision does *not* comply with the conditions to the court's satisfaction, or if the defendant is rearrested within a certain period of time after completion, a formal execution of the sentence ensues and a record of the conviction is reinstated. Examples of diversion programs can be found in Figure 1–2. The most common example is deferred probation supervision, or perhaps the defendant may be ordered to complete community service hours, or agree to mediation sessions with the victim or even to attend treatment programs through a problem-solving court. These diversion programs are all considered part of the corrections system and will be discussed in more detail in Chapter 5.

For defendants who do not qualify for diversion, prosecutors will often offer the defendant a plea agreement to entice the defendant to plead guilty over asking for a trial. Most defendants plead guilty and take the plea agreement, after which they

What is the sequence of events in the CJ system?

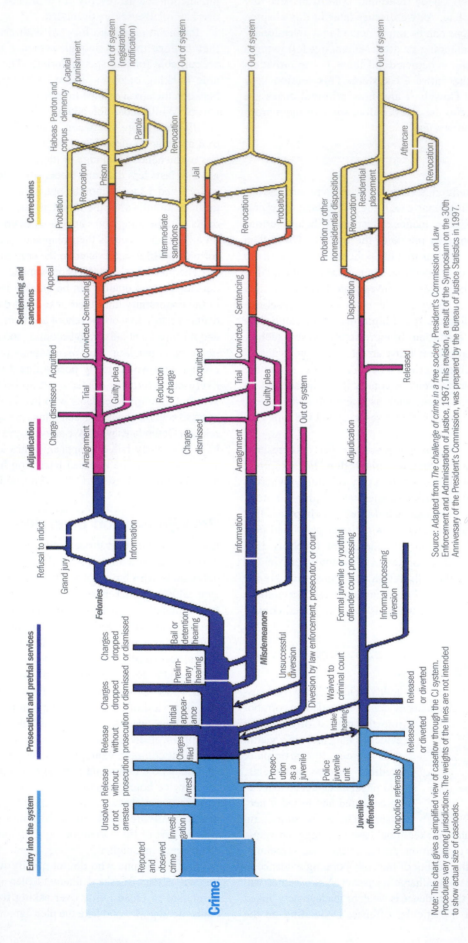

Source: Adapted from *The challenge of crime in a free society*. President's Commission on Law Enforcement and Administration of Justice, 1967. This revision, a result of the Symposium on the 30th Anniversary of the President's Commission, was prepared by the Bureau of Justice Statistics in 1997.

Note: This chart gives a simplified view of caseflow through the CJ system. Procedures vary among jurisdictions. The weights of the lines are not intended to show actual size of caseloads.

FIGURE 1–1 **Criminal Justice System Flowchart.**

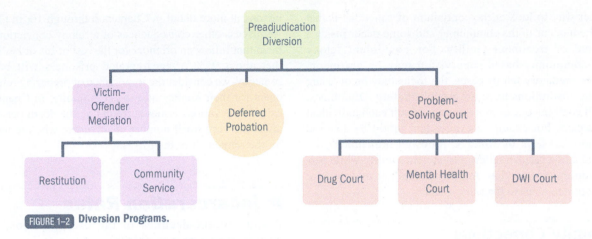

FIGURE 1-2 **Diversion Programs.**

are formally sentenced by the court. Where the law allows, plea agreements can involve community supervision over jail, or involve considerably less prison time.

▶ Corrections as Community-Based or Institutional

A wide variety of sentencing options are available, particularly for misdemeanors and nonviolent felony offenses. For serious

felony offenses, the judge considers the law in conjunction with the individual case circumstances to decide whether the offender is eligible for a community sentence or whether incarceration is more appropriate. The **continuum of sanctions**, as shown in Figure 1–3, refers to the options that are available by law or available to the judge to select for each individual offender so that the appropriate sentencing goals will be achieved. Sentencing goals or philosophies of punishment, such as rehabilitation and deterrence, will be discussed in Chapter 2.

FIGURE 1-3 **Postsentencing Correctional Sanctions.** Following sentencing, the judge decides whether the offender is eligible for a community sentence. Note that the sanctions within the orange boxes can be used in conjunction with probation, parole, jail, and prison as long as they are related to the crime itself or the risk the offender poses.

Another way to look at the continuum of sanctions is that some of them occur in the community and some occur inside a correctional or treatment facility. For nonviolent felony offenses, community-based supervision may be an option, whereas for predatory felony cases, the focus may be on using correctional institutions to achieve public safety. Oftentimes, judges will combine one or more options to suit each individual offender's case. For example, a defendant might be deterred from a short jail term of 30 days, followed immediately by three months in a residential drug treatment facility while performing community service. Another defendant may require only probation to achieve the same goals.

Community Corrections

Community corrections programs depend on correctional resources available in the community to assist the offender in

 **LEARNING OUTCOMES 2** Compare and contrast institutional and community-based corrections.

seeking help and abiding by certain conditions. The philosophy behind community corrections assumes that most offenders have made poor decisions along the way, but their need to retain responsibility and/or change overrides their threat to public safety and therefore they do not require incarceration. Community correctional programs are more likely, than jails and prisons, to offer rehabilitation programs that meet the offender's court-ordered conditions. In addition, the offender can enlist the help of his or her family for support. Forms of community corrections can be residential, where the offender lives at the facility (depicted in blue in Figure 1–3) or lives at home (depicted with green boxes). Community-based options can also include add-on sanctions (depicted as orange boxes in Figure 1–3). In Chapter 5, we discuss probation, restitution, electronic monitoring, and day-reporting centers in more detail.

At times, all of these add-on alternatives may be used to excess and thus offenders on probation are required to do too much or to do more than they need for adequate punishment. Had these programs not been available, judges would have used straight probation anyway, but sometimes they have a tendency to use a tougher sanction just because it's there—not because it truly benefits an offender. This principle is called **net widening**; engaging too much in this practice is inefficient and a costly use of resources.

Institutional Corrections

Institutional corrections house offenders in an institutional environment, apart from their community, friends, and family. Visits are restricted to weekends if at all. Institutional corrections operate under the philosophy that some people need to be separated from the elements of daily life to protect others' safety or to pay for their crimes by having their freedom taken away. Jails are primarily for pretrial detainees who have not been convicted of a crime. Jails also detain people convicted of misdemeanors who are serving less than one year of time. Prisons are long-term institutions designed to house convicted felons who are serving more than one year of time. We delve into jails and

prisons in more detail in Chapters 6 through 10. In Chapter 11, we discuss other consequences of a felony conviction, some of them that follow an offender for the rest of his or her life. Given that about 95% of incarcerated prisoners will be released someday, we consider the importance of preparing released prisoners for their reentry into the community. In Chapter 12, we explore the various issues surrounding the death penalty, which affect the very small number of offenders who are incarcerated for the remainder of their lives.

▶ Incarceration Rates

Despite recent declines in the use of prison, the U.S. **incarceration rate** per 100,000 people remains significantly higher than that for most other countries in the world. U.S. incarceration rates were not always that high. In fact, the United States used prisons at a rate similar to European countries until the 1970s. Incarceration and crime policy became part of the political agenda as a platform for reelection campaigns to a public who thought that little could be done to reform criminals. The United States used mass incarceration in an attempt to curb drug possession, sales, and manufacturing, and lengthened sentences for repeat and violent offenders. The war on drugs had a pronounced effect on the federal prison system, and greatly increased the number of incarcerated women. While researchers and analysts long criticized the ineffectiveness of U.S. drug policy (Bagley, 1988), enforcement and punishment activities continued unabated. States began to consider the utility of marijuana for medical benefits and proceeded to pass legislation that decriminalized marijuana possession in small amounts, regulated the sale of marijuana for medical patients (in about half of all states), and legalized marijuana for recreational purposes in a handful of states. In 2010, the United States reached an incarceration rate high of over 750 people per 100,000, before decreasing down to the current rate of 698. While the federal government eventually declared that mass arrests and incarceration for drug possession was a failed effort, federal efforts to decrease incarceration rates have been challenging given its new war on immigration. Figure 1–4 shows how the U.S. incarceration rate compares to those for other countries, such as China, India, Mexico, Iran, and Iraq.

The disproportionately high number of U.S. prisoners deeply affects Latino and African-American communities. Using arrest and incarceration as a control mechanism dates back to the end of the Civil War. Although slavery had ended, many people of color were incarcerated for

 **LEARNING OUTCOMES 3** Explain the effect that rising incarceration rates between 1970 and 2010 had on racial and economic disparity.

minor offenses and treated differently from Caucasians. Historians contend that dehumanization and differential treatment was simply transferred from slavery on plantation farms to prisons. Then it took a different form with regard to the southern states' use of the convict leasing system. By the 1950s, African-Americans constituted about one-third of inmates admitted to prison (Mauer, 1999). People of Latino descent

A dubious distinction

In 2007, the U.S. had about 723,000 inmates in jails and 1.6 million in prisons, more prisoners than any other country.

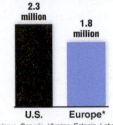

U.S. vs. all other nations
Nations with the largest prison populations, latest available data (rate per 100,000 residents)

Country	Prison population	(rate)
U.S.	2.3 million	(751)
China	1.6 million	(119)
Russia	888,200	(628)
Brazil	419,600	(219)
India	358,400	(32)
Mexico	217,400	(198)
Thailand	165,300	(253)
S. Africa	163,000	(341)
Ukraine	160,000	(345)
Iran	158,400	(222)

U.S. vs. Europe
Total U.S. inmate population compared to the 36 largest European inmate populations

U.S. 2.3 million — Europe* 1.8 million

*Countries (in order of incarceration rate): Russia, Belarus, Georgia, Ukraine, Estonia, Latvia, Moldova, Poland, Lithuania, Azerbaijan, Czech Rep., Hungary, Slovakia, Romania, England & Wales, Bulgaria, Spain, Scotland, Albania, Netherlands, Portugal, Serbia, Turkey, Austria, Armenia, Germany, Croatia, Greece, Switzerland, Norway, Finland, Italy, Denmark

Source: Pew Center on the States, World Prison Brief: King's College London
Graphic: Pat Carr   © 2008 MCT

FIGURE 1–4 **Incarceration Rates (per 100,000 Persons) Around the World.**
Source: Bar chart created from data provided by World Prison Brief (2016), http://www.prisonstudies.org/highest-to-lowest/prison_population_rate.

have also experienced hardships within the CJ system on account of their heritage.

One perspective on why this is the case is that the police may target people of a certain race or ethnic group more often than Caucasians, and that increased police contact results in a greater likelihood of an arrest for some people because of their race or ethnicity. Studies investigating the "driving while black" (or "driving while brown") phenomenon and various points in the CJ system, such as the charging decision or sentencing, support a view of racial bias in some jurisdictions. Another view suggests that although young males across all racial groups engage in criminal offenses in their teens and early 20s (as suggested by self-report data), African-American males engage in more violent felony offenses and continue offending behavior for a longer duration than males of other racial groups (Walker, Spohn, & Delone, 2012). A third observation suggests that the war on drugs has worsened racial disparities in that it has affected both men and women from low-income, urban communities. These views by themselves clearly do not explain all cases, nor are they limited to African-Americans. History shows that arrest and incarceration has long been a tool to control and limit the lives of Native Americans, Latinos, and, most recently, undocumented immigrants (Walker et al., 2012).

Racial disparities in corrections continue to widen and affect entire communities, many of which are poor communities that lack political influence. The corrections system, especially incarceration, hinders the **economic mobility** of individuals and their children, and thus hinders their ability to move up the economic ladder (Pew Charitable Trusts, 2010). These disparities, in turn, reinforce stereotypes that some people hold about dangerousness and who is perceived to be a criminal. It is precisely for these reasons that in this book, one common underlying theme that runs throughout is drawing attention to the history and contemporary situation of racial disparity and socioeconomic differences in the correctional system, where applicable.

Think About It…

Over 7 million people are *currently* under some form of correctional supervision in the United States. Of this number, 2 million are serving time in local, state, and federal institutions, like the prisoners pictured here. These numbers don't even count the estimated 20 million people with felony records and the millions of people who have misdemeanor criminal records but are not currently in the system. The grand total could be as many as 100 million people nationwide with a criminal record of some kind (Cassidy, 2010). Does knowing this change your perception of offenders?

A. Ramey/PhotoEdit

▶ *Media Influence on Public Opinion and Correctional Policy*

The **mass media** provide us with global news, entertainment, and education, and have perhaps the greatest influence on how most people learn and develop opinions about various social issues. The media also play a significant role in influencing public opinion and encouraging political involvement in the punishment of offenders. Public opinion on crime and punishment issues remains deeply rooted in Hollywood movies, documentaries, and television programs depicting rogue police officers, crime scene investigations, courtroom dramas, and scenes of the agitated, difficult prisoner. News programs and newspapers remain wedded to headlining only the most horrific crimes that have occurred that particular day, while at the same time ignoring more common crimes (Cecil, 2015). This creates a public perception that violence is random and frequent, while ignoring the true likelihood of victimization of violence and its contributing factors.

Despite concerns about the economy, employment, education, health care, and dwindling social security, violent crime in the urban core dominates local news stations' aims to increase ratings for a specific target audience (Yanich, 2004). When it comes to discussing punishments for particular crimes, the media are not privy to attorney conversations about the lack of evidence that lead to possible dismissals, charge reductions, and plea bargaining, so only the maximum possible penalty is reported. When the actual sentence is later publicized, it is not surprising that citizens feel angered or disconnected with what they perceive as injustice. Being that crimes are rarely followed throughout the entire justice process, people rely on what they see on the latest episode of *Law and Order* or read on the latest blog and personal website page as representative of the "real" judicial process. Few people actually understand the realities of sentencing options and the correctional process. Yanich (2004) warns that

> viewers think that they are getting information about public issues when, more often than not, they are simply gathering factoids that have no useful purpose in public debate. . . . But, the news system communicates them to make us think that they do. Who among us can take the time to deconstruct a news story about a violent crime when we are bombarded by images of victims, suspects, and yellow crime scene tape? To understand that the reality that we are being shown is designed to hold us as consumers until the next commercial break and not to inform us as citizens? The danger is that we think that we are being informed, when in fact, we are only being sold. (p. 560)

Yanich's observations are backed up by empirical research that found that the *more* reliant a person is on the media for crime and criminal justice issues, the *less* knowledgeable he or she is about sentencing and punishment facts (Pickett, Mancini, Mears, & Gertz, 2015).

Research on media influence and crime indicates support for **cultivation theory**, otherwise known as the "mean world syndrome." Cultivation theory suggests that violence in the media, by itself, does not cause individuals to become violent. Rather, repeated and cumulative exposure to violence eventually creates a sense of insecurity and irrational fear of violent victimization and anxiety about certain types of people (Gorham, 2006). This leads to a potential for widespread "moral panic" about child abductions, child molestations, and homicides (Zgoba, 2004).

Most images of the corrections system focus heavily on maximum security prisons and administrative segregation, and do not show images of probation and other more common community-based supervision options. Prison imagery narrowly and stereotypically characterizes men's prisons as places rampant with violent gangs, rape, and sadistic guards, which is more likely to invoke public fear of prisoners and the sense that prisoners may have it too easy. Films about women prisoners are characterized primarily in sexual terms for entertainment value, while the few documentaries that do exist depict women prisoners as being emotionally unstable (Cecil, 2015). With their focus on maximum and supermaximum units, the media present a one-dimensional and incomplete picture of prison life, ignoring complicated past issues of prisoners' lives and not showing prisoners who are actively trying to improve their lives or trying to get through their sentence in the most expedient and nonviolent way possible. It is no wonder that few people are hesitant to accept or hire former felons.

When it comes to public opinion on punishments and treatment for people who break the law, the majority of the general public favor rehabilitation over punitive crime policies for most offenders (Applegate & Davis, 2006; Applegate, Davis, & Cullen, 2009), but that fear of crime, perceived racial threat, and perceived risk of victimization increase the likelihood of favoring punitive policies (Baker, Metcalfe, Berenblum, Aviv, & Gertz, 2015). Researchers found that public support for the death penalty is more strongly related to resentment and the inability to connect with racial minorities than to views on the moral decline of society or fear of uncontrolled violence (Unnever & Cullen, 2010).

Crime Control Policy

Media influences and public opinion are also related, in part, to the formation of **crime control policy**. Many crime control policies were developed in piecemeal fashion by state and federal legislatures for responses to an immediate problem or in reaction to something other states were LEARNING OUTCOMES 4 — Analyze the relationships among mass media, public opinion, and the making of correctional policy.

doing. There is still enormous variation among the states with respect to level of punitiveness. Most research suggests that the more punitive states tend to also have higher rates of poverty, more persons who are African-American, lower percentage of voter turnout, and less generous welfare payments for impoverished persons (Neill, Yusuf, & Morris, 2015). The authors suggest that punitive correctional policies are a way to control populations of people who are perceived as threats to the status quo.

In Table 1–1, we examine reasons why crime policies in the United States appear to be distinctly different—more punitive—from crime policies in other Western countries in the world. These reasons indicate that crime policy in the United States is more decentralized and tied to political/elected positions within all three branches of the government—the legislative, judicial,

TABLE 1–1 · MAKING CRIME POLICY: WHY THE UNITED STATES IS DIFFERENT

	United States	Other Westernized Countries
Judges and prosecutors	Elected at state and local levels—influenced by politics and short-term terms	Career civil servants—receive special training and remain there as a career
Legislative organization	Vulnerable to voting according to party lines or according to what other states are doing	Various parties are present
Funding	Reliance on federal funding; vulnerable to loss of federal funding; 50 state systems	Centralized single system
Sentencing and release decisions	Micromanaged by legislators	Managed by the courts and corrections system
Legislative style of decision making	Political action committees; lobbyists; appeal to human emotions	Rational decision making

Source: Information derived from Tonry (2004).

and executive—in a more significant way than in other countries, which are more likely to rely on career employees who take a more long-term approach to prosecution, sentencing, and corrections management.

The more punitive crime policies in the United States have led to CJ responses that have relied substantially on incarceration. This has caused correctional spending to increase faster than spending for most other government budget items. Correctional spending is now the fourth largest line item in most states' budgets, after education, health care, and transportation (Vera Institute of Justice, 2010). Annual corrections' costs account for over *$173 billion* at state and local levels. These expensive approaches, coupled with our recent economic troubles, have led to budget shortfalls and underfunded community supervision programs left to supervise a high number of clients. Despite increasing corrections expenditures, recidivism rates remain high, with about half of all persons released from prison returning within three years. To complicate the problem, offenders cycle in and out of the justice system from the same communities that are also underserved and impoverished.

▶ Evidence-Based Practices

Around 2009, the term **evidence-based practice** (EBP) first surfaced on the CJ scene. EBP had already been used in fields such as medicine, education, social work, and mental health, but now the term was being applied to all aspects of criminal justice. According to Figure 1–5, there are essentially two parts to EBP. First, the academic side of EBP is about researchers carefully designing methodologically strong program evaluations to determine what works, what is promising, and what does not work. The second part, "applying the techniques," is when practitioners are to use only correctional practices and program elements that have been

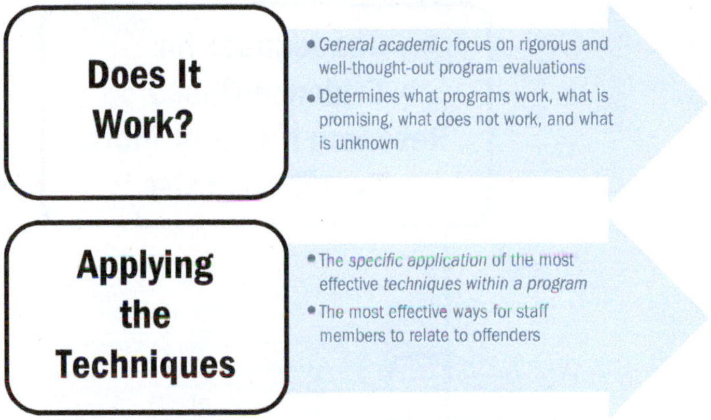

Does It Work?
- *General academic* focus on rigorous and well-thought-out program evaluations
- Determines what programs work, what is promising, what does not work, and what is unknown

Applying the Techniques
- The *specific application* of the most effective *techniques within a program*
- The most effective ways for staff members to relate to offenders

FIGURE 1–5 Two Parts to Evidence-Based Practice.

proven to work, and also permanently discard programs that do not work.

Before EBP, practitioners "evaluated" their own programs based on anecdotal evidence and may have been reluctant to try anything new because "this is what we've always done." EBP challenges anecdotal evidence by requiring programs to prove with statistical evidence that what they do works.

EBP allows academics and practitioners to come together with programs that work and make a difference on intended outcomes. In corrections, the chief concerns (and thus the intended outcomes) are achieving public safety through offenders committing no new crimes while on supervision and reducing offender recidivism after supervision. Although reducing recidivism remains important, EBP allows for the possibility of examining other ways to measure whether a program or practice works. Outcomes are typically focused on the offender and may vary depending on the program to include the following:

- Offender change in thinking patterns
- Increased number of drug-free days

- Increased number of days offender is working or employed while on supervision
- More effective assessments—matching risk and need with supervision levels

How to Determine What Works

EBP requires agency practitioners to use programs that have been empirically shown through methodologically sound academic research to meet the intended outcome. Each chapter of the text has at least one box entitled "Evidence-Based Practice—Does It Work?" to demonstrate which correctional programs have had the greatest effect on decreasing recidivism. So, only studies conducted with a strong methodology and those that have found a true difference are counted. This is harder to determine than it sounds, as only a small percentage of published studies meet all the criteria for a quality study. Figure 1–6 shows how researchers identify rigorous studies with strong methodology. A program evaluation is judged to be of highest quality if all six conditions exist in the way that the study itself is carried out, from the group selection method, to the number of people in the sample, all the way to the validity of the testing instrument. Programs that are evaluated using poor measures and small samples are not valid or reliable enough to be judged with certainty that they really work, or that there is some other reason why participants did so well.

When at least one high-quality or rigorous study shows a program to be effective, that program is considered to be "promising." When the same correctional program has two or more independent and rigorous studies showing a significant difference between the treatment group and the control group, that program "works" and is judged to be effective. A program or intervention that "doesn't work" has at least two rigorous studies showing no significant difference between program participants and an equivalent comparison group that did not receive the intervention.

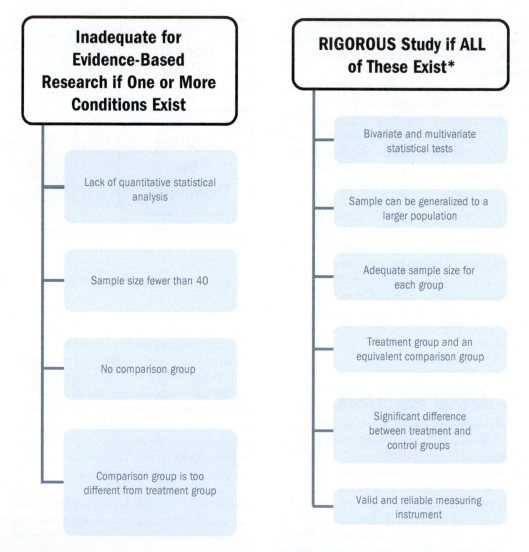

Inadequate for Evidence-Based Research if One or More Conditions Exist

- Lack of quantitative statistical analysis
- Sample size fewer than 40
- No comparison group
- Comparison group is too different from treatment group

RIGOROUS Study if ALL of These Exist*

- Bivariate and multivariate statistical tests
- Sample can be generalized to a larger population
- Adequate sample size for each group
- Treatment group and an equivalent comparison group
- Significant difference between treatment and control groups
- Valid and reliable measuring instrument

* True random assignment is rare in the social sciences, so there are plenty of quasi-experimental and matched group designs that are still considered rigorous.

FIGURE 1–6 **How to Identify RIGOROUS Academic Studies Used to Evaluate Effective Correctional Programs.**

EBP Techniques

Using EBP techniques, however, is more specific to *how* practitioners implement offender treatment interventions when time and resources are limited. For example, treatment interventions should be focused toward the highest-risk clients based on correcting problems that most likely contribute to criminal behavior, such as drug use, anger management, and the like. Agencies are increasingly required to measure what they do through an independent evaluator who collects and statistically examines their data.

The principles of EBP are shown in Figure 1–7. Applying EBP techniques in corrections (pretrial or postconviction) begins with a valid assessment instrument to measure the level of risk the offender poses and the problem areas (needs) that should be emphasized with the offender during his or her sentence. Two valid assessment instruments are the Level of Service Inventory-Revised and the Ohio Risk Assessment System. Once the risk and needs are accurately measured, correctional supervision and treatment can commence. Risk and needs assessments are also used to make decisions about prison custody level, housing, and institutional release.

Another technique of EBP is that intervention should be based on **social learning** and/or **cognitive behavioral approaches**. Treatment interventions should also match the learning styles, abilities, and demographics of the offender. For example, treatment interventions that are gender focused seem to be more effective than programs developed to help both men and women simultaneously.

Treatment interventions should target risk factors that are most closely associated with criminal behavior for the greatest gains in recidivism reduction. These factors include the following:

LEARNING OUTCOMES 5 Characterize the meaning of evidence-based practice and explain how it can improve the correctional system.

- Antisocial attitudes, values, beliefs, and emotional states (criminal thinking)
- Pro-criminal associates and isolation from pro-social associates

FIGURE 1–7 **EBPs that Correctional Practitioners Use.**
Source: Adapted from Crime and Justice Institute (2004).

- Egocentrism, weak problem-solving and self-regulation skills
- Criminal history
- Familial factors (low levels of affection and cohesiveness, poor parental supervision and discipline practices, neglect and abuse)
- Low levels of personal, vocational, and educational achievement
- Substance abuse

Correctional treatment should target higher-risk offenders. Intensive treatment for lower-risk offenders can actually *increase* the likelihood of recidivism.

Finally, how staff members relate to offenders is extremely important to achieving lasting behavioral change. Staff should be well trained in recognizing criminal thinking errors, establishing rapport, increasing offender motivation, and using positive reinforcement with rewards and incentives over the use of instilling fear through negative reinforcement. The quality of the visit or appointment is more important than the quantity. EBP would also favor graduated sanctions over incarcerating someone for violating his or her probation or parole.

At least 12 states—California, Florida, Indiana, Iowa, Kansas, Louisiana, Nevada, New Hampshire, Oregon, Pennsylvania, South Carolina, and Virginia—implemented EBP for offender supervision.

In conclusion, the complexity of public opinion, the interests of the media, and the factors that influence passing or not passing crime control legislation are indeed important considerations as you read this book. Further, understanding the importance of using programs and strategies that work is part of the evidence-based approach. A final goal of this book is to provide a base for that knowledge so that you can intelligently engage in a discussion of both philosophies of punishment and effective and salient correctional strategies.

Using EBP to Address Racial Disparities

Cases that are brought into the corrections system depend on decision making that occurs beforehand. No one knows that better than Milwaukee County District Attorney John Chisholm. Chisholm was interested in collecting and analyzing evidence-based data to identify possible racial or ethnic bias in cases originating out of his Wisconsin county between arrest and sentencing. The ultimate goal was to build public confidence in the CJ process and to explain case outcomes from the courts to the corrections system.

This was quite challenging because most case information in his office was maintained as hard-copy files, and none of it was kept at any one agency. A team of experts listed key data that were necessary to assemble for each individual defendant to determine how a system operated during key discretion points in the process: arrest, initial case screening, charging, plea offers, and sentencing. Data were entered in a single computerized database, not only by individual defendant, but also including multiple charges, some of which were dismissed and others that were charged. The database also accounted for the various charges that may lead to different plea agreements and different sentences.

The data revealed a disparity in misdemeanor cases involving possession of drug paraphernalia. About 73% of non-white defendants charged with possession of drug paraphernalia were prosecuted, compared to only 59% of white defendants. Upon closer examination of the data, the disparity originated with differences in perceptions between prosecutors. Prosecutors with less experience aggressively prosecuted individuals arrested for possession of crack pipes but not individuals in possession of other forms of paraphernalia. More experienced prosecutors decided against pursuing most drug paraphernalia cases, seeing them as too minor and not worth the effort. Once the source of the disparity was identified, District Attorney Chisholm encouraged his junior prosecutors to view possession of paraphernalia as a treatment issue that qualified for dismissal or diversion rather than prosecution. He also implemented a policy that required prosecutors to seek a supervisor's approval if they wanted to prosecute such charges.

Following that change in policy and practice, racial disparities in possession of drug paraphernalia disappeared.

Source: McKenzie, Stemen, and Coursen (2009).

The case in Milwaukee County raises several interesting questions:

1. Given that district attorneys like Chisholm are elected to their position, what are the potential ramifications for one's political career of doing a study such as this? Is Chisholm a change agent, or is he destined to end his district attorney career prematurely?

2. Decisions made by prosecutors are considered to be one of the most influential in the system, yet these decisions are rarely scrutinized. Should the scrutiny applied to Milwaukee County prosecutors be expanded to other counties and even other states?

3. When it comes to issues of racial/ethnic disparity, how important is it that the public has confidence in our CJ system?

LEARNING OUTCOMES 1   Describe how corrections is part of the larger CJ system that is dependent on decisions made earlier in the process by the police and the courts.

The three main social control agencies of the CJ system are the police, the courts, and the corrections system.

The police are the gatekeepers of the system.

The courts depend on the efficiency and professionalism of the police to determine whether the suspected lawbreaker is the right suspect and whether this suspect broke the law in the manner that he or she is being accused of by the police.

Corrections serve to carry out the sentence of the court.

1. What role do local police play, if any, in racial and economic disparity in jails and prisons?

2. Do gender disparities exist in the corrections system? If so, where, and how can these disparities be corrected?

3. What circumstances about an offender's past might make him or her a good candidate for pretrial community supervision?

corrections The network of government and private agencies responsible for the pre- and postconviction custody, supervision, and treatment of persons accused or convicted of crimes.

police Law enforcement officials who are sworn to uphold the law, keep social order, and preserve public safety.

citation A police-issued ticket ordering a citizen to pay a fine for a minor law violation.

booked When a suspect is identified and fingerprinted in jail after being arrested for an alleged crime.

jurisdiction A predefined geographic area.

dismissed When a case is dropped for lack of evidence and does not proceed any further.

pretrial supervision The community supervision of a defendant who has not yet been convicted but is waiting for his or her next court hearing date.

LEARNING OUTCOMES 2   Compare and contrast institutional and community-based corrections.

Corrections programs involve the community supervision of diverted individuals who have not yet been sentenced, as well as misdemeanants and felons who have been formally convicted or have pled guilty.

Offenders who are in jail or prison are separated from the elements of daily life to protect the safety of others or to pay for their crimes by having their freedom taken away.

1. What factors determine if a case or an offender is qualified for diversion, and who makes the decision?

2. Which crimes and/or offender situations would be best suited for community supervision, and why?

3. What crimes and/or offender situations would best qualify for institutional corrections, and why?

diversion A form of community supervision for individuals who have not been formally sentenced, but who agree to complete stipulations, such as treatment or community service, in exchange for having their charges dropped.

continuum of sanctions One or more sentencing options within the community or an institution that can be combined with one another to achieve a range of sentencing goals.

community corrections Court-ordered supervision and treatment while the offender remains at liberty in the community.

net widening When offenders receive a level of correctional control or punishment that is greater than what they really require, resulting in bringing more people into the system.

institutional corrections Incarceration of offenders in a jail or prison, apart from the community.

LEARNING OUTCOMES 3   Explain the effect that rising incarceration rates between 1970 and 2010 had on racial and economic disparity.

The U.S. incarceration rate per 100,000 men and women remains the highest in the world, yet incarceration is the most expensive option and yields only a small impact on the crime rate.

Incarceration negatively affects the economic mobility of individuals and can impact entire communities, especially those areas that are underserved and are composed primarily of families of Latino and African-American heritage.

Increases in the prison population were related to the politicization of criminal behavior based on emotions, changes in sentencing laws for drug and violent offenses, decreased rates of release on discretionary parole, and decisions made about responding to parole and probation violators.

1. How can the police, prosecutors, and/or judges correct racial and economic disparities that exist in their jurisdiction?

2. If the United States has the highest incarceration rates in the world, is it because Americans are just more violent or criminal than the rest of the world, or are there other reasons? If so, what are some possible reasons?

3. Why did incarceration rates have such a small impact on crime rates?

incarceration rate The proportion of people in jail and prison per 100,000 residents in a given area.

economic mobility The likelihood that individuals can rise and maintain a higher socioeconomic status than they were born into, through employment and earnings.

LEARNING OUTCOMES 4

Analyze the relationships among mass media, public opinion, and the making of correctional policy.

Media sources inform public opinion of crime and responses to it more often than do learning experiences at school, home, or other settings.

Citizens are generally in favor of rehabilitation and prevention programs and support alternatives to incarceration when available.

U.S. crime policymaking is unique compared to other Westernized countries, due to its system of electing or appointing state/local judges and prosecutors, legislative micromanagement of sentencing/parole, and state reliance on federal funding.

Correctional policy trends may not be representative of public opinion in the long term, but they have affected the overall expansion of the corrections system, the increase in the number of women under correctional supervision, the high incarceration rate, and the burgeoning cost of the system.

1. In what other ways do the media inform public opinion on social issues?
2. How have legislators been major definers of the "crime problem"?
3. If citizens are in support of alternatives to prison, why haven't we developed more programs and options in this direction?
4. What other ways exist to develop rational crime policies?

mass media Broadcast and print forms of expression for consumer news, education, and entertainment, such as television, movies, the Internet, DVDs, video games, radio, books, newspapers, and magazines.

cultivation theory Repeated viewing and cumulative exposure to violence in the media eventually creates a sense of insecurity and irrational fear of violent victimization and about people in the world in general.

crime control policy A course of action to respond to criminal behavior in the best interest of the public.

LEARNING OUTCOMES 5

Characterize the meaning of evidence-based practice and explain how it can improve the correctional system.

EBP requires agencies to use programs that have been empirically shown through methodologically sound academic research to work, thus becoming more effective over time at reducing recidivism.

Specific EBP techniques for lasting behavior change include assessing risk/needs, using cognitive behavioral approaches, having a program duration between three and nine months, targeting high-risk offenders, being responsive to the demographics of the population, using motivational interviewing, and using rewards/incentives.

It is important that EBPs are continually measured through data collection, evaluation, and dissemination of that EBP practice or intervention so that minor adjustments may be made.

1. How does EBP help achieve public safety?
2. How is EBP different from the type of correctional supervision used two decades ago?
3. Is EBP applicable to correctional officers in prison who are tasked with supervision of inmates but not treatment? If so, how? If not, why not?
4. Is EBP seen as more demanding for offenders overall or as an intervention that is less punitive?

evidence-based practice Correctional interventions for which there is consistent and solid scientific evidence showing that they work to meet the intended outcomes, such as recidivism reduction.

social learning Changing old behavior through modeling new skills and desirable behavior.

cognitive behavioral approaches Changing an individual's thinking patterns and habits that lead to criminal behavior through techniques such as self-control, anger management, social perspective taking, moral reasoning, problem solving, and attitudinal change.

Additional Links

Visit the National Conference of State Legislature website at **www.ncsl.org** and click on the "Issues and Research" tab. Then click on the "Civil/Criminal Justice" committee to see what correctional policies and correctional topics were a part of the most recent legislative session in your state.

Visit the VERA Institute of Justice's Center on Sentencing and Corrections at **www.vera.org** to review recent legislative trends in reducing prison populations.

View *The Mean World Syndrome*—a video by George Gerbner and Michael Morgan about the effect of media violence on perceptions of the world that uses cultivation theory. A shortened explanation of this video is on YouTube at **www.youtube. com** and is entitled *Media as Storytellers: Nothing to Tell, but a Lot to Sell*.

Visit the FrameWorks Institute at **www.frameworksinstitute.org** to learn more about how people cognitively process media information, and how this exposure shapes public opinion.

Watch a short video explaining evidence-based practices from George Keiser, the division chief of the National Institute of Corrections, at **http://nicic.gov/EvidenceBasedPractices**.

Listen to how EBP can be applied in community corrections and to treatment programs by scrolling down to the list of previous podcasts from July 6, 2009, at **http://media.csosa.gov/podcast/audio/**.

2

Why Do We Punish?

1 Describe the five primary punishment philosophies.

2 Discuss the deterrence philosophy of punishment by understanding the effects of specific and general deterrence.

3 Compare and contrast selective and general incapacitation.

4 Summarize rehabilitation's development from a reclamation focus to a reentry emphasis.

5 Explain the key ways in which retribution differs from revenge.

6 Describe how restorative justice principles are used in sentencing, during community supervision, and in prison.

James Steidl/Shutterstock

WHAT DOES SOCIETY HOPE TO ACCOMPLISH WHEN PUNISHING CRIMINAL OFFENDERS?

In recent years, in different U.S. jurisdictions, the following sentences were imposed:

- As part of a probation agreement for causing an accident that killed Army Sgt. Thomas E. Towers, Jr., Andrew Gaudioso was ordered to send the soldier's family a postcard, via the probation department, every week for 15 years. If he fails to send the postcards, he could be sent to prison for the remainder of the 15 years. Towers's father agreed to the unusual stipulation because he thought it would force Gaudioso to think about what he did at least once a week (Hudak, 2010).

- A federal judge ordered Grammy-winning rap artist T.I. (Clifford Harris, Jr.) back to prison for 11 months. He violated the terms of his supervised release on federal weapons charges when he was arrested on suspicion of drug possession. T.I. said that he had now learned his lesson ("T.I. says new prison sentence is his final lesson," 2010).

- Tyler Alred, 17, pleaded guilty to manslaughter after crashing a pickup truck and killing the passenger—Alred's 16-year-old friend. Alred had been drinking and, although not drunk, was considered to have been driving under the influence because he was underage. The victim's family viewed the incident as an accident and didn't want to see two lives wasted as a result. The Oklahoma judge was accordingly lenient and sentenced Alred to a list of conditions (e.g., graduate from welding school and attend church) to meet over the next 10 years in order to stay out of prison (Goforth, 2012).

Allstar Picture Library/Alamy Stock Photo

DISCUSS **Do we punish in order to force an offender to remember the wrong, to learn a lesson, to follow victim preferences, or for some other reason?**

▶ Why Punish?

Important implications result from asking why we are punishing someone. The answers we come up with, independently or collectively, help us determine whether justice has been done. Equally important is how our view of punishment's goals affects the correctional process and helps us evaluate the success of correctional programs. This chapter directs our attention to those issues by describing key reasons for punishment.

In our representative democracy, the people's will is expressed through elected legislators. That means we should be able to identify punishment philosophies in each state and at the federal level by finding the relevant statutes or other legislative documents. Unfortunately, not all legislators have put into writing their understanding of their constituencies' reasons for applying criminal punishment. A few states that have done so provide interesting variation:

Alabama: The Alabama Sentencing Commission is directed to consider sentencing laws and practices that, in part, (a) promote respect for the law, (b) provide just and adequate punishment for the offense, (c) protect the public, (d) deter criminal conduct, and (e) promote the rehabilitation of offenders (Alabama Sentencing Commission, 2000).

California: The court rules for California identify the general objectives of sentencing as (a) protecting society, (b) punishing the defendant, (c) encouraging the defendant to lead a law-abiding life in the future and deterring him or her from future offenses, (d) deterring others from criminal conduct by demonstrating crime's consequences, (e) preventing the defendant from committing new crimes by isolating him or her for the period of incarceration, (f) securing restitution for the victims of crime, and (g) achieving uniformity in sentencing (Judicial Council of California, 2013).

Colorado: The Colorado Revised Statutes explain that the purposes of sentencing are (a) to punish a convicted offender, (b) to assure fair and consistent treatment of all convicted offenders, (c) to prevent crime and promote respect for the law, (d) to promote rehabilitation, (e) to select a sentence that addresses the offender's individual characteristics and reduces the potential, and (f) to promote acceptance of responsibility and accountability by offenders and to provide restoration and healing for victims and the community (State of Colorado, 2013).

Texas: The Texas penal code's provisions are intended to ensure public safety through (a) the deterrent influence of the penalties provided in the code, (b) the rehabilitation of those convicted of violations of the code, and (c) such punishment as may be necessary to prevent likely recurrence of criminal behavior (State of Texas, 2009).

There is an interesting connection among these four states' reasons for punishing offenders. Especially similar are references to

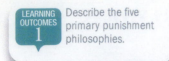
deterring the offender from future criminal acts (including people who have not yet offended, California adds), protecting the public (specifically for California, through incarceration), rehabilitating the offender, and punishing the offender (justly and adequately, Alabama notes). Also mentioned are goals of promoting respect for the law (Alabama and Colorado), facilitating uniformity in sentencing (California and Colorado), securing restitution for the victim (California), and providing restoration and healing (Colorado).

Those objectives provide the broad base from which a discussion of punishment rationales builds. Specifically, this chapter discusses the reasons for punishment as primarily focused on **deterrence** (discouraging future criminal acts by both the offender and others in the population), **incapacitation** (isolation of the offender from the general population), **rehabilitation** (providing the offender with skills, attitudes, and norms that enable him or her to be law-abiding), **retribution** (just and adequate punishment), and **restoration** (restoring the victim, community, and offender through accountability, respect for the law and the legal process, and attention to victim needs).

The concepts of deterrence, incapacitation, rehabilitation, retribution, and restoration provide the structure for society's system of penal sanctions and for this book. Their importance in understanding the theory and practice of corrections is emphasized by how they relate to the main ideas in several chapters of this book. In Chapter 3, for example, the philosophies help explain the development of correctional practices over time. Throughout the textbook, the philosophies provide an important perspective when discussing what, if anything, works in corrections.

▶ Deterrence

The deterrence philosophy of punishment assumes that actions serving a useful function (i.e., they are utilitarian)

are desirable when they benefit the general welfare of society. Figure 2–1 identifies Bentham and Beccaria as key figures in applying this utilitarian aspect. Reducing crime, the argument goes, certainly benefits the general welfare, so punishment that serves to reduce crime is utilitarian and desirable.

The aim of punishment is to prevent future offenses by example to both the offender and others. When applied to the offender, punishment is said to be acting as a **specific deterrent** by showing the criminal that his or her action brought more pain than pleasure. When others hear about a criminal being punished, that punishment serves as a **general deterrent** by showing people who might be considering a criminal act the consequences they will suffer. Both specific and general deterrence are important when understanding the deterrence philosophy.

Specific Deterrence

When punishment is applied to someone who has already misbehaved, it is acting as a specific deterrent with the goal of discouraging that person from offending again. It is assumed that punishment will have that effect because proponents of the deterrence philosophy believe everyone is a rational, pleasure-seeking, and pain-avoiding person with free will.

This doctrine, that punishing persons for their misdeeds will make them less likely to commit the misdeeds again, is a guiding principle for many (maybe most) Western criminal justice systems. The proposition seems intuitively correct, but contemporary research has failed to find consistent evidence of the deterrent effects of punishment (Fagan & Meares, 2008, p. 182). It seems that formal punishment alone has a very limited ability to deter crime. As shown in Figure 2–2, the lack of a specific deterrent effect might be due to problems society has in achieving three key requirements of an effective deterrence system:

Jeremy Bentham was an eighteenth-century British philosopher who argued that actions are moral if they are useful or utilitarian and benefit the general welfare.

Cesare Beccaria was an eighteenth-century Italian criminologist who believed that punishment should only be used to achieve good.

Building on Bentham and Beccaria, the deterrence philosophy argues that punishment is utilitarian and desirable since it benefits the general welfare by helping to reduce crime.

FIGURE 2–1 **How Utilitarianism Influenced the Deterrence Philosophy.**
Source: Classic Image/Alamy Stock Photo and Universal Images Group/Superstock

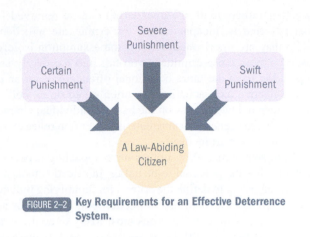

FIGURE 2–2 **Key Requirements for an Effective Deterrence System.**

DISCUSS Do you think humans mostly have free will and behave in a rational manner after weighing the consequences of their actions? How should the answer to that question affect punishment decisions?

- *Certainty:* This is problematic because certainty is realistically achieved only if citizens are willing to be constantly monitored so that all criminal acts are known to the authorities and can thereby be punished. However, less intrusive tactics such as hot spot policing (focusing police resources on a small geographic area where crime is high or increasing) can be effective by increasing the perception that criminals will be caught and punished (Nagin, 2013).

- *Severity:* This requirement may be possible, but there is the problem that "severe" for one person may be "mild" to another. In addition, research shows that increasing the severity of punishment does little to deter crimes since criminals generally know little about the punishment attached to specific crimes. As Nagin (2013) puts it, a criminal is more likely to be deterred by seeing a police officer with handcuffs and a radio than through the passage of a new law increasing penalties.

- *Swiftness:* Swiftness will likely be achieved only by restricting the due process currently provided to defendants and the rights to appeal now granted to convicted offenders.

Applying these key requirements means, for example, that having caught offender Jones—and wanting to deter him from future acts—society's punishment must be unavoidable, it must be severe enough (but not disproportionately severe) that Jones considers it more painful than any pleasure he got from the act, and it must be applied to Jones soon after the crime occurred. Each of these conditions is problematic, and as a result **specific deterrence** is hard to accomplish.

Even if specific deterrence is not as effective in reducing reoffending as we might hope, deterrence theory may still be a desirable punishment rationale if it has a general deterrent effect.

General Deterrence

When the aim of punishment is to discourage other people from committing a crime in the first place, it is said to have a **general deterrence** function. For example, as the holiday season approaches, local department stores may seek to deter shoplifting by increasing their willingness to press charges against shoplifters. The store manager believes that the publicity resulting from shoplifters being prosecuted and punished will discourage other people from shoplifting.

In order for punishment of one offender to have a deterrent effect on others, the others must believe that they will be punished, that the punishment will be more painful than any pleasure they get from the act, and that the punishment will be administered soon after their wrongful act. In addition to those conditions, Newman (1985) adds the requirement of publicity because that condition is necessary for others to know about the punishment someone else received.

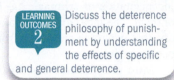

LEARNING OUTCOMES **2** Discuss the deterrence philosophy of punishment by understanding the effects of specific and general deterrence.

Just as certainty, severity, and swiftness are difficult to achieve for purposes of specific deterrence, they are also problematic for general deterrence. Publicity, however, is more attainable today with our advanced media technology. But if the public is informed less about criminals being punished and more about the problems of making arrests and getting convictions (a lack of certainty), the increased use of what are seen as lenient penalties (a lack of severity), and the excessive time it takes for punishment to actually be applied (a lack of swiftness), publicity may be more harmful than helpful in having punishment be a general deterrent.

We have used the concepts of certainty, severity, swiftness, and publicity to show some of the problems of using punishment, either specific or general, to deter behavior. Of course, it is also possible that the deterrence philosophy of punishment suffers from a more fatal problem—its very core assumptions may be wrong. Maybe people are not rational, calculating individuals using free will to achieve pleasure and avoid pain. If this is the case, then all the certainty, severity, and swiftness

Think About It…

If people refrain from committing a crime because they fear the punishment they might receive, that punishment is serving a deterrent function. Do you think signs such as this one can deter someone from distributing drugs near a school? Is anything really accomplished if drugs are distributed instead to persons under age 18 when they are more than 1,000 feet from a school?

Source: Chris DeRidder and Hans VandenNieuwendijk/ Shutterstock

that society can muster will be to no avail. Irrational people, or those whose behavior is determined by biological, psychological, or social factors rather than through free will, are not going to be deterred by punishment (Katz, 1988).

▶ Incapacitation

When incapacitation is used as a punishment, a person's ability to move about freely is impaired or restricted. Historically, the incapacitation of criminals has been achieved through imprisonment. The idea is that by removing a criminal from free society, that person is prevented from continuing to cause harm to people or property.

Most people agree that prison is necessary for some criminals. Where we disagree is about the size of that "some" category. One group would reserve imprisonment for those very few offenders who must truly be locked away for society's protection. Imprisonment, in other words, is acceptable on a limited scale. "Confine only specific offenders or offender types," say these folks. Others see imprisonment as acceptable and desirable on an extensive scale for a wide range of offenders. This "lock 'em all up" approach views imprisonment as protecting society from criminals whether or not any rehabilitation or specific deterrence occurs. Zimring and Hawkins (1995) refer to the limited approach as **selective incapacitation** and the expansionist approach as **general incapacitation** (see Figure 2–3).

Both selective incapacitation and general incapacitation are based on the premise that a particular group of offenders is responsible for a large percentage of crime. If that group

(whether rather small or rather large) can be removed from society—that is, incapacitated—the crime rate will decline while they are imprisoned. Even if the assumption is correct, distinguishing those criminals who fall into the overly active population from the more occasional offenders is not an easy task. Selective incapacitation has often relied on an ability to distinguish the two groups on the basis of individual characteristics, whereas general incapacitation more often relies on characteristics of the crime itself.

Both sentencing philosophies have appealing aspects, but each also has the potential to be unfair. In selective incapacitation, when trying to define the criteria for identifying individual dangerousness, bias and discrimination play a role. For argument's sake, assume that persons most likely to continue their criminal behavior will be those who come from a low-socioeconomic area of the inner city, are high school dropouts, and are unemployed. If these characteristics are included among those used to identify persons likely to continue committing crime, there is a potential for discrimination by race and ethnicity. Unfortunately, in contemporary U.S. society, there is a disproportionate number of African-Americans and Latinos who are unemployed high school dropouts living in low-income inner-city areas. Not all of them, however, commit crimes. Even those who are criminal may not be any more likely to continue their criminal involvement than would be a European American offender with a high school diploma who is living in suburbia.

Redding (2009, fn. 14) reminds us that there is considerable research identifying the risk factors associated with criminal behavior (e.g., criminal history, early age of criminal offending

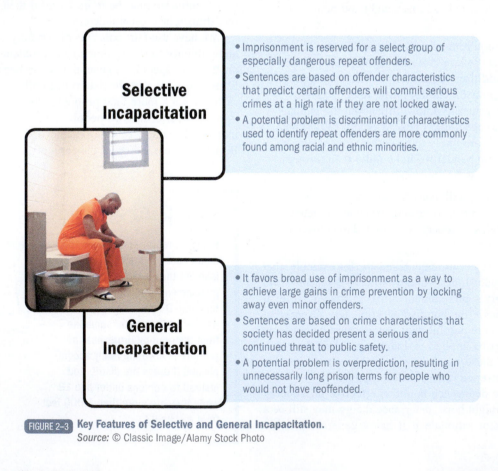

Selective Incapacitation

- Imprisonment is reserved for a select group of especially dangerous repeat offenders.
- Sentences are based on offender characteristics that predict certain offenders will commit serious crimes at a high rate if they are not locked away.
- A potential problem is discrimination if characteristics used to identify repeat offenders are more commonly found among racial and ethnic minorities.

General Incapacitation

- It favors broad use of imprisonment as a way to achieve large gains in crime prevention by locking away even minor offenders.
- Sentences are based on crime characteristics that society has decided present a serious and continued threat to public safety.
- A potential problem is overprediction, resulting in unnecessarily long prison terms for people who would not have reoffended.

FIGURE 2–3 **Key Features of Selective and General Incapacitation.**
Source: © Classic Image/Alamy Stock Photo

onset, substance abuse, association with deviant peers), but it remains difficult to accurately identify those people most likely to continue their criminal ways—some of them may commit serious crimes over a prolonged period, but many may not. However, as discussed in Chapter 4, increased reliance on evidence-based practices when sentencing may be changing this problem.

General incapacitation may avoid the problem of racially and ethnically biased sentencing by imposing prison sentences based on what offenders did rather than who they are. For example, if members of a community decide that drug offenders present a serious and continued threat to the public safety, they can develop a policy of longer prison terms for anyone convicted of a drug offense. In this manner, Anglo drug dealer Patterson and Hispanic drug dealer Jaramillo both receive long prison sentences. Presumably, Patterson's and Jaramillo's educational level, employment status, and neighborhood will not influence the length of imprisonment. In this manner, Patterson and Jaramillo are punished because the community believes that drug offenders are dangerous—not because it thinks either Patterson or Jaramillo is necessarily a dangerous individual.

Zimring and Hawkins (1995) agree that the policy of general incapacitation may resist stereotypes of dangerousness, but they are not so sure that it can avoid the problem of false positives wherein an offender is incorrectly included among the likely-to-repeat group. This overpredicting will mean that some people will be imprisoned for an unnecessarily long time. Even ignoring the ethical aspects of that situation, the mere cost involved in constructing prisons to house these offenders presents a problem to proponents of general incapacitation.

LEARNING OUTCOMES 3 — Compare and contrast selective and general incapacitation.

The value of selective and general incapacitation as punishment rationales continues to be debated. As with all the rationales, a key to deciding if incapacitation is a desirable basis for making punishment decisions will ride on how effectively it achieves its goal. The answer may depend on what is meant by "effective." Consider, for example, the problem of replacement. If Patterson completes 100 drug deals a year in his community, the effect of his imprisonment would be 100 fewer drug deals in that community. But what if drug dealer Tanaka begins to service Patterson's former clients and essentially makes 100 more drug sales than he does when Patterson is around? The community has lessened Patterson's criminal behavior but has not lowered the amount of crime occurring because Tanaka has replaced Patterson. Has imprisonment achieved the goal of incapacitation? The answer seems to be yes regarding Patterson, but no regarding the community's crime rate.

However, even Patterson's punishment may cause other problems because incapacitation may provide him with opportunities to learn techniques for committing other offenses. To the extent that prisons might be "schools for crime," offenders may complete their prison sentences with greater knowledge about ways to commit an even wider variety of crimes. Although incapacitation may have temporarily disabled Patterson's drug dealing, it could have introduced him to auto theft or burglary.

Incapacitation Through Technology

Although imprisonment is the classic way to incapacitate offenders, recent technological advances offer other ways to restrict an offender's freedom of movement. As shown in Figure 2–4, examples of this **technological incapacitation** include critical organ surgery, chemical treatment, and electronic monitoring.

This chapter's Voices in Corrections feature "*How has GPS tracking of probationers affected the way probation officers do their job?*" provides an example of electronic monitoring's role in probation. Figure 2–5 highlights one technique, castration of male sex offenders, that continues to receive considerable attention and can involve either surgery or chemical treatment. Although females also commit sex offenses, treatment responses for them rely on psychological (Gannon & Cortoni, 2010) rather than technological measures. As such, this particular example of technological incapacitation is relevant only to male sex offenders.

Seven states currently allow chemical or surgical castration of sex offenders being released from prison into the community. Four of those states (California, Florida, Iowa, and Louisiana) authorize either voluntary surgical or chemical castration, two allow only chemical castration (Montana and Wisconsin), and one (Texas) provides for only voluntary surgical castration (Chism, 2013; Vaillancourt, 2012).

Proponents of chemical castration argue that it is a humane and effective treatment for some sex offenders when used in conjunction with counseling therapy. The medication decreases offenders' sexual drive and provides an opportunity for them to engage in cognitive behavioral tasks that recognize and control unacceptable sexual urges. Opponents respond by noting that the medication decreases—but does not prevent—erections and ejaculation, so chemical castration is not appropriate for all sex offenders. In addition, some sex offenders are motivated by anger, hatred, or power rather than by sex. Those people will not be affected by chemical castration because their crimes do not stem from sexual urges or fantasies.

Chemical Treatment

- This includes chemical intervention such as Antabuse for alcoholics and methadone for heroin addicts in an attempt to force abstinence or to reduce sexual drive or interest (that is, chemical castration).

Critical Organ Surgery

- This includes operating on specific regions of the brain in an attempt to lessen a propensity toward violence (that is, psychosurgery) or surgical removal of both testicles in order to reduce sexual drive or interest (that is, surgical castration).

Electronic Monitoring

- Freedom to move about is restricted through the use of monitoring devices that inform authorities of the offender's location and/or movements.

FIGURE 2–4 Common Types of Technological Incapacitation.

Use of Surgical and Chemical Castration in the Twentieth and Twenty-First Centuries

1966
Czechoslovakia authorizes surgical castration for sex offenders who volunteer for the procedure (Council of Europe, 2009).

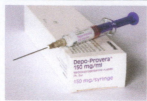

Visions of America, LLC/Alamy Stock Photo

1996
California passes the nation's first law requiring chemical castration of repeat child sex offenders on parole. Offenders may opt for surgical castration (Norman-Eady, 2006).

1997
Texas allows voluntary surgical castration of incarcerated sex offenders and Florida requires chemical castration for certain repeat offenders (Norman-Eady, 2006).

FIGURE 2–5 **Timeline: Use of Surgical and Chemical Castration in the Twentieth and Twenty-First Centuries.**
Council of Europe. (2009). Report to the Czech government on the visit to the Czech Republic carried out by the European Committee for the Prevention of Torture and Inhuman or Degrading Treatment or Punishment (CPT). Retrieved from http://Council of Europe website: www.cpt.coe.int/documents/cze/2009-08-inf-eng.htm; Castration of sex offenders. Connecticut General Assembly, OLR Research Report 2006-R-0183. Retrieved from https://www.cga.ct.gov/2006/rpt/2006-R-0183.htm.

It is difficult to determine whether castration effectively reduces recidivism. Studies of both surgical and chemical castrations have shown lower reoffense rates by offenders undergoing the treatment in comparison with either control groups or with the reported pretreatment behavior of the offenders themselves (Chism, 2013; Meyer & Cole, 1997). However, such studies are few in number and often rely on self-report data. Although its 1999 authorizing law was repealed in 2011, Oregon's chemical castration treatment program resulted in a more rigorous study than most. Three groups were studied: men judged to need the chemical treatment and who actually received it; men who were recommended for the treatment but, for a

Voices in Corrections

How has GPS tracking of probationers affected the way probation officers do their job?

Mr. Craig Spingarn, a former Probation Supervisor in Colorado, is currently a Crime Analyst for the Denver Police Department.

It was nearly midnight when the first call came in. A victim of a sexual assault was reporting that the defendant in her case had just been seen leaving the area in front of her home. She was afraid, and wanted the offender locked up for violating the no-contact order that was in place. The police dispatch center contacted me, as I was the assigned probation officer (PO) in this matter. I explained that I had not received an alert on this individual, but I could verify his location.

Quickly, while still on the phone with the police dispatcher, I connected a wireless laptop to a secure Internet site that provides GPS tracking for the sex offenders on my caseload. In a matter of minutes, I located the offender at his home, scanned a quick history, and found that he had not changed location for more than four hours. I was also able to verify that he had not consumed any alcohol, by a quick scan of the sobriety-monitoring device attached to his ankle, also done remotely from my laptop. With this information, the victim was reassured that the offender was well away from her and that it must have been someone else who was observed.

That was an interesting experience and an excellent example of how new technology has affected the offender, victim, community, and the probation officer. During the last 15 years, the influence of technology on community-based corrections has grown exponentially. It was not too long ago that a PO would rely on a field book, card files, and leg work. Today we have the benefit of integrated information systems, global satellite surveillance, and instant drug recognition, to name just a few.

Officers now take mobile computing devices into the field and link up to their office network via a broadband cellular network. Here they can take the office to the offender and observe more of their behavior in a natural setting. The clients in turn are able to meet with their PO while remaining at home or at a job site, saving them time and money. Technology has allowed the PO to move away from the office and have a greater presence in the community.

The use of new technology offers safety to the community while holding the offenders more accountable for their behavior; at the same time allowing the offender the benefit of remaining in the community. In the past, the offender in the scenario above may have been free to harass the victim without the risk of being caught, and the probation officer would have to venture out into the field in the middle of the night to learn much of the information now provided by technology. Many of the offenders who in the past would have been incarcerated are allowed to be in the community while being monitored by one of several electronic methods. This in turn saves the resources of jails and prisons for the most dangerous high-risk offenders.

Source: From Corrections: A Contemporary Introduction by Leanne F Alarid and Philip L Reichel. Copyright © 2008 by Pearson Education.

2008	2009	2010	2015
Louisiana allows judge to order chemical castration for convicted rapists and other sex offenders (Millhollon, 2008).	**Poland becomes** the only European country making chemical castration mandatory for adults who rape children or immediate family members (Easton, 2009).	**South Korea enacts** mandatory chemical castration of child sex offenders upon court order. This can include first-time offenders (Hyun-jung, 2010).	**Guam becomes** the only U.S. territory to adopt chemical castration for persons convicted of sex crimes and who are eligible for parole or post-prison supervision (KUAM News, 2015).

variety of reasons, did not receive it; and men deemed not to need the treatment. Results of the study found significant differences among the groups, with men actually receiving the treatment committing no new sexual offenses and committing fewer overall offenses and violations compared with the other two groups (Maletzky, Tolan, & McFarland, 2006). Results such as these suggest that at least some versions of technological incapacitation of male sex offenders may hold promise for the future.

▶ Rehabilitation

Some people do not consider rehabilitation as either a form of or justification for punishment. It just does not seem right to think of efforts to "restore someone to good health" as being a type of punishment. But consider the point raised by Weihofen (1971), who argues that any measure that deprives people of their liberty against their will is essentially punitive in nature, no matter how well intentioned are the authorities who administer the measure. When the choice of where and how you will spend Wednesday afternoons for the next nine months is your probation officer's rather than yours, it makes the sentences no less punitive just because the goal is to help you earn a high school equivalency diploma. The point is, someone else is making the choice for you. So, let's consider how rehabilitation operates as a punishment rationale.

The idea of punishment for purposes of rehabilitation is possibly the newest of the five punishment rationales. This newcomer, as Figure 2–6 reviews, has a lengthy history, from the Quakers' desire to reclaim the offender's soul to the contemporary version of rehabilitation as a way to reintegrate the offender back into society.

The contemporary approach to rehabilitation is likely linked to what Travis (2005) calls the **iron law of imprisonment**, meaning that essentially all prisoners—except the few who die in custody—will return to live in free society. The extensive use of imprisonment since the 1980s has resulted in a dramatic increase in the number of prisoners flowing back into the community after their release from prison. In fact, Figure 2–7 shows that in recent years prisons have released more prisoners than they have admitted. As the reality of the iron law of imprisonment sinks in, community members seem increasingly concerned about the type of neighbors these former prisoners are going to make. The community is, in other words, interested in having as neighbors people who have been rehabilitated from their previous law-violating ways. However, contemporary rehabilitation seems less treatment-based and more reentry-based. That is to say, whereas traditional rehabilitation followed a medical model that focused on the offender's diagnosis and treatment plan, reentry programs focus on both offender and community to provide programs geared toward reintegration or restoration of the offender into the community.

The need for this emphasis on rehabilitation as reentry becomes apparent upon seeing statistics showing that prisoners today are ill-prepared for life on the outside. The Justice Policy Center at the Urban Institute, which is actively involved in

TIMELINE	The History of Rehabilitation as a Punishment Philosophy		
Late Eighteenth Century	**Late Nineteenth Century**	**Twentieth Century** (especially 1960s & 1970s)	**Twenty-First Century**
Rehabilitation as reclamation aimed to rescue wrongdoers from the evil that had overcome them. Pennsylvania Quakers believed imprisonment would bring the offender back to the correct way of living.	**Rehabilitation as reformation** saw offenders as responsible for changing themselves. Society should provide opportunities from among which offenders must select those most helpful to them.	**Rehabilitation as individualized treatment** viewed criminal behavior as similar to a treatable illness. Following a medical model, the offender was examined, diagnosed, and then treated.	**Rehabilitation as reentry** is a contemporary view that focuses less on offender treatment and more on how the offender can be reintegrated into the community.

FIGURE 2–6 Timeline: The History of Rehabilitation as a Punishment Philosophy.

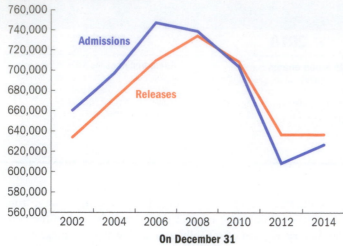

Number of sentenced prisoners

FIGURE 2-7 **Sentenced Prisoners Admitted to and Released from State and Federal Prisons, 2002–2014.**
Source: Created from data in Table 7 in Carson (2015). Prisoners in 2014. (NCJ 248955). Retrieved from Bureau of Justice Statistics website, www.bjs.gov/index.cfm?ty=pbdetail&iid=5387; Table 9 in Carson (2014). Prisoners in 2013 (NCJ 247282). Retrieved from Bureau of Justice Statistics website, www.bjs.gov/index.cfm?ty=pbdetail&iid=5109; and Tables 12 and 13 in Carson and Sabol (2012). Prisoners in 2011 (NCJ 2398808). Retrieved from Bureau of Justice Statistics website, http://www.bjs.gov/index.cfm?ty=pbdetail&iid=4559.

conducting and reporting on prisoner reentry research, notes that the challenges confronting men and women when they enter prison remain—and may even be worse—upon their release. For example, despite the need for employment assistance, few prisoners receive employment-related training in prison. Similar problems are found in the lack of adequate mental and physical health care either in prison or after release, and in the limited or temporary living options available to returning prisoners (Urban Institute, 2006).

Even as the realization that inmates must be prepared for postincarceration life gathers momentum, there remains the feeling that offenders must also be punished for having committed a crime in the first place. It can be argued that this desire to punish a wrongful act is a basic aspect of society. And that point brings us to the punishment philosophy called retribution.

LEARNING OUTCOMES 4 Summarize rehabilitation's development from a reclamation focus to a reentry emphasis.

▶ *Retribution*

Retribution is sometimes mistakenly assumed to be the same as revenge. As Table 2–1 explains, the two concepts, although related, actually differ in several key ways. In its more crude form, retribution was the revenge exhibited in feuds between individuals and families. Today, retribution—but not revenge—is considered a legitimate punishment philosophy because it includes three key elements: (1) formal penal sanction, (2) equity, and (3) just deserts.

In addition to distinguishing retribution and revenge, we can also set retribution apart from the other punishment philosophies by noting retribution's lack of interest in preventing crime. Deterrence, incapacitation, and rehabilitation all have a utilitarian aspect—that is, each hopes that punishment will achieve some goal, have some utility. Figure 2–8 shows that for deterrence, punishment is imposed to either keep criminals

TABLE 2-1 | WHAT RETRIBUTION IS AND ISN'T

Elements of Retribution	How It Differs from Revenge
Formal penal sanction	Informal sanction
Retribution is applied in the name of the public when a law has been violated. For example, a judge sentences Lynn to prison for committing theft.	Revenge is applied individually in retaliation for a perceived wrong. For example, Laura spreads rumors about Lynn as payback for Lynn snubbing Laura.
Equity	Irregular
Retribution maintains that similar crimes and similar criminals should be treated alike. Two people committing burglary for the first time should receive similar sentences and a person committing burglary for the first time should not be punished as harshly as persons committing their third burglary.	When revenge is sought, there can be considerable variation in what is considered appropriate retaliation for similar wrongs. Even the mistreated individual may retaliate differently from separate wrongdoers. Both Scott and Mary push Tammy into the mud, but Tammy pushes Scott back and simply frowns at Mary.
Just deserts	Unbalanced
Punishment must be proportional to the seriousness of the offense and the culpability of the offender. A person who commits assault should be punished more severely than one who damages property, and a person who purposefully struck another in the head with a beer bottle should receive a harsher penalty than one who recklessly ran toward a door and unintentionally hit another in the face with a book.	The person seeking revenge often favors a punishment that is disproportionate to the harmful act. Steal my neighbor's car and I think you should be placed on probation; steal my car and I want you to be put in jail for three years.

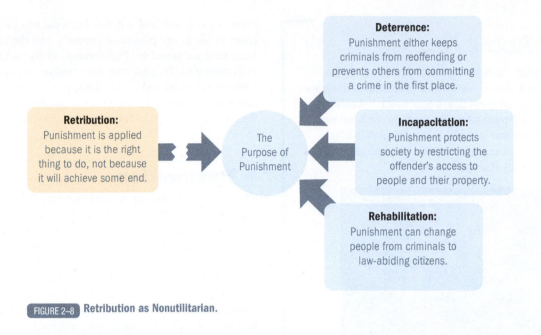

Deterrence:
Punishment either keeps criminals from reoffending or prevents others from committing a crime in the first place.

Retribution:
Punishment is applied because it is the right thing to do, not because it will achieve some end.

The Purpose of Punishment

Incapacitation:
Punishment protects society by restricting the offender's access to people and their property.

Rehabilitation:
Punishment can change people from criminals to law-abiding citizens.

FIGURE 2–8 Retribution as Nonutilitarian.

from reoffending or to prevent others from committing a crime in the first place. Proponents of incapacitation believe punishment can be used to protect society, for at least the period of incapacitation, from the continued misbehavior of the criminal. And the followers of rehabilitation propose that punishment can change people from criminals to law-abiding citizens. Retributivists, however, do not care if criminals or others are deterred, if society is safer while a criminal is locked up, or whether offenders are rehabilitated. Their concern is simply that society carries out its moral obligation to punish people who commit a crime. To be fair, it should be noted that retributivists certainly do not mind if punishment results in crime prevention. However, any prevention that occurs as a result of imposing punishment on an offender is simply a secondary result that is welcome but was neither sought nor intended.

Probably the most difficult problem presented by a retributive philosophy of punishment is determining exactly what the just punishment is for a particular offense. Ellis and Ellis (1989) note that both the crime and the penalty must somehow be measured—crime for its seriousness and penalty for its desert. Of course, deterrence theorists had a similar problem because that philosophy also required a correspondence between crime and penalty—that is, for deterrence to occur, the penalty had to be fixed at a level just harsh enough to convince the offender, or potential offender, that the pain would outweigh the pleasure. There is a difference, however, between the deterrence and retribution view of how a crime and its appropriate penalty are linked. Where deterrence requires correspondence in order to accomplish a goal of crime prevention or reduction, retribution requires correspondence in the sense that an offender justly deserves a certain severity of punishment (Ellis & Ellis, 1989). So, we are back to the problem of deciding which penalty a crime deserves or merits.

Determining when a penalty has provided criminals with their just deserts is no small task. We could ask the public to rate the unpleasantness of a given penalty or to rank penalties according to their level of severity. Neither of these techniques accounts for the individual differences that certainly arise when one person's penalty is another person's mere inconvenience. But more important, these approaches seem better suited to deterrence purposes when trying to find a penalty to prevent or reduce crime. What is really needed is a way to determine what kind (type, level, etc.) of penalty a particular criminal act deserves.

So far, the closest retributivists have come to matching the penalty to the crime is the principle of *lex talionis*, or the law of retaliation. The classic example of this principle is stated in the Bible: "And if any mischief follow, then thou shalt give life for life, eye for eye, tooth for tooth, hand for hand, foot for foot, burning for burning, wound for wound, stripe for stripe" (Exodus 21:23–25). A similar principle is stated in the Koran: "And [as for] the man who steals and the woman who steals, cut off their hands as a punishment for what they have earned" (5:38).

LEARNING OUTCOMES 5 Explain the key ways in which retribution differs from revenge.

This goal of having a punishment equivalent to the crime is infrequently found in U.S. jurisdictions today. The death penalty for homicide is the best example, but more often retribution seeks proportional rather than equivalent punishment.

Nigel Walker (1991) has succinctly described, in the form of two ladder-like scales whose rungs correspond, how retributivists conceive of proportionality (see Figure 2–9). On the penalty ladder, each rung indicates different levels of severity increasing in order from the lowest rungs to the higher ones. Unfortunately, we cannot assume that the distance between each rung indicates any standard progression. In this manner, the third rung might indicate a fine, the fourth could mean a probation sentence, and the fifth could require nine months in jail. But is the progression of severity between the third and

fourth rungs, or even between the fourth and fifth, of similar degree? Possibly more important, is a jail sentence always more severe than a fine or probation? Maybe an offender would actually choose confinement in order to avoid financial hardship. In other words, the ladder's rungs are not only loose, but they may also be interchangeable.

The other ladder is a harm ladder, in which the rungs are well-defined harms. But this ladder remains poorly defined by retributivists. Instead, the second structure more often is a crime seriousness ladder. Its rungs consist of offenses distinguished by their legal definitions: murder, robbery, theft, and so on. Again, the rungs may imply a rank order of seriousness (although, as on the penalty ladder, individuals may differ in their assessment of seriousness), but the distance between rungs cannot be taken to show similar degrees.

To achieve proportionality according to the retributivist, the two ladders are fitted together so that a rod of proportionality could be balanced on corresponding rungs of the two ladders. In this way, the punishment (penalty rung) will match the offense (harm rung). But because of problems such as inconsistent intervals among rungs within and between the ladders, the best a retributivist can claim is that the ladders provide consistency among judges using the ladders—that is, when several judges use the coupled ladders to determine sentences, the penalties will be similar as the harm rung and penalty rung match up. But consistency is not the same as proportionality, and Walker suggests the retributivists have been unable thus far to provide a way to measure both crimes and penalties in order to ensure that offenders get their just deserts.

Another aspect of retributive philosophy deserves mention. It is possible to view the norm of reciprocity as trying to restore equilibrium. Just as the balance is unequal when your friend has invited you to dinner but you have not yet returned the favor, so is it unequal when a criminal has caused the victim harm to his or her person or property and the criminal has not been held accountable. Punishment, in its reciprocal role, can help restore the balance that the criminal has upset. When punishment is considered in this light, a new aspect of the sanction and a new rationale under which it can be discussed emerge as the fifth, and last, punishment philosophy: restoration.

▶ Restoration

The focus of punishment philosophies thus far has been on either the offender (rehabilitation) or the crime (deterrence, incapacitation, and retribution). Increasingly in U.S. jurisdictions, calls are made for a penal philosophy that considers the harm done to the victim when deciding an appropriate punishment for the offender. Restoration is a punishment rationale that attempts to make the victim and the community "whole again" by restoring things, as much as possible, to how they were before the crime occurred. This return to equilibrium provides a link between retribution and restoration because each philosophy is based on the **norm of reciprocity** wherein punishment is a natural response, or reciprocation, to a wrongful act (Newman, 1985). In addition, restoration incorporates reentry (rehabilitation) as a key ingredient for achieving equilibrium.

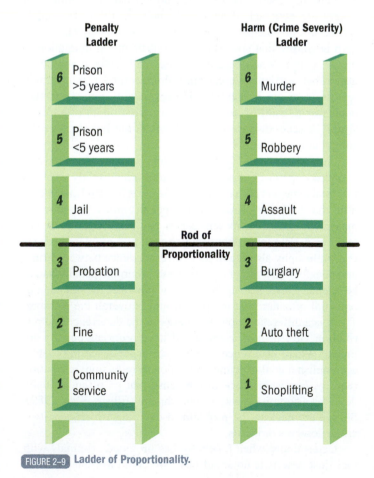

FIGURE 2–9 **Ladder of Proportionality.**

Restorative Practices in Sentencing

- **Victim–offender mediation**
  - This is a process wherein the victim, offender, and community representative work out their version of what would be a fair or just way to restore the balance that the crime upset. The emphasis is less on the sanction (for example, apology, financial compensation, and community service) than on getting the offender to take responsibility, express remorse, and repair the damage.

Restorative Practices in the Community

- **Community reparation boards**
  - This is a postconviction use of restorative justice wherein board members meet with the offender and victim to determine how the offender will repair the harm done and to identify strategies for reducing future offending. These trained board members also monitor and supervise the offender's progress.

- **Citizen circles**
  - During parole, a group comprised of the offender, the offender's family, ex-convicts, employers, victims, the police, and faith-based staff, joins to assist in the reentry process by providing employment opportunities and positive social support.

Restorative Practices in Prison

- **Victim impact classes**
  - These are sessions attended by prisoners while incarcerated where violent crime survivors share their experiences with the hope of effecting positive change in the offender.

FIGURE 2–10 Examples of Restorative Justice Practices.

There is increasing indication that a penal philosophy of restoration will take a prominent role in the twenty-first century. The label attached to this philosophy is **restorative justice** or community justice, and its initial proponents include people such as Howard Zehr (1985) and Mark Umbreit (1989). Although the terms *restorative justice* and *community justice* are used interchangeably in many U.S. communities, this text prefers *restorative justice* since the philosophy is applied in both community and incarceration settings.

Figure 2–10 shows that restorative justice principles are used today for sentencing, during community supervision of the offender, and even in prison. At the sentencing stage, mediation sessions involving both offender and victim take the place of traditional sentencing by a judge. These **victim–offender mediation** programs are most often used with misdemeanor offenses or felony property offenses—especially when the offender is a juvenile or first-time adult offender (Umbreit, Vos, Coates, & Brown, 2003). A unique example of this type of restorative justice is the sentencing circle based on the customs of Native American and Canadian tribal peacemaking. Forming the circle are the offender, the victim, and family, friends, and coworkers of both the offender and the victim; social service personnel; juvenile justice personnel; and interested community members. The judge, prosecutor, and defense attorney may even be present. The group discusses the event and eventually comes to an agreement regarding the best resolution. The "sentence" is either accepted within the group or recommended to the judge at the next court appearance (Kurki, 1999).

Restorative justice programs are used in the community in both postconviction (e.g., community reparation) and prisoner reentry (e.g., citizen circles) formats. An example of the postconviction type is Vermont's statewide **reparative probation program** (one form of probation in Vermont), which combines a suspended probation sentence by the court with elements of community reparation boards. Those boards, numbering 76 across the state, draw on citizen volunteers and corrections employees to place less serious offenders in a situation where they come to understand the consequences of their actions and move toward restoring the community. As long as the probationer completes the reparation board's contract terms and conditions and stays out of trouble for a specified time, the probationer's sentence will be expunged. If an offender does not complete the reparation board conditions, he or she is referred back to court for an executed sentence of probation that remains permanently on his or her criminal record (Humphrey, Burford, & Huey, 2007; Vermont Department of Corrections, 2010). The program, as reviewed in Figure 2–11, is promising.

Prisoner reentry under restorative justice is the process by which incarcerated prisoners get reacquainted with living a regular life in the larger society. Reentry is not an easy process, so restorative justice methods can be used to help ease that transition. In Ohio, **citizen circles** developed with the goal of community collaboration with offenders during their supervision. Parole officers lead the circles, which comprise the offender, the offender's family, ex-convicts, employers, victims, the police, and faith-based staff. The thinking behind this

The Indianapolis (Indiana) Family Group Conferencing Experiment implemented a restorative justice diversion program for young, first-time juvenile offenders. CrimeSolutions.gov (Office of Justice Programs, 2013b) gives the program an evidence rating of "promising" based on a study by McGarrell and Hipple (2007) finding that, compared with a control group, persons in the treatment program were rearrested at a significantly lower level (8% versus 15%) during the period of 13 to 26 weeks following initial arrest. Another program identified as "promising" is the Clarke County (Georgia) Victim Impact Panels (VIPs), which is a restorative justice program operated through the courts (Office of Justice Programs, 2013a). The program's goal is to keep offenders convicted of driving under the influence (DUI) from drinking and driving in the future. Rojek, Coverdill, and Fors (2003) found that after five years, 16% of the offenders who attended victim impact panels were rearrested, compared with 34% of the offenders who did not attend.

FIGURE 2–11 Evidence-Based Practice—Does It Work? Research Supporting Restorative Justice Programs.

is that ex-convicts are less likely to return to crime if they feel accepted by their community rather than shunned. Like all other restorative justice programs, the offender must voluntarily participate and be willing to set goals that focus on productive legitimate behavior. The community board assists the offender in employment opportunities and positive social support. In turn, the offender comes to understand that being a positive community member demands responsibility and obligation (Rhine, Matthews, Sampson, & Daley, 2003; State of Ohio, 2007).

Many predatory criminals who commit violent crimes are able to victimize other people because they reduce them to objects or in some way justify that the crime has little impact on the victim (e.g., the victim is insured or the victim deserved it). A common complaint of traditional methods of punishment for violent crimes is that offenders rarely understand how their actions affected the victims' lives and their loved ones. Restorative practices in prison attempt to remedy these concerns by encouraging or requiring that prisoners attend **victim impact classes** while incarcerated. The session leaders are violent crime survivors and have agreed to come forward in an educator role to share their experiences with groups of offenders in hopes that their story will make a difference in offenders' lives. Although the victims may not be necessarily matched with their actual offenders, the participants represent all crime survivors and their families.

More than 70% of U.S. jurisdictions have victim impact classes in place, and the effects of these programs are quite promising. Participation in Connecticut Department of Corrections victim impact classes showed significant improvement in offenders' understanding of victimization facts, knowledge of victims' rights, and sensitivity to the plight of victims when compared with a matched control group that did not attend the classes. A separate study in Iowa and another that involved four states (California, Ohio, Tennessee, and Virginia) had similar results, leading researchers to believe that the classes are reinforcing the message that being victimized is a traumatic experience (Office for Victims of Crime, 2010).

LEARNING OUTCOMES 6 Describe how restorative justice principles are used in sentencing, during community supervision, and in prison.

Criticism of Restorative Justice

It is appropriate to briefly note here some of the criticisms directed at the restoration philosophy. For example, retributivists often see it as too lenient, proponents of deterrence do not think it can deter (either specifically or generally), and those favoring incapacitation fail to see how society is protected from continued harm. Some people are concerned that restorative justice will unnecessarily increase the number of people brought under the net of social control. That situation—referred to as net widening—expresses a concern that programs designed as alternatives to the traditional process actually end up bringing more people into the system.

Another criticism of restorative justice is that it can promote discrimination. Some critics of the restorative process warn that it may perpetuate existing social inequities when one party has greater economic, intellectual, political, or physical power than the other. Proponents respond that the restorative process relies on all participants negotiating in good faith and not using mediation to legitimize an unfair solution. Critics feel that relying on good faith and achieving fairness are not always compatible.

Think About It…

A criticism of restorative justice is that it may not work when one person is in a subordinate position. For example, weaker victims may be under pressure to accept too little in the hope of

Keith Publicover/Shutterstock

quickly obtaining an agreement and being left alone—or, they may argue for what they think they can get rather than what they think is fair. Is this a legitimate criticism of restorative justice? What procedures could be used to lessen the likelihood that weaker parties may accept agreements that give them less than they could have obtained if the power imbalance did not exist?

People in a weaker or subordinate position (such as students to school officials or employees to employers) may be under pressure to accept too little in the hope of obtaining an agreement and being left alone. Or weaker parties (such as persons with fewer financial resources) may argue for what they think they can get rather than what they think is fair. In other words, weaker parties, whether victim or offender, may accept agreements that give them much less than they could have obtained if the power imbalance did not exist. Even mediators could influence the outcome if they are of a higher social standing than one or both participants. For example, mediation sessions could end up simply providing opportunities for predominantly middle-class helping professionals to supervise and control the private lives of the working class (Merry, 1989).

These are valid concerns, and proponents of restorative justice note that the programs and procedures must be continually evaluated to make sure that they are operating in as nondiscriminatory a fashion as possible. Some authors have also noted that restorative justice is certainly no more likely to discriminate than is the traditional formal justice process. In fact, it may even have the potential to be more responsive to cultural diversity. Maxwell and Morris (1996), for example, suggest that restorative justice processes may challenge misconceptions in cases involving racial strife and could even increase understanding among different subcultures—goals the traditional justice system does not even attempt.

As Bright (1997) reminds us, social injustices in society are bound to influence any system of justice, including restorative justice. However, because restorative justice involves the community members in an attempt to resolve the problem, the possibility for engagement and interaction may provide opportunities to address even broader issues such as inequalities, discrimination, and prejudice.

Despite those valid concerns, restorative justice has its proponents and has been shown to have positive outcomes. Also, its ability to incorporate aspects of retribution and rehabilitation suggest to some that the restorative philosophy may foretell the twenty-first century's response to the question "Why do we punish?"

Make the Punishment Fit the Crime

A distinguishing feature of retribution as punishment is the goal of just deserts—that is, the offender receives a punishment that is deserved and proportional to the crime. Some judges have come up with quite unique sentences when trying to determine what particular punishment an offender deserves. For example, an Ohio woman who drove on the sidewalk to get around a school bus as children were getting off was ordered to stand on a Cleveland street corner during rush-hour traffic holding a sign that said, "Only an idiot would drive on the sidewalk to avoid a school bus" (Edwins, 2013). For a man who had called an officer a "pig" during a confrontation with the police, the judge gave the choice of three days in jail or two hours standing next to a 350-pound pig with a sign saying, "This is not a police officer." The offender chose the pig option (Libaw, 2002).

Punishments meant to shame offenders were common in colonial America when criminals were sentenced to the pillory, the stocks, or to be branded. Today, the public nature of those punishments is still reflected in sentences such as those where offenders are required to hold signs announcing their crime.

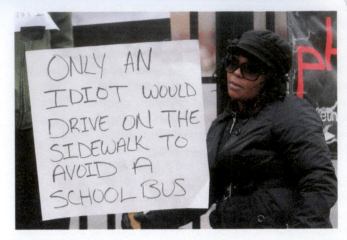

Tony Dejak/AP Images

The use of shaming punishments raises several interesting questions:

1. **Are shaming punishments still appropriate in modern society? Why or why not?**

2. **Might shaming punishments support any other punishment philosophies than retribution? If so, which ones and why?**

3. **If shaming punishments were used as an alternative to imprisonment, would they provide a more equitable, or even less abusive, punishment than does imprisonment?**

4. **Check the last several days of your local newspaper and find details of some minor crime that was committed. Propose a unique sentence for the offender(s) that you believe would provide just deserts.**

LEARNING OUTCOMES 1

Describe the five primary punishment philosophies.

The five punishment philosophies—or reasons for punishment—are deterrence (both specific and general), incapacitation (both selective and general), rehabilitation, retribution, and restoration.

1. Which punishment philosophy is being used when a judge sentences a thief to three years in prison as a way to discourage other people from stealing?

2. Which punishment philosophies are reflected in the court rules for California?

3. Which punishment philosophy does Colorado emphasize that is not so clearly found in Alabama, California, or Texas?

deterrence Discouraging future criminal acts by both the offender and others in the population.

incapacitation Restricting an offender's freedom of movement through isolation from the general population.

rehabilitation Providing the offender with skills, attitudes, and norms that enable him or her to be law-abiding.

retribution Just and adequate punishment.

restoration Restoring the victim, community, and offender through accountability, respect for the law and the legal process, and attention to victim needs.

LEARNING OUTCOMES 2

Discuss the deterrence philosophy of punishment by understanding the effects of specific and general deterrence.

In order for a punishment to deter an offender or others from committing a crime, the punishment must be certain, severe, and swiftly applied.

1. How does specific deterrence differ from general deterrence?

2. Why would certainty of punishment require constant monitoring of people?

3. If one person views probation as a minor nuisance and another person sees it as a major inconvenience, how can severity be achieved in sentencing?

4. Is it possible for punishment to be swift and still protect the rights of suspects and defendants?

5. Publicity is considered an important, but not a key, element for successful deterrence. Should it be given greater weight and actually be a fourth key element? Why or why not?

specific deterrence Seeks to prevent crime by using punishment to discourage a person from committing additional crimes.

general deterrence Seeks to prevent crime by using punishment to discourage people from committing a crime in the first place.

LEARNING OUTCOMES 3

Compare and contrast selective and general incapacitation.

Selective incapacitation relies on characteristics of the criminal to identify which offenders need to be in prison, whereas general incapacitation emphasizes crime characteristics when sentencing to prison.

1. What is the common premise upon which both selective and general incapacitation are based?

2. Name five personal characteristics you believe many or most criminals have in common. If these characteristics were used to identify people who should be sentenced to prison, could sentencing end up being unfair to a particular segment of society?

3. Would justice be served by using technological incapacitation to temporarily disable (e.g., make blind or deaf, or confine to a wheelchair) a person as punishment for a crime?

selective incapacitation Imprisonment is reserved for those very few offenders who must truly be locked away for society's protection.

general incapacitation Imprisonment is acceptable and desirable on an extensive scale for a wide range of offenders as a means of crime prevention.

technological incapacitation Using technologies such as critical organ surgery, chemical treatment, and electronic monitoring to restrict an offender's freedom of movement.

LEARNING OUTCOMES 4

Summarize rehabilitation's development from a reclamation focus to a reentry emphasis.

The concept of rehabilitation began with an eighteenth-century belief that criminals had to be rescued from evil ways, and then progressed through nineteenth-century views of offenders as responsible for reforming themselves and twentieth-century ideas that criminals were ill and needed individualized treatment. Today's view is that rehabilitation should focus on how the offender can be reintegrated in the community.

1. How did the belief in reclamation differ from the idea of reformation?

2. How could one argue that the twentieth-century view of rehabilitation followed a medical model?

3. What is the "iron law of imprisonment," and is it likely to always be true?

4. Is it possible to achieve the goal of rehabilitation while implementing the goal of incapacitation?

iron law of imprisonment The realization that almost all prisoners will return to free society.

LEARNING OUTCOMES 5

Explain the key ways in which retribution differs from revenge.

Although closely related, retribution is distinguished from its better known cousin by noting that retribution, but not revenge, is a legitimate punishment philosophy requiring formal penal sanction, equity, and just deserts.

1. Should revenge, rather than retribution, be a punishment philosophy? Why or why not?

2. Design your own ladder of proportionality and describe how you matched the rungs on the harm ladder with the proportional rungs on the penalty ladder.

3. Some people argue that retributionists must favor the death penalty for homicide. Others suggest that as long as society's most severe penalty is applied to its most serious crime, retribution is achieved. That could mean that a retributionist favors life imprisonment rather than death as a proportional punishment if society chose life imprisonment as its most severe penalty. Do you agree with this assessment of retribution?

lex talionis The law of retaliation.

LEARNING OUTCOMES 6

Describe how restorative justice principles are used in sentencing, during community supervision, and in prison.

Restorative justice can be found at every stage in the justice process because it can be used to determine the appropriate penalty (as is done in mediation sessions), while an offender is at liberty in the community (reparative probation programs are an example), or even when the offender is in prison (as is shown with victim impact classes).

1. Explain the norm of reciprocity.

2. Why is restorative justice said to place more emphasis on the victim than do other punishment philosophies?

3. Why is victim–offender mediation considered a good way to achieve restorative justice?

4. In what way can the use of restorative justice principles help make the community whole again after a crime has occurred?

5. What is net widening, and do you think it is a legitimate concern?

6. Describe how restorative justice could be used even in situations where one of the involved parties is in a subordinate position to the other.

norm of reciprocity The view of punishment as a natural response, or reciprocation, to a wrongful act.

restorative justice The process, also called community justice, wherein victim, offender, and community representatives determine a fair or just way to restore the balance that the crime had upset.

victim–offender mediation An application of restorative justice principles at the sentencing stage by having mediation sessions involving both offender and victim take the place of traditional sentencing by a judge.

reparative probation program A Vermont restorative justice program at the postconviction stage that combines a suspended probation sentence with elements of community reparation boards.

citizen circles An Ohio restorative justice program at the prisoner reentry stage that encourages community collaboration with offenders during their supervision in the community.

victim impact classes Restorative justice program, typically offered in prison, wherein prisoners hear violent crime survivors share their experiences with the hope of effecting positive change in the offender.

Additional Links

Go to **http://topics.law.cornell.edu** and find the "State Law Resources" section; then click on "listing by jurisdiction" to find the link for your state. Try to find a section that explains the punishment philosophies that should be guiding sentencing.

Visit **www.urban.org** and do a search for "reentry mapping." Find and read about the Reentry Mapping Network, which helps in understanding the spatial dynamics of incarceration and prisoner reentry.

The National Association of Community and Restorative Justice (NACRJ) promotes forms of social and restorative justice that are equitable, sustainable, and socially constructive. Find examples on its website at **www.nacrj.org/**.

3

Correctional Practices from Ancient to Contemporary Times

1 Describe key features of the Code of Hammurabi, Mosaic Law, Roman law, and law during the Middle Ages.

2 Discuss the use of transportation to handle criminal offenders and identify the two important themes in the development of imprisonment as punishment.

3 Compare and contrast the Pennsylvania and Auburn prison systems in terms of their architecture, orienting strategies, and advantages/disadvantages.

4 Describe how men's and women's prisons differed during the reformatory movement of the nineteenth century.

5 Explain how penal systems in the South and West differed from those in the East and summarize reasons for those differences.

6 Summarize the development of prison programs and the treatment of women and other minorities during the early, middle, and late twentieth century.

7 Explain the effects of changing public opinion on the use of imprisonment and prison alternatives in the twenty-first century.

Hernan H. Hernandez A./Shutterstock

INTRO SENTENCE FOR SHOPLIFTING? A TRIP TO THE COLONIES!

On January 16, 1760, Joseph Tedar, 32 years old, was tried at London's Old Bailey. He was charged with stealing one pair of silver shoe buckles worth 10 shillings from Robert Parr's shop. The shop clerk explained to the court that Tedar asked to be shown some silver buckles: "I shew'd him some, and he chose out a pair . . . He stood at the door some time to look at them, then put them into his pocket, and went away with them. . . I went out from behind the counter and cry'd stop thief." Tedar was caught and found guilty of shoplifting and sentenced to be transported (Old Bailey Proceedings Online, n.d.).

Most likely, Tedar would have ended up in Virginia Colony or Maryland Colony. At either location, he would have been sold as a convict servant to private individuals soon after he landed. Buyers were typically plantation owners looking for persons with skill sets that would prove useful on the plantation. Because most convicts had no identifiable skills, they were generally forced to work as common field hands alongside slaves or laboring in the iron mines. Because Tedar announced in court that he had been a sailor, he may have been more fortunate and ended up on a boat (Vaver, 2009).

The American colonists did not have transportation available to them as a way to handle criminal offenders. They did, however, make use of the other common British

sentences: corporal and capital punishment. But this chapter is mostly concerned with punishments, such as long-term imprisonment, that were developed in nineteenth-century America and how those developments influenced what has come since.

 **Is there a place in today's society for such punishments as transportation and banishment?**

Concepts of crime and punishment have evolved over the centuries from the ancient blood feuds sparked by harm done to a person or property to today's complex legal systems that distinguish among categories of crime and varieties of punishment. A key point in this developmental process occurred when responsibility for punishing antisocial behavior moved from being an obligation of the harmed person or family to being the responsibility of the entire community.

As Roth (2011) explains, the mode of revenge was taken from a victim and placed in the collective hands of the community. This process is typically established with a written code describing desirable behavior and specifying punishment for those not complying. Key features of law in ancient Babylonia, Hebrew law, Roman law, and law during the medieval period provided the basis for society's response to criminal offenders in modern times.

▶ Corrections in the Ancient and Medieval World

The **Code of Hammurabi**, as identified in Figure 3–1, provided the basis for Western criminal and civil law, and defined procedures for commerce and trade. It also introduced the concept of *lex talionis*, which is commonly known as "eye for an eye" justice. The Hebrew legal system (**Mosaic Law**) started when God gave Moses two stone tablets containing the Ten Commandments. Those religious and moral imperatives are recorded in the book of Exodus, which—along with Genesis, Leviticus, Numbers, and Deuteronomy—makes up the first five books of the Bible. These books, known as the Torah to Jewish people, provided the base for the Hebrew legal system. Mosaic Law continued the principle of *lex talionis,* with such proclamations as "life for life, eye for eye, tooth for tooth" (Exodus 21:23–24), but expanded it to include the concept of proportionality(recall Chapter 2's discussion of proportionality as a key aspect of retribution). Rather than literally requiring an eye for an eye, scholars of Jewish law understand the proclamation as setting

forth a commandment that the punishment should be no more severe than the crime. In that manner, "an eye for eye, or a tooth for a tooth" is seen as limiting what kind of response the injured party could expect (Roth, 2011).

The earliest form of written Roman law dates to about 450 BCE, when a council of 10 men inscribed the rights of Roman citizens on 12 bronze tablets. The **Twelve Tables**, which provided the basis for private rights of Roman citizens, consisted mainly of ancient custom and concerned procedural more than substantive law. Nevertheless, it added to the legal base and punishment types for what eventually became sophisticated legal systems and a greater variety of punishments. Developments continued into the Middle Ages as societies struggled to establish just systems

> LEARNING OUTCOMES 1 Describe key features of the Code of Hammurabi, Mosaic Law, Roman law, and law during the Middle Ages.

1800–1600 BCE	1200 BCE–100 CE	500 BCE–550 CE	400–1400 CE
Legal Systems in Babylonia King Hammurabi (reign circa 1792–1750 BCE) provides one of the first known bodies of law. The Code of Hammurabi introduces the concept of *lex talionis* (the law of retaliation).	**Mosaic Law** Moses receives from God two stone tablets containing the Ten Commandments and these along with the entire Torah provide a base for the Hebrew legal system. Mosaic Law continues the principle of *lex talionis*, but expands it to include the concept of proportionality.	**Roman Law** The Twelve Tables (451–450 BCE) provide the basis for private rights of Roman citizens. Prescribed punishments include the death penalty, early forms of imprisonment, and some compensation penalties.	**Law in the Medieval Period** Increased attempts to move conflict resolution out of the hands of individuals and into the courts. This is reflected in the increased importance of the British justices of the peace, who are authorized to hear misdemeanor cases and the occasional felony.

FIGURE 3–1   Timeline: Ancient and Medieval Times.

for responding to law violators and experimented with other punishment types.

The Middle Ages, the medieval period from the fifth century to the early fifteenth century, saw changes to crime and punishment throughout Europe. Developments in England were especially important to the correctional systems in the United States because colonial America was heavily influenced by British custom and practice. Upon his arrival in England, William the Conqueror (reigning from 1066 to 1087) established a system of royal courts with primary interest in settling disputes of landholders. By the mid-1300s, the justice of the peace was becoming the cornerstone of British law and played a major role in maintaining law and order. Punishments during this period moved away from capital punishment and toward mutilation, although convicted offenders often still died from such punishments as having their eyes put out or their testicles cut off (Roth, 2011). By the end of the Middle Ages, punishment became less cruel and there was a movement toward exhibitory punishments, such as stocks and pillories and other shame punishments.

▶ Corrections in Seventeenth- and Eighteenth-Century England

Many histories of American correctional practices begin with happenings in seventeenth-century Europe because that is when we start seeing punishment types that are more familiar to us today. It is during these centuries that we see the first widespread use of transportation to handle criminal offenders and the institutional base for what would become long-term imprisonment was laid.

Transportation

Attempts to rid a community of crime by tossing out the criminals have a certain appeal. This "out of sight, out of mind" philosophy had its initial form in the **banishment** of wrongdoers from the village, expulsion to sea as a galley slave, and

eventually through **transportation** to faraway lands. Banishing misbehaving villagers meant there was no need to worry about that person's future behavior. Similarly, transportation of criminals had as one goal the removal of criminals to a place where they could do no harm. But, although banishment had little economic impact on the sending village other than being a very cheap method of social control, transportation was touted as having specific economic benefits.

Transportation was used by European countries such as France (especially to French Guiana), Russia (to Siberia), Portugal (to places such as Mozambique and Brazil), and Italy (to islands off the Tuscan coast). South American countries such as Chile and Ecuador (to islands in the Pacific) also transported criminals (Barnes & Teeters, 1943). But the country attracting the most attention has been England, which used transportation for economic purposes.

> **LEARNING OUTCOMES 2** Discuss the use of transportation to handle criminal offenders and identify the two important themes in the development of imprisonment as punishment.

The first indication of transportation's use in England was in 1598 when, plagued by unemployment at a time when labor was lacking in the new American colonies, officials decided to ship some offenders to the colonies. Although such activity continued on a primarily informal basis, transportation did not become an official aspect of England's punishment system until specific laws were passed by Parliament in the seventeenth century. The acts provided that persons found guilty of just about any felony could be sent to the West Indies or to American plantations as laborers. But despite the existence of such laws, transportation as a major component of the British penal system did not occur until the eighteenth century. With the passage of the Transportation Act of 1718, transportation became a possible substitute for execution or was used as a punishment in its own right.

The actual transporting of the criminal was a duty given to individuals, usually ship captains, who contracted for rights to the prisoner's labor. Ship captains could transfer that right to another person, so when transport ships arrived in the colonies, the captains auctioned prisoners off to the highest bidders. Historians estimate that some 50,000 prisoners were transported, primarily from England and Ireland, to the American colonies before 1775 (Christianson, 1998; Hughes, 1987; Shaw, 1966).

When the American Revolution stopped transportation to England's former colony in North America, the British turned to their new colony of Australia. In the United States, the prisoners had become indentured servants, and the British government gave up all responsibility for them. In Australia, the government took responsibility for shipping the prisoners and continued to have control over them after their arrival in Australia.

From 1788 to 1868, over 160,000 convicts were transported from England and Ireland to the British colonies in Australia. As Figure 3–2 shows, women were included among the offenders eligible for transportation. During the entire transportation period, about 24,000 of the transportees were women, typically in their teens and early twenties. The percentage of women was especially high during the first decade of the 1800s, when more than 80% of all convicts transported were women, but fell to less than 20% in the 1820s ("Convicts in Australia," 1987).

The initial increase in women transportees was linked in part to a hope that the women would act as a moralizing influence over Australia's coarse masculine society of settlers and ex-convicts. But the expected positive influence did not materialize, and one colonial official admitted, "The influence of female convicts is wholly valueless upon male convicts; women of depraved character do them no good whatsoever" (quoted in Zedner, 1995, pp. 330–331). Apparently, such officials did not see the assignment of the transported women to brothel work, or simply marrying them off to male convicts and settlers, as playing a role in the women's self-concept and in how they were perceived by others. As Zedner explains, life in the Australian colonies for transported women made it all but impossible for even well-intentioned women to retain their character (1995, p. 331). Disillusioned with the inability of the women to have a positive influence, fewer and fewer provinces would accept female transportees, and by mid-century, they were not accepted anywhere in Australia.

Although the felons transported to Australia remained prisoners rather than becoming indentured servants, the penal colony governor could assign a convict to a free settler who would put the prisoner to work. Most convicts were lent out as laborers to the settlers, who then gave the prisoner food and shelter in return for his or her work. Those prisoners who were left unassigned—maybe 1 in 10—were kept by the British government in penal colonies and put to work on public projects (Hughes, 1987).

Prisons Before the Prison

There are examples of imprisonment being used as punishment in ancient times, but secure confinement was more typically used to prepare offenders for the torture that would soon extract a confession, to await their execution or banishment, or even to coerce payment of debts. The idea of using long-term imprisonment in a secure facility as a punishment for convicted felons did not fully occur until the nineteenth century. But the pre-nineteenth-century institutions serving as forerunners to the modern penitentiary provided important philosophies and practices that continue to have an impact today. Notable examples of those forerunners include **hospice facilities** and **houses of correction**, as shown in Figure 3–3. Together these institutions gave rise to two important themes in the development of imprisonment as punishment. One was the idea that convicts should be isolated in order to encourage penitence and to prevent cross-contamination of evil ideas. A second theme was that prisoners should be required to work at hard labor on the assumption that such labor would deter them from future crime and could provide a profit for the institution. These themes had parallel development during the sixteenth and seventeenth centuries and can be traced through the hospice facilities (representing the isolation theme) and the houses of correction (representing the work theme). The idea of isolation continues today, but primarily for purposes of discipline or protection, as reflected in the Voices in Corrections feature.

With the procedures developed at the hospice facilities and the houses of correction providing the ideas of separating prisoners and putting them to work, the concept of punishment through imprisonment was ready to move to the next stage. In England, this was accomplished through the efforts of John Howard, who is credited with formalizing the penitentiary system.

In 1773 John Howard, often considered the greatest prison reformer of modern times, was elected high sheriff of Bedfordshire, England. Through this position, he was made aware of the deplorable conditions existing in the English gaols (jails) and **prison hulks** of his day. The hulks, which were old merchant and naval ships that had been converted into floating prisons, came into use after the American colonies declared

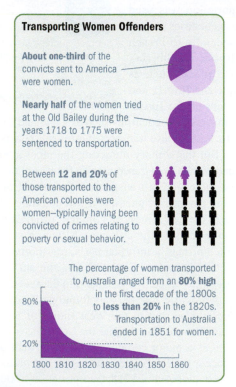

FIGURE 3–2 **Transporting Women Offenders.**
References: Convicts in Australia. (1987). In J. C. R. Camm & J. McQuilton (Eds.), Australians: A historical atlas (pp. 200–201). New South Wales, Australia: Fairfax Syme & Weldon Associates; Zedner, L. (1995). Wayward sisters: The prison for women. In N. Morris & D. J. Rothman (Eds.), The Oxford history of the prison (pp. 229–361). New York, NY: Oxford University Press.

Convicts should be isolated to encourage penitence and prevent cross-contamination of evil ideas.

Represented by hospice facilities first used in Europe during the sixteenth century.

Hospice of St. Michael provides an especially good example.
- Built in 1704 in Rome for misbehaving boys
- Boys worked together at hard labor during the day and were locked alone in their cells at night
- Architectural forerunner to penitentiaries with outside rooms or cells arranged on three tiers of a rectangular structure
- Not truly a penitentiary since other parts of the facility housed orphans and infirmed elderly men and women

Prisoners should be required to work hard at disagreeable tasks.

Represented by houses of correction (or workhouses) that began appearing in the late sixteenth century.

Bridewell House provides an especially good example.
- Former palace converted in 1557 as England's first workhouse
- Held London's vagrants, beggars, and corrupt men and women sent by the courts
- Husbands, parents, and masters could have disobedient and wayward wives, children, and servants taken to the workhouse
- Proved successful and spread throughout England and across the European continent

FIGURE 3–3 **Development of Imprisonment as Punishment.**

References: Barnes, H. E., & Teeters, N. K. (1943). New horizons in criminology: The American crime problem. New York, NY: Prentice Hall.; Dobash, R. P., Dobash, R. E., & Gutteridge, S. (1986). The imprisonment of women. New York, NY: Basil Blackwell.; Eriksson, T. (1976). The reformers: An historical survey of pioneer experiments in the treatment of criminals (C. Djurklou, Trans.). New York, NY: Elsevier.; Johnston, N. (1973). The human cage: A brief history of prison architecture. Philadelphia, PA: American Foundation Inc.; Spierenburg, P. (1995). The body and the state: Early modern Europe. In N. Morris & D. J. Rothman (Eds.), The Oxford history of the prison (pp. 49–77). New York, NY: Oxford University Press.

their independence from England and closed their ports to British prisoner transportation ships. Although envisioned as a temporary measure, the act authorizing use of prison hulks lasted for 80 years and many prisoners served their entire sentence on the hulks. Most of the 6,000 convicts imprisoned on hulks at any given time during the 80-year period were taken off the ships by day to perform hard labor. Hygiene standards on the hulks were so poor that disease spread quickly and mortality rates of around 30% were quite common (PortCities London, n.d.).

Because of Howard's attacks on the prevailing system, in 1774, Parliament corrected some abuses and tried to improve the sanitary conditions of the gaols. Howard, however, believed there still had to be better ways to house offenders. In 1775, he visited institutions in Paris, Amsterdam, Mannheim, Ghent, and Rome to see what could be learned from the institutions operating there. In some parts of Europe, he found conditions that were as bad as those in England, but other places impressed him with their treatment of the convicts.

In one European house of correction, for example, Howard noted that the prisoners' cells had a sleeping bench and appropriate bedding, and that the prisoners themselves were given adequate food, were allowed to perform work, and could attend daily religious services. Such procedures stood in stark contrast to conditions in England, where Howard had found prisoners being forced to sleep on damp dungeon floors or required to go hungry because they could not afford to buy food from their jailers. At the Hospice of St. Michael, Howard was quite taken with the monastic philosophy of doing penance in seclusion. He returned to England with a wealth of new information and immediately set about advocating changes to the operation of English gaols and prisons.

In 1777, Howard published a book entitled *The State of Prisons in England and Wales.* Eventually, the English Parliament used Howard's book to provide the basic principles underlying the **1779 Penitentiary Act** (Barnes & Teeters, 1943; Dobash, Dobash, & Gutteridge, 1986):

- Prisoners should be housed in secure and sanitary facilities.
- Those facilities should undergo systematic inspection.
- Fees for basic needs and services, such as food, should be abolished.
- Discipline at the facilities should follow a reformatory regime.

Voices in Corrections

What was segregation like?

ARDITH "SUNSHINE" SMITH was incarcerated over eight years in state and federal prison institutions. She earned a Bachelor of Arts degree in criminology/criminal justice from the University of Missouri–Kansas City. She remains devoted to helping former inmates and others in need to achieve acceptance back into society.

In prison, you have little control over other people's actions, and sometimes inmates are forced into situations that require a strong defense. Acts of violence, theft, attitude adjustments, or numerous punitive infractions can result in solitary confinement, single cell segregation, or strip cell segregation. The type of infraction determines which type of segregation you receive and whether you walk to segregation, escorted by the guards, or whether you are physically subdued and dragged to confinement.

You may request segregation from general population if you need to get yourself together. When my children's birthdays, my birthday, or holidays came around, I would request administrative segregation so that the other inmates did not see my pain. In each type of segregation, the length of confinement is determined by the administration and case managers. The guards can make recommendations since they interact with you on a daily basis.

The worst type of segregation is strip cell, where you are put naked in a bare cell. There is a hole in the floor for a toilet and no toilet tissue. You are not allowed personal items, and if you do not [know] someone who works in the kitchen, you should fast until they move you to a different level of segregation. Your food can be tampered with by inmates who either don't like you or have received compensation from another inmate.

After a period of time in single cell segregation, you can request television, radio, writing materials, or library books. In this type of cell, you have a bed and combination water fountain, sink, and toilet. You leave the cell for showers once a week and recreation amounts to one hour a week. I requested recreation at night while the "camp" was locked in their rooms so I could breathe fresh air and look at the stars.

Solitary confinement has several cells in a pod with women of infractions of a less serious nature. You cannot see each other but can talk as long as the noise level stays reasonable. It requires cooperation from each inmate to achieve this form of communication. If you need a guard, you must yell "guard" into a speaker located in the ceiling of your cell. They get to you when they get to you!

To keep track of the days without writing materials, you can rub your toothbrush onto the wall to count the days. Other women have usually already made marks on the walls, and you can work out your own system so you do not lose track of what day or how many days you have been in segregation. Reflections of why you are in segregation and struggling with the feelings of isolation consume your thoughts. To pass the time, you can also count the bricks on the wall and floor. After a few days, a few weeks, or in some cases months, most women leave segregation and return back to general population. Some inmates choose to repeatedly return to segregation as a way of escaping the pressures of general population.

Source: From Corrections: A Contemporary Introduction by Leanne F Alarid and Philip L Reichel. Copyright © 2008 by Pearson Education.

- The facilities should be built for solitary confinement and operated on the basis of silent contemplation and continuous labor.

Those basic principles brought positive change in England and would also influence the development of corrections in the American colonies.

▶ Corrections in Eighteenth- and Nineteenth-Century America

Corporal and capital punishment remained the primary sentence types well into eighteenth-century America. Legislators in the new country were hesitant to replace those tried-and-

TIMELINE

A Timeline of Early American Jails and Prisons

1635	1773	1776	1785
Boston Prison (Boston, Massachusetts)—Operates as a jail with both criminal (holding prisoners and persons awaiting trial or sentencing) and civil (holding persons who had not paid a debt, taxes, fines, or court costs) functions.	**Newgate Prison** (Simsbury, Connecticut)—Located in an old copper mine with an underground dormitory for prisoners.	**Walnut Street Jail** (Philadelphia, Pennsylvania)—Houses petty offenders and debtors as well as more serious offenders awaiting trial or sentencing.	**Castle Island** (Boston, Massachusetts)—The first "state prison" in the sense of a facility housing only convicted offenders (not those simply accused of crime) from all over the state.

FIGURE 3–4 Timeline: Early American Jails and Prisons.
Source: REICHEL, PHILIP L. CORRECTIONS: PHILOSOPHIES, PRACTICES, AND PROCEDURES, 2nd, ©2001. Printed and Electronically reproduced by permission of Pearson Education, Inc., Upper Saddle River, New Jersey.

true methods with the untested idea of long-term imprisonment as punishment. Rather than completely changing the criminal codes to make imprisonment the only punishment option, incarceration was more often an alternative to, rather than a replacement for, the old corporal punishments. For example, when Massachusetts established Castle Island (see Figure 3–4) as the state prison, the sanction of imprisonment and hard labor was often just one of several options available to the judge. Arson against a building other than a dwelling, for example, had always been punished by whipping. The revised statute of 1785 allowed sentences to include hard labor (either for life or for a specified number of years), the pillory, whipping, imprisonment, a fine, or some combination of these (Hirsch, 1992).

The new ideas of imprisonment and hard labor as alternatives to corporal and capital punishment were especially evident in the activities of the **Pennsylvania Quakers**. In 1787, the Quakers (the Society of Friends) argued that solitude and hard labor were humanitarian alternatives to the existing punishments. And they believed Philadelphia's Walnut Street Jail provided the perfect setting to test those ideas.

> **LEARNING OUTCOMES 3** Compare and contrast the Pennsylvania and Auburn prison systems in terms of their architecture, orienting strategies, and advantages/disadvantages.

When it first opened in 1776, Philadelphia's **Walnut Street Jail** housed in large rooms rather than cells petty offenders and debtors on one side and more serious offenders waiting to be tried or sentenced on the other side (McKelvey, 1977). Men and women prisoners intermingled freely; one critic of the sexually mixed jail commented on its universal debauchery and the promiscuous nature of its inhabitants (Freedman, 1974, p. 78). Not helping the situation was the common practice of allowing jail keepers to sell alcohol to the inmates. Terror reigned among the prisoners as exemplified by the pastime known as "strip or pay." For that activity, newly admitted inmates could choose between treating all the other inmates to a drink and stripping themselves of their clothes, which were then sold to pay for a round or two (Eriksson, 1976).

With the new penal code of 1786, Quakers and others suggested that the Walnut Street Jail be expanded to have a new role. The pleas were successful, and in 1790, the legislature ordered that a special block of cells be built at the Walnut Street Jail. Construction was completed in 1792, and the new penitentiary house confined the most hardened criminals in single cells. In theory, if not in practice (see Eriksson, 1976, p. 46), the prisoners were kept strictly isolated from each other and from other prisoners and were made to work at hard labor.

As the eighteenth century came to a close, the dual themes of solitude and labor—first seen in the English and European hospice facilities and the houses of correction—were firmly established, and each theme continued to be important as two parallel views of operating a prison emerged in the United States. Both were based on the idea that regimens of silence and penitence would prevent cross-infection and encourage positive changes in behavior. The systems' names come from the first locations of their use: Pennsylvania and Auburn (New York).

The Pennsylvania System

Eastern State Penitentiary opened in 1829 in Philadelphia, Pennsylvania. As shown in Figure 3–5, it was designed with seven cell blocks radiating from a hub-like center. A corridor ran down the center of each cell block, with the cells positioned on each side of the corridor. Each cell had a back door to a small, uncovered yard where prisoners were allowed to exercise for two brief periods each day. The prison's design was important to the idea that correction was best achieved when prisoners were kept separate from each other and required to remain silent. This **separate and silent** strategy, key words distinguishing the **Pennsylvania system**, assumed that offenders would more quickly repent and reform if they could reflect on their crimes all day.

Critics of the Pennsylvania system argued that the practice of separation (termed *solitude* by the system's proponents) produced insanity in the prisoners. This argument was difficult to refute because reality kept providing examples of prisoners who developed mental problems during their incarceration. The system's founders were admittedly ignorant of the basic tenets of disciplines such as psychology, sociology, and social work. But those disciplines were not well established in the early and mid-1800s, so it is probably more appropriate to view the Pennsylvania system

---

1792

Walnut Street Jail's Penitentiary House
(Philadelphia, Pennsylvania)—Special block of cells constructed to confine the most hardened criminals under a "separate and silent" system.

1800

Virginia and Kentucky Prisons
(Richmond, Virginia, and Frankfort, Kentucky)—These states, the first in the South to open prisons, are unusual in this region of the country where justice and punishment tends to be handled more at the local level.

1817

Auburn Prison (Auburn, New York)—After an unsuccessful attempt to implement the "separate and silent" system borrowed from the Walnut Street Jail's Penitentiary House, Auburn turns (in 1821) to a "congregate and silent" model that came to be known as the Auburn system.

1825	1828	1829
Auburn Prison's Women's Unit (Auburn, New York)—Female offenders are accepted in Auburn but are confined to a third-floor attic above the prison kitchen.	**Sing Sing** (Sing Sing, New York)—Built by convict labor, Sing Sing refines the Auburn system into an especially repressive disciplinary regimen.	**Eastern State Penitentiary** (Philadelphia, Pennsylvania)—Built to implement the "separate and silent" system, which came to be called the Pennsylvania system and found greater success than it had at Auburn prison.

FIGURE 3–4 **Early American Jails and Prisons. (continued)**

FIGURE 3–5 **Eastern State Penitentiary.** The penitentiary was designed with cell block spokes jutting from a central hub to make it easier for guards to watch the inmates and to implement the philosophy of solitary confinement and silence.
Source: Library of Congress

silent system soon proved a failure, although some could argue it never received a fair chance.

Criticism that the separate and silent system caused mental problems in the inmates and the inability to maintain separation of prisoners were important factors in the Pennsylvania system's demise. But another criticism seemed to take priority in the debates between its champions and its critics: The separate and silent system was very costly. As the system developed at Eastern State Penitentiary, prisoners were allowed to work in their cells at various handicrafts. They made shoes, caned chairs, and knitted hose, but the cell size (18 feet long, 8 feet wide, and 16 feet high) made it difficult to get much production from its single occupant. Even when two prisoners were working in the cell, the profits that could be gained by the prison for their labor were small. Fortunately, for those wanting an economically self-supporting prison, another option was developing in Auburn, New York.

backers as well intentioned rather than as inhumane. Mental retardation and mental disease were considered the same by most laypeople, and attempts to explain how either version of this "insanity" came about were difficult.

Borrowing the concept of solitude from the workhouses of England and Europe, proponents of the Pennsylvania system had hoped to stop what they saw as the training in crime that prisoners received at those institutions where inmates had close and constant contact with each other. But, as Barnes and Teeters (1943) note, it was physically impossible to keep prisoners entirely apart. Inmates developed ingenious methods to communicate with each other (such as tapping out codes on the water pipes within the cells), but even such shrewdness was soon unnecessary because the officials themselves provided contact among the prisoners. From the beginning, convicts were used as servants in the warden's home, and very soon two men were put in each cell so that one might learn a trade from the other. Possibly most important in affecting how the prison was made to operate, the legislature's building appropriations never kept pace with the ever-increasing prison population, so doubling of prisoners in single cells became necessary. The separate and

Think About It...

During its earliest days, the rule of silence was strictly followed at Eastern State Penitentiary, as inmates were not allowed to see or talk with each other. The idea was, in part, to prevent cross-contamination among the prisoners—that is, preventing them from sharing criminal values and techniques. However, maintaining complete separation and silence quickly became impossible for prison administrators. If complete and continued solitude and silence could be achieved in prisons today, do you think the result would have more positive or negative consequences?

Source: Library of Congress (Photoduplication)

Sing Sing Women's Unit (Sing Sing, New York)—Women offenders are placed in a separate cell block in a partially isolated corner of the yard at Sing Sing. (Some sources use 1835 as the date this occurred).

Indiana Reformatory Institution for Women and Girls (Indianapolis, Indiana)—The first completely independent and physically separate prison for women in the United States.

Elmira Reformatory (Elmira, New York)—Specifically built to implement the progressive ideas, known collectively as the Irish system, of people such as Alexander Maconochie and Sir Walter Crofton.

The Auburn System

The Auburn prison opened in 1817 in Auburn, New York. In 1821, Auburn officials borrowed the separate and silent strategy from the Walnut Street Jail for use at the new prison. This meant that the Auburn prison actually used the Pennsylvania system before the Eastern State Penitentiary even opened, but it did not prove very successful in New York. The Auburn design, with cells built back-to-back on five tiers within a hollow building and doors opening out on galleries, did not allow for individual exercise yards. Continual confinement in their cells without access to an outside area and without the distractions of work created mental and physical problems for the inmates. Officials soon decided that the separate and silent strategy from Pennsylvania was not working and the experiment was abandoned as a failure in 1823.

The alternative that Auburn officials turned to was a modification of the Pennsylvania system in which inmates were locked in separate cells at night but allowed to work and eat together, in silence, during the day. This **congregate and silent** policy, which was often enforced with flogging, distinguished the **Auburn system**. The spread of evil ideas among prisoners could be prevented, Auburn proponents argued, by separating prisoners at night and enforcing strict silence in the shops and dining hall during the daytime. That silence was enforced through regulations such as lockstep marching, downcast eyes, constant activity when out of the cells, and prohibitions against prisoners ever being in face-to-face contact (Barnes & Teeters, 1943). Eventually, the Auburn model was adopted in states across the country because it produced more money for the state. The craft-oriented labor at Eastern State Penitentiary was considered an outdated labor system when compared with the factory-oriented labor at Auburn.

The Pennsylvania Versus Auburn Debate

Between the 1820s and 1860s, the merits of the Pennsylvania and Auburn systems were hotly debated. Proponents of the Pennsylvania strategy claimed that it was superior because it was easier to control prisoners, it provided more opportunity

for meditation and repentance, and it avoided cross-contamination of prisoners by maintaining strict separation. The single cells for sleeping, eating, and working; the solitary exercise yards; the restricted and carefully selected visitors; and even the hood placed over the head of a new prisoner being marched to his cell were all precautions against contamination (Rothman, 1971). The end result, in theory, was an opportunity to reform because the prisoner's solitude not only halts the progress of corruption, but also encourages the prisoner to recognize the wrongs of his ways.

Figure 3–6 contrasts the advantages of the Pennsylvania system against those of the Auburn system, which supporters claimed was superior because it was cheaper to construct and operate, it provided better vocational training, it was less damaging to the prisoner's mental health, and it produced more money for the state. On this last point, Conley (1980) contrasts the craft-oriented labor at Eastern State Penitentiary with the factory-oriented labor at Auburn and concludes that Pennsylvania had adopted an outdated labor system. The Auburn model, on the other hand, proposed a labor system that could provide the state

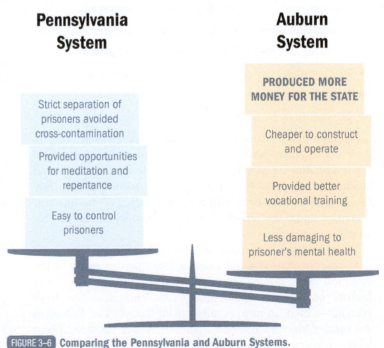

Pennsylvania System

Strict separation of prisoners avoided cross-contamination

Provided opportunities for meditation and repentance

Easy to control prisoners

Auburn System

PRODUCED MORE MONEY FOR THE STATE

Cheaper to construct and operate

Provided better vocational training

Less damaging to prisoner's mental health

FIGURE 3–6 Comparing the Pennsylvania and Auburn Systems.

with a way to exploit convict labor in order to defray institutional expenses, and possibly earn a profit for the state. This economic point tipped the balance in favor of the Auburn system.

By the mid-1800s, long-term imprisonment as designed in the United States was influencing the spread of penitentiaries in Europe and other parts of the world. However, the next steps for America's penal system were heavily influenced by activities in European countries. There were, of course, home-grown efforts as well, but the reformatory movement in America owes a great deal to activities that first occurred in other countries.

The Reformatory Movement

The United States was at the forefront of putting into operation the first penal philosophies for long-term imprisonment. But after about 50 years of little more than debate about the merits of the Auburn and the Pennsylvania systems, things were stagnating in the United States and some prison reformers began looking for new approaches. It soon became apparent that since the 1830s, some people had focused their attention less on handling the prisoner in confinement and more on ways to prepare the prisoners for their eventual return to the community. This new focus, which was appealing to many in post–Civil War America, featured an approach that came to be called the reformatory movement.

When reviewing the history of penal institutions, the term **reformatory** refers to a system of prison discipline that incorporates a more humanitarian approach to confinement and has an interest in preparing inmates for their eventual return to the community. Reformatory procedures and institutions called *reformatories* presented different views about prison discipline and administration than were found in the penitentiaries that developed in the first half of the nineteenth century. The first American reformatory, which was in Elmira, New York, opened in 1876 and received offenders ranging from 16 to 30 years old who were serving their first prison term.

The reformatory differed from existing prisons by

- Using indeterminate sentences with fixed minimum terms

- Allowing the possibility of early release on parole

- Placing greater emphasis on reforming the inmates

- Providing more extensive trade training

- Increasing opportunities for academic education

Inmates were placed into one of three classes depending on their achievement and conduct. They entered at the second grade and after six months were demoted to third grade for bad conduct or promoted to first grade as they earned marks. Only those at first grade were eligible for parole. Paroled inmates remained under the jurisdiction of reformatory authorities for another six months.

That emphasis on education and trade training, indeterminate sentences, and early release from prison came to the attention of Americans by way of Ireland and, as such, these factors comprised what came to be known as the Irish system—which, in turn, resulted from the work of Scotsman Alexander Maconochie and Irishman Walter Crofton. These men are discussed more fully in Chapter 10 because their efforts were especially relevant to the development of discretionary parole.

In 1870, Americans got a chance to hear firsthand about the Irish system when the American Prison Association (now the American Correctional Association) met in Cincinnati for its first National Prison Congress. In attendance were 130 delegates from 24 states who heard some 40 papers presented by penal reformers and administrators. As one of the presenters, Crofton's arguments were well received and they clearly influenced both the direction of the meeting and the development of a reformatory philosophy in the United States.

Another presenter, Zebulon Brockway, also made quite an impact on the delegates at the Congress. Since 1861, Brockway had been director of the Detroit House of Correction, which several people had noted as being a praiseworthy institution. Brockway advocated classification of prisoners by age, sex, and offense and saw great benefit in the use of indeterminate sentences. By the meeting's end, the views of people such as Crofton and Brockway had been adopted in a declaration of principles and the view that society should take responsibility for its criminals and their rehabilitation began to take hold. The reformation of offenders would be achieved through religion, education, industrious work habits, and supervision of the prisoners after their release from prison (Sullivan, 1990). The enthusiasm generated at the meeting resulted in the 1876 opening of a facility in Elmira, New York, specifically built to carry out the progressive ideas from Maconochie and Crofton.

▶ *Segregating the Sexes*

As the reformatory movement began taking hold in the 1860s, there was an interest in reforming female as well as male prisoners. Feminists of the time worked hard to get all-male legislatures to fund separate reformatory prisons for women. The call was for different responses to women and men prisoners. Women were worthy of reform, they argued, and that reform was best achieved in separate facilities operated by women. There were certainly opponents to such a change, with the argument of both sides shown in Figure 3–7, but prisons or reformatories specifically for women began operating when Indiana opened the Women's Prison in 1873 and Massachusetts opened the Reformatory Prison for Women in 1877. The women reformers who had argued for these facilities often became administrators in the new reformatories. In doing so, they were able to put into practice the principles they had argued in the legislatures—women inmates should be treated differently from male prisoners.

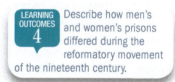

LEARNING OUTCOMES 4 — Describe how men's and women's prisons differed during the reformatory movement of the nineteenth century.

The new women's facilities differed from those for men in four important ways (Freedman, 1974; Rafter, 1990, 1993):

1. **Architectural style:** The women's reformatories were built in a cottage plan with inmates living in relatively small individual units (cottages) that created an atmosphere more like a home than a cell block. The cottages

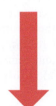

Arguments Favoring

(1) Assigning the blame for female criminality to men instead of to the women themselves

(2) Proposing rehabilitation as being best achieved by removing the women from the evil influences of men

(3) Stressing the ability of women to control and reform their sisters

Arguments Against

(1) Women were incapable of controlling, let alone reforming, female criminals

(2) Female-controlled prisons would not have a familial, or home-like, structure

(3) Women's institutions could reduce male dominance in society and would destroy femininity

FIGURE 3–7 **Arguments for and Against Separate Facilities for Women.**
Reference: Freedman, E. B. (1974). Their sisters' keepers: An historical perspective on female correctional institutions in the United States: 1870–1900. Feminist Studies, 2(1), 77–95.

themselves could be set up in dormitory style or with individual rooms having windows, bedspreads, rugs, and wooden doors instead of iron bars. The goal was to project a domestic atmosphere that would focus the women's attention and interests on their expected role in society.

2. **Programs:** Programs for women were consistent with the cottage atmosphere by emphasizing domesticity. In their new reformatories, the women prisoners mainly received training in sewing, cooking, washing and ironing clothes, gardening, and farming. The reformers, who were primarily middle-class women, seemed intent on putting female offenders into a homemaker mold despite the fact that most of the prisoners would have to support themselves after release from prison.

3. **Sentencing disparity:** For the reform efforts to be successful, it was necessary to have access to the offenders over a long time. As a result, the legislation establishing women's reformatories allowed them to hold misdemeanor offenders on sentences that were equivalent to those given to felons serving time at the state prison.

4. **Racial bias:** The reformers establishing the new reformatories were not much interested in dealing with felons. Those serious offenders, many of whom were black, did not draw much empathy from the middle-class and essentially white women reformers. The "preferred" clientele for reform efforts were white women convicted of misdemeanors. Although the lack of clear records makes it hard to substantiate, there is good reason to suspect that black women prisoners did not benefit as much from the reformatory movement. Nineteenth-century women's reformatories may have accepted only white women, leaving black female offenders to serve their sentence in the women's—and sometimes men's—custodial prisons. In the twentieth century, black women were more likely to be admitted to reformatories but were usually segregated in cottages of their own.

Separate and different-style prisons, different programs, and different sentencing practices are just some of the areas indicating

Think About It...

Over the years, the male model of imprisonment has become the measuring rod for what is considered equal treatment of women offenders. That is, if the standard punishment for male offenders is imprisonment, equal treatment makes imprisonment the standard for female offenders. Some critics of equalization argue that an undesirable consequence has been few non-prison alternatives for women. What arguments can be made for treating women offenders differently from men offenders? Can an equitable response to both men and women offenders be a "fair" response yet not necessarily the same response?

a **differential response** to women offenders during the reformatory movement. In many ways, the result was a clear improvement over the neglect and mistreatment women prisoners suffered when they were housed in male-dominated prisons. But in highlighting the special needs of women prisoners and in encouraging a different response, reformers created a new set of problems by assuming that women inmates could all be treated alike through methods aimed at reinforcing "true womanhood" in an era when a "new woman" was emerging (Freedman, 1974).

By the end of the nineteenth century, enthusiasm for the reformatory concept had been dampened. One reason the reformatory ideals had trouble was the setting in which they were being tried. The first three reformatories (Elmira, New York; Concord, Massachusetts; and Huntingdon, Pennsylvania) were all opened in buildings that were originally built as maximum-security prisons for adult felons. The economic benefits of using existing structures meant that many states tried the reformatory ideas in settings that were more conducive to tight security and hard labor than to progressive stages and vocational training. Barnes and Teeters (1959) attribute the decay of the reformatory program to the forbidding atmosphere of steel cages and high, gloomy walls that made it impossible to develop true reformatory ideals. Reformatories became more like junior prisons than the enlightened alternative proposed by reformers at the Cincinnati Congress. As the century ended, vocational training was about the only aspect of the reformatory philosophy that officials stressed—but even that survived less for purposes of education and training than as a way for the prison to make a profit.

▶ Prison Development in the South and West

The history of America's prison development was not restricted to the northeastern part of the country. Obviously, the rest of the country did not just wait around for the northeastern states to

LEARNING OUTCOMES 5 Explain how penal systems in the South and West differed from those in the East and summarize reasons for those differences.

decide what form U.S. imprisonment would take. The other states and territories were certainly influenced by what was happening in places, such as Massachusetts, New York, and Pennsylvania, but they also realized that there were unique circumstances at home that often required modification, replacement, and even rejection of the prison systems developing in the Northeast. In this section, we consider the history of state prisons in the South and the West.

Developments in the American South

While penitentiaries and reformatories were developing in the North during the nineteenth century, the South found little advantage to building large prison facilities—whether based on the Pennsylvania, Auburn, or reformatory model. Table 3–1 summarizes some reasons for that lack of interest in penitentiaries.

By 1835, most of the states had revised their criminal codes to substitute imprisonment for the traditional corporal punishments. But in many of those jurisdictions, the administration of justice was left to local authorities instead of being centralized at the state level. The reliance on local authority was especially entrenched in the South, where the role of county government and the position of sheriff were of greater consequence than either was in the North. A few states tried the penitentiary idea, with Virginia, Kentucky, and Maryland opening state prisons during the first decade of the nineteenth century. Georgia established a prison in 1817, Tennessee in 1831, and Louisiana in 1835, but by the mid-1800s, state prisons in the South were still more talk than reality (Colvin, 1997). The South still preferred to have justice and punishment dispensed at the county rather than the state level.

But the principle of **decentralization** was not the sole or even primary cause of differences between southern and northern penal developments. Religion also played a role—with groups such as the Quakers in the North supporting penitentiaries and religious beliefs in the South being more inclined to follow the Bible's lead and rely on corporal and capital punishment.

Economic differences between the North and the South also influenced developments in punishment (Colvin, 1997; McKelvey, 1977). While the industrial North put its prisoners to work under labor systems designed to produce a product, the agricultural South was making greater use of a **lease** system that provided labor to plantation owners and others. In fact, arguments have been made that imprisonment in the postwar South quickly came to take the place held by slavery in the antebellum South (Colvin, 1997; Hindus, 1980). Statistics showing that African-Americans soon made up over 90% of the total criminal population in the Deep South help to support that thesis. The lease system put convicts in the role of exploited laborer and prison wardens in the role of slaveholder. By 1880, all the former Confederate states and Kentucky had leased out a major portion of their criminal populations. When reformers sought to end leasing, the taxpayers prevented any change. The tragic system continued as former slaves found themselves now shackled to penal slavery rather than plantation slavery.

Leasing's end was brought about not so much by new humanitarian concerns as by reduced profits. By the end of the nineteenth century, states were finding that other labor systems were proving beneficial. Experiments with penal plantations were especially encouraging. Louisiana, Mississippi, and Texas were among the first states to experiment with the use of prisoners on large farms and plantations. These states began purchasing farmland and buying plantations where prisoners would work for the state rather than for private contractors or lessees. The penal plantation became entrenched in southern penology and influenced the direction imprisonment would take in the twentieth-century South.

Developments in the American West

The earliest prisons in the West were not strongly influenced by the developments in New York and Pennsylvania. California opened San Quentin prison in 1852 and Folsom in 1880, and the total prison population was soon double capacity. But as bad as the crowding in California prisons was, the conditions to the north were of even greater concern. To handle its law violators, the Washington Territory started leasing prisoners to a mill owner who worked the prisoners during the day and then herded them through a trapdoor into a log pit to spend the nights. Conditions in the pit were so terrible that they were believed by some to have been the worst since those of a century earlier (McKelvey, 1977).

TABLE 3–1 | CORRECTIONS IN THE NINETEENTH-CENTURY SOUTH

Southern reliance on decentralization to local authorities	Political authority in the South was spread more across rural areas than centralized at the state level. As a result, justice and punishment was dispensed at the county rather than state level.
Absence of religious support in the South	Several religious groups in the North promoted penitentiaries as a means of salvation, but southern evangelicals preferred instead the application of corporal and capital punishment—as directed in the Bible.
Southern agricultural economy	Agricultural labor such as farm work, road construction, and turpentine extraction required that workers be dispersed over a wide area. Rather than being conveniently housed in a big building, prisoners needed to be where the crops were grown, the roads built, and the pine trees sapped. Rather than putting prisoners in a single state penitentiary, it was more reasonable and economical to have smaller work camps from which prisoners could be transported to the work site each day.

One explanation for California's overcrowding was the lack of satisfactory classification procedures. Because of inadequate classification, California tended to place a larger portion of its lesser offenders into prisons than was the practice in the East. Problems were aggravated when the criminally naïve were mixed with the more hardened offenders and no system of correctional discipline was used to control, reward, or encourage the inmates.

Some of the territories chose to transfer their criminals to other states rather than build their own prisons. Wyoming Territory contracted first with the Nebraska state prison, and then with the Illinois prison at Joliet, to house its criminals. Oklahoma's criminals—who multiplied even more rapidly than its citizens (McKelvey, 1977)—were sent off to the penitentiary in Kansas, where they were jammed into crowded cells when they were not digging coal in the mine pits.

Possibly the most successful states to develop stable prison systems in the West were Colorado, Utah, and the Dakotas. McKelvey (1977) suggests that the success of these states was due to their ability to keep open the channels of eastern influence and their participation in the congresses of the National Prison Association. From each source, these western states were kept informed about eastern debates, experiments, and theories regarding penal administration. For example, when the National Prison Association held its 1895 Congress in the Rocky Mountain West, Colorado officials were able to brag about having the first adult reformatory, the first board of charities, the only separate prison building for women, the only effective parole law, and the only genuine grading system west of the Mississippi River.

During the twentieth century, other western states, most notably California, came to play a prominent role in directing penal policies and procedures across the nation. The East no longer had a hold on innovation, and both independent and collaborative efforts by each of the 50 states created facets of the U.S. penal system. But while this brief history is informative, its importance for this chapter is to remind us about the cycle of history. Problems of crowding, complaints about prison conditions, and concerns over prison labor systems are not new in American history. Although it would be nice to explain that society has learned from history and can now handle these problems with efficiency and expertise, it is more accurate to say that society has not. Contemporary problems are typically seen by the media, the public, legislators, and even corrections professionals as being unique to this time.

▶ Corrections in the Twentieth Century

Throughout the twentieth century, dramatic changes occurred in all aspects of America's prison system. Figure 3–8 summarizes many of them, but here we highlight changes in prison programs.

 **LEARNING OUTCOMES 6** Summarize the development of prison programs and the treatment of women and other minorities during the early, middle, and late twentieth century.

In the 1890s, a general reform movement known to history as **progressivism** began sweeping the country. For the next 30 years, America would undergo dramatic changes to the nation's political, social, and economic arenas. By the end of the progressive era, women had won the right to vote, child labor was restricted, general working conditions were improved, citizens had more direct control over their government, business practices were better regulated, and the sale of alcohol was prohibited. The efforts of progressives to reform institutions for delinquent youth, the mentally ill, and prisoners are especially relevant for our purposes.

The reformatories, asylums, and prisons that had been established as mechanisms of social control were viewed by the progressives as misguided. Instead, these benevolent and optimistic social reformers believed that people could be cured of delinquency, insanity, and crime through an individualized program of treatment (Smith, 1997). These reformers differed from those in earlier decades by being professional experts rather than amateur volunteers. As such, the progressives collected and analyzed data using social science methods and made treatment decisions based on scientific understanding of the time. The belief that criminal behavior is influenced by sociological, psychological, and biological factors—rather than simply being the result of misdirected free will on the part of the criminal—came to define the correctional practices during much of the twentieth century.

One of the clearest examples of progressivism's influence during the twentieth century is seen in the general development of prison programs and the specific influence of the rehabilitation philosophy. The progressive reformers saw themselves as impartial experts gathering and analyzing social data that would allow them to uncover laws of human behavior. Newfound knowledge in medicine, such as the germ theory of disease, bolstered the idea that individuals are not totally responsible for what happens to them. Illness began to replace free will as an explanation as to why antisocial behavior occurs.

Reforms initiated by the progressives at the century's start gave rise, in the 1930s, to a medical model that presented criminal behavior as pathological. Criminals were not so much "bad" as they were "ill." Because of that, offenders should be referred to as people who are sick (physically, mentally, and/or socially), and their crimes are symptoms of their sickness. This **medical model** approach argued that society's response to the criminal should include the three stages, shown in Figure 3–9, of examination, diagnosis, and treatment (Abadinsky, 1994). Following these stages, professionals could, for example, conclude that an offender has committed a crime because he or she came from a dysfunctional family (the source of the illness) and then dropped out of school and began using drugs (placing him or her in a category holding other offenders with similar "symptoms"). Such an offender may be assigned to a treatment program that includes academic instruction and therapy for substance abuse.

Many types of treatment programs were developed during the 1950s and 1960s. Academic programs treated persons lacking basic educational abilities, whereas vocational training was the remedy for those presumably choosing a career

	Early Century	Mid Century	Late Century
Prison Architecture	• Prison camps and farms continue to dominate in the South. • Some states build "big house" prisons holding more than 2,500 inmates (for example, Stateville prison in Illinois and San Quentin prison in California).	• Most southern states had at least one centrally located penitentiary, but most prisoners were still on large prison farms. • "Telephone pole" prison design flourished (for example, Vacaville, CA and Ferguson Unit, TX).	• Super-maximum security prisons (known as super-max prisons) are built by the federal government (for example, in Florence, CO) and by some states (for example, California's Pelican Bay state prison).
Prison Programs	• Social and behavioral scientists are introduced in the prison environment to help implement basic concepts of classification. • Educational and vocational training programs are introduced in prisons. • The Federal Bureau of Prisons is established in 1930 and quickly takes the lead in new methods and programs (for example, improved training of correctional officers and enhanced vocational training).	• Classification of inmates is implemented throughout the country's prisons. • Diagnosis is added to the classification process to determine appropriate treatment plans.	• The rehabilitation model falls out of favor and a new reliance on incapacitation turns to warehousing serious offenders as a way to protect society. • Restorative justice procedures receive increased attention as a way to recognize concerns of victims.
Women Offenders	• As male inmates were providing prison labor that gave them some marketable skills and had economic advantage for the prison, female inmates were delegated to domestic chores and training that resulted in neither economic advantage for the prison nor for the inmate upon her release.	• Calls are made, and action taken, toward equal treatment of male and female inmates in such areas as opportunities to participate in similar vocational and treatment programs.	• A new approach to female offenders recognizes differences between women and men and argues for deciding appropriate responses toward women offenders from a female orientation. For example, since women present low risk to public safety they should receive greater consideration for community-based sentences.
Race/Ethnicity Disparity	• Although making up only about 9% of the American adult population in the mid-1920s, African-Americans comprise 31% of the prison population.	• Foreign-born Caucasian immigrants are increasingly rare in prisons, but the proportion of African-Americans, Hispanics, and Native Americans grows.	• African-Americans comprise about 12% of the national population but represent more than 40% of the total prison population.
Key Developments	• The number of inmates employed in prison industries declines as organized labor argues that prisoner labor creates unfair business competition.	• The 1960s civil rights movement includes an interest in prisoner rights and federal courts start taking a more active role in how states treat prisoners.	• Mandatory sentencing and increased severity of drug penalties requires more jails and prisons to handle bigger prison population.

FIGURE 3–8 **Key Features of Corrections in the Twentieth Century.**

References: Chesney-Lind, M., & Pollock, J. M. (1995). Women's prisons: Equality with a vengeance. In A. V. Merlo & J. M. Pollock (Eds.), Women, law, and social control (pp. 155–175). Boston, MA: Allyn and Bacon.; Christianson, S. (1998). With liberty for some: 500 years of imprisonment in America. Boston, MA: Northeastern University Press.; Kurshan, N. (1992). Women and imprisonment in the U.S.-History and current reality. In W. Churchill & J. J. Vander Wall (Eds.), Cages of steel: The politics of imprisonment in the United States (pp. 331–358). Washington, DC: Maisonneuve Press.; Rafter, N. H. (1990). Partial justice: Women, prisons, and social control (2nd ed.). New Brunswick, NJ: Transaction Publishers.; Roth, M. P. (2011). Crime and punishment: A history of the criminal justice system (2nd ed.). Belmont, CA: Wadsworth Cengage.

in crime because they did not have marketable job skills. Others, it was argued, engaged in criminal acts because they were morally deficient (treatment = religious training), abused a variety of substances (treatment = therapy groups), or had mental health problems (treatment = group and individual counseling).

The medical model with rehabilitation as individualized treatment began falling out of favor in the 1970s. However, many of the innovations from that period continue to influence prison programs today. The major difference is that they are no longer a central theme around which prisons are organized.

Basic vocational and academic education remain popular programs in contemporary prisons. Similarly, programs focused on alcohol and drug treatment are widespread.

▶ Corrections in the Twenty-First Century

At the start of the new century, the United States had the highest incarceration rate of any country in the world, but by 2010, there were signs the prison boom was slowing—although not

Examination		**Diagnosis**		**Treatment**
A case history is developed to identify causes or sources of the illness	**+**	A particular version of the illness is identified and the offender is assigned to groups with similar problems	**=**	A plan is proposed that allows the offender to "get well" and return to the community as a law-abiding citizen

FIGURE 3–9 The Medical Model.

enough for the United States to lose its incarceration rate ranking. By 2014, the decline was the sixth consecutive reduction in the nation's imprisonment rate. Interestingly, and importantly, violent and property crime rates declined in 2014 for the fifth time in seven years (Pew Charitable Trusts, 2015). Although the declining crime rate can be attributed in part to having put so many criminals in prison, there were many other factors at work as well, including better policing and increased use of anticrime technologies (e.g., car theft prevention devices and reduced use of cash in favor of electronic payments). Similarly, the declining imprisonment rate is the result of many factors. Two of those factors, changing public opinion and decreased reliance on prisons, provide concluding topics for this chapter.

Public Opinion

The Opportunity Agenda conducted a meta-analysis of public opinion research related to criminal justice reform. Looking at studies over the last 15 years that met standards and best practices

LEARNING OUTCOMES 7 Explain the effects of changing public opinion on the use of imprisonment and prison alternatives in the twenty-first century.

for quality and objective public opinion research, some interesting conclusions can be drawn (Mizell, 2014, p. 7).

- Since the 1990s, there has been a shift in public views with people backing away from harsh sentencing policies and more likely to favor rehabilitation, treatment, and support efforts—especially for offenders with low-level drug convictions.

- Public support for rehabilitation services for convicted young people and adults is growing. Such services as treatment, job and educational training, housing assistance, and mental health or substance abuse services are viewed as vital to successful reentry.

- Although the public supports offenders making an effort to change, they prefer that the process not affect them directly and therefore hesitate to pay more taxes or to have a halfway house in their neighborhood.

- Criminal justice issues generally continue to be polarized around race. Persons of color, especially African-Americans, perceive systemic racial disparities in policing, sentencing, and overall treatment by the criminal justice system. White respondents acknowledge the disparities to some extent, but pluralities believe the system treats people of all races equally.

The conclusions drawn from that meta-analysis are reflected in a specific nationwide public opinion survey conducted in 2012 by Pew Charitable Trusts. That survey found that American voters believe too many people are in prison and too much money is being spent on imprisonment. In addition, whereas they want criminals to be held accountable and believe there must be consequences for illegal activities, they overwhelmingly support policy changes that shift nonviolent offenders from prison to more effective, less expensive alternatives (Pew Charitable Trusts, 2012). Importantly, support for sentencing and corrections reform is strong across geographical regions and age, gender, and racial/ethnic groups, and from all political perspectives.

With the twenty-first-century public being more supportive of a reduction in the use of prisons, we should begin seeing crime control policy moving away from primary reliance on imprisonment and toward greater reliance on prevention and rehabilitation—and, in fact, we have.

Decreased Reliance on Prisons

Recall from Chapter 1's discussion of the Justice Reinvestment Initiative that it relies on development and implementation of policy reforms that improve public safety and generate savings that can be reinvested into crime prevention efforts. Since 2007, more than half the states have enacted policy reforms to control growth in the corrections industry, contain taxpayer costs, and improve public safety using evidence-based policies (Pew Charitable Trusts, 2015).

In November 2000, California voters passed Proposition 36, which allows people convicted of first- and second-time nonviolent, simple drug possession to receive drug treatment instead of imprisonment. In 2002, Michigan legislators repealed almost all of the state's mandatory minimum drug statutes and replaced them with sentencing guidelines that give discretion back to judges. In 2012, Georgia enacted a law that concentrates prison space on serious offenders, expands cost-effective sentencing options, and requires government agencies to report performance outcomes. Utah has also shifted gears on sentencing and corrections policy with a sweeping reform package in 2015 that converts all first- and second-time drug possession offenses from felonies to misdemeanors and creates "re-entry specialists" to support offenders as they leave prison and return to the community (Gelb, 2015; Pew Charitable Trusts, 2013a).

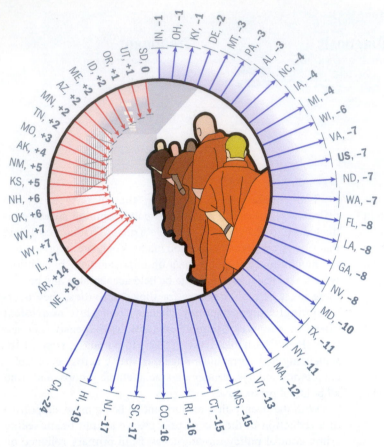

IN, -1 OH, -1 KY, -1 DE, -2 MT, -3 PA, -3 AL, -3
SD, 0 NC, -4
UT, +1 IA, -4
OR, +1 MI, -4
ID, +2 WI, -6
AZ, +2 VA, -7
ME, +2 US, -7
MN, +2 ND, -7
TN, +2 WA, -7
MO, +3 FL, -8
AK, +4 LA, -8
NM, +5 GA, -8
KS, +5 NV, -8
NH, +6 MD, -10
OK, +6 TX, -11
WV, +7 NY, -11
WY, +7 MA, -12
IL, +7 VT, -13
AR, +14 MS, -15
NE, +16 CT, -15
CA, -24 RI, -16
HI, -19 CO, -16
NJ, -17 SC, -17

FIGURE 3–10 **Percentage Change in Imprisonment Rate (per 100,000 residents) from 2009 to 2014.**
Reference: Based on data from "Imprisonment, crime rates fell in 30 states over 5 years," Pew Charitable Trusts, September 2015.

release policies, but financial pressures alone cannot explain the decline in state prison populations.

- *Fewer prison admissions.* A drop in prison admissions actually began in 2007—well before the economic collapse—and (except for a slight increase in 2013) continued through 2014 (Carson, 2015). Importantly, the crime rate fell by 13% in the 10 states that reduced imprisonment rates the most, while dropping only 8% in the 10 states where imprisonment rates rose the most (Gelb, 2015).

- *States began to realize they could get taxpayers a better return on their public safety dollars.* Several states, including those with the largest prison population declines (e.g., California, Michigan, and Texas), have enacted reforms that reduced the number of prisoners without sacrificing public safety. Texas, for example, invested in residential and community-based treatment and diversion programs to provide non-prison options for probation violators, whereas Mississippi implemented a new risk assessment tool that helps distinguish between inmates who can be safely paroled and those needing to remain behind bars (Pew Charitable Trusts, 2010b).

- *Public opinion supports reform efforts, especially with the growing awareness that there are research-based alternatives that cost less than prison and work better to reduce recidivism (Pew Charitable Trusts, 2013b).* In fact, survey respondents believe about 20% of the current prison population could be released from prison and not pose a threat to overall public safety (Pew Charitable Trusts, 2012). Examples of these evidence-based programs are offered throughout this text and especially in the "Evidence-Based Practice—Does It Work?" boxes like Figure 3–11.

In the remaining chapters of this book (especially Chapter 5), you will find examples of these prison alternatives and will come to appreciate why many people believe American crime policy is ready to move toward less dependence on prison and more reliance on alternatives that will provide for public safety, hold criminals accountable, and reduce recidivism.

Reasons for the decreasing use of imprisonment by the states are clearly linked to economic conditions. But, there are other reasons as well that are too often overlooked. The following are typically included when discussing factors driving the decline in imprisonment:

- *State budget deficits have forced states to reduce prison populations in an attempt to save money.* The fiscal crisis clearly prompted states to reconsider their sentencing and

One reason cited for the decreased reliance on prisons is the realization that there are research-based alternatives that cost less than prison and work better to reduce recidivism. One example, which has received an evidence rating of "promising" by CrimeSolutions.gov (Office of Justice Programs, 2013), is the Drug Treatment Alternative to Prison (DTAP) program in Brooklyn, New York. DTAP attempts to reduce recidivism and drug use by diverting nonviolent felony drug offenders to community-based residential treatment. The program incorporates three fundamental components of effective treatment: a high level of structure, a long period of intervention, and flexibility. Research by Dynia and Sung (2000) found that program participants had a significantly lower rearrest rate compared to nonparticipants, and a study by Belenko, Foltz, Lang, and Sung (2005) found that overall participation in the DTAP program led to a reduction in the prevalence and rate of recidivism and delayed time to first rearrest.

FIGURE 3–11 **Evidence-Based Practice—Does It Work? Public Safety Doesn't Require Prison.**

From Eastern State Penitentiary to Alcatraz of the Rockies

What do a shoe bomber, the Unabomber, a 9/11 conspirator, and a Federal Bureau of Investigation (FBI) agent turned Russian spy have in common with prisoners serving time at Eastern State Penitentiary in the 1830s? They have all experienced prison under the separate and silent system.

The Administrative Maximum (ADX) facility in Florence, Colorado, is the most secure facility in the federal prison system—and possibly the most secure in the world. Called Supermax, or the Alcatraz of the Rockies, some of the country's most notorious prisoners are housed here, including would-be airline shoe bomber Richard Reid, "Unabomber" Ted Kaczynski, the self-confessed al-Qaeda operative Zacarias Moussaoui, and former FBI agent turned Russian spy Robert Hanssen.

These and the other inmates housed at ADX find themselves for 23 hours a day in a 7' × 12' soundproofed cell furnished with a poured concrete bed slab where they can sleep on a thin green mattress or lay to watch selected programs on a 12" black-and-white television set. Or, they can sit on a poured cement stool to read books or write letters at a concrete desk. Stainless steel toilets and sinks provide what is probably a welcome color and texture contrast. Each cell has a slit window, only a few inches wide, providing a view of an inner courtyard and maybe a patch of sky—but no one has a view of the surrounding Rocky Mountains (Cohen, 2007; Schuster, 2007).

Inmates who have been abiding by the rules may get about 10 hours per week of outside recreation in an area that Olympic

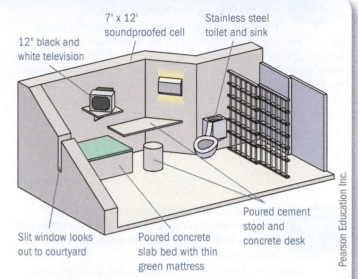

Labels: 7' x 12' soundproofed cell · Stainless steel toilet and sink · 12" black and white television · Slit window looks out to courtyard · Poured concrete slab bed with thin green mattress · Poured cement stool and concrete desk

Pearson Education Inc.

Zacarias Moussaoui—the only person who has been tried in a U.S. court on charges of involvement in the September 11, 2001, attacks—pleaded guilty in 2005 on charges of involvement in the strikes. In 2006, he was taken to ADX Florence to begin serving a life sentence. The graphic shows a typical cell at ADX Florence.

Park bomber Eric Rudolph describes as a large empty swimming pool divided into dog-kennel style cages (Rappold, 2006). Other inmates are under Special Administrative Measures (SAMs) and they may get only 90 minutes of exercise 5 days a week in a caged courtyard.

The contemporary use of separate and silent conditions raises several interesting questions:

1. ADX inmate Eric Rudolph wrote to a Colorado Springs newspaper that Supermax was designed to isolate inmates from social and environmental stimuli, with the ultimate purpose of causing mental illness and a variety of physical ailments (Rappold, 2006). Similar arguments were made by detractors of Eastern State Penitentiary's version of separate and silent. *Do you think such descriptors are exaggerations or reasonably accurate? Is a separate and silent regimen cruel and unusual punishment?*

2. ADX officials point out that although the prisoners have no authorized contact with each other, they are in contact with prison staff during the day. *Should contact with prison staff be sufficient to counter criticism that ADX is creating a situation of sensory deprivation?*

CHAPTER 3 Correctional Practices from Ancient to Contemporary Times

LEARNING OUTCOMES 1

Describe key features of the Code of Hammurabi, Mosaic Law, Roman law, and law during the Middle Ages.

The Code of Hammurabi introduced the concept of *lex talionis,* and Mosaic Law expanded on it by including the concept of proportionality. The Twelve Tables, the earliest form of written Roman law, provided the basis for private rights of Roman citizens. During the Middle Ages, courts rather than individuals began taking a greater role in conflict resolution.

1. Explain the principle of *lex talionis.*
2. Why is Hebrew law called Mosaic Law?

3. What serves as the earliest form of written Roman law?
4. What are some examples of exhibitory punishments?

Code of Hammurabi The first known body of law, established by King Hammurabi about 4,000 years ago, which lays out the basis of criminal law.

Mosaic Law The Hebrew legal system, which started when God gave Moses two stone tablets containing the Ten Commandments.

Twelve Tables The earliest form of written Roman law, which provided the basis for private rights of Roman citizens.

LEARNING OUTCOMES 2

Discuss the use of transportation to handle criminal offenders and identify the two important themes in the development of imprisonment as punishment.

The sixteenth-century ideas that prisoners should be isolated (taken from hospice facilities) and should be required to work (taken from houses of correction) provided themes that would continue to influence penal philosophy into the nineteenth century.

1. What are some countries besides England that used transportation?
2. Transported prisoners to Australia remained the responsibility of the British government. How did that differ for the prisoners transported to the American colonies?
3. What were "prison hulks"?
4. Explain three of the basic principles underlying the 1779 Penitentiary Act.

5. Are the themes that prisoners should be isolated and prisoners should work still important today? If so, in what way, or why not?

banishment The permanent expulsion of criminals to remote locations.

transportation The removal of criminals to a remote location where they could be used as laborers.

hospice facilities Late-sixteenth and early-seventeenth-century institutions that promoted the idea of isolating offenders from each other.

houses of correction Sixteenth-century institutions for offenders that emphasized the importance of hard work at disagreeable tasks.

prison hulks Eighteenth-century British merchant and naval ships converted into floating prisons.

1779 Penitentiary Act Passed by the English Parliament, this act relied on John Howard's ideas to make significant reforms to the prison system.

LEARNING OUTCOMES 3

Compare and contrast the Pennsylvania and Auburn prison systems in terms of their architecture, orienting strategies, and advantages/disadvantages.

The Pennsylvania system was used at Eastern State Penitentiary, which followed a separate and silent strategy. The prison, which was built with this strategy in mind, had individual cells with a small outside recreation yard for each prisoner. The Auburn prison, on the other hand, followed a congregate and silent strategy because its architecture was better suited for prisoners to leave their cells and work together during the day. The Pennsylvania system allowed easier control of the prisoners and had the advantage of avoiding cross-contamination because prisoners had no contact with each other. It also provided more opportunities for meditation and repentance. The Auburn system was more widely adopted by other states because it was deemed less damaging to the prisoner's mental

health, provided better vocational training, was cheaper to construct and operate, and—most important—produced money for the state.

1. What role did the Pennsylvania Quakers play in instituting long-term imprisonment as an alternative to corporal and capital punishment?
2. Highlight what you consider to have been the major advantages of both the Pennsylvania and Auburn systems.
3. Why did most American states choose to follow the Auburn model rather than the Pennsylvania model?
4. In what way was the 1870 meeting of the American Prison Association important for the development of American corrections?
5. What were the key characteristics of the reformatory movement?

Pennsylvania Quakers Members of the Society of Friends who, in 1787, argued that solitude and hard labor were humanitarian alternatives to the existing punishments.

Walnut Street Jail Opened in Philadelphia in 1776 to house petty offenders, debtors, and serious offenders and operated only as a jail until 1792 when a penitentiary addition was completed.

separate and silent Key words distinguishing the Pennsylvania system, which sought to keep prisoners separate from each other and required them to remain silent.

Pennsylvania system Prison system established with the Eastern State Penitentiary in 1892 in Philadelphia that assumed offenders would more quickly repent and reform if they could reflect on their crimes all day in silence and separated from others.

congregate and silent Key words distinguishing the Auburn system, which required prisoners to remain silent, even while working and eating together.

Auburn system Prison system established with the Auburn prison in New York, which used a modified version of the Pennsylvania system wherein prisoners were kept separate from each other at night but allowed to work and eat together, in silence, during the day.

reformatory A system of prison discipline that incorporates a more humanitarian approach to confinement and has an interest in preparing inmates for their eventual return to the community.

LEARNING OUTCOMES 4

Describe how men's and women's prisons differed during the reformatory movement of the nineteenth century.

Rather than following the architectural style of big prisons, women's reformatories were built in a cottage plan wherein small individual units created a more home-like than cell-like atmosphere. The programs for women were consistent with the cottage atmosphere and emphasized domestic activities rather than vocational training. In order to have more time to reform women offenders, state laws allowed them to be put in the reformatories for less serious crimes than those required for men to be sent to prison. That disparity was even more apparent for black women, who were more likely to be put in custodial prisons than in the reformatory.

1. What were three arguments favoring separate prison facilities for women in the nineteenth century?
2. What were three arguments against separate prison facilities for women in the nineteenth century?
3. What are the four ways in which women's facilities differed from men's during the reformatory movement?

differential response Term applied to society's response to women offenders when emphasis was on having separate and different-style prisons, different programs, and different sentencing practices for women offenders.

LEARNING OUTCOMES 5

Explain how penal systems in the South and West differed from those in the East and summarize reasons for those differences.

Whereas the northern states were developing large central prison facilities to hold offenders from throughout the states, southern states relied on prison farms distributed in rural locations across the states. The large penitentiaries did not catch on in the South because of the South's preference to let local authorities handle issues of justice and punishment and because the South's rural economy made prison farms and work camps more convenient sites for convict labor. In addition, there wasn't religious support for penitentiaries in the South as there was in the North. The penal system in the West often suffered from overcrowding to a greater extent than was present in the East, and some of that was the result of inadequate classification procedures that put low-level offenders into prison. The western states that had stable prison systems were those that kept informed about what was happening in the East and were willing to implement those more professional procedures.

1. Religion was important in both the North and the South, but the result in terms of penal philosophy was different. Why?
2. How did economic differences between the North and the South influence the resulting punishments in each region?
3. Do you think that imprisonment took slavery's place in the post–Civil War South? Explain.
4. In what ways did classification procedures affect imprisonment in California during the nineteenth century?
5. What explanations are offered for why Colorado, Utah, and the Dakotas had reasonably stable prison systems in the late 1800s?

decentralization A principle popular in the South during the first half of the nineteenth century wherein the administration of justice was left to local authorities instead of being centralized at the state level.

lease system Prison officials lease a prisoner to a private contractor to do labor for a specified sum and for a fixed time.

LEARNING OUTCOMES 6

Summarize the development of prison programs and the treatment of women and other minorities during the early, middle, and late twentieth century.

During the twentieth century, prisons began using information from the social and behavioral sciences to provide for basic classification of prisoners and to introduce more educational and vocational training. Classification became more sophisticated as the century progressed and rehabilitation took hold as the orienting philosophy. But by late century, rehabilitation had fallen out of favor and a preference for warehousing offenders took priority. Vocational training throughout the century was geared primarily toward male offenders, whereas women prisoners received domestic training at the century's start and were only able to participate in some of the more marketable training in middle and late century. By the 1990s, arguments were being made for providing more non-prison sanctions for women offenders. Throughout the century, African-Americans, Hispanics, and Native Americans were disproportionately represented in the nation's prison population.

1. What was progressivism?
2. What role did the Federal Bureau of Prisons play in moving prison programs forward in the early twentieth century?
3. Is there any advantage to providing women offenders with vocational training in nondomestic skills when they are in prison? Explain.
4. In what ways, if any, did racial disparity in imprisonment change from the early to late twentieth century?
5. Using information from other classes in sociology, psychology, criminal justice, and social work, what are some arguments supporting the basic concepts of the medical model?

progressivism Reform movement that began in the 1890s and resulted in widespread, significant political and social reforms in many social institutions, including prisons.

medical model An orienting philosophy that views criminals not so much as "bad" but as "sick" and in need of treatment.

LEARNING OUTCOMES 7

Explain the effects of changing public opinion on the use of imprisonment and prison alternatives in the twenty-first century.

During the first decade of the twenty-first century, opinion polls indicated that the American public was interested in strengthening the probation and parole system and in decreasing reliance on prisons—especially for low-risk, nonviolent offenders. Legislators are responding to the public's interest in prison alternatives—and to state budget deficits—by reducing the number of people being sent to prison and increasing the number of inmates released from prison.

1. Why does the United States have the highest incarceration rate of any country in the world?
2. Was the public opinion survey showing Americans favoring less reliance on imprisonment a fluke or the start of an ongoing trend?
3. Do you think treatment in the community or imprisonment is a better response to drug offenders? Why?
4. Looking at the states that had the greatest drop in prison populations from 2006 to 2011 and the three states with the greatest increases, what cultural or social differences in those states might explain the differences?
5. Do you agree that as much as 20% of the current prison population could be released from prison without jeopardizing public safety? Is that reason enough to release those people?

Additional Links

Visit **www.earlyamerica.com/review/2010_winter_spring/female-convicts-tables.html** to learn more about the crimes and sentences that resulted in women being transported to the American colonies.

Search the records of the Old Bailey, London's central criminal court, from 1674 to 1913 at **www.oldbaileyonline.org/**. Maybe you'll find some ancestors who were transported to the American colonies.

The official website of the historic Eastern State Penitentiary at **www.easternstate.org** includes a virtual tour of the prison and many other items of interest.

Get the most recent midyear report on jail and prison populations at **http://bjs.ojp.usdoj.gov/index.cfm?ty=pbse&sid=38** to see if the decline has continued.

Watch the CBS *60 Minutes* episode "Supermax: A Clean Version of Hell" about the Administrative Maximum (ADX) federal penitentiary at Florence, Colorado (Supermax) at **www.cbsnews.com/video/watch/?id=5101352n**.

Test your knowledge about crime and imprisonment in the United States with a 10-question quiz developed by the PEW Charitable Trusts at **http://www.pewtrusts.org/en/multimedia/surveys-and-quizzes/2015/what-do-you-know-about-us-crime-and-imprisonment**.

Check out some of the Justice Reinvestment Initiative success stories at **https://www.bja.gov/programs/justicereinvestment/success_stories.html**.

4

Sentencing

1 Discuss the severity of different sentence types and the importance of having access to presentence investigation reports.

2 Explain the two basic sentencing systems used in the United States.

3 Explain three sentencing practices.

4 Describe three techniques used to reduce the length of a sentence.

5 Explain the use of evidence-based sentencing to improve the quality of judicial decision making.

6 Describe two types of sentencing injustice.

7 Explain sentencing trends over the last five decades and discuss the current movement away from mandatory penalties.

SENTENCED TO 1,000 YEARS (IN ONE'S MIND)

Scholars at Oxford University in England have been thinking about ways futuristic technologies might transform sentencing and punishment. In one scenario, life extension technology could keep the worst criminals alive indefinitely in conditions deemed appropriate to their crime. If society doesn't want to wait for technology that can extend life, how about just

altering the criminal's perception of time? Philosopher Rebecca Roache, who leads the team at Oxford, points out that psychoactive drugs that distort people's sense of time already exist. She imagines a pill or a liquid that distorts prisoners' sense of time, leading them to feel as though they are condemned to eternal torment (or 500 years or 1,000 years of torment). Other scenarios are linked to technology that scans and maps human brain procedures. As that technology improves, it may be possible to upload human minds to a supercomputer or the cloud. Once uploaded, the criminal's mind could be sped up or slowed down. If run a million times faster than normal, the uploaded mind could serve a 1,000-year sentence in eight and a half hours. Or, maybe future sentences will emotionally enhance convicts who exhibit a neurologically stunted capacity for empathy. The genuine remorse felt by these newly empathetic criminals may be a punishment worse than prison (Andersen, 2014; West, 2014; Zolfagharifard, 2014).

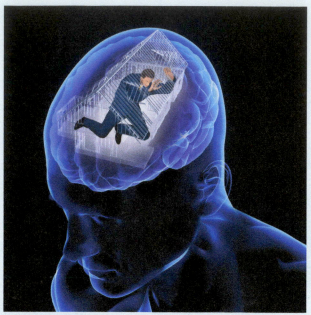

BSIP SA/Alamy Stock Photo

DISCUSS What are some of the ethical issues to consider regarding these punishments? Is it less humane to lock someone up for the best part of their life, or might it be more humane to tinker with their brains and set them free?

This chapter is concerned with the topic of **sentencing**, which refers to the process of a court imposing a penalty on a person convicted of a crime. There are a variety of penalties or punishments that a judge might apply, and that makes sentencing policy very complex. Sanctions can include fines, community service, probation, electronic monitoring, imprisonment, and several others—including combinations of the penalties. Adding to that complexity, the perceived severity of various sentences is not easily determined. This makes it difficult, for example, to decide whether a particular punishment will be considered severe enough by an offender to deter his or her continued criminal behavior.

▶ Sentence Severity and Types

 LEARNING OUTCOMES 1 Discuss the severity of different sentence types and the importance of having access to presentence investigation reports.

Presumably, the penalty applied to a convicted offender will be of increasing severity as the seriousness of the offense increases. We say "presumably" because punishment continuums are proposed by legislators and practitioners rather than being based on the experiences of people who actually serve the sentence. In fact, several studies (see, e.g., Wodahl, Ogle, Kadleck, & Gerow, 2009) suggest that imprisonment is not always viewed as the most punitive sanction.

As shown in Figure 4–1, when three categories of offenders were surveyed (prisoners in Oklahoma, probationers in Indiana, and both probationers and parolees in Kentucky), researchers found rather different views about punishment rankings. Despite general agreement by lay public and offenders that community service and regular probation are not very severe punishments, the offenders saw jail and boot camp as being more severe penalties than prison. Some offenders prefer time in jail to such community-based sanctions as electronic monitoring and time in prison to such alternatives as boot camp. Maybe some offenders view a relatively short jail sentence as a welcome break from the stressors of employment and family obligations. Possibly other offenders prefer the structure and clear-cut expectations of prison to having to put forth the greater personal responsibility needed to successfully complete a community-based penalty.

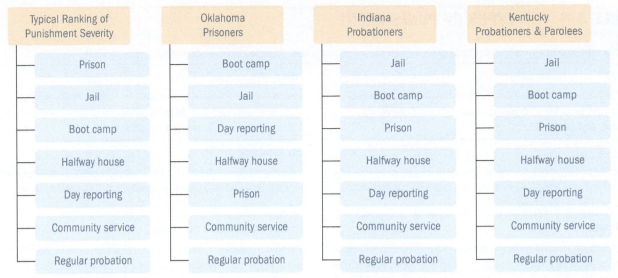

Typical Ranking of Punishment Severity	Oklahoma Prisoners	Indiana Probationers	Kentucky Probationers & Parolees
Prison	Boot camp	Jail	Jail
Jail	Jail	Boot camp	Boot camp
Boot camp	Day reporting	Prison	Prison
Halfway house	Halfway house	Halfway house	Halfway house
Day reporting	Prison	Day reporting	Day reporting
Community service	Community service	Community service	Community service
Regular probation	Regular probation	Regular probation	Regular probation

FIGURE 4–1 **Differing Views on the Severity of Punishment.** Although many people view the punishments listed in the first column as clearly descending from the most severe to the least severe, prisoners, probationers, and parolees may have different perceptions.
Source: Reprinted from Ranking Correctional Punishments: Views from Offenders, Practitioners, and the Public © 2010 by David C May and Peter B Wood. Published by Carolina Academic Press, Durham, NC. Reprinted by permission of published. All Rights Reserved.

DISCUSS **Meet with three or four other students and build your own ranking of sentence types from most to least serious. What arguments were used when people disagreed on the rankings?**

The research on punishment ranking is careful to point out that people receiving identical punishments may perceive the severity of that punishment very differently. May and Wood (2010) explain that factors such as age (e.g., older offenders perceive brief imprisonment as less severe than community-based sanctions of longer length) and experiences in the system (e.g., those with experience serving time in prison are more likely than those without prison experience to view a jail term as less severe than a longer time of close supervision in the community) will affect one's punishment ranking. Also, race, ethnicity, and gender are found to influence views about the severity of various punishments. In several studies, blacks have been found to be more likely than whites to choose prison over community-based sanctions (see May & Wood, 2010, p. 63). One explanation for this might be that blacks perceive prison alternatives such as boot camp, halfway houses, and even day reporting as too much of a hassle (e.g., abusive program officers and rules that are too hard to follow) compared with prison. But, regardless of the reason, the important point made by punishment-ranking research is that common assumptions about imprisonment being the most severe penalty and community-based punishment being less severe might be incorrect—at least in the calculation of some offenders. It will be helpful to keep this in mind as various punishment types are discussed and the sentencing process is reviewed.

Although there may be disagreement about how various penalties rank in severity, there is general agreement as to what each type involves. Table 4–1 briefly describes the major types of punishment. There may be restrictions placed on the options a judge has when sentencing an offender (such as those mentioned later in this chapter), but judges typically have some discretion in the sentencing process. Importantly, judges are not restricted to using just one sentence type. Some types obviously cannot occur together (e.g., a person could not be executed and placed on probation), but for the most part several different sentence types can be included as part of the actual sentence. Consider Keith's case, for example. After Keith's conviction for burglary, Judge Swanson requests a presentence investigation from the probation department. The results of that investigation tell Judge Swanson that this is Keith's second conviction for burglary in the past three years. For the first conviction, Keith was placed on probation for nine months, and he successfully completed that sentence without incident. Believing that this second conviction requires a harsher punishment, Judge Swanson sentences Keith to probation again, but with the special condition that he reside at the local halfway house. The sentence also requires Keith to perform 50 hours of unpaid labor that will benefit his community. This sentence, which uses probation, residential community corrections, and community service, is a reasonable example of combining sentence types. For a more complete understanding of how the sentencing process works, we will begin with that presentence investigation that Judge Swanson ordered.

Presentence Investigation Reports

In order to determine the most appropriate sentence type, it is vital that sentencing judges have access to information about the crime and the offense. The **presentence investigation report** is an important informational source on which judges base their sentencing decision for adult felony offenses. Writing a presentence report first requires a **presentence investigation (PSI)**,

TABLE 4–1 | TYPES OF PUNISHMENT

The primary sentences are briefly described here although each receives greater attention in other chapters.

Boot Camp

A form of short-term imprisonment that emphasizes a military-like philosophy and includes a combination of hard work, physical conditioning, and treatment

Prison

A sentence to confinement in a state or federal facility (typically for more than one year) that could be under minimum-, medium-, or maximum-security supervision conditions

Jail

A sentence to confinement in a city or county facility (typically for one year or less) that could be under minimum-, medium-, or maximum-security supervision conditions

Day Reporting

A nonresidential community-based sanction that blends high levels of supervision with the delivery of specific services needed by the offender

Halfway House

Community-based residential facilities that house offenders and serve as midpoints between liberty in the community and deprivation of liberty in a prison

Intensive Supervision Probation

A form of probation that requires closer supervision of the offender under increased rules and regulations governing the offender's movement and behavior

Community Service

Requirements for the offender to do unpaid work for the general good of the community

Regular Probation

Community supervision of an offender under court-imposed conditions for a specified time period during which the court can modify conditions as needed

Electronic Monitoring

Community-based sanction that requires the offender to wear an electronic device that can be used to monitor the offender's location and help ensure compliance with conditions of probation

Fines

A financial penalty that requires the offender to pay a specified sum of money within limits set by law

---

which is an inquiry interview and data-collection method used by a probation officer to summarize information about a convicted offender. As shown in Figure 4–2, the PSI is comprised of information about the offender's prior record as well as relevant personal and family data. In addition, information about the crime's impact on the victim is included. Because of the wealth of information, most well-researched PSIs for state cases are between 8 and 10 pages in length, with federal PSIs standardized at about 15 to 20 pages. A concluding summary provides the probation officer's sentence recommendation to the judge.

One study in Ohio found that sentencing judges followed the probation officer's recommendation in 66% of the cases when prison was recommended and in 85% of the cases when probation was recommended. Another study in Utah found that the court agreed with the probation officer's recommendation about 91% of the time in felony and misdemeanor cases (Norman & Wadman, 2000). Such a high level of concurrence may be influenced by factors such as probation officers recommending what they have learned a particular judge is likely to do anyway, might reflect the probation officer conforming to a

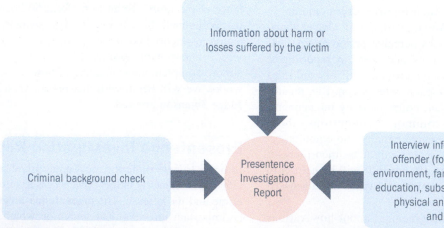

FIGURE 4–2 **PSI (Presentence Investigation).** The PSI requires the probation officer to gather information that might influence the sentencing decision but was not available to the judge during the plea-bargaining or trial proceedings.

plea agreement that was struck with the prosecutor, or might simply reflect a set of sentencing standards developed by a courtroom workgroup (Leifker & Sample, 2010). But in fairness to the hard work and dedication of probation officers charged with producing PSI reports, it must also be acknowledged that judges recognize those efforts and express their confidence in the probation officers by agreeing with recommended sentences. While keeping in mind the purposes of punishment, judges are influenced by the presentence investigator's report along with the wishes of the victim, prosecutor, and defense attorney.

Although the PSI report's primary use is to assist judges in determining the most appropriate sentence for a particular offender, it is also helpful to probation officers charged with supervising the offender in the community. Probation and parole supervisors use the PSI when assigning offenders to officers' caseloads. Field probation and parole officers use the PSI when writing a treatment or program plan (Norman & Wadman, 2000).

Despite its importance in the process, the use of the PSI at sentencing for felony crimes has declined in many states due to funding cuts and the increased use of determinate sentencing. Approximately 64% of all felony cases nationwide included a PSI prior to sentencing. About half of all states required a presentence investigation in all felony cases, whereas a PSI was discretionary in 16 states and nonexistent in 10 states (Petersilia, 2002). Probation officers in jurisdictions that do not have PSIs (e.g., Minnesota) complete a guidelines or sentencing worksheet to calculate the sentence based solely on prior criminal history and the severity of the current offense. This short form unfortunately deprives correctional agencies of valuable information about the offender.

▶ Basic Sentencing Systems

Describing how sentencing is accomplished across the country is not easily done. Each state and the federal government have developed their own specific procedures for determining and assigning the type and severity of punishment given to convicted offenders. Rather than trying to describe 51 different systems, the various approaches are typically grouped into one of two basic types—but with the important caution that there are hybrids (called **structured sentencing**) within each of the two systems, making it difficult to flatly say that a particular state is a pure example of one type or the other. The two broad approaches are **indeterminate sentencing** and **determinate sentencing**.

During the first hundred years of sentencing in the United States, the various states took the position that offenders should be sentenced to a specific penalty (a determinate sentence). Typically, that sentence was either corporal or capital punishment. With the growing use of prisons for punishment, the idea of specific penalties remained and offenders were sentenced to prison for a definite time period. A prisoner was

LEARNING OUTCOMES 2 Explain the two basic sentencing systems used in the United States.

released from confinement only when he or she had completed the years, months, and days stipulated in the judge's sentence. By the mid-nineteenth century, some prison officials were convinced that a fixed penalty prevented the reformation of offenders by keeping prisoners confined regardless of their efforts toward improvement. A new sentencing strategy—indeterminate sentencing—developed that allowed people other than a judge to determine when a prisoner should be released from confinement. Although it followed determinate sentencing in U.S. history, indeterminate sentencing provides the background for an understanding of today's resurgence of fixed or specific penalties, so we begin with the indeterminate type.

Indeterminate Sentencing

With indeterminate sentencing, legislatures assign wide sentencing ranges to offenses and judges have broad discretion in assigning sentence type (e.g., community supervision or a prison term) and sentence length. Because of that discretion to apply a sentence that best fits the individual case and offender, indeterminate sentencing is often linked to rehabilitation goals. Conceivably, one burglar could be released after one year whereas another offender convicted of a similar crime could spend several more years in prison.

Today, both state legislatures and judges provide limits to indeterminate sentencing in the United States. State legislatures are responsible for enacting criminal laws and penalties in their respective jurisdictions, and the resulting **statutory penalties** are linked to specific crimes or to classes of felonies or misdemeanors. With the state legislatures typically identifying a minimum and maximum time period, a person convicted of auto theft, for example, may be sentenced to at least one year but no more than five years. The sentence imposed by the judge must fall within the statutory penalty set by the legislature. If, for example, the statutory penalty requires that an auto thief receive a punishment between one and five years, the judge must impose a minimum and maximum somewhere between those numbers. Once the sentence is given, a parole board determines an offender's progress toward the goal of rehabilitation and behavioral change and decides when the offender has served sufficient time in prison and can safely be released on parole.

DISCUSS **The assumption underlying indeterminate sentencing is that corrections personnel, such as paroling authorities, are better able to determine when an offender is ready to be released than is a judge. Does that mean it would be even better to simply sentence a person to prison without any minimum or maximum and leave sentence termination entirely up to corrections officials? The result, of course, could mean that some offenders would be released after only a few days or weeks in prison whereas others would never be released.**

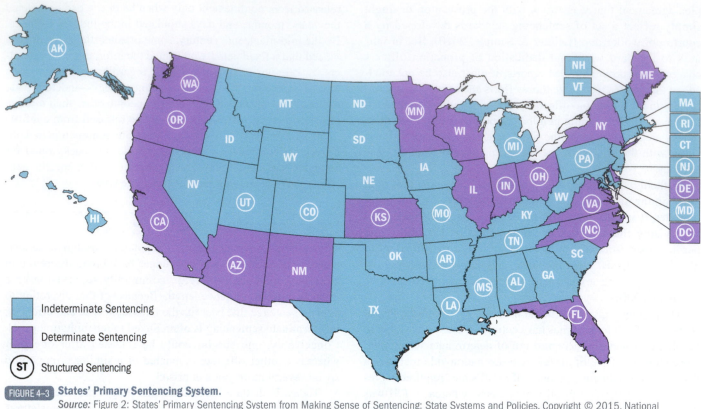

FIGURE 4–3 **States' Primary Sentencing System.**
Source: Figure 2: States' Primary Sentencing System from *Making Sense of Sentencing: State Systems and Policies.* Copyright © 2015, National Conference of State Legislatures. Used by permission of National Conference of State Legislatures.

As shown in Figure 4–3, currently 33 states use a primarily indeterminate sentencing system.

Determinate Sentencing

Dissatisfaction with indeterminate sentencing first surfaced in the early 1970s, when the American Friend's Service Committee (1971) published an attack on indeterminate sentencing and parole. The criticism struck at the very heart of indeterminate sentencing—the idea of individualized sentences. Although the proponents of indeterminate sentencing praised the notion that sentences should vary according to individual needs, the American Friend's Service Committee complained that poverty was ignored and discrimination was rampant. Furthermore, despite their best efforts, behavioral sciences had not advanced to the point that a parole board could tell when a person had been rehabilitated and therefore was ready for release to the community.

The attack on rehabilitation programs, excessive discretion by parole boards, and apparent sentencing inequalities seemed to leave indeterminate sentencing with few supporters. People on the political right asserted that the parole boards were releasing prisoners too early. Those on the political left said persons convicted of the same crime received very different sentences. The result was a return in many states to determinate sentencing in which the judge sentenced offenders to a fixed period of time—to community supervision or prison—within narrow statutory limits determined by the legislature. Release is determined by the percentage of sentence completed rather than whether a person has been rehabilitated. For example, if the statutory penalty is two to five years, sentences such as two and a half years' probation or four years' imprisonment would be acceptable. Sentences of one year or of five and a half years would not be possible because the time falls outside the statutory penalty. Figure 4–3 shows that today, 17 states and the District of Columbia have found determinate sentencing to be a satisfactory way to restore justice by reducing discretion and increasing the likelihood that the length of time actually served is closer to the time imposed by the courts.

Structured Sentencing

Although each state can be characterized as primarily indeterminate or determinate, no state is a pure example of either system (Lawrence, 2015). Half of the states include a structured component to their primary sentencing system in order to provide guidance to the judges as to the type and length of sentence to impose. As shown in Figure 4–3, this structured sentencing occurs in both indeterminate and determinate sentencing states.

Sentencing guidelines and presumptive sentencing (see the next section) are examples of a structured component. The rationale for structured sentencing is to enhance fairness and to provide consistency in sentences for similar crimes and categories of offenders. Where such components exist, release from prison is still determined by the state's primary sentencing system—a parole board in indeterminate systems and completion of the fixed prison term in determinate systems (Lawrence, 2015).

▶ *Sentencing Practices*

Variation among the sentencing procedures is the result of how jurisdictions modify their indeterminate or determinate

sentencing system using one or more special sentencing practices. The specific practices covered here are sentencing guidelines, mandatory sentencing, and aggravating/mitigating factors. The first two are tied to a just deserts philosophy and to general incapacitation (see Chapter 2) because they require similar sentences for comparable offenses. The use of aggravating or mitigating factors is a strategy that allows judges to increase or decrease a sentence because of special conditions associated with the offense, the offender, or the victim.

Sentencing Guidelines

Sentencing guidelines impose a predefined sentence length based on crime severity and prior criminal history, with the opportunity for the judge to depart (impose a greater or a lesser sentence) from the guidelines when circumstances warrant. When indeterminate sentencing states use guidelines that retain a parole board, the judge is recommended to use a range of years deemed appropriate for the case at hand. When guidelines are used in determinate sentencing jurisdictions, the judge sets a very narrow range or fixed sentence.

The two types of sentencing guidelines are voluntary and presumptive. In states with **voluntary sentencing guidelines**, possible sentences are suggested, but judges are not required to follow those suggestions. In states with **presumptive sentencing guidelines**, judges are required to issue a sentence that falls in a range established for a particular crime; they may even be required to provide written reasons for deviating beyond the customary limits. The presumptive model has been endorsed by the American Bar Association and in the American Law Institute's revised Model Penal Code (Frase, 2012). In addition, research suggests that presumptive guidelines may be more effective than voluntary guidelines in eliminating racial and ethnic disparities (Wang, Mears, Spohn, & Dario, 2013, p. 107).

One jurisdiction using presumptive guidelines has received considerable attention and will be used here to describe more fully the use of such guidelines. Minnesota uses sentencing guidelines that arrange presumptive penalties in the cells of a matrix or grid. The guidelines are created by a sentencing commission that determines suitable sentences for particular crimes and offenders.

Minnesota's presumptive sentencing guidelines system has been adopted in several other jurisdictions and is often identified as the premier example of this structural model (Frase, 2013). As shown in Figure 4–4, the grid is composed of 11 rows identifying crime severity levels ranging from those at the lower level of 1 to the higher level of 11. The grid's seven columns identify the offender's criminal history score, which is based on items such as number of prior misdemeanors and felony convictions, whether the offender was under correctional supervision when the current offense occurred, and prior

juvenile adjudications (Minnesota Sentencing Guidelines Commission, 2013). In the boxes where these two dimensions intersect are numbers that tell judges what the sentencing commission considers the ideal sentence (in months) for a particular crime committed by an offender with a particular criminal history score. Dividing the grid is a solid line that distinguishes sentences where imprisonment is presumed or mandatory (boxes above and to the right of the line) from sentences that are presumed will involve a stayed sentence (either the imposition or execution is stayed) and could include community sanctions, such as probation.

As an example of how a Minnesota judge might use the grid, look at Figure 4–4 and consider a robbery involving two offenders with similar criminal histories. If offender "A" (the leader/instigator) had a criminal history score of 2 and was convicted of aggravated robbery, he could receive a sentence of between 58 and 81 months in prison. The accomplice, offender "B" with a criminal history score of 2, is convicted of simple robbery because she had a minor role of driving the getaway car. She could receive a prison sentence of 28 months that is stayed as long as she successfully completes a period on probation.

Guidelines in other states vary with respect to the offense severity ranking and also the way the criminal history score is calculated. There are also different regulations that govern the circumstances in which a judge may depart from the guideline ranges.

Mandatory Sentencing

The possibility of a judge imposing probation or some other form of community-based sentence rather than prison time did not always agree with "get tough on crime" supporters, who often criticized judges' decisions to impose a non-prison sentence on offenders who were viewed as deserving or needing prison. Complaints were especially forceful in indeterminate sentencing states because those judges had the most discretion. Lawmakers responded by passing legislation to make a prison sentence mandatory for some crimes and offenders.

The theory behind **mandatory sentencing** is crime prevention through the use of general incapacitation and "just deserts" sentencing. According to Alarid (2004), proponents of general incapacitation believe that an increase in the use of prison will lead to a decrease in crime rates. All states, the District of Columbia, and the federal government presently employ some version of mandatory sentencing laws. Under those laws, persons convicted of particular crimes (e.g., drug possession/trafficking) or for crimes of increased danger (e.g., use of a deadly weapon) must be sentenced to a minimum number of years in prison—regardless of circumstances.

Once mandatory sentencing began, America's prison population increased dramatically, and there is reason to believe that this policy contributed to the decline in crime that began in the 1990s. However, there was also a dramatic increase in costs to taxpayers as more prisons were built and quickly filled. Importantly, many of those prisoners were nonviolent drug offenders, and citizens increasingly questioned whether it was sound policy to be using such an expensive sanction as

4.A. Sentencing Guidelines Grid

Presumptive sentence lengths are in months. Italicized numbers within the grid denote the discretionary range within which a court may sentence without the sentence being deemed a departure. Offenders with stayed felony sentences may be subject to local confinement.

SEVERITY LEVEL OF CONVICTION OFFENSE (Example offenses listed in italics)		CRIMINAL HISTORY SCORE						
		0	**1**	**2**	**3**	**4**	**5**	**6 or more**
Murder, 2nd Degree (intentional murder; drive-by-shootings)	11	306 *261–367*	326 *278–391*	346 *295–415*	366 *312–439*	386 *329–463*	406 *346–480[2]*	426 *363–480[2]*
Murder, 3rd Degree Murder, 2nd Degree (unintentional murder)	10	150 *128–180*	165 *141–198*	180 *153–216*	195 *166–234*	210 *179–252*	225 *192–270*	240 *204–288*
Assault, 1st Degree Controlled Substance Crime, 1st Degree	9	86 *74–103*	98 *84–117*	110 *94–132*	122 *104–146*	134 *114–160*	146 *125–175*	158 *135–189*
Aggravated Robbery, 1st Degree Controlled Substance Crime, 2nd Degree	8	48 *41–57*	58 *50–69*	68 *58–81*	78 *67–93*	88 *75–105*	98 *84–117*	108 *92–129*
Felony DWI; Financial Exploitation of a Vulnerable Adult	7	36	42	48	54 *46–64*	60 *51–72*	66 *57–79*	72 *62–84[2, 3]*
Controlled Substance Crime, 3rd Degree	6	21	27	33	39 *34–46*	45 *39–54*	51 *44–61*	57 *49–68*
Residential Burglary Simple Robbery	5	18	23	28	33 *29–39*	38 *33–45*	43 *37–51*	48 *41–57*
Nonresidential Burglary	4	12[1]	15	18	21	24 *21–28*	27 *23–32*	30 *26–36*
Theft Crimes (Over $5,000)	3	12[1]	13	15	17	19 *17–28*	21 *18–25*	23 *20–27*
Theft Crimes ($5,000 or less) Check Forgery ($251–$2,500)	2	12[1]	12[1]	13	15	17	19	21 *18–25*
Sale of Simulated Controlled Substance	1	12[1]	12[1]	12[1]	13	15	17	19 *17–22*

[1] 12[1] = One year and one day

☐ Presumptive commitment to state imprisonment. First-degree murder has a mandatory life sentence and is excluded from the Guidelines under Minn. Stat. § 609.185. See section 2.E, for policies regarding those sentences controlled by law.

▨ Presumptive stayed sentence; at the discretion of the court, up to one year of confinement and other non-jail sanctions can be imposed as conditions of probation. However, certain offenses in the shaded area of the Grid always carry a presumptive commitment to state prison. See sections 2.C and 2.E.

[2] Minn. Stat. § 244.09 requires that the Guidelines provide a range for sentences that are presumptive commitment to state imprisonment of 15% lower and 20% higher than the fixed duration displayed, provided that the minimum sentence is not less than one year and one day and the maximum sentence is not more than the statutory maximum. See section 2.C.1-2.

[3] The stat. max. for Financial Exploitation of Vulnerable Adult is 240 months; the standard range of 20% higher than the fixed duration applies at CHS 6 or more. (The range is 62–86.)

Effective August 1, 2015

FIGURE 4–4 **Minnesota Sentencing Guidelines Grid: Presumptive Sentence Lengths in Months.**
Source: 4.A. Sentencing Guidelines Grid from Minnesota Sentencing Guidelines and Commentary. Published by MN Sentencing Guidelines Commission.

imprisonment for persons who were nonviolent offenders. In recent years, state legislatures have been rethinking mandatory sentencing, and many states have revised those laws and are letting judges use their discretion and judgment in sentences for minor drug crimes. Even the most conservative states are considering prison alternatives. Texas, for example, has chosen to use money planned for prison construction to instead set up drug courts, electronic monitoring, and enhanced parole supervision for nonviolent offenders (Stewart, 2013). This continued movement away from heavy reliance on imprisonment and mandatory sentencing receives further discussion at the end of this chapter, in the section "Trends in State and Federal Sentencing."

Two specific sentencing practices that are linked to mandatory sentencing are truth-in-sentencing and "three strikes and you're out" laws (see Figure 4–5). The concept of **truth-in-sentencing** (TIS) refers to an attempt to reduce the apparent disparity between court-imposed sentences and the time offenders actually serve in prison. During the 1980s and 1990s, concern was expressed by citizens and legislators that offenders were not actually serving the sentences that had been imposed. For example, an offender who received a five-year prison term might be released after serving only three years. In an attempt to address such disparities, Congress authorized a grant program that provided states with federal funding assistance to build or expand correctional facilities and jails. Grants were awarded from 1996 to 2001 that allowed states to construct or renovate prisons and jails so that more violent offenders could be confined for a greater percentage of their sentences.

Eligibility for the TIS incentive funds required states to implement a so-called 85% rule, meaning that states must have or pass laws requiring serious violent offenders to serve at least 85% of their imposed sentences in prison. Grant eligibility criteria were established that allowed states with diverse sentencing structures to qualify, including those with determinate or indeterminate sentencing and those with parole release (Bureau of Justice Assistance, 2012; Ditton & Wilson, 1999; Rosich & Kane, 2005). A report after the funding program ended determined that although many states had enacted TIS laws, most of the reforms predated the federal legislation or were little more than tweaks to existing practices. By the end of the 1990s, regardless of whether they received federal TIS grants, most states—41, plus the District of Columbia—had implemented some form of TIS activity, but nine states remained without any TIS laws (Ditton & Wilson, 1999; Rosich & Kane, 2005).

In addition to the goal of attaining a closer match between sentence given and time served, TIS laws allowed states to forecast the effect of sentencing policies on the numbers of people incarcerated. Although a handful of states have successfully developed sentencing guidelines while keeping space allocation in mind, many states may have adopted TIS policies that created state fiscal problems because they have no "overcrowding release valve," such as good time or early release, to account for the new prison admissions that may enter faster than the number of available beds. One unique response to such fiscal problems is reflected in Missouri's policy of informing judges about the cost of a particular punishment. Under Missouri's sentencing procedure, a judge can learn that it could cost $37,000 to impose a prison sentence on someone convicted of endangering the welfare of a child whereas probation would cost $6,770. A second-degree robber, the judge might be told, would carry a price tag of less than $9,000 for five years of intensive probation, but more than $50,000 for a comparable prison sentence and parole afterward (Davey, 2010). The idea is to encourage judges to consider punishments that are less costly than imprisonment.

A second practice linked to mandatory sentencing is laws directed toward habitual offenders—popularly known as **three strikes and you're out** legislation. The first "three-strikes" law was passed in Washington State (1993), then a few months later in California (1994). By 1995, 24 states had enacted laws specifically addressing repeat and habitual offenders, 11 of which imposed mandatory life without parole. The "three strikes and you're out" moniker is more a catchy phrase than a helpful descriptor because the states vary widely in interpreting its meaning (in some states, two strikes are sufficient for a longer prison sentence) and implementation. Despite the differences, all three-strikes laws authorize, or in some cases mandate, longer periods of incarceration for violent felonies, such as murder, rape, robbery, arson, aggravated assault, and carjacking (Clark, Austin, & Henry, 1997). Less common are longer prison sentences for drug sales (e.g., California, Indiana, and Louisiana), escape (Florida), treason (Washington), and embezzlement and bribery (South Carolina). Some of the states that follow three-strikes legislation do not allow parole, and others allow for parole only after a minimum amount of time is served.

Truth-in-Sentencing
This guarantees that offenders who receive a prison sentence will serve at least 85% of that sentence.

Three Strikes and You're Out
These laws authorize or mandate longer periods of incarceration for persons convicted of subsequent crimes.

Mandatory Sentencing
This makes a prison sentence mandatory for some crimes and for some offenders. It is the result of such practices as truth-in-sentencing and three strikes laws.

FIGURE 4–5 Examples of Mandatory Sentencing.

DISCUSS The United States is among a minority of countries that have life without parole (LWOP) sentences (Solter, Kwon, & Isaac, 2012). Why is the United States rather unique in allowing this type of sentence?

By 2010, three-strikes laws were being viewed less as the best way to get violent offenders off the streets and more as an unfair and costly sanction without clearly shown benefits. California's three-strikes law was considered to be the country's harshest because it allowed for a life sentence to be imposed even if the third offense was a low-level felony like simple drug possession, shoplifting from a department store, or passing a bad check. As a result, by 2010, nearly 4,000 California prisoners were serving life for a third strike that was neither violent nor serious, according to the legal definition (Bazelon, 2010). In 2012, California voters opted to ease the state's three-strikes laws by ending life sentences for offenders whose third strike was not violent or serious as defined in state law (Fagan, 2013). Even in Washington State, where three-strikes law has been used so much that more than 15% of the entire prison population is serving a life sentence—the majority of whom were sentenced under three strikes—a few prosecutors and politicians are proponents of reforming the law (Sottile, 2013). As Table 4–2 shows, both proponents and critics of three-strikes legislation present strong arguments for their side, and it will be interesting to see whether these laws persevere, get repealed, or are reformed.

Aggravating and Mitigating Circumstances

A goal of sentencing guidelines and mandatory sentencing is to reduce the discretion of judges. That is partly an attempt to achieve fairness in the sentences given to different offenders convicted of similar crimes, and in the sentences given by different judges throughout a jurisdiction. In addition, reducing judicial discretion is a way the legislature can have greater impact on sentencing and presumably assure its constituents that stiff penalties will be imposed when necessary. But in most jurisdictions the judges still have some discretion available because they are often allowed to take aggravating and mitigating circumstances into consideration.

Legislatures have realized that they cannot anticipate all the different aspects of a particular case. Deciding that all

TABLE 4–2   PROS AND CONS OF THREE-STRIKES LEGISLATION

Pros	Cons
The fundamental purpose of the criminal justice system is to protect the rights and the safety of law-abiding citizens. But these citizens are not protected by "revolving-door justice," which allows criminals back on the street after repeat offenses. Three-strikes laws remove repeat offenders from society, and prevent them from committing further crimes.	Historically, judges have had discretionary powers when sentencing criminals; this practice recognizes that sentencing should take into account the circumstances of the crime, the character of the criminal, and the amount of harm caused by the crime. Mandatory sentences rob judges of those discretionary powers that are properly theirs. Indeed, mandatory sentences are imposed, in effect, by the politicians of the legislative branch of government—thus violating the independence of the judiciary and the separation of powers outlined in the Constitution.
Since three-strikes laws have been introduced across the nation, crime has dropped dramatically. The reason for this decline is obvious: Convicted recidivists are not free to commit more crimes, and felons with one or two strikes on their records are deterred by the punishment that they know will follow a third offense.	Defenders of the three-strikes laws claim that these laws have a powerful deterrent effect, and reduce the occurrence of crime. Statistics show, however, that recidivism has not been reduced by the presence of such laws, and the general reduction in crime, when and where it has occurred, is due to effective policing rather than to harsh sentencing.
The growth of the prison population has occurred alongside the decline in the crime rate; the two are clearly linked. Because those imprisoned under three-strikes laws are habitual criminals, the extra cost of holding them in prison has to balance against the economic savings to society from fewer robberies, burglaries, vandalism, violent crime (resulting in expensive hospital treatment), drug addicts, and so forth.	One effect of mandatory sentencing, and of three-strikes laws in particular, is the rapid growth of the prison population. The United States now locks up a higher proportion of its population than any comparable developed nation, yet many of those imprisoned for a great many years are nonviolent offenders convicted of relatively minor drug offenses or shoplifting. All of this comes at a very high cost to the taxpayer and is rapidly becoming unaffordable in a period of economic hardship. It is also notable that prison guard unions have spent heavily in favor of such mandatory sentencing, which favors the narrow economic interest of their members rather than the society they are meant to serve.

Source: Copyright © 2009 by International Debate Education Association.

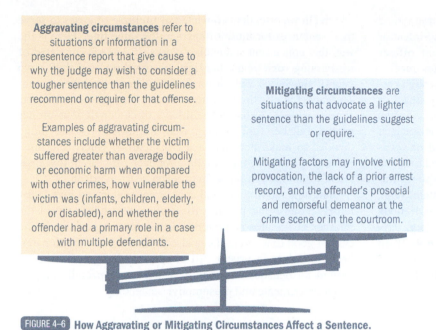

Aggravating circumstances refer to situations or information in a presentence report that give cause to why the judge may wish to consider a tougher sentence than the guidelines recommend or require for that offense.

Examples of aggravating circumstances include whether the victim suffered greater than average bodily or economic harm when compared with other crimes, how vulnerable the victim was (infants, children, elderly, or disabled), and whether the offender had a primary role in a case with multiple defendants.

Mitigating circumstances are situations that advocate a lighter sentence than the guidelines suggest or require.

Mitigating factors may involve victim provocation, the lack of a prior arrest record, and the offender's prosocial and remorseful demeanor at the crime scene or in the courtroom.

FIGURE 4–6 How Aggravating or Mitigating Circumstances Affect a Sentence.

convictions of robbery with a weapon will require a prison term of eight years may sound reasonable as a general principle. But what happens when the convicted robber not only carried a weapon, but also repeatedly kicked the victim while the victim was lying face down on the sidewalk? Is the mandatory eight-year sentence harsh enough for this case? On the other hand, what if the convicted robber had no prior criminal record and engaged in this crime only at the urging of his older brother, who has two prior robbery convictions? Should the younger brother receive the same eight-year sentence as his older brother?

Because some cases are more serious or less serious than the standard incident, legislatures often allow judges to vary from the determinate or presumptive sentence when either aggravating or mitigating circumstances are present. As highlighted in Figure 4–6, **aggravating circumstances** refer to situations that require a tougher sentence, whereas **mitigating circumstances** are situations requiring a lighter sentence. Similarly, under sentencing guidelines, the judge is often allowed to impose a sentence outside the guidelines if circumstances of the case warrant such departure. When aggravating or mitigating circumstances lead a judge's sentence to depart from the determinate or guideline sentence, many jurisdictions require the judge to provide written justification for the deviation.

► *Reducing Sentence Time*

Practices such as sentencing guidelines, truth-in-sentencing, three strikes, and aggravating circumstances have resulted in crowded prisons in many jurisdictions. As a counterbalance to those population-increasing factors, most states use little "tricks of the trade" to help make sure there is room for newly sentenced prisoners.

LEARNING OUTCOMES 4 Describe three techniques used to reduce the length of a sentence.

Jail Time

Many jurisdictions interpret the equal protection provision of the U.S. Constitution and state constitutions as requiring that punishment imposed on criminal defendants who cannot afford to post bond must be no different from punishment imposed on offenders who remain free until trial because they have the resources to make bail. Therefore, it is common for a person who was in jail prior to and during trial to have that jail time credited toward any prison sentence he or she receives.

By receiving that credit, the "jailed" offender does not receive a longer imprisonment sentence than does a similarly situated offender who remained at liberty in the community while awaiting trial. After conviction, felony prisoners may also spend time in a county jail waiting to be transferred to prison. Most states have decided that all or some of this **jail time**—either pretrial or after conviction—should be counted as time served toward their prison sentence.

Good Time

The concept of **good time** refers to a reduction of days from a sentence as a result of statutory provisions, the offender's good behavior, or extra work done by the offender. The general goal is to encourage a prisoner's good behavior by rewarding that good behavior through days off his or her length-of-stay. However, it also serves as a population management tool that can effectively, and in a low-profile way, help control prison admissions and releases (Clear & Schrantz, 2011; O'Hear, 2012).

A recent survey of state good time provisions found considerable variation in the amount of good time available (O'Hear, 2012). Some states offer day-for-day credit (or better), with the result of effectively cutting a sentence in half based on good conduct. Other states award only three or four days of credit per month, and still others have rather complex calculations that are not easily summarized. The norm, however, seems to be 10 to 20 days per month, or a reduction in sentence length of 25 to 40%.

Good time typically falls into three categories: statutory good time, earned good time, and meritorious good time. **Statutory good time** is usually given automatically (by state statute) either at the time the inmate enters prison or after monthly reviews. Although statutory good time is typically available to

DISCUSS **Should mitigating and aggravating circumstances be used for all types of crimes and criminals? For example, should sentencing in death penalty cases be influenced by mitigating and aggravating circumstances? For what other types of crimes or criminals might the use of mitigating and aggravating circumstances be controversial? (See Figure 4–6.)**

all prison inmates in those states with this provision, some states exclude inmates who have committed serious violent or sexual offenses or have killed a law enforcement officer (O'Hear, 2012). **Earned good time** is when inmates receive good time credit as the result of good behavior or through participation in work, rehabilitation, or education programs. For example, in Massachusetts an inmate may earn up to 2.5 days of good time credit per month for satisfactory performance related to a work assignment, or for an educational or vocational program (State of Massachusetts, 2013). Earned time is a prison management tool to encourage compliance with institutional rules and to keep prisoners occupied. A few states (e.g., California, Delaware, and Rhode Island) reward **meritorious good time** to inmates who perform exceptional acts (e.g., saving a life while in custody) or service (see Figure 4–7). In Rhode Island, inmates are even eligible for meritorious good time if they submit useful ideas or plans that benefit the state (State of Rhode Island, 2012).

Concurrent Sentencing

Both jail time and good time are techniques that effectively reduce the time offenders must serve on their sentences. A third way to reduce sentence time is through **concurrent sentencing**,

FIGURE 4–7 **Meritorious Good Time.** The California Department of Forestry has handpicked inmate crews that receive meritorious good time for their work. Shown here are rescue workers searching in the aftermath of a mudslide in the San Bernardino Mountains.
Source: JEBB HARRIS/EPA/Newscom

which allows offenders convicted of multiple offenses to serve their sentences for those offenses at the same time. Here is the way that concurrent sentencing works: If Anna is convicted of trespassing (one year), burglary (four years), and theft (two years), she serves only a total of four years on a concurrent sentence for all three crimes because the time clock starts simultaneously. Anna will still have three convictions on her record, but her time is increased dramatically if the judge decides to make her sentence *consecutive*, where she must serve each sentence one at a time for each offense. In this case, Anna would have to serve up to seven years in prison.

Jail time, good time, and concurrent sentencing give legislators, judges, and prison officials ways to help control the number of inmates in prison. Furthermore, especially in the case of good time, control can also be exerted over the inmates' behavior while in prison. All of these techniques have been around for decades, but they have become especially helpful under determinate and presumptive sentencing.

▶ Evidence-Based Sentencing

Sentencing policies beginning in the 1970s relied on incapacitation as the primary punishment philosophy, and those policies resulted in overcrowded prisons and skyrocketing corrections costs—second only to growth in state expenditures for Medicaid (Tierney, 2012). Criminal justice practitioners, legislators, and the general public are becoming increasingly dissatisfied with the burgeoning prison populations and their accompanying costs to state budgets. The overreliance on incarceration is increasingly viewed as having limited and diminishing effectiveness as a crime control strategy. An especially promising response is the increased reliance on evidence-based sentencing (EBS).

Evidence-based practices in corrections are those practices that have been proven through scientific research to reduce offender recidivism (Warren, 2007, p. 26). **Evidence-based sentencing**, then, involves the use of scientific research to improve the quality of judicial decision making when determining sentences and sentencing conditions (cf. Redding, 2009). In the past, judges relied on gut instinct, experience, or guidelines set by legislators when deciding an offender's sentence. Redding argues that instead of those unscientific measures, judges should be selecting the sentencing options that will best reduce recidivism through deterrence, incapacitation, or rehabilitation. By using evidence-based options, sentencing becomes a scientific question rather than one based on instinct, experience, or legislative mandate.

Evidence-based practices research has provided important information that can help judges make sentencing decisions. The following conclusions can be drawn from that research, and sentences based on the findings can reduce recidivism of felony offenders and, as a result, represent significant savings in corrections costs and the avoidance of future crime (Casey, 2010; Warren, 2009):

> LEARNING OUTCOMES 5 — Explain the use of evidence-based sentencing to improve the quality of judicial decision making.

- Effective recidivism reduction programs must target moderate- and high-risk offenders. Offenders in these risk categories have reduced recidivism when correctional interventions are provided with appropriate supervision and treatment services.

- Low-risk offenders need less supervision and fewer services. Placing low-risk offenders in structured treatment and supervision programs with higher-risk offenders may actually increase recidivism among the low-risk offenders.

- Cognitive behavioral programs that are rooted in social learning theory and address offender attitudes and thought processes are the most effective in reducing recidivism. Examples of such programs include Moral Reconation Therapy and Thinking for a Change (Milkman & Wanberg, 2007, pp. 41–47).

- Positive reinforcement is more effective than negative sanctions. Offenders respond better, and maintain newly learned behaviors longer, when approached with "carrots" rather than "sticks," or rewards rather than punishments. Research indicates that a ratio of four positive reinforcements to every negative reinforcement is effective in changing offender behavior (Crime and Justice Institute, 2004).

- Sentencing to some programs should be avoided. For example, adult boot camps, wilderness programs, domestic violence education, and life skills education typically do not reduce recidivism. Some programs, such as "scared straight," actually increase recidivism. Ineffective programs tend not to be sufficiently individualized, and are often based on inappropriate or unproven treatment approaches or are improperly implemented (National Center for State Courts, 2009; Redding, 2009, fn. 26).

How Judges Can Use Evidence-Based Research

Drawing on the results of evidence-based practices such as those described in Figure 4–8, we can identify some specific measures the judge should follow during the sentencing process (Warren, 2007):

- The judge, like the probation officer, should act as a change agent to reinforce the importance of the offender's voluntary compliance, not merely to enforce compliance.

- Judges have the opportunity to maximize the positive effect and minimize any negative effect of court processes by the way they interact with the people coming before them.

- The more offenders feel that they have been treated fairly, the more likely they will be to obey the law in the future.

- To achieve multiple sentencing objectives (e.g., deterrence, rehabilitation, and restoration), effective treatment programs must be successfully integrated with other sentencing requirements.

Evidence-based sentencing is seen as a means to smarter and more individualized sentencing and corrections policies that allow targeting of individual offenders who should be imprisoned and those who are appropriate candidates for effective treatment, intermediate sanctions, or community corrections programs (Warren, 2007). Increasingly, states are incorporating evidence-based practices into their probation and community corrections systems as a way to determine appropriate supervision and recidivism reduction strategies. Such state courts as those in Arizona, California, Idaho, Iowa, Texas, and Wisconsin are using or exploring how to use evidence-based practices to increase the effectiveness of their sentences (Casey, 2010).

▶ Unjust Justice

Unfortunately, examples of injustice can be found both in the factors used when determining a sentence and in the wrongful conviction of innocent people. The first injustice involves sentencing disparity wherein difference in sentencing may be attributed to extra-legal factors such as gender and race or ethnicity rather than to the appropriate factors such as offense severity and prior criminal record.

LEARNING OUTCOMES 6 Describe two types of sentencing injustice.

Sentencing Disparity

Today's sentencing policies do not openly target any specific groups of people, but many changes in sentencing policy have increased the disproportionality of Latinos, Native Americans, and African-Americans who are sentenced to prison throughout the country. This disproportionate representation in prison is an example of **sentencing disparity**. For example, enhanced penalty or mandatory drug laws for drug possession or distribution in public housing are more likely to target poor people living in those communities, a disproportionate number of whom also happen to be Latino or African-American. Prior to President Obama's signing of the Fair Sentencing Act of 2010 (see Figure 4–9), a person caught with five grams of crack received

In their meta-analysis of program evaluation research, the Washington State Institute of Public Policy (WSIPP) found that some programs work and some do not. Cognitive behavioral therapy programs—either in prison or the community—are among those that work. WSIPP analyzed the findings from 25 well-researched studies of cognitive behavioral programs for adult offenders in prison and community settings and found that, on average, they can be expected to reduce recidivism rates by 6.3%. In other words, one can expect recidivism to drop among offenders who participate in evidence-based cognitive behavioral treatment programs (Aos, Miller, & Drake, 2006).

FIGURE 4–8 **Evidence-Based Practice—Does It Work?** Cognitive Behavioral Programs Work!

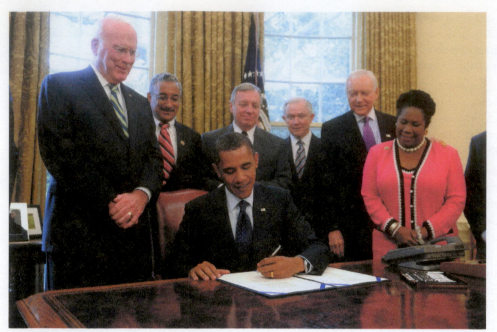

FIGURE 4–9 **The Fair Sentencing Act of 2010.** In 2010, President Obama signed a legislation that reduced, but did not eliminate, long-standing federal sentencing disparities between those caught with crack and those arrested with powder cocaine.
Source: Owen/Black Star/Newscom

In addition to the factors of race and ethnicity—and even celebrity status, as suggested in Figure 4–10—sentencing disparity is also found when gender is considered. Past beliefs about women criminals were that they were more amenable to rehabilitation than men but also seemed to have more problems than men, and thus women should actually spend *more* time in prison for the same crime. Following the 1970s, statutes that provided harsher maximum sentences for women than for men were consistently overturned by the courts, and today those kind of disparate sentencing laws no longer exist. Today's sentencing policies might still be affecting women differently than they do men—even though no gender-based differences are explicitly identified in the statutes.

a mandatory sentence of five years in prison whereas a person caught with powder cocaine had to have 500 grams to merit the same term. The new law reduces the 100-to-1 disparity to 18-to-1. A crack defendant would have to have 28 grams to trigger the five-year mandatory minimum sentence, or roughly the amount that authorities presume would indicate a dealer rather than a casual user.

Consider for a moment that the drug war may have affected female offenders more than male offenders. There are several reasons for this. First, women's drug use is more likely linked to their criminal behavior. Research shows a more consistent and significant link between drug use and female offenders than drug use and male offenders at time of arrest (Davis, Merlo, & Pollock, 2006; McShane & Williams, 2006). A similar profile is found for women in prison, particularly for the disproportionate number of African-American and

Defendant: Rapper Snoop Dogg
Crime: Felony possession of a dangerous weapon at an airport
Sentence: 160 hours of community service, three years' probation, $1,000 in fines and court costs, mandatory $10,000 donation to charity

Defendant: Actress Lindsay Lohan
Crime: Stealing a necklace from a jewelry store
Sentence: Probation with five weeks of home confinement followed by 480 hours of community service

Defendant: Financier Bernard Madoff
Crime: Fraud for giant Ponzi scheme, which judge called "extraordinarily evil"
Sentence: 150 years (thrice the length asked by the federal probation office)

FIGURE 4–10 **Sentencing Disparity and Celebrities.** In addition to sentencing disparity issues related to such extra-legal factors as race, ethnicity, and gender, an argument might be made that celebrities receive sentences that are both less and more harsh than is typical based, in part, on their celebrity status.
Source: Dee Cercone/Everett Collection Inc/Alamy Stock Photo

Hispanic women sentenced to prison for a drug offense. Reports on drug use history find that female prisoners used more drugs than did male prisoners (Greenfeld & Snell, 1999). If female offenders are more likely to have drugs linked to their criminal behavior, sentencing policies that inadvertently incarcerate small-time drug users and dealers are more likely to affect women (Mauer, Potler, & Wolf, 1999).

In mixed-gender crime partnerships, men offenders tend to operate in higher positions and in more primary criminal roles than women (Alarid, Marquart, Burton Jr., Cullen, & Cuvelier, 1996). This line of reasoning should not be confused with leniency, only to suggest that women may receive less time than men because they play a secondary role in the same criminal incident and are sentenced accordingly. Roles played in crime may not be available to sentencing researchers who are merely examining time served for various types of crime.

The courts are interested in maintaining the family unit and not punishing dependents for the actions of one offender. In the larger society, women tend to be the primary caretakers of dependent children, in terms of spending more time caring for children and being involved in domestic duties. Daly (1987) called this "familial paternalism," in which the identified primary caretaker may receive a more lenient sentence (particularly in state courts) than an offender without family or dependents. So in some courts, being a caretaker of dependent children, and assuming that the crime was not related to parental ability, judges may give leniency for this reason. The federal courts eliminated the consideration of family at the time of sentencing, which has disadvantaged primary caretakers. However, the federal sentencing guidelines do allow a very small number of women to receive more lenient sentences as a result of their family responsibilities (Morash & Schram, 2002).

The gender of the victim even makes a difference in the sentence lengths for homicide, robbery, and assault. For example, in Texas, whereas gender did not affect the incarceration decision, prison sentences were significantly longer for men who victimized women and when the victim suffered extensive injuries. Age and race or ethnicity had no effect on the sentencing outcome or sentence length for these same crimes (Curry, Lee, & Rodriguez, 2004).

Recent research on race, ethnicity, gender, and other legally irrelevant offender characteristics shows less of an interest in any direct effect those characteristics might have and considers instead their indirect or interactive effects. Spohn (2013) notes that study results have been inconsistent but generally show that certain categories of racial minorities—males, the young, and the unemployed—are singled out for harsher treatment. The combination of race or ethnicity and one or more of the other characteristics better predicts sentence severity than does any individual characteristic.

Wrongful Convictions

A second type of injustice is the wrongful conviction of an innocent person. Whether you agree with William Blackstone's ratio of "better that ten guilty persons escape than that one innocent suffer" or have some other proportion in mind, it is likely that you at least agree with the principle of punishing the guilty rather than the innocent.

Estimates of the number of wrongful convictions are complicated by definition problems (e.g., how is factual innocence best determined?) and by the absence of any official list of exonerees (for examples of unofficial online lists, see Zalman, Smith, & Kiger, 2008, p. 77). Using estimates by criminal justice experts, Zalman et al. suggest that wrongful convictions may occur at a rate of 1 to 3% in the United States. Gross (2013, p. 57) estimates that 1 to 5% of convictions for serious felonies in the United States are erroneous. If the rate is as few as 1% of serious felony convictions, there may be 10,000 to 20,000 prisoners in America who are in fact innocent of the crime for which they were convicted.

Wrongful convictions can be the result of several types of missteps or misbehavior in the criminal justice system. The Center on Wrongful Convictions (www.law.northwestern.edu/legalclinic/wrongfulconvictions/) lists erroneous eyewitness identification, false and coerced confessions, inadequate legal defense, official misconduct, and false or misleading forensic evidence as examples of such problems. Of those, erroneous eyewitness identification and false confessions are generally considered to account for the majority of wrongful convictions.

Erroneous eyewitness identification is the single greatest cause of wrongful convictions in the U.S. criminal justice system (Innocence Project, 2013). Unfortunately, despite the increased attention this problem has received, most American law enforcement agencies lack uniformity with respect to eyewitness identification procedures, nor have they fully implemented recommended federal guidelines.

A wrongful conviction based on a false confession may be even more difficult to understand than erroneous eyewitness identification. The largest category of falsely confessing suspects consists of the mentally impaired, the mentally ill, the young, and the easily led. It is not uncommon that a confession—later determined to have been false—may include a detailed and accurate account of what occurred. However, Garrett (2010) explains that such details may actually have been introduced, whether intentionally or not, by the police during interrogation.

Three decades of research has led psychologists to suggest the following steps as ways to lessen the likelihood of erroneous eyewitness identification during police lineups (Dittmann, 2004):

- Select fillers to appear in lineups that fit a witness's description of the perpetrator.

- Instruct witnesses that the person who committed the crime may not be in the lineup.

- Do not say anything that may influence the witness's decision in identifying a person from the lineup, such as by providing any information about lineup members.

- Use a sequential method by presenting photographs one at a time to witnesses and having them make a decision about a photo before viewing the next.

- Record in writing both identification and nonidentification lineup results, including witnesses' statements—in their own words—about their identification certainty.

▶ Trends in State and Federal Sentencing

The timeline in Figure 4–11 shows a five-decade period moving from harsh penalties of mandatory sentencing to a contemporary time when public opinion and many state legislatures are preferring prison alternatives over long-term imprisonment. Mandatory penalties continue to exist in every state, but increasingly states are revising those penalties—especially for nonviolent and drug offenders.

LEARNING OUTCOMES 7 — Explain sentencing trends over the last five decades and discuss the current movement away from mandatory penalties.

Reports by the Vera Institute of Justice (Subramanian & Delaney, 2014; Subramanian, Moreno, & Broomhead, 2014) identify specific ways in which state legislatures are showing a willingness to rely on carefully implemented and well-targeted community-based programs rather than on the more expensive and less productive prison option. Two of those approaches are highlighted in the next sections.

Reduce Prison Populations and Costs

Since 2000, more than 30 states have reduced their prison populations and related costs by, among others, (1) repealing or easing mandatory penalties and (2) reclassifying offenses to not require imprisonment. The mandatory penalties (such as mandatory minimum sentences and habitual offender laws) were hallmarks of the tough-on-crime era when crime control was believed to be best accomplished by "sending a message" to potential offenders. However, research consistently shows that longer sentences have little deterrent value and are not helping to reduce recidivism (see Subramanian & Delaney, 2014, fn. 8; Subramanian et al., 2014, fn. 11). Instead, mandatory penalties are major contributing factors in the growth of prison populations and costs. Facing questionable benefits and high costs, legislators are increasingly willing to rethink mandatory penalties. Recent examples of states modifying or repealing mandatory sentencing policies include Georgia and Hawaii restoring some discretion to sentencing judges for certain drug and property offenses, and Illinois and Indiana revising the criteria that trigger the mandatory sentence.

The strategy of reclassifying offenses to not require imprisonment is also a popular option for legislatures and is often linked to the concept of proportionality (see chapter 2). Imprisonment is increasingly viewed as a disproportionally severe punishment for some crime—notably some drug and property offenses. With examples of laws such as one in Indiana where possession of cocaine with intent to deliver was punished more harshly than rape leading the way, states such as Colorado, Indiana, and Maryland reclassified offenses to better align the sentence with the crime. In 2014, California reclassified six property and drug offenses from felonies to misdemeanors and eliminated prison as a sentencing option (Porter, 2015; Subramanian et al., 2014).

Expand or Strengthen Community-Based Sanctions

Encouraged by public opinion polls showing that most Americans support alternatives to incarceration for nonviolent offenses, and drawing on research that shows certain offenders can be safely and effectively supervised in the community rather than housed in prison, states have introduced or strengthened community corrections programs proven to reduce recidivism. Quite a variety of strategies are being used (see Subramanian et al., 2014), including the (1) expansion of community-based sentencing options and (2) increasing the use of incentives in community supervision.

Realistically, it is not possible for prison to be a "last resort" if there are no effective alternatives in the community. And, in turn, effective community-based supervision is possible only if programs and services, such as housing, employment, and substance abuse treatment, exist. To that end, some states have created new community-based sentences (e.g., home detention as a prison alternative) or increased the potential for success by requiring probation agencies to provide probationers with intake and orientation, substance abuse assessment, and a treatment plan (Porter, 2015; Subramanian et al., 2014).

TIMELINE	Sentencing Trends Over Five Decades					
1973	**1984**	**1994**	**1999**	**2002**	**2012**
New York's Rockefeller drug laws come into effect, establishing mandatory minimum sentences for drug offenses.	**Washington state** enacts the first truth-in-sentencing law that requires violent offenders to serve most of their sentences in prison.	**California passes** a three-strikes law enhancing mandatory penalties for third-time felony convictions.	**Twenty-four states** now have three-strikes laws and 29 states now have truth-in-sentencing laws.	**Michigan eliminates** mandatory sentences for most drug offenses.	**At least** 17 states and the federal government have partially repealed or lessened the severity of mandatory sentences.

FIGURE 4–11 **Timeline: Sentencing Trends Over Five Decades**
Source: From Playbook for Change? States Reconsider Mandatory Sentences by Ram Subramanian and Ruth Delaney. Copyright © 2014 by Vera Institute of Justice.

Positive reinforcement and the use of incentives are components of effective behavior modification, and some states have passed laws that offer offenders on probation or parole early discharge or other benefits if they comply with the conditions of their supervision. A benefit of rewarding consistently compliant offenders in that way is to allow more focus on offenders who pose greater risk to public safety. Other states award compliant offenders with an offense downgrade so that some negative consequences of their conviction may be mitigated.

Changes in Federal Sentencing

The federal government is following the state lead, and in 2013, Attorney General Holder announced that the Justice Department would no longer pursue mandatory minimum sentences for certain low-level drug offenders. U.S. prosecutors were instructed to omit the specific quantity of drugs when drafting indictments for drug defendants who meet four criteria: (1) Their conduct did not involve violence, the use of a weapon, or sales to minors; (2) they are not leaders of a criminal organization; (3) they have no significant ties to large-scale gangs or cartels; and (4) they have no significant criminal history. By omitting reference to quantity, the prosecutors would be able to sidestep federal laws that impose strict mandatory minimum sentences for drug-related offenses until the laws themselves could be changed (Savage, 2013).

In 2014, the U.S. Sentencing Commission voted to reduce sentencing guidelines for most federal drug-trafficking offenders and to make the sentencing reduction retroactive (U.S. Sentencing Commission, n.d.). Since Congress did not act to modify or disapprove the change, the policy change became effective in November 2014 and federal courts began hearing motions for retroactive sentence reductions. The change reduced penalties by an average of 11 months for 70% of drug-trafficking offenders in new cases and more than 40,000 current federal prisoners became eligible to have their sentences reduced by an average of 25 months.

The first group of prisoners receiving a sentence reduction began leaving halfway houses and prisons in November 2015. That group of about 6,000 people included foreign citizens (about 2,000) who will be deported to their home country. Among the other 4,000 are persons who will simply be released from community supervision and almost 1,000 who will be released from prison and placed in community supervision. Other groups to be released in the coming years under this sentence reduction process will follow a similar pattern.

The policy change is designed to help reduce federal prison costs and populations. The U.S. Department of Justice testified before the Sentencing Commission that the dramatic increase in the federal prison population was making prisons less safe—for both prison personnel and inmates—and made successful reentry programs more difficult. The commissioners were also swayed by the argument that increased federal prison costs meant less funding for law enforcement, prosecutors, crime prevention, victim services, and other priorities (U.S. Sentencing Commission, n.d.).

The prisoners are mostly black and Hispanic men in their early 40s and many of them had minimal or no criminal history prior to their drug conviction. Further, more than 75% of persons in federal prisons for drug offenses had no serious history of violence prior to their current offense (Taxy & Kotonias, 2015). It is this last point that highlights the reference to "nonviolent drug offender" in discussion about the need—and support—for sentencing reform. As with changes in state sentencing policy, the federal changes reflect concerns about prison costs and overcrowding that are widely shared among leaders of both political parties and by criminologists.

The remaining chapters of this book provide specifics regarding jail, prison, and community-based programs. As this chapter points out, sentence types, lengths, options allowed, and even the reason for the punishment vary over time and place. It will be helpful while reading the coming chapters to understand that the various sentencing options are not set in stone.

Mandatory Sentencing and Drug Laws

In 2000, John Horner lost his eye in an accident and was prescribed painkillers. Many years later, he met "Matt"—who, it turns out, was an informant for the Osceola Florida County Sheriff's Office. One day Matt explained that he was forced to decide between paying his rent and filling a prescription for pain pills. Matt asked John if he could buy some of John's pain pills. John, who claims that Matt looked in pain at the time of the request, agreed and over a period of several weeks provided Matt with four of his own unused bottles of prescription pain pills for a total of $1,800—part of which, John claims, was repayment of money Matt had previously lent him. After the last exchange, John was arrested and charged with dealing drugs. At the advice of his public defender, John pleaded guilty, and in 2012 was sentenced under Florida law to the mandatory minimum of 25 years in prison. John will be 72 when he is released, and his three young children will have grown up without him. Matt, who turned out to have a long history of drug offenses, received a reduced sentence of just 18 months after informing on Horner (Friedersdorf, 2013; Stewart, 2013; Walker, 2013).

The way mandatory sentencing has been implemented in some cases raises several interesting questions:

1. Matt had apparently agreed to act as a police informant in return for a reduced sentence. John was actually offered a similar deal by the prosecutor. Under the deal, John agreed to plead guilty, but if he helped make prosecutable cases against five other people on drug-trafficking charges his own sentence could be reduced from 25 years to 10. John was unsuccessful in his assigned task and therefore received the full sentence (Walker, 2013). The *Frontline* television program "Snitch" (www.pbs.org/wgbh/pages/frontline/shows/snitch/) asks whether mandatory minimum sentencing has bred a culture of snitching that ends up rewarding the guiltiest and punishing the less guilty. Assume for the moment that the threat of mandatory minimum sentences is used to encourage offenders to serve as police informants in exchange for a reduced sentence. *Is that sound policy or practice?*

2. Ignore any possible concerns that you or others may have regarding the use of "snitches" and concentrate only on the crime. Essentially, a 46-year-old employed father was caught selling four bottles of pain pills prescribed for him. Friedersdorf (2013) notes that Florida spends about $19,000 to incarcerate an inmate for a year. *Do you think keeping nonviolent drug offenders like John Horner in prison for 25 years is the best use of $475,000?*

3. A 2013 poll found that most Americans oppose prison sentences for a first-time offense of possessing powder cocaine, crack cocaine, or heroine (Flatow, 2013; Moore, 2013). In many jurisdictions, that possession—especially if prosecutors believe it was with the intent to distribute the drug—could result in lengthy mandatory sentences. *What is your opinion—if it seems clear the possession was only for personal use? How about if it is clear that the intent was to distribute? Do you think public attitudes about prison sentences for drug offenses have changed over the last few decades?*

LEARNING OUTCOMES 1

Discuss the severity of different sentence types and the importance of having access to presentence investigation reports.

Sentence types include ones as simple as fines and community service and as disruptive as jail and prison. Others, such as boot camps and halfway houses, can be alternatives to prison, whereas additional ones are considered more community-based sanctions (e.g., day reporting, regular and intensive supervision probation, and electronic monitoring). It is difficult to rank these sanctions by severity because the consequences of each are perceived differently depending on the individual.

1. Make an argument for one year on regular probation being a more severe punishment than three months in jail.

2. If you were a judge, what information would you want to have in a presentence investigation report to help you decide an appropriate sentence?

3. How does regular probation differ from intensive supervision probation?

4. Could fines be made so punitive that the public would accept them as an alternative to probation or jail? What are some problems when using fines in that way?

sentencing When a court imposes a penalty on a person convicted of a crime.

presentence investigation report A report developed from information derived through a presentence investigation that is provided to the judge to assist in sentencing decisions.

presentence investigation (PSI) An inquiry interview and data-collection method used by a probation officer to summarize information about a convicted offender.

LEARNING OUTCOMES 2

Explain the two basic sentencing systems used in the United States.

The basic sentencing systems found in the United States are indeterminate and determinate sentencing. Under indeterminate sentencing, the judge can impose a range of years (e.g., two to four years in prison), but determinate sentencing requires imposition of a specific penalty (e.g., five years in prison).

1. Some of the strongest proponents of determinate sentencing are prisoners. Why?

2. State legislators set minimum and maximum penalties for crimes, but judges must determine particular sentences for individual offenders. Wouldn't it make more sense to allow judges complete authority to determine a sentence?

indeterminate sentencing A system wherein the convicted offender receives a sentence that covers a time range rather than a fixed period.

determinate sentencing A system wherein the convicted offender receives a sentence to a specific time period rather than a time range.

statutory penalties Sentences linked via legislation to specific crimes, or to specific classes of felonies or misdemeanors, with a minimum and maximum time period.

structured sentencing A modification to either indeterminate or determinate sentencing wherein judges are provided guidance on sentence type and length.

LEARNING OUTCOMES 3

Explain three sentencing practices.

Three sentencing practices used today are sentencing guidelines, mandatory sentencing, and aggravating/mitigating circumstances. All of these can be used under either a determinate or indeterminate sentencing system and each provides a way to modify that basic system. For example, sentencing guidelines encourage or require a judge to impose a sentence within an established range. Mandatory sentencing—exemplified by three-strikes and truth-in-sentencing laws—requires prison sentences for some crimes and offenders. Aggravating and mitigating circumstances allow sentences to be increased or decreased due to particular circumstances.

1. What two factors are used in the Minnesota sentencing guidelines to calculate a sentence?

2. What are some pros and cons of three-strikes laws?

3. Why are truth-in-sentencing and three-strikes laws examples of mandatory sentencing?

4. What are some arguments for why judges should be allowed to take aggravating and mitigating circumstances into consideration when imposing a sentence? What are some arguments for why they should not?

sentencing guidelines Impose a predefined sentence length based on crime severity and prior criminal history, with the opportunity for the judge to depart from the guidelines when circumstances warrant.

voluntary sentencing guidelines Suggested, rather than required, guidelines that stipulate a time range for a judge to use when deciding a sentence.

presumptive sentencing guidelines Required, rather than suggested, guidelines for a judge to use when deciding a sentence.

mandatory sentencing Requires a prison sentence for some crimes and some offenders.

truth-in-sentencing When the length of time served in a sentence is close to the time imposed by the courts.

three strikes and you're out Laws that authorize, or mandate in some cases, longer periods of incarceration after a certain number of prior convictions ("strikes").

aggravating circumstances An event or condition that makes an offense more serious than it might otherwise be.

mitigating circumstances An event or condition that makes an offense less serious than it might otherwise be.

LEARNING OUTCOMES 4

Describe three techniques used to reduce the length of a sentence.

Sentence length can be reduced by giving credit for time spent in jail while awaiting trial (pretrial jail time), for good behavior while in prison (good time), and by serving multiple sentences all at the same time (concurrent sentencing).

1. What are some factors leading to the increase in prison populations?

2. How might correctional workers and administrators benefit from good time credits being given to prisoners?

3. Should offenders be given time off of their sentences for good behavior?

4. Is it fair to crime victims when offenders serve multiple sentences concurrently?

jail time Time spent in jail, either pretrial or after conviction, that could be counted toward a convicted offender's sentence.

good time Reduction of days from a sentence as a result of statutory provisions, the offender's good behavior, or extra work done by the offender.

statutory good time Reduction of days from a sentence usually given automatically as a prison management tool to relieve overcrowding.

earned good time Good time credits resulting from good behavior or through participation in work or education programs.

meritorious good time Good time credits given to inmates who perform exceptional acts or services such as firefighting or working in emergency conditions.

concurrent sentencing Allows an offender convicted of multiple offenses to serve the sentences for those offenses at the same time.

LEARNING OUTCOMES 5

Explain the use of evidence-based sentencing to improve the quality of judicial decision making.

Findings from evidence-based practices suggest that during the sentencing process judges should act as a change agent, rather than merely enforcing compliance, to minimize any negative effect of the court process on the offender. Further, the judge should work to assure that offenders believe they have been treated fairly and should integrate effective treatment programs with other sentencing requirements.

1. What are some things a judge can do during the sentencing process to have a positive effect on the person being sentenced?

2. Why is recidivism increased among low-risk offenders when they are put in programs designed for moderate- and high-risk offenders?

3. Why are cognitive behavioral programs especially effective in reducing recidivism?

4. Why do some people support the use of boot camps even if they cannot be shown to reduce recidivism?

evidence-based sentencing Involves the use of scientific research to improve the quality of judicial decision making when determining sentences and sentencing conditions.

LEARNING OUTCOMES 6

Describe two types of sentencing injustice.

Unjust sentencing is reflected in instances of sentencing disparity wherein members of minority groups are subject to harsher penalties, and in instances of wrongful convictions that result in innocent people being punished for crimes they did not commit.

1. What are some steps that can be taken to lessen the likelihood of erroneous or mistaken eyewitness identification during a police lineup?

2. Generally speaking, are celebrities treated differently at sentencing?

3. What would you consider to be just compensation for someone who was wrongfully convicted of a crime?

sentencing disparity A type of injustice wherein sentencing policy has the unintended effect of targeting a population group—often minority—and resulting in members of that group being disproportionately represented among persons in the correctional system.

wrongful convictions A type of injustice wherein a person is convicted and punished for a crime he or she did not commit.

LEARNING OUTCOMES 7

Explain sentencing trends over the last five decades and discuss the current movement away from mandatory penalties.

Sentencing during the last five decades has moved from a heavy reliance on harsh penalties and mandatory sentences to today's preference for prison alternatives rather than long-term imprisonment. At the state level, these changes are apparent in the movement to reduce state prison populations and their related costs by repealing or easing mandatory penalties and by reclassifying offenses to not require imprisonment. In addition, states are expanding or strengthening community-based sanctions. Similar changes are occurring at the federal level—especially in how federal drug offenders are being handled.

1. What are two ways that states have used recently to reduce their prison populations?

2. How is positive reinforcement being used to modify the behavior of offenders on probation or parole?

3. What policy changes occurring at the federal level are effecting the sentences of federal drug offenders?

Additional Links

Review the rise and fall of California's three-strikes legislation at **http://retroreport.org/crime-and-punishment-three-strikes-and-youre-out/**

Visit the Frontline site at **www.pbs.org/wgbh/pages/frontline/shows/snitch/** to learn how mandatory sentencing may be encouraging snitching as a key prosecutorial strategy in the drug war.

Visit **www.innocenceproject.org** to read about an organization dedicated to assisting prisoners who could be proven innocent through DNA testing.

At **http://webapp.urban.org/reducing-federal-mass-incarceration/**, the Urban Institute provide an interactive tool that lets you see how different policy changes will affect the federal prison population.

5

Probation and Community Supervision

1 Explain the key ways in which community supervision is beneficial to the offender, the community, and the victim.

2 Describe how probation supervision works.

3 Identify the ways that probation and community correctional sanctions can be reparative to the victim and community.

4 Discuss how intermediate sanctions created for the surveillance of community conditions reduce risk to public safety.

5 Describe the most typical community-based programs that address root causes of defendants' problems with crime.

Mikael Karlsson/Alamy Stock Photo

THE CASE OF "AFFLUENZA:" ARE WEALTHY OFFENDERS MORE LIKELY TO BE SUPERVISED ON PROBATION?

In June of 2013, 16-year-old Ethan Couch left a house party near Fort Worth Texas with seven teenage passengers, two of whom were in the bed of his pickup truck. Couch was driving too fast down a narrow residential road when he lost control of his vehicle. The pickup veered off the road, hit a parked SUV, and ran over four people, killing them instantly. Three of the four people killed had stopped or come out of their house to render assistance to the driver of the SUV, who was having mechanical difficulties (Osborne, 2015). The occupants of Couch's truck were also injured, including one friend who suffered a traumatic brain injury. Ethan Couch's blood-alcohol level registered .24, and later tests confirmed that he had ingested Valium earlier that night.

At the juvenile sentencing hearing, the Tarrant County prosecutor asked the judge for a 20-year sentence because of the severity of the situation and the previous lenient responses of Ethan's parents, Tonya and Frederick, who encouraged him to work around the consequences of his actions. Couch's attorney said in his defense that Couch suffered from "affluenza," a condition whereby his upbringing in an environment of wealth and privilege, along with poor parental role models, caused his inability to know the difference between right and wrong. Juvenile Judge Boyd reportedly said that she dismissed the affluenza comment when she made her decision to do what she thought was right in this case. With

no prior juvenile record, the judge sentenced Ethan to 10 years of probation, to not drink alcohol or use drugs, to have no contact with his parents, and to complete drug treatment through a private residential facility that his father agreed to fund. The sentence outraged area residents, who obtained over 13,000 signatures calling for Judge Boyd's dismissal (the judge retired in 2014).

While on probation, Ethan allegedly failed to show for appointments with his probation officer and was seen on YouTube drinking alcohol with friends at a house party, acts which outraged the community once more. In response to community pressure, the probation department issued a request in December 2015 to the judge for a probation violation hearing. Mother Tonya agreed to drive Ethan into Mexico before a juvenile arrest warrant was issued on December 16 so as to avoid the probation violation hearing. The pair were tracked to Puerto Vallarta, where they were apprehended by Mexican officials who agreed to hold both of them for extradition to the United States (Osborne, 2015).

Texas law allowed Ethan to be held in a juvenile detention facility until his 19th birthday, which was until April 2016. A separate hearing determined that the original case would be transferred to the adult system instead of remaining with the juvenile court. Texas law requires a minimum of 120 days of additional jail time for transferred cases. In adult criminal court, Judge Salvant decided to incarcerate Mr. Couch for 720 days (180 days for each deceased victim), and then mandate that he finish the remaining eight years of his original probation term. Tonya Couch, who had one previous probation term for reckless driving, is facing a third-degree felony charge for hindering the apprehension of a fugitive (Hanna, 2016).

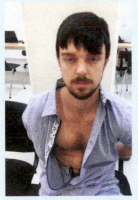

Uncredited/AP Images

DISCUSS Was the final outcome justified in this case? Are wealthy offenders more likely to be supervised on probation, or was this a rare exception?

▶ Community Corrections

As we discussed in Chapter 1, most offenders in the corrections system are *not* incarcerated in jail or prison. Nearly 70% of offenders (3.8 million on probation and 857,000 parolees) serve at least a portion of their correctional sentence through some form of community supervision or treatment program (Kaeble, Maruschak, & Bonczar, 2015). Community correction sentences provide judges with a wide range of options, which in turn become court-ordered conditions, to address individual offender circumstances (recall the ranking of these court-ordered conditions in Chapter 4) in order of least to most

restrictive, but this list varies greatly by jurisdiction and can be confusing to most people who are unsure whether they are a part of—or separate from—probation. So, to avoid confusion, this chapter is presented in a different way from most other texts.

The foundation of a community corrections sentence starts with **probation**, and then judges add conditions to that probation sentence that the offender must complete. While most conditions are added at the very beginning of the sentence, some may be added in the middle of the sentence if the offender is not progressing as expected and needs more structure or monitoring. These court-ordered conditions must be related to the crime, fulfill a specific and legitimate purpose, and/or address problems or needs that the offender has. After first discussing how probation works, this chapter categorizes the added conditions according to their intended purpose.

For example, community service, restitution, and/or fines are discussed as added monetary probation conditions for the purpose of the offender making payments to the victim, the community, or the court. For offenders who require more surveillance or structure to their probation sentence, we discuss electronic monitoring, residential community corrections facilities, and day reporting centers, where all clients in these programs are on probation, but the level of monitoring is more intensive. Finally, judges can choose treatment programs that address concerns and special needs of probation offenders, such as addiction, mental health, and anger management. These problems are addressed through problem-solving courts and community-based drug treatment facilities.

As a whole, no matter which options judges choose for each person, all community-based corrections sentences provide some important benefits. For example, community supervision is not only less expensive than jail or prison, but it also provides an opportunity for individuals to continue working, and going to school. Probationers remain productive taxpayers, rather than institutionalized tax burdens. Living at home while completing court-ordered conditions helps the offender avoid the corrupting influences and violence that may accompany a jail stay. Rather, offenders can retain ties with their own families and generate income to help support their own dependent children. Children whose parents are on probation have more stable home lives than children who have one or both parents incarcerated. An additional benefit of offenders being supervised in the community is that they have greater access to treatment programs, so their chances of making real changes are better than trying to receive help in prison. Employed probation offenders are more likely to pay their victim back than incarcerated offenders who must rely on their own family for any extra money beyond basic meals and uniforms.

The use of community sanctions is favored for women offenders because they are generally less likely to present a risk to the general public compared to men, and women offenders generally have less serious prior records. However, the vast majority of people on community supervision are men, primarily because men are arrested for crimes far more often than are women.

One problem with community-based supervision is the possibility that an offender may commit another crime. While this could potentially happen, new crimes vary widely (misdemeanors and felonies). The likelihood of committing a new crime is lower while an offender is on supervision than after correctional supervision ends. Potential problems that some offenders encounter on community supervision include having too many monetary obligations that seem overwhelming and that pull them in too many different directions. These obligations sometimes contribute to the offender's failure at meeting all of them, and ultimately ending up in prison where there is less focus on appointments, treatment, financial obligations, and pleasing family members. A second issue with having an offender living at home with other family members is that it intrudes on the privacy and civil liberties of other household members. Despite these limitations, probation restricts lawbreakers in some way, while still allowing them to retain a law-abiding life and avoid the stigmatizing effects of prison.

▶ Probation

Probation remains the most common correctional sentence for misdemeanants and felons. Deciding when probation will be used is defined by legislative statute in some states, and in others, the decision rests in the hands of the judge. Probation is intertwined with pretrial supervision because both involve supervision in the community. As depicted in Figure 5–1, community supervision can be used during different time periods, such as during pretrial supervision (after an arrest but before a plea is entered). A second time is when defendants agree to complete treatment or supervision conditions during diversion/deferred adjudication in exchange for their charges getting dismissed. A third time is following the sentencing of a convicted offender for a misdemeanor or a felony, which includes intensive or specialized probation supervision. Pretrial release and diversion have an interesting history that actually began in England before these practices were adopted in the United States.

Early English Practices that Allowed for Incarceration Alternatives

Over the course of hundreds of years, English law and judicial practices allowed for opportunities for defendants to avoid

LEARNING OUTCOMES 1 — Explain the key ways in which community supervision is beneficial to the offender, the community, and the victim.

Pretrial Supervision:	Diversion/Deferred Adjudication Probation:	Misdemeanor/Felony Probation	Intensive Probation/ Specialized Caseload: More
When courts impose supervision *before* a guilty plea so that a defendant can better assist in case preparation, and the court is assured the defendant will appear.	When defendants enter into an agreement with the court to complete various conditions so that if successfully completed, the charges will be dismissed without a conviction. If a defendant on deferred adjudication is noncompliant or commits a new crime during supervision, the courts will sentence the offender and the defendant's conviction will be permanently on record.	Community supervision of a convicted offender under court-imposed conditions for a length of time according to offense severity and completion of treatment or other court-ordered condition.	frequent contact between a convicted offender and the supervision officer, along with greater restrictions (curfew, home visits) due to a special risk or specialized needs.

FIGURE 5–1 Four Types of Probation Supervision.

Early Practices in England That Allowed for Exceptions to Incarceration

1000–1827	1275	1700s and 1800s	1700s	1700s
Benefit of clergy meant that ordained priests, monks, and nuns accused of violating common law had their cases transferred to the bishop's church court for leniency.	**Statute of Westminster** limited the offenses for which sheriffs could mandate bail (sheriffs had complete authority on the bail amounts and release decision).	A person who had pled or been found guilty and was waiting for a pardon from the Crown could receive a **Judicial reprieve** or temporary suspension of the prison sentence.	**Recognizance**—As an alternative to bail, defendant promises to appear in court at a specified time while the court allows the defendant to remain at liberty in the community.	**Surety**—Defendant's release is backed by a third party who is responsible for the defendant's next court appearance and has the duty to return the offender to court if a new offense is committed.

FIGURE 5–2 Timeline of Early Practices in England to Reduce Pretrial Incarceration.
References: Chute, C. L., & Bell, M. (1956). Crime, courts, and probation. New York, NY: The Macmillan Company; Vanstone, M. (2004). Supervising offenders in the community: A history of probation theory and practice. Burlington, VT: Ashgate.

incarceration in jail. These practices are shown as a timeline in Figure 5–2. Three situations address the time period between the defendant's arrest and the court hearings that occur prior to being sentenced. The Statute of Westminster, release on recognizance, and surety all allowed for the release of an eligible defendant without having to pay the sheriff bail money for pretrial release. Judicial reprieve allowed for a temporary suspension of sentence if a sentenced defendant was waiting for a pardon. Finally, any member of the church clergy who was accused of a crime could avoid incarceration completely by having his or her case transferred to the church for review by the bishop. This was known as "benefit of clergy." The justice practices of pretrial release and suspension of sentence made their way overseas to the East Coast of the United States, and were adopted by American judges.

John Augustus: From Shoemaker to Third-Party Surety

The biggest problem with release on recognizance or suspension of sentence was, at that time, the absence of any effective control over the offenders who were released to the community. In the mid-1800s, John Augustus owned a successful shoe business in downtown Boston, Massachusetts. Augustus was also a member of the Washingtonian Total Abstinence Society, a missionary group that believed in helping people who had drinking problems instead of harshly judging them with punishment. Augustus found himself wandering into Judge Oxenbridge Thacher's courtroom to observe court proceedings. Augustus was appalled at all the alcoholics who went to jail because they could not afford bail. He spent the next 16 years of his life voluntarily donating his own money as a third-party surety in recognizance cases to provide aid and supervision to nearly 2,000 offenders released to his care. Although at first he focused on alcohol offenders, he expanded his help to women and children accused of other offenses. Augustus assured Judge Thacher that the defendants would return for the sentencing hearings, in return for the court releasing the defendants to him instead of throwing them in jail. Even though he had many supporters, Augustus is considered the first bail bondsman and the founder of American probation. Augustus was able to help defendants find homes, secure employment, ensure school attendance, and soothe family problems in exchange for having the offenders sign a pledge that they would abstain from alcohol (Chute & Bell, 1956; Vanstone, 2004). As you can see in Figure 5–3, Augustus's efforts had a direct impact on the passage of probation laws between 1878 and 1956 that made probation a permanent option for judges.

TIMELINE

Growth of Probation in the United States

1830	1841–1859	1878	1891	1925	1956
Judge Oxenbridge Thacher first used **recognizance** in the Municipal Court of Boston. The practice, known as "release on recognizance" is still used today, but only before a guilty plea/verdict.	**John Augustus** helped men and women stay out of jail by providing surety bonds to the Boston court. His efforts inspired other volunteers and philanthropic organizations to help.	First probation law enacted by the Massachusetts legislature permitted hiring paid presentence investigation advisors to investigate cases and recommend probation, as appropriate, to the judge.	Massachusetts law mandated statewide salaried probation officers to supervise all offense levels.	Federal statute authorizing probation in federal courts was passed.	All states had enacted probation statutes for juveniles and adults.

FIGURE 5–3 Timeline of Growth of Probation in the United States.
References: Chute, C. L., & Bell, M. (1956). Crime, courts, and probation. New York, NY: The Macmillan Company; Vanstone, M. (2004). Supervising offenders in the community: A history of probation theory and practice. Burlington, VT: Ashgate.

- Obey all local, state, and federal laws.
- Answer all reasonable inquiries by the probation officer, and follow officer directives.
- Remain within the jurisdiction (county or state) at all times. Leaving the jurisdiction requires permission in advance.
- Pay all probation supervision fees, fines, and restitution as ordered by the court. Complete any court-ordered community service.
- Refrain from possessing any firearms, or any other dangerous weapon, without written permission from the court.
- Refrain from using or possessing controlled substances or dangerous drugs unless with a medical doctor's prescription. Refrain from alcohol use if under supervision for an alcohol-related offense.
- Submit to testing for controlled substances (and alcohol testing if under supervision for an alcohol-related offense).
- If there is a history of substance abuse, participate in a substance abuse evaluation and complete treatment as directed.
- Maintain suitable employment and/or educational/vocational training and notify third parties of your criminal record, as directed by the probation officer.
- Promptly inform the probation officer of any changes in residence, employment, educational status, or any contact with law enforcement.
- Allow the probation officer access to your home and workplace at reasonable times. Consent to the search of person, vehicle, or premises if the supervising officer has reasonable grounds to believe that evidence of a violation will be found.
- Support your dependents, including keeping current on any child support obligations.
- If under supervision for a sex offense, participate in an evaluation, submit to polygraph examinations, register with local law enforcement, and, if directed, successfully complete an approved sex offender treatment program.

FIGURE 5–4 **Examples of Standard Probation Conditions from Various Jurisdictions.**

Probation Conditions

As you learned about earlier, judges impose the actual length of a probation sentence, which is often less than if the offender were sent to prison. Judges rely heavily on the defendant's prior record, along with other factors such as his or her risk to the community, demeanor and cooperativeness, and community ties when deciding whether probation is appropriate. If probation is the best option, judges will order certain conditions for defendants to follow. **Standard conditions** from various jurisdictions are depicted in Figure 5–4 and include reporting to a probation officer, working or going to school full-time, remaining within the city or county limits, and agreeing to submit to drug tests, home visits, and searches.

In addition to the standard conditions of probation, **special conditions** may be required by the court that repair the harm caused to the victim or the community. These may include community service, restitution, and payment of fines. Other special conditions may be related to reducing the risk to public safety through increased surveillance, such as community-based residential facilities and electronic monitoring. A third reason for special conditions is specific to the offender's problems as related to his or her crime. These conditions require the offender to enroll in and pay for mental health evaluations, counseling, substance abuse treatment, and parenting classes. All of these special conditions described next can be mandated for diversionary programs or for any community supervision program as add-ons to probation or graduated sanctions when the offender fails to comply with the original sentence.

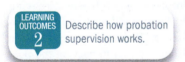

LEARNING OUTCOMES 2 Describe how probation supervision works.

The average time people spend on probation nationwide is about 22 months. About 64% of probationers who leave probation during any given year complete supervision successfully, and some may even be discharged earlier than expected (Kaeble et al., 2015). Judges may further modify the length of probation after initial sentencing as the offender shows improvement or digresses. For example, if a probationer is showing improvement but the probation officer wants to keep him or her on probation until a new treatment program is completed, some jurisdictions allow judges to extend the probation term before sentence expiration.

Current national data indicate that most people are on probation for property offenses or alcohol- and drug-related crimes (80%). Nearly 20% of all offenders on probation have been convicted of a violent offense against a person, such as assault, domestic violence, sexual offense, or murder, as you read about at the beginning of the chapter (Kaeble et al., 2015). This surprises some people who think that offenders who have committed a violent act are in prison, whereas nonviolent offenders are on probation.

What Does a Probation Officer Do?

To carry out all the expectations of a community-based sentence, probation officers have multiple roles that are depicted in Figure 5–5. These roles include gathering information to complete a presentence investigation report prior to sentencing, managing each case to ensure that the offender is fulfilling his or her court-ordered conditions, referring offenders to treatment programs, and monitoring the offender's whereabouts in the community through home visits, searches, and office visits. In some ways, these roles seem to conflict with each other. On one hand, probation officers are expected to be a supportive confidante to turn to for advice or to help offenders obtain jobs, education, or reapply for other government benefits for which they are eligible. On the other hand, the probation officer is the court's representative, charged with enforcing the conditions of the offender's sentence and with bringing violations of those conditions to the court's attention—thereby placing the offender at risk of losing his or her liberty. It is not easy to serve simultaneously as advisor and enforcer, but doing both well is indeed important.

Using Evidence-Based Principles in Community Supervision

At the first meeting, offenders are typically assessed by a trained officer using a reliable and objective assessment instrument to

1. **Presentence investigator**: Interviews convicted felons and gathers information prior to court sentencing to determine the offender's suitability for probation.

2. **Caseworker**: Provides mentoring and advice to clients in areas such as time management, talking to other family members, and budgeting. Most prevalent in juvenile probation.

3. **Broker of Services**: Refers offenders to court-ordered services such as anger management, drug and alcohol treatment, and parenting classes.

4. **Surveillance**: Monitors the whereabouts of the probationer and ensures that the conditions of probation are being followed. In some jurisdictions, the officer carries a firearm.

FIGURE 5–5 Four Hats a Probation Officer Wears.

identify the potential threats or problems that the offender may pose, along with the offender's needs that should be addressed through treatment. These objective instruments are scored quantitatively based on preassigned points for offender characteristics such as gender, age, education level, and mental stability. Other factors that are considered in the assessment are behaviors such as substance use, work history, number of previous times on probation, and probation outcomes.

After the initial interview and screening, individuals on probation are assigned to a particular officer's **caseload** depending on the nature of the case and intensity of supervision required. Individuals requiring more individualized attention are assigned to an officer with a smaller caseload (between 25 and 50 offenders), whereas individuals requiring minimal supervision may be assigned to an officer with a caseload of 200 to 300 people. Through **motivational interviewing**, each

officer uses the risk/needs assessment score to devise an individualized case plan with the offender—one that the offender agrees to do. Table 5–1 lists and describes all the possible services that probation officers use to assist offenders during community supervision.

If an offender on community supervision commits a new crime, it is known as a **legal violation**. In this case, the local prosecutor has the authority to charge and prosecute the offender on that new crime but cannot order the offender's probation revoked. Prosecutors may be willing to avoid prosecution of the new crime in exchange for the offender having probation revoked and being sent to prison for the crime for which he or she was originally placed on probation.

If the probationer repeatedly fails to abide by any of the court-ordered standard (or special) conditions of probation, this is considered a **technical violation**, which is the more common

TABLE 5–1	COMMUNITY-BASED SOCIAL SERVICES USED DURING CORRECTIONAL SUPERVISION

Services to Assist Offenders	Description
Navigating basic services offered by the government and nonprofit organizations	Offenders may need help applying for welfare, food stamps, or to make arrangements for emergency temporary housing and financial assistance for the purchase of necessities, such as food, clothing, medicine, and child care. In addition, referrals may be made for transportation to treatment facilities, medical visits, or other placement programs.
Employment assistance	Probation officers may refer offenders for testing and work skills evaluations, preemployment training, and skill-development courses, or directly to certain employers or job placement agencies.
Literacy, education, and vocational training	Literacy, General Educational Development (GED), and vocational training programs are available, as is access to higher education institutions.
Diagnostic assessments	Assessments may be conducted by a licensed professional for substance abuse, mental health, and/or developmental disabilities. The assessment is followed by a prognosis report and treatment plan.
Detoxification	Probation officers may request inpatient and outpatient detoxification services. Such services may include, for example, a physical examination and report; medication, such as methadone, Antabuse®, or naltrexone hydrochloride; laboratory work; and a residential placement.
Substance abuse treatment	This includes substance abuse prevention and treatment readiness groups; individual, family, and group substance abuse counseling; intensive outpatient group or individual treatment; short-term residential treatment; longer-term placement in a therapeutic community setting; and methadone maintenance.

Source: From Prisoners Releases: Trends and Information on Reintegration Programs, GAO-01-483 by Laurie E Ekstrand by Danny R Burton. Published by U.S. Government Accountability Office.

of the two. Probation officers report the violations to the court and recommend a course of action. The judge makes the final decision regarding the revocation, choosing to retain the original sentence with modifications, or revoke probation completely and incarcerate.

▶ Probation Conditions that are Reparative to the Victim or Community

Community Service

In its most general meaning, **community service** mandates that offenders labor in unpaid work for the general good of the community. As early as the seventeenth century, community work was used in Germany as a separate sentence and as the default for an unpaid fine (van Kalmthout & Tak, 1988). However, it was not until 1966 that community service appeared in the United States as a sanction receiving serious attention for traffic offenders, misdemeanants, and juvenile delinquents. Community service developed as an alternative to jail, fines, or as an additional condition of probation. As shown in Figure 5–6, community service was found to have a number of benefits, including providing much needed assistance to nonprofit organizations, and it allowed offenders to work off the punishment

if they could not afford paying a fine. Performing community service has been effective as a character-building exercise for wealthy offenders who could easily afford paying fines. Despite these noted benefits, community service is underutilized in adult probation, with judges requiring community service in only about 25% of felony cases (Bonczar, 1997). Community service is used more frequently in juvenile probation (Thomas & Hunninen, 2008).

Of the judges who order community service, offenders labor between 40 and 1,000 hours before their service is considered complete. There are generally three types of community service: individual placement to a particular agency, assignment to a work crew, and placements with a service-learning component. Completion rates varied from 50 to 75%, depending on the type of work performed and how well community service is enforced by the courts (Durkin et al., 2009). Placements that are considered more meaningful—when the offender realizes that the work is meant to restore the harm he or she caused—have higher completion rates than those designed to be punitive, such as roadside litter crews (Thomas & Hunninen, 2008). The most common problem is failure to show up and failure to complete community service hours, both of which may constitute a technical violation of probation. One challenge with evaluating community service is that most programs lack clear goals and objectives, such as whether they aim to divert offenders from a formal sentence, serve as an additional compliance tactic during probation, reduce recidivism, or change offender attitudes. Community

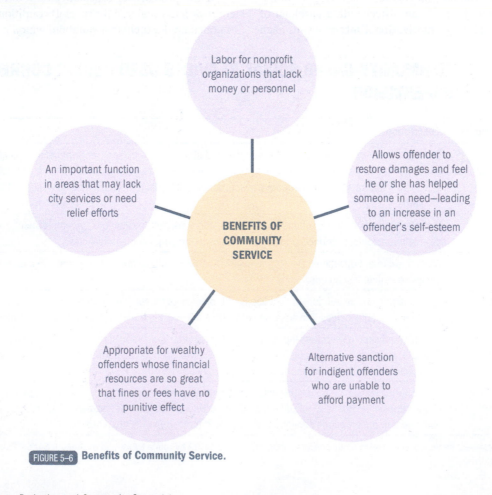

FIGURE 5–6 Benefits of Community Service.

service orders had no significant effect on recidivism when compared with fines or electronic monitoring, but the programs are cost-effective. For example, if we consider minimum wage rates for just the state of Florida, offenders in Florida completed the equivalent of over $3.3 million in wages in a single year in community service (Harris & Lo, 2002). As community corrections programs continue to expand in the future, community service certainly has the potential to be a part of this growing trend.

Restitution

Compensating crime victims is one of the oldest principles of justice, dating back to the Old Testament and to ancient codes such as the Code of Hammurabi. In the mid-1800s in the United States, Quaker prison reformer Elizabeth Fry viewed repaying the victim as a step toward offender rehabilitation, and the practice was known as **restitution**. However, widespread enforcement of restitution did not occur until the 1970s due to more active victim advocacy efforts. Yet, victims forfeited restitution if offenders went to prison. That changed when a series of federal acts in the 1980s broadened the use of restitution to include offenders who went to prison and those who owed back child support. Restitution also became mandatory in crimes such as sexual abuse, sexual exploitation of children, domestic violence, and Title 18 property offenses (Shephard, 2014).

In restorative justice cases, restitution amounts are determined at victim–offender mediation sessions. In conventional misdemeanor and felony courts, judges order restitution at the time of sentencing. The more active that victims were about demanding restitution, the more likely that it was ordered (Ruback, Schaffer, & Logue, 2004). Restitution amounts are based on the following:

> **LEARNING OUTCOMES 3** Identify the ways that probation and community correctional sanctions can be reparative to the victim and community.

- Amounts are based on the crime for which an offender is formally convicted.
- Amounts are based on the cost of replacement value or actual losses suffered.
- Amounts do not involve money for "pain and suffering."

Just because restitution is court ordered does not mean that a victim will necessarily receive restitution. Part of the problem lies with probation officers enforcing its collection from the offender while on community supervision. Indigence does not entitle the offender to immunity from restitution, but failure to pay restitution because of indigence by itself is not a jailable offense. The court differentiates *inability* to pay from *unwillingness* to pay (*Bearden* v. *Georgia*, 461 U.S. 660, 1983).

In cases where the losses incurred by the victim are substantial, the state attorney general provides money to qualifying victims of violent crimes through a **victim compensation** fund. A victim could potentially obtain both compensation and restitution if the victim agrees to prosecute. For example, in a sexual assault case, potential costs incurred may include hospital bills for physical injuries, lost income from work, court transportation, child care during litigation, counseling sessions, sexual assault exams, HIV testing, rehabilitative therapy, and moving expenses (Office for the Victims of Crime, 2010).

Fines

Another monetary sanction that the offender typically pays is a fixed **fine**. Fines are determined by the severity of the offense and, like restitution, can be paid in installments. The idea of punishing offenders financially predates the Code of Hammurabi and is widely used in many countries throughout the world as the primary means of punishment. The benefits and problems of fixed fines are listed in Figure 5–7. Although U.S. jurisdictions use the fine as a sole sanction for most traffic offenses and ordinance violations, fines for misdemeanors and felonies, if used at all, are typically an add-on to probation (Vigorita, 2002). Morris and Tonry (1990, p. 111) observed the irony that "a society that relies so heavily on the financial incentive in its social philosophy and economic practice [like the United States] should be so reluctant to use the financial disincentive as a punishment of crime."

Fines average $1,000 for felony cases and $100 for misdemeanor cases and are largely based on the defendant's ability to pay (Vigorita, 2002). This means that the courts consider employment status at arrest, future employment status, current financial status, and future bills.

Think About It…

To increase community service completion rates, some jurisdictions have opted to allow misdemeanor offenders the option to donate an amount of money equal to the number of service hours multiplied by the minimum wage. The offender merely buys a new product from a preapproved list and brings in the purchases with receipts to fulfill community service hours. On the other hand, other states allow the judge to substitute eight community service hours for one day in jail, or eight hours of unpaid labor can pay off between $60 and $80 of fines (Texas Code of Criminal Procedure, Article 42.036).

Do you think substitutions like charitable donations should be allowed in lieu of community service? Should community service be substituted for a day in jail?

Pressmaster/Shutterstock

BENEFITS	PROBLEMS
• Fines can be combined with other sanctions when multiple sentencing goals are sought.	• There are possible credibility issues in the public's eyes.
• Fines can be tailored to the offender's assets and income to make up roughly comparable financial burdens.	• This is a form of discrimination against the poor.
• Fines can be collected with the same vigor and ruthlessness that characterize finance companies.	• Collecting small fines is more trouble than it is worth.
• Fines do not necessarily undermine the offender's ties to family and community.	• Debt might be shared by others in the household who had nothing to do with the crime but who combine their assets with the offender.

FIGURE 5–7 **Benefits and Problems of Fixed Fines.**
References: Ashworth, A. (2015). Sentencing and criminal justice (6th ed.). New York, NY: Cambridge University Press; Morris, N., & Tonry, M. (1990). Between prison and probation: Intermediate punishments in a rational sentencing system. New York, NY: Oxford University Press.

Think About It...

Ruback and colleagues (2004) found that while on supervision, the likelihood of rearrest lessened as the proportion of restitution paid increased, but it was difficult to determine cause and effect. In another study, offenders with strong community ties to employment, school, and the neighborhood were more likely to fully pay restitution than offenders without such ties (Davis, Smith, & Hillenbrand, 1991). Based on these two conclusions, how might payment of restitution lower recidivism?

Corepics VOF/Shutterstock

▶ Intermediate Sanctions that Reduce Risk to Public Safety

Some community conditions ordered by the court may require more surveillance than probation alone, so intermediate sanctions were created to fill that gap to reduce the risk to public safety. Figure 5–8 considers three strategies that probation officers use for surveillance: verifying employment to ensure the offender is actually working, conducting drug testing to ensure the offender remains clean of drugs and alcohol, and requiring the offender to remain at home when he or she is not working or attending treatment. Increased surveillance programs discussed in this section include residential community corrections facilities, electronic monitoring, and day reporting centers.

Residential Community Corrections Facilities

In the mid-1800s, halfway houses first opened to assist men and women who were released from jails and prisons with housing and clothing, until they found more permanent jobs and were able to transition out to living independently (Goldfarb & Singer, 1973). Many of the earlier facilities were nonprofit and supported through private donations and faith-based organizations.

Beginning in the 1960s with federal support, halfway houses expanded their mission to include an intermediate sanction option for probationers who needed increased surveillance. Today, halfway houses are called **residential community correction facilities (RCCFs)** and are places in which the offender lives under supervision and must obtain permission to leave for work, treatment, and occasional leisure passes. RCCFs exist at the federal, state, and local levels and include profit-oriented companies that contract with the government. RCCFs are considered to be a type of minimum-security facility with large, open, dormitory-style rooms where clients can freely interact. Others have private rooms where prisoners are allowed keys to their own rooms.

The exact number of RCCFs at the state and local level is unknown, but any facility classified as work release, prerelease, a restitution center, or a community facility for mothers and infants is a type of RCCF. The most promising intervention strategies for female offenders include skill building to teach economic and emotional independence (van Wormer, 2010). One example of an RCCF for women leaving prostitution is called "safe house." Women can stay for up to 18 months and are provided with job skills training, food, and counseling for domestic violence, drug abuse, and

> **LEARNING OUTCOMES 4** Discuss how intermediate sanctions created for the surveillance of community conditions reduce risk to public safety.

Employment Verifications

- Probation officers may periodically verify employment through talking to employers and by monitoring pay stubs/paychecks.

Drug and Alcohol Detection

- Probation officers and service providers may collect urine specimens or use portable drug testing devices, breathalyzers, and saliva swabs. Some use vehicle ignition locks, which link a breathalyzer to an offender's vehicle so that the ignition cannot be started unless the offender blows into the device and registers a breath alcohol content level below legal limits.

Community and Home Confinement

- Probation officers may recommend that the court requires an offender to reside in a community corrections center or remain in his or her residence for all or part of the day. Both of these options are used as alternatives to incarceration, permitting the officer to work with the offender in the community.

FIGURE 5–8 **Supervision Strategies Used for Community-Based Sanctions.**
Source: From Prisoners Releases: Trends and Information on Reintegration Programs, GAO-01-483 by Laurie E Ekstrand by Danny R Burton. Published by U.S. Government Accountability Office.

sexual assault victimization (Tsenin, 2000). Some programs are culturally focused to meet the needs of African-American and Latina clients.

When not working, residents at all RCCFs have assigned chores, and some perform community service and attend drug treatment programs if court ordered. Residents submit to random drug testing and Breathalyzers, and subsidize some of the daily costs by paying rent. As detailed in Table 5–2, most RCCFs operate on a **levels system,** which is a behavior modification program that increases a client's community freedom depending on the amount of time spent in the program and the client's behavior, employment status, and amount of money saved. Notice that Table 5–2 shows five different levels, beginning with Level 5 and progressing to Level 1, which has the

TABLE 5–2   EXAMPLE OF A RESIDENTIAL COMMUNITY CORRECTION FACILITY LEVELS SYSTEM

Characteristic	Level 5	Level 4	Level 3	Level 2	Level 1
Minimum time residing at RCCF to be at this level	Client placed on hold for up to 24 hours	Two weeks	Four weeks	Six weeks	Eight weeks
Requirements client must meet to be on this level	Complete intake assessment with case manager	Part-time or full-time employment	Full-time employment; no disciplinary reports for two weeks	Full-time employment; no disciplinary reports for two weeks; rent is current	Full-time employment; no disciplinary reports for two weeks; rent is current; $200 in savings
Reasons client could leave RCCF	N/A—client cannot leave facility	Work/school, treatment, medical/doctor, religion	Work/school, treatment, medical/doctor, religion, store, leisure/family	Work/school, treatment, medical/doctor, religion, store, leisure/family	Work/school, treatment, medical/doctor, religion, store, leisure/family
Length of daily leisure pass with family	N/A	N/A	Four hours	Six hours	Eight hours
Weekday curfew	N/A	N/A	10:00 PM	11:00 PM	11:59 PM
Weekend furlough	No	No	No	No	6:00 PM Friday to 11:59 PM Sunday
Driving privileges	No	No	No	No	Yes

most freedoms and privileges. Preapproved daytime visits to a pass address (a family member's home) are allowed, provided the clients return to check in at the RCCF after work. Clients out on pass must be available by phone at all times and must produce receipts to verify their whereabouts. Clients who receive a disciplinary report for misconduct or who fall behind on making rental payments to the facility will lose privileges and their levels will change.

Research shows that employment is a key factor in a client's success. It follows, therefore, that halfway houses that are located close to public transportation/ bus lines are critical to getting to work. Critics contend that halfway houses are located primarily in urban and minority communities and seem to be absent in communities that have strong community opposition such as in suburban or Caucasian communities. However, through a tax incentive program that benefits local government, halfway houses may be able to increase tax revenue in areas with a high number of vacant buildings that were previously not generating any tax revenue (Costanza, Kilburn, & Vendetti-Koski, 2013).

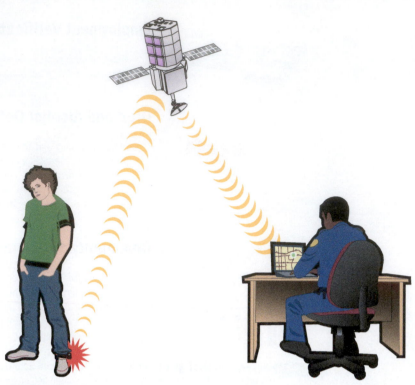

FIGURE 5–9 **How Electronic Monitoring Works.** An electronic monitoring device on an individual's ankle communicates with GPS satellites. After detecting the location of the person's ankle device, the GPS satellite transmits the information to a centralized database that the probation officer can access via a laptop. This process is repeated once every 10 to 15 minutes continuously throughout the day.

Electronic Monitoring

Technological advancements in the last several decades have encouraged people to think of how limited movement can be accomplished in the community without the use of high walls or razor-wire fences. **Electronic monitoring (EM)** is a community-based tool that is increasingly used in a wide variety of situations, such as during pretrial release, as a condition of diversion, or following sentencing. Sentences may include EM as a condition for a placement on work release, furlough, or at a residential facility, or as a parole condition following a prison sentence.

Although there are several types of EM, all EM devices have a unique transmitter device that is permanently attached to the offender (usually around the ankle) that emits a continuous signal to a receiving device (see Figure 5–9). For radio frequency devices, the receiver is attached to the offender's home telephone and can only detect transmissions when the offender is within 500 feet. Radio frequency devices are used for offenders who are court ordered to **home detention**. When enforced with EM, home detention is stricter than curfew and affords greater control over offenders' activities.

EM units suffer from the same limitations as cell phones when it comes to picking up satellite signals and keeping batteries properly charged. For example, if the signal is not received when it should be because the battery weakens or the offender is in a "dead zone" that is unable to pick-up the signal, a computer sends a report of the violation to a central computer accessed by corrections officials. The EM user is warned about these violations and instructed how to avoid these signal losses. If too many lost-signal violations continue after the warnings, the offender may lose his or her chance at this method of supervision.

Other EM devices emit a signal only in response to a random computer phone call. The offender verifies his or her presence at home by placing the transmitter on the verifier box. Alternative methods of confirmation allow the offender to provide voice verification or visual verification by still-picture video phone.

The advent of global positioning system (GPS) technology changed the face and the capabilities of EM technology. Instead of limiting tracking to the home, GPS technology uses military satellites to pinpoint locations anywhere in the world using specific data coordinates that communicate with each receiver (DeMichele & Payne, 2009). The newest technology has the transmitter and receiver built in the same ankle device, as opposed to being two separate devices. The microprocessor also allows the probation officer to program in places where the offender is not allowed, such as near a victim's house or near a school. The newer systems allow authorities to know an offender's whereabouts at all times. The main drawback of GPS technology is the occasional loss of GPS signal and "dead spots," when the offender's receiver is unable to make the repeated cell phone calls to the central station with updates (DeMichele & Payne, 2009). As the number of dead spots and technology costs decrease in the future, GPS technology will likely be expanded to other types of offenders.

Day Reporting Centers

The **day reporting center (DRC)** is a nonresidential alternative to incarceration that blends high levels of control with the delivery of specific services needed by offenders. Officials in Connecticut and Massachusetts initially adopted the idea in the 1990s from England. DRCs are typically used as a "graduated sanction" for probationers who violate conditions of supervision, most

Characteristics of Day Reporting Centers

- Provide treatment and other services on-site to address clients' employment, education, and counseling needs and to reduce jail or prison crowding.
- Accept probation or parole violators for an average duration of five months.
- Three phase system: During the most intensive phase, offenders report daily and are tested for drug use about once per week. Offenders monitored for 70 hours per week.
- Offenders are required to perform community service.
- Offenders are progress with increasingly less-stringent requirements.

FIGURE 5–10 **Characteristics of Day Reporting Centers.**
Source: Craddock, A. (2000). Exploratory analysis of client outcomes, costs and benefits of day reporting: Final report. Federal Grant 97_IJ_CX_0006. Washington, DC: National Institute of Justice.

commonly for drug use, but need to be in a treatment program or kept in the community. As shown in Figure 5–10, most DRCs have a levels system of progression that includes drug testing and performing community service. Clients live at home and report to the DRC five days during the workweek and attend classes such as anger management and cognitive behavior modification (Kim, Joo, & McCarty, 2008). Terri Broadus provides her perspective on what working in a DRC is like.

In a random assignment experiment, men on traditional parole supervision in New Jersey who had technically violated a condition of their parole (but not committed a new crime) were randomly assigned to either the DRC or continued on regular parole supervision (Boyle, Ragusa-Salerno, Lanterman, & Marcus, 2013). Both groups were followed for a period of 90 days. No significant differences existed for either group on the 50% rate that each completed their respective conditions. Of the half who did not make it beyond the 90-day mark, there was a significant difference concerning what happened to each group. The

Voices in Corrections

What was it like to work in a day reporting center?

Terri L. Broadus, formerly a DRC staff member, is now employed with the Wyandotte County Juvenile Detention Center in Kansas City, Kansas.

The day reporting center (DRC) in which I worked offered adjudicated juveniles a last chance to remain in the community for six months as an alternative to being in youth detention. We had youths who were adjudicated for all kinds of offenses, such as auto theft, burglary, theft, and truancy. I began working for the DRC as a case manager. At that time, the DRC was considered to be one of the most structured community correctional programs for youth that were lacking parental supervision and stability at home.

All referred DRC youth were initially accompanied by a parent or guardian for enrollment. Each morning, case managers reported the status of their "clients" to the program director. Some clients would be visually checked to see if they were in school that day. In addition to attending school, all clients were mandated to take weekly drug screenings. Juveniles who attended community schools would be picked up from school by the "YWCA van" and returned to the DRC for evening programming.

Evening programming consisted of tutoring, arts and crafts, mentorship, and field trips. All clients were fed dinner prior to going home, due to some of them living in alternative situations where they had no food in the home. Many times, we had clients who did not eat until they returned to the center the next evening. It was those times that the DRC staff went above and beyond the call of duty and ensured that the family had

groceries and each child had lunch money. By making these sacrifices, I felt that it led to a higher success rate from the program. Our completion rate was about 70%. Anything that I could do, I was more than happy to do for the success of my client. I really felt that I held up to that motto until the end, because I see former clients in the community from time to time.

Two clients that I will never forget are Jershawn and Vincent. Jershawn was a DRC client for nine months because of auto theft. Jershawn stayed with the DRC for an additional three months because of his inability to follow the rules. He is currently a father of four and is working in the community. I see Jershawn and his children on a regular basis, due to him often returning to me for advice in his everyday life.

Vincent came to our DRC for six months for drug usage and auto theft. He ultimately went to the Youth Detention Center because he refused to "work the program," which resulted in violations. He is employed at a local nursing home and is currently taking courses to become a nurse. I talk to Vincent on a regular basis and he attends church and many family functions, due to his mom being killed shortly after he completed the program. He is now 25 years old and on the road to success. He always thanks me for believing in him.

The biggest challenge of the DRC was the lack of parental involvement and a deficiency of a common goal and objective among all parties involved in the center. I would wholeheartedly say that in order for this type of program to be successful, the staff members have to be very dedicated in what they do.

Source: From Corrections: A Contemporary Introduction by Leanne F Alarid and Philip L Reichel. Copyright © 2008 by Pearson Education.

parole violators who were assigned to the DRC were more likely to be arrested and convicted for a new offense, whereas the unsuccessful parolees on regular supervision were more likely to violate parole rules, such as by not attending drug treatment or missing too many appointments with their parole officer, which is considered significantly less serious than committing a new crime. The failure of DRCs to reduce recidivism was due in part to the program's structure, which the researchers observed to encourage parolees to socialize and network with each other. Traditional parolees had significantly less contact with each other in an organized setting.

▶ Community Corrections Programs that Address Root Causes

There are many potential reasons why people commit crime, and these reasons are addressed through the many criminological theories that are present in the field. These reasons can include adverse early childhood experiences such as loss, neglect or abuse, lack of available opportunities, deficiency of meaningful ties to parents or legitimate mentors, impulsivity, perceived stress to achieve, living in distressed communities, greed, associating with others who are already involved in criminal activity, sheer disregard for others, failure to control violent tendencies, or addiction to alcohol, drugs, or gambling. Of all of the possible reasons, anger management and **substance abuse** seem to be two common problems that are correlated with peo-

LEARNING OUTCOMES 5 Describe the most typical community-based programs that address root causes of defendants' problems with crime.

ple who end up on community correctional supervision. We discuss problem-solving courts and drug treatment as two programs designed to address common root causes of crime.

Problem-Solving Courts: Drug, Mental Health, and Veteran's Courts

One of the noted problems with the U.S. criminal justice system is the long period of time that passes from arrest to sentence, and then another delay from sentencing until court-ordered treatment commences. **Problem-solving courts** are an alternative process to traditional criminal court for people who have been arrested for misdemeanors, nonviolent felonies, and have a history of alcohol or drug abuse, or who have committed a crime and have a mental illness. The primary goals of these courts are to increase treatment services, stabilize clients faster, and reduce recidivism.

The most common problem-solving courts are drug court, domestic violence court, veteran's court, and mental health court (Kaiser & Holtfreter, 2016). Each problem-solving court involves a specially trained team for each particular issue (either addiction or mental illness) and consists of collaborative efforts by the judge, prosecutor, defense attorney, probation officer, and various treatment providers who all act in the client's best interest. All clients in a problem-solving court sign a contract to

agree to the treatment or medication. Problem-solving courts are primarily pre-plea/diversionary, but a small number carry a conviction. Both types of courts seek for the offender to avoid jail and to obtain treatment as quickly as possible. The court team reviews the progress of each individual case every two to four weeks, and decides when the client has earned the privilege to progress to the next level (Kaiser & Holtfreter, 2016).

Drug courts can be used successfully with juveniles who have substance abuse problems. Family support and parental involvement are associated with youth program completion and reduced recidivism after the program is over (Alarid, Montemayor, & Dannhaus, 2012). Of course, the degree of abuse (occasional, moderate, severe), length of abuse, and type of substances vary greatly. Individuals who committed a crime to support a drug habit or criminals who were heavily under the influence of drugs when they committed their crime qualify at some level. Given the high percentage of convicted offenders who have a substance abuse or dependency problem, it is ironic that so few drug treatment programs exist in jails and prisons. Thus, offenders with substance abuse problems are more likely to receive alcohol and drug treatment while under community corrections supervision.

Two other types of problem-solving courts are the mental health court and veteran's court. Detailed in Figure 5–11, mental health courts frequently address offenders with **co-occurring disorders**, both a substance abuse problem and a mental health diagnosis. While there are many types of mental health disorders, mental health court funding is limited to individuals with bipolar disorder, major depression, schizophrenia, and schizoaffective disorder (Axis 1 disorders).

Veteran's court evolved in response to the high numbers of military veterans who developed substance abuse problems and post-traumatic stress disorder (PTSD), and were arrested for driving while intoxicated, possession, domestic violence, or theft. Since PTSD is not listed as an Axis 1 disorder, people with PTSD symptoms were not able to receive help at mental health courts. About 92% of participants in veteran's court are males, 62% are Caucasian, 30% are African-American, and 8% are Latino. There are nearly 130 veteran's courts nationwide that link nearly 4,000 veterans to counseling and drug treatment offered by the Veteran's Administration. Most use peer mentors, who are fellow veterans who have experienced similar circumstances and have overcome their challenges (Baldwin, 2013).

The dropout rate is about 20% of individuals who did not want to commit to treatment or to sobriety. These individuals opted instead to go through traditional criminal court and probation. In sum, all problem-solving courts have voluntary participation as their foundation, with the belief that coerced treatment does not work. While most drug courts and mental health courts are diversionary, veteran's court requires a plea of guilty and that participants have been honorably discharged (Baldwin, 2013).

Community Drug Treatment Programs

Community-based treatment programs exist alongside or contract with problem-solving courts, DRCs, and residential facilities. They are specifically for convicted offenders who have abused drugs and alcohol but who the courts feel would benefit more from treatment rather than incarceration

As many as 400 mental health courts (MHC) operate as jail diversion options across the country. Typically, rather than having a trial and conventional sentence, defendants agreeing to the mental health court option attend court-mandated treatment for 12 to 24 months. They must also appear regularly at status hearings in the courtroom and may be sent to jail for noncompliance with treatment. For her doctoral dissertation, Christine Sarteschi wanted to know if mental health courts made a difference for mentally ill offenders with respect to increasing their quality of life, decreasing substance abuse, and decreasing crime after supervision. To do this, she collected all existing studies of adult mental health courts in the United States. From that body of research, 23 studies met the "rigorous" criteria for meta-analysis. These 23 studies examined more than 11,000 offenders and could then be compared with each other. Sarteschi (2009) found that ". . . recidivism, quality of life, and mental health outcomes were positively influenced by the participation in an MHC program. Substance abuse outcomes were found not to have been significant" (p. 113). A later study compared persons in four different mental health courts with persons receiving treatment as usual in the conventional court system. MHC participants had significantly better outcomes on arrests and number of incarceration days than the jail comparison group (Steadman, Redlich, Callahan, Robbins, & Vesselinov, 2011). So, it seems that mental health courts work to reduce recidivism and increase quality of life, but have no effect on later drug use.

FIGURE 5–11 **Evidence-Based Practice—Does it Work?**
Are Mental Health Courts Effective?
Source: Sarteschi, C. M. (2009). Assessing the effectiveness of mental health courts: A meta-analysis of clinical and recidivism outcomes. An unpublished doctoral dissertation. Retrieved from http://d-scholarship.pitt.edu/9275//.; Steadman, Redlich, Callahan, Robbins, & Vesselinov (2011).

(Gainey, Steen, & Engen, 2005). Some modalities exist exclusively in the community, whereas others begin in prison and continue out in the community. Certain treatments are residential (in-patient), which means that a resident lives at the facility during the most crucial treatment periods and gradually transitions out. Other treatment facilities and modalities are nonresidential, where the client lives at home and comes to the facility for meetings and treatment. According to Gainey et al. (2005), community drug treatment modalities include the following:

1. **Detoxification** is an entry-point measure for chronic drug users where the body is cleansed of drugs so that treatment while sober can begin.

2. **Therapeutic communities (TCs)** are long-term peer-led programs that force chronic addicts to face their addiction using group confrontational methods. TCs are based in the community and in prison, with 9 to 12 months of residential treatment followed by outpatient treatment. Confrontational style peer-led encounter groups are the hallmark for clients to learn how to express their feelings constructively and to improve their interpersonal skills. As individuals progress through the program, they become role models for newer members.

3. **Short-term inpatient residential programs** are three to six months in length and are for less severe drug abusers. These programs can exist in both the community and behind walls. In the community, the most well-known example is Treatment Alternatives to Street Crime (TASC), which has about 130 programs in 25 states.

4. **Outpatient treatment** is where participants are involved in activities while they live and work independently in the community. Outpatient treatment may be used during transition from inpatient drug treatment, transition from prison, or solely as a part of probation conditions. Forms of outpatient treatments include one or more (in combination) of the following:

   - *Methadone or naltrexone maintenance:* a prescribed substance to help fight cravings for illegal opiate drugs
   - *Antabuse:* a prescribed substance that deters alcoholics from ingesting alcohol

   - *Relapse prevention:* a form of aftercare for recovering addicts who have completed a TC or other residential program that continues enforcing the principles of the previous treatment modality
   - *Alcoholics Anonymous/Narcotics Anonymous meetings:* a support system of recovery using a designated sponsor and integrating faith-based beliefs with a 12-step program of taking responsibility for actions
   - *Drug education classes:* teaching the recreational or occasional drug user on probation the effects and dangers of using various illegal drugs through 25 to 35 contact hours (Welsh & Zajac, 2004)

Long-term programs for addiction have been conducted in prisons since the late 1960s. This sounds impressive until we point out that less than 15% of offenders who have a problem actually receive treatment while incarcerated (Welsh & Zajac, 2004). Available drug treatment is not near enough to cover the offenders in correctional facilities with alcohol or drug-related problems, making community-based interventions crucial for offenders as a part of their probation (or parole conditions once they leave prison). As you can see, there are several options available for drug treatment. This is because some modalities are more effective for chronic abusers whereas others are tailored for occasional users. The type of drug used or abused, along with the reasons behind the drug abuse, may dictate the treatment modality as well.

The Future of Community Corrections

In earlier chapters, we discussed recent modifications in federal sentencing laws, decriminalization of marijuana for medical use, and alignment efforts to reduce prison populations in over half of all states. Alignment essentially means to move drug and nonviolent criminals from prison to community-based settings. Given this situation, the use of all community corrections programs is predicted to significantly increase in the future. This also means that specialized drug treatment and problem-solving courts will be necessary to support the influx of offenders with treatment needs that are related to their crimes. At the same time, RCCFs, EM/GPS, and DRCs will be used to increase structure and graduated sanctions if needed.

Applying Evidence-Based Practices in a Community-Based Therapeutic Community

Lisa M. is 22 years old and has been using drugs since age 14. She began with alcohol and inhalants, but switched to methamphetamine by the age of 18 to stay awake. Lisa was sexually abused by her father at the age of 13 and when she confronted her mother about the situation, Lisa was called a liar. Lisa ran away multiple times between the ages of 13 and 15 to minimize the abuse. She dropped out of school in her senior year when she moved in with an older man who was her boyfriend. Within a year, he turned her on to methamphetamine. Lisa was arrested and jailed for prostitution multiple times between the ages of 18 and 21—yet, her chronic drug habit made relapse likely.

On Lisa's latest arrest, an understanding judge ordered her to treatment for the first time at an all-female community-based residential therapeutic community. The TC was regimented, highly structured, and led by ex-addicts and licensed counselors so that clients could identify with someone who had been through the same experience. Participants lived together and were expected to help each other recognize and change negative beliefs and behaviors that had contributed to excessive drug use. Treatment was based on cognitive behavioral components and encounter groups, where participants confronted Lisa's thinking patterns and behaviors and resocialized her thinking into positive and new ways of thinking and behaving (Greenfield et al., 2007).

As she progressed through the program, Lisa began to understand that she, like many other women, was socialized not to express her anger outwardly. Instead, Lisa found that she turned her anger inward and became severely depressed about abandonment, but covered those feelings with drugs. Lisa learned that she was also acting in a "codependent" role—she allowed

WAVEBREAKMEDIA/SHUTTERSTOCK

her boyfriend to continue using by taking on his problems as her own and prostituting herself to support both of them, never asking that he help. Lisa learned how her situation led to a greater likelihood of arrest and how she could break the cycle. After eight months, Lisa is still learning how to express her feelings constructively and hopes to soon become a role model for newer clients. But first, she must transition out on her own and learn how to use her new skills in the real world.

TCs have shown through evidence-based research to significantly reduce relapses and return to criminal behavior. Treatment programs that address these issues in a single-sex environment have a greater likelihood of retention and completion than those in a co-ed program (Grella, 1999). An eight-month stay in a community-based TC costs about $21,000 per year per person (French, Popopvici, & Tapsell, 2008).

Lisa's situation raises several interesting questions:

1. Researchers found that women are actually less likely over their life to enter treatment compared to men. Like Lisa, many women enter through a court order. What other efforts could be made to encourage women to seek community-based treatment?

2. In order for the TC to be effective, Lisa must assume responsibility for her own actions. Do you think the community-based TC was an appropriate placement, or should she have gone to jail?

3. Do you think that treatment for substance abuse in community settings can work to reduce reoffending?

LEARNING OUTCOMES 1 **Explain the key ways in which community supervision is beneficial to the offender, the community, and the victim.**

Offenders continue to be productive, retain family ties, continue to support dependent children, and avoid corrupting influences, stigmatizing effects, and physical and psychological damage that might accompany a stay in jail or prison. Taxpayers enjoy cost savings and victims are more likely to receive restitution.

1. Which standard probation conditions emphasize deterrence?

2. Which standard conditions have a rehabilitative aspect?

3. Which probation conditions are incapacitative, in the sense that they limit the offender's freedom while in the community?

4. Who benefits most from a community-based sentence, and why?

probation The court-ordered community supervision of an offender by an officer who enforces conditions for a specified length of time.

standard conditions Commitments every probationer agrees to abide by in return for remaining at liberty in the community.

special conditions Requirements in addition to the standard conditions, such as paying fines or undergoing electronic monitoring.

 LEARNING OUTCOMES 2 **Describe how probation supervision works.**

Offenders are assessed for their risks and needs, and assigned to a caseload to best meet these needs. A case supervision plan is drafted to incorporate the special conditions.

1. Why is assessing offender risk important to community supervision?

2. If the courts already order the treatment programs, why are offender needs still assessed?

3. If a crime wasn't committed, why do probation officers report technical violations to the court?

caseload The number of individuals that one probation officer can effectively supervise based on predefined risks and needs posed.

motivational interviewing A style of personal interaction between the officer and client that involves rapport, trust, and persuasion to help bring about positive behavior change.

legal violation When a probationer commits a new criminal act, and the original probation sentence can be revoked.

technical violation When a probationer repeatedly fails to abide by conditions of probation, and the probation sentence can be revoked.

 LEARNING OUTCOMES 3 **Identify the ways that probation and community correctional sanctions can be reparative to the victim and community.**

Offenders are responsible for repaying the harm caused through unpaid labor to nonprofit organizations, payment of fines to reimburse the court for some of the expenses the system incurs, and payment of restitution to directly compensate the victim.

1. What ideas do you have for how restitution rates can be increased to make completing the payment more attractive?

2. How can community service hours be more readily completed?

3. Should the victim compensation fund be expanded for victims of other types of crimes? If so, what types of crime, and how would you decide who is eligible?

community service Court-ordered special condition that mandates that offenders complete unpaid work for nonprofit organizations.

restitution A court-ordered cash payment that an offender makes to the victim to offset some of the losses incurred from the crime.

victim compensation A general fund by which state governments disperse money to qualifying victims of violent crimes for payment of bills and lost wages.

fines A fixed financial penalty imposed by the judge, with the amount determined by the severity of the offense.

Discuss how intermediate sanctions created for the surveillance of community conditions reduce risk to public safety.

Reducing the risk to public safety while keeping an offender in the community requires more surveillance through intermediate sanctions such as residential community corrections facilities, electronic monitoring, and day reporting centers.

1. What are some of the graduated sanction options available for probation violators?

2. How can residential community corrections facilities use technological advances to monitor offenders when they leave the facility?

3. Do you believe that monitoring using GPS may one day replace prisons? Why or why not?

residential community correction facility (RCCF) A modern term for *halfway house*; a community-based correctional center in which the offender lives under supervision and must obtain permission to leave for work and leisure.

levels system A behavior modification program that increases a client's community freedom with good behavior.

electronic monitoring When a probationer or parolee is monitored in the community by wearing an electronic device that tracks his or her location.

home detention Requires offenders to remain at home at all times, except for such purposes as employment, school, treatment, medical emergencies, or approved shopping trips.

day reporting center A nonresidential community corrections sanction that blends high levels of control with the delivery of specific services needed by offenders.

Describe the most typical community-based programs that address root causes of defendants' problems with crime.

Community-based treatment programs focus primarily on reducing substance abuse and stabilizing persons who have mental illnesses to break the cycle of recidivism.

1. Attend a session of drug court and compare it to a session in a regular criminal court. What main differences do you observe?

2. If a treatment is court ordered, is it truly voluntary? Is court-ordered treatment implemented against a person's free will?

3. For an offender who is nonviolent and has a substance abuse problem, how many chances do you think would be acceptable to provide him or her another chance to reenter treatment and get clean?

4. For an offender who has violent tendencies while inebriated, how many chances do you think would be acceptable to provide him or her another chance to reenter treatment and get clean?

5. How do you define "relapse"? How is relapse similar to "recidivism"?

substance abuse When the use of one or more chemical substances disrupts normal living patterns.

problem-solving courts An alternative court process for people who get arrested and have a history of alcohol or drug abuse, or a mental illness.

co-occurring disorders A client with a mental disorder and a substance abuse problem.

detoxification A process of sudden withdrawal from all drugs and alcohol so that treatment can begin.

therapeutic communities Long-term peer-led programs for chronic addicts using group confrontational methods.

short-term inpatient residential programs Drug treatment programs of three to six months in length for less severe drug abusers.

outpatient treatment Drug treatment programs for participants who live and work independently in the community.

Additional Links

Visit the National Center on Institutions and Alternatives, a nonprofit policy and research organization, for more information on community sanctions: **www.ncianet.org/**.

Visit the Arkansas Department of Community Correction **www.dcc.arkansas.gov/** and click on "programs and services" to see examples of community-based programs in each county.

Go to the Office for the Victims of Crime website at **http://ovc.ncjrs.gov/HelpVictim.aspx**, and scroll down to the 12-minute video entitled "Recovering from Your Crime-Related Injuries" to find out more information about victim compensation.

Go to the National Criminal Justice Reference website **www.ncjrs.gov** and read report #198805 about various instruments that assist in screening inmates for drug and alcohol problems at **www.ncjrs.gov/pdffiles1/nij/grants/198805.pdf**.

6

Jails and Pretrial Release

1 Discuss the pretrial release and detention systems developed to balance the interests of both the community and the suspect.

2 Distinguish the functions and purposes of jails from prisons.

3 Summarize the characteristics of the jail population.

4 Discuss the two key aspects that new-generation jails provide for better jail management.

AMERICA'S TOUGHEST SHERIFF

That's how Sheriff Joe Arpaio of Maricopa County, Arizona, is introduced on radio and television shows—and how he identifies himself on the sheriff's office website (www.mcso.org/). At that same website (under the Jail Information tab), you will see the "Mugshot of the Day!" and can click on a crime to view mugshots. Or, under the Patrol Operations tab, find a link to the Deadbeat Parents page where you can see a photo of the person along with their bond amount.

Sheriff Joe's "tough-on-crime" philosophy is probably best known from his operation of the county's jails—especially the internationally known Tent City Jail that opened in 1993. Vowing to not release any inmates due to jail overcrowding, Sheriff Joe obtained surplus military tents and set them up in an area adjacent to one of the existing county jails. The Tent City Jail can currently hold up to 2,000 inmates.

Inmates range from persons awaiting their trial to convicted celebrities such as former world heavyweight boxing champion Mike Tyson, who was sentenced in 2007 to three years' probation and 24 hours at Tent City Jail for drug possession and driving under the influence. Whether unconvicted or convicted, all the inmates wear black and white striped uniforms with pink underwear. They eat two meals a day that cost the taxpayers about 35 cents each—tasting as one would expect a 35-cent meal to taste. However, inmates can pay 40 cents for a condiment packet (salt, pepper, mustard, mayonnaise, ketchup) if they would like to enhance the flavor. Inmates are entertained by watching TV (as long as it is on a network such as the Disney Channel and C-SPAN) or the

Jim West/Alamy Stock Photo

occasional "Inmate Idol" extravaganza. The first idol show was held in 2007 (including Alice Cooper as a judge) and another was held in December 2010 with a Christmas caroling contest. The Christmas winner (Jodi Arias, who was awaiting trial for the murder she was eventually convicted of in 2013) received a full turkey dinner with all the trimmings for herself and her entire housing unit.

DISCUSS **Do you think persons who spend time in a Maricopa County jail are less likely to commit another crime because of the conditions Sheriff Joe imposes on the inmates?**

This chapter focuses on jail as a key feature of the American justice system and the correctional process. Some suspects and defendants, however, never see much more of a jail than the booking area. That is because, as shown in Figure 6–1, not everyone who has been arrested or is awaiting trial is required to stay in jail. Instead, the majority of persons arrested technically have the opportunity to remain at liberty in the community while their cases are prosecuted. It's important to note, however, that those defendants released to the community are increasingly being monitored by justice officials rather than simply roaming at will. It seems appropriate, therefore, to consider the topic of pretrial release before concentrating on the jail and its place in American corrections.

▶ Pretrial Release

When authorities arrest a person suspected of having committed a crime, two conflicting goals are put in motion: those of the community and those of the suspect. The community, which believes it has been harmed by the suspect, is interested in ensuring that the suspect will appear for trial and, meanwhile, will refrain from harming members of the public and their property. The suspect is, among other things, interested in preparing a defense against the charges brought by the community and in avoiding damage to such areas as employment, school, and family life. The community's goals seem best achieved if the suspect is confined in a jail or is at least closely monitored in the community. The suspect's goals are most easily realized if he or she has complete freedom of movement and choice of associates. The resulting dilemma has forced jurisdictions to develop systems of pretrial release and pretrial detention that try to balance the interests of both the community and the suspect. This section looks at approaches that have been tried, discarded, modified, or proposed to accomplish those goals.

Types of Pretrial Release

According to a national sample of state felony cases, 62% of all defendants were released before case disposition and 38% were detained (Reaves, 2013). The released defendants returned to the community as the result of incurring some financial obligation (38%) or because they simply promised

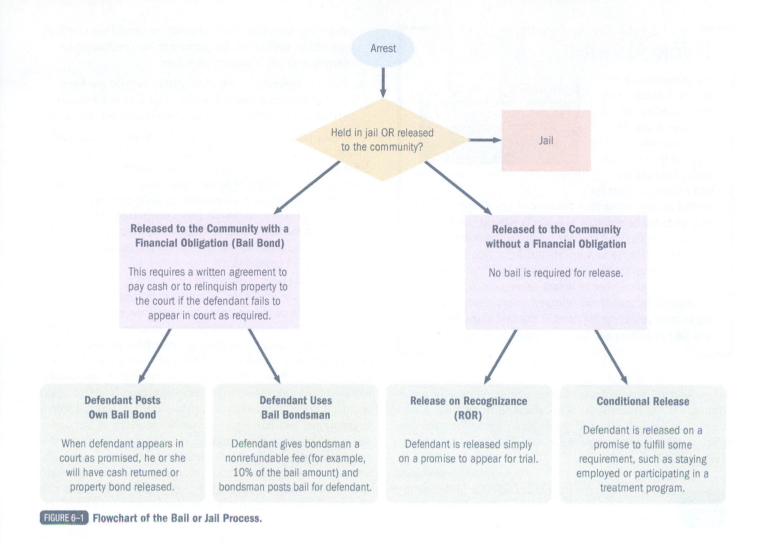

FIGURE 6-1 Flowchart of the Bail or Jail Process.

---

to return to court for all required appearances (24%). Those who were not allowed to remain in the community were kept in jail because they were unable to meet the required financial obligation (34%) or because the court had denied their release (4%). We consider first those who are released to the community.

Pretrial release occurs when efforts to balance community and suspect interests result in the suspect's release in the community. Under pretrial release, the suspect is released from custody for all or part of the time before or during prosecution. That release is conditional upon the defendant's agreement to return to court at the appointed day and time. When the agreement is backed by a financial obligation, it involves a **bail bond**, which is a written agreement by the defendant to pay cash or relinquish property to the court if the defendant fails to attend required court appearances. Because not all defendants have the money or property necessary to secure bail, another person, acting as surety, is allowed to pay the money or put up the property for the defendant. Of course, just as the defendant may not have the necessary money or property, neither may the defendant's family or friends. In those cases, it may be possible for a bail bondsman to secure the defendant's release by telling the court that the bondsman will pay the required sum if the defendant fails to appear. Bondsmen make money this way because

the defendant must pay the bondsman (usually 10% of the bail amount) to gain the bondsman's financial support.

The most frequent nonfinancial release procedure is **release on recognizance (ROR)**, which is based only on the defendant's promise to appear for trial (not backed with money or property). The other primary type of nonfinancial pretrial release is **conditional release**, wherein the defendant is released on a promise to fulfill some requirement such as staying employed, maintaining a curfew, or participating in a treatment program. In some jurisdictions, defendants may be released without having to make any payment but are liable for the full bail amount if they fail to appear (called release on an **unsecured bond**).

Behavior of Pretrial Release Defendants

As noted at this section's start, the community's goals when considering pretrial release are (1) that the defendant refrain from causing further harm in the community and (2) that the defendant appear in court at the required time. Whether the pretrial release procedures are effective in achieving those goals of community safety and court appearance depends on how much compliance is expected. Data from a sample of state court felony cases show that 71% of defendants who were released prior to case disposition made all scheduled court appearances and

had no pretrial misconduct, such as being arrested for a new offense. Of the defendants who were rearrested for a new offense (16% of all released defendants) while they were on pretrial release, about half were arrested for a new felony (Reaves, 2013).

LEARNING OUTCOMES 1 Discuss the pretrial release and detention systems developed to balance the interests of both the community and the suspect.

There is no agreed-upon percentage for determining successful pretrial release policies. As a result, some people will focus on the 29% who missed a court appearance or were rearrested for a new crime—especially the 16% who were rearrested for new crimes—and determine that pretrial release is not meeting court appearance or community safety needs. Others will view the 71% court appearance rate and the 84% who did not get rearrested while on pretrial release as proportions representing an acceptable risk. These people argue that in exchange for living in a society where persons merely accused of a crime have the ability to maintain their family, work, and community ties while assisting in the preparation of their defense, citizens must be willing to accept a procedure that is less than 100% effective—although we should always strive to do better. This is where programs and services designed to further reduce the community's risk come into play.

Pretrial Services

Pretrial service programs are designed to achieve two goals (Stevenson & Legg, 2010; VanNostrand, 2007):

1. *Pretrial Assessment:* The intended outcome is to reduce the number of pretrial defendants who fail to make required court appearances by providing the court official, who is making the pretrial release decision, with information

about the defendant. That information should help the judicial officer decide whether release in the community or detention in jail is more appropriate.

2. *Pretrial Supervision:* Provide pretrial service workers with information that will assist in monitoring and supervising pretrial defendants who are released pending trial.

For the pretrial assessment, a team of workers gathers information from and about a defendant and then evaluates the defendant in terms of the risk of failure to appear in court and the danger he or she poses to the community during the pretrial stage. Typically the risk assessment is accomplished using an objective and research-based instrument that evaluates the defendant on the basis of factors shown to be good predictors of court appearance and/or danger to the community—such as those shown in Figure 6–2.

The supervision goal of pretrial services provides an opportunity to motivate offenders to make behavioral changes while assuring court appearances and community safety. During this period of pretrial release in the community, offenders may participate in treatment programs, hold down a job, attend classes, take anger management classes, and generally show themselves to be capable of responsible behavior. At the other extreme, they could fail to make required court appearances, ignore any treatment referral suggestions, and basically present themselves as uncooperative. In either case, the pretrial case managers will be able to provide sensible and practical sentencing recommendations to judges, prosecuting attorneys, and the offender's defense attorney (Stevenson & Legg, 2010). Positive pretrial performance reports may lead to opportunities for non-prison sanctions, whereas negative reports could bolster arguments for incarceration or close supervision in the

- Current charges
- Outstanding warrants at time of arrest
- Pending charges at time of arrest
- Active community supervision at time of arrest (e.g., pretrial release, probation, and parole)
- History of criminal convictions
- History of failure to appear
- History of violence
- Residence stability
- Employment stability
- Community ties
- History of substance abuse

DISCUSS Using at least seven of these factors, describe a person you think would be a good candidate for pretrial release. If that person were granted pretrial release and you were his or her case manager, what pretrial supervision conditions would you recommend?

Reference: From Legal and Evidence Based Practices: Application of Legal Principles, Laws, and Research to The Field of Pretrial Services by Marie VanNostrand. Published by U S Department of Justice.

FIGURE 6–2 Risk Factors Considered Good Predictors of Court Appearance and Danger to the Community.

community. In fact, a study of cases from two federal district courts found that successfully completing a term of pretrial services supervision was associated with shorter sentence length (Oleson, Lowenkamp, Cadigan, Van-Nostrand, & Wooldredge, 2014).

Consequences of the Jail-Versus-Bail Distinction

About 40% of defendants are kept in jail while awaiting their case disposition. That pretrial detention will obviously affect such things as a person's work, school, family life, and—even under the best of jail conditions—their physical and psychological well-being. But, there seems to be another negative consequence of pretrial detention in comparison with being released in the community to await trial: Those detained are more likely to be convicted and incarcerated.

Data from several sources consistently show that detained defendants are more likely to be convicted than are released defendants, and, when convicted, are more likely to receive a jail or prison sentence (Lowenkamp, VanNostrand, & Holsinger 2013; Phillips, 2008; Reaves, 2013). Of course, the higher conviction rate and increased likelihood for incarceration may simply reflect a more serious criminal history or a more serious felony charge for the detained defendants. However, Lowenkamp and his colleagues, as well as Phillips, found that detention had an adverse effect on outcomes in felony cases beyond that explained by such variables as criminal history, offense type, and charge severity. The implication is that persons who were detained in jail suffered more negative consequences as a result of that detention than did similarly situated defendants who were released to the community to await trail. If research continues to find that detention itself, rather than factors, such as criminal history and seriousness of charges, increases the likelihood of going to jail or prison—as well as increasing the length of sentence—attention must be given to issues such as the fairness of jail versus bail or of pretrial services supervision.

DISCUSS What is it about detention that could explain the harsher penalties? Might a jailed defendant be more likely to plead guilty than a defendant under pretrial release—thereby explaining the greater likelihood of conviction? Do released defendants benefit from being able to show the judge that they can hold a job and stay out of trouble—thereby getting a probation sentence rather than a jail or prison sentence?

▶ Jail Function and Purposes

Jails, which Figure 6–3 shows are distinguished from prisons in several important ways, are confinement facilities usually operated by city or county governments and typically managed by that government's law enforcement agency. For example, the city police department administers the city jail, and the county sheriff manages the county jail. Not all cities and counties operate their own jails, but those that do not have made some arrangement with another entity for jail services. The Federal Bureau of Prisons operates nine jails (called federal detention centers or metropolitan detention centers) in locations around the country and in Puerto Rico, but those facilities typically are not included in reports and statistics on jails.

In the United States, six states have state jail systems (also called **integrated jail–prison systems**) rather than the more typical local jail systems. In those states—Alaska, Connecticut, Delaware, Hawaii, Rhode Island, and Vermont—the state government is responsible for the administration and operation of jails located throughout the state (Carson & Golinelli, 2013).

You might think of jails only as places where persons are held awaiting trial or serving short-term confinement sentences, but contemporary jails serve many purposes, including the following:

- Receive individuals pending arraignment and hold them while awaiting trial, conviction, or sentencing

JAILS	PRISONS
• Operated by local government (except in AK, CT, DE, HI, RI, and VT)	• Operated by the state or federal government
• Hold convicted misdemeanants (usually on sentences up to one year)	• Hold convicted felons (usually on sentences of one year and more)
• Typically hold males and females in separate units of the same facility	• Typically hold males and females in separate facilities
• Serve as a detention facility for persons not yet convicted of a crime	• Serve as a custody facility for persons already convicted and sentenced

FIGURE 6–3 Some Differences Between Jails and Prisons.

- Readmit probation, parole, and bail-bond violators and absconders
- Temporarily detain juveniles pending transfer to juvenile authorities
- Hold mentally ill persons pending their movement to appropriate health facilities
- Hold individuals for the military, for protective custody, for contempt, and for the courts as witnesses
- Release convicted inmates to the community upon completion of sentence
- Transfer inmates to federal, state, or other authorities
- House inmates for federal, state, or other authorities because of crowding of their facilities
- Sometimes operate community-based programs as alternatives to incarceration (Minton & Zeng, 2015).

LEARNING OUTCOMES 2 — Distinguish the functions and purposes of jails from prisons.

As that list suggests, a person in jail could be unconvicted and awaiting trial, waiting for a transfer to another agency or jurisdiction, or being held for possible revocation of his or her probation or parole. Similarly, a jail resident could be convicted but not yet sentenced or convicted and waiting for transfer to a prison. In fact, during the last decade, most people in jail have not been convicted of a crime. Typically about 60% of the nation's adult jail inmates are unconvicted (awaiting court action on their current conviction), and the other 40% are serving a jail sentence, awaiting sentencing, or serving time for probation or parole violation (Minton & Zeng, 2015, Table 3). It is clear that jails hold persons under a variety of statuses, but they can be described according to particular characteristics.

▶ Characteristics of the Jail Population

Many of the local jails around the country are rather small (holding fewer than 50 inmates), but several are **"mega" jails**, holding over 1,000 people. The nation's two largest local jail jurisdictions, Los Angeles County and New York City, together hold about 30,000 inmates—about 4% of the national total (Minton, 2011a).

DISCUSS **Although jail inmates are predominantly male, the adult female jail population has increased each year (see Table 6-1). What explanations can you offer for this phenomenon? More than half of the jail inmates are members of racial or ethnic minorities. However, since 2000 the percentage of non-Hispanic African-Americans has declined whereas the percentage of Hispanics has remained constant. What are some possible explanations?**

From 2000 to 2008, the number of inmates held in the nation's jails increased from 621,000 to 785,000. The growth began slowing in 2005, and the population actually declined between 2009 and 2013. The 2013 population of 731,000 jail inmates was the lowest it had been since 2005, but the 2014 population showed an increase to 745,000 (Minton & Zeng, 2015).

In addition to the inmates held in jail, there are others under jail supervision, but they are supervised outside of a jail facility. In 2014, there were more than 63,000 people in this category across the country and most of them were on electronic monitoring or doing community service under the supervision of jail authorities (Minton & Zeng, 2015).

Females as an Increasing Percentage of Jail Inmates

As shown in Table 6–1, the percentage of white non-Hispanic/Latino inmates has increased since 2000, whereas the percentage of black/African-American inmates has decreased. Hispanic/Latino inmates have maintained a rather steady 15% during that period. However, and despite the overwhelmingly large percentage of males, the proportion of female jail inmates shows a steady increase. If we go back as far as 1990, when women were 9% of the jail population, the increase is even more dramatic (Gilliard, 1999). Because of their increasing numbers, it is becoming more difficult for jail administrators to ignore the problems associated with female inmates. Although there are several gender-specific concerns associated with female inmates (e.g., high rates of substance abuse and mental illness, physical health problems, and parenting and child-care issues), problems associated with histories of physical and sexual abuse are often highlighted in the literature.

Veysey, De Cou, and Prescott (1998) suggest that the coercive environment and procedures in jails present particular problems for women inmates who have histories of abuse. This is because those women may perceive the environment and procedures as dangerous and threatening. In response to that misperception, the women may withdraw, fight back, experience a worsening of psychiatric symptoms or physical health problems, engage in self-injury, or find access to illegal substances. Veysey et al. argue that it behooves jail administrators to understand the genesis of these behaviors in order to respond appropriately or, better yet, reduce the likelihood they will even appear.

Because they were created with male inmates in mind, the security and treatment practices in jails may unintentionally create crisis situations for female inmates. Examples of standard procedures that are harmless, even if irritating, for male inmates but that may remind women of prior experiences of abuse might include intimate touching (e.g., strip searches); threatening use of force (e.g., crisis response teams); observing threats, assaults, or use of physical force (e.g., inmate–inmate or inmate–staff violence); isolation (e.g., administrative or medical isolation); and locked rooms or spaces and the use of restraint devices (e.g., handcuffs or shackles). Add to those jail features the appearance of uniforms and male officers and the presence of fear based on lack of information, and it is not surprising that women with histories of physical and sexual abuse experience increased stress and vulnerability. When the

TABLE 6–1

PERCENTAGE OF INMATES IN LOCAL JAILS, BY CHARACTERISTICS, MIDYEAR 2000–2014

Characteristic	2000	2005	2006	2010	2014
Sex					
Male	89	87	87	88	85
Female	11	13	13	12	15
Status					
Adult	99	99	99	99	99
Juvenile*	1	1	1	1	1
Race/Hispanic Origin					
White, non-Hispanic	42	44	44	44	47
Black/African-American, non-Hispanic	41	39	39	38	35
Hispanic/Latino	15	15	16	16	15
Other**	2	2	2	2	2

Note: *Includes juveniles held as adults and juveniles held as juveniles in adult jail.

**Includes American Indians, Alaska Natives, Asians, Native Hawaiians, other Pacific Islanders, and—from 2005 forward—those self-identifying as "two or more races."

Source: From Jail Inmates at Midyear 2014, NCJ 248629. Published by Bureau of Justice Statistics.

response to these triggers is turned outward, there may be an escalation of violence in the women's unit of the jail.

As more research is conducted on women involved in the criminal justice system (see Figure 6–4), it becomes increasingly clear that there are differences in male and female pathways to criminality and in how men and women respond to custody and supervision. Those differences should be responded to by applying gender-informed interventions and treatments that can yield better results and contribute to more successful outcomes for women offenders. As a bonus, gender-informed responses can enhance the safety and security of jails and prisons (Ney, 2014).

Accommodating the Needs of Women in Jail

Jails have a mandate to provide secure and humane conditions of confinement, but doing so for female inmates may require modifying the jail environment and procedures. Veysey and her colleagues (1998, pp. 52–53) offer a few suggestions for how this might be accomplished:

- *Information disclosure.* Both women and men should have a detailed understanding of what will happen during their time of incarceration, but jail administrators should be aware that each group may need different kinds of information. For example, female inmates especially will want information regarding their children and what child-care arrangements have been made.

- *Regimentation, lack of privacy, and unquestioned response to authority.* Jails must provide a secure environment for the safety of both inmates and staff. However, security measures developed to control male inmates may not be

necessary or appropriate for female inmates. Because most female offenders are arrested for nonviolent crimes, they may not need the same high-security supervision that men require. Keeping cell doors unlocked or open, allowing greater interaction among the women inmates, and training staff in nonthreatening management techniques may actually result in a more tranquil women's unit.

- *Treatment services.* Incarcerated women, more so than incarcerated men, report that they want someone to talk to—not necessarily someone to solve their problems, just someone who will listen. Women inmates, especially those who are victims of abuse, also tend to find single-gender group treatment activities preferable to mixed-gender groups. Recognizing and responding to these preferences may allow jail staff to provide a more effective treatment response to their female inmates.

Jails in Indian Country

U.S. law recognizes as **Indian country** the land within an Indian reservation or land that is technically owned by the federal government but held in trust for a tribe or tribal member. Law enforcement services in Indian country, which consists of some 56 million acres of land in 35 states, is provided by the Bureau of Indian Affairs (BIA) through direct assistance to tribes on reservations (U.S. Department of the Interior, 2004).

As part of those law enforcement services, the BIA operates or funds detention facilities throughout Indian country, and, unfortunately, those jails are among the worst in the nation. A U.S. Department of the Interior report (2004) that evaluated these facilities was titled "Neither Safe Nor Secure" and declared the BIA detention program to be a national disgrace.

1. Women, who typically enter the criminal justice system for nonviolent crimes that are often drug and/or property related, pose a lower public safety risk than do men. Incidents of violence and aggression committed by incarcerated women are extremely low.

2. The pathways taken by women into the criminal justice system are different from those taken by men. Women entering jails are much more likely to have experienced poverty, intimate partner violence, sexual abuse, and/or other forms of victimization often linked to their offending behavior.

3. Their exposure to dysfunctional and abusive relationships throughout their lives can elevate women's risk for future victimization, and their often unhealthy relationships (with men or others) can lead to their own involvement in crime and criminal justice.

4. Women entering jails and prisons often report histories of victimization and trauma, and continue to be vulnerable to victimization within correctional settings. In addition, incarcerated women with a history of trauma and accompanying mental health concerns are more likely to have difficulties with jail and prison adjustment and misconduct.

5. Because they have largely been developed with male inmates in mind, the policies and practices in jails do not reflect an understanding of the risk and needs of female offenders. Gender differences may be ignored or not adapted for women during classification, screening, and assessment.

6. Most jail classification systems have not been normed and validated specifically for women; yet they are often used to guide key housing and security decisions. A typical result is unreliable custody designations and over-classification of female inmates. Women classified as high-risk actually have reoffense and misconduct rates that are more similar to medium-risk men and medium-risk women look more like low-risk men.

7. Gender-informed risk assessment tools that include risk factors such as depression, psychotic symptoms, housing safety, and parental stress are needed to more accurately identify women's risk and needs.

8. When jail staff members understand trauma and its effects on women, use trauma-informed strategies when interacting with female inmates, and engage in cognitive problem solving with female inmates, facility safety and security is enhanced for both staff and inmates.

9. Because of their overwhelming needs, transition and reentry from jail can be especially challenging for women. In addition, women are more likely than men to have primary child-rearing responsibilities and are often single parents. Finding "safe" housing where women can live and support their children is very challenging.

10. When women released from incarceration are rearrested and returned to confinement, it is most often for technical violations rather than new crimes. The incidents often stem from unmet "survival needs," such as difficulty meeting financial obligations, lower employment skills, or the inability to secure safe housing. Implementing gender-responsive practices can help reduce women's involvement in the criminal justice system, and that benefits women and their families, their communities, and society in the long term.

FIGURE 6–4 **Ten Things We Know About Women in Jails.**
Source: From "10 Facts About Women in Jails" by Becki Ney in American Jails, Vol. 27, Issue. 06, pp. 08-10. Copyright © 2014, American Jail Association. Used with permission of American Jail Association.

Many facilities had conditions comparable to those found in third-world countries and were considered a hazard to both inmates and staff alike.

About 2,400 inmates are held in 79 Indian country jails, with more than 10,000 persons admitted to the jails during a typical year. The expected average length of stay at admission is about six days. Females are 25% of the inmate population (up from 20% in 2000), whereas the juvenile population has declined from 16% in 2000 to 8% in 2014 (Minton, 2015).

Two types of Indian offenders are detained in Indian country jails: those who have committed crimes under federal law and those who have committed crimes under tribal law (Summerill, 2005). The federal law offenses are more serious crimes (e.g., murder, rape, and aggravated assault) and the tribal law violations are less serious acts that are subject to a maximum $5,000 fine or one year of incarceration.

About 30% of inmates in Indian country jails are confined for a violent offense—with domestic violence and aggravated or simple assault accounting for the largest percentage of those offenses. After reaching a high of 20% in 2007, confinement for domestic violence fell to 12% in 2014 (Minton, 2011b, 2015). The decline of domestic violence is especially promising because American Indian women suffer domestic violence and physical assault at rates far exceeding those of women of other ethnicities. In fact, 39% of American Indian women nationally report being victims of domestic violence (Fletcher, 2009), and American Indian and Alaska Native women are more than twice as likely to be victims of violent crime compared to other women in the U.S. general population (Perry, 2004).

Although domestic violence statistics across tribal communities specifically have not been compiled (National Institute of

Justice, 2016), there is consensus that women living in Indian country are also victimized at rates higher than women in the general U.S. population (National Coordination Committee, 2014). The Tribal Law and Order Act of 2010 and the Violence Against Women Reauthorization Act of 2013 are examples of legislative efforts intended to assist in combating sexual and domestic violence against American Indian and Alaska Native women. These laws give tribal governments greater authority to prosecute both Indians and non-Indians who commit acts of domestic violence or dating violence and more clearly specify actions to be taken by the federal government in combating sexual and domestic violence in Indian country and in Alaska Native villages.

Jailing the Mentally Ill

Today, there are more mentally ill people in jails than there are in hospitals. Specifics vary depending on the definition of mental illness that is used in the study, but there is general agreement that America's jails and prisons have become our new mental hospitals. Torrey and his colleagues (Torrey, Kennard, Eslinger, Lamb, & Pavle, 2010) put this in historical perspective by noting that we have returned to the state of the early nineteenth century, when mentally ill people filled our jails and prisons.

The rate of mental illness in America's state prisons and local jails is at least three times the rate in the general population. When the nation's three biggest jail systems are combined (Cook County, in Illinois; Los Angeles County; and New York City), they represent the largest mental health treatment facilities in the country (Fields & Phillips, 2013). Los Angeles County Jail alone holds more people with mental illness than does any state hospital or mental health institution in the United States (Council of State Governments, 2002, pp. xii–xiii). Using the broad criterion of self-reported mental health problems—including clinical diagnosis or treatment by a mental health professional—64% of jail inmates had symptoms of a **mental health disorder** (James & Glaze, 2006). Using a more stringent definition, 17% of jail inmates suffer from a **serious mental illness** such as bipolar disorder, schizophrenia spectrum disorder, or major depression (Steadman, Osher, Robbins, Case, & Samuels, 2009). That percentage is believed to be four to six times that of the general population (Glazer, 2015). With either definition, the problem is obvious because our nation's jails were not designed as mental health facilities. The number of people with serious mental illness or mental health problems is substantial, and these individuals require complex treatment, services, and supervision that jails were neither designed nor equipped to provide.

The high rate of mental health disorder and serious mental illness among jail inmates reflects the role of local jails in today's criminal justice system, but, as Figure 6–5 shows, there are several things that may help us understand the disproportionate number. As locally operated facilities, jails hold—along with other offenders—mentally ill persons pending their movement to appropriate mental health facilities. The percentage of jail inmates identified as having a mental health problem was especially high for white non-Hispanics (71%), females (75%), and persons aged 24 or younger (70%). In addition, inmates with a mental health

Most mentally ill jail inmates are picked up for minor nonviolent crimes. Some studies have found persons with mental illnesses to be slightly more likely than other offenders to have committed violent offenses, but that alone does not explain their overrepresentation in jail. More likely explanations include (Council of State Governments, n.d.; Ditton, 1999; Glazer, 2015) the following:

- The behavior resulting in arrest and jail is often less indicative of criminal behavior than it is of untreated mental illness (e.g., experiencing delusions, being immobilized by depression, and suffering the consequences of inadequate treatment).
- Nearly 75% of jail inmates with mental illness also suffer from drug or alcohol addiction and are therefore more likely to be arrested for drug-related crimes.
- People with serious mental illness are often unable to access affordable housing and homelessness is frequently associated with arrest. This is especially true where persons are arrested for "quality of life" crimes (as a strategy for preventing more serious offenses) since the homeless are more likely to be found peeing in the street, panhandling, sleeping in subways, etc.
- Despite being picked up for minor offenses, mentally ill inmates tend to stay longer than the average inmate—possibly because they are less skilled at obtaining bail and more likely to commit infractions while in jail.
- Police may find it easier to catch mentally ill offenders, juries might be more willing to convict them, and judges may be more inclined to sentence them to jail or prison than to release them on probation.

DISCUSS Which of these explanations do you find most persuasive? What other explanations can you think of for why the mentally ill are overrepresented in the jail population?

FIGURE 6–5 **Why the Disproportionate Number of Mentally Ill People in Jail?**
Source: Pearson Education Inc.

problem were more likely than those without a mental health problem to have been homeless in the year before their incarceration and to have lived in a foster home, agency, or institution while growing up (James & Glaze, 2006).

Having a period of homelessness in the year prior to their arrest emphasizes the lack of appropriate facilities in the United States for many of our mentally ill citizens. Belcher (1988) studied homeless mentally ill people in an effort to understand the interactions those people have with the criminal justice system. The difficulties of street life, the tendency not to comply with aftercare arrangements, and the problems associated with impaired mental functioning often result in displays of odd behavior by many of these people. That odd behavior places homeless mentally ill people in direct conflict with many societal norms, and as a result, they are frequently involved with the criminal justice system. In many states, unless individuals are overtly suicidal or homicidal, the state hospitals will not admit them. Police officers are left to decide whether to let the people wander back to the void of street life or detain them in jail.

The jail may be a refuge for the homeless mentally ill, but it is a refuge without treatment or even prolonged shelter because these people are quickly released—55% of convicted jail inmates with mental problems serve six months or less

(James & Glaze, 2006). Belcher (1988) explains that for chronically homeless mentally ill people who wander aimlessly in the community, are psychotic much of the time, and are typically unable to manage their internal control systems, the criminal justice system functions as an asylum of last resort. Unfortunately, the jail serves more as a shelter for these people than a treatment facility. James and Glaze (2006) report that 83% of jail inmates with a mental health problem received no treatment for their condition after admission to jail.

Bleak as this may sound, there is reason for hope. One option is to divert people with mental illness from jail to community-based services—and doing so has had positive results. A multisite national study of persons who participated in postbooking jail diversion programs found that persons with serious mental illness who are diverted to community-based services experience fewer arrests and days in jail in the 12 months following their diversion than in the prior 12 months (Case, Steadman, Dupuis, & Morris, 2009). Another possibility is to provide jail-based treatment programs. Although such programs are infrequently found and those that are operating need additional study, an evaluation of a therapeutic program for mentally ill adult male inmates in the Broward County (Florida) Jail suggests that providing jail-based mental health programming services for inmates with mental illness can stabilize psychiatric symptoms and support effective jail operations (Hagar, Ludwig, & McGovern, 2008).

► New-Generation Jails

For more than 200 years, America's jails were designed in a consistent style and the inmates were managed in a common manner. The typical architectural design had cells placed sequentially along a hallway. Inmates were monitored by correctional officers patrolling the hallway and looking into each cell. These two key features of jail management—facility design and inmate supervision—began changing in the mid-1970s when the Federal Bureau of Prisons opened three detention centers that featured a more residential type of design and operated under a management system that gave correctional officers more direct contact with inmates (Wener, 2005).

This innovative design and supervision model was adopted by some cities and counties, and by 1995 the National Institute of Corrections had identified 199 jails across the country that used the new model. Today, the more than 350 jails implementing this design and supervision philosophy are known as **new-generation jails** (National Institute of Corrections, 2006). The two key ingredients of the new-generation approach are architectural design and inmate supervision.

Architectural design may seem like a strange thing to concentrate on, but it has been accepted as an integral part of jail and prison construction since the nineteenth century. Also, some people may view inmate supervision as being little more than a couple of guards watching a group of prisoners. But, like architectural design, inmate supervision is more complicated than it first appears. Although new-generation jails are identified by the integration of both design and supervision aspects, we separate them here for discussion purposes.

Jail Design

Prior to the mid-1970s, jails throughout the United States had much in common with their historical ancestors—in fact, some of them were old enough to have been those very ancestors. A jail reform movement was attempted in the 1970s when 1,000 new jail facilities were built (Zupan, 1991). But the design of those facilities was basically the same as those of the jails built in the eighteenth century, and the end result was more of the same rather than the beginning of a new era. Specifically, jails were configured as **linear facilities** in which single- or multiple-occupancy cells are aligned along corridors—similar to a hospital in which long rows of rooms are placed along a hallway.

Security in the linear jails relied on physical containment rather than active supervision and management of inmates. Heavy metal doors, bars, and other security devices were considered necessary to prevent inmate escapes and assaults on staff. To observe inmates, the officer had to patrol the hall and look into individual rooms. The result was infrequent inmate supervision, making it difficult to monitor inmate behavior and to anticipate problems. The absence of active supervision resulted in such problems as assaults on inmates and staff, introduction of dangerous contraband, and inmate disregard for staff-imposed rules (Bowker, 2002).

LEARNING OUTCOMES 4 Discuss the two key aspects that new-generation jails provide for better jail management.

New-generation jails take a dramatically different approach to architectural design. Specifically, they use a layout consisting of a triangular or pie-shaped pod that has its walls lined with cells or rooms arranged around a common area. That common area, or dayroom, is where the inmates converge to watch television, play board games, and socialize. In many podular jails, inmate meals are delivered to the dayroom rather than having to move the inmates to a remote location three times a day.

The living area and cells in new-generation jails are likely to have comfortable furniture, tile or carpet floors, access to telephones, and basically a normalized living environment when compared with linear facilities. The goal is to provide an incentive for inmates to behave—because misbehavior results in placement in a less desirable part of the jail with fewer privileges. In fact, studies have found a decrease in property destruction and reduced levels of vandalism in new-generation jails (Senese, 1997; Wener, 2006).

With the elimination of the old physical barriers, the inmates and officers can now intermingle in relative freedom. In this way, control lies in the hands of the institutional staff rather than with the inmates, as it often does when officials rely too much on things (bars, indestructible furniture, etc.) rather than people (correctional staff) to control inmate behavior.

Inmate Supervision

The linear facility design made it difficult—impossible, even—for custodial staff to continuously supervise inmate activities. Inmate supervision in such facilities is described as being **intermittent**, as jail staff could observe or interact

Oftentimes, when students tour a facility using the podular direct approach, they are surprised to find a single correctional officer in the pod with supervising responsibility for the many inmates also in the pod. Can such a setup really be safe for both officer and inmates?

Mr. Rick Dill is the retired Chief of the Offender Supervision Bureau at the Weld County (CO) Sheriff's Office.

Touring a direct supervision facility for the first time is probably surprising. How could one officer working in a housing unit filled by a virtual sea of inmates be safe? It might not be safe without jail operations being effectively integrated with the principles of direct supervision.

Direct supervision housing units are designed with good lines of sight, natural light, and sound attenuation. Each unit includes security features appropriate for the custody level of offenders to be housed there, and all offenders are assigned housing based upon objective classification. The officer-to-inmate ratio must allow the officer to interact with every inmate during the course of a shift.

In addition to basic training, there is extensive initial and ongoing training in interpersonal communication, conflict management, situational leadership, and problem solving. Staff is well trained in the recognition and effective response to symptoms of drug abuse, mental illness, and self-harming behaviors.

Experience has shown that the best-performing officers are articulate and have the abilities to work well with others, take command when appropriate, and comfortably relate to a wide range of people from differing backgrounds. During the initial transition from indirect to direct supervision, some attrition occurred because not all of the current staff had these abilities. Finding the right people remains a challenge.

An officer is vested with broad authority and inmates must know the officer is the unit leader. Effective control requires authority be exercised in a fair, firm, and consistent manner. Well-documented procedures and directives give boundaries to the officer. Directives also maintain consistency and provide structure for inmates.

Inmates cannot know when a supervisor disagrees with an officer's decision without the officer's authority being eroded. The perception that an officer lacks authority within a housing unit will quickly translate into a loss of control. Initially, supervisors had to adjust their supervision style, and conflict between supervisors and officers was common until everyone became more comfortable.

Prior to direct supervision, nonviolent conflict between inmates would go unnoticed. The most dominant inmate filled the void in housing unit leadership and that quickly could escalate violence. Since direct supervision was implemented, there are fewer assaults, inmate-on-inmate victimizations, and escapes. Countless suicide attempts have been interrupted or prevented. The facility is cleaner, and easier to maintain with less vandalism.

The difference between the staff of indirect and direct supervision facilities was clear in a recent event. Officers at our jail volunteered to work at another county jail for a few hours so that some of the on-duty officers at that facility could attend a funeral. The other jail was an indirect supervision facility.

Local officers became very uncomfortable because the visiting officers were frequently going into units and working with offenders. The visiting officers were equally uncomfortable not having contact with offenders inside the units because they felt the inmates were in control and not the staff.

The positive reaction from my staff was the real indicator of effectiveness.

Source: From Corrections: A Contemporary Introduction by Leanne F Alarid and Philip L Reichel. Copyright © 2008 by Pearson Education.

---

with inmates only on an irregular or sporadic basis. As a result, the inmates were left unsupervised for long periods. In addition, inmates had to be moved from their cells to other locations for various activities. For example, it would not be unusual to have hundreds of inmates gather together on the "big yard" for recreation or in the mess hall for meals—and both of those locations could become dangerous places for inmates and staff.

In addition to a unique architectural design, the new-generation jails provide an alternative to the intermittent supervision model. Initially, the podular design included an observation area (typically at the hub from which the various pods flow out) where correctional officers engaged in remote

observation and supervision of the inmates (e.g., issuing commands to the inmates in each pod via an intercom system). This system, which Figure 6–6 identifies as podular **indirect supervision** (also called remote supervision), increased visual surveillance over what was possible in linear facilities but allowed less frequent verbal interaction with the inmates. Watching through windows (typically one-way) and listening via microphones in the living area, the officers monitored inmate behavior and conversation.

Beginning in the 1970s, design and supervision were further refined, and the result is today's podular **direct supervision** wherein custodial staff are placed—for their entire shift—in the inmates' living area. In this way, the officer has immediate

Intermittent Supervision

- This is used in linear style jails.
- Surveillance is intermittent and security relies more on physical barriers than on active supervision on inmates.

Podular Indirect Supervision

- This is used in new-generation jails.
- Surveillance is continuous observation of inmates from an officer's station in a secure room separated from the inmate living area.

Podular Direct Supervision

- This is used in new-generation jails.
- Surveillance is continuous and supervision is direct as officers intermingle with inmates.

FIGURE 6–6 **Types of Jail Supervision.**

visual observation of inmates and has the ability to interact freely with them. This style of inmate supervision provides for continuous rather than intermittent or indirect supervision. By placing the officer in the pod, there is an increased awareness of the behaviors and needs of the inmates. This creates a safer environment for both the staff and the inmates. Because interaction between inmates is constantly and closely monitored, dissension can be quickly detected before it escalates. Inmates who show signs of becoming unruly also can be quickly identified and moved to a more secure living unit/pod (Beck, 2006). Figure 6–7 points out that studies of direct supervision have mixed results, but the trend definitely is one of increased use of this supervision type.

The confinement function provided by jails is certainly important, but when the general public thinks of incarceration it is probably the prison that comes to mind. We turn to prisons in the next chapter as we consider the facilities designed for long-term confinement and some of the issues faced by officials charged with the management of those facilities and their prisoners.

Think About It...

Incorporating ideas from social and environmental psychology, new-generation jails are designed to maximize the power of expectations as a way to encourage positive behavioral norms (Wener, 2005). The idea is that rather than

Source: Philip L. Reichel

challenging someone to break or damage an item designed to be unbreakable, surround them instead with more normal furnishings that provide no challenge or gratification when vandalized. So, a well-lit and colorful area with carpeting and upholstered furniture should encourage caretaking among the inmates. Do the potential benefits of putting inmates in a less-institutionalized setting outweigh any retributive or deterrent benefit that might result from placing them in a harsher environment?

Assuming that jail staff have received the appropriate training and have the necessary interpersonal and communication skills to successfully implement direct supervision—admittedly, not always a safe assumption—we should expect new-generation jails to be a safer environment for both staff and inmates. For the most part, research supports this expectation. In his review of some 20 years of direct supervision literature, Wener (2006) concludes that direct supervision design and management results in reduced levels of serious and violent incidents, fewer inmate assaults on staff, and a diminished number of inmate–inmate assaults. However, there are mixed results regarding the quality of the working environment (e.g., stress levels and job satisfaction) among jail staff in new-generation jails (Wener, 2006), and one study suggests direct supervision can be used without negative effects on staff regardless of the facility's architectural design (Applegate & Paoline, 2007). Another study found that suicide may be more affected by the institutional living environment than by the use of direct supervision (Tartaro & Levy, 2010). Despite the mixed results, we believe the research to date indicates that direct supervision looks promising.

FIGURE 6–7 **Evidence-Based Practice—Does It Work? Direct Supervision**
Source: Leanne Fiftal Alarid.

Do People with Mental Illness Belong in Jail?

A Harris County (Texas) Jail inmate sat at a picnic table and explained to a reporter that he is extremely mentally ill and extremely intelligent. The *New York Times* reporter describes the inmate as veering in and out of reality during the interview. Sometimes he talked lucidly about taking medication for his severe bipolar disorder; at other times, he described how Vice President Joseph Biden spoke to him through the television or explained that Pope Benedict XVI is his grandfather (Grissom, 2011).

The Harris County Jail houses more than 10,000 inmates and about 2,400 of them are taking psychotropic medications. Some of the inmates with mental health problems say the jail—which is essentially the largest mental institution in Texas—provides the best mental health care available to them in the Houston area. Community mental health care suffered major cuts in 2003 as a result of the state budget crisis, and more cuts seem likely under the current crisis. The situation is not much different in other states, and across the country more mentally ill people are likely to end up on the streets or behind bars.

The large number of mentally ill persons in jail raises several interesting questions:

1. It is important for public safety that persons with mental illness who commit serious crimes be held responsible for their actions. However, many people with mental illness who wind up in jail have committed low-level, nonviolent crimes, often as a result of their untreated mental illness or co-occurring substance abuse. Both jail officials and community-based treatment providers will often agree that the jail environment is not the best treatment setting for persons with mental illness. *Do you think people with mental illnesses belong in jail? If budget cuts continue to reduce community-based mental health programs, might jail be the best available option?*

2. The proportion of women with serious mental illness in jails is double that of men (Steadman et al., 2009). The cause of the disparity awaits additional research, but some have suggested that early childhood experiences and higher rates of trauma exposure may explain some of the variation (Council of State Governments, n.d.). *Might experiences with physical or sexual abuse be a factor? Are men and women affected differently by such childhood experiences as growing up in homes where a parent or guardian abused alcohol or drugs? What other childhood experiences might explain the phenomenon?*

LEARNING OUTCOMES 1

Discuss the pretrial release and detention systems developed to balance the interests of both the community and the suspect.

Pretrial release can be of either a financial or a nonfinancial type. When release is backed by a financial obligation, it involves an agreement to pay cash or relinquish property to the court if the defendant fails to make required court appearances. Under nonfinancial release, the defendant either makes a simple promise to appear for trial or may be released under specific conditions such as a promise to participate in a treatment program.

1. Four states (Illinois, Kentucky, Oregon, and Wisconsin) have abolished commercial bail bonds and rely on the defendant's promise to return for trial or on deposits to courts instead of payments to private businesses. What are some pros and cons of abolishing commercial bail?

2. Seventy-one percent of defendants on pretrial release made all scheduled court appearances and had no pretrial misconduct. Twenty-nine percent of defendants on pretrial release missed court appearances or were rearrested for new crimes. Which of those statistics is more important to you when deciding whether to support pretrial release?

bail bond　A written agreement by the defendant to pay cash or relinquish property to the court if the defendant fails to attend required court appearances.

release on recognizance (ROR)　Pretrial release based only on the defendant's promise to appear for trial (not backed with money or property).

conditional release　The return of prisoners to the larger community with a brief period of supervision with rules, such as curfew, treatment completion, and maintaining employment. Can be used either pretrial or postconviction.

unsecured bond　When a defendant is released without having to make any payment but is liable for the full bail amount if required court appearances are missed.

LEARNING OUTCOMES 2

Distinguish the functions and purposes of jails from prisons.

Whereas jails are operated by local governments, detain persons not yet convicted of a crime, and hold convicted misdemeanants, prisons are operated by the state or federal government, hold only persons already convicted and sentenced, and provide custody for convicted felons. Jails typically hold both males and females in separate units of the same facility, but prisons usually hold males and females in separate facilities. Jails serve several purposes, including detention of persons awaiting trial and the temporary holding of persons awaiting transfer to other agencies or facilities.

1. What are some pros and cons of having jails operated by the local government rather than the state government?

2. Many of the people in jail have not been convicted of a crime. Should those who are awaiting trial be treated differently while in jail from those who have been convicted? Do people who have not yet been found guilty have more "rights" than those who have been found guilty?

3. Should governments invest in separate jail facilities for men and women rather than simply have separate units within the same facility? What advantages and disadvantages might result from this arrangement?

jails　Confinement facilities usually operated by city or county governments and typically managed by that government's law enforcement agency.

integrated jail–prison systems　A state government, rather than the more typical local government agency, is responsible for the administration and operation of jails located throughout the state.

LEARNING OUTCOMES 3

Summarize the characteristics of the jail population.

Most jail inmates are African-American and Hispanic males, but the percentage of females has increased since 1990 and along with that increase comes a need for greater attention to such gender-specific concerns as high rates of substance abuse, mental illness, and problems associated with physical and sexual abuse. The number of inmates in Indian country jails has also increased in recent years and they are often kept in facilities that are neither safe nor secure. Most of the inmates are adult males convicted of assault, domestic violence, and driving while intoxicated/driving under the influence (DWI/DUI) offenses. There are more mentally ill people in jail today than in hospitals. Some 17% of jail inmates suffer from a serious mental illness and as many as 64% have symptoms of a mental health disorder.

1. What are some explanations for the gender, racial, and ethnic characteristics of jail inmates?

2. Why is the percentage of female jail inmates increasing?

3. Veysey et al. (1998) have suggested modification to the jail environment that can better accommodate the special needs of women detainees and convicts. Argue for why such modifications should be done. Why should they not be done?

4. Why are jail facilities in Indian country in such poor condition? Why should we care?

5. Discuss the extent to which you believe homeless mentally ill people in your community are involved with the criminal justice process. What options should the police have when dealing with such people?

mega jails The country's largest jails, holding over 1,000 people each.

Indian country Land within an Indian reservation or land that is technically owned by the federal government but held in trust for a tribe or tribal member.

mental health disorder A broad category used to identify convicted offenders who are considered to have mental health problems as a result of self-reported clinical diagnosis or treatment by a mental health professional.

serious mental illness A narrow category used to identify convicted offenders suffering from such conditions as bipolar disorder, schizophrenia spectrum disorder, or major depression.

LEARNING OUTCOMES 4

Discuss the two key aspects that new-generation jails provide for better jail management.

Prior to the mid-1970s, jails were designed in a linear style with inmate supervision being only intermittent as officers strolled the cell block. With the advent of new-generation jails, designs were based on pie-shaped pods with cells arranged in tiers around a central living area. This design allows inmate supervision to be either indirect (from an observation point separated from the living area) or direct (officer stays in the living area with the inmates).

1. How are the concepts of jail design and inmate supervision interrelated?

2. Why is it said that control lies in the hands of inmates in linear facilities, but in the hands of officers in new-generation facilities?

3. Distinguish between indirect and direct supervision.

4. Do you accept or reject the idea that jail inmates are less likely to damage more normal furnishings than items designed to be unbreakable? Why?

5. If you were a jail correctional officer, which work environment would you prefer: a linear facility, a podular facility with indirect supervision, or a podular facility with direct supervision? Why?

new-generation jails Facilities using a specific architectural design and inmate supervision model in order to reduce violent and destructive behavior by the inmates.

linear facilities Jails and prisons designed with single- or multiple-occupancy cells aligned along corridors that, in turn, are often stacked in tiers.

intermittent supervision Inmate supervision method wherein custodial staff members are able to observe or interact with inmates only on an irregular or sporadic basis.

indirect supervision Inmate supervision method wherein custodial staff observe and interact with inmates remotely by watching through windows and listening via microphones.

direct supervision Inmate supervision method wherein custodial staff are placed—for their entire shift—in the inmates' living area.

Additional Links

Watch the slide show and listen to the audio file about a bail bondsman at **www.nytimes.com/packages/html/us/20080128_BAIL_FEATURE/index.html**.

Use the interactive map provided at **www.ncsl.org/research/civil-and-criminal-justice/pretrial-policy-search-by-state.aspx** to read about pretrial policies in your state.

Visit the National Institute of Corrections Jails Division at **http://nicic.gov/JailsDivision** and look at some of its initiatives and training programs.

The American Jail Association (AJA) at **www.aja.org** is a national nonprofit organization dedicated to supporting those who work in and operate our nation's jails.

Listen to the National Public Radio (NPR) story on the role of jails in treating the mentally ill at **www.npr.org/2013/09/15/222822452/what-is-the-role-of-jails-in-treating-the-mentally-ill**.

Visit the website for *The Released*, a PBS Frontline show about mentally ill offenders struggling to make it on the outside, at **www.pbs.org/wgbh/pages/frontline/released/**.

At **http://nicic.gov/library/030135**, watch the video *Jails in America: A Report on Podular Direct Supervision*, which provides an introduction to podular direct supervision.

7

Managing Prisons and Prisoners

1 Outline the development and organization of the federal prison system.

2 Outline the development and organization of the state prison systems.

3 Distinguish between administrative and disciplinary segregation and describe solitary confinement.

4 Explain how prisoners are classified and assigned in prisons.

5 Describe the various jobs and functions of prison staff.

6 Summarize the privatization of prisons.

STARTING A PRISON SENTENCE

As the bus pulled up to the prison, John wasn't sure what he was feeling. He tried not to show that he was scared, but he was. He tried to act like he was just going to the mall. He wanted very much to be somewhere else. John figured that he deserved all that he got, but it was a traumatic day that lives in his memory years later. As the bus filled with new prisoners neared the entryway, you could see the razor wire on the fences surrounding the place. You could have heard a pin drop inside the bus. Nobody made a sound.

That is how an inmate—who we'll call John—describes his initial reactions as he arrived at the state reception facility to be processed into the prison system. John will stay at this initial facility, where he will be interviewed and tested, before being sent to the state prison, where he will begin serving his sentence. As John might explain it, "You'll be in this reception center for a few weeks. Then, one day, they will inform you that you'll be leaving in the morning for whatever institution that they've decided to send you. Don't try to fight them, because you can't. They make all the decisions for you now. If you make a fuss, they will still send you to the prison they chose, but because you fought them you'll start off in that prison's hole. That's

Angelo Gilardelli/Shutterstock

not good, 'cause it's always better to start off with a clear record."

DISCUSS Does the prison, or any specific prison employee, have an obligation to help newly arrived prisoners feel less anxious and to adjust as quickly as possible to the new environment? Or, could it be to the prison's advantage to keep newly arrived prisoners as nervous as possible? Explain your reasoning.

Contemporary prisons have two primary purposes. First, they must provide security to the general public by keeping the prisoners confined, but must also provide a safe environment for the staff and inmates working and living there. Second, most prisons try to provide inmates with opportunities to change and thereby reduce the likelihood of them continuing their criminal behavior. The second goal is the more controversial (some people would prefer that prisons do no more than incapacitate or provide an experience that serves as a deterrent), but we see in this chapter that prisons mostly accept both security and treatment obligations.

This becomes apparent as we see the importance of both security and treatment in the federal and state prison systems, and especially when we consider the importance of inmate classification in meeting prison security and treatment goals. The chapter continues with attention to the prison staff members who have responsibility for the security and treatment tasks and concludes with a look at how private prisons are taking over some of the responsibilities previously held by the government.

▶ The Development and Organization of the Federal Prison System

The Federal Bureau of Prisons (BOP) was established in 1930 as part of the Department of Justice. The bureau had three goals:

1. To ensure consistent, centralized administration of the federal prison system
2. To professionalize the prison service
3. To provide more progressive and humane care for federal inmates

For more than 80 years, the BOP has sought to achieve these goals and in doing so has often served as a model for state correctional systems (Federal Bureau of Prisons, 2015a).

A Brief History of the BOP

Prior to the creation of the BOP, most offenders convicted of violating federal laws were placed in state prisons and county jails. After the Civil War, the number of federal offenders began expanding, and the states and counties increasingly complained about the burden of housing federal criminals. In 1891, Congress responded by authorizing the construction of three federal penitentiaries for men: one in Atlanta, Georgia; one in Leavenworth, Kansas; and one in McNeil Island, Washington. Later, a detention center, a youth facility, and the first federal women's reformatory opened as part of the federal prison system under the authority of the Justice Department.

By the 1920s, the federal prisons were experiencing crowding problems and were plagued by inconsistent, haphazard administration. Much of the blame for that condition was due to the wardens, who were political appointees operating with no central direction as they applied their individual policies and procedures. Finally, in 1930, Congress decided to provide the needed centralization by establishing the BOP to manage and regulate all federal prisons. The new bureau quickly began to build or acquire new institutions in an attempt to relieve the crowding—including abandoned military barracks on Alcatraz Island (see Figure 7–1).

The first federal women's reformatory officially opened in 1928 in Alderson, West Virginia. Dr. Mary B. Harris was the first warden who insisted that this showcase prison's goal was not to punish but to maximize rehabilitation. Sixteen redbrick cottages, each with separate kitchens and sewing areas, were situated in the mountains of rural West Virginia on beautiful grounds that resembled a college campus. The prison had no fences, no walls, and no armed guard towers, but successful escape was difficult because of the remote location. Over time, as the redbrick cottages became too expensive to keep repairing, a new four-story facility replaced the cottages. Alderson now holds approximately 900 women and remains a minimum-security facility. Today there are 27 facilities housing female inmates. Most of those are actually mixed facilities for both men and women.

FIGURE 7–1 **The U.S. Penitentiary at Alcatraz.** Until its closing in 1963, the U.S. Penitentiary at Alcatraz served as a maximum-security, minimum-privilege prison holding federal prisoners considered especially troublesome and dangerous.
Source: Tomasz Szymanski/Shutterstock.

The BOP Today

Today, the BOP consists of 122 institutions and is responsible for almost 200,000 prisoners. As Table 7–1 shows, those prisoners, who are primarily white males with U.S. citizenship, are dealt with by a staff that is also mostly white and male. From the bureau's central office in Washington, D.C., the director and

LEARNING OUTCOMES 1 Outline the development and organization of the federal prison system.

TABLE 7–1 — QUICK FACTS ABOUT THE BUREAU OF PRISONS*

Inmates by gender	Male: 93%	Staff by gender	Male: 73%
	Female: 7%		Female: 27%
Inmates by race	White: 59%	Staff by race/ethnicity	White (Non-Hispanic): 63%
	Black: 38%		African-American: 21%
	Native American: 2%		Hispanic: 12%
	Asian: 2%		Asian: 2%
			Native American: 1%
Inmates by ethnicity (could be any race)	Hispanic: 34%		
Inmates by citizenship	United States: 77%		
	Mexico: 15%		
	Remainder: 8%		
Inmates by offense	Drug Offenses: 47%		
	Weapons, Explosives, Arson: 17%		
	Immigration: 9%		
	Sex Offenses: 8%		
	Extortion, Fraud, Bribery: 7%		
	Robbery: 4%		
	Burglary, Larceny, Property Offenses: 4%		
	Homicide, Aggravated Assault, and Kidnapping Offenses: 3%		
	Other: 1%		

Reference: From About Us. Published by Federal Bureau of Prisons.

*All data as on December 26, 2015. Totals may not equal 100% due to rounding.

Are you surprised by which offense types are the top two and bottom two categories (excluding "other")? Why are these most and least frequent offenses categories for federal prisoners?

assistant directors oversee BOP activities around the nation. For management purposes, the country is divided into six geographic regions, each with a regional director.

An indication of the changing nature of federal corrections is the influx of persons linked to terrorism. In 2011, the BOP housed more than 360 persons convicted in terrorism-related cases. Management of these offenders is comprehensive and includes such things as coordinated information sharing with relevant agencies, close monitoring of general correspondence and social telephone calls, and staff training on identifying recruitment and radicalization activities (Shane, 2011).

Many of those convicted in terrorism cases are held in special units, called communication management units

(CMUs), at the federal prisons in Terre Haute, Indiana, and Marion, Illinois. The strict monitoring of CMU inmate mail, e-mail, and phone calls is intended to prevent those inmates from radicalizing others and illuminate plotting from behind bars. Visits are allowed at the CMU, but non contact visiting booths must be used (Shane, 2011).

Security Levels at Federal Facilities

The security level of a prison is determined by such features as the prison's design, perimeter, and staff-to-inmate ratio. The more elaborate a prison's design and perimeter, and the higher its staff-to-inmate ratio, the more secure the prison is said to be. As shown in Figure 7–2, the BOP classifies its prisons by five security levels (minimum, low, medium, high, and administrative). Administrative facilities (which include those with special missions, such as detaining pretrial offenders or offenders with serious medical problems) can actually hold inmates in all security levels. An exception is the administrative-maximum penitentiary, which is an administrative facility but holds only those inmates who are extremely dangerous, violent, or escape-prone. As such, these inmates are under the tightest security available in the BOP.

In addition to the more distinctive facility types, the BOP also operates satellite camps that are small, minimum-security units adjacent to a main facility with a higher security rating. Inmates at these camps provide labor to the main institution and to off-site work programs. For example, the Federal Correctional Institution in Jesup, Georgia, is a medium-security facility housing male offenders. It has one adjacent low-security satellite facility and a minimum-security prison camp, both housing male inmates.

A final type of BOP facility to mention is actually a grouping of facilities. In 1991 the BOP began constructing the first Federal Correctional Complex (FCC). The complex, located in Florence, Colorado, used a new design concept with several correctional facilities of different security levels at a single site. Benefits of the complex include the obvious financial savings due to lower construction and operating costs, but also have personnel advantages, as staff members can have career mobility without making geographic moves. Today there are 15 such complexes located across the country, each with at least two main facilities.

Minimum Security facilities, also called Federal Prison Camps (FPC), have dormitory housing, limited or no perimeter fencing, and a relatively low staff-to-inmate ratio. FPCs are work- and program-oriented and their inmates often work at nearby military bases or at other federal prisons.

Low Security Federal Correctional Institutions (FCIs) have double-fenced perimeters. Most use dormitory or cubicle housing and include strong work and program components. The staff-to-inmate ratio is higher than in FPCs.

Medium Security FCIs and some U.S. Penitentiaries housing medium-security inmates use this security level. These facilities have double-fenced perimeters with electronic detection systems and use mostly cell-type housing. They have a higher staff-to-inmate ratio and provide a variety of work and treatment programs.

High Security institutions are called U.S. Penitentiaries (USPs) and they have highly secured perimeters featuring walls or reinforced fences. Inmate housing is in multiple- or single-occupant cells and the staff-to-inmate ratio is the highest of all facilities.

Administrative facilities are institutions with special missions, such as the detention of pretrial offenders (e.g., Metropolitan Detention Centers), treatment of inmates with serious medical problems (Federal Medical Centers), or for holding extremely dangerous or escape-prone inmates (Administrative Max USP).

FIGURE 7–2 **The Five BOP Security Levels.**
Source: From About Our Facilities. Published by Federal Bureau of Prisons.

▶ The Development and Organization of State Prison Systems

State prison systems are typically operated by the state's **department of corrections** (DOC) or a state agency with a similar name (e.g., Hawaii's Department of Public Safety, New York State's Department of Correctional Services, and Ohio's Department of Rehabilitation and Correction). Each state's DOC manages at least the state's adult prison facilities and may also be responsible for parole services and community corrections.

At the time of the last national census of state correctional facilities (Stephan, 2008), there were about 1,700 state correctional facilities with nearly 1,200 identified as confinement facilities (e.g., prisons, penitentiaries, and work camps) and about 500 as community-based facilities (e.g., halfway houses, restitution centers, and residential treatment centers). Some states have as few as 6 or 7 correctional facilities (e.g., Maine, Rhode Island, South Dakota, Utah, and Wyoming), whereas others have 100 or more (California, Florida, and Texas). Most state correctional facilities hold fewer than 500 inmates, although some have a daily population exceeding 2,500 prisoners (examples include some prisons in California, Florida, Pennsylvania, and Texas).

Overcrowding is a problem in many states, as determined by one or more of three measures: **operational capacity** (based on the ability of the staff, programs, and services to accommodate a certain size population); **design capacity** (the number of inmates that facility planners or architects intended for the facility); and **rated capacity** (the maximum number of beds or inmates allocated by a rating official to institutions in the states). Data from 2014 show that the federal system and 28 states had more prisoners in custody than their rated capacity (Carson, 2015). The problem is especially notable in Illinois, where some 48,000 inmates are held in facilities with a rated capacity of 32,000 and a design capacity of 28,000. Other states housing notably more inmates than their operational,

rated, or design capacity include Massachusetts, Nebraska, and Ohio—each at about 130% of its maximum capacity.

Security Levels at State Facilities

The actual terms used to designate the security levels of state correctional facilities vary by state, as does the number of levels used. Figure 7–3 uses the most basic of distinctions: minimum (including low or no security designations), medium, or maximum (including those identified in some states as supermaximum, close, or high-security). Some facilities mix several security levels, whereas others house a single level. Most of the prisoners held in the country's state prisons (Stephan, 2008) are in medium-security facilities (42%), followed by those in maximum-security facilities (36%) and minimum-security facilities (22%).

Inmates assigned to **minimum-security facilities** have the most freedom and privileges afforded any state prisoner. These facilities, some of which resemble residential houses and even college campuses, are typically dormitory-style barracks or small rooms for which inmates have their own key. The absence

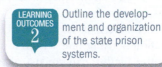

LEARNING OUTCOMES 2 — Outline the development and organization of the state prison systems.

of walls, fences, guarded towers, and obvious physical barriers is not unusual. Such facilities are desirable for offenders who have earned a transfer there based on good behavior and who show little threat to themselves or others. Minimum-security facilities are often used for inmates nearing their release date and who are eligible to participate in work- or education-release programs to help prepare them for return to the community.

Prisoners at **medium-security facilities** are not allowed to leave the institution grounds without an escort. The perimeter is lined with chain-link fences, razor wire, and electronic sensors, and the staff-to-inmate ratio is higher than in minimum-security facilities. However, there is relatively free movement of the inmates within the confines of the prison itself as they move around the living quarters, walk to work assignments, and visit programming areas.

Traditionally, **maximum-security facilities** were built as fortress-like structures with high stone walls surrounding groupings of buildings that served as cell blocks, chow halls, auditoriums, laundry rooms, gymnasiums, and chapels. Guard towers were attached to the walls at the corners and other strategic places, such as at the front and back entrances. Although some of those early prisons still exist, the more recently constructed maximum-security prisons tend to rely on a double-fence perimeter (usually including coiled razor wire) or an electric

Minimum

Minimum security includes both institutional and community-based institutions, such as prerelease/work-release centers, restitution centers, trusty units, large drug rehabilitation centers, community corrections facilities, forestry or wilderness camps, and honor camps. Inmates have considerable personal freedom and are often given opportunities on a time-restricted basis for work furloughs and educational release outside the institution.

Medium

These prisons may resemble higher-security prisons from the outside, but inmates in a medium-security facility have more freedom of movement inside the walls. Although most prisoners spend most of the day outside their housing area, they are still locked in their housing area at night after curfew.

Maximum

The "Big House," as the nineteenth-century maximum-security prisons were often called, was designed for the fullest possible supervision, control, and surveillance of inmates. Contemporary maximum-security prisons forego the high walls and rely instead on fenced perimeters with electronic sensing devices and video surveillance to alert officials about perimeter breaches.

FIGURE 7–3 **Three General Security Levels for State Facilities.**
Source: bibiphoto/Shutterstock.

fence rather than high walls. Prisoners are housed in single or double cells, and time out of the cell is structured and controlled with passes for a specific purpose. Security takes priority over rehabilitation, so fewer treatment and work programs are present. The theory behind this is that maximum-security inmates have shown through their attitudes and behavior that they need more regulation in their daily lives.

A small number of prisons at the highest security level are known as **supermax prisons**, or what some states call "control units" or "secured housing units." The first supermax prison was the U.S. Penitentiary at Marion, Illinois, which converted to permanent lockdown status in 1983 due to the murder of two correctional officers. Since then, many states have followed the federal lead and have modified existing prisons or built new ones to allow implementation of the control-unit philosophy. Because Marion was not built as a lockdown facility (but was being used as one), the federal government eventually constructed an administrative-maximum penitentiary (ADX) prison in Florence, Colorado, that was specifically designed as a supermax facility.

A supermax facility can be either an administrative segregation housing unit within a maximum-custody facility or the entire facility can consist of prisoners at the highest custody level who are isolated from the general population of prisoners and from each other. Inmates assigned to these units are believed to pose a threat to other prisoners and/or correctional officers based on gang membership or behavior while incarcerated. Supermax prisoners may have killed someone while in custody, have a pattern of assaulting correctional officers, have attempted or completed escape from a high-custody facility, or have incited or threatened to incite a disturbance in a correctional facility.

The growth of supermax facilities for troublesome inmates indicates a prison management trend away from a **dispersion approach** and toward a **concentration approach**. In the dispersion approach, prison administrators spread troublemakers around the system or in various units of the prison. Sometimes they might even be sent to other states or to the Federal Bureau of Prisons. The goal is to prevent troublemakers from collaborating, and it enables officials to break up cliques and gangs. In many cases, the dispersion approach backfires and actually assists prison gang recruitment—leaders start a chapter in each new location.

Under a concentration approach, prisoners are grouped together, and their activities and movements are severely restricted and highly monitored. As a result, the general prison population is more easily and safely managed because the most ardent troublemakers have been removed.

▶ Segregation and Solitary Confinement

Segregation of an inmate from the general prison population is used as either a disciplinary or a management tool in both federal and state prisons (as well as in jails). Prisoners placed in segregation are moved to housing units with high levels of restrictions and control. Although often referred to as special housing units (SHUs), in some jurisdictions they are called security housing units (SHUs), intensive management units (IMUs), restricted housing units (RHUs), or communication management units (CMUs).

Segregation is used in prisons of all security levels and conditions of the housing, the duration of the segregation, and restrictions on the inmate will all vary. Although inmates may be housed either alone or with other inmates in the SHU (pronounced like "shoe"), solitary confinement is the more typical and controversial condition.

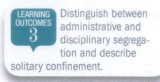

As noted in Chapter 3, isolation has been used in American prisons since the late 1700s. After passing out of favor for several decades, it was revisited in the twentieth century at the federal prisons on Alcatraz Island and in Marion, Illinois. Maintaining control of those prisoners posing the greatest behavioral and management concerns was seen as best accomplished through isolation. State departments of correction began following the federal lead and segregation units were added to house the most dangerous and threatening inmates.

Variations in how records are kept and in what constitutes solitary confinement make it difficult to determine the extent of its use across the country. One frequently cited estimate (The Liman Program, & Association of State Correctional Administrators, 2015) suggests that between 80,000 and 100,000 persons are held in some form of isolated confinement in the United States (not including people in local jails, juvenile facilities, or military and immigration detention). Data from the *National Inmate Survey* (Beck, 2015) show that nearly 20% of state and federal prison inmates had spent time under disciplinary or administrative segregation or in solitary confinement (all conditions that the survey refers to as "restrictive housing") in the 12 months preceding the survey or since coming to their current facility, if that time was shorter. Highlights of findings from the survey are shown in Figure 7–4.

Administrative and Disciplinary Segregation

Administrative segregation, which is often for an indeterminate period, is considered nonpunitive in nature—although the conditions and results of the segregation may be detrimental to the inmate. Prisoners could be placed in administrative segregation while awaiting classification, transfer to another facility, or while a reported prison rule violation is being investigated. They could also be segregated in order to provide for their special needs (e.g., medical or mental health) or to ensure the safety, security, and orderly operation of the facility. For example, a gang leader thought to be coordinating gang activities within the prison might be placed in administrative segregation even without violating any rules. Protective custody is a type of administrative segregation wherein inmates are segregated for their own safety. For example, they may be considered to be at risk in the general prison population due to physical characteristics, other individual factors, or because they have

- Younger inmates, inmates without a high school diploma, and lesbian, gay, and bisexual inmates were more likely to have spent time in restrictive housing than older inmates, inmates with a high school diploma or more, and heterosexual inmates.
- Inmates held for a violent offense other than a sex offense and inmates with extensive arrest histories or prior incarcerations were more likely to have spent time in restrictive housing than inmates held for other offenses and inmates with no prior arrests or incarcerations.
- Use of restrictive housing was linked to inmate mental health problems: 29% of prison inmates with current symptoms of serious psychological distress had spent time in restrictive housing units in the past 12 months.
- In prisons, black inmates (21%) were somewhat more likely than white inmates (16%) to have spent time in restrictive housing. Inmates of other races (including American Indians and Alaska Natives; Asians, Native Hawaiians, and other Pacific Islanders; and those reporting two or more races) were more likely than white inmates to have spent time in restrictive housing (20% in prison). Hispanic inmates (16%) were as likely as white inmates in prison to report having spent time in restrictive housing.
- Among prison inmates who had spent 30 or more days in restrictive housing in the past 12 months or since coming to the facility, 54% had been in a fight or had been written up for assaulting other inmates or staff.
- Prison facilities varied widely in their rates of use of restrictive housing. In 17% of prisons, fewer than 5% of inmates spent time in restrictive housing. However, in another 38% of prisons at least 25% of the inmates had spent such time.
- Prisons with higher rates of restrictive housing had higher levels of facility disorder; lower levels of inmate trust and confidence in staff; higher concentrations of violent inmates (other than sex offenders) and inmates with longer criminal histories; higher percentages of inmates with mental health problems; and higher percentages of lesbian, gay, and bisexual inmates.

FIGURE 7–4 **Characteristics of Prisoners Reporting Time Spent in Administrative or Disciplinary Segregation or Solitary Confinement.**
Source: From Use of Restrictive Housing in U.S. Prisons and Jails, 2011–12. Published by Bureau of Justice Statistics.

provided information to prison officials about violations committed by other inmates (Beck, 2015; Browne, Cambier, & Agha, 2011).

Inmates under **disciplinary segregation** are being punished for rule violations that occurred in the prison setting. For example, a prisoner could be placed in segregation for assault, possession of contraband, or for violating a direct order. The period of disciplinary segregation is usually for a specific time, but could be hours, days, months, or years. Solitary Watch (http://solitarywatch.com/), a web-based project providing original reporting and background research on solitary confinement in the United States, argues that rather than being a last-resort measure reserved for the worst-behaving prisoners, solitary confinement has become a control strategy of first resort in many prisons. Inmates are placed in complete isolation not only for violent acts but for possessing contraband, testing positive for drug use, ignoring orders, or using profanity (Rodriguez, 2015).

Solitary Confinement and Other Conditions of Segregation

Segregation typically involves intense control and isolation. Prisoners usually spend at least 23 hours a day in a cell—generally measuring 6 × 9 to 8 × 10 feet—with a built-in bed, a toilet–sink unit, a small molded desk bolted to the wall, and a narrow slit for a window. Some cells have bars, but more often they have solid metal doors. Meals are typically passed through slots in the door and, when visits are allowed, they often take place via closed-circuit television. Persons confined to segregation are usually restricted from work opportunities and prison programming. They may have access to televisions, radios, art supplies, or even reading and writing materials in their cells, but those items can also be restricted or removed for rule violations (Cloud, Drucker, Browne, & Parsons, 2015; Rodriguez, 2015).

Prisoners are allowed out of their cell for recreation or a shower for as little as 3 to 7 hours per week—maybe 1 hour per day or, in some systems, once a week for 5 hours. Before being moved from their cells, prisoners are cuffed and often shackled at the waist and placed in leg irons. Recreation usually occurs outdoor in an open cage or an indoor area (Cloud et al., 2015).

The condition of **solitary confinement** is especially controversial due to its apparent negative impact on psychological and physical health, its cost, and the possibility that it does not achieve the goal of deterring or reducing prison misconduct. Research on health consequences has found that exposure to solitary confinement leads to such conditions as severe headaches and heart palpitations, confusion and impaired concentration, hallucinations, illusions, and paranoid ideas, impulsive actions, as well as lethargy and debilitation. More specifically, Smith's (2006) meta-analysis of research on the effects of solitary confinement led him to conclude that solitary confinement produces a higher rate of psychiatric and psychological health problems than does regular imprisonment.

Cost-related concerns note that, where information is available, solitary confinement is more expensive that costs related to general confinement. The increased costs are related to construction (SHUs are simply more expensive to build) and to staffing (close and constant observation requires more staff per inmate). In his summary of state data, Rodriguez (2011) reports that solitary confinement cost California taxpayers an additional $175 million a year, Illinois paid two to three times more to keep an inmate in solitary confinement than at the state's other maximum-security prisons, and that the additional annual cost of solitary confinement in Colorado exceeded $20 million.

Presumably, concerns of health and cost could be accepted as unfortunate consequences if solitary confinement served to provide a safer environment and effectively deterred misbehavior. That does not, however, seem to be the case. In an attempt to determine the effect short-term solitary confinement has on subsequent prison misconduct, Morris (2015) tracked the behavior of male inmates who had engaged in violent misconduct at least once during the first two years of their incarceration. The results indicated that exposure to short-term solitary confinement as a punishment for an initial violence did not increase or decrease the probability, timing, or development of future misconduct. As Morris notes, if these findings are validated, there should be discussion regarding the utility of solitary confinement policies under certain contexts.

Less Reliance on Segregation

Action to reduce the use of segregation, and specifically solitary confinement, began in earnest in 2011 when a United Nations expert on torture called on all countries to ban solitary confinement of juveniles and the mentally ill and when Washington state initiated a program relying more on rehabilitation than lockdown—resulting in a 50% drop from 2011 to 2015 in the number of inmates kept in isolation (Glazer, 2015; Neyfakh, 2015). In 2014, Colorado stopped long-term solitary confinement for mentally ill. In 2015, Massachusetts limited solitary confinement for the mentally ill, and New York state agreed to overhaul the way solitary confinement is administered in the state's prisons. New York's goal is to significantly reduce the number of inmates held in isolation, cutting the maximum length of stay, and improving their living conditions (Glazer, 2015; Schwirtz & Winerip, 2015). In 2016, President Obama banned federal prisons from holding juveniles in solitary confinement, and across the country other states are reevaluating how solitary confinement is being used.

If prisons come to rely less on segregation and isolation, how will troublesome inmates be handled? Washington state certainly provides a model (Neyfakh, 2015) but so too does Great Britain. According to Gawande (2009), beginning in the 1980s, British authorities gradually adopted a strategy that focused less on the use of solitary confinement and more on preventing prison violence. With an understanding that prisoners who are unmanageable in one setting often behave perfectly reasonably in another, the British reduced isolation and offered prisoners opportunities for work, education, and special programming to increase social ties and skills. Small housing units (Close Supervision Centres) of fewer than ten people in individual cells provide opportunities to receive mental health treatment and earn rights for more exercise, more phone calls, and contact visits. The results have been impressive. The use of long-term isolation in England is now negligible and the Inspectorate of Prisons (2015) has deemed the Close Supervision Centres to be a well-run system that contains dangerous men safely and decently. Further, other European countries have, with a similar focus on small units and violence prevention, achieved a similar outcome (Herrman, 2015).

▶ Inmate Classification

When the courts sentence offenders to imprisonment, the judge has no control over the facility at which the offenders will serve time or the treatment programs in which they will participate. Those tasks belong to a team of correctional experts made up of members who specialize in determining the risk each offender poses to the community and within the prison, as well as the offender's treatment needs. The process and procedures by which this is accomplished are called **classification**.

Classification in the Early Years

The earliest versions of classification were to separate prisoners on the basis of such simple and obvious criteria as gender, age, and offense seriousness. It was not until the twentieth century that classification was viewed as a crucial element in prison management. This began in the late 1920s with the efforts of F. Lovell Bixby, a psychologist in charge of the classification division for New Jersey's prisons.

In the late 1920s, Bixby developed a classification procedure that standardized the testing of newly sentenced offenders throughout New Jersey's diverse prison facilities. He prepared various reporting forms in order to standardize information that had been gathered on each new arrival and tried to identify some of their personality traits, work skills, and educational needs. Using the collected data for each prisoner, Bixby divided them into groups requiring minimum, medium, or maximum security (McKelvey, 1977). By the 1950s, classification was being implemented throughout the country's prisons as a way of separating inmates based on the security risk they presented and to determine what treatment programs might benefit them the most.

Although the classification process provided more standardization in prisoner placement, the procedures remained primarily subjective in nature. Decisions about which prisoners needed what services were made in the "professional opinion" of treatment personnel, whereas decisions about offender custody level were based on the "experiences" of the security staff. In the mid-1970s, a move toward greater objectivity in classification helped bring the process into the modern era.

Increasing Objectivity in Classification

As the concept of rehabilitation was increasingly criticized and as the focus shifted to public safety and victims' rights, classification was also modified to better fit the changing penal philosophies. Classification procedures used in prison and in community corrections were increasingly concerned with the risk that offenders posed to public safety and to other prisoners. Treatment needs were of secondary concern.

In the latter half of the 1970s, court decisions directed prison officials to make significant changes in the classification process. Federal courts ruled that classification, although not constitutionally required (*French* v. *Heyne,* 547 F.2d 994, 1976), must be rational  and reasonable rather than arbitrary and capricious (*Laaman* v. *Heigemore,* 437 F.Supp. 269, 1977; *Pugh* v. *Locke,* 406 F.Supp. 318, 1976).

In the 1980s, the courts continued to agree that there was no constitutional requirement for a classification system, but they

LEARNING OUTCOMES 4 — Explain how prisoners are classified and assigned in prisons.

Think About It...

Classification committees have operated in federal and state prisons since the mid-twentieth century. Composed of professionals representing a variety of areas, the committee members review reports on newly arrived inmates and decide such things as the inmate's work area, treatment programming, and security level. What disciplines do you think should be represented on a classification committee? What would people with undergraduate majors in sociology, criminal justice, psychology, rehabilitation, education, religion, or other areas be able to add to the discussion about the most appropriate custody level and treatment program for an inmate?

also recognized that there may be times when classification is necessary to ensure inmates' constitutional rights to a safe and secure living environment (*Grubbs* v. *Bradley*, 552 F.Supp. 1052, 1982). The rational and reasonable requirement did not provide specific criteria that prison officials could use to meet those conditions, but the implication was that procedures should be more objective than subjective—and that is exactly the direction in which the states moved.

Table 7–2 summarizes the distinguishing features of **objective classification systems**, which are ones that have a factual, impartial, and observable base rather than the intuitive footing of subjective systems. The goals of classification remain the same—determining risk and needs. The classification procedures are often described as falling into two stages: external prison classification and internal prison classification. **External classification** determines a prisoner's custody level, which in turn determines the prison where the inmate begins serving the sentence. **Internal classification** establishes the prisoner's housing, program, and work assignments. Both of these classification systems deserve some elaboration.

External Prison Classification

As Figure 7–5 shows, upon receiving a prison sentence, felony offenders are transferred to a facility where they are officially turned over to the state's DOC. This facility, which is typically called a reception and diagnostic unit or reception and orientation unit, will house the newly sentenced prisoners for several weeks as they undergo a variety of tests and interviews. The tests may include those measuring intelligence quotient (IQ), reading comprehension, and the grade level at which the inmate is operating. Complete medical and dental exams will be conducted along with a determination of any medicine that must be continued or should be started. Interviews with psychologists, clergy, vocational rehabilitation professionals, and others are also likely.

Of particular importance at this stage is determining the risk posed by the inmate. Austin (2003) points out that the risk being assessed here (**prison risk assessment**) is different from that which may have been assessed earlier (**public risk assessment**). For example, when probation officials were making a sentence recommendation the concern was with the level of risk the offender posed to the public. That is, was this person likely to continue engaging in criminal behavior if allowed to remain in the community? Prison risk assessment, however, is less interested in the risk posed to the public (given the offender's removal from the public) and more interested in identifying those prisoners who pose a risk to escape or may cause management problems. As a result, the purpose of prison risk assessment is to determine the custody level to which a prisoner should be initially assigned. That assignment allows officials to

TABLE 7–2   DISTINGUISHING FEATURES OF AN OBJECTIVE CLASSIFICATION SYSTEM

Reliability and validity	The use of criteria that have been proven through research to use both reliable and valid factors to assess a prisoner's custody level
Professionalism	A centralized classification unit that is adequately staffed with well-trained professional personnel who have control over all interagency transfers
Continuity	A centralized classification unit that is responsible for monitoring the classification unit and preparing all policies and procedures that pertain to classification
Transparency	A fully automated classification system such that each classification decision, and the factors used to make each decision, is recorded and available for analysis
Reclassification	An initial and reclassification process where all prisoners are reviewed at least annually to update and possibly modify the prisoners' current classification level
Discretion	The use of overrides to allow staff to depart from the scored classification level for reasons approved by the agency

Source: From Findings in Prison Classification and Risk Assessment. Published by National Institute of Corrections.

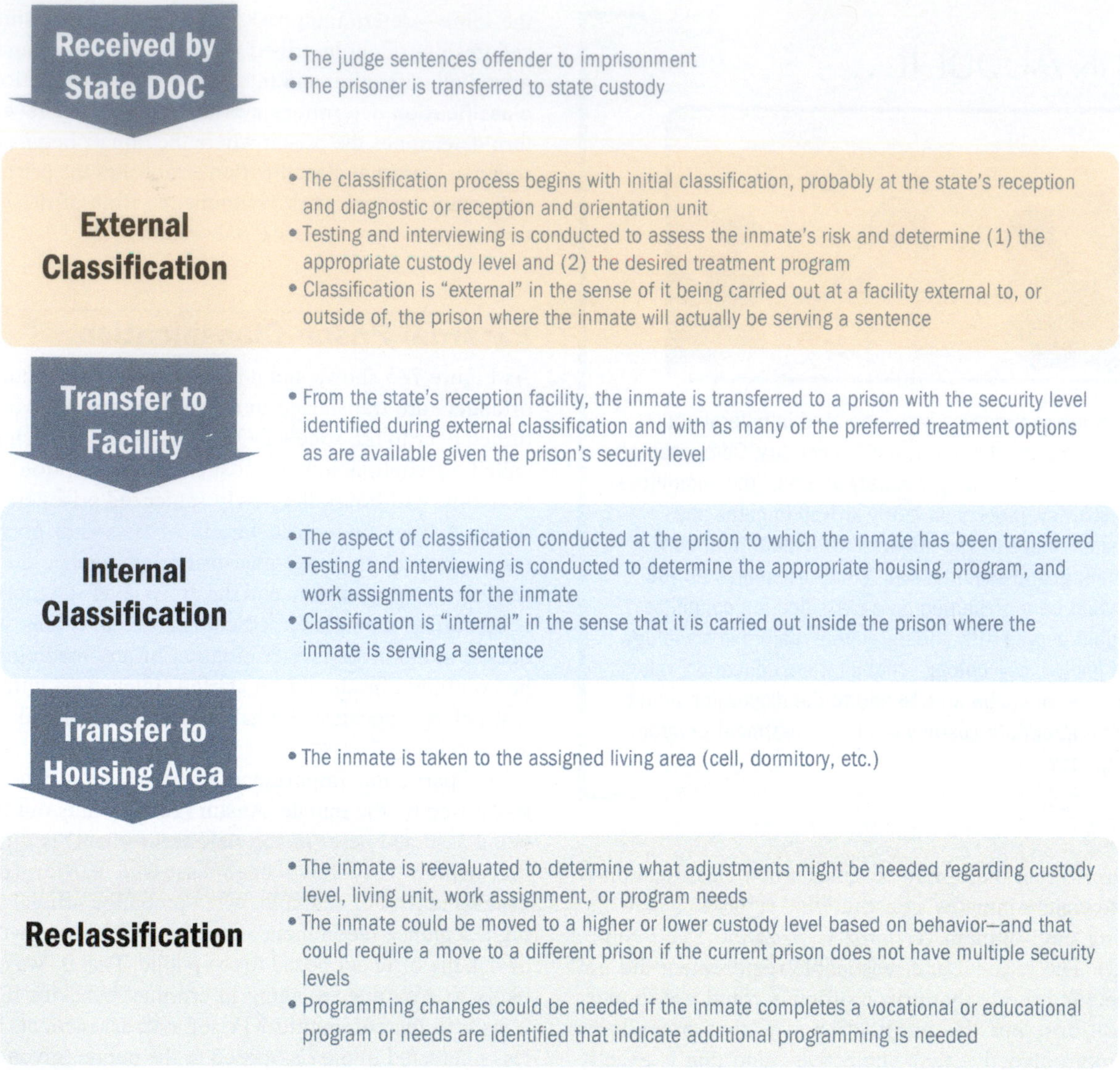

Received by State DOC
- The judge sentences offender to imprisonment
- The prisoner is transferred to state custody

External Classification
- The classification process begins with initial classification, probably at the state's reception and diagnostic or reception and orientation unit
- Testing and interviewing is conducted to assess the inmate's risk and determine (1) the appropriate custody level and (2) the desired treatment program
- Classification is "external" in the sense of it being carried out at a facility external to, or outside of, the prison where the inmate will actually be serving a sentence

Transfer to Facility
- From the state's reception facility, the inmate is transferred to a prison with the security level identified during external classification and with as many of the preferred treatment options as are available given the prison's security level

Internal Classification
- The aspect of classification conducted at the prison to which the inmate has been transferred
- Testing and interviewing is conducted to determine the appropriate housing, program, and work assignments for the inmate
- Classification is "internal" in the sense that it is carried out inside the prison where the inmate is serving a sentence

Transfer to Housing Area
- The inmate is taken to the assigned living area (cell, dormitory, etc.)

Reclassification
- The inmate is reevaluated to determine what adjustments might be needed regarding custody level, living unit, work assignment, or program needs
- The inmate could be moved to a higher or lower custody level based on behavior—and that could require a move to a different prison if the current prison does not have multiple security levels
- Programming changes could be needed if the inmate completes a vocational or educational program or needs are identified that indicate additional programming is needed

FIGURE 7–5 The Classification Process from Intake to Reclassification.

match the inmate's custody level with a prison's security level—for example, a minimum-custody prisoner goes to a minimum-security prison whereas a close-custody prisoner will go to a high-security prison.

Many of the assessment instruments used to determine prison risk during the external classification process are the same as those used to determine public risk. The Level of Services Inventory-Revised (LSI-R), mentioned in Chapters 1 and 5, is a good example, but Austin (2003) notes that several factors important for public risk assessment are irrelevant for prison risk assessment (e.g., current employment status and current marital status) or have no predictive value regarding prison conduct (e.g., age at first arrest and associations with criminal peer groups). As such, work is needed on developing assessment instruments for prison risk specifically.

In some states, the external classification process is the same for both men and women despite studies showing that the systems are invalid for women. A common result is that prison staff members make extensive use of overrides wherein a staff member's subjective opinion is relied upon rather than an objective instrument to determine a woman prisoner's custody level.

Validation studies often find statistically significant differences in the predictive power of risk factors for men and women offenders. For example, criminal history factors are poor predictors of prison adjustment for women offenders and education factors appear to be an indicator of stability among men but not women offenders. Classification systems that ignore such gender differences will not provide accurate custody predictions for women prisoners (Hardyman & Van Voorhis, 2004; Van Voorhis, Wright, Salisbury, & Bauman 2010). In addition, current assessment scales do not include risk and need factors that may be especially relevant to women offenders. These may include needs related to abuse, relationships, parenting, self-esteem, and victimization. Omitting such factors may result in the absence of essential programs for women—although see Figure 7–6 for more on this topic.

The Level of Services Inventory-Revised (LSI-R) is a highly regarded classification tool that is used in both community corrections and institutional settings to identify such things as the supervision or custody level that is most appropriate for an offender. However, the LSI-R, as with most such instruments, was developed based on data from males and may not be valid when applied to females. That is because some criminologists believe that men and women get involved in crime differently (i.e., the pathways to crime are "gendered") and that men and women are exposed to different risk factors (e.g., factors such as victimization, abuse, and low self-esteem may have greater impact on women). When classification tools that ignore or avoid these points are used to determine needed supervision levels and service types, the result may not be accurate for women offenders.

Vose, Lowenkamp, Smith, and Cullen (2009) tested the LSI-R's applicability to women offenders in terms of the LSI-R's ability to accurately predict recidivism (higher LSI-R scores are considered to predict persons most likely to recidivate). Their results indicate that the LSI-R is a valid instrument for predicting recidivism with both male and female offenders and should be considered a useful resource in corrections.

FIGURE 7–6 **Evidence-Based Practice—Does It Work?** Classifying Women with the LSI-R

Internal Prison Classification

Once custody level has been determined and the prisoner has been transferred to a prison with the appropriate security level, another type of classification becomes important. This internal classification system governs facility-specific decisions such as where and with whom the prisoner will be housed, the types of programs and services to be made available to the prisoner, and the prisoner's work assignment.

As with the assessment instruments used for external classification purposes, those that provide objectivity for internal classification remain rather closely tied to instruments designed more for community corrections than for institutional placement. Exceptions include the Adult Internal Management System (AIMS), which identifies inmates who are likely to be incompatible in terms of housing and those most likely to pose risk to the safety and security of the facility.

Identifying the prisoner's program needs can also rely on evaluation instruments used for community corrections, but an obvious weakness of doing so is that many programs available in the community are not available in the confines of a prison. The Case Needs Identification and Analysis (CNIA) instrument is designed to assess inmate needs at admission, and the Prison Inmate Inventory (PII) measures such items as truthfulness, self-esteem, and stress-coping abilities in order to identify inmate needs. These and other reliable and valid classification instruments are careful to address dynamic rather than static factors because the dynamic factors are those to which treatment programs are most effectively directed. This focus on dynamic factors is best understood in the context of criminogenic needs.

Criminogenic Needs

Research has identified a variety of factors that predict recidivism—the likelihood that an offender will repeat his or her criminal behavior. Among those predictors are the person's gender, age at first arrest, number of prior arrests, and alcohol/substance abuse history. An interesting thing about those factors is that they are all constant or happened in the past and cannot be changed. They are, in other words, **static factors**. Developing treatment programs that try to affect these unchangeable factors are, of course, useless. But, there are also other predictors of recidivism, such as antisocial attitudes, values and beliefs, poor self-control, criminal peers, and criminal thinking patterns. These are **dynamic factors** because they can be changed.

Both static and dynamic factors can be **criminogenic** in the sense that they cause or tend to cause criminal behavior. The interviews, tests, and evaluation instruments used during the internal classification process help identify these criminogenic factors or needs. When considered in conjunction with the risk an inmate poses to reoffend and to the safety and security of the facility, the base is established for what is called the Risk-Need-Responsivity (RNR) model. Prisoners are assigned to treatment programs that match the program to the offender's risk of reoffending and that are designed to address their particular set of dynamic criminogenic needs. Linking the risk and need principles to the treatment intervention results in the **responsivity** principle.

Andrews and Dowden (2007, p. 446–448) provide several examples of how the RNR model might be used. Research has shown that key risk/need factors associated with criminal behavior include an antisocial personality pattern and antisocial cognition. Applying the RNR model to the antisocial personality pattern would mean that offenders characterized as being adventurous and pleasure seeking, with weak self-control, and being restlessly aggressive, will need a treatment program that builds problem-solving, self-management, anger management, and coping skills. Similarly, the antisocial cognition factor is characterized by attitudes, values, beliefs, and rationalizations that support criminal behavior. Offenders showing antisocial cognition, therefore, should have a treatment program that allows them to recognize risky thinking and feeling, then builds up alternative, less risky options.

Two other risk/need factors that have been well documented in the research are a history of antisocial behavior and having antisocial associates. Treatment programs designed to address those factors might include interventions that provide early-stage offenders with low-risk non-criminal alternatives and that reduce association with criminal others while enhancing association with persons who are not supportive of criminal activity (Andrews & Dowden, 2007).

Reclassification

Because criminogenic needs are dynamic, the classification process must include procedures to keep pace with the changing risks and needs of prisoners. The **reclassification** procedures provide an opportunity to reevaluate the inmate's prison risk assessment (possibly, good behavior may allow a custody level change from medium to minimum) and current needs assessment (perhaps the inmate completed his or her General Education Development [GED] and can now enter a vocational training program).

Austin (2003) suggests that no later than 12 months after prison admission, a reclassification form should be used to score the prisoner on factors such as the type and number of misconduct reports lodged against the prisoner, the prisoner's participation in treatment programs, and the prisoner's work performance. In this way, the inmate's risk status (custody level) and programming needs are kept current and relevant.

▶ Prison Staff

Figure 7–7 shows that a prison operates only through the efforts of people in a wide variety of occupations. Even in smaller facilities, the warden manages employees with responsibilities in areas ranging from laundry and food services to facility maintenance and recreation. As facility size increases, there may be positions related to prison industries and the need for medical services. We cannot give the deserved attention to all these staff members, so instead we concentrate on those linked to the two more well-known aspects of prison work: employees responsible for security and employees responsible for treatment.

Correctional Officers

Correctional officers (COs) maintain order within the institution and enforce rules and regulations. In this way, they are responsible for public safety (ensuring that criminals confined to an institution stay there) and institutional security (guaranteeing that prisoners and staff members are safe while in the institution). Although they have no law enforcement responsibilities outside the institution where they work, COs maintain security and

LEARNING OUTCOMES 5 — Describe the various jobs and functions of prison staff.

Correctional officers are responsible for institutional security by ensuring a safe environment for both prisoners and staff.

inmate accountability in prisons to prevent disturbances, assaults, and escapes.

This occupational group, which accounts for more than 60% of prison staff at both state and federal levels, is mostly white non-Hispanic males (Camp, 2003; Stephan, 2008). Exceptions (American Correctional Association, 2007; Stephan, 2008) include Mississippi, where more than 60% are female, and a few states where the majority of COs are minority-group members. For example, in Hawaii more than 80% are "Other" (presumably, Asian-Pacific Islanders), and in Alabama, Arkansas, Georgia, Louisiana, Mississippi, and South Carolina, the majority of COs are African-American.

Although females are more frequently found among today's correctional officer ranks, access to that occupation was hard fought. The earliest prisoners, both male and female, were guarded by men. The first female prison guards were hired in 1832 to work in the women's wing of Auburn prison. In the late nineteenth and early twentieth centuries, as states built facilities specifically for women offenders, some legislatures required the institutions to be administered and staffed entirely by women. Later much of that legislation was repealed (because of a shortage of qualified women managers and a lack of faith by male legislators in the administrative abilities of women), thus allowing males to assume administrative positions in facilities for women (Zupan, 1992). The situation improved in the 1970s when women began more forcefully asserting their rights to job and advancement opportunities. In 1972, Congress added the Title VII amendment to the 1964 Civil Rights Act and in doing so prohibited sex-based employment discrimination by public employers at state, county, and local levels. As a result of Title VII, the courts have generally upheld a woman's right to employment. For example, in *Grummet* v. *Rushen* (587 F. Supp. 913, 1984) a woman's right to employment in all-male institutions was recognized as taking precedence over inmates' rights to privacy.

Female COs have experienced resistance to their presence in male prisons—from male inmates, but especially from male officers. Reasons offered for the hesitancy some

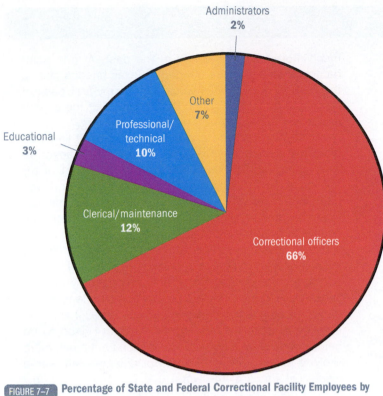

Administrators
2%

Other
7%

Professional/
technical
10%

Educational
3%

Clerical/maintenance
12%

Correctional officers
66%

FIGURE 7–7 **Percentage of State and Federal Correctional Facility Employees by Occupational Category.**
Reference: Stephan, J. J. (2008). Census of state and federal correctional facilities, 2005 (NCJ 222182). Washington, DC: U.S. Department of Justice, Bureau of Justice Statistics.

male COs have about female COs include an argument that the use and threatened use of physical force over inmates is needed to maintain control over the inmates. Female COs, the argument continues, do not possess the necessary physical attributes or attitudes to accomplish that task. The argument has been weakened as more female COs perform their duties without compromising their own or their fellow officers' safety. In fact, female COs are assaulted less often than are male officers, and there is no evidence that male COs are assaulted more frequently when there are more women working in the prison (Lawrence & Mahan, 1998). That may be a result of what research suggests is a calming effect that female officers have on male prisoners and a belief that the presence of female COs tends to reduce tension and hostility in the institution.

As is true for most occupations, this is not a job for everyone. As this chapter's Voices in Corrections points out, working in prison as a correctional officer changes a person just as serving time in prison changes an inmate. Seiter (2002) notes that many people receiving a two- or four-year college degree do not seriously consider CO positions because those positions are viewed as unskilled and poorly paid. The unskilled perception is unfortunate and inaccurate because today's CO must be intelligent, are well trained, and have extensive interpersonal skills. Unfortunately, the poorly paid part seems to be true. Using salary averages from the Bureau of Labor Statistics (2015), in 2014 correctional officers nationally had an average salary of $44,800 compared with $59,600 for the police and sheriff patrol officer category. Salary amounts continue to increase for these occupation

categories, but until the gap between correctional officer and police officer earnings closes, it seems unlikely that college graduates will pursue CO positions with the same enthusiasm they have for police officer positions.

Lack of interest in becoming a CO means the entry-level requirements for the position might be less stringent than is desirable. To encourage a larger pool of applicants, education requirements tend to be high school graduate (or GED or certain work experiences) rather than any college credits or degrees. In those states requiring prehire testing, applicants must pass physical agility, psychological evaluation, reading comprehension, report writing, and drug screening tests. Oral interviews and background checks are also typical (American Correctional Association, 2013).

Treatment Staff

Correctional officers may be expected to actively support treatment goals as they ensure a safe and secure environment; however, persons more directly charged with carrying out treatment duties range from full-time psychiatrists, psychologists, and social workers to other professionals working with prisoners on health, ethical, educational, vocational, and recreational issues. Table 7–3 briefly describes some of the duties related to each of these positions. The programs through which treatment objectives are achieved are also quite varied. A more complete understanding of treatment in a prison environment is found in Chapter 9, but in this chapter we briefly consider the people responsible for implementing the treatment programs. Those people, after all, may play a key role in reducing recidivism. For our purposes, treatment staff members include those persons in positions related to counseling, recreation, religion, and education.

Members of the counseling staff are responsible for providing such programs as cognitive behavioral therapy, anger management, substance abuse therapy, and others. These prison employees will typically have specific training (received as part of a graduate education in such disciplines as psychology or social work, or as part of a prison's in-service training program for employees interested in broadening their education and expertise) that enables them to provide particular treatment modalities.

Some prison counselors work specifically with prisoners having mental health problems—an increasingly important and time-consuming inmate category. Adams and Ferrandino (2008) note that the problem of mentally ill prisoners is serious and substantial and by all indications is likely to worsen. The first steps in working with these inmates are to identify which ones may need mental health services and to link them with the appropriate staff. A national survey (American Correctional Association, 2008) found that all prison systems do **mental health screening** (80% do this at intake and the remainder within 24 hours to 14 days of intake), but the bigger problem is having sufficient numbers of staff qualified to work with the

Research and media portrayals of prisons often concentrate on how prison changes prisoners—more often for the worse rather than the better. Does prison change correctional officers? How and in what manner?

Mr. Alarid is a former correctional officer for the Texas Department of Criminal Justice-Institutional Division. He worked in a maximum-security unit for five years, three of which he was also a member of the Special Operations Response Team. He has since earned his MBA, and buys/sells real estate through his own company.

The changes that take place for officers working in an institutional correctional setting are subtle but over time become very profound. First of all, my friends changed. Within six months of working at the prison, I found that I was closer to some officers than others and eventually began to spend time away from work with my new friends, so much so that we became somewhat of a clique. We would always assist other officers outside our clique and had a "pro-officer mentality." It wasn't long before I found that I spent almost no time with friends that I had before beginning to work in the prison system. Because of the common experience shared with my co-workers, other changes occurred that were reinforced by this relationship.

Among those changes were that I found myself drinking much more in both frequency and quantity. It was common to meet at someone's home or just go out to the woods and drink beer with a few others and talk about all that happened that day or what was going on at work recently. Also, I found myself smoking cigarettes much more than I ever had in the past. At one point before all smoking was banned in Texas prisons, during the 6 AM to 2 PM shift, I would smoke my first pack of cigarettes by 10:00 AM and the second over the course of the rest of the day before bed that evening.

Frustration became a very common part of life. This often manifested itself verbally. I found that I began to swear and use foul language as a regular part of my speech pattern. I also became much louder and was often told by my wife that I didn't need to "talk so loud." I also became very argumentative, and would challenge people on even the most trivial of issues. This increased verbal aggressiveness was, at times, the cause of conflict in some of my personal relationships. This type of interaction was common and acceptable amongst my friends. Those who did not work in a prison found it offensive.

As far as positive changes are concerned, I find that I am more assertive and confident than I used to be before working as a correctional officer. I am much more likely to speak up when I agree or disagree with some issue. Let's face it; the worst that could happen in my current daily life is really nothing when compared with what I dealt with on a daily basis while working in prison. I am also more outgoing and capable of public speaking than I ever would have dreamed before. This is due to the need to yell and announce various things to groups of inmates, a much more hostile audience than I will ever see in the free world. I can recognize and subvert mind games and manipulation techniques. I have a more complete understanding of people from a variety of backgrounds who face different challenges in their lives.

Source: From Corrections: A Contemporary Introduction by Leanne F Alarid and Philip L Reichel. Copyright © 2008 by Pearson Education.

---

mentally ill. The same survey found that most prison systems consider their number of staff dealing with mentally ill offenders to be inadequate.

Recreation is an essential part of prison operations, and a well-run recreation program is an important goal of every prison or jail administrator (Kahler, 1999). That position may seem at odds with media reports and legislator comments that purport to reflect public dissatisfaction with inmates being allowed to lift weights, attend movies, participate in sporting events, and make ceramic pottery. "Where is the punishment in such coddling?" voters seem to ask. But corrections professionals have a more supportive view of recreation programs and are more appreciative of the staff providing those programs. As Kahler (1999) notes, it might be appropriate to question prison recreation programs if they were solely for the benefit of inmates. However, most correctional managers support these programs and consider them to be important management and rehabilitation tools that benefit the inmates as well as the staff and even the public.

Members of the clergy were probably the first non-guard occupation group to work regularly in prisons. Dammer (1996) explains that most state and federal correctional institutions provide support for the four traditional religious denominations—Catholic, Protestant, Muslim, and Jewish. Regional variation and inmate interest also result in representation in some prisons by faiths, such as Buddhist, Rastafarianism, Jehovah Witness, Native American Church, Moorish Temple, and Black Hebrew Israelite Nation. The chaplains, volunteers, and spiritual advisers representing the various faiths may be assigned to the prison facility itself (especially for the major denominations) or might be regular visitors from the outside (for those denominations with fewer adherents in the prison).

Inmates have a variety of reasons for involvement in religious activities while in prison (Dammer, 1996). In some cases, the inmates believe that religion provides direction and meaning for their lives and is a source of hope that their future holds more promise than their past. Inmates also report that religion improves their self-concept because the core of many

TABLE 7–3 | **PRIMARY TREATMENT STAFF POSITIONS**

Case managers	Case managers, also called caseworkers, are charged with guiding inmates through all aspects of their prison sentence and may serve as a liaison between inmates and the outside community. More specific duties may include inmate classification (if that is the only or primary duty, the position may be called *classification officer*), social service support (e.g., facilitating contact with family and appropriate others in the outside community), institution program planning (e.g., assisting with work assignments, educational/vocational classes, and group counseling sessions), and release preparation (e.g., helping inmates with postrelease living and employment arrangements).
Correctional educators	All correctional educators must be certified to provide instruction in either academic or vocational areas. These educators provide instruction in such areas as literacy, secondary education, GED preparation, vocational training, and special education.
Counseling staff	Members of the counseling staff include those working with prisoners having mental health problems or simply needing assistance working through problems, such as poor life skills, alcohol and drug dependence, or employment-related issues. The mental health counseling is provided by employees who may be psychiatrists, licensed professional counselors, clinical social workers, psychologists, and others. More general counseling and/or assistance could be provided by college graduates with degrees in criminal justice, sociology, and other social sciences.
Recreation staff	Members of the recreation staff provide recreation programs that teach and develop the social skills necessary for participation in free society. They organize outdoor group intramural activities (e.g., flag football and baseball), indoor group activities (e.g., card games and board games), individual activities (e.g., playing musical instruments, making crafts and performing in talent shows), and club activities (e.g., Jaycees and stamp club). As a result of these efforts, inmates learn the value of teamwork, fair play, and anger management, and have a constructive way to use idle time and relieve the stress and tension of incarceration (Kahler, 1999).
Religious staff	Religious staff members provide religious services, counsel troubled inmates, and advise inmates of "bad news" from home or from prison authorities. More recently, their role has expanded to include organizing volunteers, facilitating religious furlough visits, contracting for outside religious services, and training prison staff about the basic tenets and rituals of the different faith groups, especially the nontraditional ones about which some staff members may have limited or no knowledge (Dammer, 1996; Schwartz & Fewell, 1999).

Think About It...

SHERRY LAVARS/MCT/ Newscom

Should religious instruction and practices be allowed in prison? Some people argue that if the offenders were all that religious to begin with, they wouldn't be in prison. And, if you allow some religions, won't you have to allow all of them—including Satanism, Wicca, and others outside the mainstream?

religious beliefs is acceptance and love from a higher being and from members of the faith group. Still others (sex offenders, for example) affiliate with faith groups as a way to gain protection. For some, religious involvement is a way to access things that would otherwise be too difficult or costly to obtain (such as free food and coffee, holiday items, and even musical instruments).

People in prisons are among the most educationally disadvantaged groups in the nation, and the important task of providing academic and vocational education typically falls to correctional educators. Their efforts are not in vain, as the research shows that correctional education reduces recidivism and enhances postrelease employment (Gaes, 2008). Academic education programs in prisons may be accredited through affiliation with local school districts, community colleges or universities, or a private educational agency. In some instances, the correctional system is large enough to be legislated as a distinct school district.

▶ Private Prisons

The last topic for this chapter is actually a variation on the management theme. Prison management in the twentieth century was primarily carried out by public employees in public facilities. In the twenty-first century, it appears that prison management increasingly may be the responsibility of corporate employees in private facilities.

LEARNING OUTCOMES 6 — Summarize the privatization of prisons.

In other books, you might have read about the volunteer and private law enforcement techniques that preceded modern policing and the early reliance on victims or privately run prosecution societies to prosecute offenders. You may also have read about the historical and continued role of private bondsmen and the early use of the jail as a way for keepers to earn fees for providing services, such as bedding and food. In this book, we reviewed examples of the important role that private groups, such as the Quakers in Pennsylvania, played in developing the new sanction of long-term imprisonment and the significance of private businesses' role in influencing a preference in the United States for the Auburn-style prison philosophy. Specific aspects of penal philosophies have been linked to prison labor, which in turn has ebbed and flowed as support from private businesses fluctuates. In the area of intermediate sanctions, the direct tie to private individuals (e.g., John Augustus in Boston) makes clear the widespread impact of private individuals, associations, and businesses in the area of corrections. This reminds us that privatization in corrections is much more an old concept than a new one, but is certainly one of growing importance.

Privatization in the United States Today

A **private prison** is a correctional facility operated by a nongovernmental organization that is under contract with federal or state authorities to provide security, housing, and programs to adult offenders. The organization is often a for-profit company using state-owned institutions or facilities built by the company to house prisoners and using its own employees to provide the needed management, security, and programming. As Figure 7–8 describes, the use of private prisons has both proponents

Private prisons have greater flexibility and can respond quickly to problems and opportunities because they are not encumbered by government "red tape"

The use of private prisons reduces the pressure and costs of overcrowding in the public sector

As a private enterprise, private prisons can be more creative and innovative

Private prisons are motivated to provide good quality at a reasonable cost in order to secure repeat contracts

Punishing criminal offenders is a core function of government and should be administered only by government agencies

Contracting with private business is more expensive because it adds a profit margin to all other costs

Sentencing- and prison-related legislation may be influenced by private companies wishing to improve their profit margin

Contracting diffuses responsibility allowing government and private entities to blame each other

FIGURE 7–8 **Debating Private Prisons.**

DISCUSS **Which arguments in Figure 7-8 (name one or two) do you find most compelling? Why?**

and detractors. The largest private prison company is Corrections Corporation of America (CCA), which manages more than 75,000 inmates and detainees in more than 60 facilities across the country (Mason, 2012).

About 131,000 state and federal prisoners are held in privately operated corrections facilities—7% of all state prisoners and 19% of federal prisoners (Carson, 2015). Of the many issues to discuss in relation to privatization, we look at where privatization is especially popular, the characteristics of persons held in private facilities, and the issue of cost savings.

Privatization has certainly increased over the last several decades, but much of the growth has been in particular geographic areas (see Figure 7–9). About 20 states have no prisoners in private facilities; however, 7 states have at least 20% of their prison population housed in private facilities. At the end of 2014 (Carson, 2015), approximately 60% of state inmates held in private facilities were held in six states—Texas (14,400), Florida (12,400), Georgia (8,000), Oklahoma (7,400), Arizona (7,000), and Ohio (5,400).

This geographical distribution of the private prison population (the majority of the nation's privately held state prisoners are in southern and western states) is consistent with the historical evolution of private prisons, which was in the South and West. The lack of private prisons in the Midwest and Northeast is, according to Austin and Coventry (2003), directly related to the strength of labor unions in those regions and their successful resistance to any significant attempts to privatize.

The characteristics of persons held in private prisons are generally consistent with those in public prisons. Blakely and Bumphus (2004) found that both private and public facilities house a large percentage of African-American offenders (43% for private and 47% for public). However, more females were in private-sector facilities (10%) than in the public sector (6%), the average length of sentence for all offenders was less in private facilities (11 months versus 28 months in public facilities), and the custody level was generally lower in private facilities—90% of the private sector's inmates were at the medium- or minimum-security levels compared with 69% at the same levels in the public sector. This point of private facilities tending to have more females and having prisoners with lower average sentences and custody levels has led to charges that comparing the cost-effectiveness of private facilities with public facilities is unfair (Oppel, 2011). "Give us prisoners with the same characteristics and we'll look more cost effective too," say the public facilities.

The cost-effectiveness argument is especially relevant because cost savings to taxpayers is a primary claim made by supporters of privatization. Presumably, private firms can finance and construct prisons more quickly than can the government; are more likely to design efficient operations; and are freed from the cumbersome bureaucracy, restrictive personnel policies, and union contracts that add expenses for government agencies (Austin & Coventry, 2003; Logan, 1990). There are, however, a variety of methodological problems that make it very difficult to compare cost savings. For example, because private prisons have not been used to any significant

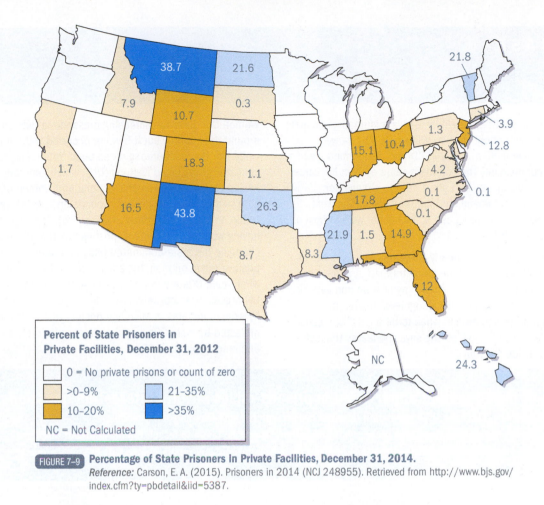

Percent of State Prisoners in Private Facilities, December 31, 2012

- ☐ 0 = No private prisons or count of zero
- ☐ >0–9%
- ☐ 10–20%
- ☐ 21–35%
- ☐ >35%

NC = Not Calculated

FIGURE 7–9 **Percentage of State Prisoners in Private Facilities, December 31, 2014.**
Reference: Carson, E. A. (2015). Prisoners in 2014 (NCJ 248955). Retrieved from http://www.bjs.gov/index.cfm?ty=pbdetail&iid=5387.

extent in those states with the more expensive prison systems (i.e., the Midwest and Northeast), it has been difficult to clearly determine if there can actually be cost savings with privatization (Austin & Coventry, 2003). Similarly, deciding how—or even if—to count indirect costs (e.g., contract writing and financial liability) and some direct costs (e.g., medical care, construction, and renovation) makes study comparison problematic.

After reviewing more current studies on cost savings from privatization, Austin and Coventry (2003) found little, if any, evidence that private prisons are cheaper to operate. Even studies that found cost-effectiveness have shown only minimal savings (5 to 15%), so it is difficult for there to be any significant impact on a state prison budget when private prisons continue to reflect such a small proportion of the overall prison population. A meta-analysis by Lundahl and his colleagues (Lundahl, Kunz, Brownell, Harris, & Van Vleet, 2007) led to a similar conclusion (i.e., cost savings from privatizing prisons are not certain and appear minimal), and, most recently, an Arizona report found that it can often be more expensive to house inmates in private than in state prisons (Newton, Rough, & Hensley, 2010).

Mixed-Gender Supervision in Prison

Correctional Officer Barbara Williams tells a journalist of a male inmate's comment about the way Williams's hips swayed beneath her blue uniform. He said, "Damn! You remind me of a pantyhose commercial." The comment came early in her career and Williams quickly saw that she'd have to change her demeanor, be more forceful, and harden herself. She went home that evening and practiced stiffening her walk in front of a mirror (Hauser, 2008).

Since that event, Williams's nearly 20 years of experiences as a correctional officer (CO) include being trapped in a mess hall with rioting inmates and being thrown against an iron gate by a man twice her size. She tells her daughters, "In life, you have to know when to be a woman and when to be a lady." She doesn't believe ladies belong in jail, so she says she leaves that softer part of her outside the walls.

Women COs have an increasing presence in jails and prisons around the country, but it has not occurred without controversy. Not the least among those organizations expressing concern is the United Nations (UN), which generally opposes having male COs in women's prisons and women COs in men's—that is, mixed-gender supervision (United Nations Office on Drugs and Crime, 2008, p. 36). Although noting that having women COs in men's prisons has the advantages of changing the male-dominated prison culture and having a positive effect on men, the same does not seem to be true when male COs are in women's prisons. In those cases, the UN argues, risks outweigh any advantages. Lawsuits in 2009 by women inmates in Michigan prisons who were raped and molested by male COs would certainly support the UN's argument (Seidel, 2009).

The use of mixed-gender supervision in prisons raises several interesting questions:

1. Do you support or reject the UN's opposition to mixed-gender supervision? Explain your reasoning.
2. If mixed-gender supervision does take place, what precautions should be taken to lessen the likelihood of problems?
3. Are different precautions needed for situations of men COs in women's prisons versus women COs in men's prisons?

LEARNING OUTCOMES 1

Outline the development and organization of the federal prison system.

Although the federal government operated prisons beginning in the 1890s, it was not until the Bureau of Prisons (BOP) was created in 1930 that a true federal prison system began. Since that time, the BOP has grown to an organization with more than 100 institutions responsible for more than 200,000 prisoners. The BOP's central office is in Washington, D.C., but for management purposes the country is divided into six geographic regions, each with a regional director for all facilities in that region. Federal facilities are identified by their security level: minimum, low, medium, high, or administrative.

1. What are the top three offenses for which persons are in a federal prison?

2. After the United States, of which country are federal prisoners most likely to be citizens?

3. Describe characteristics of prisons at each of the five federal prison security levels.

4. What role is the BOP playing in the fight against terrorism?

LEARNING OUTCOMES 2

Outline the development and organization of the state prison systems.

State prisons are operated by a state agency (usually called the department of corrections) that manages all prisons in the state and may also be responsible for community corrections and parole services. There are about 1,700 state correctional facilities across the country, but the number in each state varies considerably from as few as 6 or 7 in some states to more than 100 in others. As in the federal prison system, state prisons identify their facilities by security level. The level names and the number of levels vary by state, so it is easiest to simply refer to state security levels as being minimum, medium, and maximum. There are, however, some state prisons identified as "supermax" because they house the most dangerous or troublesome prisoners at the tightest security levels available in the state.

1. Of the 1,700 state correctional facilities across the country, about how many of them are community-based facilities?

2. Distinguish operational capacity, design capacity, and rated capacity. What do you suppose are some reasons for having three types of prison capacity?

3. Describe characteristics of prisons at the minimum, medium, and maximum levels.

4. What is meant by saying that the growth of supermax facilities indicates a trend away from a dispersion approach and toward a concentration approach for handling troublesome inmates?

department of corrections The state agency responsible for managing and operating the state's adult prison system.

operational capacity A measure of prison facility capacity based on the ability of the staff, programs, and services to accommodate a certain size population.

design capacity The number of inmates that facility planners or architects intended for the facility.

rated capacity The maximum number of beds or inmates allocated by a rating official to institutions in the states.

minimum-security facility Institutions where inmates have considerable personal freedom and more relaxed supervision.

medium-security facility Institutions where inmates receive more supervision than at minimum-security prisons, but still have considerable freedom to move around to work assignments and programming activities.

maximum-security facility Designed for the fullest possible supervision, control, and surveillance of general-population inmates. Also known as *close-security prisons*.

supermax prison Prisons at the highest security level, with prisoners isolated from the general population and from each other. Also known as *control units* or *secured housing units*.

dispersion approach Prison administrators spread troublemakers to prisons throughout the system or in various units of the prison.

concentration approach Prisoners are grouped together in special prisons or special units within a prison, and their activities and movements are severely restricted and highly monitored.

Distinguish between administrative and disciplinary segregation and describe solitary confinement.

When inmates are segregated from the general prison population, they are placed in housing units with high levels of restriction and control—often involving solitary confinement. When the segregation is done for administrative purposes, it is to ensure the safety, security, and orderly operation of the facility. Persons might be placed in administrative segregation because they are awaiting classification, transfer to another facility, or while a reported prison rule violation is being investigated. They could also be segregated in order to provide for their special needs (e.g., medical or mental health). When the segregation is done for disciplinary purposes, the inmate is being punished for rule violations that occurred in the prison setting. In both instances, the segregation may include solitary confinement—isolation from other prisoners. Solitary confinement is increasingly controversial since it has been shown to have negative effects on prisoners' physical and psychological health, is very expensive, and may not achieve the intended results of deterring or reducing prison misconduct. As a result, solitary confinement policies are being adjusted at the federal level and in many of the state prison systems.

1. Describe the difference between administrative and disciplinary segregation?

2. Do you think administrative segregation is really nonpunitive?

3. Given the characteristics of persons likely to experience segregation of either type, or solitary confinement, do you believe segregation and isolation are used in a fair manner?

4. Discuss the phrase "Offenders are sent to prison as punishment, not for punishment" in the context of solitary confinement.

special housing unit An area of the prison, or a separate prison, where inmates are held under high levels of restriction and control.

administrative segregation A management tool wherein prisoners are placed in a special housing unit, often under solitary confinement, for the security and safety of the prison or the inmate.

disciplinary segregation A management tool wherein prisoners are placed in a special housing unit, often under solitary confinement, as punishment for rule violations within the prison setting.

solitary confinement The placement of a prisoner in a separate cell or other location that isolates the prisoner from other inmates.

Explain how prisoners are classified and assigned in prisons.

In order to achieve their security and treatment obligations, prison systems must have a way to identify how much risk an inmate presents and what needs the inmate has that can be addressed in the prison environment. In the past, those decisions were made very subjectively, but today there is increased reliance on objective classification methods that allow for more accurate assessment of both risk and needs.

1. How do objective classification procedures differ from subjective ones?

2. List and explain at least three features of an objective classification system.

3. Distinguish between external and internal prison classification systems.

4. Explain how both static and dynamic factors can be criminogenic, but successful treatment programs need to focus on dynamic factors.

5. What is meant by the term *reclassification*? Do you think reclassification is necessary to do on a regular basis, or could it be done only upon request from the prisoner or treatment staff?

classification The process and procedures by which prison officials determine the risk posed by each offender and the offender's individual treatment needs.

objective classification system Classification procedures that have a factual, impartial, and observable base rather than the intuitive footing of subjective systems.

external classification A stage in the classification process wherein a prisoner's custody level is determined and, based on that custody level, in which the prison inmate begins serving the sentence.

internal classification Establishes the prisoner's housing, program, and work assignments within the prison.

prison risk assessment A determination of the risk an offender poses to escape or to be a management problem for prison officials.

public risk assessment A determination of the risk posed by an offender to the general public.

static factors Individual characteristics that are constant or happened in the past and cannot be changed, such as a person's gender, age at first arrest, or number of prior arrests.

dynamic factors Individual characteristics that can be changed, such as antisocial attitudes, values and beliefs, poor self-control, criminal peers, and criminal thinking patterns.

criminogenic Factors that cause or tend to cause criminal behavior.

responsivity The process in which prisoners are assigned to treatment programs designed to address their particular set of dynamic criminogenic needs.

reclassification A stage in the classification process wherein an inmate's custody level, treatment program, or work assignment is reevaluated to be sure it is still appropriate.

Describe the various jobs and functions of prison staff.

Of the many occupational areas represented by prison staff, two are of particular importance in this chapter. Prison staff members responsible for security are the correctional officers (COs) who maintain order and enforce prison rules and regulations. Nationwide, this group is mostly white, non-Hispanic, and male, but in some states women and minorities represent a large proportion of COs. The second group of prison staff highlighted in this chapter is made up of members of the treatment staff. These people are responsible for such areas as counseling, recreation, religion, and education.

1. About what percentage of prison staff members are correctional officers (COs)?

2. Would you consider a career as a CO? Why or why not?

3. Under what legal precedents are women allowed to work as COs in a men's prison?

4. Do, or should, COs have a treatment role in addition to their security role?

5. Describe the possible benefits of having education, religious, and recreation programs in a prison environment.

correctional officer The person responsible for maintaining order within the institution and enforcing prison rules and regulations.

mental health screening An examination performed on each newly admitted inmate that usually includes a review of the medical screening, behavior observations, an inquiry into any mental health history, and an assessment of suicide potential.

Summarize the privatization of prisons.

Traditionally prison management has been carried out by public employees in public facilities, but that is changing in the twenty-first century. Not all, but most states today have some prison facilities operated by private for-profit companies. The companies make money by contracting with federal, state, or local government to provide the housing, security, and programming for prisoners. About 9% of all prisoners in the country are now held in private facilities. A major argument for privatization is that private prisons are cost-effective, but some research suggests there is little evidence that private prisons are cheaper to operate.

1. Define the term *private prison*.

2. Why have private prisons been more accepted in some regions of the country than others?

3. Give two arguments favoring and two opposing the use of private prisons.

private prison A correctional facility operated by a nongovernmental organization that is under contract with federal or state authorities to provide security, housing, and programs to adult offenders.

Additional Links

Follow the development of the BOP with the timeline at **www.bop.gov/about/history/timeline.jsp**.

Find information about each federal correctional facility at **www.bop.gov/locations/list.jsp**.

Visit Solitary Watch, a web-based project, and read stories by prisoners about their experiences in solitary confinement at **http://solitarywatch.com/category/projects/voices/**.

Read about employment opportunities for correctional officers at **www.bls.gov/ooh/Protective-Service/Correctional-officers.htm**.

The National Institute of Corrections has information on the jail, prison, and community corrections system of each state at **http://nicic.gov/StateStats/**.

Read the Sentencing Project's report about prison privatization in other countries at **http://sentencingproject.org/doc/publications/inc_International%20Growth%20Trends%20in%20Prison%20Privatization.pdf**.

8

Prison Life

1 Discuss the evolution of prison norms and the changes in mainstream prison culture.

2 Explain the benefits and challenges of assigning jobs to incarcerated inmates.

3 Compare and contrast prison gangs and play families in terms of their structure, purpose, and management.

4 Discuss the incidence of sexual assault and violence in prisons.

In 2015, a New York correctional officer named Joyce Mitchell helped inmates David Sweat and Richard Matt escape from the Clinton Correctional Facility by smuggling hacksaw blades inside frozen meat. Mitchell was having a sexual relationship with Matt, who used charm and flattery to convince her to smuggle in tools and then, after a series of months, directed her to pick up both escapees. When Mitchell refused to pick them up for fear that the escapees would kill her and her husband, the two men lived as fugitives in cabins in a wooded area for three weeks before one was captured and the other killed. Mitchell was sentenced to seven years in prison and ordered to pay over $100,000 in restitution (Morgenstein, 2015).

A similar situation occurred in 2016 when a part-time teacher named Nooshafarian Ravaghi, who taught English as a second language, aided in the escape of three men from the Orange County Jail in California. The prison teacher was convinced to bring in maps and tools for one of the inmates with whom she was having relations (Winton & Queally, 2016). The inmates rappeled four stories down the outside of the building, but were eventually caught within eight days.

In that same year, 46 former and current correctional officers from 11 different Georgia prisons were arrested in a two-year FBI undercover sting that involved drug trafficking and contraband smuggling activities for personal profit. Some officers smuggled in tobacco, alcohol, drugs, and cell phones to prisoners, while other officers wore their uniforms to knowingly transport drugs across the state of Georgia. Most officers arrested were line officers in their mid-20s, and five were members of a tactical team. There were 21 women and 25 men indicted (Egan, 2016). Research shows that in most cases, inmates initiate intimate relationships with prison staff who are in unhappy marriages, lonely, and vulnerable (Worley, 2015). Inmates also target officers for inappropriate economic relationships if they perceive that the person is having financial problems.

References: Egan (2016); Morgenstein (2015); Winton & Queally (2016); Worley (2015).

G.N. Miller/New York Post/AP Images

DISCUSS Despite an organizational environment that strongly discourages interpersonal relationships between prisoners and staff, why do some correctional officers cross the boundaries and engage in inappropriate relationships with inmates? How can this problem be reduced?

You learned in the last chapter that prison facilities exist at both the state and federal levels for incarcerating people for terms longer than one year. Each individual inmate is classified to live at a particular security level according to his or her treatment needs and the risks posed. Regardless of where a prisoner does time, the prison experience permanently changes a person. The adjustments many individuals make in order to endure a prison sentence too often result in greater social challenges, anger, and individuals who are released with the same problems (drug abuse, parenting, job skills, etc.) that they had before they were arrested. One explanation for the negative impact prison has on many inmates is the social structure and environment of the prison itself. We will discuss this explanation later in the chapter, but first we examine who is in prison.

► Who Is in Prison?

Individuals in prison originate from all kinds of family backgrounds, nationalities, occupations, and socioeconomic levels. However, prisoners also share some similarities. First, most prisoners must overcome specific challenges to rebalance their lives in some way. They have either become excessively focused on a single behavior—such as drug addiction, money, or power—or they lack a fundamental skill or ability that has affected their lives in a significant way—such as their inability to control their emotions, lack of education, or employment in which they can make a livable wage. Many times, people who

end up in prison are in both groups—they have lived a life of excess and of deficits.

When we consider demographics, most prisoners are young men between the ages of 18 and 35. The average age of prisoners is actually 35, but averages factor in both the younger crowd and those between 35 and 75 years of age. The number of women in the prison population has always been **disproportionately** less than their percentage in the general population. For example, if women prisoners were proportional to the percentage they represent in the general population, we would expect female prisoners

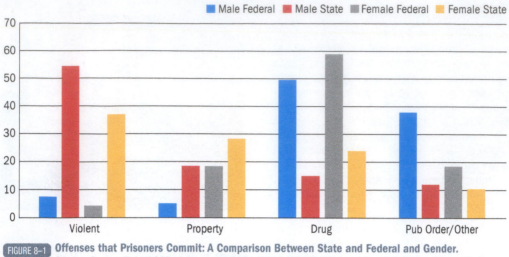

Offenses that Prisoners Commit: A Comparison by State
and Federal and by Gender (%)

Male Federal ■ Male State ■ Female Federal ■ Female State

FIGURE 8–1 **Offenses that Prisoners Commit: A Comparison Between State and Federal and Gender.**
Source: Carson, E. A. (2015). Prisoners in 2014 (NCJ 248955). Retrieved from http://www.bjs.gov/index.cfm?ty=pbdetail&iid=5387.

to comprise about 51% of the prison population. However, women accounted for only 7% of all prisoners nationwide, which makes women *disproportionately underrepresented* in prison. The types of offenses that prisoners commit are depicted as pie charts in Figure 8–1, separated by gender.

Most prisoners tend to come from impoverished backgrounds riddled with childhood abuse, from parents who neglected them, and from underfunded school districts. Related to socioeconomic status is race/ethnicity—a disproportionate number of African-American and Hispanic individuals are in prison. For females, the national average was 21.2% African-American, 50% Caucasian, and 16.8% Hispanic. For men, 36.9% were African-American, 32.3% were Caucasian, and 22% were Hispanic, with the remaining percentage as "Other," which included Asians, Pacific Islanders, American Indians, and persons of two or more races (Carson, 2015). Of

all race/ethnic groups, however, black men had the highest incarceration *rates* compared to their numbers in the general population. According to national statistics (Carson, 2015, p. 15), "Imprisonment rates for black males were 3.8 to 10.5 times greater at each age group than white males and 1.4 to 3.1 times greater than rates for Hispanic males. The largest disparity between white and black male prisoners occurred among inmates ages 18 and 19. . . . Black females were between 1.6 and 4.1 times more likely to be imprisoned than white females of any age group."

Federal Prisoners

Individuals who have committed a serious federal offense are under authority of the **Bureau of Prisons (BOP)**. Examples of federal (and state) offenses are depicted in Figure 8–2. Federal

Offense Type	State Offenses	Federal Offenses
VIOLENT	• Murder/manslaughter • Robbery • Rape/sexual assault • Assault	• Kidnapping • Bank robbery • Explosives
PROPERTY	• Larceny/motor vehicle theft • Burglary • Fraud/forgery	• Extortion • Bribery • Fraud
DRUG	• Possession • Selling	• Trafficking • Organized distribution
PUBLIC ORDER	• Driving while intoxicated • Commercialized vice/indecency	• Immigration-related • Weapons offenses

FIGURE 8–2 **Examples of Common Felony Offenses.**
References: 1. Federal Bureau of Prisons. (2011). Quick facts about the Bureau of Prisons. Retrieved from http://www.bop.gov/news/quick.jsp.
2. Carson, E. A. (2015). Prisoners in 2014 (NCJ 248955). Retrieved from http://www.bjs.gov/index.cfm?ty=pbdetail&iid=5387.

offenses include drug trafficking/distribution, kidnapping, bank robbery, weapons offenses, bribery, fraud, and extortion. Federal prisoners comprise 9% of all prisoners held in the United States. As of 2016, there were about 195,000 federal offenders; 93% were in a prison and 7% in a community-based or other short-term residential facility (Federal Bureau of Prisons, 2016). The BOP inmate population is changing in composition as well as in number. Although drug offenders still account for half of all federal offenses, more than one out of every four federal prisoners was *not* a U.S. citizen. BOP prisoners who were non-U.S. citizens had citizenship in Mexico, Colombia, the Dominican Republic, or Cuba (Federal Bureau of Prisons, 2016). Some non-U.S. citizens were convicted of felony crimes for which they must serve time before being deported. Others were detained longer in an Immigration and Customs Enforcement (ICE) facility, to investigate suspected roles in human trafficking, illegal drug distribution, and identity fraud. Some offenders are detained because of repeat immigration offenses, such as arriving without proper documents or overstaying a visa. Immigration offenses comprised 11% of all federal offenses.

▶ *Learning Prison Norms*

Every society has a set of norms and values that are considered "mainstream," defined by those wielding the most power and influence. Individuals who operate inside mainstream norms are rewarded and those who do not are considered "deviant" and ostracized. For first timers, prison is a new experience that takes some time to adjust to; it is a learning process of mainstream prison culture. Clemmer (1966) used the term **prisonization** to explain the process by which prisoners were socialized into prison life, or the **inmate subculture** with its own norms, values, and beliefs. Although prison society shares many aspects of the dominant culture, prisoners have developed their own informal rules, language, economic systems, and groups that exhibit a strong influence on life in prison (Santos, 2004). The degree to which prisoners adopt prison values as their own largely depends on the length of their sentence and the custody level of the prison to which they are assigned (Dye, Aday, Farney, & Raley, 2014; Terry, 2003). Short-term prisoners serving two years or fewer are typically housed in lower-custody facilities and within that span can resist the pressures of the prison environment and not become a "regular" or a convict. Individuals with longer sentences often find it difficult to remain connected to the world outside for that long, and may succumb to norms of their situation to make their own lives easier. Others become involved in religion and spirituality to help themselves and other inmates with abandonment, depression, and stressful daily experiences. For example, one female prisoner stated,

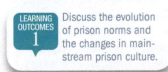

Discuss the evolution of prison norms and the changes in mainstream prison culture.

"Coping with prison life tests your religion. Imagine being forced to interact with others—some of whom are less than desirable company. The peace of my beliefs helps me cope by being able to meditate and separate my thoughts from the chaos that others tend to bring . . ." (Dye et al., 2014, p. 400)

Deprivations of the Big House

During the **Big House** era, when prisons were located in remote areas, routines were highly disciplined and prisoners lacked access to media sources. Prisons were **total institutions** and convicts and building tenders were in charge at the top of the social and political hierarchy. Building tenders controlled the housing units and were rewarded through informal accommodations and staff favoritism. The focus of prison at that time was on the **deprivation model**, which assumed that prison culture developed as a response to procure the things that prisoners did not have anymore. As depicted in Figure 8–3, these deprivations were identified as "pains of imprisonment" by Gresham Sykes (1958) and included disruptions in normal sexual relationships, security needs, autonomy, liberty, and goods and services.

Once the courts mandated the end of the building tender system (where building tenders were replaced with new-generation correctional officers) and facilitated the rise of the rehabilitative ideal, this created a very different culture. Many senior guards retreated to positions where they could continue to avoid contact with prisoners (similar to when the building tenders were in charge), some out of resentment and others out of fear. The prison environment was open for a new group of prisoners—prison gangs—to take over. Unlike the elite convicts and building tenders who had the same goal of controlling the masses, prison gangs were in competition with each other for scarce resources and prisons became less safe. The Big House era and its traditional convict code were replaced by a new code of conduct that provided predatory inmates the opportunity to exploit vulnerable fellow inmates (Winfree, Newbold, & Tubb, 2002). Understanding mainstream prison culture turned toward the **importation model**, in which inmate attitudes and behaviors are an extension of their life before prison and adapted to the prison environment where toughness and exploitation are necessary to survive. For example, individuals who were willing to use violence before they entered prison will continue to respond in violent ways if provoked.

FIGURE 8–3 **Deprivations and "Pains of Imprisonment."**
Reference: Sykes, G. M. (1958). The society of captives. Princeton: Princeton University Press.

Current theoretical models of understanding prison culture incorporate a mix of deprivation and importation theories, along with the influence of administrative and staff control. In other words, prisoner social systems, norms, and behaviors are not only adaptive responses to restrictive conditions and deprivations that prisons are expected to have, but prisoners themselves, long before they came to prison, have experienced trauma, violence, addiction, and engaged in predatory and manipulative behavior at disproportionately higher rates than other lawbreakers. Finally, prison life can also be defined by organizational characteristics such as custody level, institutional policies, budgets and resources, quality and training of staff, and level of professional staff/inmate interactions (Ricciardelli & Sit, 2016). We begin the following section with an explanation of prison life via the inmate code.

Mainstream Prisoner Code for Women
1. Follow institutional rules. Discipline yourself.
2. Stay to yourself. Do your own time.
3. Use religious influences for inner strength (pray, read the Bible, turn to a higher power).
4. Keep busy in programs (school, job, meetings).
5. Don't trust anyone, especially other inmates.
6. Keep your head up. Respect yourself.

FIGURE 8–5   **Mainstream Prisoner Code for Women.**
Reference: Alarid, L. F. (1996). Women offenders' perception of confinement: Behavior code acceptance, hustling, and group relations in jail and prison (Unpublished doctoral dissertation). Huntsville, TX: Sam Houston State University.

Inmate Code

The **inmate code** is an informal, unwritten set of ideal norms that directs an inmate's behavior. But unlike formal prison rules, the inmate code is learned by word of mouth, and if not followed, inmates enforce the norms via bullying, harassment, or violence. The principles of the code, shown in Figure 8–4, have remained fairly constant for male prisoners over the last 60 years (Sykes & Messinger, 1960; Winfree et al., 2002). The inmate code is strikingly similar across many prisons in the world.

Code of Conduct for Women

Women prisoners seem to have a slightly different inmate code than men. As Figure 8–5 illustrates, violence to obtain respect is not glorified, nor is there necessarily a need to join gangs for protection. Women also seem to be more tolerant of mixed-race groupings than are men (Alarid, 1996). Pollock (2002) observed

that women were less likely than men to "do their own time," as the subcultural norms in women's prisons did not prohibit or discourage individuals from getting involved in another woman's problems. Women were more likely than men to "spread rumors and gossip about one another's activities as a form of social control or merely as a social pastime" (Pollock, 2002, p. 131). Interaction with correctional officers is not prohibited for female inmates—it is more casual and social. There is even some indication that female prisoners look to staff, as well as to each other, for support. As a result, staff may be more likely to bend the rules. As one woman explained, a main part of the code is "don't snitch," but, she quickly added, "It is good to tell for certain things, like if someone gets jumped or somebody got stabbed" (Owen, 1998, p. 178).

Prison Argot

Prison argot or "prison-proper" is the language, slang, and physical gestures used to communicate meaning in prison. According to Encinas (2001), argot is influenced by the region of the country or the dominant race/ethnic group incarcerated in that area. For example, prisons in the Southwest that are populated mainly with Latino prisoners use slightly different slang than prisons dominated by African-American prisoners. Argot terms describe the inmate world as one that is hardened, lacks tolerance, and is filled with racist and sexist terminology. K.C. Carceral (2004), now a former prisoner, provides more detail:

Prison-proper perpetuates prejudice and stereotyping based on skin color. For example, African-American prisoners call whites Square Johns, crackers, peckerwoods, white boyees, and honkies. . . . Of course, I see the same prejudicial attitude when white prisoners look at black prisoners. Both groups justify their hatred because of ignorance and intolerance of diversity. . . . There are [also] many terms that are derogatory toward women. It helps create and support an uncaring place

Mainstream Prisoner Code for Men
1. "Don't snitch" on other inmates.
2. Don't make friends with the prison staff. That leads to others labeling you as a snitch.
3. "Do your own time"—Mind your own business. Don't get involved.
4. Maintain yourself and keep your dignity—"Be tough." "Don't whine."
5. Don't allow yourself to get taken advantage of. "Be sharp."
6. If someone tries (or succeeds) in getting over on you, react immediately and with violence. Never ask for protective custody.

FIGURE 8–4   **Mainstream Prisoner Code for Men.**
References: 1. Sykes, G. M., & Messinger, S. (1960). The inmate social system. In Theoretical studies in social organization of the prison (pp. 5-19). New York, NY: Social Science Research Council.
2. Winfree, L. T., Newbold, G., & Tubb, S. H. (2002). Prisoner perspective on inmate culture in New Mexico and New Zealand: A descriptive case study. The Prison Journal, 82(2), 213-233.

where feminine qualities are seen as a target for predatory behavior. (p. 28)

Carceral's observations support how race/ethnic identification and separatism become a primary characteristic that defines the prison experience, particularly for men (Alarid, 2000a). Although some prisoners enter the institution with racist attitudes, Carceral's view suggests that most prisoners simply give in to the norms that staying with one's own race is the only way to avoid trouble, and do not go against the norms because of the bullying and potential violent consequences: "The prison identity is grounded in hatred, learned racism, and a willingness to resort to violence when necessary" (Carceral, 2004, p. 127).

A study of prison argot provides a window into understanding what qualities are valued and what is despised. For example, Figure 8–6 shows that individuals who are prison gang leaders, organized crime figures, or traffickers are given the most respect by other inmates. Prison gang members are second because they are part of the networked power structure. The vast majority of individual prisoners fall into one of two groups: They are either **players** or **squares**, as every prisoner chooses whether to embrace the mainstream norms or oppose prison culture (Terry, 2003). At the bottom of the hierarchy are inmates who have committed sex-related crimes against children or who are perceived as **snitches** or **punks** (Carceral, 2004).

It seems that the individuals who undergo the most radical transformations in prison come in as **fish**, make the key connections with the players, and decide to fully assimilate themselves into the prison world. Inmates who choose not to assimilate to convict norms do harder time as outcasts, but because they've been "living on the outside in their head," they will likely remain free after release (Terry, 2003, p. 74). An explanation of the classic outcasts is protective custody inmates who are ". . . generally the nonviolent intelligent ones, have to live with limited privileges, whereas the regular inmates, who are generally the violent ones and losers, have all the privileges permitted" (Harkleroad, 2000, p. 164).

Gang leaders, organized crime, traffickers

Gang members

Players, crews; Embraced maintream prison culture

Gleaners, squares, cave dwellers; Opposed maintream prison culture

Punks

Snitches, Player haters, Sex offenders

FIGURE 8–6 Prisoner Hierarchy.

▶ Prisoner Job Assignments

American culture is an occupation-dominated one in which a job organizes routines, behavior, and even one's identity. In prison culture, administrators initially used inmates for cheap labor to decrease incarceration costs and to make a profit through the leasing system and through manufacturing prison-made goods. The timeline in Figure 8–7 shows that prison-made goods were first subjected to limitations by the states during the Great Depression so that free-world citizens would not have to compete with prisoner labor. Later,

Think About It...

A prison's physical structure restricts a person's freedom of movement and ability to control what he or she eats, where he or she lives or works, and even the ability to control the room temperature. To most prisoners, not having independence or control greatly affects their sense of dignity, their emotional well-being, and, over time, their decision-making ability. On the one hand, some call this situation "punishment," whereas others believe it severely prevents inmates from learning the tools they need to keep a job and control their behavior after they leave prison. What can be done to teach prisoners what they need to learn to be successful in mainstream America while being incarcerated as punishment?

CAN BALCIOGLU/Shutterstock

Timeline of Prison Labor Laws

1929	**1935**	**1940**	**1979**
Hawes-Cooper Act	**Ashurst-Sumners Act**	**Ashurst-Sumners Amendment**	**Prison Industries Enhancement (PIE) Act**
Prison-made goods were subjected to control of the receiving state's laws.	It became a federal offense to transport prison-made goods into states that had barred them under Hawes-Cooper.	This allowed state *agricultural* prison products to be sold in other states.	This increased opportunities for public–private cooperation.
One state can prohibit another state from selling its prison-made goods there.		Twenty-two states mandated that state agencies purchase certain products made at state prisons.	It restricted the number of jurisdictions and industries.

FIGURE 8–7 **Timeline of Prison Labor Laws.**
Source: Hawes-Cooper Act,1929; Ashurst-Sumners Act 1935; Ashurst-Sumners Amendment 1940; Prison Industries Enhancement (PIE) Act 1979.

working became an important source of informal social control and a method of keeping inmates occupied, but the Prison Industries Enhancement Act of 1979 restricted the number of private factories that could be operated inside prison facilities. However, the main challenge today is that there are more prisoners than work available to keep each occupied for eight hours per day; therefore, the work is spread around so that most inmates actually work two to three hours per day.

Figure 8–8 shows the types of jobs that inmates work today. Most inmates are assigned to **institutional maintenance** jobs that help to operate and maintain the prison in areas, such as food preparation, laundry, cleaning of all surfaces and floors, and lawn care. Specialty maintenance jobs exist—in which **trustys** can be promoted— that offer more freedom of movement or access to information. These jobs include hall janitors, porters, stock clerks, barbers, warden's assistants, and library clerks (Alarid, 2005).

A second category of prison jobs exists primarily in southern regions of the United States, where there is open land for agriculture—growing crops and raising cattle and pigs. This work is traditionally for inmates with disciplinary problems. **Agricultural work** is hard and hot—as it is done using shovels and sharp pitchforks—and the inmates work in rows under the watchful eye of armed officers on horses (Alarid, 2005). Some states offer good time, but do not pay prisoners for institutional maintenance or agricultural jobs, whereas others offer wages, such as $0.10 per hour.

Prison industry jobs are highly competitive and are sought after by inmates because they provide the most realistic work environment of six- to eight-hour days and the best pay. There are few slots available for these jobs only because they are highly regulated by the government. The prison industry is typically a manufacturing plant or factory that produces prison-made goods for either **open markets** or **sheltered markets** (see Figure 8–9). The greatest concern is that prisoner labor might

LEARNING OUTCOMES 2 — Explain the benefits and challenges of assigning jobs to incarcerated inmates.

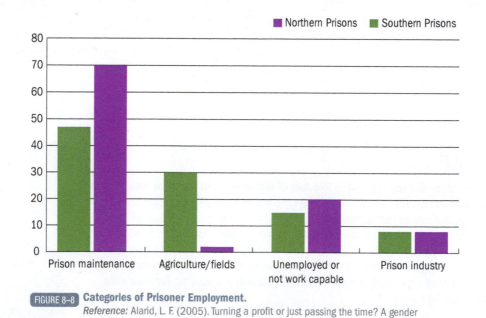

FIGURE 8–8 **Categories of Prisoner Employment.**
Reference: Alarid, L. F. (2005). Turning a profit or just passing the time? A gender comparison of prisoner jobs and workplace deviance in the sub rosa economy. Deviant Behavior, 6, 621–641.

System	Market	Control	Product Examples
Government use or state use	Sheltered	Government 100%	Traffic signs, license plates, furniture, dairy
Joint-venture	Sheltered	Government 50% (wage scales, hiring) Private firm 50% (product design, marketing, distribution)	Joint Venture Program (California) Corcraft (New York)
Corporate	Open	Private more control than government	PRIDE (Florida) UNICOR (Federal BOP)
Free enterprise	Open	Private sector 100%	PIE products Prison Blues® (Oregon)

FIGURE 8–9 **Contemporary Prison Industry Systems.**
Reference: Adapted from Dwyer & McNally (1993).

again unfairly compete with free-world labor, so restrictions were placed on the prison industry that operates under a **free-enterprise** system.

Federal Prison Industries, Inc. (FPI) was established by Congress in 1934 to provide prison-made goods for all federal agencies. In the 1970s, FPI introduced the name "UNICOR" as its new corporate identity. UNICOR is not only self-sustaining, but it makes significant profits every year. For example, during 2015, UNICOR employed about 6% of federal inmates in 80 factories and 3 farms across the country. The prisoners are paid between $0.23 and $1.15 per hour to make such things as clothing, office furniture, electronics, fleet management and vehicular components, and industrial products (UNICOR, 2016).

Another open-market system is the heavily restricted PIE prison industry programs that operate with private business in up to 50 jurisdictions around the United States. The PIE program allows preselected inmates to work in a realistic environment, get paid for their efforts at wages that are equal for similar work elsewhere, and learn a trade. The inmates must be at minimum-custody level, hold at least a General Education Development (GED) or a high school diploma, and have not received a disciplinary report for six months. The government also requires the following of PIE programs (National Correctional Industries Association, 2011):

- They must not displace private-sector workers.
- Inmates apply voluntarily and are selected based on predefined standards.

- Inmate wages must be similar to those paid to private-sector employees.
- Up to 20% of inmate wages goes to pay court fines, victim restitution, or child support.

Many of the PIE program jobs are skilled and require job training. Figure 8–10 examines the extent to which prisoner job training programs reduce recidivism after release from prison.

Having prisoners work while incarcerated involves a number of benefits and challenges that are illustrated in Figure 8–11. The benefits include reduction of idleness, learning of employable skills, and the maintenance of facility operations. In addition, for jobs in which prisoners earn wages, the wages can be garnished to pay victim restitution, child support, and court-ordered fines. In addition, private businesses receive tax incentives for agreeing to open a factory inside a prison instead of sending the jobs overseas to another country. A previous study conducted by the Bureau of Prisons found that UNICOR contributed to lower recidivism and increased job-related success of male inmates upon release (UNICOR, 2016). A similar study with female inmate federal prison industry programs found that UNICOR jobs did not necessarily advantage women inmates in the same way they did men, in that the skills that women were learning might not transition over as well to jobs they sought in the community (Richmond, 2014).

The next section discusses how prisoner labor may be used as a source of personal profit for inmates to use their jobs to move around contraband in the sub rosa economy.

Until recently, data on job training program results were either anecdotal or based on less rigorous methodological studies. In past evaluations, the groups of prisoners who received job training differed from comparison groups of prisoners who did not seek out training because the trained groups already had more motivation while incarcerated, making evaluation of results difficult. Eight job training programs that used *random group assignment* were analyzed to look at whether the programs reduced rates of rearrest after release. Job training programs for ex-offenders had *no significant effect* on the likelihood that the treatment subjects would be rearrested compared to the group who did not receive such services.

FIGURE 8–10 **Evidence-Based Practice—Does it Work? Prisoner Job Training.**
Source: Visher, C. A., Winterfield, L., & Coggeshall, M. B. (2005). Ex-offender employment programs and recidivism: A meta-analysis. *Journal of Experimental Criminology, 1*(3), 295–316.

Prisoner Labor Benefits	Challenges of Prisoner Labor
• Offsets the cost of cleaning and maintaining the institution	• Prisoners can use their jobs to profit by moving contraband and commissary.
• Maintains day-to-day facility operations	• Private companies feel that it is unfair to compete with prison-made goods.
• Cost-effective goods can be made.	• Congress passed legislation restricting prison-made products and made it difficult for prisons to be too profitable.
• Government profits	
• Victim restitution, child support, and court-ordered fines can be garnished from wages.	• Many inmates do not get paid at all for their labor or payment is not enough to garnish wages.
• Reduces idleness during incarceration	• Idleness still exists when there are more prisoners than jobs—unemployment rate of 10–30%.
• Choice jobs that inmates earn reduce institutional misconduct.	• Behavioral problems with the lower-ranked jobs (hoe squad, field work)
• Private businesses receive tax incentives, avoid payment of employee benefits such as retirement, vacation, and sick leave; and they have a reliable workforce.	• Prison spends much effort with job placement, promotions, demotions, and getting work crews to work on time; work schedule revolves around prison security; occasional work stoppages occur.
• Inmates learn employable skills.	• May interfere or compete with the free labor market.

FIGURE 8–11 Benefits and Challenges of Prisoner Labor.

▶ Sub Rosa Economy

Every jail and prison has a bartering system of reciprocity based on negotiation and exchange of goods and services between prisoners without the use of cash. This illicit, underground economy is forbidden, and is known as the **sub rosa economy**. Prisoners secure items of value through favors and trades. Most of the items are state supplies and are considered more of a nuisance for prison officials than a real security threat. Thus, officers may disregard or overlook minor acts that do not interfere with institutional security. Some inmates provide **commissary** such as hygiene products, office supplies, and snack foods or loan items to friends on disciplinary status or as a form of resistance to control (Smoyer, 2016). Other individuals are well known in the prison for their entrepreneurial spirit. For example, **merchants** control scarce resources by running illegal prison stores by selling excess commissary from their cells. **Jailhouse lawyers** are not licensed attorneys, but use their legal knowledge and skills to conduct legal research and write writs and grievances. Other inmates perfect a skill such as artwork, making cards, and writing poems and sell, trade, or barter that skill for goods (such as snacks or stamps) or services (such as ironing a uniform, cleaning a cell, or cooking a late-night meal). For example, one female inmate shares a story in which she was preparing stolen food in her cell:

"The lieutenant came to take my blow dryer 'cause I was cooking a bagel with it. . . . He be up in my room talking shit. . . . He knew what I was doing so he came downstairs and was like 'What are you cooking? Give it to me.' I was like 'Hell, no! I ain't giving it to you.' Cause I had some contraband roast beef with a poppa on a bagel. . . . So. . . . the lieutenant came and took my blow dryer. I was mad! I did get a ticket too. . . ." (Smoyer, 2016, p. 204).

Alarid (2005) found that about 27% of men and women inmates admitted to using their assigned prison job to yield a personal profit, and that prison industry workers were the least likely to participate in the sub rosa economy. Skimming and pilfering of food, laundry bleach, and office supplies were group efforts carried out in maintenance jobs. Other inmates admitted to using their freedom of movement in their jobs to pass contraband, food, and information (Smoyer, 2016; Santos, 2004). Terry (2003, p. 64) described how he used his job as a receiving clerk for profit:

This position gave me access to information about who would be arriving in the institution the day before they arrived. One of the things I was expected to do [by inmates included] . . . making three lists of these soon-to-be-new prisoners . . . of their names, race, county of origin, and crime. Once completed, I gave a copy to a black, brown, and white prisoner. . . . In return, I was rewarded with something tangible, such as cigarettes or a small amount of marijuana, and social status. This process served the purpose of screening incoming prisoners . . . for determining who could stay, or who had to go.

Prisoner Misconduct

Prisoners who are caught engaging in economic activities for profit risk a written disciplinary report that remains permanently in their file. Figure 8–12 illustrates a broader range of prisoner misconduct, which ranges from failure to follow rules and policies to unauthorized staff contact, refusing to follow staff orders, and destroying facility property. Prisoner misconduct is of interest because of its association with adjustment to prison, readiness for early release, and, possibly, future recidivism upon release. Inmates who behave according to institutional rules and avoid misconduct while incarcerated generally seem to transition easier and avoid future rearrest. It seems that younger males with a history of drug use are more prone to misconduct, especially at the beginning of their sentence (Kuanliang & Sorensen, 2008). The conditions of confinement also predicted misconduct. Prisoners who were concerned with their safety, had interpersonal conflicts with staff, and considered lengthy periods of boredom and idleness to be stressful were more likely to engage in misconduct and violence

(Rocheleau, 2013). Finally, reclassification and a change in supervision levels to a different custody level seemed to increase inmate misconduct. Inmates who transferred to a higher or a lower custody level (e.g., from a medium down to a minimum, or from a medium up to a maximum) engaged in more misconduct following their transfer (Kigerl & Hamilton, 2016). Perhaps movement to a different institution necessitated the need for the inmate to establish his or reputation to avoid being bullied or harassed by the more established inmates at that unit.

A more serious form of prisoner misconduct is smuggling in **contraband** that proves to be lucrative, such as metal tools, drugs, cell phones, cigarettes, or cash. Unauthorized cell phone use poses a huge problem inside every correctional facility in the country. Currently, federal and state correctional officials are unable to convince the Federal Communications Commission to block satellite signals to jails and prison institutions. Other than cell phones, some prisoners may feel obligated to hide weapons or other contraband for gangs if they happen to be housed in a certain cell that has a particular known hiding place for certain items. For example, one non-gang member said,

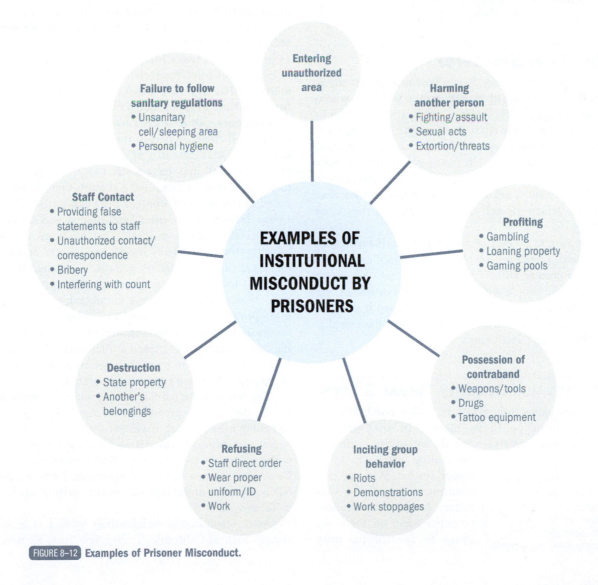

FIGURE 8–12 Examples of Prisoner Misconduct.

"The cell I was in had a space about that big at the bottom of the toilet. Just big enough to fit some steal [sic] under. When I got on the range and somebody said 'Bro listen, your cell is the cell, can you take care of this? It was like 'Yeah-yeah, sure.' I had no choice I didn't want to touch that thing. I was trying to get parole, the last thing I wanted was for them to search me cell and find this steal. But at the same time what am I going to say? 'Oh, sorry bro, can't do it'' Well, [if I Said that] I was going to be wearing that piece of jewelry to the frigging medical wing . . . if it means I have to take a fall, or take a charge, or not parole to stay solid, well that's part of the life in there." (Ricciardelli, 2014, p. 423).

The extent of contraband in each prison is more dependent on the level of staff enforcement rather than the custody level.

Movement of contraband typically involves **crews**, but a large amount of the most lucrative part of the illegal economy is claimed by prison gangs (Santos, 2004). Gangs control the institution's drug transactions, gambling, loans, prostitution, and debt-collection rackets. In addition, they increase an inmate's status, provide protection from other gangs, and instill a sense of camaraderie like a second family, which is the subject of the next section.

▶ *Collective Behavior*

In prisons, like anywhere else, people tend to seek out others with whom they have something in common and from whom they can expect support. There are opportunities to join religious groups, such as Bible study groups and choir. There are athletic leagues that have organized teams that play basketball, volleyball, or flag football, for example. There are chess clubs and groups such as Alcoholics Anonymous that address addiction. These groups are allowed by the prison because they aid in the prisoner's self-development, and they keep prisoners busy.

Another reason to be part of a crew is for self-protection. Ross and Richards (2002, p. 133) observed that in some prisons "you absolutely need to affiliate with a group that will protect you. The loners, the people without social skills or friends, are vulnerable to being physically attacked or preyed upon." We begin first by discussing men's prison gangs, and then we discuss groups in women's institutions.

Prison Gangs and Security Threat Groups

Growth of prison gangs throughout the 1960s and 1970s was closely tied to racial conflicts among African-American, Latino, and Caucasian prisoners and the instability caused by

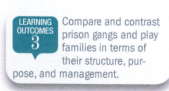
LEARNING OUTCOMES 3 Compare and contrast prison gangs and play families in terms of their structure, purpose, and management.

the ending of the building tender system. With the dismantling of the convict subculture, Latino prisoners saw potential early on for using gangs to control the drug economy in prison and, at the same time, protect them from being victimized by outsiders (Irwin, 1980). As the numbers of Latino gang members increased and became a perceived threat, black and white prisoners responded by creating their own groups. In the 1980s and 1990s, gangs continued to recruit **state-raised youth** who were waived to adult institutions. State-raised youth grew up in youth facilities that were racially segregated and hostile, and where violence earned respect and stealing was necessary for survival.

Gangs are organized criminal enterprises that attempt to maximize power and profit through contraband and drug-trafficking movement in prison. Prison gangs are also known as **security threat groups (STGs)** because their activities are predatory and their presence poses a threat to the security and safety of staff and inmates. Although most STGs are prison gangs, the definition of *STG* applies to over 1,000 groups (examples are listed in Table 8–1) consisting of street gangs, motorcycle clubs, militias, mafia families, Asian triads, and occult groups—all of which require constant monitoring (Winterdyk & Ruddell, 2010).

Ways that STGs are structured vary greatly. Some groups, such as the Mexican Mafia, are paramilitary, which is ". . . a hierarchical structure with clear distinction between ranks, and often include military titles such as general, captain, lieutenant, sergeant, and soldier. Senior leaders are able to issue orders to subordinates, which are carried out as instructed." (Texas Joint Crime Information Center Intelligence and Counterterrorism Division, 2015, p. 33). **Paramilitary STGs** have a constitution and require membership for life. Other groups, such as the Texas Syndicate, operate as a **regional cell STG** because they ". . . are composed of several cells that are part of the same organization, but generally act independently of one another at an operational level. Each cell may have a strict internal hierarchy similar to a paramilitary model, even though there is little coordinated command and control between cells" (Texas Joint Crime Information Center Intelligence and Counterterrorism Division, 2015, p. 33). Most other groups are more loosely structured. They have a designated leader, but are less rigid than paramilitary groups. The Tango Blast STG is the most loosely structured group of all, given the absence of a constitution, no lifetime membership requirement, and a temporary and ever-changing leadership hierarchy that seems to depend on who is incarcerated in a particular housing unit in each jail or prison at that time. Most Tango members leave the group once they are released, only to rejoin the group if they are ever reincarcerated.

The threat that each STG poses within correctional facilities is defined by prevalence/strength of numbers, active recruiting efforts, level of violent activities, level of domestic and/or transnational criminal activity, and the group's alliance with other gangs and/or cartels (Texas Joint Crime Information Center Intelligence and Counterterrorism Division, 2015). The STGs that present the highest threat to prisons are highlighted in Table 8–1.

Active membership varies widely by each state, with some states—such as California, Texas, New York, Florida, Illinois,

TABLE 8–1 | EXAMPLES OF SECURITY THREAT GROUPS

Group Formation	Latino Groups	Caucasian Groups	African-American Groups
1950s	Latin Kings	Hell's Angels MC	Vice Lords
	Mexican Mafia (CA)	Pagans MC	
1960s	Texas Syndicate	Diablos MC	CRIPs/Folk Nation
	Nuestra Familia	Sons of Silence MC	Bloods/People Nation
	Sureños	Warlocks MC	Black Guerilla Family
		Vagos MC	Black Panther Party
	18th Street	Brother Speed MC	Black P Stones
	Bandidos MC	Aryan Brotherhood	
	Mongols MC		
1970s	Neta	Nazi Low Riders	DC Blacks
	Norteños	Simon City Royals	El Rukns
	Mexikanemi (TX)	Skinheads	
1980s	Barrio Azteca	Peckerwoods	Gangster Disciples
	Raza Unida	Aryan Circle	Nation of Islam
	Hermanos de Pistoleros Latinos	Public Enemy Number One	Five Percenters
	Border Brothers	Dirty White Boys	
	Mara Salvatrucha 13	White Knights	United Blood Nation
1990s	Tri-City Bombers	Dead Man, Inc.	Fruits of Islam
	Texas Chicano Brotherhood	United Aryan Brotherhood	
	Partido Revolucionario Mexicano	White Aryan Resistance	
	Tango Blast	The Order	
2000s	Gulf Cartel	Christian Identity	Jam'iyyat Ul-Islam Is-Saheed (JIS)
	Sinaloa Cartel	World Church of the Creator	Moorish Science Temple
	Zetas		Prison Islam Groups
	Juarez Cartel		
	Paisas/Mexicles		

Notes: MC = Motorcycle club; the groups highlighted in green above represent a significant threat inside U.S. prisons nationwide at the current time.

Sources: 1. Barker, T. (2012). North American criminal gangs: Street, prison, outlaw motorcycle, and drug trafficking organizations. Durham, NC: Carolina Academic Press. 2. Griffin, M. L., Pyrooz, D., & Decker, S. H. (2013). Surviving and thriving: The growth, influence, and administrative control of prison gangs. In J. L. Wood & T. A. Gannon (Eds.), Crime and crime reduction: The importance of group processes (pp. 137–156). New York, NY: Routledge. 3. Texas Joint Crime Information Center Intelligence and Counterterrorism Division. (2015). Texas gang threat assessment. Austin, TX: Texas Department of Public Safety.

and Wisconsin—having more significant STG problems than others. An average of between 19 and 26% of prisoners were gang members before imprisonment (Winterdyk & Ruddell, 2010), while more were recruited into an STG during imprisonment (Alarid, 2000a). At this time, the loosely structured situational STG model seems more popular than joining an STG for life.

There are an estimated 500,000 STG members currently in jail and prison throughout the United States. However, the number varies because some members are more active than others, making it difficult for prison authorities to confirm memberships. When a gang member enters a prison where there are very few members from his own group, he will temporarily align himself or become a hybrid gang member with

another preaccepted group for protection. For example, the Mara Salvatrucha have aligned themselves with the Latin Kings, and many smaller Latino STGs temporarily join the Tangos while incarcerated and return to their street gang upon release. Concern remains that prisons may be possible breeding grounds for future terrorists, particularly by religious extremist groups during chapel services.

Gang intelligence officers (GIs) collect information on suspected gang members using the list of gang identifiers (shown in Figure 8–13), along with information from correctional officers and other inmate informants (Knox, 2005). Once active STG members are identified, prison officials place restrictions on them, such as removal from the general prison population, reclassification to a higher

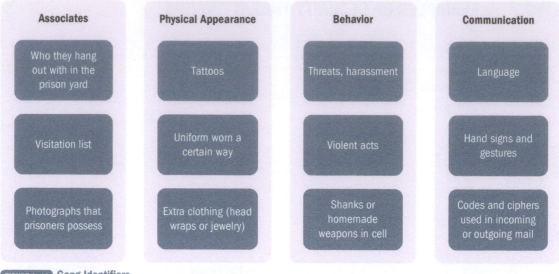

FIGURE 8–13 **Gang Identifiers.**
Source: From The Problem of Gangs and Security Threat Groups (STG's) in American Prisons Today: Recent Research Findings From the 2004 Prison Gang Survey by George W Knox. Copyright © 2004 by George W. Knox. Used by permission of National Gang Crime Research Center.

custody level, and placement in administrative segregation for the remainder of their prison terms (Winterdyk & Ruddell, 2010). Figure 8–14 illustrates the various ways that gang intelligence officers constantly work at managing the effect of STGs. A few prisons have programs that encourage members to permanently renounce their gang membership and "debrief," which means to share confidential information. However, less than 10% of validated gang members renounce their membership because of the consequences of assault or death (Knox, 2005). Despite efforts to control STGs, prison gangs maintain a stronghold in maximum-security and supermax prisons throughout the United States. Unfortunately, drugs are brought in primarily by visitors and the occasional corrupt prison employee or naïve volunteer. That situation makes it even more difficult for prison administrators to control the introduction of drugs into the prison and to negatively impact the growth of prison gangs (Winterdyk & Ruddell, 2010).

Groups in Women's Prisons

Although their numbers are growing, women tend to recruit less actively and are less likely to make group membership a security threat issue. Less than 4% of female inmates are recruited into a gang during imprisonment, and 6.3% of female prisoners were gang members before imprisonment (Knox, 2005). Female gang members seem to be less active while incarcerated, as the environment inside the institution does not support gang behavior (Petersen, 2000). Instead, female groups were organized based on make-believe families, friendships, and couples that crossed racial lines. Small, close-knit make-believe families were encouraged because being well connected was important to being part of "the drama" or "the mix." "Their advocacy is emotional and personal; their allegiance is to a few rather than to many" (Pollock, 2002, p. 138).

Close friendships were the most prevalent type of relationship found in women's prisons. Most women had between 1 and 10 close friends whom they considered to be trustworthy, with an average of 2 close friends. Friendships allowed women to share problems and commissary, but were not used very often for hustling goods and services or for protection (Alarid, 1996). Only 12% of adult women reported being loners. These women were not necessarily social outcasts or unable to form social bonds. Rather, loners chose a different path, after deciding that "commissary and sex games" were not the way to do time (Alarid, 1996).

One of the most widely documented aspects of the social structure of women's prisons is a fabricated kinship network that has been called *pseudofamilies*, *make-believe families*, or *prison families*. The most common term is **play families**, which refers to relationships among women prisoners that borrow the structure, terminology, and function of families in larger society. About 4 in 10 women joined play families in prison, whereas only 12% reported doing so in jail. Play families shared commissary, persuaded members to be compliant with prison rules, and protected each other from predatory inmates. Most play families existed as mentoring relationships, where the play mother is the family's center (Alarid, 1996). The most common roles are mother–daughter and sister–sister. Mothers, especially, may have several daughters for whom they listen to problems and offer advice. The relationships created in the play family likely do not represent the women's previous familial experiences. Instead, the play mother may be a better mother to her inmate daughters than her real-life mother was to her while growing up, or better than the inmate was to her own children before imprisonment. Generally, women's prisons had less incidents of serious misconduct than men's facilities.

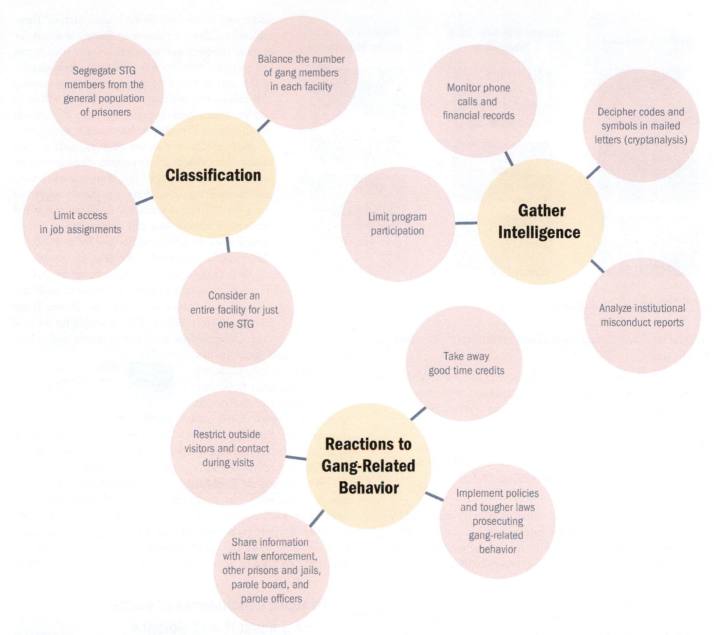

FIGURE 8–14 **Ways of Managing Security Threat Groups (STGs).**
References: 1. Knox, G. W. (2005). The problem of gangs and security threat groups (STGs) in American prisons today: Recent research findings from the 2004 prison gang survey. Retrieved from http://www.ngcrc.com. 2. Winterdyk, J., & Ruddell, R. (2010). Managing prison gangs: Results from a survey of U.S. prison systems. Journal of Criminal Justice, 38(4), 730-736.

▶ *Prison Violence*

Potential for violence exists in all institutions, but violence is clearly concentrated in higher-security jail and prison units in part because inmates experience more deprivations and more stress in higher custody units, and also because a disproportionately higher number of inmates perceive violence as an acceptable way to solve problems (Ricciardelli & Sit, 2016). Environments that encourage using violence to create a reputation, bullying or harassing as a show of power, imposing fear when necessary to avoid being victimized, and settling problems without staff are all circumstances that sustain violent behavior (Carceral, 2004). As shown in Figure 8–15, causes of violence can be in response to any number of events, including stress, hostility, interpersonal conflict, and to keep a strong reputation.

In some cases, even mild-mannered prisoners feel like they had no choice but to fight a certain prisoner or group to avoid future harassment, bullying, assaults, or property theft (Ricciardelli, 2014). Prison officials have a duty under the Eighth Amendment to keep prisoners safe from violence by other prisoners, but staff is not liable for assaults unless the prisoner can prove that staff exhibited **deliberate indifference**, which is when staff completely ignore or fail to respond after it becomes clear the staff became aware of and/or witnessed the behavior.

The most common acts of violence involving two people are inmate–inmate threats, assaults, and sexual assault. Threats are the most common, but are undocumented in official statistics. Cases of assault and sexual assault/rape are underreported out of fear of further retaliation and harassment (Miller, 2010). Documented cases are therefore the worst ones that involve

Individual Response	Response to Subcultural Expectations	Response to Avoid Further Victimization

Individual Response
- Stress (prisoner "snaps")
- Jealousy, low self-esteem
- Learned way to deal with interpersonal conflict

Response to Subcultural Expectations
- Boredom; to impress peers; to establish a reputation
- Gambling or other unpaid debts
- Racial hostility/gang hit ordered

Response to Avoid Further Victimization
- To avoid further harassment/insults/threats
- Get staff attention to get placed in protective custody

FIGURE 8–15 Causes of Individual-Level Violence.

medical attention. Some known facts about assault in prison are as follows:

- A poor prison environment characterized by dissatisfaction with treatment by prison staff contributed to increased physical victimization of other inmates (Wolff, Shi, & Siegel, 2009).

- Inmates housed in larger and more crowded facilities generated more opportunities for undetected assaults, with less chance of being officially caught for assault (Wooldredge & Steiner, 2009).

- Women prisoners reported being physically assaulted by another inmate at the same rate as men prisoners, but women reported nearly double the rate of property theft than did men (Wooldredge & Steiner, 2016).

- Incidents of assault in women's prisons were less likely to involve deadly weapons and less related to race/ethnic tension than for men. Jealousy, sexual pressuring, and unreciprocated attention were the most frequently cited reasons that led to assault (Alarid, 2000b).

- Inmates with mental illnesses were more likely to be assaulted and to assault others (Wood & Buttaro, 2013).

- For men, STG members committed acts of violence at two to three times the rate of inmates who were not STG members in units of the same security level.

Sexual Assault and Rape

Sexual behavior between inmates, and especially between inmates and staff members, has always been prohibited—this includes sexual assault (intentional touching) or nonconsensual sexual acts. In the past, a climate of acceptance that rape and sexual harassment were part of the punishment

dominated prisons across the United States. "Turning out" a vulnerable inmate by force was a way for another prisoner to enhance his or her own status among peers, whether it was blatantly through rape or through more subtle strategies such as loaning new prisoners more than they could ever afford to pay back and then demanding payment through sex (Santos, 2004). Sexual harassment, derogatory or profane comments, or acts of staff sexual misconduct (indecent exposure, voyeurism, or requested sexual acts) had few, if any, negative consequences. Prison conditions have greatly improved since the 1970s, but anecdotal evidence suggested that sexual assault was still entrenched in prison culture because it was overlooked by correctional officers and encouraged by the prisoner subculture.

Reducing sexual victimization of prison inmates became a priority nationwide with the passage of a federal act called the Prison Rape Elimination Act (PREA). PREA sought for the first time to measure the incidence of prison rape in federal, state, and local institutions, and to provide guidelines to protect prisoners from rape. The provisions of the act are shown in Figure 8–16 and included staff training on the new law, a zero-tolerance policy of sexual misconduct and rape incidents, and victim access to counseling and protective custody housing (PREA, 2003).

LEARNING OUTCOMES 4 — Discuss the incidence of sexual assault and violence in prisons.

Five years after PREA's passage, the nationwide rate of inmates who, when surveyed, reported sexual victimization at least once within a prior 12-month period was still 4.4% in prisons and 3% in jails. This equated to 88,500 incidents every year. At some units around the country, rates ranged from less than 1% to a high of nearly 20% (Beck, Harrison, & Guerino,

To reduce incidences of prison sexual assault and violence

- Separate predatory inmates from targeted inmates
- Provide prisoner and staff training on sexual assault
- Encourage staff to be part of the solution (rather than the problem)
- Provide counseling intervention for sexual assault victims
- Encourage consistent rule enforcement by staff
- Aggressively investigate and prosecute rapes
- Provide protective custody for inmates targeted for sexual assault
- Use video cameras to prevent sex abuse
- Allow housing changes and facility transfers for victims
- Implement criminal sanctions for any inmates or staffers engaging in abuse

FIGURE 8–16 Reducing Incidents of Sexual Assault and Violence in Correctional Institutions.
References: 1. Austin, J., Fabelo, T., Gunter, A., & McGinnis, K. (2006). Sexual violence in the Texas prison system (NCJ 215774). Washington, DC: U.S. Department of Justice and The JFA Institute.

2. Zweig, J. M., Naser, R. L., Blackmore, J., & Schaffer, M. (2007). Addressing sexual violence in prisons: A national snapshot of approaches and highlights of innovative strategies (NCJ 216856). Washington, DC: National Institute of Justice.

2010). Facilities with higher rates of sexual abuse had a higher number of violent offenders, high racial conflict, dormitory housing, and areas without video surveillance, and were understaffed compared to the number of offenders (English, Heil, & Dumond, 2010). About 90% of these incidents that inmates anonymously reported to researchers were *not* reported to prison officials, in part because few incidents could be substantiated (proven that they occurred) due to lack of evidence.

About 45% of youth sexual victimization in correctional facilities involved staff-on-youth while the remaining were youth-on-youth (Beck & Rantala, 2016). However, about 70% of reported incidents of adult sexual abuse of inmates were committed by staff members rather than by other inmates. In both men's and women's units, staff member sexual abusers were more likely to be of the opposite sex relative to the inmate victim (Beck et al., 2010). The unequal power relationship that exists between correctional staff and confined prisoners is particularly important to address due to these findings. All sexual acts involving staff are considered to be forms of coerced sexual misconduct and may result in termination and/or additional criminal charges.

Adult inmate *perpetrators* of sexual assault tend to have spent time in juvenile facilities, have committed a violent crime as an adult, be gang affiliated, be more likely to be involved in all types of misconduct, and be under age 30. Targeted inmate *victims* tended to be young, first-time, nonviolent, Caucasian, and from a middle-class background. Individual characteristics that increased victimization even more (whether they were actual or perceived by others) were those who were developmentally disabled or mentally ill, unaffiliated with a group, known to be gay or bisexual, perceived to be a snitch, possessed certain physical traits (effeminate traits if a man and masculine traits if a woman), and those who were convicted of a crime against a minor (English et al., 2010). Victims who reported being sexually abused were targeted between three and five times during that year. Most sexually coerced incidents by other inmates involved sexual harassment or forced sexual assault. Sexual coercion led to incidents of sexual assault when other prisoners perceived their advances were being ignored. In women's facilities, once a woman was targeted for physical and/or sexual violence, it was difficult to escape the situation. If rape occurred, it involved a group of women (Alarid, 2000b).

In general, across the United States, sexual victimization reporting rates in prison have increased since PREA, as expected. PREA provides victims with more options and has changed the culture of prisoner sexual victimization to one that punishes prison staff for looking the other way.

▶ Collective Violence

Most acts of collective violence are for the purpose of prisoners vehemently communicating some form of change. Prisoners have engaged in group hunger strikes, work stoppages, and **voluntary lockdowns**. Acts of collective violence in prison can be differentiated into disturbances and riots. **Disturbances** are quite common—occurring once or twice per week in maximum-security institutions and once every few months in minimum-security correctional facilities throughout the United States. Most disturbances involve fighting/assault because of racial tension, gang rivalries, or retaliation. Other incidents were disruptive, meaning they involved noise and property damage, including banging on cell doors, flooding cells (by stopping up toilets), setting fire to property, throwing feces/urine at officers, and cell extraction problems. Most disturbances occur in large areas where many inmates congregate, such as the prison yard, the chow hall, the dormitories, and the dayroom. Most disturbances can cause injury to inmates and property damage, but they usually end within minutes. Most important, with disturbances, the prison remains in control by the staff at all times. Disturbances in female prisons occur less often than with men and are most often group strikes, fires, and fights.

Prison Riots

More attention has been paid to **prison riots** because they involve a large number of inmates who plan to forcibly take control of the prison. Once the control of the prison changes hands from officers to prisoners, a disturbance officially becomes a riot. Causes of riots are shown in Figure 8–17. Rioting stems from prisoners viewing violence as their best response to adverse conditions or the way to achieve change of **predisposing factors** that, over an extended period of time, provide the riot's foundation. The predisposing condition could

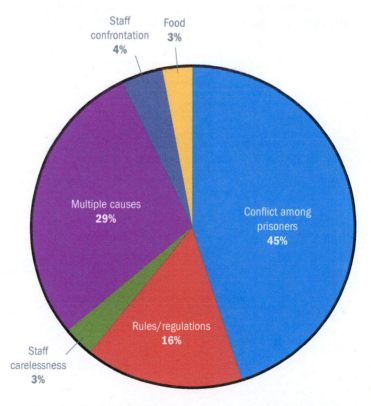

*Note: Some of the causes were triggering events, while others were predisposing factors

FIGURE 8–17 **Causes* of Prison Riots and Disturbances.**
Source: Reprinted with permission of the american correctional association,alexandria, VA from a History of Correctional Violence: an Examination of Riots and Correctional Disturbances by Reid H Montgomery and Gordon A. Crews.

be administrative breakdown, severe staff shortages, perceived oppressive conditions, continuous staff confrontation, or ongoing racial tension. Predisposing factors are more likely to occur in higher-custody-level prisons than in medium- or minimum-level facilities.

The **triggering event** is what actually starts the riot, *but is not the cause*. For example, the triggering event in a 2009 riot in Chino, California, was racial tension in the dayroom, but the riot was planned because of oppressive conditions due to overcrowding and idleness. Once a riot has begun, some inmates will seek safety and remove themselves from the rioters. Others will rejoice in their newfound freedom and partake in binges of drinking, drug use, and property damage. There may also be violence among inmates as old grudges are settled or snitches are harmed or even killed.

Nearly all riots today are contained in a small area of the prison and never make it to a full-scale organized plan because they are extinguished by prison officials within a few hours. Riots between the 1950s and 1970s, however, lasted longer and involved organized negotiation by a few inmate leaders who challenged abuses of power by corrections officers. For example, the Attica, New York, riot in 1971 was a complete prison takeover; it lasted five days and involved negotiations between inmate leaders and prison authorities to improve prison conditions and inmate treatment. In the eager attempt to reclaim the prison, law enforcement officers killed 39 inmates and 10 correctional officers, and wounded more than 80 others. Three inmates were intentionally killed at the hands of other inmates, and one officer died two days later of head wounds inflicted when the inmates took his keys (Wicker, 1994).

The Santa Fe riot provides an interesting contrast to the Attica riot. On February 2, 1980, inmates at the New Mexico State Penitentiary began what would be a 36-hour riot. Before it was over, 33 inmates were dead and over 100 others were beaten and sexually assaulted by fellow prisoners. There were some similarities in the predisposing conditions (Colvin, 1997), but the biggest differences were the absence of organization and the brutal violence that took place against other inmates. Property damage amounted to over $100 million, and a new prison had to be built to replace the one that was destroyed.

Montgomery and Crews (1998) examined 255 U.S. prison riots between 1900 and 1995, and found that 7 out of 10 riots did not involve hostages, most riots involved a small area of the prison that was taken over (as opposed to the whole prison), the inmates conceded within a one- to five-hour span after the riot began, and the reasons for the riot varied widely—likely because some of what was reported were triggering events whereas others were predisposing factors. Although riots still happen from time to time, more is known today about how to respond and, most important, how to prevent riots from occurring in the first place. Figure 8–18 lists all the practical methods that prisons utilize to prevent prison riots, which include consistent and fair rule enforcement, quality food, open lines of communication, and continuous staff training. Clearly, prison staff play an important role in setting the tone and reducing tension and potential violence in the prison environment by treating inmates and other staff professionally and with respect (Trammel & Rundle, 2015).

- Consistent and fair rule enforcement by staff
- Adequate ratios of both treatment and security staff per inmate
- Quality food
- Vigilance for abrupt changes in prisoner or staff behavior (inmates requesting transfers, staff who call in sick)
- "No hostage" policy—administrators will not negotiate if hostages are taken
- Riot plan and continuous training
- Open lines of communication among management, staff, and inmates (decreases rumors)
- Good classification system

FIGURE 8–18 **Preventing Prison Riots.**

Decreasing Violence Through the Inmate Subculture

The Resolve to Stop the Violence Project (RSVP) began in a San Francisco jail to decrease violence among prisoners with a history of street violence or institutional misconduct. RSVP is different from most programs in that it changes the institutional subculture of violence within one dorm through peer mentoring, direct and consistent staff supervision, and a race/ethnic composition that reflects the composition of program participants. RSVP is known as a peer-mentoring program because it uses more senior-level clients as change agents for newer participants and also focuses on changing the *institutional culture* that permeates the problem.

The second main component in RSVP is its restorative justice concepts that aim to bring about victim empathy, repair the harm done to others, and repair harm done to the inmates themselves. Part of behavioral change in RSVP mandates that the offender apologize to people he or she has hurt or victimized. Exposure to the program is for 12 hours per day for 6 days per week. The length of stay is dependent largely on the inmate's sentence, but it averages 165 days (most range from 2 to 6 months).

RSVP has support from community groups including the District Attorney's Office, the Probation Department, domestic violence shelters, and other victim advocate groups. The community groups developed concrete ways that violent offenders convicted of domestic violence, robbery, assault, rape, and terrorist threats can take responsibility for their actions and restore the harm they caused to their victims, their own families, and the larger community.

The first way is that as inmates progress through the program, each inmate is expected to take on a greater leadership role with newcomers. The senior-status inmates confront newcomers about their violent behavior in a controlled group setting and help them to recognize how their early gender socialization, such as suppressing their feelings and expressing a tough macho image, has contributed to their anger problems.

The second phase is victim impact, in which victims of violent crime describe in vivid detail how that crime

McClatchy-Tribune/Tribune Content Agency LLC/Alamy Stock Photo

has devastated their lives. This phase also allows the inmates to begin to reflect on how they have been victimized and witnessed violence in their own lives. The third phase involves artistic expression through a one-act play that each inmate writes that represents a traumatic incident that led him or her to become a violent person. The play is performed by inmates, and could have alternate endings. The final step is the continued participation in group sessions for one year after returning to the community. Since the program began, violent incidents in the rest of the jail have decreased because the predatory inmates are transferred to the program dorm. As program duration increases from 8 weeks to 16 weeks, rates of recidivism significantly decrease when the RSVP group is compared to a group not exposed to RSVP. Over 4,000 offenders have participated, and 87% of participants have *not* been rearrested for another violent offense.

References: 1. Lee, B., & Gilligan, J. (2005). The resolve to stop violence project: Transforming an in-house culture of violence through a jail-based programme. Journal of Public Health, 27(2), 149–155. 2. WABC-TV/DT. (2008, June 10). RSVP program helps inmates with anger. Eyewitness News, WABC, New York. Retrieved from http://abclocal.go.com/wabc/story?section=news/ local&id=6197063.

RSVP provides hope for change, but consider the following questions:

1. What characteristics do peer-mentoring programs (such as therapeutic communities for drug addicts and RSVP for violent offenders featured here) share in common?
2. Can you think of any challenges with the use of peer-mentoring programs?
3. What other programs could be modeled after RSVP to change other undesirable behaviors in the prisoner subculture?

Discuss the evolution of prison norms and the changes in mainstream prison culture.

Prisoners are primarily young men who lack skills and education. Women account for a disproportionately small group of offenders compared to men, but are still growing at a greater rate. Non-U.S. citizens and aliens, detained in special ICE units, now comprise one out of four federal prisoners. The norms and values of the inmate subculture are the result of a combination of losses inherent in prison conditions and importation of street norms and behaviors that represent the code of the streets. The elements of prison life that define the incarceration experience include socialization, the inmate code, language, group membership, working a job, disciplinary reports, and involvement in the sub rosa economic system.

1. Why do prisoners tend to come from impoverished communities, and why do they lack education?

2. How would a new prisoner best learn the ropes of prison life without getting victimized in the process?

3. Are there ways that staff members can influence or change the inmate subculture? If so, how? If not, why not?

4. Which theory (deprivation or importation) best explains the sub rosa economy?

5. Which theory (deprivation or importation) best explains women's play families? Why?

disproportionate When the group under study has a substantially greater or lesser percentage than exists in the larger population.

Bureau of Prisons (BOP) Where federal prisoners go when they have violated an incarcerable federal offense.

prisonization The process by which the prisoners learn the norms of life in prison.

inmate subculture A society with its own norms and values defined by inmates with the most power and influence.

Big House A maximum-security penitentiary with a convict subculture, lasting from the early 1800s until about 1980.

total institution A regimented facility that is physically separate from the larger society and meets the survival needs of its occupants.

deprivation model Assumes that prison culture developed out of the pains of imprisonment through adaptations that prisoners make to circumvent these losses.

importation model Assumes that prison life is an extension of street life of marginalized people from impoverished communities who dominate the prison.

inmate code A system of unwritten rules that directs inmate behavior.

prison argot or "prison-proper" The language, slang, and physical gestures used to communicate meaning in prison.

players Prisoners who embrace mainstream prison culture that values manipulating and intimidating others.

squares Inmates who oppose mainstream prison culture by being well behaved and who take advantage of every self-improvement program they can to keep themselves busy. Also known as *bootlickers*.

snitches Inmates who are targeted by predatory inmates because they have passed along information to staff that has gotten another inmate in trouble. Also known as *player haters*.

punks Inmates who are targeted by predatory inmates because they are perceived as physically or mentally weak and afraid to fight back.

fish A first-time inmate who is vulnerable because he or she has not yet been prisonized.

Explain the benefits and challenges of assigning jobs to incarcerated inmates.

Most prisoners are assigned to work a part-time maintenance job, and have the opportunity to attend school or other programs. Working life closely resembles outside society for only a chosen few prisoners who work full-time in prison industry. Prison-made goods are mainly sold in sheltered markets, but some private businesses partner with prisons to sell goods on the open market. A substantial number of prisoners use the sub rosa economy illicitly for personal profit and to obtain goods and services in an environment that lacks access to resources. More lucrative smuggling and movement of contraband is controlled by prison gangs.

1. Although prisoner labor should not compete with free-world labor, with all the private businesses relocating to other countries, isn't the relocation (e.g., to India and China) a greater threat than simply allowing U.S. prisoners that same opportunity?

2. What would happen if our government increased the number of jurisdictions that could have a private factory inside a prison from 50, across the whole United States, to 500?

3. Would you support paying all inmates a wage for their work, and then deducting that money for rent, utilities, and paying restitution? Debate the pros and cons of this policy.

4. If it is known that stealing and other workplace deviance exist in prisoner jobs, then why have prisoners work at all?

5. How can common illicit behaviors—such as loaning, gambling, extortion, and running commissary stores—be minimized?

6. How much illicit behavior is tolerated simply because officers are so outnumbered by inmates?

institutional maintenance Unskilled jobs that inmates are assigned in order to assist with daily prison operations (food preparation, laundry, cleaning).

trustys Minimum-security-level inmates who earn this status through not causing behavioral problems.

agricultural work Outdoor fieldwork jobs involving prisoners' growing crops and raising livestock; prevalent in southern states.

prison industry A skilled job within the prison that provides inmates training while incarcerated (manufacturing, construction, auto repair, welding, etc.).

open market Prison-made products are sold, either by private companies or by the state, to prospective buyers.

sheltered market Restricts the sale of prison-made products only to other state and local government markets. Also known as *government or state-use models*.

free enterprise A private-sector entrepreneurial model of doing business.

sub rosa economy Underground economy based on negotiation and exchange of goods and services between prisoners without the use of cash.

commissary Snacks, hygiene items, and other items available for purchase at the prison store.

merchants Inmates who control scarce resources by running a prison store.

jailhouse lawyers Inmates who use their legal knowledge and skills to write writs and grievances, but who are not legally permitted to practice law.

contraband Forbidden items that compromise institutional safety and security.

crews Small cliques of prisoners who spend time together, but there is no initiation or formal alliances. Some crews can be networked and predatory, but they are more loosely associated and are not an institutional security threat.

Compare and contrast prison gangs and play families in terms of their structure, purpose, and management.

The social structure of men's prisons is built on crews and gangs—many of which are racially and ethnically segregated. *Security threat groups* are widespread in men's prisons and have a formalized structure and constitution with rigid rules. In some states, active STG leaders and members are segregated in an attempt to decrease prison violence. The social structure of women's prisons is less influenced by violence, gangs, and race/ethnicity. *Play families* reflect an informal structure built on bonding, social control, and economic assistance; they do not pose an institutional threat, so fewer attempts are made to control them.

1. Given what you know about the prisoner subculture and the limited freedoms of prison life, how can racial hostility in jails and prisons be realistically reduced?

2. Can prison gangs be abolished in prisons, or are they just too powerful?

3. Which strategies do you think are most effective in managing security threat groups?

4. Are play families problematic in women's prisons? If so, how? If not, why not?

state-raised youth Inmates who grew up in youth prisons and who tend to be more violent than the average prisoner.

security threat group (STG) An organized group whose activities are predatory and criminal and whose presence in a correctional institution/agency poses a real and imminent threat to the security and safety of staff and inmates.

paramilitary STG A prison gang with a formal and centralized hierarchical structure, a rigid division of labor, and a written constitution detailing penalties for disloyalty, and requiring membership for life.

regional cell STG A prison gang with a decentralized hierarchical structure that is authorized to act independently for the good of the entire group, but there is little coordination between cells.

play families Relationships among women prisoners that mimic the structure, terminology, and function of families in general society.

Discuss the incidence of sexual assault and violence in prisons.

Individual-level violence for men is most often caused by personality clashes, racial tensions, unpaid debts, sexual assault, and retaliation. Violence for women is caused most often by jealously, unreciprocated love, and sexual coercion/harassment. The PREA act was passed to further prevent inmates from getting sexually assaulted and harassed. Most acts of collective violence are classified as disturbances involving small groups of prisoners or security threat groups. Disturbances are different from riots in that they do not involve any intent to take over a prison. Riots have the intent of prisoners taking over the control of a prison.

1. What forms of individual-level violence do you see as most problematic and why?

2. Discuss how the following three policies for *staff* would or would not reduce prisoner sexual assault in prisons on their own merit:
   a. Provide staff training on sexual assault
   b. Mandate staff intervention for sexual assault victims
   c. Encourage staff to consistently enforce the rules for predatory inmates

3. Discuss how the following three policies for *prisoners* would or would not reduce sexual assault in prisons on their own merit:
   a. Provide prisoner training on sexual assault
   b. Provide condoms to inmates
   c. Increase conjugal visitation

4. Can disturbances lead to riots, or are they completely different events?

5. How can prison riots be decreased or prevented?

deliberate indifference When officers know about a situation and fail to take action to prevent it.

voluntary lockdown When prisoners refuse to leave their cells.

disturbance An altercation involving three or more inmates resulting in official action, but where staff control of the facility is maintained.

prison riot A situation involving a large number of inmates making a forcible attempt to take control of a sizable area of the prison for a substantial amount of time.

predisposing factors Underlying conditions that occur over an extended period of time and provide the foundation for a riot.

triggering event One or several specific events that spark a riot.

Additional Links

Visit the YouTube website at **www.youtube.com/watch?v=PAS4uSDJe9k&feature=relmfu** and watch National Geographic's "First-Time in Prison: Learning the Ropes." (3 minutes)

Visit the YouTube website to see Lockup Raw's (2012) footage on the inmate code of conduct (9 minutes) **https://www.youtube.com/watch?v=DRsy1a4K8Wo.**

Visit the YouTube website to view a 9-minute video of Lockup's Raw footage of how prisoner sexual relationships differ by gender **https://www.youtube.com/watch?v=iczUVzrEbDI.**

Visit the YouTube website at **www.youtube.com/watch?v=uvcMvn9azxc** and watch how prison commissary is used in the sub rosa economy (National Geographic—3 minutes).

Visit the YouTube website at **https://www.youtube.com/watch?v=zJd2oClnGYs.**

Visit the YouTube website at **www.youtube.com/watch?v=PrZx2YdZFOk** and watch "The MS-13 Gang from El Salvador" documentary (60 minutes).

Visit the YouTube website at **www.youtube.com/watch?v=vRMq0umehWk&feature=related** and watch the "Nuestra Familia Prison Gang" video (age-appropriate video that users must sign in to watch).

Visit the YouTube website at **https://www.youtube.com/watch?v=sBjxzZmyoy0** for debriefing from gangs.

Visit the YouTube website at **https://www.youtube.com/watch?v=HDAelT3K5w4** and view the 29-minute video about the RSVP violence reduction program in correctional facilities (featured as a case study at the end of the chapter) entitled "Visionaries with Sam Waterston: Resolve to Stop the Violence."

Visit the National Correctional Industries Association at **www.nationalcia.org** and click on the "News" section to see "CI videos" of all the prisoner-made goods: **http://www.nationalcia.org/ci-videos-and-studies**.

9

Special Correctional Populations

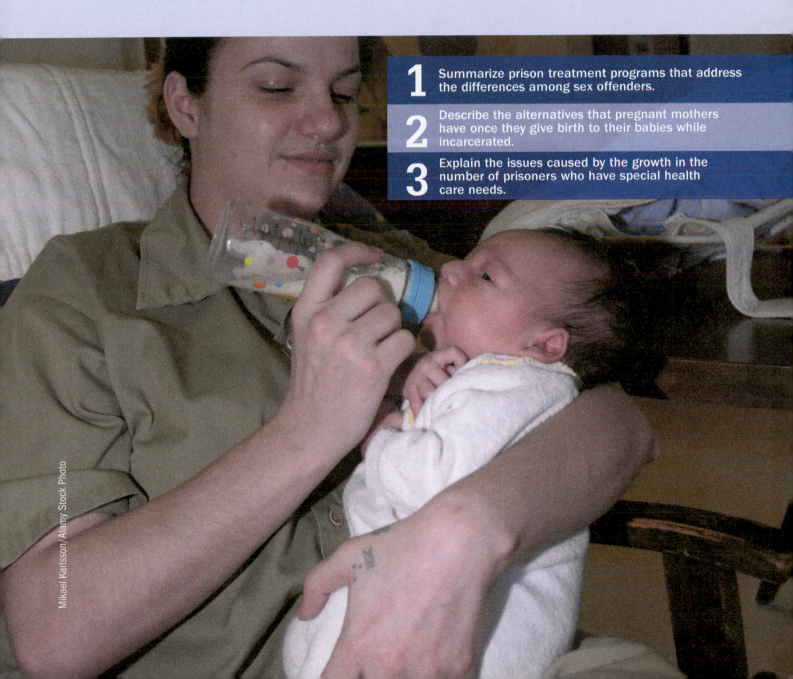

1 Summarize prison treatment programs that address the differences among sex offenders.

2 Describe the alternatives that pregnant mothers have once they give birth to their babies while incarcerated.

3 Explain the issues caused by the growth in the number of prisoners who have special health care needs.

WAS THE SENTENCE APPROPRIATE FOR THIS STUDENT FOR A FIRST-TIME MISDEMEANOR SEX OFFENSE?

Owen Labrie was looking forward to his upcoming graduation from St. Paul's, an elite private preparatory school in New Hampshire. As captain of the soccer team, Labrie was a well-known and popular student. He was looking forward to attending Harvard University in the fall on a scholarship. On the surface, the 18-year-old had everything going for him. However, Labrie's Harvard plans and scholarship were cancelled when he was accused of raping a 15-year-old classmate. Labrie took his case to a jury trial. At the trial, the jury heard about a twisted tradition at St. Paul's that Labrie and his friends called "senior salute," which involved high school senior males engaging in sex with younger female classmates before graduation. Labrie posted his list of sexual conquests on social media and used derogatory terms to refer to his conquests. Using the computer to communicate, he attempted to lure a fellow classmate. When the female victim, age 15, initially turned him down, he referred to her in an angry message as a "slut" and "dumb cum-bucket" (Bidgood, 2015). He later convinced the same victim to go with him to the rooftop of a school building and they engaged in sexual intercourse, which Labrie boasted about on social media but later denied at the trial (and which the victim said was nonconsensual). Although Labrie was acquitted of rape, he was found guilty of misdemeanor sexual assault, endangering a child, and using a computer to lure a victim for sex. The victim

Jim Cole/AP Images

says she remains traumatized by the incident. Labrie was sentenced in October 2015 to one year of jail, followed by five years of probation. The judge acknowledged that intelligence and charisma were common traits of sexual predators. He was court ordered to complete a sex offender treatment program and register as a sex offender for life (Stevens, 2015).

DISCUSS **Do you think the judge's sentence was appropriate under the circumstances? Why or why not?**

▶ Treatment Programs in Prison

One of the main purposes of the corrections system is rehabilitation, which was described in Chapter 2 as helping offenders to understand how they ended up in prison and to motivate them to change their attitudes and behavior through self-improvement and/or treatment programs. There are many interpersonal challenges that offenders face and just as many paths to achieve rehabilitation. For example, involvement in religion and spiritual groups not only assists in adjusting to prison during incarceration, but it provides mental and emotional strength and hope for the future (Dye, Aday, Farney, & Raley 2014). One of the prerequisites, however, is for offenders to admit that something within themselves needs to be changed and then to be open to redefining what those new values and possibilities might be.

In-prison treatment programs based on cognitive behavioral interventions can reduce future recidivism between 20 and 30% within the general prisoner population (Landenberger & Lipsey, 2005). These interventions assume that thought patterns and feelings determine behavior and that identifying and changing **thinking errors** will ultimately change

an offender's behavior. Examples of criminal thinking errors are presented in Figure 9–1 and include blaming others, seeing oneself as a victim, and use of intimidation or threats as a way of controlling others. The key in the treatment process is for the offender to admit how thinking errors resulted in failure to accept responsibility and in dysfunctional habits, addictions, and criminal behaviors. Other principles of becoming socially competent are presented in Figure 9–2 and include considering the consequences before acting, including how one's actions will affect others. Psychologists who work with offenders describe them as emotionally and cognitively immature. Exposure to thinking errors is a starting point for change, but true change comes from the individual's genuine willingness to become a better person.

Some treatment programs address offender needs that require specialized treatment, attention, and/or medical care. These specialized treatment programs can include offenders with mental illness, which was

LEARNING OUTCOMES 1 Summarize prison treatment programs that address the differences among sex offenders.

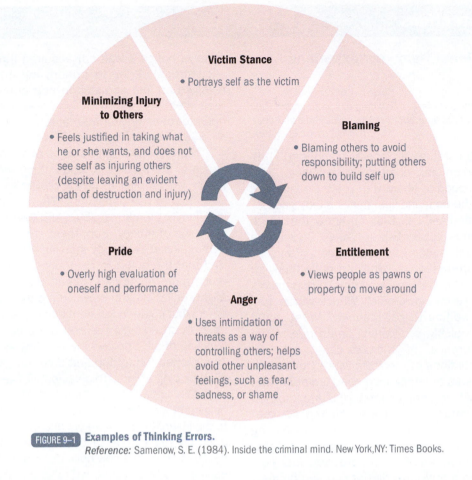

FIGURE 9–1 Examples of Thinking Errors.
Reference: Samenow, S. E. (1984). Inside the criminal mind. New York, NY: Times Books.

fully covered in Chapter 6, so it will not be covered here. In this chapter, we address sex offenders, pregnant and parenting inmates, offenders with chronic or terminal health conditions, and aging prisoners.

▶ Treatment That Addresses Sex Offending

One of the principles of evidence-based practices (EBP) is that treatment interventions should target higher-risk offenders and behaviors most closely associated with criminal activity. Sex offenders meet both of these criteria. Furthermore, mandatory

I will recognize my own patterns of thinking, feeling, and perceiving.
I will differentiate my healthy thoughts, feelings, and perceptions from my dysfunctional ones.
Through repetitive modelling, role playing, and rehearsal, I will learn how to change the dysfunctional thought processes by stopping them when they occur.
I will stop and consider the consequences before acting.
I resolve to consider various alternatives of responding and how my behavior may impact someone else.

FIGURE 9–2 Evidence-Based Practices—Applying the Techniques.
Principles of Becoming Socially Competent
Source: From "Probation and Cognitive Skills" by Frederick R Chavaria in Federal Probation, Volume 61, Number 2, pp: 57-60. Published by United States Courts, © 1997.

polygraph testing as part of the treatment makes sex offender treatment unique from all other types. In this section, the antisocial attitudes, thinking errors, and treatment of different types of sex offenders are discussed.

Sex offenses are inappropriate sexual acts against children or sexual acts against a victim's will. The three main types of sexual offenders are child molesters, incest offenders, and rapists (Harris, 2004). Victims of sex offenses can be children or adults—in both cases, victims more often already know their perpetrator, rather than it being a stranger whom they've never previously met. Roughly one-third of all sex offenses are reported to the police, based on comparing arrests and convictions with self-reported information gathered from polygraphs of known sex offenders. Sex offenses are more often reported when the perpetrator is a stranger than when the perpetrator and the victim know each other.

Sex offenders are a very heterogeneous group, each having different motivations, thinking patterns, targeted victims, and personality styles. Three typical profiles of sex offenders (child molesters, incest offenders, and rapists) are depicted in Figure 9–3. Child molesters require resolution for their own victimization, as well as intense behavioral modification to change their focus from children to adults. Child molesters seem to start their deviant sexual behavior as adolescents, so they have an earlier age of onset. Incest offenders are the most socially competent and secretive, and many of them have children of their own, so they are the most difficult to identify.

Voices in Corrections

What did you learn from your experience in prison?

Dr. Daniel S. Murphy is Professor Emeritus at Appalachian State University. He serves as a board member for Federal Cure, a prisoner advocacy group.

Formerly, my master status was federal prisoner #03439-090. Yes, I've lived on both sides of the razor wire. Thus, I am uniquely equipped to share with you the reality, the duality of prison: the bad, and yes, the rarefied "good."

Prison is spelled H-E-L-L. Did you know that there are 86,400 seconds in twenty-four hours? Believe me it's true. When each second ticks off a unit of misery, one becomes acutely familiar with the daily time-line ("turning calendars" equals marking time). Then there's the things that time cannot predict. What's worse, getting stabbed, or waiting to get stabbed? What would you prefer, dying quickly, or awaiting death due to the "deliberate indifference" of "medical care" (not) provided within the confines of the razor wire? Other problems include the loss of family, increased isolation, and hunger. Ninety-five percent of men who are married when they enter prison are divorced by the five-year mark. The isolation prisoners endure is from feeling completely alone even though surrounded by thousands; can you imagine? Furthermore, you feel constantly hungry with a repetitive diet of rice and beans.

This said, is it all bad? Mostly. But, there are those incredible rays of enlightened hope. Those moments of prophetic realization: my epiphany! My count of conviction was medical marijuana. In truth, I was addicted to money (though it was not acquired through the sale of illicit drugs). Prior to prison, my myopic world-view revolved around acquisition and amassment of fiscal resources. To this end, I was a successful owner and operator of an environmental law consulting firm. I lived for $$$$; what a fool I was.

The most important outcome of my incarceration experience is that I came to understand many of the things I most valued prior to prison proved to be meaningless. Does money buy happiness? No. I came to understand that family, friends, laughter, and love so far outweighed the value of money; truly, there is no comparison. Thus, I am an incredibly happy starving professor who has realized that the quest to contribute to a better world is a much more admirable pursuit than amassing the "all mighty dollar." Prison provided me the opportunity to help others, but not for any recompense: just the opportunity to help. In so doing, I realized the greatest (unexpected) blessing of all: I helped myself grow as a human being. This showed me for the first time that the greatest joy of all is helping others. This valued life's-lesson determined my future. I now live what I learned. My life revolves around helping others, doing my best to make a positive change to the insanity we call prison, and striving for excellence in each pursuit I undertake. Think about it dear reader, because of prison I now have this opportunity to challenge each of you to do your best, to go out and make it a good day, to contribute to the improvement of what we call humanity, to smile at yourself and help others to laugh.

Source: From Corrections: A Contemporary Introduction by Leanne F Alarid and Philip L Reichel. Copyright © 2008 by Pearson Education.

Child Molesters	Incest Offenders	Rapists
Low self-esteem, socially awkward as children, not married	Socially competent and most resembles other law-abiding citizens	Have experienced violence and/or sexual abuse in the past
Were likely sexually victimized as a child and did not resolve or cope	Married/cohabitating and has children or step-children	Share similar characteristics to other non sexual violent offenders
Earlier age of onset (molesting starts as an adolescent)	60% are adults and 40% are adolescents when offending first occurs	Later age of onset
Highest use of deviant or child pornography	Most secretive and most difficult to identify; victim least likely to report	Most likely (compared to incest and CM) to abuse substances

FIGURE 9–3 **Three Typical Sex Offender Profiles.** *Reference:* Harris, D. A. (2004). A typological approach to exploring pathways for rapists, child molesters, and incest offenders(Unpublished master's thesis). University of Maryland.

Rapists have typically experienced previous violence and/or sexual abuse themselves, but have a later age of onset. People who commit rape need help with managing their anger, chemical dependency, and choosing nonviolent responses. Treatment approaches must reflect these differences in offender types. Sex offender treatment programs use multiple regimens that include cognitive behavioral therapy to address thinking errors and minimization, victim empathy, polygraph to avoid denial and aid in divulging previous sex offenses, and **aversive conditioning**. Medications such as **antiandrogens** or **selective serotonin reuptake inhibitors** may be used along with therapy (Harris, 2004).

Treating sex offenders in a separate therapeutic environment is very important to reduce anxiety and threats to one's safety that would arise if sex offenders were housed within the larger prisoner population. A therapeutic environment is one that promotes the most significant change in the shortest possible time frame (Blagden, Winder, & Hames, 2016). Finally, how staff relate to sex offenders is extremely important to achieving lasting behavioral change. Understanding criminal thinking errors, requiring polygraphs and drug testing, and disapproving of the behavior—not the person—is important to reducing recidivism for this group of offenders. Perhaps Robert Johnson (2002, p. 12) summarized it best when he said, "Yet whatever criminals do—and criminals do some terrible things—they remain human beings, however miserable or flawed. . . . Prisons, then, pose difficult tests of our values because the conditions of our prisons are a measure of our capacity to recognize and respect the humanity of offenders, people we fear and hate." Figure 9–4 asks you to consider whether sex offenders can be rehabilitated.

The Static-99 is known as a valid risk assessment instrument that measures the risk of reoffending for adult sex offenders. The assessment is based on current age, prior criminal history, living arrangements, and preferred victim. Sex offenders who began illegal sexual activity as an adolescent, who are currently between 18 and 30 years old, who lived less than 2 years with another adult in an intimate relationship and targeted male victims who were unknown to them had the highest risk of recidivism compared to other sex offenders (Hanson, Harris, Helmus, & Thornton, 2014). How much does risk level matter? And, can sex offenders be successfully treated? Researchers seem to think that completion of cognitive behavioral treatment significantly reduces later rearrest: "For each additional month spent in the TC [the sex offender therapeutic community], inmates increase their chances of success upon release by one percent" (Lowden et al., 2003, p. 17). To answer the question about whether risk level mattered, 7,740 sex offenders were tracked over a 20-year period of time. Recidivism for low-risk offenders (older, few previous convictions, and targeted females who were known to them) consistently ranged between 1 and 5%. Recidivism for high-risk offenders was at 22% for the first five years, and then decreased down to 4.2% over ten years (Hanson et al., 2014). For some sex offenders, then, treatment can work, and recidivism seems to vary greatly according to risk level.

FIGURE 9–4 *Evidence-Based Practices—Does It Work?*
Can Sex Offenders Be Rehabilitated?

Think About It...

pefostudio5/
Shutterstock

Polygraphs for Treatment? Most sex offender treatment programs require participants to undergo polygraphs to acknowledge all prior sex offenses and do not guarantee immunity against prosecution for such confessions. Prisoners who refuse to cooperate are removed from the program and reclassified to a maximum-security unit with reduced privileges. A Kansas prisoner challenged the polygraphs, saying that they violated his Fifth Amendment privilege against self-incrimination. The U.S. Supreme Court ruled in favor of the prison system's confessionary requirement, citing that accepting responsibility is the first step in the rehabilitation process and that the program was developed for treatment, not for law enforcement or investigatory purposes (Warden v. Lile, 2002). Based on the court's ruling, should polygraphs be used with other types of offenders, such as with domestic violence offenders who attend battering treatment, or with drug offenders in substance-abuse treatment programs?

▶ *Pregnant Women and Parents of Minor Children*

Over half of all male prisoners and 75% of female prisoners have dependent children under the age of 18, but just over half of these parents provided primary financial support before they were arrested. The parents who could not provide financial support were likely to be homeless or suffer from mental health or medical problems. According to Table 9–1, mothers in prison were more likely to have experienced past physical or sexual abuse, medical problems, and homelessness than were incarcerated fathers (Glaze & Maruschak, 2008).

All people who are incarcerated, particularly parents with young children, miss important milestones in their children's lives or in the lives of other family members—births, baby's first steps, first days of school, birthdays, proms, graduations, weddings, and even funerals. Incarceration is particularly difficult for single-parent caretakers who become dismayed and overcome by feelings of failure and guilt at not being there for their children. The children and their nonincarcerated caregivers are also affected when the family support system is disrupted (Turanovic, Rodriguez, & Pratt, 2012).

Prisoners are encouraged to remain in contact with family or friends by writing letters/sending cards, or calling collect on the phone, but prisoners on disciplinary status may not make phone calls or receive personal visits (Pierce, 2015). According to Table 9–1, mothers were generally more likely to keep in

TABLE 9–1

BACKGROUNDS OF PRISONERS WHO WERE PARENTS AND LIVED WITH MINOR CHILDREN

	Fathers	Mothers
Has another family member ever been incarcerated?	48.9%	58.4%
Did you ever experience physical or sexual violence?	16.1%	59.7%
Were you homeless in the year before your arrest?	4.0%	8.5%
Any substance dependence/abuse?	65.0%	63.6%
Any current medical problems?	39.7%	50.0%
Contact/Communicate with Your Children While Incarcerated?		
Yes, at least once a week	38.5%	55.7%
Yes, once a month or less	39.6%	29.3%
No contact/communication	11.9%	15.0%

Source: Glaze, L. E., & Maruschak, L. M. (2008). Parents in prison and their minor children (NCJ 222984). Washington, DC:U.S. Department of Justice.

contact with family members. Having contact with outside family members can be a double-edged sword. Although it gives some prisoners something to hold on to, others find it more bearable to do time if they cut off all family ties while incarcerated (Crawley & Sparks, 2006).

For prisoners who look forward to visits, visits are stressful on family because of the long distance, the cost, the lack of transportation, and the painful reminder of seeing their family members locked up. For example, for one person to take a bus round-trip to a prison located 250 miles away, and to be there for the predefined visiting hours, the visitor needs to leave around 5:00 AM, with needed $150–$200 for transportation, food, and any gifts. Visits are also stressful on inmates, from the anticipation leading up to the visit, to the depression that immediately follows (Pierce, 2015). While maintaining contact with outside family members can provide emotional and instrumental support (Barrick, Lattimore, & Visher, 2014), visitation has a small to modest effect in reducing later recidivism for inmates who are serving shorter sentences (Mears, Cochran, Siennick, & Bales, 2012). Some prisons are now experimenting with "virtual visits" (similar to Skype) that allow children to see their parents on a computer screen from home while communicating with them on the telephone.

Being Pregnant While Incarcerated

A related problem with lack of contact between parents and their outside family is infants born to incarcerated mothers. Between 6 and 10% of women enter prison pregnant, but this is a conservative estimate, as only half of all state prisons screen for pregnancy at intake. Pregnant inmates are definitely in need of special care, so they are transferred to a facility that is located near a hospital, and one where they can receive a prenatal diet. Once she is in labor, the pregnant inmate is transported to a regular hospital off facility grounds to have her baby. A correctional officer remains with her the entire time, and in some states, she may be chained to the bed, even during labor. Shackling prison inmates during labor is a safety hazard to the women and their fetuses, and the American Civil Liberties Union (ACLU) is attempting to encourage states to pass policies that ban this practice (National Women's Law Center, 2010). The new mother may only get from a few minutes to a few hours to hold her baby, depending on its health. The mother is transported back to the jail or prison the same day after giving birth to minimize the security costs.

Once the baby is ready to leave the hospital, prisons expect a temporary guardian or relative to pick up the newborn within 24 hours. If family members are unavailable or unwilling to accept the temporary custody and care of an infant born to a mother in jail or prison, the infant becomes a ward of the state (Sharp, 2003). Many incarcerated women fear losing parental rights and therefore encourage family members to take care of their children. Unfortunately, the fear of parental termination may result in a family placement that is unsafe and abusive for children (Sharp, 2003). Foster parents can be a short-term option, but in some states, there is a limit on the length of time a child can be in foster care before permanently terminating the rights of the biological parents.

The United States is one of the few developed countries that routinely separate children from their mothers upon incarceration based on two assumptions:

1. That incarceration is supposed to punish offenders by limiting freedoms and taking away what is cherished, and that includes family

2. That a convicted mother or father must be a bad parent

Research shows that a young infant who is unable to bond with his or her mother or father during the first two years of life suffers lifelong attachment difficulties—a situation that routinely occurs when the infant and mother are permanently separated within a few hours of birth. Compared with children who do not have an incarcerated parent,

LEARNING OUTCOMES **2** Describe the alternatives that pregnant mothers have once they give birth to their babies while incarcerated.

children who have at least one parent behind bars are more likely to experience:

- Higher levels of anxiety and depression
- Poorer academic performance
- Significantly greater risk of committing a crime before age 18
- Significantly greater chance of continuing crime patterns into adulthood (Dallaire, Zemen, & Thrash, 2014; Hahl, Alarid, Harris, & Firestone, 2016)

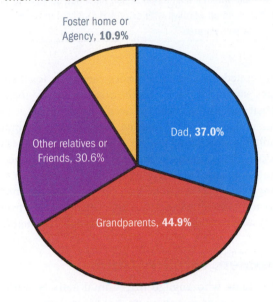

When MOM Goes to Prison, Caretakers of Children are:

Foster home or Agency, **10.9%**

Dad, **37.0%**

Other relatives or Friends, 30.6%

Grandparents, **44.9%**

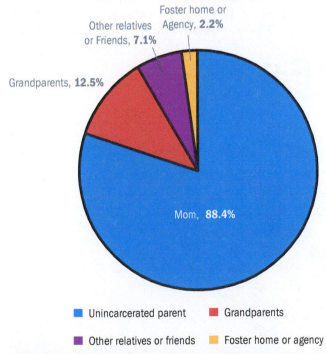

When DAD goes to Prison, Caretakers of Children are:

Foster home or Agency, **2.2%**

Other relatives or Friends, **7.1%**

Grandparents, **12.5%**

Mom, **88.4%**

- ■ Unincarcerated parent
- ■ Grandparents
- ■ Other relatives or friends
- ■ Foster home or agency

FIGURE 9–5 **Living Arrangements of Children of Incarcerated Parents by Gender.**
Source: Glaze, L. E., & Maruschak, L. M. (2008). Parents in prison and their minor children (NCJ 222984). Washington, DC:U.S. Department of Justice.

Figure 9–5 shows who takes care of dependent children when parents are incarcerated. When dad goes to prison, most children are raised by their mothers. However, when mom goes to prison, *her* parents are more likely to raise their grandchildren more often than the children's biological father. Some extended family members may not be able to afford adequate care. There is also the fear that some children will experience the physical or sexual abuse that their mother (or father) experienced when they were younger. But are young children better off living *with* their mothers when their mothers are incarcerated?

Prison Nurseries

Prison nurseries are separate facilities inside prison where each pair of infants and mothers must qualify (mothers for their offense and babies up to age five). During the day, the babies play with each other and each mom is responsible to watch her child. At night, the infant sleeps in a crib in the mother's cell. Table 9–2 lists the benefits and the concerns of prison nurseries. The strongest argument in favor of keeping mothers with their newborns is that the mother's attachment and sense of responsibility for her baby teaches her how to become a better parent. However, there is no scientific evidence that prison nurseries reduce recidivism after release. A case study of a prison nursery is described at the end of the chapter.

▶ Health Care and Medical Issues

When we incarcerate individuals, we remove the opportunity for inmates to care for themselves, so the system takes on the full responsibility for the health and welfare of every prisoner. As a result, the government must make available to inmates a level of medical care that is reasonably designed to meet routine and emergency health care needs, including physical ills, dental care, and psychiatric care. However, the prevailing principle of less eligibility suggests that jail and prison conditions must be more severe than conditions for law-abiding people. Regarding medical care, jails and prisons are not only obligated to provide medical care for incarcerated offenders, but staff can also be held legally accountable for ignoring medical conditions based on a standard of "deliberate indifference" (*Estelle* v. *Gamble*, 1976). However, inmates do *not* have the right to better medical care than free-world citizens, and the courts restrict the recourse that inmates have for inadequate medical care.

When offenders enter correctional facilities, most need immediate testing and medical attention because they have neglected their health while living on the streets and they have engaged in lifestyles that may put them at risk, such as intravenous drug use and unprotected sex. The number one issue that is linked to rising costs of incarceration is the growth in the number of prisoners who have special health care needs (Maruschak, Berzofsky, & Unangst, 2015). Jails and prisons provide all the basic health care services that an average clinic does, including examinations, diagnostic testing, and treatment. As prisoners serve longer sentences, they may contract communicable diseases and terminal illnesses, and an increasing number of

TABLE 9–2   BENEFITS AND CONCERNS ABOUT PRISON NURSERIES

Benefits of Prison Nurseries	Concerns About Prison Nurseries
Biological parent retains custody	Potential liability concerns within the facility
Child establishes a bond with his or her mother	No scientific evidence that prison nurseries lower recidivism compared to women with dependent children who do not get to take advantage of the prison nursery
Mother learns parental responsibility, positive reinforcement, and how to respond to negative behavior appropriately (consistent and assertive, but not aggressive)	The welfare of a child is the main responsibility of child protective services—it is an additional responsibility that is beyond the scope of prisons
Allows inmates to serve as positive role models for their children and each other	Questionable whether children in prison nurseries benefit significantly more than children who live with extended family or in foster care while parents are incarcerated

them have aged and now require special care. More specific treatments and procedures requiring surgery may necessitate a supervised trip to a hospital outside the prison walls. The best indicator of the types of medical needs that prisoners have is to examine causes of death. According to Figure 9–6, most prisoners die from cancer, heart disease, or other illness (such as stroke, diabetes, cirrhosis, or kidney malfunction). Only a small number of prisoner deaths are ruled as accidental, suicides, homicides, or overdoses from illegal drugs or homemade alcohol.

Due to increased health care costs and the belief that inmates should share responsibility for their own health, nearly 40 states deduct less than $20 from inmates for each infirmary visit, or a co-pay is deducted on an annual basis to curb rising health care costs (Ollove, 2015;). Charging inmates medical co-payments for requesting doctor visits while

LEARNING OUTCOMES 3 Explain the issues caused by the growth in the number of prisoners who have special health care needs.

incarcerated reduces some health care costs for taxpayers, but critics say that it passes on the costs to family members who deposit money into the offender's account and it may cause some inmates to avoid seeking medical care for more serious conditions which may lead to worse health outcomes (Fisher & Hatton, 2010). Indigent inmates who request to see a doctor cannot be denied medical treatment, according to the court's ruling in *Estelle* v. *Gamble* (1976). Collecting medical fees adds administrative costs, but also deters inmates from abusing the system through visits for frivolous or false conditions.

Prisoners with HIV/AIDS

Individuals who engage in criminal activity are also more likely to engage in behaviors that place them at risk for HIV and other communicable diseases, such as intravenous drug use. Thus, it is no surprise that there is a disproportionately higher number of HIV-positive persons in correctional facilities—1.3%—compared with 0.4% of U.S. residents

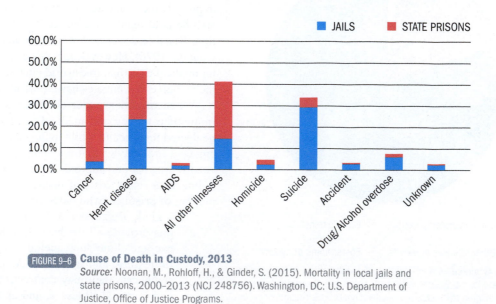

Cause of Death in Custody, 2013

FIGURE 9–6 Cause of Death in Custody, 2013
Source: Noonan, M., Rohloff, H., & Ginder, S. (2015). Mortality in local jails and state prisons, 2000-2013 (NCJ 248756). Washington, DC: U.S. Department of Justice, Office of Justice Programs.

outside of prison who are living with HIV or AIDS (Maruschak et al., 2015). The number has steadily declined since the mid-1990s due primarily to prevention efforts and improvements in care for HIV/AIDS, such as protease inhibitors and antiretroviral therapies.

HIV-infected inmates live among the general population so that they have equal opportunities and will not be treated differently or discriminated against. In 2013, an Alabama middle court judge ordered the Alabama Department of Corrections to completely desegregate all prisoners with HIV and remove all medical information from nonmedical files (Sarfo, 2013). At this time, only South Carolina continues to keep known HIV-positive prisoners separate from the general prisoner population. This is despite objections by the ACLU and possible legal consequences by the Justice Department (American Civil Liberties Union, 2010). Once HIV-infected inmates contract AIDS (about one out of four HIV-positive prisoners), they are segregated from the general prison population for their own safety—separate housing is required to be away from airborne diseases prevalent among the general population.

Certain policies may be effective in lessening the spread of HIV/AIDS, including education, testing, notifying partners, and issuing protection supplies. Examples include the following:

- Many facilities provide education programs on how HIV is transmitted and how it progresses to AIDS.

- Testing inmates for HIV occurs at admission in 28 states, at release in 6 states, and upon request. After intake, additional testing is conducted on inmate request, by a court order, by clinical judgment, or for anyone who is involved in an incident that might increase his or her risk of exposure (Maruschak et al., 2015).

- Correctional officers are issued disposable gloves for pat searches and cell searches; some have one-way face shields for performing first aid on someone with breathing difficulties (Alarid, 2009).

- Inmates are issued bleach for cleaning living areas.

Treatment of Other Communicable Diseases

Besides HIV/AIDS, inmates are tested for other communicable diseases—including tuberculosis (TB), hepatitis B, hepatitis C, syphilis, and gonorrhea—at intake and treated if necessary. As with HIV/AIDS, many of these communicable diseases exist at greater rates in correctional facilities due to their link with intravenous drug use and unprotected sex. One reason that TB rates are five times higher inside jails is that TB spreads in places of confinement where crowded conditions and poor ventilation provide ideal conditions, and inmates move around the facility as well as transfer to other facilities. Thus, inmates with active TB must be quarantined in an airtight isolated room until the TB is no longer contagious. Although correctional facilities play an important role in the reduction of TB, recovering fully from TB takes from six to nine months, which is longer than most jail sentences—inmates with active TB are released from confinement before they complete the cycle. Releasees are

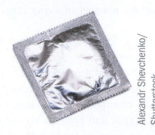

Alexandr Shevchenko/Shutterstock

Think About It...

Should Condoms Be Issued to Inmates? Sexual activity is prohibited within institutions, so providing condoms places prison officials in a predicament of approving conduct that violates prison rules. Advocates of condom distribution argue that sexual behavior is a fact of life, and prisons have an obligation to protect lives. Critics argue that condoms can also be used to pass contraband (swallowing balloons of drugs) or to fill with bodily fluids or excrement to throw at others. Should condoms be provided to all inmates, only to certain inmates at highest risk of HIV, or not at all? Defend your position.

provided with enough medication to finish the cycle, but they are no longer being supervised. For some people, the partially treated TB is still contagious and, over time, can become resistant to antibiotics (Parvez, Lobato, & Greifinger, 2010).

Hepatitis C is a virus that affects the liver and is spread primarily through injected drug use, unsafe sexual practices, and unsterile tattooing (Hellard, Aitken, & Hocking, 2007). A disproportionately high number of people with hepatitis C are arrested and incarcerated, making the rate of hepatitis C in confinement between 8 and 20 times higher than the rate in the general population. Between 23% and up to one-third of all prisoners test positive for hepatitis C (Maruschak et al., 2015). Chronic hepatitis C can be treated with antiviral medications at a cost of $7,000 to $20,000 per person for one cycle, with a success rate of 30 to 40% (Horowitz, 2014).

▶ Aging Prisoners

"Graying of U.S. prisoners" first became an issue in the mid-1980s as longer prison sentences for recidivists and reductions in the use of parole began expanding the number of inmates that remained. The National Institute of Corrections and most state prisons define an **aging prisoner** as being age 50 or over. Although this is considered "middle age" outside the prison walls, the stress of the prison experience, coupled with prisoners who led a fast life of drug use, poor health, and lack of preventive care prior to incarceration, seems to age individuals faster than their chronological age. Prisoners over the age of 50 are the fastest growing and most costly segment within the general prisoner population (Reimer, 2008). Older inmates now make up about 11% of the prisoner population, and their average cost per year is nearly $60,000, which is almost twice what it costs to incarcerate one younger prisoner per year (Horowitz, 2014). Unless changes are made, current protocol will continue to increase the number of aging inmates in prison in the coming decade.

Male prisoners over age 65 were interviewed about coping with their prison experience (Crawley & Sparks, 2006). Most were either first-timers or were at the other end of the spectrum as lifers. The older first-time felons reported being anxious and depressed by how prison disrupted their former lives, particularly the ones who had family and spouses on the outside. Lifers, or men who had spent many years in prison, had not been on the streets in so long that they lost touch with the outside world and doubted their own decision-making capabilities. At this stage of life, many prisoners reported thinking about getting medical help in the middle of the night if needed, and dying in prison. The prisoners who were most enthusiastic about release were the ones who had family waiting for them on the outside (Crawley & Sparks, 2006).

Studies have consistently shown that the vast majority of people age out of crime, which means that if and when they are released, the likelihood of continuing criminal behavior decreases as people get older. This is supported through data provided by the Illinois Department of Corrections. Older inmates are less likely to commit new offenses within three years after being released—3.6% recidivism for those 70–79 years old compared to 30% for prisoners under age 50 (Pupovac, 2011).

The number one concern of managing older prisoners is not violence or recidivism, but maintaining health. The special health needs of older prisoners cost about three times more than those of a younger inmate of average health. For example, the Illinois Department of Corrections spends about a third of its annual budget ($428 million) on aging prisoners (Pupovac, 2011). The situation in Illinois represents the situation all over the United States.

A decline in visual abilities and a loss of hearing may make the older offender more vulnerable to harm by the very structure of the prison, and it can cause depression and post-traumatic stress disorder and result in social isolation. Studies report that many older male prisoners exhibit signs of trauma, stress, and mental illness, and thus feel unsafe and vulnerable to attack by younger inmates (Haugebrook, Zgoba, Maschi, Morgen, & Brown, 2010). The physical condition and structure of many prisons are also cause for concern about physical safety. Prisons were, after all, designed for young, active inmates and have stairs in tiered cell blocks and long distances to walk from one place to the next. Possible options for housing aging prisoners are mainstreaming them completely with the general population, housing them separately at night, or completely separating older from younger prisoners in geriatric or chronic care prisons.

Geriatric prisons are separate facilities specifically designed for aging inmates with three or more chronic conditions, inmates with physical limitations, and/or inmates of any age who are terminally ill. In about half of all states, chronically ill prisoners are housed with or near aging prisoners because both groups have similar medical and dietary needs. These facilities are more like infirmaries, hospice care, or chronic care facilities that offer safety from predatory inmates. Geriatric prisons offer unique programming or services geared specifically toward this population of prisoners, who will not likely be employed (or employable) once they return to society. Thus, involvement in GED or occupational training is not offered. Instead, inmates in these facilities tend to care for each other instead of placing each other in jeopardy. Oxygen generators and wheelchairs are kept on hand, and medication time becomes as important as count time. Aging trustys complete the facility operation work, such as changing sheets, bedpans, laundry, cooking, and cleaning.

In light of high medical costs, the issue of early release of terminally ill prisoners from prison has received new attention. Many states and the Federal BOP have **compassionate release** or medical parole available on a case-by-case basis for inmates who are permanently incapacitated, those who have less than one year to live, and/or those who no longer pose an imminent danger to the community. Release must be made in most cases by the governor or a parole board, after a team of physicians makes a recommendation on the prisoner's medical condition. Currently, about 100 prisoners are released every year in this way (Reimer, 2008), but the hope is to expand the program by changing eligibility requirements. In 2016, Department of Justice Inspector General Michael Horowitz requested to the U.S. Sentencing Commission that the eligibility age be lowered from 65 to 50, and that the 10-year minimum be waived to allow more federal prisoners to become eligible (Horowitz, 2016). Table 9–3 considers the arguments in favor of and against having terminally ill prisoners released early on parole

TABLE 9–3 | SHOULD TERMINALLY ILL PRISONERS BE RELEASED ON PAROLE?

Arguments in Favor	Arguments Against
Cost savings realized with the same levels of care still offered in a community-based hospice	State prisons are shifting responsibility to Medicaid for an indigent prisoner's medical needs
The inmate is still on parole supervision	May go against victim's wishes
Chance of committing a new crime is extremely low	There is still a chance that a prisoner could feel well enough to commit a crime again
The prisoner's family could more easily visit and prepare for death	Interrupting some treatment regimens contributes to developing drug-resistant strains of bacteria/infectious diseases

or released to a community-based assisted-care living facility. Among the challenges is the problem of finding a nursing home that will accept someone with a criminal record. Another issue is re-enrolling former prisoners for Medicaid and Social Security benefits, which are automatically terminated when someone is incarcerated. Given that the re-enrollment period takes up to three months, some states have started "suspending" or temporarily freezing benefits which are easier to reinstate within a matter of weeks and do not require re-enrollment.

Prison Hospice

Hospices based inside prison are available for terminally ill prisoners whose sentences do not qualify them for medical parole or whose application was denied. The National Prison Hospice Association formed to address the large increase of AIDS-related deaths (Wright & Bronstein, 2007). Prison hospices operate similarly to community-based hospice services in that the inmates are provided with medication to manage pain; they are cared for by a team of nurses, social workers, dieticians, pharmacists, and clergy; and the environment resembles a secure hospital rather than a prison atmosphere. Some of the more unique volunteers are other able-bodied prisoners who are there to emotionally console dying prisoners when they have no family left or family members are unable or unwilling to visit. The correctional officers have respect for the care and companionship that they see as necessary to allow every person, no matter how they behaved on the streets, to die with dignity (Reimer, 2008; Wright & Bronstein, 2007).

Should Infants and Toddlers of Incarcerated Moms Be Raised in Prison?

New York's Bedford Hills opened the first prison nursery over a hundred years ago and remains the oldest operating prison nursery in the United States. Up to 29 mothers are selected if they have been convicted of a nonviolent offense and have no history of child abuse or neglect. Mothers can live with and raise their children for up to 18 months, or until the child reaches two years old—whichever occurs first. In an effort to emulate conditions in the real world, mothers return to work at the prison (or outside, if they are eligible for work release) six weeks after their babies are born (National Women's Law Center, 2010). Other inmates at the prison, who are specially trained and participate in parenting classes, may serve as caregivers. The program is thus inmate-centered, in that women prisoners teach each other about parenting. When they are not at work, the mothers assume full responsibility for their children (Kauffman, 2006). The parenting experience of most of the women is quite different from what they've ever experienced on the streets, because it is the first time they've been a parent while clean and sober.

From the early 1900s to the 1950s, most women's prisons had nurseries for the needs of babies born inside the facility. Except for Bedford Hills, all other nurseries had closed their doors by the 1970s due to litigation worries and concern for the effect it had on children. The mother/child bond during the first two years of an infant's life was important enough to convince several states to reinstitute prison nurseries programs once again (Byrne, 2006). New York expanded its nursery program across the street at Taconic Correctional Facility. Although 13 state departments of corrections claim to allow mothers access to a prison nursery, 3 allow stays up to one month, and 6 states allow infants and moms to live together in prison for up to 18 months (National Women's Law Center, 2010). Most prison nurseries limit the age of children to two or younger.

Scott Olson/Getty Images

Nurseries in women's prison raise two interesting issues:

1. What are the potential benefits for infants up to age two being raised by their mothers? What are the potential problems?
2. What are the potential benefits to mothers of raising a child while doing time? What are the potential problems?

LEARNING OUTCOMES 1

Summarize prison treatment programs that address the differences among sex offenders.

Rehabilitation requires offenders to admit that something within themselves needs to be changed and then to be open to redefining what those new values and possibilities might be. Some treatment programs address offender needs that require specialized treatment, such as for sex offenders. Other treatment programs prepare inmates for community reentry by teaching new skill sets.

Sex offenders are a heterogeneous group with different motivations, thinking patterns, targeted victims, and personality styles. The three main types are rapists, child molesters, and incest offenders.

Sex offender treatment programs use multiple regimens that include cognitive behavioral therapy to address thinking errors and minimization, victim empathy, polygraphs, and aversive conditioning. For child molesters and incest offenders, medication to decrease libido is imperative. Long-term treatment and medication regimens of sex offenders can significantly reduce rearrest rates after release.

1. What kind of staff qualifications (educational background, practical experience, type of person, personal characteristics, etc.) might be most effective for in-prison sex offender treatment?

2. Research the term "chemical castration." What is your view on chemical castration as an alternative treatment regimen for sex offenders?

3. What other types of thinking errors are typical with criminal offenders?

thinking errors Ways that people use to avoid taking responsibility for their own behavior, or ways to make themselves look good by making others look bad.

sex offenses Inappropriate sexual contact with family members/acquaintances, child molestation, sexual assault or rape of adults.

aversive conditioning The use of negative stimuli (painful thoughts, putrid smells, etc.) to reduce or eliminate sexual arousal.

antiandrogens Hormones that lower the male sex drive by decreasing testosterone levels. Examples include cyproterone acetate and medroxyprogesterone acetate.

selective serotonin reuptake inhibitors Medications that increase serotonin levels in the brain to decrease libido and cause erectile dysfunction.

LEARNING OUTCOMES 2

Describe the alternatives that pregnant mothers have once they give birth to their babies while incarcerated.

Most incarcerated parents will resume custody of their children when released, so contact with outside family members is encouraged.

Pregnant women who have their babies while incarcerated must find outside family members who are available and willing to accept temporary custody, or else the children go to foster care or become wards of the state.

A small number of states provide prison nurseries where qualified mothers can care for their newborns while incarcerated.

1. Given what you know about why family members do not visit, what ideas do you have for how prisons can increase visitation?

2. Do you agree that a pregnant prisoner should be shackled while being transported to the hospital? Should she be shackled while in labor? If so, why? If not, how are you going to assure that she doesn't escape?

3. Discuss the pros and cons of raising children in correctional institutions. How would you expand or limit such programs?

Explain the issues caused by the growth in the number of prisoners who have special health care needs.

The number of prisoners with HIV has steadily declined; however, it remains disproportionately high per 100,000 people compared to outside society. States test for HIV at admission and upon request of the prisoner, court, or a doctor. Inmates with HIV are housed in the general population until they become too weak with AIDS.

Other communicable diseases that are problematic inside correctional facilities are tuberculosis (TB), hepatitis B, hepatitis C, syphilis, and gonorrhea.

TB has become a serious problem in places of confinement where crowded conditions and poor ventilation provide ideal conditions for the spread of an infectious disease.

As prisoners serve longer sentences, they also age in prison. Prisoners over the age of 50 are the fastest growing segment in the prisoner population.

Geriatric prisons are separate facilities for aging inmates where they have no contact with the younger general population.

Terminally ill prisoners either experience prison-based hospice programs or are released through medical parole supervision.

1. Discuss the issue of patient confidentiality of medical records versus the right of staff to know of prisoner medical conditions. Under what conditions would the right to know be acceptable?

2. How would a jail or prison control an outbreak of tuberculosis in the facility if 15 people tested positive who all had casual contact with a carrier in the general population? How can prisoners be effectively quarantined to avoid infecting the whole facility?

3. What do you think about the policy of releasing terminally ill prisoners to the community?

4. What could be done to ensure that these prisoners do not pose a safety risk to the community if released?

aging prisoner A prisoner who is of age 50 or over.

geriatric prisons Separate facilities specifically designed for aging inmates where they have no contact with the younger general population.

compassionate release Available on a case-by-case basis for inmates who are permanently incapacitated, those who have less than one year to live, and those who no longer pose an imminent danger to the community. Also known as medical parole.

Additional Links

View the nine-minute YouTube video from perspectives of sex offenders who live in protective custody, and also gender differences in the inmate code at **https://www.youtube.com/watch?v=tB4Y3qU4Mt8**.

View the nine-minute video, narrated by Mary Byrne, about her research with prison nurseries at **www.youtube.com/watch?v=2GUfn1Sjic0**.

Go to YouTube and view the 27-minute video about healthcare and aging in prison entitled "Life in Prison: A Project Envision documentary" at **www.youtube.com/watch?v=alcK_QBE7h8**.

Go to YouTube and view the 23-minute video about release and hospice solutions for aging and terminally ill prisoners at **www.youtube.com/watch?v=Xvqj8hgxRfg&feature=relmfu**.

Go to YouTube and view the 23-minute video about the mentally ill in prison at **www.youtube.com/watch?v=bPUsdxMBEOQ&feature=related**.

For publications on correctional health care standards, go to the National Commission on Correctional Health Care at **www.ncchc.org/pubs/index.html**.

10

Reentry Programs and Parole

1 Describe the importance of reentry in reducing the challenges that prisoners face when they are released from prison.

2 Explain the benefits of education and vocational programs to inmates.

3 Outline the different forms of release from prison, including the evolution of parole.

FORMER GOVERNOR IS NOW EX-CON

Travis Spradling/AP Images

Former Louisiana governor Edwin Edwards was released from federal prison in 2011 after having served over 8 years of a 10-year sentence for 17 counts on activities that included mail fraud, money laundering, extortion, and racketeering in how he awarded riverboat casino contracts while in public office. Edwards, who turns 90 in 2017, was a well-known political figure over a span of nearly three decades, including four terms as governor. Over the years, he was allegedly involved in gambling, bribery, corruption, and accepting illegal campaign contributions, but was acquitted of these charges in the 1980s. Federal charges resulted in a conviction in the late 1990s. As a part of Edward's mandatory supervised release conditions, he lived under home confinement and reported to a federal halfway house three times a week for six months (Scram, 2011). Edwards successfully completed his federal sentence in 2013 and has stated his intentions to run again for governor of Louisiana. However, Louisiana currently has a statute that bars convicted felons from running for public office until 15 years have passed since sentence completion and the individual has had no new convictions (O'Brien, 2013).

DISCUSS **If the number of years were reduced by the Louisiana legislature to allow former governor Edwards to run for election sooner, do you see this as a good idea? Why or why not?**

► The Reentry Process

In the broadest sense, about 95% of all prisoners incarcerated right now will eventually return to the community. Every year, about 460,000 people are released from prison to continue supervision in the community (Kaeble, Maruschak, & Bonczar, 2015). Although short-term jail releasees may leave in the middle of the night with their own street clothes and no extra money, there is greater concern about the release of state and federal prisoners who have arguably served more time away. Long-term prisoners must go through a period of readjustment in transition from the rigidity of institutional life to living with choices in the larger society. **Reentry** is a process of release preparation that begins within the institution and continues in the community. Reentry begins by asking the question, "What is needed to effectively prepare an offender to lead a law-abiding life in the community?"

Figure 10–1, shows a model of the reentry process that was developed by the National Institute of Corrections to help state correctional departments develop their own transition programs from prison to the community. A prison case manager develops a "transitional accountability plan" that serves as an assessment of what each offender needs to accomplish prior to the release date and in the community. Offenders may be transferred to a minimum security prerelease center when they are close to release to ensure they have met some of the plan goals and to move them toward concrete strategies for obtaining employment and housing before or upon release (Cherney & Fitzgerald, 2016). To be successful, state corrections departments have formed partnerships with social services, mental health services, economic development services, health and senior services, and court administrators.

Some state correctional institutions are working more closely with community agencies in the areas of identification, clothing, housing, and employment needs. Some would say that the government has an obligation to make the reentry process less shocking from the "time warp" where prisoners are living with monotonous and restricted rules, to the immediate need many inmates have upon release to misuse leisure time that prisoners may feel they missed while incarcerated (McMay & Cotronea, 2015). Others would say that more attention needs to be paid to helping new releasees find employment, such as tax incentives to encourage businesses to hire former offenders (Cherney & Fitzgerald, 2016).

The essay by Velmarine Szabo examines issues that newly released prisoners face when they are transitioning from prison to the community. When you read the essay, you will better understand Figure 10–2. This figure divides reentry issues into three main areas: establishing more structure and stability, choosing supportive relationships with other people, and connecting to social services and other community agencies. If inmates believe

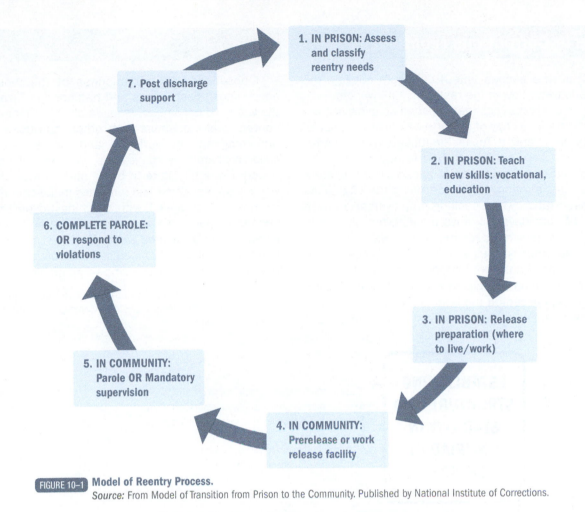

1. IN PRISON: Assess and classify reentry needs

2. IN PRISON: Teach new skills: vocational, education

3. IN PRISON: Release preparation (where to live/work)

4. IN COMMUNITY: Prerelease or work release facility

5. IN COMMUNITY: Parole OR Mandatory supervision

6. COMPLETE PAROLE: OR respond to violations

7. Post discharge support

FIGURE 10–1 **Model of Reentry Process.**
Source: From Model of Transition from Prison to the Community. Published by National Institute of Corrections.

Voices in Corrections

What did your first moments of reentry feel like?

Velmarine Szabo spent nearly 10 years on parole from 2003 to 2013 for a 1995 felony conviction, before being convicted of a new charge for aggravated assault. She has a projected mandatory release date of August 2029, but may be eligible sooner for release back out on parole.

In October 1995, I was sentenced to 25 years' imprisonment under enhanced laws for my third felony in the state of Texas. I was released from prison in August 2003 when I was 44 years old—after my second parole board hearing.

I'll never forget the strange feeling I had—a mixture of exhilaration and fear—when I walked out of the bus station after the prison bus had departed. It all seemed so surreal, handling real money after almost an entire decade, walking into the small shop to buy a cheap pair of jeans and a t-shirt.

Wearing my first pair of jeans in over eight years, I went in search of a grocery store. My own steps felt strange, foreign, and measured. Each step that I took, walking on a real, paved sidewalk with real cars zooming down the busy street beside me filled me with awe and exhilaration. There were no bars separating me from autonomous people and traffic lights. I was *in* what I'd come to know as only "the real world" for almost a decade. As I walked down that Boulevard, I secretly pinched myself a few times. Breathing fresh air unfettered by the bodily masses of prison, and walking on unsteady legs, I was completely unconcerned with the hot, August air. Upon entering the chain store grocer, I purchased fresh fruit that I'd only dreamed about for over eight years. Not wishing to appear uncouth, I waited until I had boarded the bus to gorge myself.

A few days later, I was perplexed to encounter my first heat-censored, flushing toilet. Although I wound up talking to the toilet when I couldn't figure out how to

(continued)

make it flush a second time, I did figure out how the automatic water flow in the restroom sink worked.

One of the first things that I needed upon my release from prison was a copy of my birth certificate, my social security card, and a Texas identification card. After these items were procured, I had to register with the Texas WorkSource employment agency. Unfortunately, this work registration, to include using the city buses as transportation while seeking employment an average of 14-hour days, six days a week, did nothing in producing employment for me in the Harris County, Texas, area. After one full year of futile job search and working as an occasional temporary laborer, I realized that even fast-food establishments would not hire me. At that time, I accepted the help and ideas of an associate that might enable me to become self-employed.

I possessed no nervousness at the thought of encountering past friends as I had none in Texas. Over the years, I'd become an isolated alcoholic that avoided contact and closeness with other individuals. Upon becoming an impoverished and single parent, my children shared my small world. With my release from prison, I was fortunate in being able to rebuild bonds with my two sons that had remained in the care of family members. I struggled with catching up on the past decade of political and other societal changes. It is indeed a lonely, isolated world that I navigate as I work to rebuild my life in shrouded secrecy from a society that frowns and closes doors to me—the female ex-offender.

Source: From Corrections: A Contemporary Introduction by Leanne F Alarid and Philip L Reichel. Copyright © 2008 by Pearson Education.

ESTABLISHING STRUCTURE AND STABILITY IN A MYRIAD OF CHOICES

- Finding affordable and stable housing
- Securing employment that pays a sufficient income
- Securing basic supplies (bus pass, identification, eyeglasses, clothes) with little or no money
- Making sound decisions on a daily basis
- Reliable public transportation

CHOOSING SUPPORTIVE RELATIONSHIPS

- Creating new connections that reinforces non-criminal attitudes and behaviors
- Regaining legal and physical custody of children
- Negotiating stigmatization from the community, suspicion from police, and the constant need to prove self as worthy and changed
- Making decisions about continuing prior intimate relationships, which may have been exploitative, or sexually or physically abusive

CONNECTING TO SOCIAL SERVICES AND COMMUNITY AGENCIES

- Sobriety and recovery from alcohol or drug addiction
- Parole obligations
- Reinstatement of Medicaid benefits and/or Supplemental Security Income
- Insight into problems and self understanding of behavior

FIGURE 10–2 **Challenges Offenders Face with Reentry.**
References: 1. Brown, J. D. (2004). Managing the transition to community:.A Canadian parole officer perspective on the needs of newly released federal offenders. Western Criminology Review, 5(2), 97–107. 2. Rydberg, J., & Grommon, E. (2016). A multimethod examination of the dynamics of recidivism following reentry. Corrections: Policy, Practice and Research, 1(1),40-60.

they can go back to the way things were before they were arrested or if they neglect to take these new responsibilities seriously, their lives quickly seem to become difficult to control. Former prisoners who reenter society have to change their mental health, physical health, deficits in education, underemployment, lack of social support, and dysfunctional prior relationships (McMay & Cotronea, 2015).

Professionals who work with ex-offenders report that the desire to remain free is seldom enough by itself to keep someone straight. Remaining out of prison requires revising one's community identity, along with support and guidance from others. Reentry therefore focuses on a wide variety of positive *relationships* and *community program* resources that offenders need to assist them in stabilizing their lives so that they may eventually become fully independent. To meet this goal, the **Second Chance Act** provides federal funding for reentry initiatives that include housing assistance, employment, mentoring, and substance-abuse treatment.

We know that if prisoners are not given transitional resources or if an appointment is not made prior to entering the community, many will not continue taking prescribed medications, nor will they seek out new physicians for medical or mental health care due mainly to a lack of income or a lack of available community resources. With the confidentiality of medical records, many community-based agencies are not coordinated with shared databases or medical records to directly accept former prisoners from the institution. If applicable, indigent releasees must be reenrolled for federal and/or state medical and mental health benefits following their release, as they are not eligible for federal benefits such as Medicaid, Social Security, or disability income while incarcerated. There may be a lengthy gap of time between release and the time when insurance benefits begin. Because of these gaps, offenders begin release preparation when they are within 3 to 12 months of release in state facilities and within 24 months of release in federal institutions. Although there is no uniform curriculum, reentry programs share a common set of elements (Visher, Lattimore, Barrick, & Tueller, 2016).

Elements of reentry programs are listed in Figure 10–3 and include some innovative topics for releasees. For example, representatives from the Department of Labor are invited to speak to inmates about how to initiate job searches online. A representative from the Department of Motor Vehicles might speak about how to get back a suspended license or how to apply for identification. While participating in a reentry program reduced recidivism over nonparticipation (Veysey, Ostermann, & Lanterman, 2014), the most successful reentry programs focused on individual change over learning new skills (Visher et al., 2016). Out of all the skills prisoners can learn, vocational or trade acquisition, communication skills, and postsecondary education are of greatest need and interest to inmates in reentry preparation (Neller, Vitacco, Magaletta, & Phillips-Boyles, 2016).

LEARNING OUTCOMES 1 Describe the importance of reentry in reducing the challenges that prisoners face when they are released from prison.

- Job search
- Mock job interviews
- Securing identification and vocational/educational certificates
- Credit, finance, and banking (balancing a checkbook, opening a savings account)
- Motor vehicle registration
- Consumer skills
- Goal setting
- Reaching goals
- Legal responsibilities (restitution)
- Family responsibilities (alimony, child support)
- Health education (diet, exercise, prevention, AIDS awareness)
- Anger management and controlling response
- Appreciation of diversity and cultural differences
- Information on community resources

FIGURE 10–3 Elements of Most Reentry Programs.

▶ Education and Vocational Skills in Reentry Preparation

Many students reading this book have learned how to set educational goals and reach them incrementally through taking classes part time or full time. Getting a degree is not instantaneous—it takes time, effort, and sacrifice. In comparison to college students, most former prisoners "remain largely uneducated, unskilled, and usually without solid family support systems—and now they have the added burden of a prison record and the distrust and fear that it inevitably elicits" (Petersilia, 2002, p. 154). According to national statistics (Glaze & Maruschak, 2008), about 4 in 10 of all adult inmates in jails and prisons had not completed high school nor received the equivalent General Education Development (GED). In addition, a disproportionately high number of prisoners (20%) and jail inmates (30%) have a cognitive learning disability (Bronson, Maruschak, & Berzofsky, 2015).

Being behind academically seems to start early. Juveniles who got into trouble with the law had significantly more problems in all areas of math, reading, and written and oral language skills than did juveniles who had never been in trouble. The lack of education, coupled with disabilities, makes it very difficult to find a well-paying job, and explains why other sources of income may be needed to make ends meet (see Table 10–1). Think about what it would be like to live in poverty without setting or reaching goals and yet not having the skills or motivation to improve your life the "slow" way. Instead, individuals with learning or speech disabilities lose interest and eventually drop out of school. Other reasons for leaving school early include behavioral problems, family or personal problems, socioeconomic difficulties, early entry to the workforce, and joining the military.

Evidence-based correctional practices stress the importance of increasing levels of educational achievement. At intake, inmates are given a **test for adult basic education (TABE)** to determine at what level the prisoners are functioning

TABLE 10–1 | PRE-PRISON INCOME SOURCES OF PRISONERS WHO SUPPORTED DEPENDENTS

	State Prisoners		Federal Prisoners	
	Male	Female	Male	Female
Source of Income in Month Before Current Arrest[a]				
Wages or salary	77%	61%	73%	68%
Transfer payments[b]	10	36	7	24
Family/friends	9	21	8	15
Child support/alimony	0	9	0	8
Illegal sources	24	21	36	27
Other[c]	3	3	4	0

[a]May add to more than 100% because prisoners may have had multiple sources of income; numbers in this table may be slightly different from those in the original table because of rounding.

[b]Includes welfare, Social Security, supplemental Social Security income, and compensation payments such as unemployment insurance, worker's compensation, and veteran's compensation.

[c]Includes pensions, educational assistance, investments, and other unspecified types of income.

Source: From Parents in Prison and Their Minor Children, NCJ 222984. Published by U.S Department of Justice, © 2008.

academically. The TABE score corresponds directly to the particular grade level at which a person functions (e.g., a TABE score of "12" would mean that the person functions at a 12th grade level, and is eligible to take the GED). Illiterate individuals, who have a TABE score at 6 or less, are best taught through Corrective Reading, a beginning adult reader program (Coulter & Brookens, 2003). Federal offenders who are not proficient in the English language are required to achieve at least an eighth-grade proficiency level. State prisoners are generally less educated at admission than federal prisoners, but only a small number of states established a mandatory literacy level, varying between 5th and 12th grade.

LEARNING OUTCOMES 2 — Explain the benefits of education and vocational programs to inmates.

GED and Secondary Education

Inmates who score over an 8.5 on the TABE are eligible for GED program placement. Table 10–2 displays the prevalence of educational and vocational programs offered in various correctional facilities. It seems that the best educational opportunities are offered in federal prisons, with less opportunities in state prisons, especially for special education and vocational training (Stephan, 2008). Many GED programs are self-paced so that students do not become bored or frustrated, as may happen in a traditionally structured classroom. Despite this, few inmates earn their GED while incarcerated, so some state prisons are trying to increase the educational level of inmates prior to their release. Earning a GED or diploma while incarcerated seems to improve an ex-con's chances of securing post-release

TABLE 10–2 | EDUCATIONAL AND VOCATIONAL PROGRAMS OFFERED IN CORRECTIONAL FACILITIES

Program	State Prisons	Federal Prisons
Adult literacy	66%	98%
English as a second language	31%	98%
GED/secondary education	76%	98%
College courses	32%	98%
Special education	33%	98%
Vocational training	50%	98%

Note: Percentages will not add to 100% because facilities may have more than one educational program.

References: Stephan, J. J. (2008). Census of state and federal correctional facilities, 2005 (NCJ 222182). Washington, DC: U.S.Department of Justice, Bureau of Justice Statistics.

employment compared to inmates who did not improve their education (Duwe & Clark, 2014). However, a GED or diploma does not seem to be enough to have a significant reduction in recidivism, especially compared to offenders who have achieved an associate's degree or trade certificate.

College Programs

The 1960s G.I. bill provided tuition assistance to veterans of World War II and did not limit these benefits if the vets ever became incarcerated. In the 1960s, federal grants provided assistance for tuition to low-income individuals, including inmates. These benefits provided the impetus for college programs in prison. Although prisoners received less than 1% of the Pell grants offered annually by the government, the principle of this practice became so controversial with the public that these benefits were discontinued in 1994. College-level classes became virtually extinct as a result of the provision that denied all prisoners access to federal Pell grants. Enrolling in college classes has been made possible again through online courses and correspondence programs, although prisoners are responsible for paying their own tuition and fees.

One federally funded distance-learning program called Correctional Learning Network provides general education classes that lead to an associate's degree. Earning an associate's degree or becoming certified in a trade while incarcerated was related to higher pay, more hours, and less recidivism for former offenders after release (Duwe & Clark, 2014).

Another learning program, called Inside Out, began in the mid-1990s between Temple University and Graterford State Prison in Philadelphia. Half of the students are inmates and half are college students who complete a seminar-style course together, and the semester-long course is delivered within a nearby prison. While most inmates are not getting credit for the course, they are still actively challenged and motivated to complete the readings, papers, and tests. Now, at over 200 correctional facilities nationwide, Inside Out provides a structured curriculum for interested instructors and facilitates a unique educational opportunity for college students and inmates to learn from each other.

Most prisoners who attend college classes while incarcerated are a select group and unrepresentative of most prisoners in the larger population. That said, most studies comparing recidivism of prisoners who enroll in college classes to general population prisoners suffer from self-selection bias, in that college-level prisoners already have characteristics that are different from the rest.

Vocational Programs

Vocational training efforts have a long history in prisons. Beginning in the mid-1800s, inmates received vocational training in a multitude of fields, such as welding, auto mechanics, or masonry, but it was primarily for the benefit of the institution. In the 1970s, the focus shifted to vocational training for reentry. However, vocational programs for women and men were quite different. Programs in women's prisons consisted of cosmetology, sewing, custodial, food service, horticulture, clerical, data entry/processing, and service dog trainer. Vocational programs for men included auto repair, business, barber, construction, computer repair, carpentry, culinary, drafting, furniture/upholstery, horticulture, machining, masonry, printing, and welding.

At that same time, prison administrators were criticized for not providing enough variety of opportunities for women to learn vocational skills that would assist them in obtaining good jobs. Court rulings have recognized the right to equivalent programming, but opportunities "… should be based on the interests and needs of the female inmates rather than short-sighted efforts to duplicate the programs offered at male institutions" (*Glover* v. *Johnson,* 1979 [478 F.Supp. 1075, E.D. Mich.], 1087). Women inmates are offered training in the types of jobs they want, and prison administrators are merely giving women what they want.

Another view of this issue suggests that women do not seek fields that pay better because they have never been exposed to other choices they have beyond the stereotypical low-paying service, food, and sales jobs. They either seek out familiar jobs they have been successful at in the past, or they seek an area similar to that of a fellow inmate they know. Many prison administrators, on the other hand, feel that male-dominated vocational skills are of little interest to women. This is an excuse, critics say, for not spending the money to open up more opportunities for women. "The majority of the jobs these women are being trained for are among the most underpaid and unstable jobs in society. A woman leaving prison with minimal skills, earning minimum wage, will not be able to support herself or her family, and thus may turn to the government for aid or recidivate and find herself back in prison" (Lahm, 2000, p. 45). Figure 10–4 examines the effectiveness of vocational programs compared to traditional academic programs with regard to which is better at reducing recidivism after release from prison. As it turns out, vocational programs are more marketable for postrelease employment than simply getting a GED. Until women begin to demand more valuable job skills, women's prisons will likely not provide the same opportunities for women that prisons provide men.

► *Community Corrections in Reentry*

Community corrections programs were discussed in detail in Chapter 5. Many of these programs are vitally important for persons being released from prisons or jails. The community-based programs that are most often used in the reentry process include residential community corrections facilities (halfway houses and prerelease centers), outpatient substance-abuse relapse-prevention aftercare programs, day reporting centers, electronic monitoring/global positioning devices, and reparation boards. Instead of repeating material here (refer back to Chapter 5 for descriptions of each program if needed), we will discuss a few ways that these programs are applied to reentry.

Prerelease Facilities

First, when a prisoner is getting ready for release, he or she is typically transferred to a minimum-custody facility either within the department of corrections (still considered prison-based) or to a facility in the community (prerelease center). A **prerelease center** is a minimum-security step-down facility that houses either prisoners who have not yet been granted parole or prisoners who have met with the parole board and been promised a future parole date if they can successfully complete 6–12 months in a community-based facility.

Prerelease facilities that are prison-based or community-based centers grant furloughs. A **furlough** is an authorized temporary overnight leave of absence from 24 to 72 hours. Acceptable reasons for a furlough include seeking postrelease employment or housing, attending funerals, or simply establishing community contacts and maintaining family ties. About 5% of all prerelease prisoners received at least one furlough while at a minimum-security facility. Of the ones approved for a furlough, most inmates visited family to get gradually reacquainted, and about 17% of both federal and state inmates attended a funeral. Some furloughs that are granted while the inmate is still in prison must receive special permission, and sometimes the prisoner's family must agree to pay for officer security to accompany the releasee during the leave period.

Community Reparation Boards

Restorative justice (introduced in Chapter 2) plays an important role in the reentry process. Community members and treatment providers are involved in offender reentry through **community**

There are a number of in-prison programs provided to prisoners that help with finding a job at reentry. One route is through academic education programs that ensure that students have adequate reading, math, and problem-solving skills to obtain employment. Prisons offer traditional classrooms, individual tutors, and self-paced computer-aided instruction. There was no difference in test scores for prisoners who learned with face-to-face methods compared to prisoners who used computer-aided methods. However, prisoners who used computer-aided instruction learned mathematics in a shorter period of time than with traditional classrooms or tutors (Davis, Bozick, Steele, Saunders, & Miles, 2013).

A second route of helping prisoners find employment is vocational programs that train students for a specific occupational field or career. The odds of finding a job after release from prison are 28% higher when an inmate completes a vocational program while incarcerated (Davis et al., 2013). Davis and colleagues conducted a meta-analysis that compared educational programs with vocational programs, and found that for prisoners, vocational programs were more effective than obtaining a GED for obtaining employment. However, both education and vocational programs effectively reduced recidivism. Obtaining a GED or high school diploma while incarcerated reduced the *odds* of recidivism by 30% after three years, but reduced the recidivism *rate* by 13% compared to inmates who left prison without obtaining their GED.

But there are so many levels of education—so what are we talking about here? Although college education counteracts the negative stigma of a criminal record and produced the most positive results of all education programs (Batiuk, Lahm, McKeever, Wilcox, & Wilcox, 2005), postsecondary education, in particular, received the best post-prison results for the majority compared to lesser adult basic education/literacy programs, which are only classified as "promising" (Chappell, 2004).

FIGURE 10–4 **Evidence-Based Practices—Does it Work?** Is Academic Education or Vocational Training Better for Prisoners?

reparation boards, and this process is particularly valuable for offenders. In addition to the community, crime victims have become involved with reentry to assure that the offender remains accountable for paying back victim restitution. Community reparation boards are useful in assisting the offender with finding a job, and, in turn, influence employers' perceptions of former offenders. Some reparation boards have an offender sign a contract that incrementally moves the offender toward self-sufficiency and independent living. Formal reentry partnerships that attempt to address needs while the offender is still incarcerated appear to have less of an effect on recidivism reduction than reentry programs that help offenders once they are released (Duwe, 2014). However, the majority of evaluations on reentry programs showed no significant differences on rearrest and reincarceration rates between prisoners who received reentry services compared to groups who did not (Lattimore & Visher, 2009). Some individual reentry sites were found to have modest reductions in recidivism due to employment, social support, and restorative justice methods (), or worked better with female prisoners than with male prisoners (Garland & Hass, 2015).

Now that we've discussed reentry issues and reentry programs, we move to getting released from jail and prison.

▶ Release from Prison

As shown in Figure 10–5, there are four ways to leave prison—two of which involve no supervision and two involve continued supervision in the community. **Unconditional release** refers to returning prisoners to the streets without postrelease supervision. Two reasons for unconditional release are sentence expiration and commutation. An expired sentence means that the maximum time on the prison sentence has been served. Although an attempt is made to transition prisoners down to lower security levels one to two years prior to release, prisoners with disciplinary infractions or protective custody levels may be released directly from maximum security.

Commutation of sentence involves a discretionary reduction of the sentence length by a designated individual in the executive branch. State prisoners can be commuted by a governor or a parole board, whereas federal prisoners are commuted by the president of the United States. A sentence might be commuted if it is found to be excessive or if the governor or board simply believes commutation would be in the society's best interest. Prisoners must file an application for commutation, typically after they have served a minimum amount of time. All commutations are considered, but most go to prisoners on death row who get their sentences reduced to life without parole; nonetheless, the conviction remains on record. It is rare for prisoners to be released from prison due to a commuted sentence.

Conditional release involves postrelease supervision in the community. The governing authority that releases the prisoner is the parole board in **discretionary parole** and the law in mandatory supervision. Discretionary parole is the most common release method used in northeastern states and comprises just over half of all releases in southern states. **Supervised mandatory release** includes all inmates who—by law—are automatically released to the community when they have completed their maximum prison sentence less any good time credit they have received. Mandatory parole entries are persons whose releases from prison were not decided by a parole board. This includes those entering because of determinate sentencing statutes, good time provisions, or emergency releases. But because the full sentence is not really completed, the inmate's release is conditional and requires supervision. Supervised mandatory release is the most common release mechanism in the United States today, particularly in the western and midwestern regions. We first examine the predecessors of discretionary

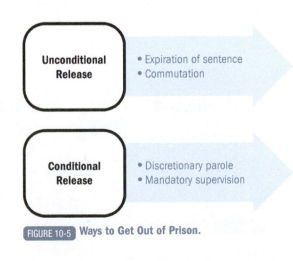

FIGURE 10-5 **Ways to Get Out of Prison.**

Predecessors of Parole in the U.S.

1800s	1817	1854	1944
British prisoners who were banished to Australia were able to work off a certain portion of their sentence before being set free.	Good time was first authorized in New York.	Sir Walter Crofton implemented the ticket-of-leave in Ireland.	All states in the United States used indeterminate sentencing and parole.
	1836–1840	**1876**	
	Captain Alexander Maconochie implemented the Marks system at Norfolk Island.	Zebulon Brockway implemented the Irish system at Elmira, New York.	

FIGURE 10-6 Predecessors of Parole in the United States.

parole in the United States, which are detailed in Figure 10–6. Parole was first influenced by the banishment of British prisoners to Norfolk Island, a small island located 1,000 miles off the coast of Australia.

History of Parole

Norfolk Island was one of the toughest penal colonies for English prisoners. Norfolk Island had a reputation for housing the most unruly and violent prisoners and for using a management style that included severe beatings and physical labor (Morris, 2002). When he arrived, **Captain Alexander Maconochie** significantly changed the way that prisoners were managed. He abolished corporal punishment and chain gangs, and rewarded positive behavior and work ethics through a daily **mark system**. Prisoners who participated in work and education programs were credited with marks, whereas marks were removed for disciplinary violations. When prisoners accumulated enough marks, they were released early from the island (Morris, 2002).

In addition to Maconochie's influence, today's version of parole owes some of its heritage to the work of Sir Walter Crofton and the application of indeterminate sentencing. Sir Walter Crofton, appointed as director of the Irish Prison System, was especially

LEARNING OUTCOMES 3 Outline the different forms of release from prison, including the evolution of parole.

intrigued with this concept of conditional release. Borrowing some ideas from Maconochie, Crofton developed a system of increasing privileges that was known as the **Irish system** (see Figure 10–7). The Irish system was a three-stage incremental process that eventually resulted in release through a ticket-of-leave.

While under a ticket-of-leave, releasees were not under supervision per se, but were expected to keep the police informed of their whereabouts. The ticket-of-leave is another one of parole's predecessors, but at that time, prisoners on leave were not being formally supervised, nor were there any revocation procedures for failing to notify law enforcement.

In the United States, prison officials realized the necessity of having ways to encourage good behavior by prisoners. With the first complaints of crowding, officials saw a need for procedures that would help control the size of the prison population by releasing some prisoners early to make room for new arrivals. The answer could be found in the Irish system's reliance on indeterminate sentencing and the ticket-of-leave. When the new institution opened at Elmira, New York, penologist **Zebulon Brockway** implemented Maconochie's mark system and Crofton's graduated release leading to a supervised ticket-of-leave. Inmates released from Elmira were supervised at first by volunteer citizens. After its successful use at Elmira, the indeterminate sentence and parole became the dominant philosophy. Figure 10–8 lists the four main uses of modern parole.

Months 0–3
Solitary confinement on reduced rations and not allowed to work

Months 4–9
Solitary confinement with full rations and allowed to work

Months 10–Release
Transferred to general population, worked with other inmates, and earned one mark per day until enough were earned for obtain a **ticket-of-leave**.

FIGURE 10-7 Walter Crofton's Irish System.

1. Assist released inmates to lead a more law-abiding life under restrictions
2. Encourage inmate conformity to prison rules
3. Backdoor prison population reduction strategy
4. Reduce judicial sentencing disparity

FIGURE 10–8 Four Uses of Parole.

The Parole Decision

Granting parole requires first that a prisoner meet the minimum eligibility criteria and second that a majority of board members agree that the prisoner is ready. Prisoners are given a date on which they are first eligible for early release on parole according to their sentence minus good time earned during the sentence. For example, consider an offender with a 6- to 10-year sentence (in which 6 is the minimum amount of time and 10 is the maximum) in a state where good time is given at a rate of one day of good time for each day served. Assuming that good time is earned every day, that inmate would be eligible for parole after serving three years in prison, because the six-year minimum sentence has been met after only three years. But the emphasis is still on the words *eligible* and *can be considered*. Parole, after all, is a privilege and not a right.

The next step in the process is to determine which of the eligible prisoners will receive a parole release. The **parole board**, appointed by the state governor, meets to review the files of those prisoners eligible for parole. In some cases, the board interviews the prisoner and reviews the file, and in other cases, the board reviews the file only. If the board members agree that a person should be released on parole, they set a specific parole date. The prisoner knows that, barring any infractions or problems with the parole plan, he or she can expect to be released on that date. If the board members do not believe the time for release is quite right, parole is deferred or delayed for 12–24 months.

The common goal, regardless of the specific criteria used, is to predict who is most likely to succeed on parole. Factors that parole boards consider in their decision are illustrated in Figure 10–9 and include the offender's prior criminal record, the offender's institutional conduct, the offender's participation in treatment programs, the offender's willingness to accept responsibility for his or her actions, and the victim's wishes. Parole boards routinely use scoring instruments to help them assess risk. Male prisoners under age 25, convicted of a property offense, with severe untreated drug addiction, and with several prior convictions represent a higher risk of recidivism than women, older prisoners, offenders with less serious drug-abuse histories, and those who were employed prior to arrest. Other factors that are important in successful reentry are being employed and having positive family support (McKiernan, Shamblen, Collins, Strader, & Kokoski, 2013; Visher, Debus-Sherrill, & Yahner, 2011).

Decrease of Discretionary Parole and Rise of Mandatory Supervision

During the 1970s, parole was attacked on the grounds that parole boards had too much discretion over a prisoner's release date, which meant persons convicted of similar crimes could end up serving very different amounts of time in prison. A second criticism centered on a perceived lack of effectiveness in treating offenders given an early release. By the 1990s, many states had revised their sentencing laws and begun using determinate sentencing for violent crimes. This change to determinate sentencing also necessitated replacing discretionary parole with supervised mandatory release. With supervised mandatory release, prisoners are automatically released to the community when they have completed their maximum prison sentence less any good time credit they have received. But because the full sentence is not really completed, the inmate's release is conditional and requires community supervision. Mandatory release takes the decision making away from a parole board and gives it to the legislators who revise sentencing laws.

The rate of supervised mandatory releases has grown significantly, and there are now more mandatory releases than discretionary, as detailed in Figure 10–10. Supervised mandatory release is used in the states where parole boards have been abolished. Mandatory release is also used in the federal system and for violent crimes in about 21 states. A small number of states reinstated discretionary release because their prisons became too crowded under mandatory release. Other

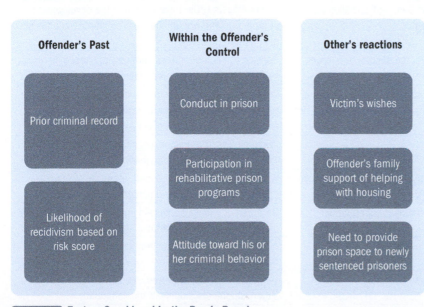

FIGURE 10–9 Factors Considered by the Parole Board.

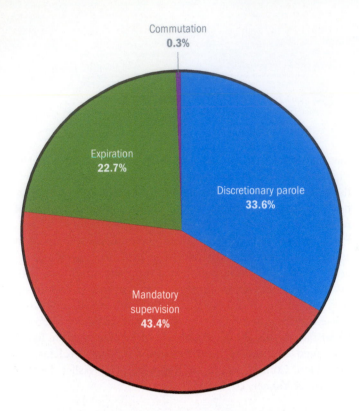

Commutation
0.3%

Expiration
22.7%

Discretionary parole
33.6%

Mandatory
supervision
43.4%

Percentages of Release from Prison

FIGURE 10–10 **Prison Release Methods.**
Source: Sabol, W. J., West, H. C., & Cooper, M. (2009). Prisoners in 2008 (NCJ 228417). Washington, DC: U.S. Department of Justice.

states, such as Alabama, have such stringent release criteria that even parole-eligible inmates serve exceedingly long sentences (Schartmueller, 2015).

Field Parole Officers and Supervision

Once the eligible offender is granted a release date on mandatory or discretionary supervision, a field officer must verify the release plan to ensure that the living arrangements are acceptable. Being that most parolees cannot afford their own place upon release, they must rely on staying with someone else. A field officer verifies that the family members agree to house the parolee and agree to parole officer visits. If housing plans are still not solidified, a halfway house facility is an available option. Once the release plan has been accepted, the offender is released from prison and is ordered to report to his or her parole officer within 24 to 48 hours. At that first visit, the offender signs a **parole agreement or parole order**. The term *agreement* is used when parole is discretionary, whereas an *order* more often suggests parole is mandatory and the parolee is aware of (although may not necessarily agree with) the rules. Parole conditions are nearly identical to those for probationers, so they will not be repeated here.

Just as there is similarity between the conditions of probation and parole, there is similarity among the duties assigned to those who manage each type of case, no matter if clients are on discretionary or mandatory parole. The two positions are enough alike that in the federal system and in many states, supervision officers have combined caseloads of probation and parole clients. Parole field officers are responsible for ensuring through supervision and assistance that the reentry plan is continued and their parolees do not pose a threat to public safety. In states with reentry initiatives, the parole officer focuses on reworking the transitional accountability plan to ensure the continuity of services the offender needs.

As detailed in Table 10–3, there are some differences between traditional parole and contemporary parole. Contemporary models of parole supervision include neighborhood-based supervision

TABLE 10–3	A COMPARISON OF TRADITIONAL AND CONTEMPORARY PAROLE	
Characteristic	**Traditional Parole**	**Contemporary Parole**
Program development	Programs should be provided through the Department of Corrections prior to being paroled.	Parole officers (POs) have input into the development of programs and are familiar with program resources in their communities.
Offender treatment plans	One size fits all and conducted for the sake of paperwork, but largely disregarded	Specific to each offender's criminogenic needs, realistic goals, and the foundation of case management
PO work with crime victims	Case managers are generally isolated from processes and information related to working with victims, and they are not entirely comfortable responding to victims or their concerns.	Case managers are trained and knowledgeable about victim issues, comfortable with issues related to confidentiality, and have tools to respond effectively to victims.
PO training	Procedures, paperwork, and rules	Evidence-based practices, cognitive behavioral interventions, motivational interviewing
PO help with employment	Unemployed offenders are encouraged to look for work.	With community workforce staff, the PO assists the offender in job search and placement.
Evaluations of POs	Based on number of contacts PO makes with offender by risk level	Based on offender's successful implementation of case plans and whether PO contacts help with treatment goals
Style of PO case management	Reactive to problems and violations	Proactive and addresses offenders' crime-producing needs to prevent new crimes or violations
Parole supervisors	Office-bound, working regular business hours	Develop partnerships with local social service agencies; supervise officers directly in the community

Source: From Parole Violations Revisited, NCJ #019833. Published by U.S Department of Justice, © 2004.

by zip code; partnerships with law enforcement; and attempting to change the offenders' lives through personal, family, and neighborhood interventions. At the core, these models move toward matching offender needs with community resources, strengthening victim services for victims who have an offender in the community, offender accountability and positive community contributions, and decreasing the number of prisoners who return to prison.

The length of time a person is on parole varies considerably, but the average time is one to two years. Looking at differences among states, we can find some examples in which time on parole cannot exceed six months or the offender's maximum sentence date, whichever comes first; in other states, parolees are discharged no later than one year after their release. States with mandatory parole typically specify time on parole as varying—for example, one to five years—depending on the crime. For instance, the state legislature might determine that conviction of a Class 3 felony will require two years on parole after completing whatever prison sentence the judge imposes. Like probationers, parolees try to complete supervision successfully through discharge rather than an unsuccessful revocation.

Parole officer responses, as in the model pictured in Figure 10–11, differentiate among low, medium, and high levels of parolee behavior. Behaviors defined as "low" are considered less consequential than "high" behaviors (Burke, 2004). The far left-hand column of this model shows how officers can reward positive behavior as well as sanction negative parolee behavior (shown in the far right-hand column). For example, a parolee who is on electronic monitoring and who is violation-free for 90 days might be eligible for regular parole supervision

LEVELS

Suggested Response	POSITIVE BEHAVIOR		NEGATIVE BEHAVIOR	Suggested Response
• Verbal recognition • Letter of recognition • Certificate of completion • 6-month compliance certificate	• 90 days clean • 90 days employed • 6 months stable residence • Completed first school semester or 30 days regular GED attendance • Outpatient program completion • 30 days electronic monitoring (EM) violation free • 2 months perfect attendance at cognitive skills course	**LOW**	• Positive drug test(s) • Program nonattendance • Failure to report • EM violations (minor) • Assessment not attended • Failure to support dependents • Unemployed (short period) • Special condition violation • Fee arrearage $60 or less • Technical violation – other	• Specific issue hearing • Outpatient program • Self-help program • PO letter of reprimand • PO verbal reprimand • Increased screening • Increased reporting • Verbal warning
• 1-year compliance certificate • Mr./Ms. Clean Award • Letter of recognition • EM early termination • Certificate of completion • Reduced reporting • Chief recognition • Decrease supervision level	• 12 months stability (employment and residence, few to no violations) • 6 months clean • 2 months perfect attendance at cognitive skills class • Completed 1 year of school or 6 months of regular GED attendance • 90 days EM violation-free • Outpatient program completion • Cognitive skills course completion	**MEDIUM**	• Misdemeanor arrest • Multiple positive drug tests • Multiple program nonattendance • EM violations (serious) • Unemployed (lengthy) • Assessment not attended (multiple) • Sex offender violations (minor) • Fee arrearage $100 or less	• Administrative hearing • In-house program • Restart program • EM extension • Outpatient program • Specific issue hearing • Increased screening • Increased reporting • Verbal reprimand—chief • Restorative community service work • Increase supervision level
• Commutation request • Donated gift certificate (GED/school graduation) • Cognitive skills graduation • Lifestyle Commitment Award • Second Mr./Ms. Clean Award • Reduced reporting	• 24 months stability • Completed school or GED • 12 months clean • Volunteer work, church affiliation • Prosocial activities	**HIGH**	• Felony arrest • Violent misdemeanor arrest or DUI • Positive drug tests (critical) • Program nonattendance (critical) • Sex offender violation (serious) • EM violations (critical) • Possession of a weapon • Absconding • Failure to attend administrative hearing • Unemployed (critical) • Fee arrearage over $100	• Request revocation • Short-term incarceration (local detention) • Electronic monitoring • In-house program • Administrative hearing • Outpatient program • EM extension • Whitworth Detention Center

FIGURE 10–11 **Example of a Behavior Response Guide for Parole Officers.**
Source: From Parole Violations Revisited, NCJ #019833. Published by U.S Department of Justice, © 2004.

without the electronic surveillance. However, if that same parolee had a drug test that showed he or she used multiple illegal substances (a medium-risk behavior), the parolee would be required to enroll in an in-house drug program. Most states have solid parole policies that sanction negative behavior but seem to neglect rewarding positive behavior.

Revoking Parole

Figure 10–12 shows that nearly 64% of parolees successfully discharge or complete parole without incident and about 2% are transferred to complete their parole in another jurisdiction because of a job move or other event. About one-third of parolees are revoked and return to prison primarily for technical violations, or for committing new crime. An additional 2% of parolees abscond from parole, which means they stop reporting and the officer loses track of the offender's whereabouts altogether.

In general, men on parole are more likely to be revoked than women who are more likely to take on childcare responsibilities for dependent children. Drug use was a common behavior for

those who were revoked (Huebner & Pleggenkuhle, 2015). Living near "potentially criminogenic places" such as alcohol establishments, public transportation stops, and places where drugs are sold did not seem to increase risk of failure for parolees (Miller, Caplan, & Ostermann, 2016). However, parolees were found to have committed new crimes not far from their homes, within their own neighborhoods (Hipp & Yates, 2009).

Upon becoming aware of the possible commission of a new crime or technical violations, a parole officer may wish to revoke parole, but the final decision is up to the parole board. If formal revocation is sought, there must be a preliminary hearing and a formal revocation hearing following arrest. The parolee is not entitled to many of the rights at a criminal trial, such as an attorney, a jury of peers, or privilege against self-incrimination. However, parole revocation represents a loss of liberty, so some due process rights are permitted. They are as follows:

1. Written notice of alleged parole violations

2. Disclosure of evidence against parolee

3. Opportunity to be heard in person and to present witnesses and evidence

4. Right to confront and cross-examine adverse witnesses (unless the hearing officer finds good cause not to allow such confrontation)

5. A neutral and detached hearing body

6. A written statement by the fact-finder as to the evidence relied upon and reason(s) for revoking parole (*Morrissey v. Brewer*, 1972 [408 U.S., 471])

A revocation for technical violations may not always result in removal from the community. In some jurisdictions, such as Colorado, intermediate sanctions like day reporting centers or residential community facilities are the preferred cost-effective alternative to jail or prison. If jail is inevitable, some states will limit the amount of time that can be served for a revocation. For example, Kentucky allows parole officers discretion to incarcerate a technical violator for up to 30 days per every 365-day period on parole (VERA Institute of Justice, 2010). Due to the economic deficits that most states have recently faced, many have explored reducing overall costs to the correctional system by way of increasing parole rates, increasing probation as an alternative to prison, and decreasing prison as an option for parole or probation revocation. With an increased focus on successful reentry, community corrections supervision officers understand the importance of employment and positive family support for former prisoners (McKiernan et al., 2013; Visher et al., 2011).

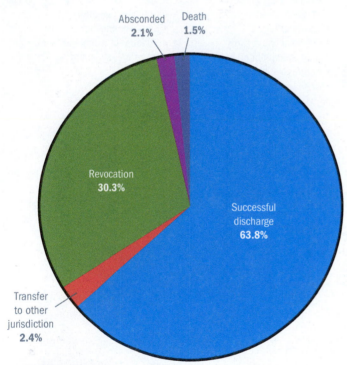

FIGURE 10–12 **What Happens to Parolees?**
Reference: Kaeble, D., Maruschak, L. M., & Bonczar, T. P. (2015). Probation and parole in the United States, 2014 (NCJ 249057). Washington, DC: U.S. Department of Justice. Retrieved from http://www.bjs.gov/content/pub/pdf/ppus14.pdf.
Note: Cases that were unknown or not reported were subtracted from the total.

Faith-Based Reentry

Correctional facilities rely on volunteers to provide a wide range of spiritual opportunities, such as worship services, Bible study, clergy visits, and publications for many denominations. Prison Fellowship Ministries (PFM), founded by ex-felon Charles Colson, provides Christian-based opportunities for prisoners and their families (Paynter, 2004). In 1997, PFM started the first Christian prison community called InnerChange Freedom Initiative (IFI) under the belief that criminal behavior, drug use, alcoholism, and dishonesty are sinful behaviors that can be cured by being saved by Jesus. Inmate volunteers are transferred to a prison unit specifically designated for the IFI program. All IFI treatment staff members and inmates are of the Christian denomination. The program has four phases:

- Phase One, Transformation (18 months): This involves intense Bible study and weekly testing on the concepts for more than 10 hours per day (Paynter, 2004). This phase includes admitting sins, taking responsibility, and seeking repentance.

- Phase Two, Reentry Preparation (6 months): This involves off-site prison work programs and involvement in reentry classes while still incarcerated. Reading the Bible, attending church service, and strengthening one's relationship with God are expected throughout all phases.

- Phase Three, Community Facility (6 months): Inmates develop a relationship with a PFM mentor who aids them in finding a more permanent job and housing.

State funds can pay only for food, security, and uniforms, so PFM must pay for all faith-based costs such as reentry classes, Bible study, and mentoring. An empirical study of

Damian Dovarganes/AP images

one IFI program in Texas compared 177 participants (75 graduates and 102 who quit or were paroled before completing) to 1,700 inmates who met the initial IFI selection criteria but did not participate. Johnson and Larson (2003) tracked recidivism rates of both groups for two years beyond their prison release dates and found no significant difference between IFI participants (36% rearrested and 24.3% reincarcerated) and nonparticipants (35% rearrested and 20% reincarcerated). A more recent study of an IFI program in Minnesota matched 366 IFI participants with a comparison group of nonparticipants. Researchers found that the IFI program participants had lower rearrest rates (42% of participants compared with 51% of nonparticipants) for new crimes (Duwe & King, 2013) and attributed the success to the mentoring phase.

The InnerChange Freedom Initiative raises some interesting issues:

1. Given that an inmate of a non-Christian religious denomination (such as Islam, Hinduism, or Buddhism) cannot openly practice at IFI, is this a violation of First Amendment rights for non-Christians? Why or why not?

2. Would you classify IFI as a reentry program? Does it work? Is it promising?

3. In tough budget times, IFI may be an attractive option for states that might want to consider using private funding assistance from PFM. Would you advocate in favor of or against expansion of IFI to other treatment programs, such as those for sex offenders? Why or why not?

LEARNING OUTCOMES 1

Describe the importance of reentry in reducing the challenges that prisoners face when they are released from prison.

Reentry programs are directed at offenders who are within 3 to 12 months of release and assist with securing identification, locating housing, finding a job, remaining sober, and making healthy decisions.

1. Should the Second Chance Act be reauthorized by Congress? Why or why not?

2. What else can we do to help former offenders who are released from prison? Make a list of as many ideas as you can think of that might help.

reentry The process of release preparation that begins within the institution and continues with community supervision.

Second Chance Act Federal legislation that authorizes reentry grants to state and local agencies and nonprofit organizations to provide employment assistance, substance-abuse treatment, housing, and mentoring to reduce recidivism for ex-offenders returning to communities from correctional facilities.

LEARNING OUTCOMES 2

Explain the benefits of education and vocational programs to inmates.

Educational programs in prison include literacy and basic education, obtaining a GED, and some college programs. Recidivism is reduced as a result of involvement in educational programs while incarcerated. Although literacy and GED programs are abundant, few college opportunities exist for prisoners.

Vocational programs are available for inmates who have at least a GED, but fewer choices exist for women than for men. Studies that have tracked inmates to see if vocational programs increased success found vocational

programs to be less successful than traditional education programs in this regard.

1. Should prisoners receive financial aid or scholarships to attend college classes while incarcerated? Why or why not?

2. In order to qualify for vocational training programs, discuss the pros and cons of requiring inmates to have a GED or diploma as a prerequisite.

test for adult basic education (TABE) Test given to inmates to determine the prisoners' level of academic ability.

LEARNING OUTCOMES 3

Outline the different forms of release from prison, including the evolution of parole.

1. Should prerelease centers be expanded in the community? Argue for or against your choice.

2. Would you be willing to volunteer on a community reparation board? Why or why not?

3. As a citizen, which form of supervised release do you think is more effective for recent releasees—discretionary parole or mandatory release? Why?

4. If you were a prisoner, would you prefer to get out early on parole supervision, or would you prefer to do all your time behind bars and get out on unconditional release? What factors weigh on this decision?

5. How does the early marks system resemble the contemporary model of responding positively and negatively to parolee behavior?

prerelease center A minimum-security prison-based or community-based facility that houses either prisoners who have not yet been granted parole or prisoners who have met with the parole board and been promised a future parole date.

furlough An authorized temporary overnight leave of absence from 24 to 72 hours.

community reparation board Group that facilitates involvement of community members in an offender's reentry to society.

unconditional release The return of prisoners to the larger community without supervision.

commutation of sentence A reduction of the sentence through action in the executive branch.

discretionary parole Conditional early release from imprisonment at the discretion of a state paroling authority and continued supervision in the community.

supervised mandatory release When an inmate is automatically released by law to the community when he or she has completed his or her maximum prison sentence less any good time credit the inmate has received.

Maconochie, Captain Alexander Governor of Norfolk Island from 1836–1840, one of the toughest penal colonies for English prisoners.

mark system Developed by Maconochie, this system rewarded positive behavior and work ethics.

Irish system Mid-nineteenth-century prison philosophy that asserted punishment's most direct purpose should be to reform the criminal.

Brockway, Zebulon Credited with implementing the Irish system in the United States at the Elmira Reformatory in Elmira, New York, in the late 1870s.

parole board Group of citizens, typically appointed by the state governor, who meet periodically to review the files of those prisoners eligible for parole.

parole agreement/order Document that the parolee signs at the first meeting with the parole officer where he or she agrees to abide by certain conditions while on parole.

Additional Links

For more information about reentry topics, visit the Council of State Government website at **https://csgjusticecenter.org/reentry**.

For more information about graduated response grids, visit the American Probation and Parole Association website **https://www.appa-net.org/eWeb/Resources/SPSP/State-Response-Guide.pdf**.

Go to YouTube at **www.youtube.com** and watch an 8 minute and 30 second video about what women offenders think about reentry programs at **www.youtube.com/watch?v=dbuav6irGJE&feature=related**.

Go to YouTube at **www.youtube.com** and watch an 8-minute video about the Second Chance Act at **https://www.youtube.com/watch?v=e_Ant1B5Uv0**.

Go to YouTube at **www.youtube.com** and watch a 19-minute video hosted by John Oliver about prisoner reentry at **https://www.youtube.com/watch?v=gJtYRxH5G2k**.

Go to YouTube at **www.youtube.com** and watch a 19-minute video about reentry programs that help with employment: **https://www.youtube.com/watch?v=xX897ZAiK2A&list=PL_TjRHVWVgUfoXVmujcs3hgFJ4E32XW82**.

Visit the Vera Family Justice Program at **www.vera.org/centers/family-justice-program** and see a variety of resources for reentry.

Visit the National Conference on State Legislatures website at **www.ncsl.org**. Type in the word "reentry" and view policymaker documents that legislatures use.

Complete the "Parole Decision Maker" to provide you with a glimpse of the factors the parole board considers at **www.insideprison.com/parole_decision_making.asp**.

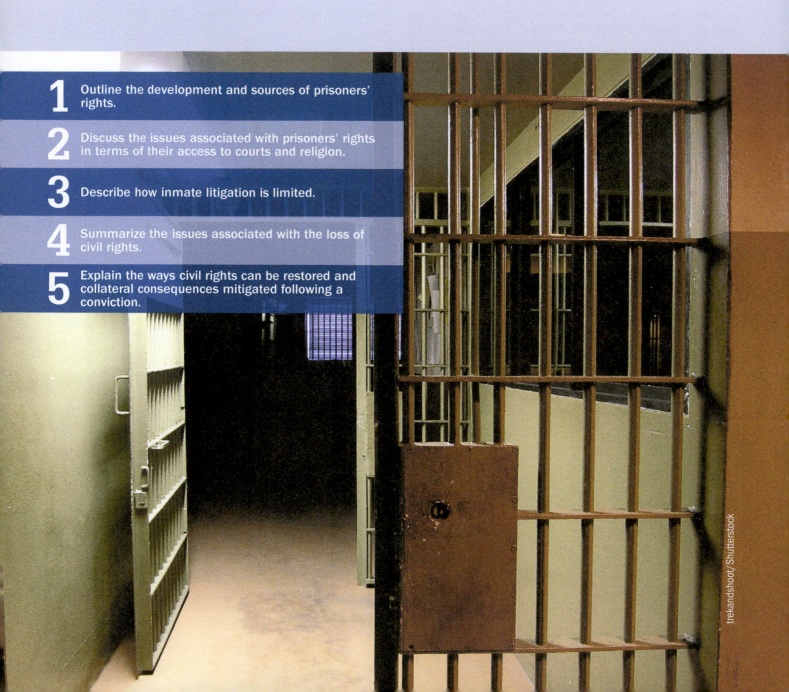

11

Legal Issues in Corrections

1 Outline the development and sources of prisoners' rights.

2 Discuss the issues associated with prisoners' rights in terms of their access to courts and religion.

3 Describe how inmate litigation is limited.

4 Summarize the issues associated with the loss of civil rights.

5 Explain the ways civil rights can be restored and collateral consequences mitigated following a conviction.

DECIDING WHAT'S RIGHT

Oklahoma City bombing conspirator Terry Nichols is serving a life sentence at the Federal Administrative Maximum prison in Colorado for conspiracy and involuntary manslaughter in the 1995 bombing of the Alfred P. Murrah Federal Building. In 2009, Nichols filed a lawsuit claiming his constitutional rights were being violated because the prison food did not meet his medical and religious needs. He claimed to need a fiber-rich diet of whole-grain foods, bran products, and unpeeled and uncooked fruits and vegetables. Nichols argued that not only does he have a medical condition requiring such a diet, but his Christian belief is that God created our foods to be consumed in their whole unrefined state. In 2010, a federal judge ruled his claims to be invalid, saying that Nichols did not prove his diet constituted cruel and unusual punishment nor did he offer proof that it violated his Christian beliefs (Doucette, 2010).

Lyralisa Stevens is one of more than 300 inmates in the California state prison system diagnosed with gender identity disorder. This psychiatric condition is treated with hormone replacement therapy and, in some cases, sex reassignment surgery. Stevens was born male but lives as a female. She is serving 50 years to life for killing a woman in a dispute over clothes. In a 2011 lawsuit, Stevens asked the court to require California to pay for a sex-change operation. She claims that removal of her penis and testicles and transfer to a women's prison are the best way to protect her from rape and abuse by male inmates (Dolan, 2011). Her fears seem well founded, as at least one study has found that transgender prisoners are 13 times more likely to suffer sexual assault than other inmates (Jenness, 2009).

Both of these cases present issues related to prisoners' rights. Nichols's argument may seem silly, but what if he

worker/Shutterstock

was of the Jewish faith and asking for kosher meals? Would that be a more legitimate request? Whether you consider the Stevens case to be frivolous or not, there certainly are issues of safety to be considered. Would it be irresponsible for prison officials to put a 17-year-old juvenile who was convicted and sentenced as an adult in a cell with a convicted child molester? Does the state have some responsibility for the safety of prisoners?

DISCUSS Are prisons obligated to meet the religious and safety needs of their prisoners?

▶ Sources of Prisoners' Rights

Two positions can be taken regarding rights of convicted and imprisoned persons:

- The **rights-are-retained position** argues that prisoners keep all the rights of an ordinary citizen, except those that are expressly or by necessity taken away from them by law.

- The **rights-are-lost position** says that prisoners are wholly without rights except those expressly conferred by law or necessity.

Importantly, but confusingly, neither position accurately identifies the approach held by the courts. Figure 11–1 reviews various stages through which the courts seem to have passed as they try to balance the retained/lost dilemma. The rights-are-retained view comes directly from a federal appeals court decision in 1944 (*Coffin* v. *Reichard*), but federal courts have issued many other decisions that suggest prisoners may only have rights that are compatible with the goals of prison administration.

In the absence of a clear and consistent approach, it is not surprising that the public, prison officials, and even judges have difficulty understanding or describing the rights of prisoners. However, before discussing how the courts have responded to this "rights-retained" or "rights-lost" dilemma, we consider from where the presumed rights come.

Proponents of having inmates retain some rights during incarceration point at state and federal constitutions and state and federal laws to support their claim. State constitutions and laws are too numerous to cover here, so we concentrate on federal-level sources. First we will look at articles of the U.S. Constitution and two of the Constitution's amendments to understand how they serve as the basis for many inmate claims. Then we consider the Civil Rights Act (U.S. Code, Title 42 Section 1983) as an example of a federal statute that is increasingly being used to support inmate claims of discrimination.

Although federal and state courts have not consistently followed either a rights-are-retained or rights-are-lost position, it is possible to identify historical periods according to the courts' willingness to be involved in prison administration issues. These periods move from an initial time of noninvolvement (called the hands-off doctrine) to a time of active intrusion (the hands-on doctrine) and most recently to a deference doctrine wherein court rulings should respect the assessment of prison officials.

1. **The Hands-Off Doctrine.** Federal and state courts, before the early 1960s, held the view that prisoners had only those rights specifically granted by statute or by policy. Prison conditions were free from outside scrutiny, and prison administrators governed without any outside interference. State and federal courts were reluctant to intervene in prison administration unless there appeared to be a clear violation of the Eighth Amendment's protection against cruel and unusual punishment. The hands-off doctrine espoused by the courts was justified on several grounds, including the argument that correctional administration was a technical matter that was best left to experts in corrections rather than to the courts, which are not equipped to make appropriate evaluations regarding the running of prisons.

2. **The Hands-On Doctrine.** After nearly 170 years of keeping the courts out of the prison management business, the hands-off doctrine began eroding. By the mid-1960s, federal district courts were seriously considering prisoners' claims. An important reason for the courts' new interest in prisoners was simply a reflection of the times, which also saw increased interest in areas such as civil rights, student rights, public welfare, and general institutional reform. Several of the earliest cases heard by the courts involved claims of racial and religious discrimination brought by Black Muslims in prison. With the new hands-on doctrine, courts (especially the lower federal courts) began supporting prisoners' claims to rights in areas such as privacy, communication, safety, and due process.

3. **The Deference Doctrine.** Since 1980, the U.S. Supreme Court and lower federal courts have based decisions regarding the constitutionality of prison restrictions with deference to the assessment of prison officials. In *Bell* v. *Wolfish* (441 U.S. 520, 1979), for example, Justice Rehnquist expressed a belief that courts had become too involved in the minutiae of prison operations. Rehnquist, writing for the majority, explained that court involvement in prison management must be limited to whether a particular prison requirement violates the Constitution. An example of the new deference to the discretion of prison authorities is *Turner* v. *Safley* (482 U.S. 78, 1987), which found that prison requirements that impinge on inmates' constitutional rights are valid if they are reasonably related to legitimate penological interests.

FIGURE 11–1 Judicial Involvement in Prison Administration.

The U.S. Constitution

When introducing the concept of individual rights under the U.S. Constitution, Ferdico (2005) states how much easier enforcing criminal laws would be if suspected criminals were presumed guilty; could be detained for long periods of time without a hearing; had no privilege against self-incrimination; and could have their bodies, vehicles, and homes searched at will (p. 4). But because the United States was founded as a direct response to what early colonists saw as British abuses in these kinds of areas, there has always been a strong commitment to protecting individual rights from government abuse. With the ratification in 1788 of the U.S. Constitution, and with the addition in 1791 of the Bill of Rights, America's commitment to individual rights was guaranteed. As a result, persons suspected of crime are presumed innocent, cannot be detained long without a hearing, are not forced to incriminate themselves, and have protection against unreasonable searches and seizures, among other rights.

In addition to concern about the rights of persons suspected and accused of crimes, the U.S. Constitution and the Bill of Rights also cover the rights of persons convicted of a crime. For example, Section 9 of Article 1 provides the privilege of the **writ of habeas corpus** (for our purposes, such a writ directs the person—the warden, for example—detaining the prisoner to show the legality of the detention). On the other hand, Section 10 of Article 1, through its prohibition against **ex post facto law**, prevents imposing a greater punishment for a crime than was in effect when the crime was committed. The Eighth Amendment's prohibition against cruel and unusual punishments is the obvious example of concern for convicted persons, but so is the Fourteenth Amendment's due process requirement. *Habeas corpus* action and complaints of *ex post facto* law violations are still brought by offenders today. But this overview concentrates on issues related to the Eighth and Fourteenth Amendments.

The Eighth Amendment to the U.S. Constitution prohibits cruel and unusual punishments. Even persons claiming that offenders forfeit all their rights after conviction are likely to make an exception to this constitutional protection. The problem is determining to what it refers. The term *cruel and unusual punishment* cannot be specifically defined because it is flexible and broadens as society pays more regard to human decency and dignity. Or, as U.S. Supreme Court Chief Justice Warren explained, the phrase "must draw its meaning from the evolving standards of decency that mark the progress of a maturing society" (*Trop* v. *Dulles* 1958, 356 U.S. at 100-101). Table 11–1 highlights some cases showing the variation in deciding what is cruel and unusual. To determine whether a punishment is cruel and unusual under this evolving standards test, the courts rely in part on public opinion as expressed in state legislation and jury decisions. For example, when finding that the death penalty for the crime of rape was cruel and unusual (grossly disproportionate and excessive in its severity), the Supreme Court noted that Georgia was the only state authorizing a death sentence for the rape of an adult woman and that juries in that state were reluctant to impose a death sentence in rape convictions (*Coker* v. *Georgia,* 433 U.S. 584 1977).

LEARNING OUTCOMES 1 — Outline the development and sources of prisoners' rights.

Does Violate the Eighth Amendment	Does Not Violate the Eighth Amendment
• The U.S. Supreme Court found that handcuffing an Alabama prisoner to a "hitching post" for two hours (the first time) and seven hours (a second time) in the hot sun without bathroom or water breaks, and taunting him by pouring water out in front of him, violated the Eighth Amendment (*Hope* v. *Pelzer*, 536 U.S. 730, 2002).	• A Kentucky jail did not violate a prisoner's Eighth Amendment rights by serving him only one meal a day for 15 consecutive days because the one meal was sufficient to maintain normal health for the 15 days involved (*Cunningham* v. *Jones*, 667 F2d 565, 1982).
• A U.S. Court of Appeals found Michigan's policy of terminating all inmate visits (except from attorneys and clergy) as a way to punish inmates with two or more violations of the department's substance-abuse policy to be an Eighth Amendment violation. The court described the ban on visits as cruel and unusual because it, in part, destroyed the social, emotional, and physical bonds of parent and child (*Bazzetta* v. *McGinnis*, 286 F.3d 311, 2002).	• When an Arkansas prison refused to allow out-of-cell exercise for the first 15 days of a prisoner's time in punitive isolation, a federal court said the policy may be severe, and even harsh, but it was neither cruel nor barbaric (*Leonard* v. *Norris*, 797 F.2d 683,1986).
• In *Knop* v. *Johnson* (667 F.Supp. 467, 1987), a federal district court ruled that Michigan had failed to provide inmates with winter coats, hats, and gloves and thereby subjected them to cruel and unusual punishment. Boots, however, were not required as long as the state provided adequate winter socks and kept the walkways and outdoor exercise areas free from snow.	• An Illinois inmate complained that the prison had failed to provide him with toilet paper for 5 days, or with soap, toothpaste, or a toothbrush for 10 days. The federal court (*Harris* v. *Fleming*, 839 F2d 1232, 1988) found that because the inmate had suffered merely some unpleasantness, the temporary neglect was not intentional and did not reach unconstitutional proportions.
	• Ohio prisoners claimed that making them share the same cell was cruel and unusual given the long prison sentences they were serving, the amount of time they must spend in their cell, and the fact that such "double celling" was not a temporary condition. The U.S. Supreme Court (*Rhodes* v. *Chapman*, 452 U.S. 337, 1981) ruled that double celling was not cruel and unusual punishment because, under the circumstances, it did not inflict unnecessary or wanton pain nor was it grossly disproportionate to the severity of the crime.

DISCUSS Can you determine from these cases just what criteria the courts are using to conclude if something constitutes cruel and unusual punishment? If more cases were cited, do you think it would be possible to identify a clear standard? Why or why not?

The Fourteenth Amendment has significant importance to the concept of individual rights. Prior to the passage of the Fourteenth Amendment, the Bill of Rights served primarily to define the relationship between citizens and the federal government. Each state had its own state constitution, and many of those identified rights held by citizens against injustices by their state government. But the U.S. Constitution's first 10 amendments referred only to the protections citizens had against the federal government. This meant that a person might have certain rights when interacting with the federal government but not have those rights when associating with the state government. Such a situation was not considered inappropriate under a federal republic in which states shared sovereignty with the federal government, nor was it necessarily confusing because many of the state constitutions were modeled after the federal constitution. There were, however, some rights guaranteed in the Bill of Rights that were being denied by some states.

After the Civil War, the Thirteenth Amendment was passed (1865) to correct the obvious violation of individual rights where states continued to allow slavery and involuntary servitude. Because other infringements on individual rights continued in some states, the Fourteenth Amendment was ratified in 1868. Its importance to individual rights is best understood through the theory of **incorporation**, which argues that all provisions of the Bill of Rights are made applicable to the states (i.e., they are incorporated) by the amendment's due process clause. So, when the amendment says that "no State shall deprive any person of life, liberty, or property, without due process of law," it is requiring each state to abide by the Bill of Rights.

The Fourteenth Amendment also prohibits any state from denying "any person within its jurisdiction the equal protection of the law." Therefore, because of the Fourteenth Amendment, individual states must abide by the Bill of Rights and must obey federal court rulings about whether the state

1. followed due process of law when depriving a person of life, liberty, or property (the **due process clause**).

2. provided equal protection of the law to all people within its jurisdiction (the **equal protection clause**).

Offenders have often used the Fourteenth Amendment's due process and equal protection clauses when claiming that their rights have been violated.

Examples of prisoner due process violation claims are those linked to whether a hearing is required before prison officials can discipline or transfer inmates. Everyone probably agrees that it would be a denial of due process to keep suspects in jail for weeks or months without having them

Important Prisoners' Rights Court Cases

1871	1958	1972	1974
Ruffin v. Commonwealth A Virginia Supreme Court ruling that prisoners are a "slave of the state" and have forfeited all personal rights except those the state chooses to give him.	**Trop v. Dulles** Determination of whether a punishment is cruel and unusual must take into consideration a society's evolving standards of decency.	**Cruz v. Beto** Prisoners with "nontraditional" beliefs, Buddhism in this case, cannot be denied an opportunity to practice their religion.	**Wolff v. McDonnell** Defined rights a prisoner retains during a prison disciplinary hearing, which include re-stating a prisoner is not stripped of his/her rights while incarcerated.

Source: Arnold Gold/New Haven Register/The Image Works

FIGURE 11–2 Timeline: Important Prisoners' Rights Court Cases.

appear before a judge to hear the charges against them and be told of their right to counsel. But what about inmates suspected of misbehavior while in prison? In its 1974 *Wolff* v. *McDonnell* (418 U.S. 539) decision, which is one of the key cases highlighted in Figure 11–2, the U.S. Supreme Court distinguished between due process requirements for a defendant at trial and those required for an inmate at a disciplinary hearing. The Court held that because "prison disciplinary proceedings are not part of a criminal prosecution, the full panoply of rights due a defendant in such proceedings does not apply" (418 U.S. at 556). However, although prison officials are not bound to the same procedures as found in criminal court, the prison disciplinary hearings must abide by some level of due process and the Court identified specific steps that must be followed:

- The prisoner must be given written notification of the charges at least 24 hours in advance of the hearing so that he or she might prepare a defense.

- There must be a written statement by the fact-finders as to the evidence relied on and the reasons for the disciplinary action.

- Inmates facing disciplinary proceedings should be allowed to call witnesses and present documentary evidence in their defense as long as it does not unduly jeopardize institutional safety or correctional goals.

- There is no constitutional requirement that prison disciplinary hearings allow for cross-examination procedures, nor does the inmate have a right to either retained or appointed counsel in the proceedings. In some cases (e.g., the inmate is illiterate or the case is particularly complex), a staff member or another inmate may act as substitute counsel.

- The inmate's hearing should be conducted by an impartial official or panel.

The Fourteenth Amendment's equal protection clause is also frequently used in inmate claims. Although this clause does not require the government to treat everyone alike in all circumstances, it does forbid unjustified or malicious discrimination or classification. Because prison officials can often articulate a rational basis for their actions, it is difficult for inmates to win an equal protection claim in a prison case. For example, the courts have not found equal protection violations when prisoners have been denied things such as temporary release programs (e.g., work release), even though other prisoners with equally—or even more—deplorable records were involved in the programs. Furthermore, having different visiting privileges for those on death row and those in the general population does not violate the equal protection clause (*Jamieson* v. *Robinson,* 641 F.2d 138, 1981), nor does a pay differential between two different prisons (*Beatham* v. *Manson,* 369 F. Supp. 783, 1973). However, as summarized in Table 11–2, courts have been sympathetic to equal protection clause claims in racial and gender-based discrimination.

The Civil Rights Act

Civil rights are those personal, natural rights that protect people against arbitrary or discriminatory treatment. Clearly the Constitution, including its Bill of Rights and other amendments, provides the first source of civil rights in the United States. However, there are civil rights not specifically mentioned in the Constitution but that are recognized by the courts, including such rights as to live and work where we wish; to marry and to have children; and to participate in the political, social, and cultural processes of society (Ferdico, 2005). Because the Constitution does not enumerate all civil rights, Americans can turn to other sources in which their rights are identified. For the purposes of discussing prisoners' rights, some of the most important relate to the Civil Rights Act, which is found in the U.S. Code as Title 42, Section 1983. For brevity, this is usually referred to as "Section 1983" and prisoner claims are typically called **Section 1983 claims**.

Early recognition that prisoners could sue for civil rights violations involved cases of religious freedom brought by Black Muslims. In 1962, Black Muslim leader Thomas X. Cooper filed suit in Illinois against Stateville Prison warden Frank Pate. Cooper claimed that his confinement in segregation was retribution for his religious beliefs. The basis for his claim was Section 1983 of the Civil Rights Act. Cooper was being denied access to the Qur'an, to Muslim literature such

Turner v. Safley Considered by some to be the most important USSC case on prison law because it sets the legal standard for judging whether prison regulations infringe on prisoners' rights. It says that prison regulations are valid as long as they are reasonably related to legitimate penological interests.

Porter v. Nussle The Prison Litigation Reform Act's requirement that inmates must exhaust all administrative grievance procedures before a lawsuit can be filed applies not only to general prison conditions, but also to individual incidents such as accusations of excessive force.

Source: Patrick Tehan/San Jose Mercury News/MCT/Newscom

Wilkinson v. Austin Although the extreme deprivation and punishment found in supermax prisons warrant protections for prisoners' due process rights, the procedures used in Ohio to transfer inmates to the supermax facility provided sufficient protection to comply with the Fourteenth Amendment.

as the newspaper *Muhammad Speaks*, and to Muslim clergy. At a 1965 trial, ordered by the U.S. Supreme Court (*Cooper v. Pate,* 378 U.S. 546, 1964), prison officials had to justify their refusal to recognize the Muslims as a religious group. Because Christian inmates were allowed to read the Bible and Jewish inmates could have Hebrew literature, the prison officials found it difficult to explain why Muslim prisoners could not have the Qur'an or receive Arabic documents (Jacobs, 1977). In the end, Cooper (*Cooper v. Pate*, 382 F.2d 518, 1967) won on some points (Muslims had to have access to the Qur'an, to communicate and visit with Muslim ministers, and to attend Muslim religious services). On other points, the court sided with prison officials (contemporary Muslim literature and Arabic textbooks did not have to be allowed).

Although the religious points were important in opening First Amendment rights to prisoner claims, *Cooper v. Pate* is important because the suit was based on a civil rights act. From the rather narrow issue of religious freedom, prisoners used Section 1983 to bring claims of civil rights violations in cases involving inadequate medical care, brutality by prison staff, and inmate-on-inmate assaults.

Think About It…

Rev. Martin Luther King, Jr.'s famed "I Have a Dream" speech galvanized the nation's civil rights movements and led to the passage of the 1964 Civil Rights Act—one of several important civil rights acts passed at the federal level. As a result of these acts, citizens (including prisoners)

files UPI Photo Service/ Newscom

have rights and privileges such as freedom from discrimination. The primary vehicle for prisoner civil rights claims is Section 1983 of the Civil Rights Act of 1871, which was designed to guarantee the rights of newly freed slaves and to allow people direct access to the federal courts. The provision has been used successfully in class-action suits challenging institutional conditions. Why do you think it is important that citizens (including inmates in state prisons) have direct access to federal courts (rather than having to progress through state courts) when they are claiming violation of their civil rights?

TABLE 11–2	FOURTEENTH AMENDMENT EQUAL PROTECTION CLAIMS
Racial/ethnic discrimination	State statutes requiring segregation of races in prisons and jails violate the Fourteenth Amendment (*Lee* v. *Washington,* 390 U.S. 333, 1968; *Holt* v. *Sarver,* 309 F. Supp. 362, 1970), as does the subjection of African-American or Hispanic prisoners to disparate and unequal treatment (*Ramos* v. *Lamm,* 485 F. Supp. 122, 1979). Importantly, the *Lee* v. *Washington* decision did say that prison officials acting in good faith, and in particular circumstances, can take racial tensions into account to maintain security, discipline, and good order. But when racial tensions are used to justify actions such as segregation, those considerations should be made after a danger to security, discipline, and good order has become apparent and not before (*Wilson* v. *Kelley,* 294 F. Supp. 1005, 1968).
Gender discrimination	In what is probably the most well-known case on women's prison issues, a U.S. district court was asked to rule on programs and facilities provided by the state of Michigan for its women prisoners compared to those for its men prisoners. Women prisoners in Michigan claimed they were not receiving access to vocational courses equal to those for male prisoners, and the numbers seemed to support the women's position. Men had access to 22 vocational courses whereas women had access to only 3. In addition, the courses available to the men led to marketable skills but those for women did not. One of the prison teachers testified that the "women were taught at a junior-high level because the attitude of those in charge was 'keep it simple, these are only women'" (Muraskin, 1993, p. 218). The court (*Glover* v. *Johnson,* 478 F. Supp. 1075, 1979) held that women inmates must be provided with treatment facilities that are substantially equal but not necessarily identical to those provided the men. As a result of the *Glover* ruling, Michigan had to provide to its women prisoners postsecondary education, counseling, vocational programs, and a legal education program.

2006	**2011**		**2015**
Beard v. Banks Denying dangerous inmates access to newspapers, magazines, and photographs does not violate the First Amendment when the prison policy meets the *Turner* v. *Safley* standard.	**Brown v. Plata** Finding that conditions in California's overcrowded prisons are so bad that they amount to cruel and unusual punishment, the U.S. Supreme Court ordered the state to dramatically reduce its overcrowded conditions through early release of prisoners, new prison construction, transfer to other states, or to county jails.	 *Source: Patrick Tehan/ MCT/Newscom*	**Holt v. Hobbs** In a unanimous decision, the USSC ruled that Arkansas corrections officials violated the religious liberty rights of Muslim inmates by forbidding them to grow beards. In doing so, the Court dismissed the security arguments that contraband could easily be hidden in a half-inch beard and that a beard made prisoner identification too difficult.

FIGURE 11–2 (Continued)

▶ A Sampling of Prisoner Rights Issues

Because of the many issues that could be addressed in this section, we review only a few. We cover those in only a cursory manner to provide a basic overview of the types of issues confronting prisoners and prison authorities. Specifically, this section considers inmate access to the courts and the issue of religion.

Access to the Courts

Possibly the most basic right for prisoners is access to the courts. Without it, any other rights would be moot because prisoners would be unable to bring their claims to the court's attention. This issue actually has two components:

1. Procedures by which inmates get their claims before the court

2. Having the necessary legal knowledge to make their access effective

The "getting a claim to court" issue was resolved in 1941 when a Michigan State Prison inmate challenged the prison policy of requiring prisoners to first submit all types of legal documents to prison authorities. The prison officials would then forward to the appropriate court those documents they considered to be properly written. The U.S. Supreme Court held (*ex parte Hull*, 312 U.S. 546, 1941) that prison authorities cannot restrict an inmate's right to apply to a federal court for a writ of *habeas corpus*.

But having direct access to courts via a writ of *habeas corpus* is only one step in the process of accessing the courts. Prisoners who are not familiar with the law may need assistance to ensure their right to access is meaningful. Similarly, prisoners who are familiar with the law can only have meaningful access if items such as law books and other legal materials are made available for their use.

In *Bounds* v. *Smith* (430 U.S. 817, 1977), the Court addressed the question of what constitutes meaningful access and ruled that prisons must provide adequate law libraries (e.g., holding such references as state statutes, court reports, legal dictionaries, and law textbooks) or adequate legal assistance from persons trained in the law (e.g., lawyers, paralegal assistants, and/or law student interns). In *Lewis* v. *Casey* (516 U.S. 804, 1996), the Court provided further explanation saying that *Bounds* did not create a freestanding right to a law library or even to legal assistance. Instead, *Bounds* simply established the right of prisoners to access the courts. So, for a violation of *Bounds* to occur, prisoners must show that the provided prison library or legal assistance program is hindering their efforts to pursue a legal claim.

Issues of Religion

Of the two religion clauses found in the First Amendment (the establishment clause and the free exercise clause), the issue of free exercise presents greater problems in a prison environment. The free exercise clause itself has been taken to have two aspects: the freedom to believe and the freedom to act. In *Cantwell* v. *Connecticut* (310 U.S. 296, 1940), the Court decided that "the first is absolute but, in the nature of things, the second cannot be. Conduct remains subject to [governmental] regulation for the protection of society" (310 U.S. at 303). With this decision, the Court understands that the First Amendment gives all people the absolute right to whatever religious beliefs they wish but not necessarily to every action they may want to carry out. The most frequent reason for limiting an inmate's religious freedom has been the duty of prison officials to maintain security within an institution. A clear example of this is found in aspects of the Black Muslims' fight for recognition and rights in prisons and jails.

Smith (1993) highlights court decisions beginning in the 1960s that allowed restrictions on the freedom of the Nation of Islam (Black Muslims) to practice their religion. Prison officials readily acknowledge that Black Muslims were not afforded the same opportunity to practice their religion as were followers of more traditional faiths. But, the officials argued, the Black Muslims presented security problems that other religions did not present, and, as a result, the officials felt restrictions were proper. For example, the California Supreme Court (*In re Ferguson,* 55 Cal.2d 663, 1961) said that prison authorities were allowed to prohibit Black Muslims from worshiping and from studying church literature because the Muslims' philosophy and assertive behavior threatened the correctional institution (Smith, 1993).

With the *Cooper* v. *Pate* decision (discussed earlier under the Civil Rights Act), Black Muslims began having some success in gaining privileges similar to those granted to the more traditional religions. And in a federal district court decision (*Northern* v. *Nelson,* 315 F. Supp. 687, 1970), the court held that the prison library was obliged to make copies of the Qur'an available and that prisoners must be allowed to receive *Muhammad Speaks* unless it could be clearly demonstrated that a particular issue would substantially disrupt prison discipline.

The requirement that prison officials must prove that an inmate's religious freedom threatens prison security and must

LEARNING OUTCOMES 2 Discuss the issues associated with prisoners' rights in terms of their access to courts and religion.

be restricted continues in more recent court decisions. In *O'Lone* v. *Estate of Shabazz* (482 U.S. 342, 1987), the court heard arguments on a New Jersey prison policy that prevented Muslim inmates from attending weekly congregational service (*Jumu'ah*). The Muslim prisoners argued that the service was central to the observation of the Muslim faith and that their participation was a necessary component to their freedom of religion. Muslim inmates with work assignments outside the prison's main buildings were unable to return for the Friday afternoon service. Seeking alternatives that would allow them to attend the services without missing any work hours, the inmates asked to be placed on inside work detail or be given substitute weekend tasks. The prison rejected these proposals as unacceptable given scarce prison personnel and potential security problems. The court, although agreeing that *Jumu'ah* was of central importance to the Islamic faith, said that the prison policy did not violate the inmates' constitutional rights because the policy was reasonably related to **legitimate penological interests**—that is, rather than being arbitrary or developed without any appreciation of the importance of the services to Muslims, the policy was established out of concern for prison order and security.

The *Turner* v. *Safley* Standards

Reference to legitimate penological interests in the *O'Lone* v. *Estate of Shabazz* is of particular importance in understanding contemporary court decisions on prisoners' rights. In its 1987

Turner v. *Safley* (482 U.S. 78) decision (made one week before *O'Lone* v. *Estate of Shabazz*), the U.S. Supreme Court laid out four factors to be considered when deciding if a prison regulation that interferes with a prisoner's constitutional rights is a valid policy:

1. Does the regulation have a valid, rational connection to a legitimate governmental interest?

2. Do inmates have available alternate means to exercise the asserted right?

3. How would accommodation of the right affect correctional officers, inmates, and prison resources?

4. Are there ready alternatives to the regulation?

The importance of *Turner* is noted by del Carmen, Ritter, and Witt (2005), who point out that the ruling provides a single test (i.e., is the restriction reasonably related to legitimate penological interests?) for responding to prisoner complaints and gives prison officials more power and authority in prison administration. Because prison officials are obliged to maintain security and discipline within the institution (making those things legitimate penological interests), prison officials may have to occasionally restrict what would otherwise be a constitutionally protected right of prisoners. As a result, when prison authorities can show that such restrictions are necessary for security and disciplinary reasons, the courts will typically approve the prison policy under the *Turner* v. *Safley* standards.

Using those standards, courts have restricted publications coming into a prison when the warden determines them to be detrimental to the security, good order, or discipline of the institution (*Thornburgh* v. *Abbott,* 490 U.S. 401, 1989; *Beard* v. *Banks,* 548 U.S. 521, 2006); restricted treating a prisoner with antipsychotic drugs against his or her will and without a judicial hearing (*Washington* v. *Harper,* 494 U.S. 210, 1990); and placed restrictions on prison visitations (*Overton* v. *Bazetta,* 539 U.S. 126, 2003) and other aspects of life in prison.

▶ *Limiting Inmate Litigation*

By the mid-1990s, prison and jail inmates were bringing annually to federal court more than 40,000 new lawsuits challenging the conditions of their confinement. The cases were noteworthy

Think About It…

Since its passage by Congress in 2000, the Religious Land Use and Institutionalized Persons Act (RLUIPA) has been the basis for many prison lawsuits related to prisoners' religious rights. The RLUIPA requires states to allow prisoners to practice their religious beliefs unless those officials can show that restricting religious practices is both necessary for an important and legitimate goal (security, for example) and that it is the least restrictive way they can achieve that goal. More states are now allowing sweat lodges, which are an important aspect of Native American spirituality. What type of religious practices do you think are probably allowed in most prisons? What do you suppose are some that could be legitimately disallowed?

Redux Pictures

for their sheer number and for being the federal court case type with the lowest plaintiff win rate. These statistics highlight two qualities long associated with prisoner lawsuits: their volume and the low rate of plaintiffs' success (Ostrom, Hanson, & Cheesman II, 2003; Schlanger, 2003).

Many of the lawsuits were filed at taxpayer expense because the prisoners claimed they lacked funds to pay filing fees (i.e., they took *in forma pauperis* status). The nature of many of the lawsuits, their growing number, the increasing burden they placed on federal courts, and the expense to taxpayers having to support the judicial system's handling of the cases resulted in strong public opinion for reform.

Congress's response to the public outcry was the **Prison Litigation Reform Act (PLRA)**. The act attempted to limit the ability of prisoners to complain about conditions of their confinement or alleging violation of their constitutional rights. That goal was to be achieved, as Figure 11–3 summarizes, by discouraging *in forma pauperis* lawsuits (frequent-filer provision), reducing meritless claims (three-strikes provision), and requiring inmates to first use the prison's grievance procedures (exhausted remedies provision).

With these provisions, the PLRA was intended to reduce the volume of prisoner litigation and to improve the merit of those claims that are filed. Research indicates that it has been successful at both, with most studies concluding that the PLRA has produced a statistically significant decrease in both the volume and trend of Section 1983 lawsuits since its passage. Similarly, research on the "more meritorious" question suggests that the PLRA has weeded out the more frivolous cases (Cheesman II, Ostrom, & Hanson, 2004; Ostrom et al., 2003; Schlanger, 2003). However, critics suggest there have also been negative, if unintended, consequences such as the inability of cases concerning, rape, assault, and religious rights violations to get filed in federal court (Alvarado, 2012).

LEARNING OUTCOMES 3 — Describe how inmate litigation is limited.

▶ Civil Disabilities and Other Postconviction Sanctions

Walter Mosley's fictional character Socrates Fortlow is an ex-con trying to readjust to life on the streets. At one point, Socrates exclaims that just because a guy's no longer in prison that doesn't mean he's free. That sentiment is shared by many released inmates who find that opportunities are blocked because of their ex-con status. In many jurisdictions, persons convicted of a felony lose some of their civil rights, meaning that they are not legally full citizens even after finishing their sentence. That status hinders full reintegration and contributes to recidivism. The sanctions imposed on convicted felons after serving time are discussed in this section. These sanctions are defined as "civil" rather than criminal in nature and as "disabilities" rather than punishments.

Under early English common law, a convicted offender might, in addition to his sentence, lose all his civil rights and have to forfeit his property. As a result of this **civil death** sanction, offenders forfeited all rights and privileges of citizenship, including things such as the right to enter into a contract (even marriage) or the right to sue. They were, in other words, civilly dead. Today, criminal offenders are more likely to suffer **civil disabilities**—that is, partial rather than absolute loss of civil rights—and, in this sense, are more civilly disabled than civilly dead. States and the federal government impose these civil disabilities in ways that can affect offenders both during incarceration and after release. The disabilities that continue to affect the offender after release from prison are the concern of this section.

Invisible Punishments

We typically think of punishments as being rather obvious—certainly to the person being punished, but also to others in society. The person who has been fined, required to report to a probation officer, or placed in jail or prison certainly considers his or her punishment to be quite apparent. The punishments

Three PLRA provisions affecting prisoner litigation may be summarized as follows:

1. *Frequent-filer provision:* To discourage prisoners from filing meritless lawsuits *in forma pauperis*, inmates must pay the full $150 fee (and costs, where applicable) when filing a complaint, or they must make an initial down payment followed by periodic installment payments. A truly indigent prisoner can still file his or her claim or appeal without paying the fee, but he or she may accumulate a substantial bill over time.

2. *Three-strikes provision:* To keep prisoners from filing meritless claims, indigent prisoners are prohibited from filing new lawsuits when they have previously filed three or more actions that were dismissed as frivolous or malicious. That provision is waived if there is an immediate threat of physical harm.

3. *Exhausted remedies provision:* Inmates must exhaust all available administrative remedies through the inmate grievance systems at their place of confinement before filing a complaint.

FIGURE 11–3 **PLRA Provisions Affecting Prisoner Litigation.**

are also made visible to anyone else who is interested enough to find out what punishments were imposed in a particular case. They could see it or hear about it through various media or might even look it up in court records. But, as shown in Table 11–3, oftentimes there are other punishments accompanying those visible ones that surprise even the offender. Did the convicted burglar realize that even after completing his sentence he will not be able to vote? Did the convicted drug distributor know that she may not be able to receive welfare or nutrition assistance as a result of that conviction? Possibly even more surprised may be the teenage daughter of that convicted drug distributor upon hearing that her mother may not be allowed to live in public housing—leaving the daughter to wonder where she and her family will live. Those examples of disenfranchisement (loss of the right to vote), being prohibited from receiving welfare, and not being able to live in public housing are examples of sanctions that Travis (2002) has termed **invisible punishments** because they operate mostly beyond public view, yet have very serious, adverse consequences for the individuals affected. Specifically, they are invisible because they (1) cannot be evaluated as to their effectiveness, impact, or even how they are implemented; (2) typically take effect outside of the traditional sentencing framework (i.e., rather than being part of a sentence, they are secondary consequences); and (3) are often created without public debate and typically remain unknown to the public (Travis, 2002, pp. 15–17).

Invisible punishments are especially important because they add **collateral consequences** to the sentence. This means that the invisible punishments have accompanying or secondary consequences beyond the actual sentence that was imposed. Those collateral effects tend to increase the negative consequences of a criminal conviction and they can be described as falling into three categories (Periman, 2007):

LEARNING OUTCOMES 4 — Summarize the issues associated with the loss of civil rights.

1. Impaired access to, or enjoyment of, the ordinary rights and benefits associated with citizenship or residence (e.g., not being allowed to vote, losing your driver's license, or having restriction placed on where you can live).

2. Impaired economic opportunity, primarily through reduction of the range of available employment (see the examples in Figure 11–4).

3. Increased severity of sanctions in any subsequent criminal proceeding brought against the offender (e.g., in some states, a prior felony conviction can trigger forfeiture of a car or boat that is used in a subsequent crime involving alcohol).

Importantly, some states are enacting policies that minimize the collateral impact of a criminal conviction (Porter, 2015, 2016). In recent years, legislatures have modified the felony

TABLE 11–3	EXAMPLES OF INVISIBLE PUNISHMENTS
Welfare benefits	The welfare reform package passed by Congress in 1996 included a lifetime ban on receiving welfare and food stamp benefits for anyone convicted of any federal or state felony drug offense (e.g., involving the use or sale of drugs). Congressional proponents of the ban argued that the government should neither feel nor have an obligation to support drug offenders—especially when the welfare benefits could be used to support drug habits.
	The bans on welfare benefits have had an especially harsh impact on women of color convicted of drug offenses. Critics of the ban argue that loss of welfare benefits makes it difficult for women to become self-sufficient, provide for their children, and be active participants in their community. Low-income women and their children are hindered in their ability to move out of poverty and as a result can increase child welfare caseloads. States can, however, opt out of the federal ban or modify it through legislation.
Public housing	Federal laws passed in the late 1990s allow public housing agencies to deny housing to anyone who had engaged in drug-related or violent criminal activity, or other criminal activity that would adversely affect the health, safety, and enjoyment of the premises of others. A tenant's and/or a tenant's visitor's possessing or using drugs on the premises is a basis for eviction from public housing. Persons convicted of drug offenses who can show that they have been rehabilitated can reapply for housing after a three-year waiting period.
Student loans	People convicted of drug offenses while enrolled in school and while receiving federal financial assistance become ineligible for federal student loans, grants, and work assistance unless they complete a treatment program. The length of the ban depends on the conviction and evidence of rehabilitation.

DISCUSS Which of these bans do you support? Why? What punishment philosophy do you feel these bans are trying to accomplish? Do you think the bans are successful in helping to achieve that penal goal?

Depending on the state, a person with a felony conviction could be prohibited from getting (or could have revoked or suspended) a license or permit to engage in certain occupations. Examples of occupations that may require a license or permit—again, depending on the state—include the following:

- Acupuncturists
- Bar tenders and managers
- Barber/beautician
- Construction contractors
- Hearing aid dealers
- Horse and dog racetrack employees
- Insurance sales people
- Interior designers
- Labor union officers
- Nurses
- Private detectives
- Real estate appraisers or brokers
- Security guards
- Social workers

Pearson Education Inc.

When a state places restrictions on entering or continuing in certain occupations as the result of a felony conviction, the restriction could be permanent or time-restricted (e.g., the prohibition is lifted five or ten years after the felony conviction).

FIGURE 11–4 Occupations That May Not Be Available to Ex-Cons.

drug bans on public assistance benefits to allow some convicted drug offenders meeting specified criteria to receive financial assistance (Alabama, California, Texas), prohibited public employers from inquiring about the criminal background of job candidates until after their first interview (Delaware), and lessened restrictions that prevented persons with felony convictions from getting occupational licenses such as cosmetology/barbering (Oklahoma) or from employment in nursing homes or long-term care facilities (Pennsylvania).

Two specific types of invisible punishments with far-reaching collateral consequences are sex offender registration and notification laws and the disenfranchisement of felons. We will take a closer look at each of these.

Sex Offender Registration, Notification, and Residence Restriction Laws

A particularly controversial topic related to restrictions placed on the ordinary rights of residency is linked to a specific type of crime—sex offenses. Collateral consequences of a sex offense conviction include **sex offender registration laws** and **public notification laws**. The former requires persons convicted of sex offenses to register in a community, even after they have completed their sentence for that conviction. The notification laws are an additional provision that requires that the public be notified of the name and location of certain sex offenders in the community. See Figure 11–5 for a discussion of whether notification laws encourage residents to modify their behavior.

Under the federal Sex Offender Registration and Notification Act (SORNA), all U.S. jurisdictions are required to pass registration and notification laws that conform to federal minimum standards or risk a penalty in receiving federal grants.

According to the Office of Justice Programs (2016), SORNA's goal is to strengthen the nationwide network of sex offender registration and notification programs by

- Extending the jurisdictions in which registration is required beyond the 50 states, the District of Columbia, and the principal U.S. territories, to also include federally recognized Indian tribes

- Incorporating a more comprehensive group of sex offenders and sex offenses for which registration is required

- Requiring registered sex offenders to register and keep their registration current in each jurisdiction in which they reside, work, or go to school

- Requiring sex offenders to provide more extensive registration information

- Requiring sex offenders to make periodic in-person appearances to verify and update their registration information

- Expanding the amount of information available to the public regarding registered sex offenders

- Making changes in the required minimum duration of registration for sex offenders

Although all states and the District of Columbia had registration and notification laws before SORNA's passage in 2006, those laws were not necessarily consistent with SORNA's minimum requirements. A 2008 national survey found inconsistencies between the federal mandates and state practices and that there are many barriers preventing states from implementing SORNA (Harris & Lobanov-Rostovsky, 2010). By February 2016, only 17 states had been identified by the Justice Department as having substantially implemented SORNA (Office of

Research on how community notification laws affect community members has consistently found that although the laws increase reported fear among residents, they have strong public support and are seen as providing an important public service. However, the research also shows that most residents do not access the available community notification information (Bandy, 2011). In addition, she explains, the findings are mixed as to whether notification prompts protective behavior. This point is important because an assumption of notification laws is that by providing people with knowledge about a person who poses a potential threat to their safety, they will change their behavior to lessen that risk.

Bandy (2011) studied that assumption with research in Minneapolis. Her results were consistent with other studies that found no statistically significant relationship between receiving notification about a high-risk sex offender and the adoption of self-protective behaviors. However, Bandy also found that parents who received information about a high-risk offender did adopt more protective behaviors to protect their children against victimization than did parents who had not received notification. So, although community members strongly support notification laws and report feeling safer as a result of knowing where sex offenders live, they engage in few protective behaviors as a result of the notification—except being slightly more likely to take protective action on behalf of their children (Levenson, 2011).

DISCUSS Because most child sexual abuse victims know the perpetrators, and because most offenders are not subject to notification laws, what do you think is gained by notification? What are some examples of protective behaviors that parents may adopt? Will those behaviors realistically protect their children from the people most likely to victimize them?

FIGURE 11–5 **Evidence-Based Practice—Does It Work?** Do Notification Laws Encourage Residents to Modify Their Behavior?

Justice Programs, 2016). Twenty-eight states are still struggling with the costs and bureaucratic bother of implementing SORNA and the other five have refused, mostly for political or fiscal reasons. One of the five states, Nebraska, stated a principled opposition to SORNA's lifetime registry requirement for juveniles (Prison Legal News, 2014). That issue is likely to present continued problems for implementation of SORNA as indicated by the Pennsylvania Supreme Court's ruling that mandatory lifetime registration of juvenile sexual offenders is unconstitutional (Prison Legal News, 2016).

Colorado, as the most recent state to be recognized as a SORNA conformer—in November 2013—provides a good example of a state's sex offender registration and notification law (see State of Colorado, n.d.).

Both adults and juveniles convicted of certain sex-related offenses in Colorado or another state are required to register at the law enforcement agency in the jurisdiction where they reside. Registration must occur within five business days of becoming a temporary or permanent resident of Colorado, of being released into the community under criminal justice supervision (probation, parole, community corrections), or of establishing an additional residence in Colorado. If released from the

Colorado Department of Corrections with no supervision, a sex offender must register the next business day.

Some sex offenders must re-register annually on their birth date, and any person convicted as an adult of especially serious offenses must register every 90 days for the remainder of his or her natural life (e.g., sexual assault on a child, incest, or a person found to be a sexually violent predator). Failure to comply with any registration requirements could result in the person being charged with the crime of "failure to register as a sex offender," which may be charged as a felony.

The community notification aspect of Colorado's law requires law enforcement agencies to release information regarding registered sex offenders that includes name, address, aliases, date of birth, photograph (upon request and if readily available), and the particular unlawful sexual behavior(s) for which the offender was convicted. No information concerning victims can be released.

In addition to the registration and notification laws, sex offenders are also subject to **residence restriction laws** that may require them to live in certain areas or restrict them from living in other areas. Tewksbury (2011) points out that limits on where registered sex offenders may live have been widely

Think About It...

Public notification of lawbreakers is designed to shame offenders and deter against future offending, as demonstrated by judges who order convicted sex offenders to display a sign in their front yard as part of the punishment. Is it sufficient to let people call their local law enforcement agency or check on a website to determine if there are registered sex offenders in their neighborhood, or would it be better to require signs to be posted? What are some of the implications of either approach?

shown to impose negative consequences on both offenders and their families. For example, registered sex offenders end up being concentrated either in very dense, socially disorganized communities or in rural communities lacking employment, treatment, and transportation options. Despite those negative consequences, residential restrictions are increasingly common across the nation.

Presumably, if residence restriction laws contributed to public safety, the negative consequences on the offenders would not be of much concern. However, existing research suggests that residential restrictions are likely to contribute very little to public safety. This is probably because of the faulty assumptions upon which residence restriction laws are based. For example, the general assumption is that all sex offenders victimize children and, most likely, children who are strangers to them. Tewksbury (2011) points out that both of those ideas are inaccurate. In addition, residence restrictions assume that if offenders live farther away from schools, day cares, and so on, they are unable or unlikely to access those facilities. That, of course, ignores the point that motivated offenders can use public transportation. When the proof of negative consequences to offenders and their families is set against the unproven assumptions that residence restrictions increase public safety, an increasing number of scholars and policymakers question the need for the residence restriction laws.

Civil Disenfranchisement

Another controversial loss that affects essentially all felons is **civil disenfranchisement**, or the loss of the right to vote. A person's eligibility to vote is regulated at the state level—even for national elections. The U.S. Constitution prohibits any state from denying the right to vote based on grounds of race, sex, or age (citizens of age 18 or older may vote), but beyond those basic qualifications, eligibility is regulated by each state. Of concern in this section is the ban that some states have imposed on persons convicted of a crime. This is no small group, with nearly 6 million Americans denied the right to vote because of laws disenfranchising people with criminal convictions (Chung, 2014). In most cases, those refer to felony convictions—and that is the general reference here—but it is important to note that 10 states and the District of Columbia also restrict some people with a misdemeanor conviction from voting (those states are listed at http://felonvoting.procon.org/).

A state-by-state breakdown of the provisions (see Table 11–4) shows that only two states (Maine and Vermont) do not disenfranchise convicted felons. In the 11 most restrictive states, a convicted felon may lose the right to vote even after serving his or her prison sentence and when the individual is no longer on probation or parole (Chung, 2014; ProCon.org, 2016).

Supporters of disenfranchisement offer several reasons for restricting a convicted felon from voting. Uggen, Behrens, and Manza (2005) discuss the primary ones as falling into the categories of retribution, deterrence, incapacitation, and rehabilitation. Felon disenfranchisement is retributive to the extent that it provides a sense of just deserts. But, as Uggen et al. note, a blanket disenfranchisement of all people convicted of felonies calls into question the proportionality of the punishment—especially when that disenfranchisement is permanent.

An argument for any deterrent effect in disenfranchisement relies on a belief that if people attach great significance to the right to vote, they will not commit another crime after having lost the right to vote while under a criminal sentence (specific deterrence) or will refrain from committing a crime for fear of losing that right (general deterrence). This point is supported by comments from George Steinbrenner, former owner of the New York Yankees baseball team. As a result of his conviction for making an illegal campaign contribution to Richard Nixon's 1972 reelection campaign, Steinbrenner lost his right to vote. Although his voting rights were restored by a pardon from President Reagan, Steinbrenner was still commenting some 30 years later about the pain caused him by the disenfranchisement (Manza & Uggen, 2006, p. 5). However, for most people losing the right to vote would likely not be the determining factor in whether they commit a crime.

It is difficult to justify felon disenfranchisement on the basis of incapacitation, as removing the right to vote cannot prevent people from committing other crimes unrelated to voting. Even for the few convicted of such crimes as electoral fraud, the ability of felon disenfranchisement to prevent repeat offending is questionable. In short, disenfranchisement prevents political participation, but not criminal activity.

The idea that disenfranchisement might be rehabilitative seems counterintuitive. Presumably, disenfranchisement could be rehabilitative if reenfranchisement was a reward for good behavior; but restoration of voting rights is rarely conditioned on good behavior. Instead, it is triggered automatically when a sentence is completed or a waiting period has passed. More likely, restricting voting rights hinders rehabilitative efforts. As Manza and Uggen (2006) suggest, it is more plausible that participation in this fundamental act of citizenship may foster respect for laws and the institutions that make and enforce them. That point is not farfetched, as at least one study has shown that, among people with an arrest history, about 27% of nonvoters were rearrested compared to 12% of voters in the sample (Manza & Uggen, 2006, p. 312). Possibly, there is at least a correlation between voting and recidivism among people who have had some official contact with the criminal justice system.

Other justifications for disenfranchisement have been offered, such as the idea that allowing criminals to vote dilutes the votes of law-abiding citizens and the suggestion that voting criminals might band together to oust government officials who are tough on crime. But those arguments are less mainstream than the others. Public opinion actually seems to favor restoring voting rights—at least for some. A Harris Interactive Poll found that only 31% of the respondents thought that people in prison should be allowed to vote, but 80% supported the right to vote for persons convicted of a crime who have served their entire sentence and are now living in the community (ProCon.org, 2009).

An argument against disenfranchisement that is considered to be especially persuasive by those favoring voting rights is that

TABLE 11–4 | FELON VOTING LAWS (CURRENT AS OF FEBRUARY 2016)

The legal ability of people with felony convictions to vote varies from state to state. Some states place no voting restriction on convicted felons, whereas other states permanently ban felons from voting even after being released from prison, parole, and probation. This table lists when, if ever, voting rights are restored in each state and the District of Columbia.

No Restrictions (2)	Restored After Term of Incarceration (15)	Restored After Term of Incarceration and Parole (4)	Restored After Term of Incarceration, Parole, and Probation (19)	May Lose Vote Permanently (11)
Maine Vermont	District of Colombia	California	Alaska	Alabama
	Hawaii	Colorado	Arkansas	Arizona
	Illinois	Connecticut	Georgia	Delaware[1]
	Indiana	New York	Idaho	Florida
	Maryland		Kansas	Iowa
	Massachusetts		Louisiana	Kentucky
	Michigan		Minnesota	Mississippi
	Montana		Missouri	Nevada
	New Hampshire		Nebraska[2]	Tennessee
	North Dakota		New Jersey	Virginia
	Ohio		New Mexico	Wyoming
	Oregon		North Carolina	
	Pennsylvania		Oklahoma	
	Rhode Island		South Carolina	
	Utah		South Dakota	
			Texas	
			Washington	
			West Virginia	
			Wisconsin	

Note: 1. Only persons convicted of murder or manslaughter, a felony offense against public administration involving bribery, improper influence or abuse of office, or a felony sexual offense are permanently disqualified from voting. People with other felony convictions are automatically eligible to vote after serving their full sentence, including incarceration, parole, and probation.

2. People convicted of a felony are automatically permitted to vote two years after completion of their sentence of incarceration and all parole and probation for all convictions except treason.

Source: ProCon.org. (2016). State felon voting laws. (February 9).Retrieved from http://felonvoting.procon.org/view.resource.php?resourceID=286.

the policy is racially discriminatory. Although felon disenfranchisement laws are race neutral on their face, their origins are tainted. After ratification of the Fifteenth Amendment (giving blacks the right to vote), many states specifically considered whether to retain the disenfranchisement of felons. Several southern state legislatures kept the felon restriction as one of several tools to lessen the ability of blacks to exercise their new right (Fellner & Mauer, 1998). A study of historical changes to state felon disenfranchisement laws concluded that states with greater non-white prison populations have been more likely to ban convicted felons from voting than states with proportionally fewer non-whites in the criminal justice system (Behrens, Uggen, & Manza, 2003, p. 596). Supporters of disenfranchisement respond to these charges with arguments that the uneven representation of black Americans among the disenfranchised felons is a result of their disproportionate representation among

persons committing felonies and not a result of racial discrimination in the laws themselves.

► Restoring Civil Rights Following a Conviction

As states and the federal government turn their attention toward reentry issues, there is increased recognition that some collateral consequences—especially those that impact employment, housing, and health—hinder the reintegration process. Between 2009 and 2014, 41 states and the District of Columbia enacted legislation designed to mitigate the burden of collateral consequences for individuals with certain criminal convictions (Subramanian, Moreno, & Gebreselassie, 2014). In some jurisdictions for some offenses, restoration of rights is automatic after sentence completion or some specific time period following sentence completion. When restoration is not automatic, the granting of a pardon was the primary method by which harsh consequences of a criminal conviction could be lessened or removed. However, the pardon power has fallen victim to political pressure, and has been used less often over the last several decades (Love, 2006; Subramanian et al., 2014). Instead, and in addition to any available automatic restoration mechanisms, a variety of new approaches are relied upon to bring relief from collateral consequences. Some of these are geared toward the individual offender whereas others affect the system more generally.

LEARNING OUTCOMES 5 Explain the ways civil rights can be restored and collateral consequences mitigated following a conviction.

Individual Restoration Methods

Pardons are certainly included in this grouping, but so too is the **expungement** or sealing of a conviction. When a conviction has been expunged or sealed, the criminal record is typically destroyed or made inaccessible to the public and the person is often able to deny his or her conviction—when completing employment forms, for example. However, the conviction normally remains available for law enforcement purposes.

Expungement or sealing is increasingly important as information technology and criminal records databases make it easier to find a person's criminal history online. Since 2009, more than 30 states and the District of Columbia have broadened the scope and impact of expungement and sealing remedies. For example, states have extended the eligibility for the remedy to more offenders, reduced the waiting periods before expungement, or sealing can be requested, or even making it automatic in some instances (National Association of Criminal Defense Lawyers, 2014; Subramanian et al., 2014).

Another individual restoration method is to offer an **offense downgrade** (e.g., from a felony to a misdemeanor conviction) to persons who have complied with conditions of supervision. In this way, compliant individuals avoid certain collateral consequences that attach to felony convictions.

One of the newer methods is to issue **certificates of rehabilitation** to people who have met certain rehabilitative standards. Also called "certificates of recovery," these documents are meant to help third parties, such as employers and landlords, make better-informed decisions about individuals with criminal records. Georgia inmates may receive certificates of program and treatment completion when they have fulfilled the terms of their treatment plans in prison and their reentry plans during probation or parole. New York's version is especially unique. Two types of certificates are offered in New York: a certificate of relief from disabilities (CRD) and a certificate of good conduct (CGC). They differ primarily in their eligibility requirements, with the CRD available to misdemeanants and first-time felons and the CGC available to repeat offenders. Both certificates have a similar legal effect in that they create a presumption of rehabilitation that must be considered by employers and licensing boards (Porter, 2015, 2016; Subramanian et al., 2014).

Systemic Relief Methods

In addition to approaches that effect persons individually, many states are using relief methods that apply more broadly. One such method is directed toward employment-related collateral consequences and is often referred to as **ban-the-box** policies because they prohibit inquiries into a job applicant's criminal history—at least upon initial application. That little box may discourage some people with convictions to even apply for a job, and those that do apply and check the box may never even get an interview. The ban-the-box initiative urges prospective employers to screen applicants based on job skills and individual qualifications before looking at criminal history. The laws take quite varied forms, however. Some apply only to public employers, whereas others include private employers. Some specify a point at which an employer is allowed to obtain criminal history information (for example, at the interview stage or after a conditional offer is made), but others establish time limits after which criminal convictions may no longer be considered at all (National Association of Criminal Defense Lawyers, 2014; Subramanian et al., 2014).

Another systemic relief method involves improved access to information. Specifically, states have enacted laws that provide convicted individuals better access to information about collateral consequences resulting from their conviction. Such measures are needed because there is no constitutional requirement that defendants be told of these consequences before being convicted. As a result, despite their availability, few offenders take advantage of—or may even be aware of—remedies to the collateral consequences of a criminal conviction. Vermont has addressed this issue with a law requiring state officials to prepare a comprehensive list of the consequences accompanying each offense in the Vermont criminal code. Not only are defendants informed of the collateral sanctions that accompany a conviction, they also are reminded of them upon release from prison and offered assistance in seeking relief from them (Porter, 2015).

The presence of collateral consequences has resulted in laws, regulations, and policies that require or allow employers, licensing agencies, landlords, and other decision makers to discriminate against applicants with criminal records. The results are significant and often insurmountable barriers for people with criminal histories as they seek housing, public benefits, employment, and even certain civil rights. Since most collateral consequences do not advance public safety—but may prevent persons with criminal records from moving on with their life—there is spreading support for the idea that punishment should end when a criminal sentence has been completed (National Association of Criminal Defense Lawyers 2014; Subramanian et al., 2014). As the criminal justice system shifts in perspective from tough-on-crime policies to having reentry and reintegration as guiding principles, there is a growing acceptance among leaders across the political spectrum—and with the public at large—that rehabilitation, treatment, and education should be important goals and that collateral consequences are not consistent with those goals.

Proof of Rehabilitation

In 2010, reporter Dawn Turner Trice brought Darrell Langdon's story to *Chicago Tribune* readers (Trice, 2010a, 2010b). It is a compelling story of a man who made a mistake two decades earlier and worked hard to pay his debt to society and to become a productive, law-abiding citizen. His success in doing so was even formally acknowledged by a court-granted certificate of good conduct that attests to a person's rehabilitation.

Langdon had been convicted of possessing half a gram of cocaine in 1985 and he was sentenced to serve six months on probation and pay a $100 fine. At the time of his conviction, he worked for the Chicago Public Schools (a job he was allowed to keep after his conviction) until 1995 when he was laid off during a major restructuring. He worked as a mortgage broker and also as a building engineer until 2008 when he applied for another job with Chicago Public Schools (CPS). His application was denied because the Illinois School Code prohibits persons with records such as Langdon from working in public schools. Langdon told Trice that he had been sober since 1988, reared two sons as a single parent, and had a very good work history since the conviction.

The desire to have some way that a person can show he or she has been rehabilitated raises several interesting questions:

1. A CPS spokesperson said, "This individual sounds like he did everything he should be doing to rehabilitate himself into professional and private community. We're glad to see that, but the delicate balance is that we need to ensure we're hiring people who won't put our children in jeopardy" (quoted in Trice, 2010a). What things could CPS or any other workplace use to determine whether someone is rehabilitated and safe to have work around children?

2. In 2010, under a newly revised law, Langdon applied for a certificate of good conduct that lifts statutory barriers to employment for persons with lower-grade felony convictions. That certificate allowed CPS to hire Langdon and, after an initial denial, CPS did so under new rules established in response to Langdon's case. Pardon and expungement of adult criminal records is becoming increasingly rare. *Do you think certificates of rehabilitation will be the main process by which civil rights are restored in the future? What do you see as some problems and benefits of this procedure?*

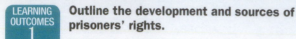
LEARNING OUTCOMES 1

Outline the development and sources of prisoners' rights.

Rather than taking an extreme position of constitutional rights being either totally lost or all retained upon entering prison, the courts have tried to determine what rights can be compatible with the goals of prison administration. When making that determination, courts turn to a variety of sources, including state constitutions and laws passed by federal and state legislators; but prisoners' rights are primarily found in the U.S. Constitution, including the Bill of Rights, and the Civil Rights Act. Courts have responded differently over the years to inmate claims as they moved from an early "hands-off" position that essentially let prison officials make decisions without interference from the courts to a period when the courts were very much involved in deciding how prisons should operate to a current position wherein the courts are more likely to defer to the reasonable assessment of prison officials as to what rights may require violation.

1. Identify and explain at least three important prisoners' rights cases.

2. How would you describe to a layperson what is meant by the phrase "cruel and unusual punishment"?

3. Explain the Fourteenth Amendment's due process clause and its equal protection clause. Give examples of how both have been used in prisoners' rights cases.

4. What are civil rights and how do they relate to prisoner claims?

5. List and explain the three eras of judicial involvement in prison administration.

rights-are-retained position Argues that prisoners keep all the rights of an ordinary citizen, except those that are expressly or by necessity taken away from them by law.

rights-are-lost position Argues that prisoners are wholly without rights except those expressly conferred by law or necessity.

writ of *habeas corpus* Judicial mandate to a prison official ordering that an inmate be brought to the court in order to determine the legality of the prisoner's detention.

***ex post facto* law** A law imposing a greater punishment for a crime than was allowed when the crime was committed.

incorporation Legal theory arguing that all provisions of the Bill of Rights are made applicable to the states through the due process clause.

due process clause That section of the Fourteenth Amendment requiring all states to abide by the Bill of Rights when depriving a person of life, liberty, or property.

equal protection clause That section of the Fourteenth Amendment prohibiting any state from denying equal protection of the law to persons within its jurisdiction.

civil rights Those personal, natural rights that protect people against arbitrary or discriminatory treatment.

Section 1983 claim A claim brought under the authority of U.S. Code Title 42, Section 1983 that civil rights have been violated.

LEARNING OUTCOMES 2

Discuss the issues associated with prisoners' rights in terms of their access to courts and religion.

Prisoners have claimed violations of many types of constitutional rights linked to such things as conditions of their confinement, lack of attention to medical needs, violation of privacy rights, and others. Of the types of lawsuits filed, those related to prisoner access to courts are particularly important because without that access prisoners would not be able to have a hearing on any of their other claims. Another important type of inmate lawsuit is when prisoners claim violation of the ability to practice their religion.

1. Why is access to courts such an important right for prisoners?

2. Summarize what steps the courts require prison officials to take so that prisoners have access to courts.

3. Distinguish the freedom to believe and the freedom to practice as they relate to freedom of religion. Which one can prison officials restrict? Why that one and not the other?

4. Explain the meaning and importance of the phrase "legitimate penological interests."

legitimate penological interests Standard used by courts to determine whether a prison policy was developed in an arbitrary manner or out of concern for prison order and security.

LEARNING OUTCOMES 3

Describe how inmate litigation is limited.

In an attempt to limit what was becoming a very large number of inmate lawsuits, Congress passed the Prison Litigation Reform Act (PLRA) in 1995. That act was intended to reduce the volume of prisoner litigation and improve the merit of those claims that are filed. Indications are that the act has succeeded at both.

1. What do you think would be examples of frivolous lawsuits that prisoners might file? Why would prisoners file such lawsuits knowing that they will likely be tossed out by the courts?

2. Explain the frequent-filer provision of the PLRA. Do you think this presents desirable and appropriate restrictions? Why or why not?

3. Explain the three-strikes provision of the PLRA. Do you think this presents desirable and appropriate restrictions? Why or why not?

4. Explain the exhausted remedies provision of the PLRA. Do you think this presents desirable and appropriate restrictions? Why or why not?

Prison Litigation Reform Act (PLRA) Intended to reduce the volume of prisoner litigation and to improve the merit of filed claims, including limiting nongovernmental organizations to legally challenge prison conditions and automatically terminating court orders after two years regardless of compliance.

LEARNING OUTCOMES 4

Summarize the issues associated with the loss of civil rights.

A criminal conviction (usually a felony, but sometimes a misdemeanor) can result in the loss of certain rights that are typically associated with full citizenship. Depending on the jurisdiction, these lost civil rights might include the ability to vote, serve on a jury, receive welfare benefits, or engage in certain occupations. Because these sanctions are less obvious than the actual sentence an offender receives, they have been called invisible punishments and are important because of the collateral consequences they add to the sentence. Examples of those invisible punishments and their collateral consequences are sex offender registration and notification laws and the disenfranchisement of felons.

1. Distinguish between civil death and civil disabilities.

2. What is meant by the concept of invisible punishments?

3. Should defendants be told of collateral consequences associated with a felony conviction—much like suspects are informed of their rights when *Miranda* warnings are read? Why or why not?

4. Distinguish between sex offender registration laws and public notification laws.

5. What are some reasons offered in support of restricting convicted felons from voting? Which, if any, do you find persuasive?

6. On what basis do some people claim that felon disenfranchisement laws were and are racially discriminatory?

civil death Convicted offenders forfeit all rights and privileges of citizenship, including things such as the right to enter into a contract or the right to sue.

civil disabilities Convicted offenders suffer a partial, rather than an absolute, loss of civil rights because of a criminal conviction.

invisible punishments Sanctions operating mostly beyond public view, yet having very serious adverse consequences for the individuals affected.

collateral consequences Secondary consequences beyond the actual sentence that was imposed.

sex offender registration laws Require persons convicted of sex offenses to register in a community, even after they have completed their sentence for that conviction.

public notification laws Require that the public be notified of the name and location of certain sex offenders in the community.

residence restriction laws Require sex offenders to live in certain areas or restrict them from living in other areas.

civil disenfranchisement The loss of the right to vote due, for example, to a felony conviction.

Explain the ways civil rights can be restored and collateral consequences mitigated following a conviction.

Increased attention to reentry has brought concern as to how collateral consequences of a felony conviction can hinder the reintegration and rehabilitation process. In some jurisdictions for some offenses, restoration of rights and mitigation of collateral consequences are automatic after sentence completion or some specific time period following sentence completion. When restoration or mitigation is not automatic, there are a variety of approaches that states may rely upon to accomplish those actions. Some of the methods, called individual restoration, include a pardon, expungement of the criminal record, an offense downgrade from a felony to a misdemeanor conviction, and the issuing of a certificate of rehabilitation. Other methods, called systemic relief, include ban-the-box policies that delay the point in a job application process when the applicant can be asked about his or her criminal record, and attempts to provide defendants with more complete information about the collateral consequences of their conviction and inform persons completing their sentence about remedies to collateral consequences.

1. It is suggested that the granting of a pardon is less frequent today than in the past because of political pressure. Do you think that is true? If not, what other reasons can explain its less frequent use?

2. When criminal records are expunged, the conviction information is often still available to law enforcement. Is that appropriate or not?

3. Explain the idea behind a certificate of rehabilitation and whether you think it can be an effective way to lessen the negative effect of collateral consequences.

4. Do you think ban-the-box policies are a good idea or do they keep important information about a job applicant hidden from the prospective employer for too long?

5. Should states be legally required to tell convicted felons who are completing their sentence about any actions they can take to get relief from the collateral sanctions that accompany a conviction?

expungement A court-ordered process for closing public access to arrest and conviction records. The term is often used interchangeably with the term "sealing."

offense downgrade A legal procedure available in some states to qualified offenders who have complied with conditions of supervision wherein felony records are reduced to misdemeanor status in order to minimize exposure to collateral consequences.

certificate of rehabilitation Generic term for an official recognition that a criminal offender has shown reliability and good character over time and deserves to regain lost civil rights.

ban-the-box Taking its name from the check box on job applications that asks about criminal convictions (and sometimes arrests), this initiative calls for delaying the point at which prospective employers can ask about an applicant's criminal history.

Additional Links

Visit the ACLU Prisoners' Rights page at **www.aclu.org/prisoners-right** for news and cases.

Read about the award-winning film *Writ Writer* at **www.writwritermovie.com/index.html** for an interesting portrayal of a self-taught jailhouse lawyer who challenged the constitutionality of prison conditions in Texas in the 1960s.

Read about the civil disabilities imposed in your state by visiting the Legal Action Center's "Roadblocks to Reentry" page at **www.lac.org/roadblocks-to-reentry/main.php?view=law**.

Get more information about felon disenfranchisement at **www.sentencingproject.org/template/page.cfm?id=133**.

Watch a video on whether ex-cons should be allowed to vote at **http://felonvoting.procon.org/view.resource.php?resourceID=005543**.

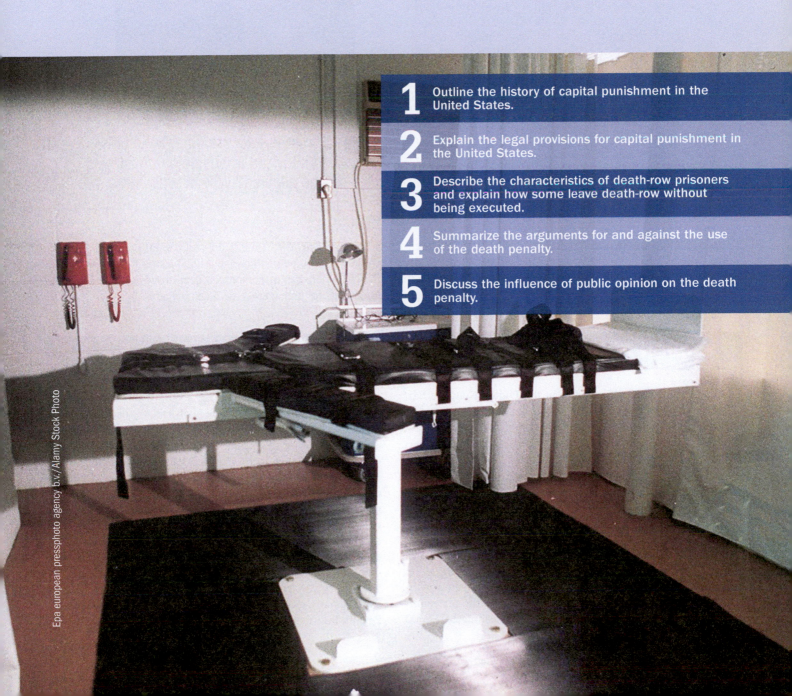

12

Capital Punishment

1 Outline the history of capital punishment in the United States.

2 Explain the legal provisions for capital punishment in the United States.

3 Describe the characteristics of death-row prisoners and explain how some leave death-row without being executed.

4 Summarize the arguments for and against the use of the death penalty.

5 Discuss the influence of public opinion on the death penalty.

LETTING THE MURDER VICTIM'S FAMILY SPEAK

On February 18, 2011, the *Lakeland (FL) Ledger* read, "Jurors Cry as Victim's Son Testifies in Leon Davis Murder Trial." The story went on to explain how several jurors dabbed at tears as 11-year-old Damon Lugo told them how lonely and sad his family was now that his mother was gone. Damon explained that they were a happy family of four but now a lonely and sad family of three (Schottelkotte, 2011). Just a few days earlier, the same jury had found Leon Davis, Jr., guilty of murdering Yvonne Bustamante, Damon's mom. The jury was now in the penalty phase and was hearing testimony from both victim and offender family members. The opportunity to speak during the penalty phase of a capital trial is provided as a way for jurors to hear thoughts and feelings that would not have been allowed during the trial.

The U.S. Supreme Court (*Payne* v. *Tennessee*, 501 U.S. 808, 1991) recognized that victims have rights in criminal cases—including the right to explain how a crime has affected their lives. In murder cases, the victim's family is allowed to tell about the victim and about the harm caused by the offender. A concern expressed by some is that allowing these victim impact statements in capital cases could arouse the emotions of jurors and bias them in favor of imposing death. A study by Paternoster and Deise (2011) suggests that this concern might be valid. According to their research, when victim impact evidence was used, the research subjects were more likely to have favorable perceptions of the victim and the victim's family and unfavorable perceptions of the offender. Those positive feelings toward the

Jenny Swanson/Getty images

victim and the victim's family were related to a heightened risk of them imposing the death penalty.

DISCUSS **If victim impact statements do bias jurors toward imposing death, should they still be allowed? Why or why not?**

The topics of capital punishment and the use of the death penalty give rise to some of the most emotional, yet academically interesting, debates of any criminal justice issue. The breadth and depth of issues are too many to tackle here, so we begin with a brief review of the history of capital punishment. Then we consider some of the related legal issues before moving to the characteristics of persons on death row. We conclude with arguments for and against the death penalty.

▶ Capital Punishment Yesterday and Today

The history of the death penalty in the United States is best understood by viewing it as two historical periods: the early period prior to 1972 and the modern period from 1972 forward. The distinguishing event was the 1972 U.S. Supreme Court decision in *Furman* v. *Georgia* (408 U.S. 238) that (as we see later) began the modern era of capital punishment. We cover these periods in a brief history of capital punishment.

A Short History of Capital Punishment in the United States

When British settlers came to the New World, they brought with them the practice of capital punishment. It had been a well-established punishment in England and during the sixteenth-century reign of Henry VIII (1509–1547), an estimated 72,000

men and women were executed for a variety of offenses. By the 1700s, more than 200 crimes were punishable by death in Britain, including stealing and cutting down a growing tree. Even into the 1800s, there were more than 100 crimes punishable by death (Death Penalty Information Center, 2016f; Kronenwetter, 1993).

With that heritage, it is not surprising that the American colonies came to rely on capital punishment as well. The first recorded execution in the colonies was in 1608 in the Jamestown Colony of Virginia when Captain George Kendall was executed for being a spy for Spain. The death penalty could also be applied in Virginia during the early 1600s for such minor offenses as stealing grapes, killing chickens, and trading with Indians. In the mid-1600s, the New York Colony punished by death such crimes as striking one's mother or father (Death Penalty Information Center, 2016f).

By the start of the American Revolution, the death penalty was used in all 13 colonies, with Rhode Island being the only colony that did not have at least 10 crimes punishable by death (ProCon.org, 2013). The colonies had fairly similar death statutes that covered arson, piracy, treason, murder, sodomy, burglary, robbery, rape, horse stealing, slave rebellion, and often counterfeiting. Hanging was the usual sentence. But it did not take long before changes began occurring in the death penalty's application.

As explained in Chapter 3, continued reliance on corporal and capital punishment as the primary sanctions for criminal behavior began falling out of favor by the middle to late 1800s. The Pennsylvania Quakers worked to have long-term imprisonment accepted as a humanitarian alternative to the existing punishments and various death penalty abolitionist societies began appearing across the country. Other key changes during the nineteenth century included making a distinction between first- and second-degree murder, a discontinuance of public executions, and a movement from mandatory to discretionary capital punishment statutes (Bohm, 2003; del Carmen, Vollum, Cheeseman, Frantzen, & San Miguel, 2005).

LEARNING OUTCOMES 1 Outline the history of capital punishment in the United States.

During the first half of the twentieth century, there were increased calls for the death penalty's abolition. However, after a period in the early 1900s, when several states abolished and then reinstated capital punishment, there was resurgence in its use from the 1920s to the 1940s. In the 1930s, there were more executions in America than there have been in any other decade—averaging 167 executions per year (Bohm, 2003). By the 1950s, public sentiment in America—and in many of the Allied nations that had fought in World War II—had turned away from the death penalty and the number of executions in the United States dropped dramatically.

Between 1608 (America's first execution) and 1972, there were more than 14,000 executions in colonial America and the United States. Forty-nine percent of those executed were black, 41% were white, and the remainder fell into the "other" category (Death Penalty Information Center, 2016c). In the period from 1930 to 1976, most of those executed were African-Americans (54%) and men (99%). Executions were typically for murder (86%, with blacks accounting for 49% of these executions), and 12% were for rape, in which blacks accounted for 90% of the executions (Office of Justice Programs, 1978).

African-Americans constituted between 10 and 12% of the total U.S. population during the twentieth century. Their 54% representation among persons executed in the mid-twentieth century was very lopsided. This disproportionate representation of African-Americans among those executed was one of the factors leading the U.S. Supreme Court to declare the death penalty unconstitutional in 1972, and that decision marked the end of capital punishment's early period in America.

Capital Punishment in the Modern Era

Specifics of the U.S. Supreme Court decision that marked the beginning of the death penalty's modern era in the United States are covered in the later section "Capital Punishment and the Law." Suffice it to say that in 1972 the death penalty was placed in a limbo status as states tried to create death penalty statutes that the U.S. Supreme Court would find to be constitutional. Here, as we cover capital punishment's history, we concentrate on how the death penalty has been implemented during this modern era from 1972 to the present.

Today, 31 states plus the federal government and the U.S. military have death penalty statutes. The most recent states to abolish the death penalty were Connecticut (2012), Maryland

Think About It…

Even brief attention to the question of who—beyond the victim and the murderer—is affected by the initial crime and an eventual execution brings to mind the victim's family and friends as well as the family and friends of the offender. Persons affected who don't come to mind as quickly are the employees charged with carrying out the execution. Every execution requires a team of employees who strap the inmate to the gurney, who insert and reinsert the needles, and who remove the inmate's body after the execution. These are the people who deal with botched executions and struggle with inmates fighting to stay alive. They are also the people who, haunted by the experience of putting people to death, have committed suicide, turned to alcohol, or suffered mental and physical health problems (Equal Justice USA, n.d.). As one former warden who supervised two executions explained, those who have been personally and

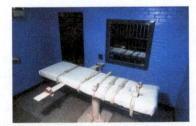

Source: Paul Harris pacificcoastnews/Newscom

directly involved in executing someone carry an immeasurable burden of awful, life-long repercussions (Thompson, 2015). There are cases of wardens, executioners, and correctional officers suffering PSTD-like symptoms as a result of their involvement with the death penalty. The experience leads to emotional and physical distress, such as mood swings, flashbacks, and nightmares. Importantly, feelings of shame and guilt last long after the employees have resigned or retired (Martinez, 2014). Should prisons simply assign execution duties to employees or should execution teams consist only of employee volunteers? Should employees (whether volunteers or not) be warned of what former warden Allen Ault says is the possibility that service on execution teams might result in life-long nagging doubt, shame, and guilt (Sackur, 2014)?

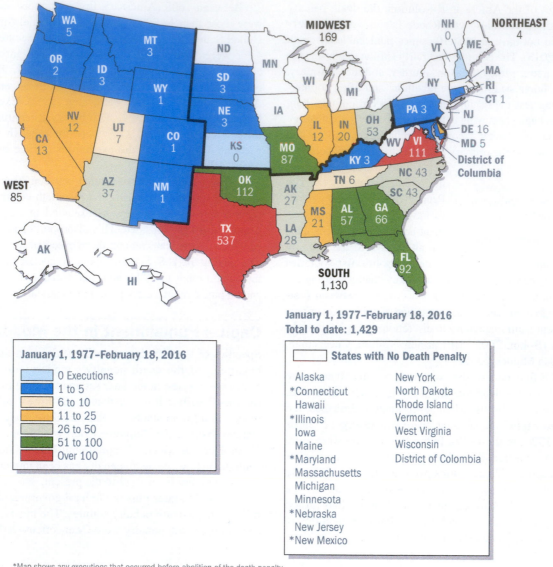

MIDWEST
169

NORTHEAST
4

WEST
85

SOUTH
1,130

January 1, 1977–February 18, 2016
Total to date: 1,429

January 1, 1977–February 18, 2016

0 Executions	
1 to 5	
6 to 10	
11 to 25	
26 to 50	
51 to 100	
Over 100	

States with No Death Penalty

Alaska	New York
*Connecticut	North Dakota
Hawaii	Rhode Island
*Illinois	Vermont
Iowa	West Virginia
Maine	Wisconsin
*Maryland	District of Colombia
Massachusetts	
Michigan	
Minnesota	
*Nebraska	
New Jersey	
*New Mexico	

*Map shows any executions that occurred before abolition of the death penalty.

FIGURE 12–1 **Executions by State, January 1, 1977–February 18, 2016.**
Source: Death Penalty Information Center. (2016e). Number of executions by state and region since 1976. (February 18).
Retrieved from http://www.deathpenaltyinfo.org/numberexecutions- state-and-region-1976.

(2013), and Nebraska (2015). The map in Figure 12–1 shows that all 33 jurisdictions retaining the death penalty (except the U.S. military, which had its last execution in 1961) have held at least one execution since 1976. Statistics from the Death Penalty Information Center (2016e) show that through February 18, 2016, 1,429 executions took place in the United States since 1976. Texas, Oklahoma, and Virginia (in order) accounted for 53% of those executions. Of the persons executed during that period, 55% were white, 35% were African-American, 8% were Latino, and 2% were of another race/ethnicity. More than 80% of the executions have occurred in the South and less than 1% have taken place in the Northeast.

The primary features of capital punishment's modern era concern legal challenges to the death penalty (as reviewed in the "Capital Punishment and the Courts" section), but a particularly interesting aspect of the period was a change in the method of execution. Figure 12–2 reviews methods of execution

popular in the twentieth century, but the preferred method in the twenty-first century is actually a return to one of the oldest—administering a lethal drug. More than 2,300 years ago, Socrates was executed by drinking a cup of hemlock, and in 1982 Charlie Brooks, Jr., received lethal injections of sodium thiopental (an anesthetic), pancuronium bromide (a muscle relaxant designed to paralyze), and potassium chloride (to stop the heart and cause death). He died, as planned, from the overdose of sodium thiopental, and dying in this way was presumed to be much like falling asleep.

The execution of Brooks made Texas the first state—and the first jurisdiction in the world—to use lethal injection as a method of execution. Figure 12–3 highlights some of the other notable events in the death penalty's history. Texas officials lauded the new technique as less painful, less offensive, and more palatable. Today, all jurisdictions with the death penalty have authorized lethal injection as a method of execution (Snell, 2014).

Hanging

- This is the primary execution method in the United States until the 1890s.
- If the inmate has strong neck muscles, if he or she is very light, if the "drop" is too short, or if the noose has been wrongly positioned, the fracture-dislocation is not rapid and death results from slow asphyxiation.
- It is currently an option in New Hampshire and Washington, but lethal injection is the primary method in both states.

Source: © Helder Almeida/Fotolia

Electrocution

- This was first used in 1888 by New York as a more humane method of execution than hanging.
- It was presumed to be a relatively painless way to die because death would be virtually immediate, but others suggested that the body fluids must heat close to the boiling point of water in order to generate the steam or wisps of smoke that were often seen after an electrocution.
- It is currently an option in nine states, but lethal injection is the primary method in each.

Source: © Helder Almeida/Fotolia

Gas Chamber

- This was introduced in Nevada in 1924 as a more humane way of execution.
- It is currently an option in four states, but lethal injection is the primary method in each.
- Crystals of sodium cyanide are released into the pail beneath a chair where the condemned prisoner is strapped. A chemical reaction occurs that releases hydrogen cyanide gas. The prisoner is instructed to breathe deeply to speed up the process, but most prisoners try to hold their breath and some struggle.
- Some have suggested that the gas chamber tortures the spectators more than the condemned because it is an unpleasant thing to watch.

Source: © Ilene MacDonald/Alamy

FIGURE 12–2 **Popular Twentieth-Century Execution Methods.**
References: 1. Death Penalty Information Center. (2016b). Description of execution methods. Retrieved from DPIC website http:// www.deathpenaltyinfo.org/descriptions-execution-methods. 2. Wikberg, R. (1992). The horror show. In W. Rideau & R. Wikberg (Eds.), Life sentences: Rage and survival behind bars (pp. 284–303). New York, NY: Times Books.

▶ Capital Punishment and the Law

The Eighth Amendment to the U.S. Constitution states that cruel and unusual punishments will not be inflicted. Unfortunately, for those preferring simple directions, the Constitution defines neither *cruel* nor *unusual*. But most constitutional scholars believe that the Founding Fathers intended to allow for the death penalty. Not only was capital punishment authorized in all 13 colonies, but there are also specific provisions in the Constitution that suggest the taking of life is possible (e.g., the Fifth Amendment's provision that no person shall be deprived of life without due process). But the ambiguous nature of the terms *cruel* and *unusual* and the Supreme Court's finding that the Eighth Amendment "must draw its meaning from the evolving standards of decency that mark the progress of a maturing society" (*Trop* v. *Dulles,* 356 U.S. at 101, 1958) have kept the topic of capital punishment at the forefront among social and legal issues. This section looks first at legal issues related to whom the death penalty applies to, and then it considers key court cases that have shaped how the death penalty is implemented.

Entering Death Row

To the surprise of some people (who, e.g., think *all* murderers should be subject to execution), the death penalty is reserved for only the most heinous crimes. Bohm (2003) notes that the U.S.

Supreme Court has ruled that the death penalty should be limited to aggravated or capital murder. In fact, all executions since 1976 have been for murder with aggravating circumstances.

Although there have been no executions since 1976 for crimes other than murder with aggravating circumstances, there are state and federal statutes that provide for the death penalty in cases other than those involving the death of the victim. State statutes for nonmurder capital crimes include the following (Snell, 2014):

- Treason (Arkansas, California, Colorado, Georgia, Louisiana)
- Aggravated kidnapping (Colorado, Idaho, Montana, and the federal government)
- Drug trafficking (Florida)
- Aircraft hijacking/piracy (Georgia, Mississippi)

Despite those statutes, the likelihood that the Supreme Court will allow someone to be executed for a crime not involving murder is very remote. The Court has already ruled in *Coker* v. *Georgia* (433 U.S. 584, 1977), *Eberheart* v. *Georgia* (433 U.S. 917, 1977), and *Kennedy* v. *Louisiana* (554 U.S. 407, 2008) that the death penalty was a disproportionate, and therefore unacceptable, punishment for the crime of rape of an adult woman who was not killed (*Coker*), the crime of kidnapping when the victim was not killed (*Eberheart*), and the rape of a child that did not result in the victim's death (*Kennedy*).

Notable People and Execution Methods

1890	1924	1936	1977		1982

At Auburn Prison in New York, William Kemmler becomes the first person executed by electrocution after killing his lover with an axe.

Source: © Richard Carson/Reuters/Corbis

Nevada becomes the first jurisdiction in the world to legally execute a person with cyanide gas.

The last public execution in the United States is a hanging in Owensboro, Kentucky.

Gary Gilmore's execution by a firing squad in Utah marks the return of the death penalty's use after a ten year pause.

Source: © Mark Jenkinson/CORBIS

Virginia executes Velma Barfield by lethal injection, and she becomes the first woman to be executed since the death penalty was reinstated in 1976.

FIGURE 12–3 Timeline: Notable People and Execution Methods.

Capital Punishment and the Courts

In the 1960s, there was a decline in use of the death penalty and an unofficial moratorium meant no executions occurred in the United States from 1968 to 1977. The moratorium resulted from increasing legal challenges to the death penalty in the 1960s. During this moratorium, the states with death penalty statutes were unsure about the Supreme Court's view of the constitutionality of the laws, so they refrained from any executions. Their concern was well founded, because the Court's 1972 *Furman* v. *Georgia* decision held that the death penalty—as it was then being used—amounted to cruel and unusual punishment. Figure 12–4 highlights this and other key Supreme Court decisions related to the death penalty.

The Furman Decision

What is referred to as the **Furman decision** actually involved three cases, each with a black defendant, that the U.S. Supreme Court heard together: *Furman* v. *Georgia*, *Jackson* v. *Georgia*, and *Branch* v. *Texas*. *Furman* v. *Georgia*, however, is the cited case when reviewing the Court's decision.

Furman, a 26-year-old black man with a sixth-grade education, tried to enter a private home at night. The homeowner surprised Furman while he was in the act of burglary. While trying to escape, Furman shot and killed the homeowner with one pistol shot fired through a closed kitchen door from the outside. At his trial, Furman said he accidentally tripped over a wire while backing away, causing the gun to fire.

Prior to his trial, Furman was committed to the Georgia Central State Hospital for a psychiatric exam regarding his plea of insanity. Initially, the superintendent reported that the diagnostic staff had concluded that Furman's diagnosis was of mild to moderate mental deficiency, with psychotic episodes associated with convulsive disorder. The physicians agreed that Furman was not presently psychotic but said he was incapable of cooperating with his counsel in preparing his defense. Furthermore, the staff believed that he needed further psychiatric hospitalization and treatment. However, at a later time, the superintendent reported that, although the staff diagnosis was the same, he concluded that although Furman was not currently psychotic, he knew right from wrong and was able to cooperate with his counsel in preparing his defense. All the jury knew about Furman was that he was black, 26 years old, and worked at an upholstery shop. After deliberating about 90 minutes, the jury returned a verdict of guilt and a sentence of death.

In *Furman* v. *Georgia* (1972), the U.S. Supreme Court determined that the death penalty was cruel and unusual. Two of the justices said it is cruel and unusual in all cases, but the majority said it was cruel and unusual because it was imposed in an arbitrary and

> LEARNING OUTCOMES 2
>
> Explain the legal provisions for capital punishment in the United States.

Key U.S. Supreme Court Cases

1775	1910		1947	1968

The death penalty is used in all 13 U.S. colonies at the outbreak of the American Revolution
Crimes typically covered were arson, treason, murder, burglary, robbery, rape, horse-stealing, and slave rebellion. Hanging was the usual method.

Weems* v. *United States In ruling that a penalty was too harsh considering the nature of the offense, the USSC establishes precedents on cruel and unusual punishment.

Source: Fotolia

Louisiana ex rel. Francis* v. *Resweber USSC finds that a second execution attempt following a technical malfunction does not constitute cruel and unusual punishment.

Witherspoon* v. *Illinois USSC forbids the dismissal of jurors based on personal opposition to capital punishment.

FIGURE 12–4 Timeline: Key U.S. Supreme Court Cases.
Source: © Natalia Bratslavsky/Fotolia

1993	1996	1999	2001	2009	2010
Maryland prisoner Kirk Bloodworth becomes the first death row inmate to be exonerated with DNA evidence.	The hanging of convicted double-murderer Bill Bailey in Delaware is America's last execution by hanging.	After twice refusing offers of lethal injection, Walter LaGrand is executed in an Arizona gas chamber and becomes America's last prisoner to be executed by the gas chamber.	Oklahoma City bomber Timothy McVeigh becomes first federal prisoner to be executed in 38 years.	Ohio becomes the first state to execute a death-row inmate with a one-drug intravenous lethal injection rather than the three-drug cocktail used in most states.	Utah death-row inmate Ronnie Lee Gardner chooses the firing squad over a lethal injection and becomes the last person in America to be executed by firing squad.

Firing Squad
Source: Leremy/Fotolia

capricious manner. Justice Douglas, taking the arbitrary-and-capricious position, said it was not possible to determine from the facts of the three cases that the defendants were sentenced to death because they were black. However, he expressed concern that the laws left the decision of death or imprisonment to "the uncontrolled discretion of judges or juries" and in doing so, "people live or die, dependent on the whim of one man or of 12" (*Furman* v. *Georgia*).

In the *Furman* case, three of the five justices in the majority took the position that the death penalty was cruel and unusual because it was applied arbitrarily. The other two justices in the majority believed the death penalty was cruel and unusual in itself. Had the majority held the second position, the death penalty would essentially have been abandoned throughout the United States. But the "arbitrary" position left the door open for laws that would allow for nonarbitrary use of the death penalty. Said differently, in the *Furman* decision, the Court's ruling was not against capital punishment itself; it was against the way it was being imposed. Under that reasoning, states assumed, death penalty statutes that removed the arbitrary nature of executions would be constitutional.

The Gregg Decision

Because each Court justice wrote a separate opinion in *Furman*, it was not immediately clear just what kind of death penalty law would be acceptable to the Court. Two major types of laws were tried by different states: mandatory and guided discretion. The

mandatory laws tried to completely eliminate discretion in capital sentencing by requiring the death penalty upon conviction of specific crimes. Those types were held unconstitutional in a series of 1976 rulings (see *Roberts* v. *Louisiana*, 428 U.S. 325, and *Woodson* v. *North Carolina*, 428 U.S. 280).

The **guided discretion** statutes require juries to administer capital punishment after considering both aggravating and mitigating circumstances. The Court upheld these statutes in several other 1976 rulings (*Gregg* v. *Georgia*, 428 U.S. 153; *Jurek* v. *Texas*, 428 U.S. 262; and *Proffitt* v. *Florida*, 428 U.S. 242), but the **Gregg decision** is typically cited as initiating the guided discretion era. The Georgia, Texas, and Florida statutes each require a **bifurcated trial**, with the first stage being the traditional trial to determine guilt. When guilt is established, the second stage takes place to decide the sentence—death or life imprisonment. It is during the second stage that guided discretion occurs; this is when the sentencing authority hears about aggravating and mitigating factors that will affect the sentencing decision.

Further refinements to the death penalty laws have included decisions such as the *Coker* v. *Georgia*, *Eberheart* v. *Georgia*, and *Kennedy* v. *Louisiana* decisions mentioned earlier. In addition, the Court has ruled that it is unconstitutional to execute persons who are mentally insane (*Ford* v. *Wainwright*, 477 U.S. 399, 1986), mentally retarded [sic] (*Atkins* v. *Virginia*, 536 U.S 304, 2002), or were younger than age 18 when they committed their crime (*Roper* v. *Simmons*, 543 U.S. 551, 2005).

1972	1976	1977	1986
Furman v. Georgia USSC determines that the death penalty does not violate the Constitution but that the arbitrary and capricious manner of its application in many states does.	**Gregg v. Georgia** Georgia's new death penalty statute is deemed constitutional, and the stage is set for capital punishment to be reinstated in other states. *Source:* ROGER L. WOLLENBERG/ UPI/Newscom	**Coker v. Georgia** USSC rules that use of the death penalty in rape cases is unconstitutional for rape of an adult woman when the victim is not killed.	**Ford v. Wainwright** USSC rules that executing the mentally insane is cruel and unusual and therefore unconstitutional.

Gregg v. Georgia
July 2, 1976–July 2, 20
30 years of blood on ou
www.ABOLITION.org

▶ Characteristics of Death-Row Prisoners

Based on the review of legal issues related to capital punishment, we know some of the characteristics of persons who are on death row in America. Basically, they are offenders who have been convicted of first-degree murder with aggravating circumstances, who are neither mentally ill nor intellectually disabled, and who were at least age 18 when committing their crime. Actually, there are questions as to whether persons who have been executed may have been mentally ill or intellectually disabled. In their review of 100 recent executions, Smith, Cull, and Robinson (2014) found that most of the executed offenders suffered from intellectual disability, borderline intellectual functioning, traumatic brain injury, or were diagnosed with or showed symptoms of mental illness. That these people were still executed speaks to the variability among jurisdictions regarding the identification of mental illness and intellectual disability. The *Atkins* v. *Virginia* decision barred states from executing persons with mental disabilities, but the Court left it to the states to determine who qualified. Florida, for example, set an I.Q. score of 70 as the cutoff—persons scoring 70 and over could be executed. Florida inmate Freddie Lee Hall (whose I.Q. had been measured various times at 71, 73, and 80) challenged that standard as inappropriately inflexible (Liptak, 2014). In *Hall* v. *Florida* (2014), the U.S. Supreme Court agreed and ruled that states cannot rely solely on a fixed I.Q. score to determine death eligibility. The extent to which that ruling affects executions remains to be seen.

Looking at demographic characteristics, we find that most (51%) of the state prisoners on death row in the United States are in the South and the fewest are in the Northeast and the Midwest (about 7% each). Thirty-five percent of death-row prisoners are in the West, but California, with more than 700, has the greatest number of prisoners under a death sentence. Almost half of all death-row prisoners are in the states of California, Texas, and Florida (Snell, 2014). As shown in Table 12–1, most of the prisoners on death row at the end of 2013 were white non-Hispanic males.

LEARNING OUTCOMES 3 — Describe the characteristics of death-row prisoners and explain how some leave death-row without being executed.

Sixty percent of the people on death row were not involved in the criminal justice system at the time of the capital offense.

TABLE 12–1 — DEMOGRAPHIC CHARACTERISTICS OF PRISONERS UNDER SENTENCE OF DEATH, 2013

Characteristic	Yearend	Admissions	Removals
Total inmates	2979	83	115
Sex			
Male	98.1%	100%	96.5%
Female	1.9	0	3.5
Race[a]			
White	55.8%	59.01%	60.9%
Black	41.9	39.8	37.4
All other races[b]	2.3	1.2	1.7
Hispanic Origin[c]			
Hispanic	14.4%	18.3%	12.1%
Non-Hispanic	85.6	81.7	87.9
Median Age	46 yr	38 yr	49 yr
Median Education Level	12 yr	12 yr	11 yr

Note: Detail may not sum to total due to rounding.

[a] Percentages for white and black inmates include persons of Hispanic or Latino origin.

[b] At yearend 2013, inmates in "all other races" consisted of 21 American Indian or Alaska Natives (AIAN); 42 Asian, Native Hawaiian, or other Pacific Islanders; and 5 self-identified Hispanics or Latinos. During 2013, one AIAN inmate was admitted, and two AIAN were removed.

[c] Calculations exclude count of inmates with unknown Hispanic or Latino origin: 278 total yearend, 1 admission, and 8 removals.

Source: Table 5, Demographic Characteristics of Prisoners Under Sentence of Death, 2013 from Capital Punishment, 2013—Statistical Tables, NCJ 248448. Published by U.S Department of Justice , © 2014.

However, those who were "in the system" were more likely to be on parole (17%) than probation (11%). A slightly higher percentage of Hispanic (32%) and black (31%) inmates were on probation or parole at the time of their capital offense, compared to 24% of white inmates (Snell, 2014).

Among death-row inmates for whom criminal history information was available, 67% had prior felony convictions, including 9% with at least one previous homicide conviction.

1988	2002	2005	2008
Thompson v. Oklahoma People aged 15 or younger when they committed a crime may not be sentenced to death.	***Atkins v. Virginia*** USSC prohibits execution of the intellectually disabled but leaves to the states the determination of what constitutes intellectual disability. ***Ring v. Arizona*** USSC rules that jurors, rather than a judge or panel of judges, must determine whether a convicted murderer should receive the death penalty.	***Roper v. Simmons*** People aged 17 or younger when they committed a crime may not be sentenced to death. Christopher Simmons was 17 when he kidnapped and killed Shirley Cook.	***Kennedy v. Louisiana*** The death penalty cannot be imposed on those convicted of raping a child when the crime did not result in the child's death.

Source: Bikeriderlondon/Shutterstock

FIGURE 12–4 (Continued)

Criminal history patterns of death-row inmates differed by race and Hispanic origin. More black inmates had a prior felony conviction (73%), compared to Hispanic (65%) or white (64%) inmates. However, similar percentages of white (9%), black (10%), and Hispanic (7%) inmates had a prior homicide conviction (Snell, 2014).

Leaving Death Row Without Being Executed

Most death-row prisoners actually leave death row without being executed. In the modern era, more than 8,000 prisoners have entered prison under sentence of death and about 16% were executed. The other 85% either remain on death row or were removed from their death sentence (Snell, 2014). The reasons for their removal include death from causes other than execution and receiving clemency, but usually it was because their sentence or conviction was overturned by an appeals or higher court.

Clemency, which is an act of leniency in the criminal justice system, typically refers to one of three things: a reprieve, a commutation, or a pardon (Burnett, 2002; VanBrocklin, 2003). A **reprieve** is a stay of sentence execution that grants time for something else to happen (e.g., pursuing an appeal); a **commutation of sentence** is a reduction of the penalty (e.g., death sentence to a life sentence); and a **pardon** releases the person (partially or fully) from the legal consequences of the crime. The clemency process varies among states (at the federal level, clemency lies with the president), but is consistently situated in the executive branch. In some states, the governor has sole authority regarding clemency and in other states clemency is granted by the governor only after receiving a recommendation from a board or advisory group. In a few states (Georgia, Nebraska, Nevada, Utah), a board or advisory group determines clemency (Death Penalty Information Center, 2016a).

Burnett (2002) and VanBrocklin (2003) explain that clemency is designed to serve as a check on the judiciary. Chief Justice Rehnquist (*Herrera* v. *Collins*, 506 U.S. 390, 1993) described executive clemency as the fail-safe mechanism in the criminal justice system wherein miscarriages of justice (e.g., an innocent person found guilty) can be corrected. For example, executive clemency is the final step prior to a death sentence being carried out and may be the only stage at which a person claiming innocence (rather than, e.g., claiming improprieties during trial) might avoid execution. Unfortunately, governors may see clemency in death sentence cases as political suicide and be unwilling to fully embrace their "fail-safe" role (Bohm, 2003; VanBrocklin, 2003).

Clemency in capital cases has been granted for such reasons as proof of actual innocence, in cases where guilt is now in doubt, and in instances when the death penalty is deemed inequitable when compared with the punishment given to equally guilty codefendants. The Death Penalty Information Center (2016a) provides a continually updated list of death sentence commutations that have been granted on humanitarian grounds. Through the end of 2015, there were 280 acts of clemency listed since 1977.

Persons more often leave death row as a result of their conviction being overturned than as a result of clemency. A serious or prejudicial error occurs when the defendant can show that something happened in the processing of a capital case that adversely affects the trial's outcome. Those errors, when accepted as such by appellate courts, provide reason for reversal of convictions and sentences and explain some of the removals from death row (Bohm, 2003).

The appeals process, which can be very lengthy, is viewed by some as a reason that the death penalty is an ineffective general deterrent (i.e., it lacks swiftness and certainty) or to explain why it creates a greater financial burden on the state than does life imprisonment without possibility of parole. Others, however, suggest that the appeals process is necessary to help assure this harshest of penalties is applied in a fair manner.

Because there are very stringent legal requirements that must be met to show that serious error occurred (see Bohm, 2003, pp. 163–165), one might think that only small numbers of death sentences are reversed on serious-error grounds. However, after reviewing 23 years of state death sentences, Liebman, Fagan, and West (2000) determined the overall rate of prejudicial error as being 68%. That is, courts found serious, reversible error in nearly 7 of every 10 capital sentences that were fully reviewed by appellate courts between 1973 and 1995. Further, 80% of state postconviction review reversals and over 70% of federal court reversals occur because of egregiously incompetent lawyering, prosecutorial misconduct or suppression of evidence, misinstruction of jurors, or judge or juror bias (Gelman, Liebman, West, & Kiss, 2004). Many of those mistakes were said by the courts to have resulted in defendants receiving a death sentence when a sentence less than death was deserved; and in 7% of the cases the defendant was determined to be innocent of the capital crime. It seems that even though the appellate process takes a long time, the goal of justice benefits from that wait.

▶ Arguments for and Against Capital Punishment

One would be hard pressed to find another criminal justice topic that occasions such passion as the death penalty. The subject has been debated on the basis of such topics as morality, deterrence, retribution, irrevocable mistake, cost comparison of death versus life imprisonment, discrimination by race and social class, and the quality of defense counsel available to capital crime defendants. A sampling of those topics is provided here.

Deterrence

The idea that people will be deterred from committing murder out of fear that they will be executed seems inherently logical and is the argument made in Figure 12–5. In fact, a belief that the death penalty provides a general deterrent is one of the oldest reasons for its use. Public executions were held to deliberately dissuade those who might be thinking about committing murder or some other capital crime of the time. But murder and

The death penalty deters.

Since people fear nothing more than death, it makes sense that nothing will deter a criminal more than the fear of death.

Ernest van den Haag

NO

The death penalty does not deter.

Research to date cannot conclusively determine whether capital punishment decreases, increases, or has no effect on homicide rates.

National Research Council

FIGURE 12–5 **Does the Death Penalty Deter?**

other crimes continued, and the public executions themselves were often a stimulus to criminal behavior.

Even when the death penalty is carried out in a private setting, reason seems to suggest that it should deter persons from doing something for which they could be executed. That belief goes back to the logic of the classical school, in which people, such as Beccaria and Bentham (see Chapter 2), argued that under conditions of certainty, severity, and swiftness, punishment can effectively keep the rational person from committing a crime. Issues of certainty, severity, and swiftness are admittedly important, but an overriding matter is the assumption of rationality. **Abolitionists** (those favoring the abolition of the death penalty) argue, for example, that murder is seldom a rational act. Quite the contrary; it typically occurs in the heat of the moment and frequently involves alcohol or drugs in the victim, offender, or both. This lethal mix does not create a setting for rational decision making. If a punishment only deters when the potential offender can rationally weigh the pros and cons of a proposed act, the death penalty will not deter the majority of murders, because they are emotional, not rational, acts.

Retentionists (those who favor keeping the death penalty) respond to the rationality argument by suggesting that the death penalty's deterrent effect is achieved through the socialization process. Throughout his or her life, the individual comes to internalize the association of act and penalty. Good behavior becomes something that occurs naturally rather than something that results from the constant weighing of pros and cons

throughout the day. Goldberg (1991) uses an analogy of angry husbands to make the point. Most husbands, he argues, slam doors, shout, or sulk when they are angry. Some husbands, when angry, murder their wives. For Goldberg, the question is not what deterred the murderer—obviously, nothing did—but rather what deterred the person who didn't murder. The slamming, shouting, sulking husband has presumably instilled a psychological resistance to murder—not because he makes a rational decision in the heat of the moment, but because he has internalized the link between killing and the death penalty.

Interesting though the philosophical debate on deterrence might be, much of the discussion about deterrence and the death penalty has relied on statistics. Use of statistical analysis is especially popular among abolitionists because the evidence has consistently supported the position that the death penalty does not serve as a general deterrent to murder—with some exceptions noted next. Kronenwetter (1993) notes that as early as 1919, statistical studies showed that there was no measurable relation between the homicide rate and the existence or absence of the death penalty. Since then, researchers have repeatedly failed to find a general deterrent effect in executions (see Table 12–2). The studies are consistent in finding that factors other than execution are responsible for the variation and trends in murder rates.

There are, however, some studies that claim to have found a deterrent effect. Sociologist Ted Goertzel (2004) explains that these studies primarily use econometric modeling wherein complex mathematical models are constructed on the assumption that the models mirror what happens in the real world. Some of these econometric models show that capital punishment deters homicide, but others do not (Fagan, 2005; Goertzel, 2004). One of the first such studies was conducted with data from the mid-twentieth-century United States. Isaac Ehrlich (1975) concluded that eight murders were prevented by each execution. His findings were roundly criticized, and attempts at replication failed to confirm a deterrent effect (Paternoster, 1991). The greatest damage to Ehrlich's study came from a board of experts commissioned by the National Academy of Sciences to review his findings. They determined that it offered no useful evidence for a deterrent effect of capital punishment (Kronenwetter, 1993).

There has been a resurgence of interest in econometric modeling to test deterrence and capital punishment. Columbia Law School professor Jeffrey Fagan reviewed more than a dozen studies published since 1995 claiming the death penalty can prevent anywhere from 3 to 32 murders (Fagan, 2005, 2006). Some of the studies claim that pardons, commutations,

Think About It...

In the third Bush–Gore debate leading up to the 2000 presidential election, George W. Bush answered the following to the question: "Do both of you believe that the death penalty actually deters crime?" Bush said, "I do, that's the only reason to be for it. I don't think you should support the death penalty to seek revenge. . . . I think the reason to support the death penalty is because it saves other people's lives" (cited at http://deathpenalty.procon.org/view.answers.php?questionID=000983). Do you agree with President Bush? Why or why not?

ZUMA Press, Inc./Alamy Stock Photo

TABLE 12–2 | DETERRENCE RESEARCH AND CAPITAL PUNISHMENT

Found Deterrent Effect?	Authors (Year)*	Findings
NO	Bailey & Peterson (1994) Peterson & Bailey (1991)	Using a monthly time-series analysis, the authors found no evidence of a deterrent effect on police killings (Bailey & Peterson 1994) nor any consistent relationship between the number of executions and the rate of felony murder (Peterson & Bailey 1991).
NO	Peterson & Bailey (1998)	After thoroughly reviewing the empirical literature on a deterrent effect of capital punishment, the authors conclude that factors other than execution are responsible for the variation and trends in murder rates.
NO	Sorensen, Wrinkle, Brewer, & Marquart (1999)	Suggesting that if the death penalty can have any general deterrent effect at all, it would have one in Texas (the most active death penalty state), researchers found that the number of executions influenced neither the rate of murder in general nor the rate of felony murder in particular.
NO	Donohue & Wolfers (2005) Donohue & Wolfers (2006)	Following a thorough assessment of the statistical evidence that claims to support a deterrent effect for capital punishment, the authors conclude that the view that the death penalty deters is the product of belief, not evidence.
YES	Ehrlich (1975)	This highly controversial study, using econometric methods, concludes the death penalty reduces homicide rates in the United States.
YES	Land, Teske, & Zheng (2009)	Based on a time-series analysis and independent-validation tests, the authors found evidence in Texas of modest, short-term reductions in homicides in the first and fourth months following an execution.
YES	Dezhbakhsh & Rubin (2010)	In disagreeing with Donohue and Wolfers (2005), these authors claim that deterrence findings based on econometric methods are, in fact, robust.

*Note: *See references section for complete citation.*

and exonerations cause murders to increase; others claim that murders of passion can be deterred; and some even claim that executions can reduce robberies and even some nonviolent crimes.

Abolitionists argue that the statistical evidence so far is on their side. Reviews of deterrence studies (Bohm, 2003; Donohue & Wolfers, 2006; Fagan, 2005, 2006; Goertzel, 2004; Radelet & Borg, 2000) consistently support Paternoster's (1991) summary that years of research with various methodologies and statistical approaches leads to the conclusion that capital punishment is not a superior general deterrent (p. 241). Or, as Donohue and Wolfers (2006) put it, empirical support for the idea that the death penalty deters is weak and inconclusive (p. 2). Importantly, however, even with statistics on their side, abolitionists have trouble responding to the retentionists' point that only the times when the death penalty has not deterred can be counted because only then is there something to count. There is no way of knowing when it did deter because there is nothing to count when the murder does not happen.

In 2012, the National Research Council of the National Academies (Daniel & John, 2012) was asked to assess whether the available evidence provides a scientific basis for answering questions of if and how the death penalty affects homicide rates. That review of more than three decades of research concluded that studies claiming a deterrent effect on murder rates from the death penalty suffer from three fundamental flaws:

LEARNING OUTCOMES 4 — Summarize the arguments for and against the use of the death penalty.

- The studies do not factor in the effects of noncapital punishments that may also be imposed.
- The studies use incomplete or implausible models of potential murderers' perceptions of and response to the use of capital punishment.
- Estimates of the effect of capital punishment are based on statistical models that make assumptions that are not credible.

As a result of those flaws, the panel of experts reported that the research to date cannot conclusively determine whether capital punishment decreases, increases, or has no effect on homicide rates. Therefore, the studies should not be used to inform judgments regarding the effect of the death penalty on homicide or influence policy judgments about capital punishment. However, as the committee report notes, the presence or absence of a deterrent effect is hardly the only point of debate regarding the death penalty. Possibly, some of these other issues are more helpful and appropriate in influencing opinion or policy.

Fairness

Several issues are raised when discussing the fairness of the death penalty. Many of those issues are based on statistics that show the death penalty applying most often to men, disproportionately to African-Americans and Latinos, and invariably to poor defendants. Women, Caucasians, and rich people also commit capital crimes, but they have not been executed quite as regularly.

Regarding fairness and gender, it is clear that the death penalty has been applied to both men and women throughout history and across cultures. There have been, however, a few capital crimes for which females were more frequently targeted. Dobash, Dobash, and Gutteridge (1986) point out that at times in history, women have been subjected to more severe punishments for the same offense as men. During the Middle Ages, women could be burned to death for adultery or murdering their spouse, but adultery was sometimes not even considered an offense for men. Even when there was equity in the death sentence, the means of execution was often hanging for men but burning (presumably a more agonizing death) for women. The charge of witchcraft, for example, was applied primarily to women who, presumably with the help of Satan, harmed people, animals, and things.

Witchcraft aside, women have not been executed in the United States as often as their number on death row suggests they could be. Women account for about 2% of all death sentences imposed in the United States. But rather than comprising 2% of the persons executed, women make up about 1% of the total. Since 1976, 16 women have been executed in U.S. jurisdictions—6 in Texas, 3 in Oklahoma, 2 in Florida, and 1 each in Alabama, Arkansas, Georgia, North Carolina, and Virginia (Death Penalty Information Center, 2016g).

In 2004, the American Civil Liberties Union released findings from the first-ever national survey of women on death row. Key findings from the survey include the following (King & Bellin, 2004):

- Women on death row often had ineffective counsel or had been subjected to official misconduct by prosecutors during their trials.

- Half of the women on death row acted with at least one other person, but in most of those cases the co-defendant received a sentence other than death—even in cases where both defendants appeared to be equally culpable.

- Nearly two-thirds of the women on death row were convicted of killing family members or people they knew. Although no one has calculated the number of men on death row for killing the same categories of people, we know from the general prison population that women who are in prison are more likely than men to have killed family members or intimates.

- Most women on death row, probably because of their small numbers, live in almost complete isolation, rarely leaving their cells. Such conditions may lead to psychosis or can exacerbate existing mental illness.

The report concludes with recommendations to ensure that women receive fair and adequate defense counsel when charged with a capital offense (e.g., train defense counsel to litigate issues of abuse in death penalty cases) and to improve conditions for women on death row (e.g., integrate women on death row into regular prison units).

A second important topic related to fairness and the death penalty concerns social class. Supreme Court Justice William Douglas commented (*Furman* v. *Georgia*) that "one searches our chronicles in vain for the execution of any member of the affluent strata of this society" (408 U.S. 251–252).

The characteristics of persons on death row seem to reflect those of the poor and lower class in society as a whole. Although most of the criminal justice system's clients are poor, death-row inmates are among the poorest. Unfortunate and unfair as it is, persons from the lower socioeconomic classes elicit little sympathy from justice system officials, jurors, or the general public. We know that punishments for other crimes, such as marijuana possession, have eased as more and more members of the middle class indulge in the behavior. Those offenders do draw sympathy from officials, jurors, and the community, with a result being a lessening of penalties associated with the behavior. One wonders how long the death penalty would have lasted if most of those executed had reflected typical middle-class characteristics.

Proponents of the death penalty argue that inequities in the application of the death penalty should draw criticism of its application, not of its use. As van den Haag (1991) argues, and as shown in Figure 12–6, just because guilty poor people are executed but guilty whites or wealthy people are not, the poor or black are no less guilty nor do they deserve less punishment (p. 158).

A good, experienced lawyer will improve the defendant's chances at each stage in the legal process, so it is not surprising that having a good lawyer also improves a defendant's chances of escaping execution. Unfortunately, almost all defendants in capital cases cannot afford their own attorney, so they are provided a public defender or court-appointed attorney. Certainly there are good, well-trained, and imminently qualified public defenders and court-appointed attorneys handling death penalty cases around the country, but there are also public defenders and court-appointed attorneys who are overworked, underpaid, or who lack the trial experience required for death penalty cases. In a study of death penalty cases in Texas, researchers found that capital defendants with court-appointed lawyers were more than twice as likely to receive a death sentence as were those able to hire their own attorneys (Kronenwetter, 1993).

As important as issues of gender and social class are, one of the most discussed areas of fairness and the death penalty deals with race and ethnicity (see Figure 12–7). Concern about the

YES

The death penalty is unfair because it is applied mostly to the lower socioeconomic class.

The death penalty is imposed mostly on society's poor and lower class because they cannot afford good lawyers. As Supreme Court Justice Ruth Bader Ginsburg explained, people with good trial lawyers don't get the death penalty (CBS News 2001).

NO

If the death penalty is applied mostly to the lower socioeconomic class that makes its application bad, not its use.

Just because guilty poor people are executed but guilty whites or wealthy people are not, the poor or black are no less guilty nor do they deserve less punishment (van den Haag, 1991).

FIGURE 12–6 **Is the Death Penalty Unfair Because of Its Discrimination by Social Class?**

FIGURE 12-7 Does Race Affect the Application of the Death Penalty?

disproportionate minority-group representation in the criminal justice system has been present for years—and especially so in how the death penalty is applied. Traditionally, the bias has been recognized as relating to the offender's race and ethnicity; more recently, attention has turned to the victim's race and ethnicity. We look first at the offender's characteristics.

In a report on race and the death penalty, Amnesty International (1999) concluded that there is no evidence that current legal safeguards have eliminated racial bias in the application of the death penalty. The report notes that the potential for racial bias is linked to prosecutorial discretion because it is unreasonable to think individual prosecutors are not influenced by the racial divisions affecting American society. Spohn (2014) also suggests that discretionary decisions by prosecutors are a source of racial and ethnic disparity. The evidence of this is dated and not entirely consistent, but studies seem to reveal that race and ethnicity affect charging and plea decisions in both capital and noncapital cases.

The racial/ethnic distribution on death row was as follows in January 2016 (NAACP Legal Defense Fund, 2016):

- 43% white
- 42% black
- 13% Latino/Latina
- 1% Native American
- 2% Asian

Of persons executed since 1976 (NAACP Legal Defense Fund, 2016), the racial/ethnic distribution is as follows:

- 56% white
- 35% black
- 8% Latino/Latina
- 1% Native American
- 0.5% Asian

Because the percentage of minorities being executed is less than it was before 1972—when minorities comprised more than half of all executions (Death Penalty Information Center, 2016c)—and because the number of minorities executed is now less than their percentage on death row, some people see improvement in the death penalty's application. Importantly, however, minorities still make up a much higher percentage of the death-row population than they do of the population as a whole. That disproportionate representation of minorities on death row has been used in court to argue that the death penalty is unconstitutional; but an even more persuasive argument has been how the victim's race might influence who receives the death penalty.

Disparity in the imposition of the death penalty has often looked at the offender's demographic factors, but more recent studies have added an interest in victim demographics. Spohn's (2014) review notes that numerous methodologically sophisticated studies have found that black and Hispanic suspects—especially those who victimize whites—are more likely to be charged and fully prosecuted than are white suspects, although African-Americans and whites each comprise about half of all homicide victims (Cooper & Smith, 2013).

Because African-Americans are about 13% of the U.S. population, it is very disproportionate for them to make up half of all homicide victims. With the racial similarity in percentage of homicide victims, one might assume that there is a similar balance in the race of the victims of persons executed. That is, about half of the persons executed since 1976 should have had white victims and the other half black victims. Actually, 76% of the people executed since 1976 were convicted of murdering white victims (NAACP Legal Defense Fund, 2016). When considering only persons executed for interracial murders since

Think About It…

Ruddell and Urbina (2004) wondered if a society's use of punishment may be linked to a desire to regulate its minority members. The authors' research found tentative evidence that countries with a more homogeneous (i.e., similar) population were more likely to have abolished the death penalty, whereas those with more racial and ethnic diversity have retained the death penalty. Might retention of the death penalty in the United States and in other countries be linked to having a racially and ethnically diverse society? Do you think the death penalty is a way to regulate society's minority members?

1976, we find that 90% of those executions were of black defendants whose victims were white whereas only 10% were of white defendants whose victims were black (Death Penalty Information Center, 2016d). Does the victim's race influence whether an offender receives the death penalty or is executed? If so, that would clearly be an extralegal factor and one that should play no role in prosecuting, adjudication, or sentencing decisions.

One of the first studies noting the predictive value of victim race in death sentences was conducted by Baldus, Pulaski, and Woodworth (1983) and was used by the U.S. Supreme Court in the case of *McCleskey* v. *Kemp* (481 U.S. 279, 1987). McCleskey, a black man who had been convicted of murdering a white police officer, used the Baldus study (as it has come to be called) in his claim that he was being discriminated against on the basis of his race and that of his victim. The Baldus study found a large racial disparity in the way Georgia juries had imposed the death penalty between 1973 and 1978. For example, Baldus and his colleagues found that offenders charged with killing a white person were 4.3 times more likely to be sentenced to death in Georgia than those charged with killing a black person.

The Court rejected McCleskey's claims, deciding that a statistical study suggesting that racial considerations entered into capital sentencing in Georgia does not establish purposeful discrimination—which the Court said a successful Fourteenth Amendment claim must show. In addition, the justices noted that although the Baldus study found a correlation between race factors and sentencing, it did not prove that race entered into the sentencing decision. For a defendant to be successful in an appeal, "exceptionally clear proof" must be provided that the decision makers had acted with discriminatory intent (*McCleskey* v. *Kemp,* 481 U.S. at 297).

Studies continue to find racial disparity when applying the death penalty. Paternoster and Brame, for example found (2003) and reaffirmed (2008) that the death penalty is more likely to be imposed in Maryland when the victim is white and in cases with black defendants and white victims. But the courts continue to find such studies lacking in "exceptionally clear proof." In 2001, a U.S. court of appeals agreed that the racial imbalance in Ohio's capital sentencing system was "extremely troubling" (*Coleman* v. *Mitchell*, 268 F.3d 417), but

it is no more so than was deemed permissible by *McCleskey*. Such decisions led Baldus, Woodworth, and Grosso (2008) to comment that for all practical purposes, the *McCleskey* decision precludes the bringing of race claims in federal courts when the evidence of discrimination is a statewide statistical study. So, despite what the research might show, the courts have not yet found the statistical analysis compelling enough to find racial disparities in capital sentencing unconstitutional. Interestingly, Figure 12–8 reports the results of a study that suggests another route to reduce the role of race in death penalty proceedings.

Retribution

Another popular capital punishment debate topic is that of *lex talionis*—the position of "an eye for an eye, a tooth for a tooth." In fact, Supreme Court Justice Stevens suggests that retribution is the primary rationale for imposing the death penalty today and that it is the grounds for much of the remaining enthusiasm for the death penalty (*Baze v. Rees*, 553 U.S. 35, 2008). In many ways, this is the most difficult topic to debate because technically it provides no basis for debate. Newman (1985) says retributivists, the prime supporters of this view, are often asked the trap question, "Why must a wrongful act be punished?" Any reply made by the retributivist will be utilitarian, and of all the punishment philosophies, retribution is the only one that is nonutilitarian. If the retributivist tries to answer a question such as "Why should the death penalty be used?" the response will inevitably lean toward things, such as deterrence, public safety, or reinforcing the moral order. But each of these answers has a utilitarian aspect, and the retributivist does not require, or even want, such a link.

Newman (1985) suggests that the only nonutilitarian response available to retributivists is "Because the act was wrong." But that response merely restates the assertion—that is, retribution claims that a wrongful act must be repaid by punishment, so saying that the reason for punishment is to repay the wrongful act is merely redundant, unless the statement "A wrongful act must be punished" is a statement of fact rather than simply an assertion. And, Newman suggests, that is exactly what the statement is. He argues that saying "A wrongful act must be punished" verges on

During the penalty phase of a capital trial, jurors are instructed to consider only legally permissible factors, such as aggravating and mitigating circumstances. Citing research that suggests juror decisions may also be influenced by such legally impermissible factors as race, researchers conducted a study to investigate the possibility of reducing juror bias toward black offenders (Shaked-Schroer, Costanzo, & Marcus-Newhall, 2008). The results suggest that by providing jurors with more simplified penalty phase instructions (e.g., definitions of legal terms and simpler sentence structure) and by using a racially diverse jury, bias against black defendants was significantly reduced. That is, the sentencing recommendation was less likely to be the death penalty and more likely to be life imprisonment. The key question, of course, is whether such recommendations could or should be put into practice. Simplifying penalty phase instructions may not be an unreasonable innovation for courts to implement, but assuring a racially diverse jury would be more problematic. But the point here is to highlight procedures that seem to work. Additional research is certainly needed, but it may be possible to reduce juror bias during the penalty phase of capital trials by providing simple instructions and by assuring a racially diverse jury.

FIGURE 12–8 **Evidence-Based Practice—Does It Work?** Can Juror Bias Be Reduced?

Think About It…

The principle of proportional retributivism suggests that a retributivist does not have to favor the death penalty—especially given the limitations presented by strict adherence to *lex talionis*. On the other hand, it may also suggest that the death

DANGER OF DEATH KEEP OUT

1000 Words/Shutterstock

penalty is appropriate for corporate leaders whose actions or inactions are shown to be responsible for the death of innocent people (see arguments in Blecker [2013]). What are your views on these two positions? Can someone be a retributivist and oppose the death penalty? Should a retributivist favor the death penalty for corporate leaders whose business practices killed people?

---

being a social law. The resulting problem is finding another position to take in order to have a debate. If retributivists say that punishment—the death penalty, for example—is inherently right, even required, the only "other side" one could take is to claim the statement is not a fact, let alone a social law. This becomes more of a philosophical discussion than a utilitarian debate. That is not a bad thing; it just means that the "discussers" must not get hung up on topics such as what punishment achieves. In other words, even if there was clear and convincing evidence that the death penalty is not needed to achieve specific deterrence, does not provide general deterrence, and is applied in a biased manner, the retributivist would still favor capital punishment because it is the "right" thing to do.

Figure 12–9 explains that because strict adherence to the principle of *lex talionis* would seemingly require that all murderers be executed—not just those who committed murder with

aggravating circumstances—and that executions be conducted in very uncivilized ways, some retributivists argue for **proportional retributivism**. Rather than requiring an exactly similar punishment for a criminal, "proportional retributivism requires only that the worst crime in any society be punished with the worst penalty" (Paternoster, 1991, p. 258). In abandoning the requirement of *lex talionis*, this version of retribution would require that a murderer receive the most severe penalty that society currently would morally tolerate. That punishment must be severe enough so as not to trivialize the victim's injury. Consider, for example, a prison sentence for rapists. Ten years in prison is not equivalent injury for one who has raped another, but it is a severe enough penalty that it does not do an injustice to the victim. Similarly, life imprisonment without the possibility for parole does not duplicate the harm to the murder victim, but it is not a penalty that is out of proportion to murder.

Innocence

As indicated in Figure 12–10, society continues to debate the question of whether the inevitability of occasionally convicting an innocent person is worth the benefit derived by having the death penalty. Between 1973 and the end of 2015, 156 people had been released from death row with evidence of their innocence (Death Penalty Information Center, 2015). In 20 of those cases, DNA was a substantial factor in establishing innocence. For the other cases, defendants must have been acquitted of all charges related to the crime that placed them on death row, or had all charges related to that crime dismissed by the prosecution, or have been granted a complete pardon based on evidence of innocence. The criteria used by the Death Penalty Information Center (DPIC) to determine the number of innocent people released from death row is criticized by some as blurring the distinction between actual innocence and legal innocence (Sharp, 2004). In one such criticism, Sharp allowed that 17 might be a credible number for actual innocents released from death row between 1973 and 2004. Whether the number is greater than 100 or fewer than 20, the possibility of executing an innocent person is reason enough for many people to be against using death sentences. Others, however, suggest that the horror of a rare mistake is outweighed by the benefits of execution when it is appropriate.

Achieving a strict principle of *lex talionis* is very difficult and, as a result, some self-described retributivists are actually against the death penalty. Paternoster (1991) offers three limitations to *lex talionis* that turn some retributivists into abolitionists:

1. Rigid adherence to the *lex talionis* principle of equality would mean that the death penalty is appropriate only for murder. Crimes of rape, kidnapping, and armed robbery would not be punished by execution, but all murders would be. Under contemporary legal requirements (i.e., only murders with aggravating circumstances are eligible for the death penalty), the principle of equity is tempered with a dose of mercy.

2. Strict following of *lex talionis* would result in ridiculous and uncivilized punishments because society cannot always treat criminals exactly as they treated their victims. We do not rape the rapists, set fire to the arsonists, or steal from thieves. Nor can we administer several executions to the serial murderer.

3. The principle of equity cannot be met in instances of brutal murder because a strict *lex talionis* would require that brutal murderers be treated brutally by tormenting those who tortured, dismembering those who cut up their victims, and so on. Such behavior by the state would require imitation of the very acts the public so intensely despises.

Sam72/Shutterstock

FIGURE 12–9 Must a Retributivist be Pro-Death Penalty?

YES
There can be no margin of error when taking a person's life.

It should not be too much to ask of a civilized society that we not kill a single innocent person.

Russ Feingold
U.S. Senator from Wisconsin

NO
The benefits of execution outweigh the horror of a rare mistake.

We don't make automobiles illegal just because there is a risk of having a fatal accident and we shouldn't eliminate the death penalty just because mistakes are inevitable.

Steven Stewart
Clark County Indiana Prosecuting Attorney

FIGURE 12–10 Should the Death Penalty Be Banned Because an Innocent Person Could Be Executed?

Although cases of innocent people being released from death row have convinced some death penalty proponents to become opponents, others simply point to these close calls as examples of the system working—they were caught in time, the argument goes. Reliance on the justice system to catch its own errors before tragedy occurs may be misplaced, however. In many of the exonerations, it was not a diligent justice system that identified the condemned person's innocence but rather an independent nonprofit organization established to assist prisoners (including those on death row) who could be proven innocent through DNA testing. **The Innocence Project** (www. innocenceproject.org/) has been instrumental in DNA exonerations of persons who have served time on death row and is actively involved in reforming the criminal justice system to prevent future injustices.

Regardless of whether the exoneration of an innocent death-row inmate resulted from a diligent justice process or a diligent nonprofit organization, the point for some capital punishment proponents is that the execution did not occur. So, they suggest, there is no reason to believe that an innocent person has ever actually been executed (Sharp, 2004). Abolitionists agree it is difficult to prove an innocent person has been executed because

courts do not generally entertain claims of innocence when the defendant is dead. Further, the need to work on cases of people living on death row who may be innocent takes precedence over cases of people already executed. The DPIC identifies 13 people executed since 1976 as possibly having been innocent, but it is especially interesting to note that the public seems to believe that innocent people have been executed. Gallup poll data from October 2009 found that 59% of Americans believe that an innocent person has been executed in the last five years, but the same poll found that 64% of the public favor capital punishment (Gallup, 2016).

Questions of whether the death penalty deters, is applied in a fair manner, provides retribution for society, or may present an irrevocable mistake due to innocence are ones with which we continue to struggle. In the end, one's position regarding the death penalty must be arrived at through personal decisions based on variables ranging from morality to assessment of statistical research.

► Public Opinion and the Death Penalty

The idea that capital punishment could be abolished because it doesn't have the public's support may seem far-fetched, but it is actually quite plausible. Because of the Supreme Court's interest in considering society's evolving standard of decency when deciding what constitutes cruel and unusual punishment, public opinion will make a difference—just as it did in the Court's decisions on executing persons who committed their crime when under age 18 (*Roper* v. *Simmons*), persons who are mentally retarded [sic] (*Atkins* v. *Virginia*), and persons who are mentally ill (*Ford* v. *Wainright*).

According to national opinion polls, in the years preceding the *Furman* decision (pre-1972), public support for the death penalty was often under 50%. The Gallup Organization, which in the 1930s began asking Americans if they are "in favor of the death penalty for a person convicted of murder," reports public support at its lowest in 1966 (42% favoring) and its highest in 1994 (80% favoring). The percentage favoring the death penalty has not been below 50% since the early 1970s. However, as Figure 12–11 shows, it has been hovering around 60% for

LEARNING OUTCOMES 5 Discuss the influence of public opinion on the death penalty.

Think About It…

Public opinion polls find that most Americans believe an innocent person has been executed in recent years, but most also favor the death penalty. Do you see this as especially inconsistent and/or troubling? Why or why not? Because of the possibility of executing an innocent person, would people be more likely to favor abolishing the death penalty if a life sentence without the possibility of parole were made the alternative?

Lightspring/Shutterstock

Death penalty poll

Americans' opinions on capital punishment over time

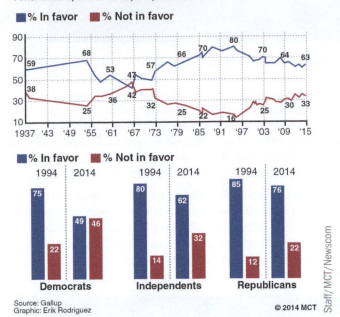

Source: Gallup
Graphic: Erik Rodriguez

© 2014 MCT

Staff/MCT/Newscom

FIGURE 12–11 **Trends in Public Opinion About the Death Penalty.**

the last several years (with the lowest level of support, 60%, occurring in 2013).

There is, however, indication that people may also be willing to have an alternative to capital punishment. When the Gallup poll asks if people believe the death penalty or life imprisonment with absolutely no possibility of parole (LWOP) is the better punishment for murder, the number choosing the death penalty has been 50% or less since 2006 (Gallup, 2016).

Some abolitionists are encouraged by the declining support for the death penalty and the rather consistent preference (42–48% since 2000) for LWOP. Possibly, the abolitionists argue, the **Marshall hypothesis** is playing a role. Supreme Court Justice Marshall, in his opinion for the *Furman* decision, said that the public lacks knowledge about the death penalty and its effects. He then suggested that an informed public generally would oppose the death penalty. Believing Justice Marshall to have been on to something, abolitionists often direct their attention toward public education. And their efforts may not be misplaced because some research suggests that educating the public can reduce support for capital punishment—but it is seldom reduced to less than a majority. Aarons (2013) reviewed more than 20 published articles describing experiments testing the Marshall hypothesis and summarized them as indicating that once informed about capital punishment's lack of

deterrence and its unequal administration, support for the death penalty falls among those who moderately support the penalty. Bohm and his colleagues have conducted several studies on this issue and found that the public lacks general knowledge about the death penalty and its administration, and that upon being informed about how the death penalty operates, support for the penalty declines among those with less prior knowledge (Bohm, Clark, & Aveni, 1991; Bohm, Vogel, & Maisto, 1993). However, persons with more prior knowledge about the death penalty are less likely to have their opinions change. Similarly, once people publically declare their support for the death penalty, they tend not to change their minds despite evidence of the penalty's bias and fallibility (Aarons, 2013; Bohm, 1990).

As the public receives more media reports about caprice, bias, and mistake in the application of death sentences, it seems possible that preference for LWOP may increase—at least among persons with only moderate support for the penalty. Unnever and Cullen (2005), for example, found that individuals who believed that innocent people have been executed are less likely to support the death penalty and more likely to support LWOP as the better punishment for murder.

Is the stage being set for a U.S. Supreme Court ruling that finds capital punishment to be cruel and unusual? As more examples of innocent people being sentenced to death (and possibly executed) come to light, it may well push public opinion against the death penalty. In the absence of clear public support, the Court may decide that society in the twenty-first century has come to view the possibility of executing innocent people as cruel and unusual punishment. Were that to happen, the death penalty would undoubtedly be ruled unconstitutional.

An alternative, of course, would be to improve the judicial process so those mistakes are never made. Or, there is always the position that the execution of the occasional innocent person is simply an unfortunate cost that is outweighed by the great benefit derived from capital punishment. One attempt at the first alternative was the passage in 2004 of the Justice for All Act. Title IV of the act, entitled the Innocence Protection Act, affects the death penalty by creating a DNA testing program and authorizing grants to states to improve the quality of prosecution and defense representation in state capital cases and to provide compensation for the wrongfully convicted. In addition, Congress increased the maximum compensation (from $5,000 to $100,000 for each 12-month period of incarceration) for any plaintiff who was unjustly sentenced to death for a federal crime. Further, state legislators are encouraged to provide reasonable compensation to any person found to have been unjustly convicted and sentenced to death.

Once again we are left with our own personal punishment philosophy to direct the choice we would make. But eventually, all those personal philosophies influence society's position, legislators' actions, and the courts' decisions.

Should You Be Able to Watch an Execution on Television or Your Smartphone?

On August 14, 1936, the last public execution was held in the United States. Rainey Bethea was hanged in Owensboro, Kentucky, for the rape and murder of a 70-year-old woman. Some 20,000 people came to witness the event, which also involved the country's first hanging conducted by a woman (National Public Radio, 2001). The carnival atmosphere—as some reporters called it—is believed by some to have encouraged the eventual banning of public executions in America. But the suitability of public executions in contemporary society still pops up on occasion, as some argue that it could increase the death penalty's deterrent effect and others say it would only serve to desensitize people to violence.

In 1991, a public television station sought permission to videotape and televise a California execution. The request was denied, in part, out of respect for the privacy of prison personnel who participate in the execution process and their concern that harm could come to themselves or their families in retaliation from those opposed to the execution. Proponents of televised executions argue that private nighttime executions leave the public uninformed about the facts surrounding capital punishment—with a result being the degrading of America's democracy by restricting public access to information and suppressing public debate.

More recently, Timothy McVeigh said he had no objection to the broadcast of his 2001 execution for the 1995 Oklahoma City bombing that killed 168 people. In the end, McVeigh's execution had a restricted broadcast to more than 200 survivors and family members who watched on a closed-circuit television feed in Oklahoma City.

The idea of having public executions raises several interesting questions:

1. A presumed benefit of public executions is to maximize the deterrent effect of capital punishment. When it is obvious to everyone that the death penalty will be used—and, humiliatingly, with thousands of others watching—it will discourage others from committing a capital offense. *Is the potential for general deterrence sufficient to reintroduce public executions?*

2. An argument against public executions is that it could desensitize people to violence. *Do you agree or disagree with that argument? What other reasons can you think of for why executions should not be public?*

3. In agreeing to a closed-circuit television broadcast of his execution, McVeigh wondered why it should not be truly public via public broadcast. *Would you have watched a televised execution of Timothy McVeigh? Why or why not?*

CHAPTER 12 Capital Punishment

Outline the history of capital punishment in the United States.

Following the British lead, American colonists relied on capital punishment as a primary punishment for criminal offenders. However, in the 1800s capital punishment began falling out of favor and by the 1940s it was used less frequently. In 1972, the death penalty was declared unconstitutional as it was then used and there was a moratorium on American executions until 1976 when new death penalty statutes were approved by the U.S. Supreme Court. Today, the death penalty is authorized in 32 states plus the federal government and the U.S. military. All those jurisdictions use lethal injection as their primary method of execution.

1. Both corporal and capital punishment were once the norm in America. Corporal punishment (e.g., whipping, branding, and the stocks) is no longer practiced but capital punishment is. Why?

2. What event distinguishes the early and modern eras of capital punishment in the United States?

3. What were the popular methods of execution during the early era of capital punishment in the United States?

4. In which area of the country are the states less likely to have death penalty statutes? Why?

Explain the legal provisions for capital punishment in the United States.

Although the Eighth Amendment prohibits cruel and unusual punishment, neither *cruel* nor *unusual* is defined in the Constitution, and the U.S. Supreme Court has determined that the terms must be considered in the context of evolving community standards. This means legal challenges to the death penalty are constantly heard by the courts. Some of those challenges focus on to whom the death penalty can apply and others center on the procedures to be used when applying it. As a result, today the death penalty may be used in cases of first-degree murder with aggravating circumstances (the "who" question) following procedures that provide for both a trial phase and a penalty phase (the "how" question).

1. What crimes other than aggravated murder are included in the death penalty statues of some states? Do you agree or disagree that those crimes should receive the death penalty?

2. Is it important that an execution method be humane? Why or why not?

3. On what basis did the U.S. Supreme Court (*Furman* v. *Georgia*) determine that the death penalty was being imposed in an unconstitutional manner?

4. Other than the *Furman* and *Gregg* decisions, what three or four U.S. Supreme Court cases do you believe have had the greatest impact on the death penalty? Why?

Furman decision In *Furman* v. *Georgia*, the U.S. Supreme Court determined that the death penalty was cruel and unusual because it was imposed in an arbitrary and capricious manner.

guided discretion A requirement that juries, after determining guilt in the first stage of a death penalty trial, consider both aggravating and mitigating circumstances during the sentencing stage of the trial.

Gregg decision Ruled that death penalty statutes that provide for bifurcated trials and that direct juries to use guided discretion in deciding the sentence are allowed under the Constitution.

bifurcated trial A requirement that death penalty cases have two stages, with the first stage being the traditional trial to determine guilt and a second stage to decide the sentence—death or life imprisonment.

Describe the characteristics of death-row prisoners and explain how some leave death-row without being executed.

Since the U.S. Supreme Court has ruled that the death penalty cannot be given to persons who are mentally ill, intellectually disabled, or were under age 18 at the time of their crime, none of the death-row prisoners should have those characteristics. Demographic descriptions tell us that those on death row are mostly white non-Hispanic males being held in a prison in a southern state. They probably were not involved in the criminal justice system at the time of the capital offense, but those who were "in the system" were more likely to have been on parole than probation. Most of the death-row inmates, especially African-Americans, have prior felony convictions, some with a prior homicide conviction. Most death-row prisoners leave death row without being executed—typically by receiving clemency or having their sentence or conviction overturned by an appeals or higher court.

1. Describe prisoners on death row in terms of their demographic characteristics. What do those characteristics tell you about persons convicted of capital murder?

2. Despite U.S. Supreme Court rulings, there are defense claims that mentally ill and intellectually disabled persons are on death row. Do you think that is true? If so, how is this possible?

3. Distinguish among the terms *reprieve*, *commutation*, and *pardon*.

4. What does it mean to say that most death-row prisoners leave death row through appellate court action or clemency?

clemency An act of leniency in the criminal justice system, such as a reprieve, a commutation, or a pardon.

reprieve A stay of execution that grants time for something, such as an appeal, to happen.

commutation of sentence A reduction of the sentence through action in the executive branch.

pardon Releases the person (partially or fully) from the legal consequences of the crime.

Summarize the arguments for and against the use of the death penalty.

Arguments for and against the death penalty are many and complex. One popular argument is centered on the question of general deterrence. That is, are others discouraged from committing murder because they could be executed? Other common debate topics concern whether execution is an appropriate way to exact retribution; whether having the death penalty is worth the risk of executing an innocent person; and whether the death penalty is handed out in a fair manner or if gender, class, and race/ethnicity issues are influencing decisions about who will be executed. As with other significant issues related to social control, we are left with our own personal punishment philosophy to influence our position on this important topic.

1. Of the four general debate topics (deterrence, fairness, retribution, and innocence), which is of most importance in forming your personal opinion about the death penalty? Why?

2. The death penalty is available only for murder with aggravating circumstances. Most murders are not of that type. Can the death penalty deter "typical" murders even though it is only used for aggravated murders?

3. Raise some capital punishment debate topics that were not covered in this chapter (e.g., cost) and present an argument favoring or opposing the death penalty based on that topic.

abolitionists Those favoring the abolition of the death penalty.

retentionists Those who favor keeping the death penalty.

proportional retributivism Requires that the worst crime in any society be punished with the worst penalty.

The Innocence Project An organization instrumental in securing DNA exonerations of persons who have served time on death row.

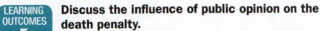

LEARNING OUTCOMES 5

Discuss the influence of public opinion on the death penalty.

The U.S. Supreme Court makes decisions as to whether a punishment is cruel and unusual by considering society's evolving standard of decency. Public opinion is one item the Court can consider when gauging that evolving standard. After reaching a low of 42% in 1964, public support for the death penalty has been above 50% since the 1970s and was especially high in the 1990s (reaching 80% in 1994). However, public support has declined in recent years and life without possibility of parole is gaining in popularity. Declining support for the death penalty may be explained in part by the Marshall hypothesis, which suggests that support will decrease as people come to realize that the death penalty may have no deterrent power and seems to be applied in an unfair manner.

1. How have public opinions about the death penalty varied over the last 60 years?

2. About what percentage of the American public currently supports the death penalty? What factors—such as age or gender—might affect one's opinion of the death penalty?

3. Explain the Marshall hypothesis and discuss whether you think it makes sense.

4. Will the Supreme Court ever rule the death penalty to be unconstitutional? Why or why not? If so, on what basis?

Marshall hypothesis Spurred by Supreme Court Justice Marshall's opinion for the *Furman* decision, it suggests that a better informed public generally would oppose the death penalty.

Additional Links

Some of the most current and comprehensive information about the death penalty is available from the Death Penalty Information Center at **www.deathpenaltyinfo.org.**

The National Center for State Courts at **www.ncsc.org/Topics/Criminal/Capital-Punishment/Resource-Guide.aspx** provides a helpful Resource Guide on capital punishment.

To review information supporting the retentionist argument, visit Pro-Death Penalty.com at **http://prodeathpenalty.com.**

Amnesty International promotes abolition of the death penalty and provides a world view on the topic at **www.amnesty.org/en/death-penalty.**

Listen to podcasts on such death penalty topics as race, representation, innocence, and victims at **www.deathpenaltyinfo.org/dpic-podcasts.**

13

Juvenile Corrections

1 Outline the development of the juvenile justice system.

2 Explain the age limits and types of offenses handled in the juvenile justice system.

3 Describe the juvenile court process and the characteristics of juvenile offenders.

4 Explain the procedures by which juveniles can be tried as adults in criminal court.

5 Describe community-based treatment programs for juvenile offenders.

6 Describe juvenile residential facilities and the treatment programs available in them.

7 Summarize the issues confronting juvenile corrections.

FROM JAIL TO YALE

You may know Charles Dutton from his television or movie roles (e.g., *Roc* or *Gothika*). What you may not know is that this respected and award-winning actor and director was sent to a juvenile reform school at age 13. When he was 17, he was convicted of manslaughter and sentenced to five years' imprisonment in the Maryland State Prison. He was released on parole, but after only a few months he returned to prison for possession of a handgun. During that return, he hit a correctional officer when a riot broke out and an additional eight years were added to his sentence.

Dutton's life began taking a more positive direction when he read a play while he was doing time in solitary confinement for refusing to clean toilets. The play sparked his interest in acting and he began participating in a prison drama program. While still in prison, he received his General Education Development (GED) degree and then an associate's degree in theater. After his release from prison, he earned a bachelor's degree in theater from Towson State University, and then went to Yale University's School of Drama for graduate work.

In 2009, Dutton and several other former juvenile offenders who went on to become productive and valued

members of society (e.g., former U.S. senator Alan Simpson [R-WY] and acclaimed writer, activist, and poet D. Luis Rodriguez) filed a brief before the U.S. Supreme Court arguing against sentences of life imprisonment without possibility of parole for juvenile offenders. Dutton and the others believe that when a juvenile commits a crime—even a serious one—the justice system should not assume there is no possibility of rehabilitation (Equal Justice Initiative, 2012).

Source: Nicolas Khayat/KRT/Newscom

DISCUSS **Should authorities estimate a juvenile's chances for rehabilitation based on the crime he or she commits?**

Juveniles (youths younger than age 18) account for about 26% of all persons arrested for property offenses (burglary, larceny-theft, motor vehicle theft, and arson) and about 16% of all arrests for violent crimes (murder, forcible rape, robbery, and aggravated assault). After remaining fairly constant in the 1980–1994 period, juvenile property crime arrests began to fall, and by 2006, they were at their lowest level since at least 1980. Although there was an increase in 2007 and 2008, the property crime index arrest rate has fallen to its lowest level in more than 30 years. A similar trend is found with juvenile arrests for violent crimes. After increases between 1980 and 1994, and again from 2004 to 2006, juvenile arrests for violent crime index offenses are at the lowest point in more than three decades (Puzzanchera, 2013; 2014).

Despite the very welcome decline in juvenile arrests for both property and violent offenses, there is a clear link between age and criminal behavior. In fact, the link is so fundamental that it is called the **age–crime curve**. This refers to the tendency for offending to rise during adolescence, peak around age 18, and then drop thereafter. The age factor is so closely tied to offending behavior that some cynics have facetiously suggested that the most effective crime policy would be to incarcerate everyone in the country on their 13th birthday and not release them until they reach age 30. Statistically, such action should dramatically reduce the nation's crime rates. Presumably, there are less dramatic proposals to consider—and we do so in this chapter. We begin with a brief overview of the decision to respond differently to juvenile offenders than we do to adult offenders.

▶ *Development and Operation of the Juvenile Justice System*

A separate system of juvenile justice did not appear in the United States until 1899, when the first juvenile court was established in Cook County (Chicago), Illinois. Other communities had made informal movements to respond differently to juvenile offenders before Cook County's formal action, but the Cook County juvenile court clearly became the model around the country. The court was established to provide for both the care and control of juveniles.

The court's "care" function was based on the concept of *parens patriae*, which is the idea that the court is the ultimate parent of all minors, and therefore has final responsibility for its younger citizens. This philosophy came from the English

system wherein children who were not receiving proper parental care could be brought before the Chancery Court. That court was concerned with protecting property rights of juveniles and with a child's general welfare. It was with this philosophy in mind that the Illinois legislators gave the juvenile court concern for, and authority over, a child's welfare. In this manner, children deemed in need of supervision—those who are dependent, neglected, or abused—are taken to the juvenile court, which has incorporated the old English Chancery Court care functions.

The need to control misbehaving young people was a second function of the new juvenile court. Prior to the court's

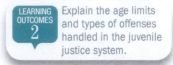

Outline the development of the juvenile justice system.

establishment, there was no age distinction (in Chicago or anywhere else in the country) as to how younger and older defendants were treated—everyone accused of a crime was handled in the regular criminal justice system. As far as the criminal courts were concerned, a 10-year-old was simply a small, misbehaving adult. But that began changing in the late nineteenth century as widespread interest in bringing about child-welfare reforms took hold across the country. The result was a desire to control misbehaving young people with more compassion than was present in the criminal justice system.

As a result, when America's version of a separate justice system for juvenile offenders began in 1899, the guiding philosophy of the new juvenile courts was clearly protective and rehabilitative. Reflecting this philosophy were terms that differed from those used in criminal court. Table 13–1 shows that rather than being a criminal who is found guilty of committing a crime, the juvenile is adjudicated a delinquent for committing a delinquent act.

Importantly, as Kurlychek (2014) notes, sentiment and terminology regarding juvenile justice have changed over the years. Today, we sometimes hear of juveniles being "arrested" and "sentenced"—terminology traditionally reserved for the criminal court. Nevertheless, the dual functions of care and control are still part of today's juvenile justice system, but the control function is not so clearly protective and rehabilitative. Instead, there has been some movement back toward a view that at least some juvenile offenders are best handled as adult offenders. But before looking at those situations, it is necessary to understand better just who comes under the juvenile justice system's jurisdiction and what happens to them once they are there.

▶ Processing Juvenile Offenders

The ways in which juvenile offenders are processed through the juvenile justice system are different enough from the ways adults are processed in the criminal court system that they are not possible to elaborate in detail here; but you can see the stages involved from the case flowchart in Figure 13–1. However, it is necessary to give brief attention to the process so that we can understand to whom this system applies and the reasons for which juvenile offenders can be processed.

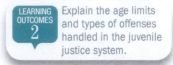Explain the age limits and types of offenses handled in the juvenile justice system.

Age Limits: Who Are the Juveniles?

Determining who will be processed in the juvenile justice system rather than the adult criminal justice system is not as easily accomplished as one might suppose. Figure 13–2 shows the oldest age at which a state's juvenile court can have jurisdiction over the juvenile. But even the map is a bit deceiving because many states have higher ages of juvenile court jurisdiction in such matters as abuse or neglect. For example, a young person identified by the juvenile court as having been neglected by his or her parents could be under the court's jurisdiction through age 20. In addition, many states exclude married or otherwise emancipated juveniles from juvenile court jurisdiction.

Juvenile Offense Categories: Reasons for Coming to Juvenile Court

Because of the *parens patriae* doctrine, the initial philosophy of the juvenile court was to assume that all the court personnel were interested in the welfare of the child and constantly had the child's best interests in mind. The result was a juvenile court system with jurisdiction over three perceived problem areas:

1. Situations wherein the child or juvenile has been neglected, abused, exploited, or in some other way mistreated

2. Certain offenses committed by juveniles that are deemed inappropriate or undesirable for persons under a certain age

3. Offenses committed by juveniles that would be a crime if committed by an adult

It is those last two items that occupy most of the juvenile court's time, because they deal with the juvenile's actual misbehavior. Misbehavior that is considered wrong only because society does not consider the juvenile old enough for certain kinds of activities is called a **status offense**; these include violating administrative rules (such as staying out past a city's curfew, skipping school, and purchasing and using alcohol and tobacco) and being "out of control" (e.g., running away from home, not obeying parents, and sexual promiscuity). Before 1974, many states responded to status offenders in the same way they responded to delinquents. It was assumed that a runaway or

TABLE 13–1	COMPARISON OF TERMS USED IN JUVENILE AND ADULT JUSTICE SYSTEMS	
	Juvenile Term	**Adult Term**
The person and the act	Delinquent	Criminal
	Delinquent act	Crime
Interaction with police	Take into custody	Arrest
	Detention facility	Jail
Interaction with courts	Petition	Charge
	Adjudication hearing	Trial
	Adjudicated delinquent	Convicted offender
Interaction with sentencing and corrections	Disposition hearing	Sentencing
	Commitment	Incarceration
	Youth Development Center, Residential Center, Youth Correctional Facility, Aftercare	Prison Parole

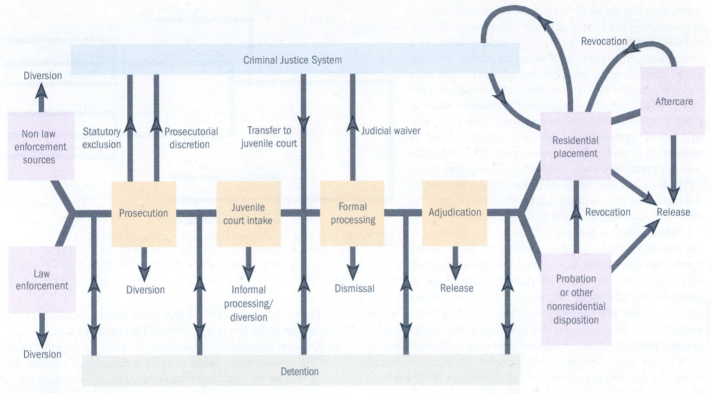

FIGURE 13–1 Case Flow Through the Juvenile Justice System.
Source: Case Flow Diagram from Statistical Briefing Book. Published by U.S Department of Justice.

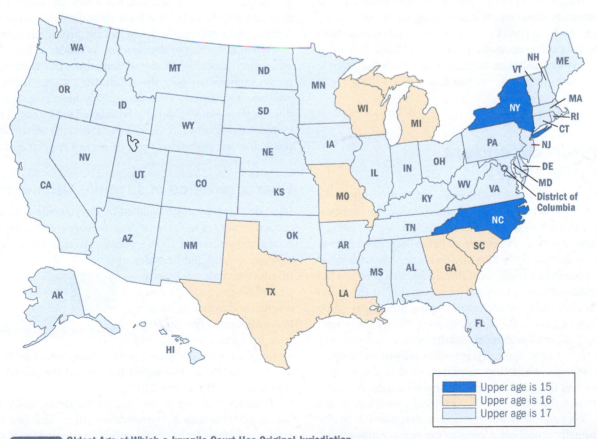

Upper age is 15
Upper age is 16
Upper age is 17

FIGURE 13–2 Oldest Age at Which a Juvenile Court Has Original Jurisdiction.
Reference: Brown, S. A. (2015). Trends in juvenile justice state legislation 2011-2015. Retrieved from National Conference of State Legislatures website http://www.ncsl.org/documents/cj/Juvenile_Justice_Trends_1.pdf.

truant would quite likely become involved in delinquent activities if some formal action was not taken. Consequently, juveniles were placed on probation or put in a correctional institution for nothing more than running away from home or being unmanageable. Today, it is more typical for status offenders to be handled separately under some nondelinquent categories such as PINS (persons in need of supervision), JINS (juveniles in need of supervision), CHINS (children in need of supervision), and MRAI (minors requiring authoritative intervention). These supervision categories allow the state to become involved in the child's life but do not confer the stigma of delinquency proceedings or the effects of such formal action as incarceration.

Status offenses present a dilemma for society. On the one hand, it is argued that young people who are truant, have run away from home, are using alcohol, or are generally beyond their parents' control are in great danger of committing crimes. Property crimes might support the runaway, vandalism may give the truant something to do, or violent acts could be a way for the ungovernable to express their continued frustration. A desire to prevent those more serious violations by "doing something" when the acts are merely at the status-offense level has been the motivation for most of the status-offense laws. But critics of those laws argue that "doing something" may actually push the offender further toward delinquency.

The third type of misbehavior that can bring a young person before the juvenile court is the one people are most familiar with—**delinquency offenses**, or committing an act that would be criminal had it been done by an adult. Such acts include both petty and serious offenses ranging from shoplifting to murder. Because this type of behavior is the one to which the juvenile corrections system responds, we use it to discuss the juvenile court's operation.

▶ Juvenile Offenders in Juvenile Court

Youths come to juvenile court officials' attention mostly as the result of police contact but also through social service agencies, schools, parents, probation officers, and victims. Upon getting a referral, an intake officer, prosecutor, or judge decides whether to handle the case informally or formally. In Figure 13–3, the informal response involves a nonjudicial disposition that is referred to as a **nonpetitioned case**. Dispositions available at this point include probation (more accurately, **informal probation**), some other sanction, or having the case dismissed. Nearly every state has authorized informal probation, and the practice is commonly used across the country. Typically, juveniles are placed on informal probation only when they have admitted to the charges against them, and they and their parents have voluntarily agreed to submit to the conditions of the informal probation. In the absence of such admission and agreement, the case will be dismissed or formally processed. Critics of the practice argue that it allows the imposition of substantial constraints on the youth's liberty without providing adequate due process safeguards.

FIGURE 13–3 **Case Flow for a Typical 1,000 Delinquency Cases in 2013.**
Source: Case Flow for a Typical 1,000 Delinquency Cases in 2013 from Delinquency cases in juvenile court, 2013 (NCJ 248899) by Julie Furdella and Charles Puzzanchera . Published by U.S Department of Justice, © 2015.

Figure 13–3 also shows that most delinquency cases are handled formally through a petition. This involves the filing of a petition that requests an adjudicatory hearing. During this hearing, the juvenile court judge or referee determines whether the youth will be adjudicated (found) delinquent. That decision is made after evidence and witnesses are presented by a prosecuting attorney (in some cases and jurisdictions this is done by a probation officer), and after the juvenile or his attorney presents evidence and cross-examines witnesses. The juvenile may admit to the charges at the hearing, but when an admission is not forthcoming, the judge or referee must dismiss the case or must find beyond a reasonable doubt that the juvenile is delinquent.

When a finding of delinquency is made, a disposition (or sentencing) proceeding follows. Sometimes the disposition stage occurs immediately after the adjudication stage—especially if a predisposition investigation has already been prepared to expedite matters—but it might also be delayed until a social history is completed. Figure 13–3 shows that most of the adjudicated cases result in either probation or placement in a residential facility.

Characteristics of Juvenile Offenders

Most delinquency cases handled by the juvenile courts involve property offenses as the most serious charge (35%), followed by public order offenses (26%), person offenses (26%), and drug offenses (13%). Public order offenses include such activities as obstruction of justice, disorderly conduct, and liquor law violations. The rankings vary by gender, by race, and by age—with the juveniles younger than age 13 at the time of their referral being responsible for 11% of the person offenses (Furdella & Puzzanchera, 2015).

LEARNING OUTCOMES 3 — Describe the juvenile court process and the characteristics of juvenile offenders.

Females make up about 28% of the delinquency caseload nationwide (Furdella & Puzzanchera, 2015). That is a relatively small proportion, but it is noteworthy that the proportion increased steadily from 19% in 1985 (Knoll & Sickmund, 2012). In recent years, the female proportion of delinquency caseload has remained

TABLE 13–2 — FEMALE PROPORTION OF DELINQUENCY CASELOAD, 2004–2013

Most Serious Offense	2004	2013
Total delinquency	27%	28%
Person	30	31
Property	27	28
Drugs	19	20
Public order	28	28

Source: Female Proportion Of Delinquency Caseload, 2004-2013 from Delinquency cases in juvenile court, 2013 (NCJ 248899) by Julie Furdella and Charles Puzzanchera. Published by U.S Department of Justice, © 2015.

around 28% and the proportion by offense type has remained steady (see Table 13–2).

Most juveniles processed through the juvenile court are white, but black youths are disproportionately represented. Although they account for 16% of the U.S. juvenile population, Table 13–3 shows that young African-Americans were 35% of all delinquency cases (Furdella & Puzzanchera, 2015). This overrepresentation is especially high for crimes against persons, but less so for drug offenses. Asian youth (including Native Hawaiian and Other Pacific Islanders) are 6% of the U.S. juvenile population, and Native American youth (including Alaska Natives) comprise 2%. The representation of Asian youth is disproportionally low for all categories, whereas Native American youth are essentially represented across all offense categories at a proportionate level.

TABLE 13–3 — RACE PROFILE OF DELINQUENCY CASES, 2013

Most Serious Offense	White	Black	Native American	Asian
Total delinquency	62%	35%	2%	1%
Person	55	42	1	1
Property	61	36	2	2
Drugs	76	21	2	1
Public order	62	36	1	1

Note: Detail may not add to totals because of rounding.

Source: Race Profile Of Cases 2013 from Delinquency cases in juvenile court, 2013 (NCJ 248899) by Julie Furdella and Charles Puzzanchera. Published by U.S Department of Justice, © 2015.

DISCUSS What explanations can you offer for why white offenders have drugs as their highest offense category and why black offenders have person offenses as their highest category? What about the respective lowest categories?

Due Process and Juveniles

The juvenile court was established without adversarial proceedings wherein a prosecutor tries to prove the defendant's guilt and the defense works to assure that the defendant has all the required legal protection. The absence of adversarial proceedings meant that due process protections for the juvenile were not really needed. After all, because the prosecution, defense, and judge were all looking out for the juvenile's rights and interests, why clog things up with procedural trappings? As a result, the juvenile court developed into a rather informal proceeding with a goal of treating rather than punishing the misbehaving juvenile.

Concern about the lack of procedural protection for juveniles did not attract much public or judicial attention until the 1960s. The U.S. Supreme Court had taken the position that the juvenile court's rehabilitative rather than penal philosophy made it an exception to the procedural guidelines of the Constitution. As Justice Blackmun said, "If the formalities of the criminal adjudicative process are to be superimposed upon the juvenile court system, there is little need for its separate existence" (*McKeiver* v. *Pennsylvania*, 403 U.S. at 551, 1971). But by the mid-1960s, it was becoming evident that in the name of treatment, juveniles were subjected to essentially the same punishments as were adult defendants.

In 1966, the U.S. Supreme Court heard the case of Gerald Gault, a 15-year-old who was taken into custody by Arizona authorities on the charge of making a lewd phone call (he was accused of asking a female neighbor, "Do you have big bombers?"). Gerald was eventually committed by the juvenile court to the State Industrial School until he reached age 21. Had Gerald been an adult making similar phone calls, Arizona law provided for a maximum penalty of a $50 fine or two months' imprisonment. Gault's parents challenged the legality of his confinement and the case eventually reached the U.S. Supreme Court. In 1967 (*In re Gault*, 387 U.S. 1), the Court reversed the Arizona court action and identified minimum due process requirements for juvenile courts to follow in cases where institutional commitment was possible. Specifically, juveniles were given the following:

1. The right to fair notice of the charges to allow sufficient time to prepare a defense
2. The right to representation by counsel
3. The right to face their accusers and cross-examine the witnesses
4. The privilege against self-incrimination

The *Gault* decision was also important for what it did not say. For example, after *Gault*, rights still unavailable to juveniles included the right to trial by jury, to release on bail, and to protection against double jeopardy. In addition, because *Gault* pertained only to juveniles whose delinquent actions may result in institutionalization, jurisdictions have differed in the extent to which they have carried out the decision. In some states, the protections provided by *Gault*, such as the right to counsel, pertain only to delinquent charges. In other jurisdictions, the protections have been expanded to apply to status offenders and in neglect and dependency proceedings.

1899	**1966**	**1967**	**1970**	**1974**
First Juvenile Court established in Cook County, Illinois. By 1925, most states have juvenile courts or probation services.	**Kent v. United States** USSC rules that courts must provide the "essentials of due process" in transferring juveniles to the adult system.	**In re Gault** USSC determines that, in hearings that could result in commitment to an institution, juveniles have four basic constitutional rights.	**In re Winship** USSC requires the state to prove its case beyond a reasonable doubt in delinquency matters. Prior to this ruling, the civil nature of juvenile court proceedings meant that the burden of proof was only a preponderance of evidence (i.e., evidence more convincing than the evidence offered in opposition).	Congress amends the 1968 Juvenile Crime and Delinquency Prevention Act to require that states keep their juvenile justice systems segregated from the adult systems and banned detention for status offenders.

FIGURE 13–4 Timeline: Key Events in the Juvenile Justice System.

In 1970, a second Supreme Court decision dealing with juveniles brought changes in juvenile court proceedings. *In re Winship* (397 U.S. 358, 1970) dealt with the burden of proof in delinquency hearings. The civil nature of the juvenile court proceedings meant that only a **preponderance of evidence**—that is, evidence having greater weight or being more convincing than the evidence offered in opposition to it—was required to establish a child's delinquency. In the *Winship* decision, the Court held that the standard of proof used in criminal court was applicable to juveniles in delinquency hearings. As a result, adjudication of delinquency required proof **beyond a reasonable doubt**—that is, fully satisfying and entirely convincing evidence establishing the accused's guilt. See Figure 13–4 for other Supreme Court decisions affecting juveniles.

▶ Juvenile Offenders in Adult Court

Even as the first juvenile courts were being established, there was concern that some of the more serious offenses by juveniles should be handled in criminal court. The issue is certainly debatable, but a rise in juvenile violence in the 1980s and 1990s brought the issue to a head. This policy shift was based largely on the assumption that there would be specific and general deterrent benefits of having the more punitive adult sanctions imposed on juvenile offenders—although Figure 13–5 suggests that assumption was incorrect. Today every state allows or requires juveniles to be tried as adults in criminal court under certain circumstances. This transfer can occur in one of three ways:

1. Judicial waiver: Juvenile court judge waives jurisdiction in the matter

2. Direct file: Prosecutor decides to try the juvenile as an adult

3. Statutory exclusion: Criminal courts have original jurisdiction for certain crimes committed by juveniles

It is possible that any particular state will have all three or just one or two of the strategies in place. In addition to these three transfer laws, some states have "once adult/always adult" laws that require criminal prosecution of any juvenile who was

- Juveniles transferred to juvenile court, particularly those convicted of violent offenses, typically receive longer sentences than those sentenced in the juvenile court for similar crimes.
- Despite the assumption that punitive adult criminal sanctions will have a *specific deterrent effect* on juvenile offenders, research finding actually show a higher recidivism rates among juveniles convicted for violent offenses in criminal court when compared with similar offenders tried in juvenile court.
- Not only has no specific deterrent effect been shown, the bulk of empirical evidence suggests that juvenile transfer laws have little or no *general deterrent effect*.
- The higher recidivism rates of violent juvenile offenders tried in criminal court as compared to those adjudicated in juvenile court may be the result of negative labeling effects, resentment felt about being tried and punished as adults, and the learning of criminal values and behavior while incarcerated with adult offenders.

FIGURE 13–5 Negative Effects of Transfer Laws.
Source: From Juvenile Transfer Laws: An Effective Deterrent to Delinquency?, NCJ 220595 by Richard E. Redding. Published by U.S Department of Justice, © 2010.

criminally prosecuted in the past—typically without regard to the seriousness of the current offense. Also, many states have "reverse waiver" provisions for transferring cases from criminal court to juvenile court under certain circumstances. Our interest is only in cases that end up in criminal court by one of the three typical strategies.

The Three Models

Transfer by **judicial waiver** is possible in most states (Griffin, Addie, Adams, & Firestine, 2011). Under this mechanism, a juvenile court judge can waive jurisdiction over a case and transfer it to criminal court. Prosecutors usually are the ones requesting such action, although in some states juveniles or their parents can request the transfer. Statutes typically limit judicial waiver by age, offense, or offense history and might also require the judge to consider the juvenile's amenability to treatment. In addition, waiver provisions are entirely discretionary in some states, whereas in others it is either presumed

1988	**2005**	**2010**	**2012**
Thompson* v. *Oklahoma USSC decides that society's "evolving standards of decency" now prohibit the execution of juveniles who committed their crime when under the age of 16.	***Roper* v. *Simmons*** USSC abolishes the death penalty for defendants who were under age 18 when they committed their crime. The decision is controversial in part because the majority of the Justices cited overwhelming international consensus against the juvenile death penalty and the dissenting Justices did not agree that U.S. law should be influenced by international opinion.	***Graham* v. *Florida*** USSC ruled that juvenile offenders may not be sentenced to life in prison without parole for nonhomicide cases.	***Miller* v. *Alabama*** USSC decides that *mandatory* life sentences cannot be given to juveniles who commit murder. The ruling left open the possibility that judges or juries, after individualized consideration of the defendant and the crime, *may choose* to give a life sentences to juvenile murderers, but they can't be required to do so.

or mandatory that the judge waive the case. Hockenberry and Puzzanchera (2014) report that about 1% of all formally handled delinquency cases are waived nationally. Most of the cases waived involve offenses against a person or property offenses, whereas drug and public order offenses are less often waived. The majority of waived cases involve males of age 16 or older, but person, drug, and public order offense cases involving black youth were slightly more likely to be judicially waived than when those cases involved white youth.

In some states, prosecutors have the authority to file certain juvenile cases in either juvenile or criminal court. This **direct file** procedure—also called *prosecutorial discretion* or *concurrent jurisdiction*—is usually limited by age and offense criteria. For example, in Virginia prosecutors can direct file against a child of at least age 14 who is charged with murder or such crimes as aggravated malicious wounding. In Florida, prosecutors have discretion to file in criminal court those cases in which juveniles of age 16 or older are charged with essentially any criminal offense and those of age 14 or older who are charged with murder, certain person offenses, and some property and weapon offenses (Griffin et al., 2011).

LEARNING OUTCOMES 4

Explain the procedures by which juveniles can be tried as adults in criminal court.

State legislatures effectively transfer young offenders to criminal court by **statutorily excluding** them from juvenile court jurisdiction. Essentially, legislators in these states have predetermined which court is appropriate and have taken the decision out of both prosecutors' and judges' hands. Although this may not technically be a transfer, the large and increasing number of juveniles affected by these statutes makes it an important strategy for getting cases to criminal court, since minors accused of certain offenses cannot have their case heard by the juvenile court. In some states, those offenses are only the most serious kind—for example, in New Mexico only first-degree murder by a child at least 15 years old is excluded. But in other states, the range of excluded offenses is quite broad. For example, in New York and California all murders and certain person offenses are excluded when committed by 13-year-olds (New York) or 14-year-olds (California). In other states, even some property offenses or drug offenses are excluded (Griffin et al., 2011).

Blended Sentencing

Comparing sentences of transferred juveniles is complicated by some states using creative alternatives that essentially mix juvenile and adult sentences. These blended sentences allow the court to impose either juvenile or adult sanctions, or a combination of these sanctions. In this manner, the blended sentence resembles transfer laws in that they define juveniles who may be treated as though they were adults (Snyder & Sickmund, 2006). Importantly, in all states where juveniles in juvenile court are at risk of receiving adult sanctions, those juveniles are entitled to the basic procedural rights afforded to criminal defendants (e.g., the right to a jury trial).

When used in juvenile court, these **juvenile blended sentences** allow the juvenile court judge to impose both juvenile and adult sanctions on certain categories of serious juvenile offenders. In most of the states using juvenile blended sentencing, any adult sanction imposed is suspended and functions as a kind of guarantee of good behavior. If the juvenile cooperates, he or she will remain in the juvenile system; if not, he or she may be sent to the adult system (Griffin et al., 2011; Snyder & Sickmund, 2006).

When juveniles are tried and convicted as adults, some states authorize their criminal courts to impose, under some circumstances, juvenile sentences that would ordinarily be available only to a juvenile court. In this way, juveniles who have left the juvenile system for criminal prosecution may be returned to it for sanctioning purposes (Griffin et al., 2011). These **criminal blended sentences** may be a combination of juvenile and criminal sanctions.

If the resulting sentence involves incarceration, there are three common ways it can be implemented:

- Straight adult incarceration: Juveniles are sentenced and imprisoned as adults with little differentiation in programming between juveniles and adults.

- Graduated incarceration: Juveniles are sentenced as adults but imprisoned in juvenile or separate adult correctional facilities until they reach a certain age. At that age, they may be released or transferred to adult facilities to serve the remainder of their sentence.

- Segregated incarceration: Juveniles are sentenced as adults but housed in separate facilities for younger adult offenders (usually 18- to 25-year-olds), and occasionally with specialized programming (Torbet, 1997).

Trends in Judicial Waiver

Transfer laws generally (including judicial waiver, direct file, and statutory exclusion) expanded dramatically during the 1980s and 1990s. Statistics are most easily kept on the waiver procedures, and the use of waivers over time reflects variation in justice policy. For example, from 1989 through 1992, drug offenses were more likely to be waived to adult court than any other offense category. Between 1993 and 2011, person offense cases were more likely to be judicially waived than cases involving other offenses (Puzzanchera & Hockenberry, 2015).

Changes are also being seen in the transfer laws themselves. In recent years, states such as Arizona, Indiana, Nevada, Missouri, Ohio, and Vermont have limited their transfer and waiver criteria, thereby creating more options for juvenile courts to handle youth. Missouri, for example, changed its "once an adult, always an adult" provisions to allow youths to return to the juvenile system who were found not guilty in adult court. Indiana now allows some youth convicted as adults to remain in a juvenile facility until age 18 and then be placed into a community-based corrections program or in-home detention. Revised statutes in California, Maryland, and Nebraska require juvenile court judges to take into account factors such as age, physical and mental health, and the possibility of rehabilitation when considering transfer. A 2015 Illinois law eliminates the automatic transfer to adult court of children aged 15 and under and allows the transfer of 16- and 17-year-olds only when charged with certain serious offenses (Brown, 2015). These changes are consistent with other reforms in the juvenile and adult justice systems as legislatures and the public place increased importance on preventive services and community-based alternatives to detention.

▶ *Community-Based Responses to Juvenile Offenders*

Several community-based programs for juvenile offenders exist for all offense types. As you will recall from Figure 13–3, most of the formally processed (petitioned) cases result in probation; but even quite a few of those that are informally processed (nonpetitioned) will also result in probation (called *informal probation* in these cases). Especially in the formally processed probation dispositions, there will also be accompanying requirements such as drug counseling, weekend confinement, or community service. The structure of juvenile probation and the work of juvenile probation officers are very similar to those of adult probation, so they do not need elaboration here. However, brief mention of some successful programs is useful.

One interesting program has the juvenile's age peers providing an alternative to formal juvenile court proceedings. In *McKeiver* v. *Pennsylvania*, the U.S. Supreme Court found no constitutional requirement to a trial by jury in juvenile court. But the justices went on to say that individual states should be free to experiment and may install a jury system or use an advisory jury to assist the judge. Some states have taken advantage of that offer (National Juvenile Defender Center, 2014). In

Massachusetts and Texas, youth are tried by jury in delinquency cases unless the child files a written waiver, but in other states the juvenile's right to a jury trial is considered waived if not demanded (e.g., Montana and New Mexico). In Michigan, youth have a right to a trial by jury if requested by a person interested in the hearing or by action of the court. More frequently, states have chosen to experiment with advisory juries composed of other juveniles. These **teen courts** (also called youth courts, peer courts, or student courts) began taking shape in the 1970s and have remained popular till today. The National Association of Youth Courts (2015) reports that there are more than 1000 youth courts in 47 states and the District of Columbia.

Although teen courts use court-like procedures, they are more accurately juvenile diversion programs. Young offenders charged with less-serious law violations (such as theft, vandalism, purchasing and using alcohol, and disorderly conduct) and school disciplinary cases can voluntarily have their case heard before a panel of age peers who take the roles of prosecuting attorney, defense lawyer, jurors, bailiffs, and clerks (Butts & Buck, 2002; Mullins, 2003). In some teen courts, the judge is also an age peer, but mostly that role is played by an adult volunteer. A few youth courts are structured to conduct trials that determine whether the charges are valid, but the majority work only with young people who have already admitted to an offense or problem behavior (Mullins, 2003; Norris, Twill, & Kim, 2011). In those cases, and also in adjudication cases, when the youth court decides the offender committed the act, the teen court determines the offender's sentence. Most often that sentence is to community service, but also popular are apologies to victims and parents, essays, teen court jury duty, curfews, and restitution.

Teen courts are widely assumed to reduce recidivism, save money for the jurisdiction, and to produce other benefits such as community service for nonprofit agencies, and provide law-related education. However, many of those assumptions remain untested or unverified. Research on teen courts is scant, and the studies that have been conducted vary widely in their methodology and type. Further, the research has produced inconsistent and conflicting findings (Norris et al., 2011; Vose & Vannan, 2013). Literature reviews find some studies where teen court participants were less likely than comparison groups to reoffend, but other studies found no such distinction. However, as Norris and his colleagues note, there seem to be no studies in which teen court groups had worse outcomes than comparison groups. Some studies have found negative effects of specific teen court sanctions (e.g., written assignments and community service), and the number of sanctions imposed, and there are concerns about net widening (see Chapters 1 and 2).

Vose and Vannan (2013) looked specifically at the number of sanctions and sanction type and found that the number of sanctions imposed was not associated with the likelihood of recidivism nor were most of the sanction types. They suggest that sanctions may have been assigned based on availability rather than on the individual's risks and needs. A preferred procedure, they argue, would be to include only treatments that have been empirically demonstrated to reduce the likelihood of recidivism, such as those reviewed next.

Community-based programs are appropriate for youths placed on either informal or formal probation, but also for those

returning to the community after residential placement. Greenwood (2008) explains that the most successful programs are those emphasizing family interactions—possibly because they include the providing of skills to the adults who supervise and train the child. Two particularly effective programs for juveniles on probation are Functional Family Therapy and Multisystemic Therapy.

Functional Family Therapy (FFT) targets youths aged 11 to 18 who are facing problems with delinquency, substance abuse, or violence. It is designed as a short-term intervention program with an average of 12 sessions over a three- to four-month period. The program can be offered in both clinic and home settings, but has also been successfully used in schools, probation offices, and mental health facilities. The focus, which is on altering interactions between family members, seeks to improve family functioning by increasing family problem-solving skills, enhancing emotional connections, and strengthening parents' ability to provide appropriate structure, guidance, and limits for their children (Functional Family Therapy, 2016; Greenwood, 2008). The program has been found to be effective for a wide range of problem youths and with different types of therapists and has received an evidence rating of "effective" from CrimeSolutions.gov (Office of Justice Programs, 2013a).

Multisystemic Therapy (MST) is also a family-based program, but it has a community-based aspect as well. MST views the individual as part of a complex network that includes his or her family, peers, school, and neighborhood. Parents learn to deal effectively with their youth's behavior problems by recognizing barriers to effective parenting and learning to address problems through collaboration with a social support network that might include other family members, teachers, or other adults supervising the youths. Intervention may be necessary in any one or a combination of the network units, so MST could be provided in the home, school, or other community locations. Master-level counselors provide 50 hours of face-to-face contact and continuous crisis intervention over four months. As with FFT, MST

> **LEARNING OUTCOMES 5** Describe community-based treatment programs for juvenile offenders.

has been proven an effective program for serious juvenile offenders aged 12 to 17 and has received an "effective" evidence rating from CrimeSolutions.gov (Greenwood, 2008; MST, 2014; Office of Justice Programs, 2013b).

There are, of course, community-based programs that focus on the individual offender rather than on the family. However, these have been found to be much less successful than the family- *and* community-based programs. Other programs such as intensive supervision probation, probation with extra services, and deterrence approaches such as Scared Straight have not been found effective (Greenwood, 2008).

An important meta-analysis by Sawyer, Borduin, & Dopp (2015) summarized evidence on psychosocial interventions and drew several interesting conclusions related to long-term reduction in youth antisocial behavior. For example, it seems that peer group interventions were less effective when samples contained more boys or older youths than when samples had fewer boys or younger youths. This suggests that peer interventions may be appropriate with younger populations but less useful for intervening with older youths who may exhibit more severe antisocial behavior or a greater number of risk factors. The meta-analysis also showed that girls benefited most from interventions involving their families and that samples with relatively high numbers of ethnic minority youths experienced the greatest benefits from parent group interventions—leading Sawyer and his colleagues to suggest that family involvement may be an especially important element for interventions serving high proportions of female and ethnic minority youths. Such conclusions speak well for current and future interventions and for the need to implement evidence-based interventions that reduce youth antisocial behavior and decrease victimization.

▶ Residential-Based Responses to Juvenile Offenders

Juvenile offenders whose disposition involves out-of-home placement are typically sent to a residential institution such as a group home, camp, or correctional facility. After reviewing the characteristics of those facilities and the juveniles in them, we consider some of the successful programs that can be used in an institutional setting.

Characteristics of Custody Facilities and the Youths in Them

Around 2,000 facilities nationwide hold about 54,000 juvenile offenders—down from more than 105,000 being held in 1997. Half of the facilities are privately operated, but most offenders are held in public facilities (either state or local). Facility type ranges from residential treatment centers and group homes (the two most frequently found facility types) to ranch/wilderness camps and shelters. Public facilities are more likely than private facilities to secure their youth by locking them in sleeping rooms at night or when the youth is out of control and to have other confinement features such as locked day rooms, floors, and corridors Hockenberry, Sickmund, & Sladky (2015).

Youths in custody are less likely to have been enrolled in school prior to being placed in custody than are their peers in the general population (76% versus 88%). In addition, about half of youths in custody are

<table>
<tr><td>LEARNING OUTCOMES 6</td><td>Describe juvenile residential facilities and the treatment programs available in them.</td></tr>
</table>

functioning below the grade level for their age compared with 28% of youth in the general population (Sedlak & Bruce, 2010). Because the link between education and delinquency is well established, an obvious need for juveniles held in residential facilities is the ability to continue their education. Most facilities evaluate the juveniles in terms of their educational needs and the majority of juveniles attend school while in the facility. Elementary level, middle school, and high school educational services are available in most facilities and many provide special education services and GED preparation. Fewer provide post–high school, vocational, or technical education (Hockenberry, Sickmund, & Sladky, 2013).

The majority of juveniles in custody facilities are being held for delinquency offenses—more often for offenses against persons (43%) than for offenses against property (26%)—and for drug offenses (10%), status offenses (10%), and public order offenses (3%). The remaining 7% are in custody for technical violations of probation or parole or some other reason (Sedlak & Bruce, 2010).

Although most of the youths in custodial facilities are male (85%), there are interesting differences between male and female offenders in terms of their offense patterns. As shown in Figure 13–6, greater percentages of males than females have murder, rape, kidnapping, robbery, drug offenses, and public order offenses as their most serious current offense. Females are more likely to be

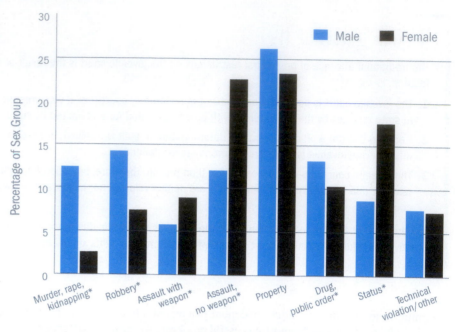

*Percentage of males and females differ significantly in these offense categories.

FIGURE 13–6 **Males and Females in Custody by Their Most Serious Current Offense.**
Source: Figure 1, Males and Females in Custody by Their Most Serious Current Offense from Youth's Characteristics And Backgrounds: Findings From The Survey Of Youth In Residential Placement by Andrea J. Sedlak and Carol Bruce. Published by U.S Department of Justice, © December 2010.

in custody as the result of a status offense or an assault without a weapon. The high proportion of female simple assault offenses is probably not so much a result of females being more violent as it is a result of mandatory domestic violence arrest laws—juvenile females are being arrested for altercations with family members whereas in the past such cases were handled informally or documented as status offenses (Sedlak & Bruce, 2010).

Think About It…

As the Justice Police Institute points out (Petteruti, Velazquez, & Walsh, 2009), youths placed in custodial facilities have a higher recidivism rate than youths who have received community-based sanctions. In addition, imprisoning youths can have

Pearson Education Inc.

severe detrimental effects on those young people and their long-term economic productivity. One reason is that imprisonment disrupts the process that normally allows many youths to "age out" of crime. What other reasons can you offer for the detrimental effects of placing young offenders in custodial facilities? Does the goal of retribution override those detrimental effects?

Institutional Programs

Treatment programs for youths in residential facilities have been evaluated over several years and some consistent patterns have emerged (Greenwood, 2008). Generally speaking,

1. Programs that support mental health issues are more successful than those focusing on punishment—so treatment programs administered by mental health professionals are more effective than similar programs administered by regular correctional staff.

2. Programs focusing on specific skills (e.g., behavior management, interpersonal skills training, family counseling, group counseling, and individual counseling) have all demonstrated positive effects in institutional settings.

3. Cognitive behavioral therapy, with its goal of changing the thinking process, has been found to work well with institutionalized youths.

4. Aggression replacement training, such as "anger control," which teaches participants what triggers their anger and how to control their reactions, has also been shown to work well with institutionalized youths.

Although effective institutional treatment programs are clearly needed—such as the one reviewed in Figure 13–7—one state has undertaken a bigger change than mere program implementation. When facilities for juvenile offenders were first considered, not much thought was given to whether they should physically resemble those for adult offenders—it was just assumed they would. They were often given nicer-sounding names (reformatories, training schools, and so on), but they were essentially large congregate-care facilities that, at best, were built on a campus-style design rather than a cell block or dormitory plan.

For many years, Missouri saw no reason to rely on anything other than the traditional congregate-care training school institution. In the 1970s, the Missouri Division of Youth Services (DYS) began questioning having youths mostly kept under the watchful gaze of correctional officers in a setting that was not especially conducive to the DYS-stated mission of rehabilitation. Instead, the DYS began experimenting with smaller correctional programs by securing small sites across the state—abandoned school buildings, large residential homes, a convent—and outfitting them to house delinquent teens. As it invested in these community-based alternatives to incarceration,

Missouri changed the philosophy and operation of its long-term secure confinement facilities to provide counseling and education in a more home-like setting. The largest of these new facilities houses only 36 juveniles (Mendel, D., 2003; Mendel, R. A., 2010).

Today, this emphasis on rehabilitation in small groups, constant therapeutic interventions, and minimal force is known as the **Missouri Model** and is influencing the direction taken by other states such as Florida, Illinois, and Louisiana (Moore, 2009) and the District of Columbia (Daly, Kapur, & Elliott, 2011). The Missouri facilities are positioned in five regions (allowing confined youths to be within driving distance of homes and family), and each facility is staffed mostly with college-educated youth specialists (selected more for their interest in nurturing than guarding) who receive extensive training. The facilities themselves are designed and furnished in a distinctly noncorrectional style. The youth, who wear their own clothes rather than a uniform, sleep in carpeted, warmly furnished dorm rooms.

More important, the approach seems to be working. Missouri has one of the lowest recidivism rates in the country, with 77% of youths released after 24 months remaining law-abiding and 68% remaining law-abiding after 36 months (Missouri Department of Social Services, 2015). R. A. Mendel (2010) points out that when measured against states that calculate recidivism in similar ways, Missouri's outcomes are far better—and they are exceptionally strong compared with states like Texas and Arizona where youth are reincarcerated for violating probation and parole rules.

▶ Issues Confronting Juvenile Corrections

The juvenile justice system as a whole is seen by many people as in urgent need of reform (e.g., Arya, 2011). Issues covered earlier in this chapter such as due process rights for juveniles, transferring juveniles to adult court, and applying adult sanctions to juvenile offenders are concerns that occasion much discussion among practitioners, policymakers, and the general public. There are other problems as well, including accusations of abuse and neglect in juvenile institutions, the

LEARNING OUTCOMES 7 — Summarize the issues confronting juvenile corrections.

The Mendota Juvenile Treatment Center (MJTC) is a secured correctional facility located in Madison, Wisconsin. MJTC provides specialized treatment and programs for delinquent youths whose behaviors present a serious problem to themselves or to others. The MJTC program has been evaluated in one quasi-experimental and two preexperimental studies and is included in the National Registry of Evidence-Based Programs and Practices (http://nrepp.samhsa.gov/) and is rated as "promising" by CrimeSolutions.gov. The program provides school services and group therapy focused on anger management, improved social skills and problem solving, and issues of substance abuse and sexual offenses. Youths in the program typically have several individual counseling sessions each week with a psychologist, psychiatrist, or social worker. The program goals are to help youths accept responsibility for their behavior, learn social skills, resolve mental health issues, and build positive relationships with families (Substance Abuse and Mental Health Services Administration, 2013).

Research findings show that the program had the greatest benefit on serious violent offenders, with those youth in the treatment group being more than six times less likely to engage in felony violence than a comparison group. Youth who received treatment in the MJTC program were also less likely than a comparison group to be involved in community violence within two years of release (Substance Abuse and Mental Health Services Administration, 2013).

FIGURE 13-7 *Evidence-Based Practice—Does It Work?*
Can Juveniles Receive Successful Treatment in an Institution?

significantly greater number of American youths in secure confinement compared with the youths of other countries (Justice Policy Institute, 2011), and the negative consequences of imprisonment on a young person's long-term economic productivity. Each of those deserves closer attention, but in this section we concentrate on the equally compelling issues of overrepresentation of minorities in the juvenile justice system and the problems of dealing with girls in a system designed for boys.

Disproportionate Minority Contact

Data from 1910 indicate that the early juvenile facilities were used more frequently for white than for black juvenile offenders. Of white youths sentenced to correctional facilities, 69% went to reformatories for delinquents, whereas 31% were sent to traditional prisons, jails, and workhouses. The reverse was true for black youths—29% were committed to juvenile facilities and 71% to prisons, jails, and workhouses (Cahalan, 1986). The discrepancy was eased as more states built facilities for juveniles and as racial segregation in public institutions was halted.

Throughout most of the twentieth century, white youths (not including Hispanics) made up the greatest percentage of the population in public and private custody facilities for juveniles, although minority youths were still confined at disproportionate levels. Today, minority youths ages 10–17 account for about one-fourth of the U.S. juvenile population but comprise more than one-third of juvenile arrests, more than one-third of the delinquency cases, and more than two-thirds of youths in residential placement facilities (Furdella & Puzzanchera, 2015; Hockenberry, 2014; Puzzanchera & Hockenberry, 2015). Non-Hispanic black juveniles make up about 16% of the nationwide juvenile population but account for 40% of juveniles in residential placement. Hispanic youths (of any race) comprise about 16% of the juvenile population but make up 23% of juveniles in residential placement (Hockenberry, 2014).

The issue of disproportionate minority representation in virtually all aspects of the juvenile justice system is referred to as **Disproportionate Minority Contact (DMC)**. For present purposes, we concentrate specifically on the disproportionate representation of minority youths in residential placement facilities. Four general factors have been suggested as contributing to minority overrepresentation (Devine, Coolbaugh, & Jenkins, 1998; Hsia, Bridges, & McHale, 2004):

1. Activities occurring in the juvenile justice system itself
2. Socioeconomic conditions
3. Educational system inadequacies
4. Family dynamics

The impact and interaction of each area is complex. Family factors such as single-parent homes, economic stress, and limited time for supervision are controversial but apparent factors. Also, the absence of school programs to adequately serve minority juveniles—or the failure of minority youths to fully participate in the educational system—can encourage involvement in delinquent behavior. And poor socioeconomic conditions likely play a role by limiting job opportunities, providing low incomes, and restricting social support services.

Finally, the juvenile justice system itself contributes to DMC through activities that occur well in advance of the actual confinement. For example, racial stereotyping and cultural insensitivity (both intentional and unintentional) seem to affect processing decisions in many juvenile justice systems. A procedure known as *selection bias* occurs when the actions or histories of minority youth are scrutinized more carefully than are the actions or histories of nonminority juveniles. For example, some studies show that police officers are more likely to stop and question a group of minority youths but only glance at a similar group of nonminority youths. According to other research, prosecutors have been found to look at a minority youth's prior system involvement as a stronger indication of a tendency toward continued crime than the same record predicts for a nonminority youth (Devine et al., 1998). When selection bias is combined with influences from the educational system, the family, and prevailing socioeconomic conditions, DMC is one of several negative consequences.

Girls in a System Designed for Boys

Girls entering the juvenile justice system are typically placed in programs that were created for delinquent boys (Bloom, Owen, Piper Deschenes, & Rosenbaum, 2002; Garcia & Lane, 2013). We know very little about the appropriateness of those programs for girls. Bloom and her colleagues explain that the "what works" literature has focused primarily on boys and men, leaving us to wonder about the applicability of the programs to girls and women. Program evaluations typically describe the proportion of girls included in the sample, but differences in outcome based on gender are not examined.

As we better understand the different developmental pathways followed by females and males, the need for gender-specific programming becomes more evident. Just as girls and boys develop physically and emotionally in different ways, their pathways to delinquency are also often gender-specific (Belknap & Holsinger, 1998). For example, scholarly work is making it increasingly apparent that girls face specific risk factors because of their gender that can derail or delay their healthy development. The American Academy of Pediatrics notes that studies of incarcerated youths report that girls are more likely than boys to have any psychiatric diagnosis and, especially, to have higher rates of mood and anxiety disorders. Further, although both genders experience sexual and physical abuse, all forms of abuse are more common in girls. As a result, post-traumatic stress disorder is more commonly diagnosed in females (Committee on Adolescence, 2011). The impact of these physical and mental health issues means that girls need programs that help them address their feelings of anger and frustration (often a contributor to involvement in criminal activity); their reluctance to trust others; and how they can develop and maintain appropriate, healthy boundaries in relationships.

Peters (1998) lists some of the things that girls need for healthy development (e.g., physical safety, validation from caring adults, and positive female role models) and some of the challenges they face (violence, substance abuse, family dysfunction, sexism, academic failure) that may put them at greater risk for delinquency. Specific risks (other than sexual and/or physical abuse) of special concern to girls include the following:

- *Substance abuse.* Psychosocial development can be interrupted by substance abuse, as suggested in the anecdote that it is not unusual for a 16-year-old girl to check into a residential drug treatment program with both her needle and syringe and a well-worn stuffed animal hidden in her backpack.

- *Teen pregnancy.* Female juvenile delinquents engage in sexual activity at an earlier age than nonoffenders, which puts them at higher risk of unwanted pregnancy. Teen mothers (most of whom drop out of high school, earn less than half the poverty-level income, and live in poor housing in poor neighborhoods) are more likely to raise a child who goes to prison than are mothers who delay having children until their early 20s.

- *Poor academic performance.* This is the most significant risk factor relating to early onset of delinquency. A disproportionate number of female juvenile offenders have learning disabilities and may have developed a negative attitude about learning.

- *Societal factors.* Girls and boys don't get into trouble for the same reasons, in the same ways, or at the same rate. Because the juvenile justice system is designed to deal with boys, community-based resources for girls are scarce. Add to that scarcity of gender-specific resources a perceived need to "protect" girls and we may have an explanation for the disproportionate number of girls who are committed to residential facilities, often for status offenses (Peters, 1998).

So, what might gender-specific programs look like? Peters (1998) explains that they involve a concentrated effort to assist all girls (not only those involved in the juvenile justice system) in nurturing and reinforcing "femaleness" as a positive identity with inherent strengths. When programming is gender-specific, girls are provided with decision-making and life skills that assist in their development into womanhood.

Essential elements of effective gender-specific programming for adolescent girls include a physically and emotionally safe space that is removed from the demands and attention of adolescent males, time for girls to talk, opportunities for them to develop relationships of trust and interdependence with other women already present in their lives, and education about women's health and female development (Peters, 1998).

Also important, but too often overlooked, is the need for specialized training for staff members who are working with adolescent girls. Because working with girls and young women presents unique challenges, staff training is especially important in terms of relationship and communication skills, gender differences in delinquency, substance abuse education, and appropriate placement (Bloom et al., 2002; Daniel, 1999).

Rather than continuing to squeeze girls into a justice system designed for boys, or to simply separate delinquents according to gender, it is necessary to have gender-specific programs for girls that provide a comprehensive approach to female delinquency rooted in the experience of girls (Peters, 1998). There is movement in that direction—for example, Indiana's Gender-Relevant Programming Initiative (Garcia & Lane, 2013)—but a long journey remains.

Should Juveniles Receive a Life Sentence?

When Terrance Graham was 16 years old, he was convicted of armed burglary and attempted armed robbery. Under a plea agreement, the Florida trial court sentenced Graham to probation, but six months later he violated that probation by committing an additional crime, a home-invasion robbery. The trial court revoked his probation and sentenced him to life imprisonment for the original armed burglary charge. Because Florida has abolished its parole system, the life sentence was essentially one without possibility of parole. Graham argued that the life sentence without possibility of parole constituted cruel and unusual punishment (Denniston, 2009; The Oyez Project, 2011). The case reached the U.S. Supreme Court in 2009 and the question before the Court was whether the Eighth Amendment is violated when a life sentence is imposed on a juvenile convicted of a nonhomicide crime. In 2010 (*Graham v. Florida*, 560 U.S. 48), the Court decided that such a sentence does indeed violate the Eighth Amendment's prohibition against cruel and unusual punishment.

If life imprisonment without parole is unconstitutional for juveniles convicted of nonhomicide crimes, might it also be uncon-stitutional for juveniles convicted of homicide crimes? Cases asking that question began making their way to the Supreme Court in 2011 when attorneys with the Equal Justice Initiative asked the U.S. Supreme Court to address whether it is constitutional to impose life imprisonment without parole sentences on juveniles convicted of homicide (Equal Justice Initiative, 2011). In one case, Evan Miller, who suffered physical and emotional abuse so severe that he tried to kill himself when he was just seven years old, was convicted of capital murder and received a mandatory life sentence without any consideration of his age or the abuse and neglect he suffered throughout his short life. The question was answered in 2012 when the Supreme Court ruled that mandatory life sentences cannot be given to juveniles who commit murder (*Miller* v. *Alabama*, 567 U.S. ___). That ruling left open the possibility that judges and juries may choose to give a life sentence to juvenile murderers, but only after they consider the characteristics of the defendant and the details of the offense.

Court decisions on life sentences for juveniles raise several interesting questions:

1. In its 2005 *Roper* v. *Simmons* (543 U.S. 551) decision, the U.S. Supreme Court ruled that it is unconstitutional to execute persons who were under age 18 when they committed their crime. In a Missouri case that resulted in mandatory life imprisonment for a 15-year-old boy convicted of killing a police officer, State Supreme Court Judge Michael Wolff wrote, "Juveniles should not be sentenced to die in prison any more than they should be sent to prison to be executed" (*Missouri* v. *Andrews*, No. SC91006; 2010). *Do you agree or disagree with Judge Wolff? Why?*

2. Some of the factors considered by the justices when ruling in favor of defendant Graham were the belief that teenagers are different from older criminals because they are less mature, more impulsive, more susceptible to peer pressure, and more likely to be rehabilitated. *Which, if any, of those reasons do you believe are especially compelling in the argument that juvenile offenders should not be given sentences of life imprisonment without parole?*

3. The *Miller* decision was made retroactive by the Supreme Court in its 2016 *Montgomery* v. *Louisiana* (577 U.S. ___) ruling. That decision requires states to remedy a *Miller* violation either by permitting juvenile homicide offenders to be considered for parole or by resentencing them. The Court said this was necessary because a remedy such as parole "ensures that juveniles whose crimes reflected only transient immaturity — and who have since matured — will not be forced to serve a disproportionate sentence in violation of the Eighth Amendment." *Does this seem fair and/or reasonable to you?*

CHAPTER 13 — Juvenile Corrections

LEARNING OUTCOMES 1

Outline the development of the juvenile justice system.

The country's first juvenile court was established in 1899 in Cook County, Illinois. The court's philosophy was based on the English concept of *parens patriae*, which meant that the court was considered to be the ultimate parent of all minors. In that role, the juvenile court came to have both a care function and a control function over children and adolescents.

1. What is meant by the *age-crime curve* concept?

2. Do you accept the legitimacy of the concept of *parens patriae*? Why or why not?

3. What is meant by the statement that the juvenile court has both a care and a control function?

age-crime curve Refers to the tendency for offending to rise during adolescence, peak around age 18, and then drop thereafter.

parens patriae The idea that the court is the ultimate parent of all minors and therefore has final responsibility for its younger citizens.

LEARNING OUTCOMES 2

Explain the age limits and types of offenses handled in the juvenile justice system.

The states vary in terms of the age for which their juvenile court has jurisdiction over juveniles, but the most typical oldest age is 17—that is, adult court starts on the defendant's 18th birthday. Although the juvenile court will hear cases in which the juvenile is more a victim than an offender (e.g., cases of neglect or abuse), the court's control function requires it to also hear cases involving certain behavior by juveniles. The types of behavior that can result in a juvenile court appearance include some actions that are perfectly acceptable when done by an adult (e.g., purchasing and using alcohol) and other offenses that would be criminal had they been done by an adult.

1. What is the youngest "age limit" for juvenile court jurisdiction in the United States?

2. Many states exclude married juveniles from juvenile court jurisdiction even if they are at an appropriate age for juvenile court. Do you agree or disagree with that exclusion? Why?

3. What term is used for cases brought to the juvenile court that involve behavior that is wrong only because the juvenile is not considered old enough for those kinds of activities?

4. What is the corresponding criminal justice term for these juvenile justice system terms: *delinquent child*, *adjudication*, *disposition*?

status offense Misbehavior that is considered wrong only because society does not consider the juvenile old enough for such activity.

delinquency offense Act that would be criminal had it been done by an adult.

LEARNING OUTCOMES 3

Describe the juvenile court process and the characteristics of juvenile offenders.

Cases come to the juvenile court primarily through referral by the police. The case can be handled either informally or formally. Formal processing means there will be a hearing at the juvenile court and a decision is made as to whether the youth will be found delinquent. When a finding of delinquency is made, the court decides what sanctions will be imposed. Most delinquency cases involve property offenses by white male youths, but the proportion of females has increased steadily over the last few decades.

1. Do you think placing a juvenile on informal probation is a fair or unfair practice? Why?

2. What are the most frequently imposed sanctions in adjudicated delinquency cases?

3. How does involvement in the four categories of delinquency cases (property, person, drugs, and public order) vary according to gender, race, and age?

4. What explanations can you offer for why female property offense cases increased during a period when male property offense cases decreased?

5. What are the four basic due process rights given to juveniles under the *In re Gault* decision?

6. Distinguish "preponderance of evidence" and "beyond a reasonable doubt" as burden-of-proof requirements.

nonpetitioned case The informal response to a juvenile court case.

informal probation Upon the voluntary agreement of the child and parents, the juvenile agrees to submit to certain probation conditions without being formally charged or adjudicated as delinquent.

preponderance of evidence Burden of proof that requires evidence supporting a charge to have greater weight or be more convincing than the evidence offered in opposition to it.

beyond a reasonable doubt Burden of proof that requires evidence supporting a claim to offer fully satisfying and entirely convincing evidence establishing the accused's guilt.

LEARNING OUTCOMES 4

Explain the procedures by which juveniles can be tried as adults in criminal court.

Responding to a rise in juvenile violence in the 1980s and 1990s, states increasingly allowed juveniles to be transferred to adult court under certain circumstances. That transfer occurs in one of three ways, with judicial waiver being the one most commonly found across the country. Judicial waiver is most often used today for cases involving person offenses, but it is important to note that judicial waiver is used less often today than it has been in the past. When juveniles who have been transferred to adult court are sentenced, it is possible that they may receive a mix of both juvenile and adult sanctions.

1. What are the three ways under which a juvenile can be transferred to adult court?

2. Which transfer model is found in all but five states?

3. Distinguish juvenile blended sentences from criminal blended sentences.

4. What are the three common ways of implementing a sentence of incarceration when a juvenile is convicted in adult court?

5. What are some of the pros and cons of transferring juveniles to adult court?

judicial waiver Juvenile court judge waives jurisdiction over a case and transfers it to criminal court.

direct file Prosecutor decides to try a juvenile as an adult.

statutory exclusion Criminal courts have original jurisdiction for certain crimes committed by juveniles.

juvenile blended sentence Juvenile court judge can impose both juvenile and adult sanctions on certain categories of serious juvenile offenders.

criminal blended sentences In cases where a juvenile is tried as an adult, the criminal court judge can impose juvenile sentences that would ordinarily be available only to juvenile court.

teen courts A juvenile court diversion program using court-like procedures and settings wherein youth sentence their age peers for minor delinquent and status offenses.

LEARNING OUTCOMES 5

Describe community-based treatment programs for juvenile offenders.

The most frequently used community sanction for adjudicated juvenile offenders is probation. As part of their probation, juveniles may also be required to participate in such programs as drug counseling or community service. The most successful community-based programs are those emphasizing family interactions. Two good examples of such programs are Functional Family Therapy and Multisystemic Therapy.

1. Although juvenile and adult probation have more similarities than differences, what do you think are some problems confronting juvenile probation officers that adult probation officers do not have?

2. Why are programs emphasizing family interactions especially successful for juvenile offenders?

3. Describe Functional Family Therapy.

4. Describe Multisystemic Therapy.

Functional Family Therapy (FFT) An effective short-term intervention program targeting youths aged 11 to 18 who are facing problems with delinquency, substance abuse, or violence.

Multisystemic Therapy (MST) An effective family-based program for serious juvenile offenders that views the individual as part of a complex network that includes his or her family, peers, school, and neighborhood.

LEARNING OUTCOMES 6

Describe juvenile residential facilities and the treatment programs available in them.

Juveniles who are placed outside the home are generally sent to a group home, camp, or correctional facility. Most of these residential facilities are small and private, but the large public facilities are where most juvenile offenders are held. Youths in these facilities are less likely than their peers to have been enrolled in school and many of them are functioning below grade level. Most facilities respond to this situation by providing educational services in the facility. Offense patterns of youths in custodial facilities show gender differences wherein females are more likely to be in custody as the result of a status offense or simple assault.

1. Because learning to interact with the opposite sex is important for all juveniles, should more juvenile residential facilities be coed? Why or why not?

2. Is a custodial facility appropriate for a juvenile whose most serious offense is a public order offense? Why or why not?

3. What are some general characteristics of successful treatment programs in residential facilities?

4. Describe the Missouri Model.

Missouri Model A model for juvenile institutions that emphasizes rehabilitation in small groups, constant therapeutic interventions, and minimal force.

Summarize the issues confronting juvenile corrections.

The juvenile justice system as a whole is confronted with questions about the need for due process rights when processing juveniles, the appropriateness of transferring juveniles to adult court, and the desirability of applying adult sanctions to juvenile offenders. Particular concerns for the corrections component of the juvenile justice system include the high number of American youth in confinement compared with the youth of other countries and the type of treatment they receive in those custodial facilities. Two issues of particular note are the disproportionately high representation of minorities in all aspects of the juvenile system, but especially in residential facilities, and the consequences of applying a system designed for boys to an increasing number of girls.

1. Describe some of the issues confronting the juvenile justice system as a whole and identify one that you consider to be especially problematic. Why did you choose that one?

2. Should we care that the United States has more youths in custody than do other countries? Why or why not?

3. What are some of the negative consequences that imprisonment can have on a young person's long-term economic productivity?

4. Explain what is meant by Disproportionate Minority Contact. Do you think this is a legitimate concern for America's juvenile justice system? Why or why not?

5. Are you convinced that there should be gender-specific programs in the juvenile justice system? Why or why not?

Disproportionate Minority Contact (DMC) Refers to the overrepresentation of minorities in virtually all aspects of the juvenile justice system.

Additional Links

The National Center for Juvenile Justice provides an online resource that profiles each state's juvenile justice system (see **www.ncjj.org/stateprofiles/**), including its transfer procedures.

Read and watch a video about Multisystemic Therapy at **www.mstservices.com/target-populations/juvenile-justice**.

Find a youth or teen court in your area at **www.youthcourt.net/?page_id=3**.

Visit the Justice Policy Institute page at **www.justicepolicy.org/research/2322** and download the Juvenile Justice fact sheet for more comparison of America's juvenile justice system with that of other countries.

14

Revisiting Evidence-Based Practices and What Works

1 Summarize evidence-based practices that work in corrections to reduce recidivism.

2 Articulate how the corrections system can become "Smart on Crime."

IS A NATIONAL CRIMINAL JUSTICE COMMISSION NECESSARY TO MAKE SYSTEM-WIDE CHANGES?

In 2015, then Michigan Senator Gary Peters reintroduced a bill in the Senate judiciary committee to create a bipartisan 14-member president's commission to examine the criminal justice system as a whole—what works, what does not work—and to make specific policy recommendations for the future. The bill was initially introduced back in 2009 by Senator Webb of Virginia. If passed, the "National Criminal Justice Commission Act" would authorize members to be appointed by the president and members of the House and Senate. Over an 18-month period, the commission would examine issues such as the over-incarceration of nonviolent and drug offenders, prison violence reduction, reentry programs, treatment of the mentally ill in the system, transnational crime, prison gangs, and drug cartels.

The only time a comprehensive study of the criminal justice system was ever commissioned by Congress was in 1965 when Congress authorized President Johnson's Commission on Law Enforcement and the Administration of Justice. This commission released its final report as a publicly available book entitled "The Challenge of Crime in a Free Society" and it was the impetus for dramatic changes in the criminal justice system for the next two decades. These changes included minimizing pretrial detention for defendants prior to conviction, installing call management and arrest records systems tied to 911 in every police department, installing mainframe computers in every courthouse to process cases, and increasing alternatives to incarceration (Blumstein, 2016).

Academics such as Professor Blumstein and members of Congress seem to recognize that a comprehensive assessment is long overdue for the criminal justice system, and there is still hope that the bill will eventually

John Rous/AP Images

pass. In the meantime, the Justice Department took it upon themselves to conduct a "Smart on Crime" assessment of the federal justice system (Department of Justice, 2013). This effort is discussed toward the end of this chapter.

References: https://www.congress.gov/bill/114th-congress/senate-bill/1119/text; Blumstein (2016); Department of Justice (2013).

DISCUSS Look up the latest version of the National Criminal Justice Commission Act. What are the arguments in favor of and the arguments against this bill? What changes could be made to increase the chances of the bill's passage by the House and the Senate?

▶ *What Works in Corrections*

This text presented an evidence-based approach to how correctional practices and research in institutional and community-based systems can be improved. We began by introducing the principles of evidence-based practice (EBP), most of which were the mechanics of how supervision and treatment in corrections is to be applied by practitioners to offenders to get the most dramatic reductions in recidivism. These principles of effective intervention include establishing rapport and positive reinforcement for offenders (Chapter 5), accurately assessing risk and needs (Chapter 7), targeting criminogenic needs using treatment (such as the violence reduction program described in Chapter 8), using cognitive behavioral methods (Chapter 9), the importance of reentry (Chapter 10), and graduated sanctions for youths and adults who may backslide while on community supervision (Chapters 10 and 13). EBP includes important methodological and evaluation considerations, which were introduced in Chapter 1 and shown throughout the text, to allow individuals to determine whether a research study is of high

enough quality to have confidence in the results. The most important thing about EBP is to use the techniques and programs that reduce recidivism and/or drug use and to discard or not use programs that do not work or those that do not reduce crime or drug use. In this chapter, the salient points of some correctional interventions will be revisited, along with examining the cost of these interventions, and how more informed decisions can be made in correctional policy.

Revisiting Correctional System Expectations Versus Stated Mission

As you learned in Chapter 2, people have many different expectations of the corrections system. These different expectations are summarized in Table 14–1 and include deterrence, incapacitation, retribution, rehabilitation, and restorative justice. The purpose or mission statements of correctional institutions still vary widely, but some philosophies are emphasized more than

TABLE 14–1 | WHAT DO WE EXPECT FROM THE CORRECTIONS SYSTEM?

Incapacitation	Implementation of court order and/or parole board orders
Community protection/ public safety	No further harm to other people while on supervision (no new criminal behaviors in the community or facility escapes)
Deterrence	Offender becomes fearful, afraid, and convinced, because of the punishment, to never commit another crime
Restoration	Victim and/or community reparations (community service and restitution completion)
Reintegration	Former offender is able to readjust into free society after a period of incarceration
Rehabilitation	Reformed offender creates a new life with changed thinking and behaviors
Retribution	Victims and others feel that the offender has received his or her just deserts

others. First and foremost, the corrections system fulfills a public safety function to keep prisoners securely locked up, or to prevent probationers and parolees from committing new offense while on supervision (Graves, 2015). The second most common mission of over half of all state systems was offender rehabilitation, followed closely by incapacitation and reintegration. Staff/inmate safety and humane treatment of inmates are two newer themes within the formal mission statements of most correctional systems (Graves, 2015). This is because correctional

institutions have the most control over the safety and treatment of people in their immediate control. Retribution through fair and just punishment and deterrence are less important today than they once were, given that both of these were listed in only one-fourth of correctional system missions. Two other new and emerging themes inherent in some correctional mission statements were the use of evidence-based techniques and cost-efficient practices (Graves, 2015).

Throughout the book, we also discussed a variety of correctional practices and programs. Figure 14–1 summarizes the correctional programs that work toward one or more correctional goals and for certain kinds of offenders. Although prison works to keep violent and predatory offenders from endangering the general public, we also know that prisons do not specifically deter most offenders. In fact, spending time in jail and prison increases the risk of felony recidivism especially for property and drug offenders (Freiburger & Iannacchione, 2011) or for individuals serving prison sentences of less than five years in length (Meade, Steiner, Makarios, & Travis, 2012). In a different study, when researchers compared two groups, matched with equivalent prior criminal records, offense severity, age, sex, and race/ethnicity, the group with a community-based sanction had lower recidivism rates than the prison-based group (Bales & Piquero, 2012). So it seems that if the decision is made to incarcerate, reductions in felony recidivism of between 10 and 15% are not achieved until individuals serve five years or more (Meade et al., 2012). While it may seem that the implications might be to increase sentence length or increase people sent to prison, the researchers concluded the opposite. They concluded that the *cost* of incarceration of sentences of less than five years with no recidivism reduction benefits is not good correctional policy. If the prison experience increases recidivism, then it makes sense to rethink who is sent to prison and for how long, and who would benefit just as well

What Works	What Does Not Work
Prison for violent and predatory offenders who endanger the public/victims	Prison for nonviolent and low-level drug offenders
Specialized case management and mental health courts	Incarceration and/or solitary confinement of mentally ill offenders
Drug courts and Therapeutic communities	Drug Abuse Resistance Education (DARE)
Reentry programs from prison	Expiration release from prison
Vocational training, job preparation, and provided work opportunities	Expecting ex-offender to find employment on his or her own
Probation or parole supervision with treatment	Long-term community supervision (more than five years)
Residential community facilities	Discipline-oriented boot camps and day reporting centers
Teen courts, diversion for low-risk juveniles	Scared Straight
Motivational interviewing and positive reinforcements to induce change	Negative punishments and threats
Cognitive behavioral, Multisystemic, and Functional Family Therapy	Psychotherapy
Graduated/progressive sanctions for technical violations and new misdemeanor crimes	Automatic revocation for technical violations

FIGURE 14–1 **Evidence-Based Practice—Does It Work?** A Summary of What Works to Reduce Recidivism in Corrections
Source: Findings from many studies are available at http://www.campbellcollaboration.org.

from a community-based sanction. It seems perhaps that prison should be reserved for those serving five years or more of a sentence and probation for those serving less than five years.

Probation and residential community facilities definitely have an important and preferred role for property, nonviolent, drug, and public order offenders. Probation and intermediate sanctions are more effective when partnered with rehabilitation programs, including problem-solving courts, vocational training, Multisystemic Therapy, and Functional Family Therapy. Other less effective correctional programs that do not work seem to be ones that involve long-term "lock 'em up" punishments without treatment, approaches based on fear and discipline only, and those that expect offenders to just "know what to do" on their own.

Cognitive Behavioral Treatment

Changing offender attitudes and behaviors through treatment is one of the main goals of the correctional system that are tied to EBP. However, not all treatment programs are equally effective. The most effective type of treatment for offenders is the cognitive behavioral approach, in that it assumes that behavioral change can only come about through the understanding that there are errors in the way offenders think about certain issues, such as the thought that violence is the way to resolve disagreements with another individual (Lipsey & Cullen, 2007).

Cognitive behavioral treatment can take place in prison, in residential community programs, or in outpatient community programs. Prison-based EBP treatment programs have been found to benefit prisoners by changing their behavior and reducing misconduct while they are still incarcerated (French & Gendreau, 2006). Community-based substance-abuse treatment in lieu of prison for drug-using offenders can save a significant amount of money and reduce criminal justice costs in the long term (Zarkin et al., 2015).

LEARNING OUTCOMES 1 — Summarize evidence-based practices that work in corrections to reduce recidivism.

Therapeutic communities (TCs) use cognitive behavioral treatment methods for drug addicts and people who have both an addiction and a mental health disorder. TC graduates had lower recidivism rates, less drug relapse, and greater improvements in mental health particularly if they received aftercare following the residential phase (Magor-Blatch, Bhullar, Thomson, & Thorsteinsson, 2014; Sacks, Chaple, Sacks, McKendrick, & Cleland, 2012).

Cognitive behavioral treatment for offenders while on community supervision is also important for change. The type and duration of treatment are more important to recidivism reduction than the probation supervision itself (intensive, regular, or electronic monitoring). More specifically, treatment that incorporates anger management and interpersonal problem solving had larger reductions in later recidivism than treatments that contained victim impact and behavioral modification (Lipsey, Landenberger, & Wilson, 2007).

How long should treatment last? The duration of treatment contact hours should be a minimum of 300 hours for high-risk offenders (who have the highest priority to get treated),

200 hours for medium-risk offenders, and 100 hours for low-risk offenders (who have the lowest priority of getting treated) for the maximum benefits (Bourgon & Armstrong, 2006; Latessa, 2004). The key to lasting change is to ensure that treatment programs are followed by an aftercare phase that continues outpatient support beyond intensive treatment.

Community Supervision

James Byrne insightfully observed that correctional academics and practitioners ". . . are better at identifying *risk level* than we are at developing strategies that result in *risk reduction*" (Byrne, 2013, p. 5). We have developed better mechanisms of identifying offenders who are high-risk and those who are low-risk offenders. For example, a low-level drug offender who was in possession of a small quantity of drugs may be identified as "high-risk" if that offender has a severe mental illness, is not capable of holding down a full-time job, is homeless, and has no family or social support. More interventions can be implemented with this offender in the community than in a correctional institution which will only exacerbate mental health problems.

Table 14–2 illustrates the kind of individual who will be more successful on probation: someone who is over age 30, has stable employment, has education of at least a high school diploma or General Education Development (GED) degree, has completed treatment, and lives in a stable housing situation surrounded by positive family support. Successful completion of probation seems to depend on continuity of supervision.

EBPs suggest minimizing treatment interventions with low-risk offenders, and keeping low-risk offenders separate from high-risk offenders. The higher-risk offenders should receive longer treatment doses of 300 contact hours and more structured supervision. Residential community corrections facilities (RCCFs), such as halfway houses and prerelease centers, can fill this role, as they cater to clients with greater needs than regular probationers or parolees. These needs are typically related

TABLE 14–2	OUTCOME ON COMMUNITY SUPERVISION	
	Successful	**Not Successful**
Age	Over age 30	Under age 30
Skills	Stable employment and educational skills	Deficient employment and educational skills
Housing	Stable housing	Mobile or transient housing
Family support	Lived with their spouses or children	No support system
Treatment	Completed substance abuse and/or sex offender treatment programs	Did not complete treatment programs

Source: Makarios, M., Steiner, B., & Travis, L. F. (2010). Examining the predictors of recidivism of men and women released from prison in Ohio. Criminal Justice and Behavior, 37(12), 1377–1391; Roy, S. (2004). Factors related to successful recidivism in a day reporting center. Criminal Jus-tice Studies, 17(1), 3–17.

to mental health or drug/alcohol abuse, and are criminogenic, in that they relate to their criminal history. RCCF offenders committed about the same number of new crimes as traditional probationers who resided at their own home. This is good news for RCCFs—showing that they work—because RCCF offenders posed no greater risk to the public despite their more complicated needs and assumed likelihood of greater failure (Lowenkamp & Latessa, 2004).

Jail and Prison

Prison and more intensive correctional interventions are reserved for those individuals who pose the highest risk to public safety, whereas community-based options are more effective for lower-risk offenders. Unlike community-based corrections and treatment programs, jails and prisons have fewer options for EBP that work to reduce long-term recidivism, so we must be extremely selective. Most correctional facilities focus on creating a safe and secure prison environment that minimizes escapes, violence, and sexual assault. As we learned in Chapter 7, risk assessments are important to manage and reduce violence among prisoners within the institutional setting. Another important element to safe prisons that are free of contraband is to value correctional staff through decent pay and benefits, and to reward them with extra bonuses for reduced violence and keeping contraband out. This will minimize the perceived need to ignore illegal activities in prison or being part of the problem. As discussed in Chapter 11, the staff members must observe prisoners' legal rights, and treat prisoners fairly and consistently. If we are truly interested in safe environments that are not mere schools of crime, we must be willing to pay for better-trained and higher-caliber staff; that is part of the solution. Finally, offenders learning new skills while incarcerated, such as increasing education levels and employment skills, is important to help with reentry. To learn more about specific programs that work, begin your search by using the interactive links provided at the end of the chapter.

▶ Cost Savings Best Practices

Now that we have a clearer idea of what correctional interventions work and what does not work, a prudent step is to factor in best practices to increase the crime reduction benefit compared to the cost to administer the program. We begin with figuring the costs of incarceration, which are shown in Figure 14–2 as rough estimates. The cost of incarceration varies widely according to the cost of living in the area and also according to the security level of the prison (cost is lower for minimum security and nearly doubles for maximum security).

About $12 million is needed each year to keep one correctional facility operational. Figure 14–3 shows how that $12 million is allocated—exactly where the money goes. Nearly

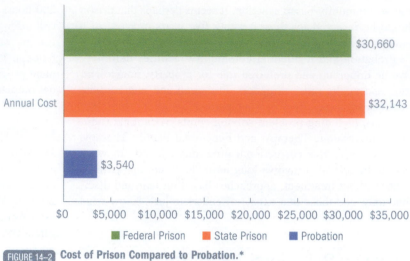

FIGURE 14–2 **Cost of Prison Compared to Probation.***
Note: *About 20% of the cost of probation detailed here is paid for by court-ordered monthly fees collected from the probationer.
Sources: (*for federal prison cost*) Federal Register, 2015. Annual determination of the Annual Cost of Incarceration. Retrieved online at https://www.federalregister.gov/articles/2015/03/09/2015-05437/annual-determination-of-average-cost-of-incarceration; (*for state prison cost*): National Institute of Corrections, Table View of Corrections Statistics by State. Retrieved online at http://nicic.gov/statestats/; (*for federal probation costs*): U.S. Courts. Supervision costs significantly less than incarceration in federal system. Retrieved online at http://www.uscourts.gov/news/2013/07/18/supervision-costs-significantly-less-incarceration-federal-system.

two-thirds of a corrections budget pays for staff members' salaries, wages, and benefits. With better facility layouts, podular-style designs that utilize less staff, and installing technology and electronic surveillance to replace personnel, a significant amount of money can be saved each year.

The entire criminal justice system (police, courts, and corrections combined) comprised about 8% of all state and local government spending, which was about the same amount spent on health care and hospitals (Kyckelhahn, 2013). The corrections system alone represented about 1.6% of local government and between 1.9 and 3.3% of state government spending. With a less stable economy, decline in tax-based revenues, and increases in health care costs, the amount spent on criminal justice is predicted to decrease. States must either raise taxes or reduce spending through program cuts and hiring freezes for state institutions, such as police, schools, universities, social services, probation, and prisons. For example, a decline in state funding for higher education has caused college tuition increases (National Association of State Budget Officers, 2011). The disjuncture between state spending on prisons and higher education is even more pronounced in California, Florida, Maryland, and New York.

When we examine state spending on prisons versus how much it costs to help people, the benefits of treatment and teaching people new skills are astounding. Table 14–3 shows that prison industry, long-term drug treatment, and education programs are the three most beneficial programs compared to their costs. To break even on the costs spent to obtain a GED, a program would need to reduce a three-year recidivism rate by only 2.5%. Davis, Bozick, Steele, Saunders, and Miles (2013) confirmed that correctional education

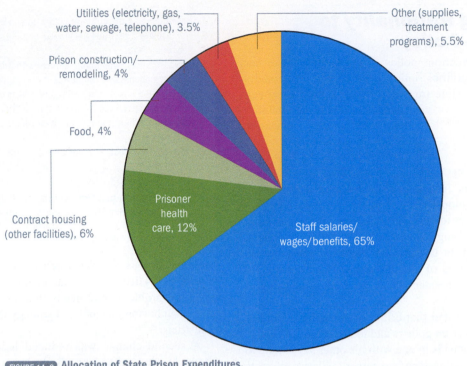

FIGURE 14-3 **Allocation of State Prison Expenditures.**
Source: Stephan, J. J. (2004). State prison expenditures, 2001 (NCJ202949). Washington, DC: Bureau of Justice Statistics.

TABLE 14-3	**PROGRAM COSTS AND ESTIMATED BENEFITS OF CORRECTIONAL INTERVENTIONS**

Program	Benefits (Value of Reduced Crime)	Initial Investment Program Costs (2007 Dollars)	Benefits Divided by Cost (Return on Investment for Every Dollar Invested)
Prison-Based			
Education	$18,621	$ 985	$18.90
Prison industry	$14,387	$ 427	$33.69
Therapeutic community	$14,357	$ 1,642	$ 8.74
Sex offender	$16,945	$12,881	$ 1.31
Violent mentally ill	$46,452	$27,617	$ 1.68
Community-Based			
Long-term therapeutic drug treatment	$12,443	$ 588	$21.16
Drug courts	$12,988	$ 4,474	$ 2.90
Work release	$ 2,904	$ 615	$ 4.72
Intensive supervision probation with no treatment	$ 0	$ 3,869	$ 0
Electronic monitoring	$ 0	$ 926	$ 0

Source: Adapted from Drake, E. K., Aos, S., & Miller, M. G. (2009). Evidence-based public policy options to reduce crime and criminal justice costs: Implications in Washington state. Victims and Offenders, 4, 170–196.

is indeed cost effective, because prisoners who obtained a GED while incarcerated reduced their own recidivism rate by 13% over a three-year period. The least beneficial programs are those that involve supervision and monitoring without help. As we learn more about reducing costs, retaining what works, and cutting what does not work, it is time to explore returning rationality to correctional policy and sentencing.

► Returning Rationality to Corrections Policy

Since the 1970s, corrections policy in the United States has become overrun by politics, union control, and emotionally based reactions to terrible tragedies, along with not enough

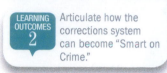

LEARNING OUTCOMES 2 Articulate how the corrections system can become "Smart on Crime."

administrative accountability and transparency. Academic scholars and not-for-profit groups such as the Pew Center, Council of State Governments, Vera Institute of Justice, and the Sentencing Project are deeply committed to rational crime control policy, which focuses on appropriate responses to the harm suffered by the victim or by communities and reducing expensive incarceration responses. The **Association of State Correctional Administrators**, whose membership is comprised of all state correctional department heads, has also taken a greater role in developing meaningful correctional policy.

Tonry (2004) suggested that crime policymaking be altogether delegated away from politics and to a specialized administrative agency. This idea is in line with his other suggestion to make prosecutors and judgeships into career civil servant tracts and to get away from the election and political appointment process. Given the current structure of the criminal justice system in the United States, Figures 14–4 and 14–5 list questions that are specific to decision makers influencing correctional policy at an earlier stage in the process. Figure 14–4 examines questions that legislators should investigate before changing existing laws or passing new laws. Figure 14–5 lists issues that prosecutors and judges should consider in the course of their occupational decisions involving criminal cases.

Being Smart on Crime

The opening story in this chapter discussed how a bill to establish a national crime commission kept getting reintroduced into Congress, but each time got blocked in committee. Given that Congress was unable to work together on such an important piece of legislation, and that the federal criminal justice system had fallen *behind* most other states, the U.S. Attorney General requested the Department of Justice immediately conduct a thorough review of the criminal justice system. This initiative became known as being "Smart on Crime" and made a series of recommendations (Department of Justice, 2013). Among the

1. Has increased use of imprisonment led to crime reductions?
2. If we completed a cost-benefit analysis of incarceration for each major class of criminal behavior, would the net effect be worth it? If not, we should devise less costly alternatives.
3. Can prisons deliver evidence-based treatment programs that will enhance public safety by reducing prisoners' later recidivism? If not, how can we be certain when and how this treatment will be received?

FIGURE 14–4 **Questions that Legislators Should Ask.**
Source: Tonry, M., & Petersilia, J. (1999). Prisons research at the beginning of the 21st century. Washington, DC: National Institute of Justice. Retrieved from http://www.ncjrs.org/pdffiles1/nij/184478.pdf.

1. How much of a direct threat is this person to the public safety?
2. How likely is it that this person will commit violent and/or predatory acts in the future?
3. What are the effects of imprisonment on prisoners' future economic mobility (income and employment opportunities)?
4. What are the immediate and future effects of imprisonment on prisoners' later physical and mental well-being?
5. What are the punishment effects on offenders' spouses, parents, and children?
6. What are the effects of punishment on the victim and the larger community?

FIGURE 14–5 **Questions that Prosecutors and Judges Should Ask.**
Source: Tonry, M., & Petersilia, J. (1999). Prisons research at the beginning of the 21st century. Washington, DC: National Institute of Justice. Retrieved from http://www.ncjrs.org/pdffiles1/nij/184478.pdf.

recommendations was decentralization—to allow each prosecutor of the 94 districts to create their own agendas for identifying crime problems and needs that are unique to their area, rather than having one national strategy that may or may not fit all districts.

A second change was reduced federal prison sentence lengths for drug offenders who had no ties to gangs, international cartels, or other large-scale criminal organizations (Department of Justice, 2013). In 2015, nearly 10,000 federal offenders qualified for this reduction, and more are expected to be released in future years (Schindler, 2015). The U.S. Sentencing Commission is currently working on reforming the mandatory minimum laws. A third change was that offenders who did not pose a threat to public safety in the federal system would be eligible for alternatives to incarceration such as diversion, drug court, and other community-based efforts. A fourth effort was to increase the eligibility for inmates seeking compassionate release because of a terminal illness or because of a dire medical need. This would allow federal judges to reconsider a sentence reduction for this purpose if the inmate committed a nonviolent crime (Department of Justice, 2013). Finally, the federal system will increase its reentry efforts by designating a "prevention and reentry coordinator" in each district's U.S. Attorney's Office. Tied to reentry is a concerted effort to reduce the collateral consequences of having a felony conviction, if that limitation does not serve a public safety purpose. For example, President Obama recommended that non law enforcement federal agencies not ask about prior criminal history prior to hiring (Schindler, 2015). More effort will be made to help former offenders who are eligible to apply for expungement and move beyond their stigma.

► The Future of Corrections

State correction department heads identified the top four critical issues to be addressed in the near future as supervision and care of mentally ill offenders, correctional staff recruitment and retention/wellness, reducing the use of administrative segregation, and better management of correctional population increases (Association of State Correctional Administrators, 2016). Three out of four of these critical issues were discussed in Chapters 6 and 7. In this section, we address innovative ways that administrators are working toward more effective management of correctional populations.

We predict that the future of corrections looks very promising, as changes are made toward the use of performance-based measures, a better understanding of factors driving jail and prison population growth, and the use of innovative solutions to reinvest in prevention factors that have a greater impact on crime. No longer will programs be funded solely on the number of persons incarcerated or on the caseload sizes on probation.

Performance-Based Measures

The model of funding that had been used historically in some jurisdictions encouraged prisons to expand and probation officers to keep their compliant probationers as long as possible for increased funding. This model of funding unfortunately never rewarded any program or system for decreasing their numbers or solving crime problems. Now, programs that receive funding are being expected to meet certain *performance-based measures*, such as recidivism reduction, decreasing revocations back to jail, increasing employment rates for offenders on supervision, increasing the amount of restitution collected, and increasing the amount of community supervision completed. This only works with accurate data, if community supervision officers are dedicated to helping offenders succeed instead of playing the **"gotcha" game**, and if parole boards and judges agree to a progressive sanction model over automatic jail or prison revocations. Ultimately, with less offenders going back to jails and prisons, the state saves a significant amount of money.

Many state and local correctional systems are hampered with outdated data systems and simply do not collect the type of data necessary to make sound policy decisions. To help this situation, the Association of State Correctional Administrators (2015)

updates a shared database and uniform definitions for a **performance-based measures system** to allow correctional administrators to use the same database platform to collect, store, and analyze data for their institution. The performance-based measures database contains seven main areas of available data primarily for jails and prisons: public safety, institutional safety, mental health, substance abuse, justice, education, and physical health. Some of these variables, featured in Table 14–4, allow one institution to compare performance against other similar institutions around the country using standardized measures that compute rates by factoring in the raw number by a standard denominator. The intent with these indicators is to help correctional institutions identify specific areas for improvement. Another purpose is to incentivize institutional and community-based departments to help increase positive behaviors such as earning a GED while incarcerated and completing community service and restitution. Private prison and probation companies should also be held to these same standards that link continued funding to quality of performance.

Justice Reinvestment Initiative

Another initiative that works alongside performance-based measures to reward states for reducing incarceration costs is the **Justice Reinvestment Initiative**. Federal financial assistance was provided to states interested in understanding factors driving jail and prison population growth in their state. Based on state-level crime, arrest, conviction, and revocation data analyzed by the Council of State Governments Justice Center, policymakers in each state then developed and implemented policy options to reduce the institutional population and generate cost savings. The savings generated by closing down prisons could be reinvested back into selected high-risk communities and other prevention-oriented strategies. The neighborhoods where most offenders were released were

TABLE 14–4 | PERFORMANCE MEASURES FOR CORRECTIONS

Public Safety	**Treatment Provided**
Facility escapes (medium custody and above)	Type and frequency of treatment programs provided
Walkaways/Absconding	Positive drug tests
Institutional Safety	Psychiatric beds
Staffing ratios (inmates for every officer)	Treatment staff (type, number of hours providing services)
Riots and disturbances	**Positive Behavior**
Prisoner homicides	Community service hours completed
Prisoner suicides	Victim restitution paid
Contraband recovered	Child support paid
Inmate-on-inmate assaults and victims	**Offender Recidivism**
Uses of force by staff	Commitment type (technical violation or new crime)
Staff injuries resulting from inmate assault	New offenses committed
Inmate-on-inmate sexual assaults	Number of crime-free days (release date to new offense date)
Staff sexual misconduct	

Source: Association of State Correctional Administrators (2015).Performance-based measures system counting rules:Revised counting rules for organization characteristics effective August 28, 2015. Hagerstown, MD: Association of State Correctional Administrators. Retrieved online at http://www.asca.net/system/assets/attachments/8868/PBMS%20KeyIndicators%20%208_28_15.pdf?1440788921.

mapped to identify which neighborhoods were in most need of the reinvestment services (Clement, Schwarzfeld, & Thompson, 2011). At least 11 states have saved taxpayer money by reducing their prison populations (including Kansas, Michigan, New York, Ohio, Oregon, and Texas). These states have been approved to use the savings on crime prevention programs in their own communities. Essentially, if prison populations dropped over time, the money saved from funds that were initially budgeted by a state to incarcerate offenders could be redirected to job training, or to support schools, libraries, public housing, and other forms of community restoration in high-crime neighborhoods (Clear, 2011). See the case study at the end of this chapter for how Kansas solved its problems of increased prison populations. Other examples of Justice Reinvestment projects include diverting people from the prison system, increasing drug treatment opportunities, closing prisons, and reducing parole and probation technical violation rates. Every intervention must use data to show measurable declines in the prison population and how the intervention affects neighborhood public safety.

As we venture into the future, we may be looking at an entire paradigm change from one that focused on an offender's deficits and shortcomings to one built on positive incentives, strengths, aspirations, and talents that have the potential of becoming exceptional and changed behavior. By focusing on positive behavior along with reinvesting in vulnerable communities, incarceration rates will be reduced without compromising public safety.

How the Prison Population Stopped Increasing and Communities became Safer: The Justice Reinvestment Experience in Kansas

Back in 2006, the Kansas Department of Corrections (KDOC) conducted a projection estimate for its prison populations based on the current rate of new admissions, which seemed to be increasing faster than in the past. The projections estimated that if nothing major changed, based on the rate they were going, within a three-year period of time, the number of prisoners would increase by 9%, and an additional 15% more by the year 2018 (Council of State Governments Justice Center, 2015). While the crime rate seemed to be stable and even going down, no one really understood exactly *why* the numbers of prisoners were increasing so rapidly.

The KDOC requested assistance from the Council of State Governments Justice Center (CSGJC) to independently analyze its data. The CSGJC collected over a million individual offender arrest and conviction records, conducted online surveys of law enforcement and probation officers, and also met with nearly 250 people in focus groups and community meetings. The CSGJC determined that the prison population growth was *not* due to a crime wave or because of longer sentences. Instead, more people were being sent to prison due to being revoked from probation and parole, primarily because of drug and/or alcohol use while on community supervision or some other pattern of technical violations. In other words, no new crimes were being committed, so offenders merely completed their original sentence behind bars. Ironically, when the drug users went to prison, few received the necessary alcohol/drug treatment or vocational education. When they left prison, there was no postrelease supervision, which created a public safety concern and a greater likelihood of recidivism.

Based on these findings, a reinvestment working group was formed. First, the group decided to reward compliant probationers with early release from probation after 12 months if they were scored as low risk, and satisfied their community service hours and restitution. For noncompliant probationers, the group decided to change the way that probation and parole officers responded to alcohol/drug use and other technical violations. Officers were allowed to impose two- to three-day jail stays for technical violations without court approval. Higher-risk offenders would receive priority for community-based resources such as alcohol/drug treatment. If that didn't work, the officer needed court permission. Judges were then required to use longer jail sanctions of 120–180 days *before* they were allowed to revoke. If revocation was inevitable, new legislation required postrelease supervision following prison. Based on this new direction, Kansas taxpayers will be saved from paying $56 million in increased prison operating costs and $25 million in construction costs over a four-year period.

The money saved ($81 million over four years) will be spent on community-based drug and alcohol treatment, increased resources for high-risk offenders on parole, and two new initiatives. First, some of the money will be reinvested into enhancing the processing speed of crime scene evidence by the Kansas Bureau of Investigation so that new evidence can be more efficiently tested, and new cases can be solved faster. Second, law enforcement agencies in Kansas will be able to improve their responses to people with mental health disorders.

The experience in Kansas raises several interesting questions:

1. If probationers were no longer getting revoked and sent to prison long term for substance use during probation, how did the probation department handle substance use with new consequences?
2. Why do you think the new consequences didn't lead to more probationers using drugs?
3. *How* do these new solutions lead to safer communities?

CHAPTER 14 — Revisiting Evidence-Based Practices and What Works

Summarize evidence-based practices that work in corrections to reduce recidivism.

Prison is recommended for those individuals who pose the highest risk to public safety, and is more appropriate for sentences of five or more years. Probation and community-based supervision are more effective for shorter sentences less than five years, and when paired with rehabilitation programs, such as drug treatment, vocational training, and cognitive-based interventions. The principles of effective intervention include establishing rapport, positive reinforcement for offenders, accurately measuring risk and needs, targeting criminogenic needs, using cognitive behavioral methods, reentry, and graduated sanctions.

Correctional interventions that are less effective involve long-term "lock 'em up" punishments without treatment, approaches based on fear and discipline, and those that provide little direction for offenders. In this age of uncertain budgets and economic shortfalls, estimating the costs and benefits of reduced crime from these programs is as important to implementing what works as it is to deciding which programs should be funded.

1. Are offenders getting exposed to enough correctional interventions to adequately change their path?

2. EBP in corrections seems to focus entirely on offenders and seems to ignore victims in this process. How can EBP be explained or sold to victims or victims' rights groups so that they will support EBP?

3. How can correctional budgets be decreased without compromising institutional safety and public safety?

Articulate how the corrections system can become "Smart on Crime."

Recommendations for the federal system include allowing each district to identify crime problems, reduce sentences for drug offenders without ties to criminal organizations, reform mandatory minimums, widen eligibility for community-based sentencing, increase compassionate releases from prison, and expand reentry efforts.

Rationality can be returned to correction through several methods. Move away from the political arena and into professionalizing key decision-making positions. Examine the broader effects of our decisions on the justice system and on communities outside the system. Reinvest dollars saved on incarceration into social service programs in low-income communities.

Future correctional budgets will fund programs that work, and will base funding on whether the system can achieve outcomes such as recidivism reduction and accounting for victim restitution and community service completion. This will necessitate transparency and access to centralized data.

1. If we are unable to separate crime policies from political influences, what limits must be set and/or standards be met for legislators and those in elected positions to minimize the irrational decisions of the past?

2. What other things need to happen in order for a new correctional paradigm to be transformed and embraced?

Association of State Correctional Administrators (ASCA) A national organization for state department of corrections directors that seeks to educate top administrators on broad correctional issues and influence correctional policy.

performance-based measures system A web-based national database that allows correctional administrators to analyze their own institutional environment and compare it to other states using standardized measures.

"gotcha" game A style of offender supervision where the officer is less interested in helping the offender succeed and is more interested in tracking failures and acting on rule violations; as a result, the officer has a high turnover of cases.

Justice Reinvestment Initiative A data-driven approach to encourage states to reduce correctional spending and reinvest savings in strategies designed to prevent crime. States and localities collect and analyze data on factors related to prison population growth and costs, implement changes to increase efficiencies, and measure both the fiscal and public safety impacts of those changes.

Additional Links

View the 60-minute Justice Reinvestment Initiative panel session on YouTube: visit **www.youtube.com/** and type in "Justice Reinvestment Panel Bureau of Justice Assistance."

View Dr. Edward Latessa's summary on YouTube of how community corrections can be strengthened using evidence-based practices: visit **www.youtube.com** and type in "Edward Latessa community corrections."

Visit the Campbell Collaboration website to look up the latest meta-analytic research on what works in the criminal justice system at **www.campbellcollaboration.org** and click on "The Campbell Library."

Look up evidence-based substance abuse and/or mental health programs that work through the U.S. Dept. of Health and Human Services Substance Abuse and Mental Health Services Administration interactive database at **http://nrepp.samhsa.gov.**

Visit the Center for the Study and Prevention of Violence to search for EBPs that work for juveniles at **www.colorado.edu/cspv/blueprints/**.

Visit the National Institute of Corrections website that has a variety of publications to help practitioners and students apply EBP, including one entitled *Tools of the Trade: A guide to incorporating science into practice*, at **https://s3.amazonaws.com/static.nicic.gov/Library/020095.pdf**.

The University of California-Irvine has a Center for Evidence-Based Corrections. Go to their main website at **http://ucicorrections.seweb.uci.edu/** and click on "Projects" or on "Publications and Presentations" for a variety of resources.

Glossary

1779 Penitentiary Act Passed by the English Parliament, this act relied on John Howard's ideas to make significant reforms to the prison system.

abolitionists Those favoring the abolition of the death penalty.

administrative segregation A management tool wherein prisoners are placed in a special housing unit, often under solitary confinement, for the security and safety of the prison or the inmate.

age–crime curve Refers to the tendency for offending to rise during adolescence, peak around age 18, and then drop thereafter.

aggravating circumstances An event or condition that makes an offense more serious than it might otherwise be.

aging prisoner A prisoner who is of age 50 or over.

agricultural work Outdoor fieldwork jobs involving prisoners' growing crops and raising livestock; prevalent in southern states.

antiandrogens Hormones that lower the male sex drive by decreasing testosterone levels. Examples include cyproterone acetate and medroxyprogesterone acetate.

Association of State Correctional Administrators (ASCA) A national organization for state department of corrections directors that seeks to educate top administrators on broad correctional issues and influence correctional policy.

Auburn system Prison system established with the Auburn prison in New York, which used a modified version of the Pennsylvania system wherein prisoners were kept separate from each other at night but allowed to work and eat together, in silence, during the day.

aversive conditioning The use of negative stimuli (painful thoughts, putrid smells, etc.) to reduce or eliminate sexual arousal.

bail bond A written agreement by the defendant to pay cash or relinquish property to the court if the defendant fails to attend required court appearances.

ban-the-box Taking its name from the check box on job applications that asks about criminal convictions (and sometimes arrests), this initiative calls for delaying the point at which prospective employers can ask about an applicant's criminal history.

banishment The permanent expulsion of criminals to remote locations.

beyond a reasonable doubt Burden of proof that requires evidence supporting a claim to offer fully satisfying and entirely convincing evidence establishing the accused's guilt.

bifurcated trial A requirement that death penalty cases have two stages, with the first stage being the traditional trial to determine guilt and a second stage to decide the sentence—death or life imprisonment.

Big House A maximum-security penitentiary with a convict subculture, lasting from the early 1800s until about 1980.

booked When a suspect is identified and fingerprinted in jail after being arrested for an alleged crime.

Brockway, Zebulon Credited with implementing the Irish system in the United States at the Elmira Reformatory in Elmira, New York, in the late 1870s.

Bureau of Prisons (BOP) Where federal prisoners go when they have violated an incarcerable federal offense.

caseload The number of individuals that one probation officer can effectively supervise based on predefined risks and needs posed.

certificate of rehabilitation Generic term for an official recognition that a criminal offender has shown reliability and good character over time and deserves to regain lost civil rights.

citation A police-issued ticket ordering a citizen to pay a fine for a minor law violation.

citizen circles An Ohio restorative justice program at the prisoner reentry stage that encourages community collaboration with offenders during their supervision in the community.

civil death Convicted offenders forfeit all rights and privileges of citizenship, including things such as the right to enter into a contract or the right to sue.

civil disabilities Convicted offenders suffer a partial, rather than an absolute, loss of civil rights because of a criminal conviction.

civil disenfranchisement The loss of the right to vote due, for example, to a felony conviction.

civil rights Those personal, natural rights that protect people against arbitrary or discriminatory treatment.

classification The process and procedures by which prison officials determine the risk posed by each offender and the offender's individual treatment needs.

clemency An act of leniency in the criminal justice system, such as a reprieve, a commutation, or a pardon.

Code of Hammurabi The first known body of law, established by King Hammurabi about 4,000 years ago, which lays out the basis of criminal law.

cognitive behavioral approaches Changing an individual's thinking patterns and habits that lead to criminal behavior through techniques, such as self-control, anger management, social perspective taking, moral reasoning, problem solving, and attitudinal change.

collateral consequences Secondary consequences beyond the actual sentence that was imposed.

commissary Snacks, hygiene items, and other items available for purchase at the prison store.

community corrections Court-ordered supervision and treatment while the offender remains at liberty in the community.

community reparation board Group that facilitates involvement of community members in an offender's reentry to society.

community service Court-ordered special condition that mandates that offenders complete unpaid work for non-profit organizations.

commutation of sentence A reduction of the sentence through action in the executive branch.

compassionate release Available on a case-by-case basis for inmates who are permanently incapacitated, those who have less than one year to live, and those who no longer pose an imminent danger to the community. Also known as medical parole.

concentration approach Prisoners are grouped together in special prisons or special units within a prison, and their activities and movements are severely restricted and highly monitored.

concurrent sentencing Allows an offender convicted of multiple offenses to serve the sentences for those offenses at the same time.

conditional release The return of prisoners to the larger community with a brief period of supervision with rules such as curfew, treatment completion, and maintaining employment. Can be used either pretrial or postconviction.

congregate and silent Key words distinguishing the Auburn system, which required prisoners to remain silent, even while working and eating together.

continuum of sanctions One or more sentencing options within the community or an institution that can be combined with one another to achieve a range of sentencing goals.

contraband Forbidden items that compromise institutional safety and security.

co-occurring disorders A client with a mental disorder and a substance abuse problem.

correctional officer The person responsible for maintaining order within the institution and enforcing prison rules and regulations.

corrections The network of government and private agencies responsible for the pre- and postconviction custody, supervision, and treatment of persons accused or convicted of crimes.

crews Small cliques of prisoners who spend time together, but there is no initiation or formal alliances. Some crews can be networked and predatory, but they are more loosely associated and are not an institutional security threat.

crime control policy A course of action to respond to criminal behavior in the best interest of the public.

criminal blended sentences In cases where a juvenile is tried as an adult, the criminal court judge can impose juvenile sentences that would ordinarily be available only to juvenile court.

criminogenic Factors that cause or tend to cause criminal behavior.

cultivation theory Repeated viewing and cumulative exposure to violence in the media eventually creates a sense of insecurity and irrational fear of violent victimization and about people in the world in general.

day reporting center A nonresidential community corrections sanction that blends high levels of control with the delivery of specific services needed by offenders.

decentralization A principle popular in the South during the first half of the nineteenth century wherein the administration of justice was left to local authorities instead of being centralized at the state level.

deliberate indifference When officers know about a situation and don't take action to prevent it.

delinquency offense Act that would be criminal had it been done by an adult.

department of corrections The state agency responsible for managing and operating the state's adult prison system.

deprivation model Assumes that prison culture developed out of the pains of imprisonment through adaptations that prisoners make to circumvent these losses.

design capacity The number of inmates that facility planners or architects intended for the facility.

determinate sentencing A system wherein the convicted offender receives a sentence to a specific time period rather than a time range.

deterrence Discouraging future criminal acts by both the offender and others in the population.

detoxification A process of sudden withdrawal from all drugs and alcohol so that treatment can begin.

differential response Term applied to society's response to women offenders when emphasis was on having separate and different-style prisons, different programs, and different sentencing practices for women offenders.

direct file Prosecutor decides to try a juvenile as an adult.

direct supervision Inmate supervision method wherein custodial staff are placed—for their entire shift—in the inmates' living area.

disciplinary segregation A management tool wherein prisoners are placed in a special housing unit, often under solitary confinement, as punishment for rule violations within the prison setting.

discretionary parole Conditional early release from imprisonment at the discretion of a state paroling authority and continued supervision in the community.

dismissed When a case is dropped for lack of evidence and does not proceed any further.

dispersion approach Prison administrators spread troublemakers to prisons throughout the system or in various units of the prison.

disproportionate When the group under study has a substantially greater or lesser percentage than exists in the larger population.

Disproportionate Minority Contact (DMC) Refers to the overrepresentation of minorities in virtually all aspects of the juvenile justice system.

disturbance An altercation involving three or more inmates resulting in official action, but where staff control of the facility is maintained.

diversion A form of community supervision for individuals who have not been formally sentenced, but who agree to complete stipulations, such as treatment or community service, in exchange for having their charges dropped.

due process clause That section of the Fourteenth Amendment requiring all states to abide by the Bill of Rights when depriving a person of life, liberty, or property.

dynamic factors Individual characteristics that can be changed, such as antisocial attitudes, values and beliefs, poor self-control, criminal peers, and criminal thinking patterns.

earned good time Good time credits resulting from good behavior or through participation in work or education programs.

economic mobility The likelihood that individuals can rise and maintain a higher socioeconomic status than they were born into, through employment and earnings.

electronic monitoring When a probationer or parolee is monitored in the community by wearing an electronic device that tracks his or her location.

equal protection clause That section of the Fourteenth Amendment prohibiting any state from denying equal protection of the law to persons within its jurisdiction.

evidence-based practice Correctional interventions for which there is consistent and solid scientific evidence showing that they work to meet the intended outcomes, such as recidivism reduction.

evidence-based sentencing Involves the use of scientific research to improve the quality of judicial decision making when determining sentences and sentencing conditions.

ex post facto law A law imposing a greater punishment for a crime than was allowed when the crime was committed.

expungement A court-ordered process for closing public access to arrest and conviction records. The term is often used interchangeably with the term "sealing."

external classification A stage in the classification process wherein a prisoner's custody level is determined and, based on that custody level, in which the prison inmate begins serving the sentence.

fines A fixed financial penalty imposed by the judge, with the amount determined by the severity of the offense.

fish A first-time inmate who is vulnerable because he or she has not yet been prisonized.

free enterprise A private-sector entrepreneurial model of doing business.

Functional Family Therapy (FFT) An effective short-term intervention program targeting youths aged 11–18 who are facing problems with delinquency, substance abuse, or violence.

furlough An authorized temporary overnight leave of absence from 24 to 72 hours.

Furman decision In *Furman* v. *Georgia*, the U.S. Supreme Court determined that the death penalty was cruel and unusual because it was imposed in an arbitrary and capricious manner.

general deterrence Seeks to prevent crime by using punishment to discourage people from committing a crime in the first place.

general incapacitation Imprisonment is acceptable and desirable on an extensive scale for a wide range of offenders as a means of crime prevention.

geriatric prisons Separate facilities specifically designed for elderly inmates where they have no contact with the younger general population.

good time Reduction of days from a sentence as a result of statutory provisions, the offender's good behavior, or extra work done by the offender.

"gotcha" game A style of offender supervision where the officer is less interested in helping the offender succeed and is more interested in tracking failures and acting on rule violations; as a result, the officer has a high turnover of cases.

Gregg decision Ruled that death penalty statutes that provide for bifurcated trials and that direct juries to use guided discretion in deciding the sentence are allowed under the Constitution.

guided discretion A requirement that juries, after determining guilt in the first stage of a death penalty trial, consider both aggravating and mitigating circumstances during the sentencing stage of the trial.

home detention Requires offenders to remain at home at all times, except for such purposes as employment, school, treatment, medical emergencies, or approved shopping trips.

hospice facilities Late-sixteenth and early-seventeenth-century institutions that promoted the idea of isolating offenders from each other.

houses of correction Sixteenth-century institutions for offenders that emphasized the importance of hard work at disagreeable tasks.

importation model Assumes that prison life is an extension of street life of marginalized people from impoverished communities who dominate the prison.

incapacitation Restricting an offender's freedom of movement through isolation from the general population.

incarceration rate The proportion of people in jail and prison per 100,000 residents in a given area.

incorporation Legal theory arguing that all provisions of the Bill of Rights are made applicable to the states through the due process clause.

indeterminate sentencing A system wherein the convicted offender receives a sentence that covers a time range rather than a fixed period.

Indian country Land within an Indian reservation or land that is technically owned by the federal government but held in trust for a tribe or tribal member.

indirect supervision Inmate supervision method wherein custodial staff observe and interact with inmates remotely by watching through windows and listening via microphones.

informal probation Upon the voluntary agreement of the child and parents, the juvenile agrees to submit to certain probation conditions without being formally charged or adjudicated as delinquent.

inmate code A system of unwritten rules that directs inmate behavior.

inmate subculture A society with its own norms and values defined by inmates with the most power and influence.

institutional corrections Incarceration of offenders in a jail or prison, apart from the community.

institutional maintenance Unskilled jobs that inmates are assigned in order to assist with daily prison operations (food preparation, laundry, cleaning).

integrated jail–prison systems A state government, rather than the more typical local government agency, is responsible for the administration and operation of jails located throughout the state.

intermittent supervision Inmate supervision method wherein custodial staff members are able to observe or interact with inmates only on an irregular or sporadic basis.

internal classification Establishes the prisoner's housing, program, and work assignments within the prison.

invisible punishments Sanctions operating mostly beyond public view, yet having very serious adverse consequences for the individuals affected.

Irish system Mid-nineteenth-century prison philosophy that asserted punishment's most direct purpose should be to reform the criminal.

iron law of imprisonment The realization that almost all prisoners will return to free society.

jail time Time spent in jail, either pretrial or after conviction, that could be counted toward a convicted offender's sentence.

jailhouse lawyers Inmates who use their legal knowledge and skills to write writs and grievances, but who are not legally permitted to practice law.

jails Confinement facilities usually operated by city or county governments and typically managed by that government's law enforcement agency.

judicial waiver Juvenile court judge waives jurisdiction over a case and transfers it to criminal court.

jurisdiction A predefined geographic area.

Justice Reinvestment Initiative A data-driven approach to encourage states to reduce correctional spending and reinvest savings in strategies designed to prevent crime. States and localities collect and analyze data on factors related to prison population growth and costs, implement changes to increase efficiencies, and measure both the fiscal and public safety impacts of those changes.

juvenile blended sentence Juvenile court judge can impose both juvenile and adult sanctions on certain categories of serious juvenile offenders.

lease system Prison officials lease a prisoner to a private contractor to do labor for a specified sum and for a fixed time.

legal violation When a probationer commits a new criminal act, and the original probation sentence can be revoked.

legitimate penological interests Standard used by courts to determine whether a prison policy was developed in an arbitrary manner or out of concern for prison order and security.

levels system A behavior modification program that increases a client's community freedom with good behavior.

lex tallonis The law of retaliation.

linear facilities Jails and prisons designed with single- or multiple-occupancy cells aligned along corridors that, in turn, are often stacked in tiers.

Maconochie, Captain Alexander Governor of Norfolk Island from 1836 to 1840, one of the toughest penal colonies for English prisoners.

mandatory sentencing Requires a prison sentence for some crimes and some offenders.

mark system Developed by Maconochie, this system rewarded positive behavior and work ethics.

Marshall hypothesis Spurred by Supreme Court Justice Marshall's opinion for the Furman decision, it suggests that a better informed public generally would oppose the death penalty.

mass media Broadcast and print forms of expression for consumer news, education, and entertainment, such as television, movies, the Internet, DVDs, video games, radio, books, newspapers, and magazines.

maximum-security facility Designed for the fullest possible supervision, control, and surveillance of general-population inmates. Also known as *close-security prisons*.

medical model An orienting philosophy that views criminals not so much as "bad" but as "sick" and in need of treatment.

medium-security facility Institutions where inmates receive more supervision than at minimum-security prisons, but still have considerable freedom to move around to work assignments and programming activities.

mega jails The country's largest jails, holding over 1,000 people each.

mental health disorder A broad category used to identify convicted offenders who are considered to have mental health problems as a result of self-reported clinical diagnosis or treatment by a mental health professional.

mental health screening An examination performed on each newly admitted inmate that usually includes a review of the medical screening, behavior observations, an inquiry into any mental health history, and an assessment of suicide potential.

merchants Inmates who control scarce resources by running a prison store.

meritorious good time Good time credits given to inmates who perform exceptional acts or services such as firefighting or working in emergency conditions.

minimum-security facility Institutions where inmates have considerable personal freedom and more relaxed supervision.

Missouri Model A model for juvenile institutions that emphasizes rehabilitation in small groups, constant therapeutic interventions, and minimal force.

mitigating circumstances An event or condition that makes an offense less serious than it might otherwise be.

Mosaic Law The Hebrew legal system, which started when God gave Moses two stone tablets containing the Ten Commandments.

motivational interviewing A style of personal interaction between the officer and client that involves rapport, trust, and persuasion to help bring about positive behavior change.

Multisystemic Therapy (MST) An effective family-based program for serious juvenile offenders that views the individual as part of a complex network that includes his or her family, peers, school, and neighborhood.

net widening When offenders receive a level of correctional control or punishment that is greater than what they really require, resulting in bringing more people into the system.

new-generation jails Facilities using a specific architectural design and inmate supervision model in order to reduce violent and destructive behavior by the inmates.

nonpetitioned case The informal response to a juvenile court case.

norm of reciprocity The view of punishment as a natural response, or reciprocation, to a wrongful act.

offense downgrade A legal procedure available in some states to qualified offenders who have complied with conditions of supervision wherein felony records are reduced to misdemeanor status in order to minimize exposure to collateral consequences.

objective classification system Classification procedures that have a factual, impartial, and observable base rather than the intuitive footing of subjective systems.

open market Prison-made products are sold, either by private companies or by the state, to prospective buyers.

operational capacity A measure of prison facility capacity based on the ability of the staff, programs, and services to accommodate a certain size population.

outpatient treatment Drug treatment programs for participants who live and work independently in the community.

paramilitary STG A prison gang with a formal and centralized hierarchical structure, a rigid division of labor, a written constitution detailing penalties for disloyalty, and requiring membership for life.

pardon Releases the person (partially or fully) from the legal consequences of the crime.

parens patriae The idea that the court is the ultimate parent of all minors and therefore has final responsibility for its younger citizens.

parole agreement/order Document that the parolee signs at the first meeting with the parole officer where he or she agrees to abide by certain conditions while on parole.

parole board Group of citizens, typically appointed by the state governor, who meet periodically to review the files of those prisoners eligible for parole.

Pennsylvania Quakers Members of the Society of Friends who, in 1787, argued that solitude and hard labor were humanitarian alternatives to the existing punishments.

Pennsylvania system Prison system established with the Eastern State Penitentiary in 1892 in Philadelphia that assumed offenders would more quickly repent and reform if they could reflect on their crimes all day in silence and separated from others.

performance-based measures system A web-based national database that allows correctional administrators to analyze their own institutional environment and compare it to other states using standardized measures.

play families Relationships among women prisoners that mimic the structure, terminology, and function of families in general society.

players Prisoners who embrace mainstream prison culture that values manipulating and intimidating others.

police Law enforcement officials who are sworn to uphold the law, keep social order, and preserve public safety.

predisposing factors Underlying conditions that occur over an extended period of time and provide the foundation for a riot.

preponderance of evidence Burden of proof that requires evidence supporting a charge to have greater weight or be more convincing than the evidence offered in opposition to it.

prerelease center A minimum-security prison-based or community-based facility that houses either prisoners who have not yet been granted parole or prisoners who have met with the parole board and been promised a future parole date.

presentence investigation (PSI) An inquiry interview and data-collection method used by a probation officer to summarize information about a convicted offender.

presentence investigation report A report developed from information derived through a presentence investigation that is provided to the judge to assist in sentencing decisions.

presumptive sentencing guidelines Required, rather than suggested, guidelines for a judge to use when deciding a sentence.

pretrial supervision The community supervision of a defendant who has not yet been convicted but is waiting for his or her next court hearing date.

prison argot or "prison-proper" The language, slang, and physical gestures used to communicate meaning in prison.

prison hulks Eighteenth-century British merchant and naval ships converted into floating prisons.

prison industry A skilled job within the prison that provides inmates training while incarcerated (manufacturing, construction, auto repair, welding, etc.).

Prison Litigation Reform Act (PLRA) Intended to reduce the volume of prisoner litigation and to improve the merit of filed claims, including limiting nongovernmental organizations to legally challenge prison conditions and automatically terminating court orders after two years regardless of compliance.

prison riot A situation involving a large number of inmates making a forcible attempt to take control of a sizable area of the prison for a substantial amount of time.

prison risk assessment A determination of the risk an offender poses to escape or to be a management problem for prison officials.

prisonization The process by which the prisoners learn the norms of life in prison.

private prison A correctional facility operated by a nongovernmental organization that is under contract with federal or state authorities to provide security, housing, and programs to adult offenders.

probation The court-ordered community supervision of an offender by an officer who enforces conditions for a specified length of time.

problem-solving courts An alternative court process for people who get arrested and have a history of alcohol or drug abuse, or a mental illness.

progressivism Reform movement that began in the 1890s and resulted in widespread, significant political and social reforms in many social institutions, including prisons.

proportional retributivism Requires that the worst crime in any society be punished with the worst penalty.

public notification laws Require that the public be notified of the name and location of certain sex offenders in the community.

public risk assessment A determination of the risk posed by an offender to the general public.

punks Inmates who are targeted by predatory inmates because they are perceived as physically or mentally weak and afraid to fight back.

rated capacity The maximum number of beds or inmates allocated by a rating official to institutions in the states.

reclassification A stage in the classification process wherein an inmate's custody level, treatment program, or work assignment is reevaluated to be sure it is still appropriate.

reentry The process of release preparation that begins within the institution and continues with community supervision.

reformatory A system of prison discipline that incorporates a more humanitarian approach to confinement and has an interest in preparing inmates for their eventual return to the community.

regional cell STG A prison gang with a decentralized hierarchical structure that is authorized to act independently for the good of the entire group, but there is little coordination between cells.

rehabilitation Providing the offender with skills, attitudes, and norms that enable him or her to be law-abiding.

release on recognizance (ROR) Pretrial release based only on the defendant's promise to appear for trial (not backed with money or property).

reparative probation program A Vermont restorative justice program at the postconviction stage that combines a suspended probation sentence with elements of community reparation boards.

reprieve A stay of execution that grants time for something, such as an appeal, to happen.

residence restriction laws Require sex offenders to live in certain areas or restrict them from living in other areas.

residential community correction facility (RCCF) A modern term for *halfway house*; a community-based correctional center in which the offender lives under supervision and must obtain permission to leave for work and leisure.

responsivity The process in which prisoners are assigned to treatment programs designed to address their particular set of dynamic criminogenic needs.

restitution A court-ordered cash payment that an offender makes to the victim to offset some of the losses incurred from the crime.

restoration Restoring the victim, community, and offender through accountability, respect for the law and the legal process, and attention to victim needs.

restorative justice The process, also called community justice, wherein victim, offender, and community representatives determine a fair or just way to restore the balance that the crime had upset.

retentionists Those who favor keeping the death penalty.

retribution Just and adequate punishment.

rights-are-lost position Argues that prisoners are wholly without rights except those expressly conferred by law or necessity.

rights-are-retained position Argues that prisoners keep all the rights of an ordinary citizen, except those that are expressly or by necessity taken away from them by law.

Second Chance Act Federal legislation that authorizes reentry grants to state and local agencies and nonprofit organizations to provide employment assistance, substance-abuse treatment, housing, and mentoring to reduce recidivism for ex-offenders returning to communities from correctional facilities.

Section 1983 claim A claim brought under the authority of U.S. Code Title 42, Section 1983 that civil rights have been violated.

security threat group (STG) An organized group whose activities are predatory and criminal and whose presence in a correctional institution/agency poses a real and imminent threat to the security and safety of staff and inmates.

selective incapacitation Imprisonment is reserved for those very few offenders who must truly be locked away for society's protection.

selective serotonin reuptake inhibitors Medications that increase serotonin levels in the brain to decrease libido and cause erectile dysfunction.

sentencing disparity A type of injustice wherein sentencing policy has the unintended effect of targeting a population group—often minority—and resulting in members of that group being disproportionately represented among persons in the correctional system.

sentencing guidelines Impose a predefined sentence length based on crime severity and prior criminal history, with the opportunity for the judge to depart from the guidelines when circumstances warrant.

sentencing When a court imposes a penalty on a person convicted of a crime.

separate and silent Key words distinguishing the Pennsylvania system, which sought to keep prisoners separate from each other and required them to remain silent.

serious mental illness A narrow category used to identify convicted offenders suffering from such conditions as bipolar disorder, schizophrenia spectrum disorder, or major depression.

sex offender registration laws Require persons convicted of sex offenses to register in a community, even after they have completed their sentence for that conviction.

sex offenses Inappropriate sexual contact with family members/acquaintances, child molestation, sexual assault or rape of adults.

sheltered market Restricts the sale of prison-made products only to other state and local government markets. Also known as *government or state-use models*.

short-term inpatient residential programs Drug treatment programs of three to six months in length for less severe drug abusers.

snitches Inmates who are targeted by predatory inmates because they have passed along information to staff that has gotten another inmate in trouble. Also known as *player haters*.

social learning Changing old behavior through modeling new skills and desirable behavior.

solitary confinement The placement of a prisoner in a separate cell or other location that isolates the prisoner from other inmates.

special conditions Requirements in addition to the standard conditions, such as paying fines or undergoing electronic monitoring.

special housing unit An area of the prison, or a separate prison, where inmates are held under high levels of restriction and control.

specific deterrence Seeks to prevent crime by using punishment to discourage a person from committing additional crimes.

squares Inmates who oppose mainstream prison culture by being well behaved and who take advantage of every self-improvement program they can to keep themselves busy. Also known as *bootlickers*.

standard conditions Commitments every probationer agrees to abide by in return for remaining at liberty in the community.

state-raised youth Inmates who grew up in youth prisons and who tend to be more violent than the average prisoner.

static factors Individual characteristics that are constant or happened in the past and cannot be changed, such as a person's gender, age at first arrest, or number of prior arrests.

status offense Misbehavior that is considered wrong only because society does not consider the juvenile old enough for such activity.

statutory exclusion Criminal courts have original jurisdiction for certain crimes committed by juveniles.

statutory good time Reduction of days from a sentence usually given automatically as a prison management tool to relieve overcrowding.

statutory penalties Sentences linked via legislation to specific crimes, or to specific classes of felonies or misdemeanors, with a minimum and maximum time period.

structured sentencing A modification to either indeterminate or determinate sentencing wherein judges are provided guidance on sentence type and length.

sub rosa economy Underground economy based on negotiation and exchange of goods and services between prisoners without the use of cash.

substance abuse When the use of one or more chemical substances disrupts normal living patterns.

supermax prison Prisons at the highest security level, with prisoners isolated from the general population and from each other. Also known as *control units* or *secured housing units*.

supervised mandatory release When an inmate is automatically released by law to the community when he or she has completed his or her maximum prison sentence less any goodtime credit the inmate has received.

technical violation When a probationer repeatedly fails to abide by conditions of probation, and the probation sentence can be revoked.

technological incapacitation Using technologies such as critical organ surgery, chemical treatment, and electronic monitoring to restrict an offender's freedom of movement.

teen courts A juvenile court diversion program using court-like procedures and settings wherein youth sentence their age peers for minor delinquent and status offenses.

test for adult basic education (TABE) Test given to inmates to determine the prisoners' level of academic ability.

The Innocence Project An organization instrumental in securing DNA exonerations of persons who have served time on death row.

therapeutic communities Long-term peer-led programs for chronic addicts using group confrontational methods.

thinking errors Ways that people use to avoid taking responsibility for their own behavior, or ways to make themselves look good by making others look bad.

three strikes and you're out Laws that authorize, or mandate in some cases, longer periods of incarceration after a certain number of prior convictions ("strikes").

total institution A regimented facility that is physically separate from the larger society and meets the survival needs of its occupants.

transportation The removal of criminals to a remote location where they could be used as laborers.

triggering event One or several specific events that spark a riot.

trustys Minimum-security-level inmates who earn this status through not causing behavioral problems.

truth-in-sentencing When the length of time served in a sentence is close to the time imposed by the courts.

Twelve Tables The earliest form of written Roman law, which provided the basis for private rights of Roman citizens.

unconditional release The return of prisoners to the larger community without supervision.

unsecured bond When a defendant is released without having to make any payment but is liable for the full bail amount if required court appearances are missed.

victim compensation A general fund by which state governments disperse money to qualifying victims of violent crimes for payment of bills and lost wages.

victim impact classes Restorative justice program, typically offered in prison, wherein prisoners hear violent crime survivors share their experiences with the hope of effecting positive change in the offender.

victim–offender mediation An application of restorative justice principles at the sentencing stage by having mediation sessions involving both offender and victim take the place of traditional sentencing by a judge.

voluntary lockdown When prisoners refuse to leave their cells.

voluntary sentencing guidelines Suggested, rather than required, guidelines that stipulate a time range for a judge to use when deciding a sentence.

Walnut Street Jail Opened in Philadelphia in 1776 to house petty offenders, debtors, and serious offenders and operated only as a jail until 1792 when a penitentiary addition was completed.

writ of *habeas corpus* Judicial mandate to a prison official ordering that an inmate be brought to the court in order to determine the legality of the prisoner's detention.

wrongful convictions A type of injustice wherein a person is convicted and punished for a crime he or she did not commit.

References

Chapter 1, An Evidence-Based Approach to Corrections

Applegate, B. K., & Davis, R. K. (2006). Public views on sentencing juvenile murderers. *Youth Violence and Juvenile Justice, 4*(1), 55–74.

Applegate, B. K., Davis, R. K., & Cullen, F. T. (2009). Reconsidering child saving. *Crime & Delinquency, 55*(1), 51–77.

Bagley, B. M. (1988). U.S. foreign policy and the war on drugs: Analysis of a policy failure. *Journal of Interamerican Studies and World Affairs, 30*(2/3), 189–212.

Baker, T., Metcalfe, C. F., Berenblum, T., Aviv, G., & Gertz, M. (2015). Examining public preferences for the allocation of resources to rehabilitative versus punitive crime policies. *Criminal Justice Policy Review, 26*(5), 448–462.

Cassidy, R. T. (2010). *Collateral consequences of criminal convictions: Our law is a tragedy*. Retrieved from http://onlawyering.com/2010/06/collateral-consequences-of-criminal-convictions-our-law-is-a-tragedy/.

Cecil, D. K. (2015). *Prison life in popular culture: From the big house to orange is the new black*. Boulder, CO: Lynne Rienner.

Clement, M., Schwarzfeld, M., & Thompson, M. (2011). *The national summit on justice reinvestment and public safety: Addressing recidivism, crime, and corrections*. Lexington, KY: Council of State Governments Justice Center. Available at https://www.bja.gov/Publications/CSG_JusticeReinvestmentSummitReport.pdf.

Crime and Justice Institute. (2004). *Implementing evidence-based practice in community corrections: The principles of effective intervention*. Longmont, CO: National Institute of Corrections.

Gerlinger, J., & Turner, S. F. (2015). California's public safety realignment: Correctional policy based on stakes rather than risk. *Criminal Justice Policy Review, 26*(8), 805–827.

Gorham, B. W. (2006). News media's relationship with stereotyping: The linguistic intergroup bias in response to crime news. *Journal of Communication, 56*(2), 289–308.

Lawrence, S., & Travis, J. (2004). *The new landscape of imprisonment: Mapping America's prison expansion*. Washington, DC: Urban Institute.

Lowenkamp, C. T., & Whetzel, J. (2009). The development of an actuarial risk assessment for U.S. pretrial services. *Federal Probation, 73*(2), 33–36.

Martinez, C. (2014). The death penalty and its inexcusable burden on prison workers. *NCADP Blog,* October 30. Retrieved from http://www.ncadp.org/blog/entry/the-death-penalty-and-its-inexcusable-burden-on-prison-workers.

Mauer, M. (1999). *The crisis of the young African-American male and the criminal justice system*. Retrieved from http://www.sentencingproject.org/doc/publications/rd_crisisoftheyoung.pdf.

McKenzie, W., Stemen, D., & Coursen, D. (2009). *Prosecution and racial justice: Using data to advance fairness in criminal prosecution*. New York, NY: Vera Institute of Justice. Retrieved from http://www.vera.org/centers/prosecution-and-racial-justice.

Neill, K. A., Yusuf, J., & Morris, J. C. (2015). Explaining dimensions of state-level punitiveness in the U.S.: The roles of social, economic, and cultural factors. *Criminal Justice Policy Review, 26*(8), 751–772.

Pew Charitable Trusts. (2010). *Collateral costs: Incarceration's effect on economic mobility*. Retrieved from http://www.pewtrusts.org.

Pickett, J. T., Mancini, C., Mears, D. P., & Gertz, M. (2015). Public (mis)understanding of crime policy: The effects of criminal justice experience and media reliance. *Criminal Justice Policy Review, 26*(5), 500–522.

Sackur, S. (2014). Electric chair haunts US former executions chief. *BBC News Magazine,* February 23. Retrieved from http://www.bbc.com/news/magazine-26273051.

Saslow, E. (2015). A virtual get out of jail free card: A new California law to reduce prison crowding keeps one addict out of jail, but not out of trouble. *The Washington Post,* October 10. Retrieved from http://www.washingtonpost.com/sf/national/2015/10/10/prop47/.

Thompson, F. (2015). Ex-warden: Death penalty doesn't make guards safer. *DelawareOnline,* April 1. Retrieved from http://www.delawareonline.com/story/opinion/contributors/2015/04/01/ex-warden-death-penalty-make-guards-safer/70791272/.

Tonry, M. (2004). *Thinking about crime: Sense and sensibility in American penal culture*. New York, NY: Oxford University Press.

Unnever, J. D., & Cullen, F. T. (2010). The social sources of Americans' punitiveness: A test of three competing models. *Criminology, 48*(1), 99–129.

Vera Institute of Justice. (2010). *The continuing fiscal crisis in corrections: Setting a new course*. New York, NY: Vera Institute of Justice.

Walker, S., Spohn, C., & Delone, M. (2012). *The color of justice: Race, ethnicity, and crime in America* (5th ed.). Belmont, CA: Cengage.

World Prison Brief. (2016). *Incarceration rates around the world*. Retrieved from http://www.prisonstudies.org/highest-to-lowest/prison_population_rate.

Yanich, D. (2004). Crime creep: Urban and suburban crime in local TV news. *Journal of Urban Affairs, 26*(5), 535–563.

Zgoba, K. M. (2004). Spin doctors and moral crusaders: The moral panic behind child safety legislation. *Criminal Justice Studies, 17*(4), 385–404.

Chapter 2, Why Do We Punish?

Alabama Sentencing Commission. (2000). Statute creating the Alabama Sentencing Commission. Retrieved from http://sentencingcommission.alacourt.gov/statute.html.

Alarid, L. F., & Reichel, P. L. (2008). *Corrections: A contemporary introduction*. Boston, MA: Allyn & Bacon.

Bright, C. (1997). *Victim offender mediation*. Retrieved from www.restorativejustice.org/university-classroom/01introduction/tutorial-introduction-to-restorative justice/processes/vom.

Carson, E. A. (2014). *Prisoners in 2013* (NCJ 247282). Retrieved from http://www.bjs.gov/index.cfm?ty=pbdetail&iid=5109.

Carson, E. A. (2015). *Prisoners in 2014* (NCJ 248955). Retrieved from http://www.bjs.gov/index.cfm?ty=pbdetail&iid=5387.

Carson, E. A., & Sabol, W. J. (2012). *Prisoners in 2011* (NCJ 239808). Retrieved from Bureau of Justice Statistics website: http://www.bjs.gov/index.cfm?ty=pbdetail&iid=4559.

Chism, L. S. (2013). The case for castration: A "shot" towards rehabilitation of sexual offenders. *Law & Psychology Review, 37*, 193–209.

Easton, A. (2009, November 27). Poland chemical castration is law. Retrieved from http://news.bbc.co.uk/2/hi/europe/8383698.stm.

Edwins, L. (2013). Woman ordered to hold "idiot" sign. Retrieved from http://www.csmonitor.com/USA/Justice/2013/0109/10-weird-criminal-sentences/Woman-ordered-to-hold-idiot-sign.

Ellis, R. D., & Ellis, C. S. (1989). *Theories of criminal justice: A critical reappraisal*. Wolfeboro, NH: Longwood Academic.

Fagan, J., & Meares, T. L. (2008). Punishment, deterrence, and social control: The paradox of punishment in minority communities. *Ohio State Journal of Criminal Law, 6*, 173–229.

Gannon, T. A., & Cortoni, F. (Eds.). (2010). *Female sexual offenders: Theory, assessment, and treatment*. Oxford, UK: Wiley-Blackwell.

Goforth, D. (2012, November 13). No jail time for teen in fatality. *Muskogee Phoenix*. Retrieved from http://muskogeephoenix.com/local/x1021804092/No-jail-time-for-teen-in-fatality.

Hudak, S. (2010, October 28). Creative sentences a growing trend, but legal experts question effectiveness. *Standard-Examiner*. Retrieved from http://www.standard.net/.

Humphrey, J. A., Burford, G., & Huey, M. P. (2007). *Reparative versus standard probation: Community justice outcomes*. Retrieved from www.doc.state.vt.us/about/reports/.

Hyun-jung, B. (2010, June 30). Child rapists to get chemical castration. *The Korea Herald*. Retrieved from http://www.koreaherald.com/national/Detail.jsp?newsMLId=20100630000789.

Judicial Council of California. (2013). California rules of court. Rule 4.410. General objectives in sentencing. Retrieved from http://www.courts.ca.gov/rules.htm

Katz, J. (1988). *Seductions of crime: Moral and sensual attractions in doing evil*. New York, NY: Basic Books.

KUAM News. (2015, September 9). Guam adopts chemical castration for sex offenders. Retrieved from http://www.kuam.com/story/29986555/2015/09/09/guam-adopts-chemical-castration-for-sex-offenders.

Kurki, L. (1999). *Incorporating restorative and community justice into American sentencing and corrections* (NCJ 175723). Retrieved from http://www.ncjrs.gov/pdffiles1/nij/175723.pdf.

Libaw, O. (2002). Judicial power, from prayers to pigpens. Retrieved from http://abcnews.go.com/US/story?id=91434&page=1.

Maletzky, B. M., Tolan, A., & McFarland, B. (2006). The Oregon Depo-Provera program: A five-year follow-up. *Sex Abuse, 18*(3), 303–316. doi:10.1177/107906320601800308

Maxwell, G., & Morris, A. (1996). Research on family group conferences with young offenders in New Zealand. In J. Hudson, A. Morris, G. M. Maxwell, & B. Galaway (Eds.), *Family group conferences: Perspectives on policy & practice* (pp. viii, 240 p.). Monsey, NY: Criminal Justice Press.

McGarrell, E. F., & Hipple, N. K. (2007). Family group conferencing and re-offending among first-time juvenile offenders: The Indianapolis experiment. *Justice Quarterly, 24*(2), 221–246.

Merry, S. (1989). Myth and practice in the mediation process. In M. Wright & B. Galaway (Eds.), *Mediation and criminal justice* (pp. 239–250). London, UK: Sage.

Meyer, W. J., III, & Cole, C. M. (1997). Physical and chemical castration of sex offenders: A review. *Journal of Offender Rehabilitation, 25*(3–4), 1–18.

Millhollon, M. (2008). Jindal signs chemical castration bill. *The Advocate*, June 26. Retrieved from http://www.bishop-accountability.org/news2008/05_06/2008_06_26_Millhollon_JundalSigns.htm.

Nagin, D. (2013). Deterrence in the 21st century. In M. H. Tonry (Ed.), *Crime and justice in America: 1975–2025* (pp. 199–263). Chicago: University of Chicago Press.

Newman, G. R. (1985). *The punishment response* (2nd ed.). Albany, NY: Harrow and Heston.

Office for Victims of Crime. (2010). *The case for evidence-based programming*. Retrieved from http://www.ovcttac.gov/victimimpact/evidence_based.cfm.

Office of Justice Programs. (2013a). *Clarke County (Georgia) victim impact panels*. Retrieved from http://www.crimesolutions.gov/ProgramDetails.aspx?ID=52.

Office of Justice Programs. (2013b). *Indianapolis (Indiana) family group conferencing experiment*. Retrieved from http://www.crimesolutions.gov/ProgramDetails.aspx?ID=250.

Redding, R. E. (2009). Evidence-based sentencing: The science of sentencing policy and practice. *Chapman Journal of Criminal Justice, 1*(1), 1–19. Retrieved from http://ssrn.com/paper=1424008.

Rhine, E., Matthews, J. R., Sampson, L. A., & Daley, R. H. (2003). Citizen's circles: Community collaboration in reentry. *Corrections Today, 65*(5), 52–64.

Rojek, D. G., Coverdill, J. E., & Fors, S. W. (2003). The effect of victim impact panels on DUI rearrest rates: A five-year follow-up. *Criminology, 41*(4), 1319–1340. doi:10.1111/j.1745-9125.2003.tb01021.x

State of Colorado. (2013). Colorado revised statutes (18-1-102.5). Retrieved from http://www.lexisnexis.com/hottopics/colorado/

State of Ohio. (2007). Citizen circles. Retrieved from http://www.drc.ohio.gov/web/Citizen/citizencircle.htm.

State of Texas. (2009). Chapter 1. General provisions; Sec. 1.02. Objectives of code. Retrieved from http://www.statutes.legis.state.tx.us/.

T.I. says new prison sentence is his final lesson. (2010, October 19). *USA Today*. Retrieved from http://www.usatoday.com/.

Travis, J. (2005). Prisoner reentry: The iron law of imprisonment. In R. Muraskin (Ed.), *Key correctional issues* (pp. 64–71). Upper Saddle River, NJ: Pearson Prentice Hall.

Umbreit, M. S. (1989). Crime victims seeking fairness, not revenge: Toward restorative justice. *Federal Probation, 53*(3), 52–57.

Umbreit, M. S., Vos, B., Coates, R. B., & Brown, K. A. (2003). *Facing violence: The path of restorative justice and dialogue*. Monsey, NY: Criminal Justice Press.

Urban Institute. (2006). *Understanding the challenges of prisoner reentry: Research findings from the Urban Institute's prisoner reentry portfolio*. Retrieved from http://www.urban.org/UploadedPDF/411289_reentry_portfolio.pdf.

Vaillancourt, S. P. (2012). *Chemical castration: How a medical therapy became punishment and the bioethical imperative to return to a rehabilitative model for sex offenders*. Wake Forest University, Z. Smilth Reynolds Library. Retrieved from http://wakespace.lib.wfu.edu/handle/10339/37658.

Vermont Department of Corrections. (2010). *Facts and figures 2010*. Retrieved from http://www.doc.vermont.gov/about/reports.

Walker, N. (1991). *Why punish?* Oxford, England: Oxford University Press.

Weihofen, H. (1971). Punishment and treatment: Rehabilitation. In S. E. Grupp (Ed.), *Theories of punishment* (pp. 255–263). Bloomington, IN: Indiana University Press.

Zehr, H. (1985). *Retributive justice, restorative justice*. Elkhart, IN: Mennonite Central Committee, Office of Criminal Justice.

Zimring, F. E., & Hawkins, G. (1995). *Incapacitation: Penal confinement and the restraint of crime*. New York, NY: Oxford University Press.

Chapter 3, Correctional Practices from Ancient to Contemporary Times

Abadinsky, H. (1994). *Probation and parole: Theory and practice*. Englewood Cliffs, NJ: Prentice Hall.

Alarid, L. F., & Reichel, P. L. (2008). *Corrections: A contemporary introduction*. Boston, MA: Allyn & Bacon.

Barnes, H. E., & Teeters, N. K. (1943). *New horizons in criminology: The American crime problem*. New York, NY: Prentice Hall.

Barnes, H. E., & Teeters, N. K. (1959). *New horizons in criminology* (3rd ed.). Englewood Cliffs, NJ: Prentice-Hall.

Belenko, S., Foltz, C., Lang, M. A., & Sung, H.-E. (2005). Recidivism among high-risk drug felons: A longitudinal analysis following residential treatment. *Journal of Offender Rehabilitation, 40*(1–2), 105–132.

Carson, E. A. (2015). *Prisoners in 2014* (NCJ 248955). Retrieved fromhttp://www.bjs.gov/index.cfm?ty=pbdetail&iid=5387.

Chesney-Lind, M., & Pollock, J. M. (1995). Women's prisons: Equality with a vengeance. In A. V. Merlo & J. M. Pollock (Eds.), *Women, law, and social control* (pp. 155–175). Boston, MA: Allyn and Bacon.

Christianson, S. (1998). *With liberty for some: 500 years of imprisonment in America*. Boston, MA: Northeastern University Press.

Cohen, A. (2007, September 12). My morning at Supermax. *CBS News*. Retrieved from http://www.cbsnews.com/8301-500803_162-3253653-500803.html.

Colvin, M. (1997). *Penitentiaries, reformatories, and chain gangs: Social theory and the history of punishment in nineteenth-century America*. New York, NY: St. Martin's Press.

Conley, J. A. (1980). Prisons, production, and profit: Reconsidering the importance of prison industries. *Journal of Social History, 14*(2), 257–275.

Convicts in Australia. (1987). In J. C. R. Camm & J. McQuilton (Eds.), *Australians: A historical atlas* (pp. 200–201). New South Wales, Australia: Fairfax Syme & Weldon Associates.

Dobash, R. P., Dobash, R. E., & Gutteridge, S. (1986). *The imprisonment of women*. New York, NY: Basil Blackwell.

Dynia, P., & Sung, H.-E. (2000). The safety and effectiveness of diverting felony drug offenders to residential treatment as measured by recidivism. *Criminal Justice Policy Review, 11*(4), 299–311.

Eriksson, T. (1976). *The reformers: An historical survey of pioneer experiments in the treatment of criminals* (C. Djurklou, Trans.). New York, NY: Elsevier.

Freedman, E. B. (1974). Their sisters' keepers: An historical perspective on female correctional institutions in the United States: 1870–1900. *Feminist Studies, 2*(1), 77–95.

Gelb, A. (2015). *State criminal justice reforms build the case for data-driven federal legislation*. Retrieved from http://www.pewtrusts.org/en/research-and-analysis/analysis/2015/07/30/state-criminal-justice-reforms-build-the-case-for-data-driven-federal-legislation.

Hindus, M. S. (1980). *Prison and plantation: Crime, justice, and authority in Massachusetts and South Carolina, 1767–1878*. Chapel Hill, NC: University of North Carolina Press.

Hirsch, A. J. (1992). *The rise of the penitentiary: Prisons and punishments in early America*. New Haven, CT: Yale University Press.

Hughes, R. (1987). *The fatal shore* (1st American ed.). New York, NY: Alfred A. Knopf.

Johnston, N. (1973). *The human cage: A brief history of prison architecture*. Philadelphia, PA: American Foundation Inc.

Kurshan, N. (1992). Women and imprisonment in the U.S.—History and current reality. In W. Churchill & J. J. Vander Wall (Eds.), *Cages of steel: The politics of imprisonment in the United States* (pp. 331–358). Washington, DC: Maisonneuve Press.

McKelvey, B. (1977). *American prisons: A history of good intentions*. Montclair, NJ: Patterson Smith.

Mizell, J. (2014). Overview of public opinion. In The Opportunity Agenda (Ed.), *An overview of public opinion and discourse on criminal justice issues* (pp. 7–49). New York, NY: The Opportunity Agenda. Retrieved from http://opportunityagenda.org/files/field_file/2014.08.23-CriminalJusticeReport-FINAL_0.pdf.

Office of Justice Programs. (2013). *Drug treatment alternative to prison (DTAP)*. Retrieved from http://www.crimesolutions.gov/ProgramDetails.aspx?ID=89.

Old Bailey Proceedings Online. January 1760, trial of Joseph Tedar (t17600116-17). Retrieved from http://www.oldbaileyonline.org.

Pew Charitable Trusts. (2010a, September 14). *National research of public attitudes on crime and punishment*. Retrieved from http://www.pewstates.org/research/analysis/public-attitudes-on-crime-and-punishment-85899424314.

Pew Charitable Trusts. (2010b, April 1). *Prison count 2010: State population declines for the first time in 38 years*. Retrieved from http://www.pewtrusts.org/our_work_report_detail.aspx?id=57797.

Pew Charitable Trusts. (2012, March 30). *Public opinion on sentencing and corrections policy in America*. Retrieved from http://www.pewstates.org/research/analysis/public-opinion-on-sentencing-and-corrections-policy-in-america85899380361.

Pew Charitable Trusts. (2013a, July). *A matrix of sentencing and corrections policies passed in states that have participated in the "justice reinvestment" process*. Retrieved from http://www.pewstates.org/uploadedFiles/PCS_Assets/2013/PSPP_Sentencing_and_Corrections_Reform_Matrix.pdf.

Pew Charitable Trusts. (2013b, August 9). *U.S. prison population drops for third year as states adopt new policy strategies*. Retrieved from http://www.pewstates.org/news-room/press-releases/us-prison-population drops-for-third-year-as-states-adopt-new-policy-strategies85899496150#

Pew Charitable Trusts. (2015, September 17). *State, federal prison population decline simultaneously for first time in 36 years*. Retrieved from http://www.pewtrusts.org/en/research-and-analysis/analysis/2015/09/17/state-federal-prison-populations-decline-simultaneously-for-first-time-in-36-years.

PortCities London. (n.d.). *Prison hulks on the River Thames*. Retrieved from http://www.portcities.org.uk/london/server/show/ConNarrative.56/Prison-hulks-on-the-River-Thames.html.

Rafter, N. H. (1990). *Partial justice: Women, prisons, and social control* (2nd ed.). New Brunswick, NJ: Transaction Publishers.

Rafter, N. H. (1993). *Equality of difference? Female offenders: Meeting needs of a neglected population*. Laurel, MD: American Correctional Association.

Rappold, R. S. (2006, December 10). Bomber expresses no remorse for victims. *The Gazette*. Retrieved from http://www.gazette.com/articles/rudolph-11114-wrote-supermax.html.

Reichel, P. L. (2001). *Corrections: Philosophies, practices, and procedures* (2nd ed.). Upper Saddle River, NJ: Pearson Education, Inc.

Roth, M. P. (2011). *Crime and punishment: A history of the criminal justice system* (2nd ed.). Belmont, CA: Wadsworth Cengage.

Rothman, D. J. (1971). *The discovery of the asylum*. Boston, MA: Little, Brown, and Company.

Schuster, H. (2007, October 14). Producer's notebook: My trip to Supermax. *CBS News*. Retrieved from http://www.cbsnews.com/stories/2007/10/13/60minutes/main3364113.shtml?tag=contentMain;contentBody.

Shaw, A. G. L. (1966). *Convicts and the colonies*. London, UK: Faber & Faber.

Smith, M. L. (1997). Progressives. In F. Schmalleger (Ed.), *Crime and the justice system in America: An encyclopedia* (p. 198). Westport, CT: Greenwood Press.

Spierenburg, P. (1995). The body and the state: Early modern Europe. In N. Morris & D. J. Rothman (Eds.), *The Oxford history of the prison* (pp. 49–77). New York, NY: Oxford University Press.

Sullivan, L. E. (1990). *The prison reform movement: Forlorn hope*. Boston, MA: Twayne Publishers.

Vaver, A. (2009, June 10). Transported convicts in the New World (6): Adjusting to America. *Convict transportation*. Retrieved from http://www.earlyamericancrime.com/convict-transportation/in-the-new-world/adjusting-to-america.

Zedner, L. (1995). Wayward sisters: The prison for women. In N. Morris & D. J. Rothman (Eds.), *The Oxford history of the prison* (pp. 229–361). New York, NY: Oxford University Press.

Chapter 4, Sentencing

Alarid, L. (2004). Incapacitation (collective and selective). In J. M. Miller & R. Wright (Eds.), *Encyclopedia of criminology*. New York, NY: Routledge.

Alarid, L. F., Marquart, J. W., Burton Jr., V. S., Cullen, F. T., & Cuvelier, S. J. (1996). Women's roles in serious offenses: A study of adult felons. *Justice Quarterly*, *13*(3), 431–454.

American Friends Service Committee. (1971). *Struggle for justice*. New York, NY: Hill and Wang.

Andersen, R. (2014). Hell on earth. *Aeon*, March 13. Retrieved from https://aeon.co/essays/how-will-radical-life-extension-transform-punishment.

Aos, S., Miller, M., & Drake, E. (2006). *Evidence-based public policy options to reduce future prison construction, criminal justice costs, and crime rates*. Retrieved from http://www.wsipp.wa.gov/pub.asp?docid=06-10-1201.

Bazelon, E. (2010, May 21). Arguing three strikes. *New York Times*. Retrieved from http://www.nytimes.com.

Bureau of Justice Assistance. (2012). Report to Congress: Violent Offender Incarceration and Truth-in-Sentencing Incentive Formula Grant Program. Retrieved from https://www.bja.gov/Publications/VOITIS-Final-Report.pdf.

Casey, P. M. (2010). *Reducing recidivism with evidence based sentencing*. Retrieved from http://contentdm.ncsonline.org/cdm4/item_viewer.php?CISOROOT=/criminal&CISOPTR=187&REC=1

Clark, J., Austin, J., & Henry, D. A. (1997, September). "Three strikes and you're out": A review of state legislation. *Research in Brief*. Retrieved from https://ncjrs.gov/pdffiles/165369.pdf.

Clear, T. R., & Schrantz, D. (2011). Strategies for reducing prison populations. *The Prison Journal*, 91(3 suppl), 138S–159S. doi:10.1177/0032885511415238

Crime and Justice Institute. (2004). *Implementing evidence-based practice in community corrections: The principles of effective intervention*. Retrieved from http://nicic.gov/Library/019342.

Curry, T. R., Lee, G., & Rodriguez, S. F. (2004). Does victim gender increase sentence severity? Further explorations of gender dynamics and sentencing outcomes. *Crime & Delinquency*, 50(3), 319–343. doi:10.1177/0011128703256265

Daly, K. (1987). Structure and practice of familial-based justice in a criminal court. *Law & Society Review*, 21(2), 267–290. doi:10.2307/3053522

Davey, M. (2010, September 18). Missouri tells judges cost of sentences. *New York Times*. Retrieved from http://www.nytimes.com.

Davis, S. M., Merlo, A. V., & Pollock, J. M. (2006). Female criminality: Ten years later. In A. V. Merlo & J. M. Pollock (Eds.), *Women, law, and social control* (2nd ed., pp. 191–210). Boston, MA: Pearson/Allyn and Bacon.

Dittmann, M. (2004). Accuracy and the accused (article sidebar: Recommendations for police lineups). *Monitor on Psychology*, 35(7). Retrieved from http://www.apa.org/monitor/julaug04/lineups.aspx.

Ditton, P. M., & Wilson, D. J. (1999). *Truth in sentencing in state prisons* (NCJ 170032). Retrieved from http://www.bjs.gov/index.cfm?ty=pbdetail&iid=820.

Fagan, K. (2013, October 2). 20 years after Polly Klaas killing, attitudes change. *SFGate*. Retrieved from http://www.sfgate.com/crime/article/20-years-after-Polly-Klaas-killing-attitudes-4861976.php#page-1.

Flatow, N. (2013, December 18). Majority of Americans oppose jail time for cocaine, heroin possession, poll finds. Retrieved from http://thinkprogress.org/justice/2013/12/18/3082061/majority-americans-oppose-jail-time-cocaine-heroine-possession-poll-finds/.

Frase, R. S. (2012). *Just sentencing #4: Existing sentencing structures—Which are the best?* Retrieved from http://sentencing.typepad.com/.

Frase, R. S. (2013). *Just sentencing: Principles and procedures for a workable system*. New York, NY: Oxford University Press.

Friedersdorf, C. (2013, April 3). A heartbreaking drug sentence of staggering idiocy. *The Atlantic*. Retrieved from http://www.theatlantic.com/politics/archive/2013/04/a-heartbreaking-drug-sentence-of-staggering-idiocy/274607/.

Garrett, B. L. (2010). The substance of false confessions. *Stanford Law Review*, 62(4), 1051–1119.

Greenfeld, L. A., & Snell, T. L. (1999). *Women offenders* (NCJ 175688). Retrieved from http://www.ncjrs.gov/App/Publications/abstract.aspx?ID=175688.

Gross, S. (2013). How many false convictions are there? How many exonerations are there? In C. R. Huff & M. Killias (Eds.), *Wrongful convictions and miscarriages of justice: Causes and remedies in North American and European criminal justice systems* (pp. 45–59). New York, NY: Routledge.

Innocence Project. (2013). *Eyewitness misidentification*. Retrieved from http://www.innocenceproject.org/understand/Eyewitness-Misidentification.php.

Lawrence, A. (2015). *Making sense of sentencing: State systems and policies*. Retrieved from http://www.ncsl.org/documents/cj/sentencing.pdf.

Leifker, D., & Sample, L. L. (2010). Do judges follow sentencing recommendations, or do recommendations simply reflect what judges want to hear? An examination of one state court. *Journal of Crime and Justice*, 33(2), 127–151. doi:10.1080/0735648X.2010.9721290

Mauer, M., Potler, C., & Wolf, R. (1999). *Gender and justice: Women, drugs, and sentencing policy*. Retrieved from http://www.sentencingproject.org/doc/publications/dp_genderandjustice.pdf.

May, D. C., & Wood, P. B. (2010). *Ranking correctional punishments: Views from offenders, practitioners, and the public*. Durham, NC: Carolina Academic Press.

McShane, M. D., & Williams III, F. P. (2006). Women drug offenders. In A. V. Merlo & J. M. Pollock (Eds.), *Women, law, and social control* (2nd ed., pp. 211–226). Boston, MA: Pearson/Allyn and Bacon.

Milkman, H., & Wanberg, K. (2007). *Cognitive-behavioral treatment: A review and discussion for correctional professionals*. Retrieved from http://nicic.gov/Library/021657.

Minnesota Sentencing Guidelines Commission. (2013). Minnesota sentencing guidelines & commentary (effective August 1, 2013). Retrieved from http://mn.gov/sentencing-guidelines/images/2013%2520Guidelines.pdf.

Moore, P. (2013, November 25). Poll results: Drug penalties. *YouGov*. Retrieved from https://today.yougov.com/news/2013/11/25/poll-results-drug-penalties/.

Morash, M., & Schram, P. J. (2002). *The prison experience: Special issues of women in prison*. Prospect Heights, IL: Waveland Press.

National Center for State Courts. (2009). *Evidence-based sentencing to improve public safety & reduce recidivism: A model curriculum for judges*. Retrieved from National Center for State Courts Digital Archive http://contentdm.ncsonline.org/cdm4/item_viewer.php?CISOROOT=/criminal&CISOPTR=185&REC=3.

Norman, M. D., & Wadman, R. C. (2000). Probation department sentencing recommendations in two Utah counties. *Federal Probation, 64*(2), 47–51.

O'Hear, M. M. (2012). Solving the good-time puzzle: Why following the rules should get you out of prison early. *Faculty Publications* (Paper 553). Retrieved from http://scholarship.law.marquette.edu/facpub/553.

Petersilia, J. (2002). *Reforming probation and parole in the 21st century.* Lanham, MD: American Correctional Association.

Porter, N. D. (2015). *The state of sentencing 2014: Developments in policy and practice.* Retrieved from http://sentencingproject.org/doc/publications/sen_State_of_Sentencing_2014.pdf.

Redding, R. E. (2009). Evidence-based sentencing: The science of sentencing policy and practice. *Chapman Journal of Criminal Justice, 1*(1), 1–19. Retrieved from http://ssrn.com/paper=1424008.

Rosich, K. J., & Kane, K. M. (2005). Truth in sentencing and state sentencing practices. *NIJ Journal, 252,* 18–21. Retrieved from http://www.nij.gov/journals/252/pages/sentencing.aspx.

Savage, C. (2013, August 12). Justice dept. seeks to curtail stiff drug sentences. Retrieved from http://www.nytimes.com/2013/08/12/us/justice-dept-seeks-to-curtail-stiff-drug-sentences.html?_r=0.

Solter, A., Kwon, S.-R., & Isaac, D. M. (2012). *Cruel and unusual: U.S. sentencing practices in a global context.* Retrieved from http://cpcjalliance.org/wp-content/uploads/2013/04/Cruel-And-Unusual.pdf.

Sottile, L. (2013, December 12). Three-strikes law causing pricey glut of lifers without parole. *Al Jazeera America.* Retrieved from http://america.aljazeera.com/articles/2013/12/12/three-strikes-lawcausingglutofliferswithoutparole.html.

Spohn, C. (2013). The effects of the offender's race, ethnicity, and sex on federal sentencing outcomes in the guidelines era. *Law & Contemporary Problems, 76*(1), 75–104.

State of Massachusetts. (2013). Code of Massachusetts regulations. *103 CMR 411.09.* Retrieved from http://www.lawlib.state.ma.us/source/mass/cmr/index.html.

State of Rhode Island. (2012). General laws. *§ 42-56-26 Additional time allowed for meritorious service.* Retrieved from http://webserver.rilin.state.ri.us/Statutes/.

Stewart, D. (2013, September 14). Rethinking mandatory sentencing. *The Week.* Retrieved from http://theweek.com/article/index/249578/rethinking-mandatory-sentencing.

Subramanian, R., & Delaney, R. (2014). *Playbook for change? States reconsider mandatory sentences.* Retrieved from: http://www.vera.org/sites/default/files/resources/downloads/mandatory-sentences-policy-report-v2b.pdf.

Subramanian, R., Moreno, R., & Broomhead, S. (2014). *Recalibrating justice: A review of 2013 state sentencing and corrections trends.* Retrieved from: http://www.vera.org/pubs/state-sentencing-and-corrections-trends-2013.

Taxy, S. A., & Kotonias, C. (2015). Who gets time for federal drug offenses? Data trends and opportunities for reform. Retrieved from http://www.urban.org/research/publication/who-gets-time-federal-drug-offenses-data-trends-and-opportunities-reform.

Tierney, J. (2012, December 11). For lesser crimes, rethinking life behind bars. *New York Times.* Retrieved from http://www.nytimes.com.

U.S. Sentencing Commission. (n.d.). Sensible sentencing reform: The 2014 reduction of drug sentences. *Policy Profile.* Retrieved from http://www.ussc.gov/sites/default/files/pdf/research-and-publications/backgrounders/profile_2014_drug_amendment.pdf

Walker, R. (2013, March 26). The trouble with using police informants in the US. *BBC News Magazine.* Retrieved from http://www.bbc.co.uk/news/magazine-21939453.

Wang, X., Mears, D. P., Spohn, C., & Dario, L. (2013). Assessing the differential effects of race and ethnicity on sentence outcomes under different sentencing systems. *Crime & Delinquency, 59*(1), 87–114. doi:10.1177/0011128709352234

Warren, R. K. (2007). Evidence-based practice to reduce recidivism: Implications for state judiciaries. Retrieved from http://nicic.gov/Downloads/PDF/Library/023358.pdf.

Warren, R. K. (2009). Arming the courts with research: 10 evidence-based sentencing initiatives to control crime and reduce costs. *Public Safety Policy Brief, 8.* Retrieved from http://www.pewcenteronthestates.org/report_detail.aspx?id=51750.

West, N. (2014). Biotech seeking ways to make people suffer eternally. *Activist Post,* March 14. Retrieved from http://www.activistpost.com/2014/03/biotech-seeking-ways-to-make-people.html.

Wodahl, E. J., Ogle, R., Kadleck, C., & Gerow, K. (2009). Offender perceptions of graduated sanctions. *Crime & Delinquency.* doi:10.1177/0011128709333725

Zalman, M., Smith, B., & Kiger, A. (2008). Officials' estimates of the incidence of "actual innocence" convictions. *Justice Quarterly, 25*(1), 72–100. doi:10.1080/07418820801954563

Zolfagharifard, E. (2014). Could we condemn criminals to suffer for hundreds of years? *The Daily Mail,* March 15. Retrieved from http://www.dailymail.co.uk/sciencetech/article-2580828/Could-soon-create-hell-EARTH-Biotechnology-let-extend-criminals-lives-makes-suffering-HUNDREDS-years.html.

Chapter 5, Probation and Community Supervision

Alarid, L. F., Montemayor, C. D., & Dannhaus, S. (2012). The effect of parental support on juvenile drug court completion and postprogram recidivism. *Youth Violence and Juvenile Justice, 10*(4), 354–369.

Alarid, L. F., & Reichel, P. L. (2008). *Corrections: A contemporary introduction.* Boston, MA: Allyn & Bacon.

Ashworth, A. (2015). *Sentencing and criminal justice* (6th ed.). New York, NY: Cambridge University Press.

Baldwin, J. M. (2013). *Executive Summary: National Survey of Veterans Treatment Courts.* Posted on Social Science

Research Network. Available at http://papers.ssrn.com/sol3/papers.cfm?abstract_id=2274138.

Bonczar, T. P. (1997). *Characteristics of adults on probation, 1995.* Washington, DC: U.S. Department of Justice.

Boyle, D. J., Ragusa-Salerno, L. M., Lanterman, J. L., & Marcus, A. F. (2013). An evaluation of day reporting centers for parolees: Outcomes of a randomized trial. *Criminology and Public Policy*, 12(1), 119–143.

Chute, C. L., & Bell, M. (1956). *Crime, courts, and probation.* New York, NY: The Macmillan Company.

Costanza, S. E., Kilburn, J. C., & Vendetti-Koski, S. (2013). Are minority areas disproportionately targeted for halfway house placement? *Journal of Ethnicity in Criminal Justice*, 11(4), 256–276.

Craddock, A. (2000). *Exploratory analysis of client outcomes, costs and benefits of day reporting: Final report.* Federal Grant 97_IJ_CX_0006. Washington, DC: National Institute of Justice.

Davis, R. C., Smith, B., & Hillenbrand, S. (1991). Increasing offender compliance with restitution orders. *Judicature*, 74(5), 245–248.

DeMichele, M., & Payne, B. (2009). *Offender supervision with electronic monitoring: Community corrections resource* (2nd ed.). Washington, DC: Bureau of Justice Assistance, Office of Justice Programs.

Durkin, M., Cheesman, F., Maggard, S., Rottman, D., Sohoni, T., & Rubio, D. (2009). *Process Evaluation of the Philadelphia Community Court.* Williamsburg, VA: National Center for State Courts.

Ekstrand, L. E., & Burton, D. R. (2001). *Prisoner releases: Trends and information on reintegration programs.* Publication GAO-01-483. Washington, DC: U.S. General Accounting Office.

French, M. T., Popovici, I., & Tapsell, L. (2008). The economic costs of substance abuse treatment: Updated estimates and cost bands for program assessment and reimbursement. *Journal of Substance Abuse Treatment*, 35(4), 462–469.

Gainey, R. R., Steen, S., & Engen, R. L. (2005). Exercising options: An assessment of the use of alternative sanctions for drug offenders. *Justice Quarterly*, 22(4), 488–520.

Goldfarb, R. L., & Singer, L. R. (1973). *After conviction.* New York, NY: Simon & Schuster.

Greenfield S. F., Brooks, A. J., Gordon, S. M., Green, C. A., Kropp, F., McHugh, R. K., et al. (2007). Substance abuse treatment entry, retention, and outcome in women: A review of the literature. *Drug and Alcohol Dependence*, 86(1), 1–21.

Grella, C. E. (1999). Women in residential drug treatment: Differences by program type and pregnancy. *Journal of Health Care for the Poor and Underserved*, 10(2), 216–229.

Hanna, J. (2016, April 14). 'Affluenza' teen Ethan Couch gets tentative order for 2-year jail term. CNN. Retrieved at http://www.cnn.com/2016/04/13/us/texas-affluenza-ethan-couch/.

Harris, R. J., & Lo, T. W. (2002). Community service: Its use in criminal justice. *International Journal of Offender Therapy and Comparative Criminology*, 46(4), 427–444.

Kaeble, D., Maruschak, L. M., & Bonczar, T. P. (2015). *Probation and parole in the United States, 2014* (NCJ 249057). Washington, DC: U.S. Department of Justice. Retrieved from http://www.bjs.gov/content/pub/pdf/ppus14.pdf.

Kaiser, K. A., & Holtfreter, K. (2016). An integrated theory of specialized court programs: Using procedural justice and therapeutic jurisprudence to promote offender compliance and rehabilitation. *Criminal Justice and Behavior*, 43(1), 45–62.

Kim, D., Joo, H., & McCarty, W. P. (2008). Risk assessment and classification of day reporting center clients: An actuarial approach. *Criminal Justice and Behavior*, 35(6), 795–812.

Morris, N., & Tonry, M. (1990). *Between prison and probation: Intermediate punishments in a rational sentencing system.* New York, NY: Oxford University Press.

Office for the Victims of Crime. (2010, April). OVC fact sheet: What is the Office for Victims of Crime? Retrieved from http://www.ovc.gov/publications/factshts/what_is_OVC2010/fs_000321.html.

Osborne, R. (2015). Tarrant district attorney investigating alleged Ethan Couch partying video. *The Ft. Worth Star-Telegram*, December 3. Retrieved from http://www.star-telegram.com/news/local/community/fort-worth/article47748570.html.

Ruback, R. B., Schaffer, J. N., & Logue, M. A. (2004). The imposition and the effects of restitution in four Pennsylvania counties: Effects of size of county and specialized collection units. *Crime and Delinquency*, 50(2), 168–188.

Sarteschi, C. M. (2009). Assessing the effectiveness of mental health courts: A meta-analysis of clinical and recidivism outcomes. An unpublished doctoral dissertation. Retrieved from http://d-scholarship.pitt.edu/9275//.

Shephard, B. (2014). Classifying crime victim restitution: The theoretical arguments and practical consequences of labeling restitution as either a criminal or civil law concept. *Lewis & Clark Law Review*, 18, 801–812.

Thomas, D., & Hunninen, M. (2008). Making things right: Meaningful community service for juvenile offenders. *Technical Assistance to the Juvenile Court Bulletin*. Pittsburgh, PA: National Center for Juvenile Justice.

Tsenin, K. (2000). One judicial perspective on the sex trade. *Research on women and girls in the justice system: Plenary papers of the 1999 conference on criminal justice research and evaluation—Enhancing policy.* Washington, DC: National Institute of Justice.

van Kalmthout, A. M., & Tak, P. (1988). *Sanctions-systems in the member-states of the Council of Europe, part I.* Norwell, MA: Kluwer Law and Taxation Publishers.

van Wormer, K. (2010). *Working with female offenders: A gender-sensitive approach.* New Jersey: John Wiley and Sons.

Vanstone, M. (2004). *Supervising offenders in the community: A history of probation theory and practice.* Burlington, VT: Ashgate.

Vigorita, M. S. (2002). Fining practices in felony courts: An analysis of offender, offense, and systemic factors. *Corrections Compendium*, 27(11), 1–5, 26.

Welsh, W. N., & Zajac, G. (2004). A census of prison-based drug treatment programs: Implications for programming, policy, and evaluation. *Crime and Delinquency*, *50*(1), 108–133.

Chapter 6, Jails and Pretrial Release

Alarid, L. F., & Reichel, P. L. (2008). *Corrections: A contemporary introduction*. Boston, MA: Allyn & Bacon.

Applegate, B., & Paoline, E. (2007). Jail officers' perceptions of the work environment in traditional versus new generation facilities. *American Journal of Criminal Justice*, *31*(2), 64–80. doi:10.1007/s12103-007-9005-z

Beck, A. R. (2006). *Deciding on a new jail design*. Retrieved from http://www.justiceconcepts.com/design.htm.

Belcher, J. (1988). Are jails replacing the mental health system for the homeless mentally ill? *Community Mental Health Journal*, *24*(3), 185–195.

Bowker, G. M. (2002). *Jail resource issues: What every funding authority needs to know*. Washington, DC: National Institute of Corrections.

Carson, E. A., & Golinelli, D. (2013). *Prisoners in 2012: Trends in admissions and releases, 1991–2012* (NCJ 243920). Retrieved from http://www.bjs.gov/index.cfm?ty =pbdetail&iid=4842.

Case, B., Steadman, H. J., Dupuis, S. A., & Morris, L. S. (2009). Who succeeds in jail diversion programs for persons with mental illness? A multi-site study. *Behavioral Sciences & the Law*, *27*(5), 661–674. doi:10.1002/bsl.883

Council of State Governments. (2002). *Criminal justice/mental health consensus project report*. Retrieved from http:// csgjusticecenter.org/jc/publications/the-consensus project-report//.

Council of State Governments. (n.d.). *Frequently asked questions about new study of serious mental illness in jails*. Retrieved from http://csgjusticecenter.org/wp-content/ uploads/2012/12/Psy_S_FAQ.pdf.

Ditton, P. M. (1999). *Mental health and treatment of inmates and probationers* (NCJ 174463). Retrieved from http://bjs. ojp.usdoj.gov/index.cfm?ty=pbdetail&iid=787.

Fields, G., & Phillips, E. E. (2013, September 25). The new asylums: Jails swell with mentally ill. *The Wall Street Journal*. Retrieved from http://online.wsj.com.

Fletcher, M. L. M. (2009). *Addressing the epidemic of domestic violence in Indian Country by restoring tribal sovereignty*. Retrieved from http://www.law.msu.edu/ foundations/6-section-2-fletcher-issue-brief.pdf.

Gilliard, D. K. (1999). *Prison and jail inmates at midyear 1998* (NCJ 173414). Retrieved from http://bjs.ojp.usdoj. gov/content/pub/pdf/pjim98.pdf.

Glazer, S. (2015). Prisoners and mental illness. *CQ Researcher*, *25*(11), 241–264.

Grissom, B. (2011, February 24). As mental health cuts mount, psychiatric cases fill jails. *New York Times*. Retrieved from http://www.nytimes.com.

Hagar, G. M., Ludwig, T. E., & McGovern, K. (2008). Program evaluation for a jail-based mental health treatment program. *Journal of Correctional Health Care*, *14*(3), 222–231. doi:10.1177/1078345808318257

James, D. J., & Glaze, L. E. (2006). *Mental health problems of prison and jail inmates* (NCJ 213600). Retrieved from http://bjs.ojp.usdoj.gov/index.cfm?ty=pbdetail&iid=789.

Lowenkamp, C. T., VanNostrand, M., & Holsinger, A. (2013). *Investigating the impact of pretrial detention on sentencing outcomes*. Retrieved from http://www.arnoldfoundation. org/research/criminaljustice.

Minton, T. D. (2011a). *Jail inmates at midyear 2010 – Statistical tables* (NCJ 233431). Retrieved from www.bjs.gov/ index.cfm?ty=pbdetail&iid=2375.

Minton, T. D. (2011b). *Jails in Indian country, 2009* (NCJ 232223). Retrieved from http://bjs.ojp.usdoj.gov/index. cfm?ty=pbdetail&iid=2223.

Minton, T. D. (2015). *Jails in Indian country, 2014* (NCJ 248974). Retrieved from http://www.bjs.gov/index.cfm?ty= pbdetail&iid=5414.

Minton, T. D., & Zeng, Z. (2015). *Jail inmates at midyear 2014* (NCJ 248629). Retrieved from http://www.bjs.gov/ index.cfm?ty=pbdetail&iid=5299.

National Coordination Committee. (2014). *Report to the U.S. Attorney General on improving federal agency response to sexual violence in tribal nations: Issues and recommendations*. Office for Victims of Crime. Retrieved from http://ovc.gov/AIANSane-Sart/pdf/NCC_June2014_ FinalReport_508.pdf.

National Institute of Corrections. (2006). *Direct supervision jails: 2006 sourcebook*. (Accession Number: 021968). Retrieved from http://nicic.gov/Library/021968.

National Institute of Justice. (2016). *Tribal crime and justice*. Office of Justice Programs. Retrieved from http://nij.gov/ topics/tribal-justice/Pages/welcome.aspx.

Ney, B. (2014). 10 facts about women in jails. *American Jails*, *27*(6), 8–10.

Oleson, J. C., Lowenkamp, C. T., Cadigan, T. P., VanNostrand, M., & Wooldredge, J. (2014). The effect of pretrial detention on sentencing in two federal districts. *Justice Quarterly*, 1–20. doi:10.1080/07418825.2014.959035

Perry, S. W. (2004). *American Indians and crime: A BJS statistical profile, 1992–2002* (NCJ 203097). Retrieved from http://www.bjs.gov/index.cfm?ty=pbdetail&iid=386.

Phillips, M. T. (2008). Bail, detention, & felony case outcomes. *CJA Research Brief* (No. 18). Retrieved from http:// www.cjareports.org/reports/brief18.pdf.

Reaves, B. A. (2013). *Felony defendants in large urban counties, 2009 – Statistical tables* (NCJ 243777). Retrieved from http://www.bjs.gov/index.cfm?ty=pbdetail&iid=4845.

Senese, J. D. (1997). Evaluating jail reform: A comparative analysis of podular/direct and linear jail inmate infractions. *Journal of Criminal Justice*, *25*(1), 61–73. doi:10.1016/ s0047-2352(96)00052-9

Steadman, H. J., Osher, F. C., Robbins, P. C., Case, B., & Samuels, S. (2009). Prevalence of serious mental illness among jail inmates. *Psychiatric Services*, *60*(6), 761–765. doi:10.1176/appi.ps.60.6.761

Stevenson, B., & Legg, S. (2010, April). Pretrial services agencies: The first responders in the reentry process. *Corrections Today, 72*(2), 104–107.

Summerill, J. (2005, February). The state of Indian jails in America. *Corrections Today, 67*(1), 64–67.

Tartaro, C., & Levy, M. (2010). The impact of jail environment on inmate suicide. *American Jails, 24*(1), 48.

Torrey, E. F., Kennard, A. D., Eslinger, D., Lamb, R., & Pavle, J. (2010). *More mentally ill persons are in jails and prisons than hospitals: A survey of the states*. Retrieved from http://www.treatmentadvocacycenter.org/storage/documents/final_jails_v_hospitals_study.pdf.

U.S. Department of the Interior. (2004). *Neither safe nor secure: An assessment of Indian detention facilities* (NCJ 207148). Retrieved from https://www.ncjrs.gov/App/Publications/abstract.aspx?ID=207148.

VanNostrand, M. (2007). *Legal and evidence based practices: Application of legal principles, laws, and research to the field of pretrial services*. Retrieved from http://www.cjinstitute.org/boxset.

Veysey, B. M., De Cou, K., & Prescott, L. (1998, May/June). Effective management of female jail detainees with histories of physical and sexual abuse. *American Jails*, 50–54.

Wener, R. (2005). The invention of direct supervision. *Corrections Compendium, 30*(2), 4–7, 32–34.

Wener, R. (2006). Effectiveness of the direct supervision system of correctional design and management. *Criminal Justice and Behavior, 33*(3), 392–410. doi:10.1177/0093854806286202

Zupan, L. L. (1991). *Jails: Reform and the new generation philosophy*. Cincinnati, OH: Anderson.

Chapter 7, Managing Prisons and Prisoners

Adams, K., & Ferrandino, J. (2008). Managing mentally ill inmates in prisons. *Criminal Justice and Behavior, 35*(8), 913–927. doi:10.1177/0093854808318624

Alarid, L. F., & Reichel, P. L. (2008). *Corrections: A contemporary introduction*. Boston, MA: Allyn & Bacon.

American Correctional Association. (2007). Correctional officers—Hiring requirements and wages: Survey summary. *Corrections Compendium, 32*(3), 12–13.

American Correctional Association. (2008). Inmate mental health care: Survey summary. *Corrections Compendium, 33*(5), 12–13.

American Correctional Association. (2013, Fall). Correctional officer education and training: Survey summary. *Corrections Compendium, 37*(3) 13–25.

Andrews, D. A., & Dowden, C. (2007). The risk–need–responsivity model of assessment and human service in prevention and corrections: Crime-prevention jurisprudence. *Canadian Journal of Criminology & Criminal Justice, 49*(4), 439–464.

Austin, J. (2003). *Findings in prison classification and risk assessment*. Retrieved from http://nicic.gov/Library/018888.

Austin, J., & Coventry, G. (2003). A second look at the private prison debate. *The Criminologist, 28*(5), 1, 3–9.

Beck, A. J. (2015). *Use of restrictive housing in U.S. prisons and jails, 2011–2012* (NCJ 249209). Retrieved from http://www.bjs.gov/index.cfm?ty=pbdetail&iid=5433.

Blakely, C. R., & Bumphus, V. W. (2004). Private and public sector prisons—A comparison of select characteristics. *Federal Probation, 68*(1), 27–31.

Browne, A., Cambier, A., & Agha, S. (2011). Prisons within prisons: The use of segregation in the United States. *Federal Sentencing Reporter, 24*(1), 46–49. doi:10.1525/fsr.2011.24.1.46

Bureau of Labor Statistics. (2015, March 25). Occupational employment and wages news release. Retrieved from http://www.bls.gov/news.release/ocwage.htm.

Camp, C. G. (Ed.). (2003). *The 2002 Corrections Yearbook: Adult Corrections*. Middletown, CT: Criminal Justice Institute.

Carson, E. A. (2015). *Prisoners in 2014* (NCJ 248955). Retrieved from BJS website http://www.bjs.gov/index.cfm?ty=pbdetail&iid=5387.

Cloud, D. H., Drucker, E., Browne, A., & Parsons, J. (2015). Public health and solitary confinement in the United States. *American Journal of Public Health, 105*(1), 18–26.

Dammer, H. R. (1996). Religion in prisons. In M. D. McShane & F. Williams III (Eds.), *Encyclopedia of American prisons* (pp. 399–402). New York, NY: Garland.

Federal Bureau of Prisons. (2015a). *About the Federal Bureau of Prisons*. Retrieved from http://www.bop.gov/resources/publications.jsp.

Federal Bureau of Prisons. (2015b). *By the numbers*. Retrieved from www.bop.gov/about/statistics/.

Gaes, G. G. (2008, February 18). The impact of prison education programs on post-release outcomes. Retrieved from http://www.ceanational.org/docs/Gaes.pdf.

Gawande, A. (2009, March 30). Hellhole: Annals of human rights. *The New Yorker, 85*(7), 36.

Glazer, S. (2015). Prisoners and mental illness. *CQ Researcher, 25*(11), 241–264.

Hardyman, P. L., & Van Voorhis, P. (2004). *Developing gender-specific classification systems for women offenders*. (NIC Accession Number 018931). Retrieved from http://nicic.gov/Library/018931.

Hauser, B. (2008, September 28). The changing of the guard. *New York Times*. Retrieved from http://www.nytimes.com.

Herrman, C. (2015). *Dispatches from Germany: Is solitary confinement necessary?* Vera Institute of Justice. Retrieved from http://www.vera.org/blog/dispatches-germany-solitary-confinement-necessary.

Inspectorate of Prisons. (2015). *Close Supervision Centres - a well run system which contains dangerous men safely and decently*. Retrieved from https://www.justiceinspectorates.gov.uk/hmiprisons/media/press-releases/2015/08/close-supervision-centres-a-well-run-system-which-contains-dangerous-men-safely-and-decently/.

Kahler, H. L. (1999). Prison recreation. In P. M. Carlson & J. S. Garrett (Eds.), *Prison and jail administration: Practice and theory* (pp. 94–99). Gaithersburg, MD: Aspen Publishers.

Lawrence, R., & Mahan, S. (1998). Women correctional officers in men's prisons: Acceptance and perceived job performance. *Women & Criminal Justice, 9*(3), 63–86.

Logan, C. H. (1990). *Private prisons: Cons and pros.* New York, NY: Oxford University Press.

Lundahl, B., Kunz, C., Brownell, C., Harris, N., & Van Vleet, R. (2007). *Prison privatization: A meta-analysis of cost effectiveness and quality of confinement indicators.* Retrieved from http://ucjc.law.utah.edu/wp-content/uploads/86.pdf.

Mason, C. (2012). *Too good to be true: Private prisons in America.* Retrieved from http://www.sentencingproject.org/doc/publications/inc_Too_Good_to_be_True.pdf.

McKelvey, B. (1977). *American prisons: A history of good intentions.* Montclair, NJ: Patterson Smith.

Morris, R. G. (2015). Exploring the effect of exposure to short-term solitary confinement among violent prison inmates. *Journal of Quantitative Criminology* (Published online, January 24), 1–22. doi:10.1007/s10940-015-9250-0

Newton, C., Rough, G., & Hensley, J. J. (2010, August 22). Arizona inmate escape puts spotlight on state private prisons. *The Arizona Republic.* Retrieved from http://www.azcentral.com/.

Neyfakh, L. (2015). What do you do with the worst of the worst? *Slate,* April 3. Retrieved from http://www.slate.com/articles/news_and_politics/crime/2015/04/solitary_confinement_in_washington_state_a_surprising_and_effective_reform.html.

Oppel, R. A., Jr. (2011, May 18). Private prisons found to offer little in savings. *New York Times.* Retrieved from http://www.nytimes.com/2011/05/19/us/19prisons.html.

Rodriguez, S. (2011). Fact sheet: The high cost of solitary confinement. *Solitary Watch.* Retrieved from http://solitarywatch.com/wp-content/uploads/2011/06/fact-sheet-the-high-cost-of-solitary-confinement.pdf.

Rodriguez, S. (2015). Solitary confinement: FAQ. *Solitary Watch.* Retrieved from http://solitarywatch.com/facts/faq/.

Schwartz, D., & Fewell, T. (1999). Religious programs. In P. M. Carlson & J. S. Garrett (Eds.), *Prison and jail administration: Practice and theory* (pp. 117–122). Gaithersburg, MD: Aspen Publishers.

Schwirtz, M., & Winerip, M. (2015). New York state agrees to overhaul solitary confinement in prisons. *New York Times,* December 16. Retrieved from http://www.nytimes.com/2015/12/17/nyregion/new-york-state-agrees-to-overhaul-solitary-confinement-in-prisons.html?_r=0.

Seidel, J. (2009, January 7). Female inmate described rapes in lawsuit against state. *Detroit Free Press.* Retrieved from http://www.freep.com.

Seiter, R. P. (2002). *Correctional administration: Integrating theory and practice.* Upper Saddle River, NJ: Prentice Hall.

Shane, S. (2011, December 10). Beyond Guantánamo, a web of prisons for terrorism inmates. *New York Times.* Retrieved from http://www.nytimes.com/2011/12/11/us/beyond-guantanamo-bay-a-web-of-federal-prisons.html?pagewanted=all&_r=0.

Smith, P. S. (2006). The effects of solitary confinement on prison inmates: A brief history and review of the literature. *Crime and Justice, 34*(1), 441–528. doi:10.1086/500626

Stephan, J. J. (2008). *Census of state and federal correctional facilities, 2005* (NCJ 222182). Retrieved from Bureau of Justice Statistics website http://bjs.ojp.usdoj.gov/index.cfm?ty=pbdetail&iid=530.

The Liman Program, & Association of State Correctional Administrators. (2015). *Time-in-cell: The ASCA-Liman 2014 national survey of administrative segregation in prison.* Retrieved from http://www.asca.net/articles/3685.

United Nations Office on Drugs and Crime. (2008). *Handbook for prison managers and policymakers on women and imprisonment.* New York, NY: United Nations.

Van Voorhis, P., Wright, E. M., Salisbury, E., & Bauman, A. (2010). Women's risk factors and their contributions to existing risk/needs assessment. *Criminal Justice and Behavior, 37*(3), 261–288. doi:10.1177/0093854809357442

Vose, B., Lowenkamp, C. T., Smith, P., & Cullen, F. T. (2009). Gender and the predictive validity of the LSI-R. *Journal of Contemporary Criminal Justice, 25*(4), 459–471. doi:10.1177/1043986209344797

Zupan, L. L. (1992). The progress of women correctional officers in all-male prisons. In I. Moyer (Ed.), *The changing role of women in the criminal justice system* (pp. 323–343). Prospect Heights, IL: Waveland.

Chapter 8, Prison Life

Alarid, L. F. (1996). *Women offenders' perception of confinement: Behavior code acceptance, hustling, and group relations in jail and prison* (Unpublished doctoral dissertation). Huntsville, TX: Sam Houston State University.

Alarid, L. F. (2000a). Along racial and gender lines: Jail subcultures in the midst of racial disproportionality. *Corrections Management Quarterly, 4*(1), 8–19.

Alarid, L. F. (2000b). Sexual assault and coercion among incarcerated women prisoners: Excerpts from prison letters. *The Prison Journal, 80*(4), 391–406.

Alarid, L. F. (2005). Turning a profit or just passing the time? A gender comparison of prisoner jobs and workplace deviance in the sub rosa economy. *Deviant Behavior, 26*(6) 621–641.

Austin, J., Fabelo, T., Gunter, A., & McGinnis, K. (2006). *Sexual violence in the Texas prison system* (NCJ 215774). Washington, DC: U.S. Department of Justice and The JFA Institute.

Barker, T. (2012). *North American criminal gangs: Street, prison, outlaw motorcycle, and drug trafficking organizations.* Durham, NC: Carolina Academic Press.

Beck, A. J., Harrison, P. M., & Guerino, P. (2010). *Sexual victimization in prisons and jails reported by inmates, 2008–2009.* Washington, DC: U.S. Department of Justice.

Beck, A. J., & Rantala, R. R. (2016). *Sexual victimization reported by juvenile correctional authorities, 2007–2012* (NCJ 249145). Washington, DC: U.S. Department of Justice.

Carceral, K. C. (2004). *Behind a convict's eyes: Doing time in a modern prison*. In T. J. Bernard, L. F. Alarid, B. Bikle, & A. Bikle (Eds.). Belmont, CA: Wadsworth.

Carson, E. A. (2015). *Prisoners in 2014* (NCJ 248955). Washington, DC: U.S. Department of Justice. Retrieved from http://www.bjs.gov/index.cfm?ty=pbdetail&iid=5387.

Clemmer, D. (1966). *The prison community*. New York, NY: Holt.

Colvin, M. (1997). *Penitentiaries, reformatories, and chain gangs: Social theory and the history of punishment in nineteenth-century America*. New York, NY: St. Martin's Press.

Dwyer, D. C., & McNally, R. B. (1993). Public policy, prison industries, and business: An equitable balance for the 1990s. *Federal Probation, 57*(2), 30–36.

Dye, M. H., Aday, R. H., Farney, L., & Raley, J. (2014). The rock I cling to: Religious engagement in the lives of life-sentenced women. *The Prison Journal, 94*(3), 388–408.

Egan, L. (2016). Officers arrested: Names of 49 Georgia officers and prisoners involved in FBI sting released. *Inquisitr*, February 12. Retrieved from http://www.inquisitr.com/2790070/officers-arrested-names-of-49-georgia-officers-and-prisoner-involved-in-fbi-sting-released/.

Encinas, G. L. (2001). *Prison argot: A sociolinguistic and lexicographic study*. Lanham, MD: University Press of America.

English, K., Heil, P., & Dumond, R. (2010). *Sexual assault in jail and juvenile facilities: Promising practices for prevention and response*. Denver, CO: Colorado Division of Criminal Justice. Retrieved from http://dcj.state.co.us/ors/pdf/PREA/FINAL%20PREA%20REPORT%20June%2028%202010.pdf.

Federal Bureau of Prisons. (2011). *Quick facts about the Bureau of Prisons*. Retrieved from http://www.bop.gov/news/quick.jsp.

Federal Bureau of Prisons. (2016). *Quick facts about the Bureau of Prisons*. Retrieved from http://www.bop.gov/news/quick.jsp.

Griffin, M. L., Pyrooz, D., & Decker, S. H. (2013). Surviving and thriving: The growth, influence, and administrative control of prison gangs. In J. L. Wood & T. A. Gannon (Eds.), *Crime and crime reduction: The importance of group processes* (pp. 137–156). New York, NY: Routledge.

Harkleroad, J. (2000). Prison is a place. In R. Johnson & H. Toch (Eds.), *Crime and punishment: Inside views* (pp. 163–164). Los Angeles, CA: Roxbury.

Irwin, J. (1980). *Prisons in turmoil*. Boston, MA: Little, Brown, & Company.

Kigerl, A., & Hamilton, Z. (2016). The impact of transfers between prisons on inmate misconduct: Testing importation, deprivation, and transfer theory models. *The Prison Journal, 96*(2), 232–257.

Knox, G. W. (2005). *The problem of gangs and security threat groups (STGs) in American prisons today: Recent research findings from the 2004 prison gang survey*. Retrieved from http://www.ngcrc.com.

Kuanliang, A., & Sorensen, J. (2008). Predictors of self-reported prison misconduct. *Criminal Justice Studies, 21*(1), 27–35.

Lee, B., & Gilligan, J. (2005). The resolve to stop violence project: Transforming an in-house culture of violence through a jail-based programme. *Journal of Public Health, 27*(2), 149–155.

Miller, K. L. (2010). The darkest figure of crime: Perceptions of reasons for male inmates to not report sexual assault. *Justice Quarterly, 27*(5), 692–712.

Montgomery, R. H., & Crews, G. A. (1998). *A history of correctional violence: An examination of riots and correctional disturbances*. Lanham, MD: American Correctional Association.

Morgenstein, M. (2015). Joyce Mitchell, who aided prison break, going to prison herself. *CNN*. Retrieved from http://www.cnn.com/2015/09/28/us/ny-prison-break/.

National Correctional Industries Association. (2011). *Prison Industry Enhancement (PIE) Certification Program*. Retrieved from http://www.nationalcia.org/wp-content/uploads/2008/10/pie-overview-final2.pdf.

Owen, B. (1998). *In the mix: Struggle and survival in a women's prison*. Albany, NY: State University of New York.

Petersen, R. D. (2000). Gang subcultures and prison gangs of female youth. *Free Inquiry in Creative Sociology 28*(2), 27–42.

Pollock, J. M. (2002). *Women, prison & crime* (2nd ed.). Belmont, CA: Thomson/Wadsworth.

Prison Rape Elimination Act. (2003). 108th Congress, 2003, 117 Stat. 972.

Ricciardelli, R. (2014). Coping strategies: Investigating how male prisoners manage the threat of victimization in federal prisons. *The Prison Journal, 94*(4), 411–434.

Ricciardelli, R., & Sit, V. (2016). Producing social (dis)order in prison: The effects of administrative controls on prisoner-on-prisoner violence. *The Prison Journal, 96*(2), 210–231.

Richmond, K. M. (2014). The impact of federal prison industries employment on the recidivism outcomes of female inmates. *Justice Quarterly, 31*(4), 719–745.

Rocheleau, A. M. (2013). An empirical exploration of the pains of imprisonment and the level of prison misconduct and violence. *Criminal Justice Review, 38*(3), 354–374.

Ross, J. I., & Richards, S. C. (2002). *Behind bars: Surviving prison*. Indianapolis, IN: Alpha Books.

Santos, M. G. (2004). *About prison*. Belmont, CA: Wadsworth/Thomson.

Smoyer, A. B. (2016). Making fatty girl cakes: Food and resistance in a women's prison. *The Prison Journal, 96*(2), 191–209.

Sykes, G. M. (1958). *The society of captives*. Princeton: Princeton University Press.

Sykes, G. M., & Messinger, S. (1960). The inmate social system. In *Theoretical studies in social organization of the prison* (pp. 5–19). New York, NY: Social Science Research Council.

Terry, C. M. (2003). *The fellas: Overcoming prison and addiction*. Belmont, CA: Wadsworth.

Texas Joint Crime Information Center Intelligence and Counterterrorism Division. (2015). *Texas gang threat assessment*. Austin, TX: Texas Department of Public Safety.

Trammell, R., & Rundle, M. (2015). The inmate as the nonperson: Examining staff conflict from the inmate's perspective. *The Prison Journal*, *95*(4), 472–492.

UNICOR. (2016). *2015 annual financial management report*. Retrieved from http://www.unicor.gov/publications/corporate/FY2015_AnnualReport.pdf.

Visher, C. A., Winterfield, L., & Coggeshall, M. B. (2005). Ex-offender employment programs and recidivism: A meta-analysis. *Journal of Experimental Criminology*, *1*(3), 295–316.

WABC-TV/DT. (2008, June 10). RSVP program helps inmates with anger. Eyewitness News, WABC, New York. Retrieved from http://abclocal.go.com/wabc/story?section=news/local&id=6197063.

Wicker, T. (1994). *A time to die: The Attica prison revolt*. University of Nebraska Press.

Winfree, L. T., Newbold, G., & Tubb, S. H. (2002). Prisoner perspective on inmate culture in New Mexico and New Zealand: A descriptive case study. *The Prison Journal*, *82*(2), 213–233.

Winterdyk, J., & Ruddell, R. (2010). Managing prison gangs: Results from a survey of U.S. prison systems. *Journal of Criminal Justice*, *38*(4), 730–736.

Winton, R., & Queally, J. (2016). Woman who worked at jail arrested for allegedly helping inmates escape. *Los Angeles Times*, January 28.

Wolff, N., Shi, J., & Siegel, J. (2009). Understanding physical victimization inside prisons: Factors that predict risk. *Justice Quarterly*, *26*(3), 445–475.

Wood, S. R., & Buttaro, A. (2013). Co-occurring severe mental illnesses and substance abuse disorders as predictors of state prison inmate assaults. *Crime and Delinquency*, *59*(4), 510–535.

Wooldredge, J., & Steiner, B. (2009). Comparing methods for examining relationships between prison crowding and inmate violence. *Justice Quarterly*, *26*(4), 795–826.

Worley, R. M. (2015). Fishing for favors: How inmates lure prison staffers. *ACJS Today*, *40* (4), 15–17.

Zweig, J. M., Naser, R. L., Blackmore, J., & Schaffer, M. (2007). *Addressing sexual violence in prisons: A national snapshot of approaches and highlights of innovative strategies* (NCJ 216856). *Washington, DC:* National Institute of Justice.

Chapter 9, Special Correctional Populations

Alarid, L. F. (2009). Risk factors for potential occupational exposure to HIV: A study of correctional officers. *Journal of Criminal Justice*, *37*(2), 114–122.

Alarid, L. F., & Reichel, P. L. (2008). *Corrections: A contemporary introduction*. Boston, MA: Allyn & Bacon.

American Civil Liberties Union. (2010, April 14). *ACLU and Human Rights Watch report calls on South Carolina and Alabama to stop segregating prisoners with HIV*. Retrieved from http://www.aclu.org/hiv-aids-prisoners-rights/aclu-and-human-rights-watch-report-calls-south-carolina-and-alabama-stop-s.

Barrick, K., Lattimore, P. K., & Visher, C. A. (2014). Reentering women: The impact of social ties on long-term recidivism. *The Prison Journal*, *94*(3), 279–304.

Bidgood, J. (2015). Owen Labrie gets year in jail for St. Paul's school assault. *New York Times*, October 29. Retrieved online at http://www.nytimes.com/2015/10/30/us/owen-labrie-st-pauls-school-sentencing.html?_r=0.

Blagden, N., Winder, B., & Hames, C. (2016). "They treat us like human beings"—Experiencing a therapeutic sex offenders prison: Impact on prisoners and staff and implications for treatment. *International Journal of Offender Therapy and Comparative Criminology*, *60*(4), 371–396.

Byrne, M. W. (2006). *Responsive parenting support during the prison nursery and reentry years: Highlights from a study in progress: Maternal and child outcomes of a prison nursery program* (Nov. 6, PowerPoint presentation). Retrieved from http://archives.drugabuse.gov/meetings/children_at_risk/pdf/Byrne.pdf.

Chavaria, F. R. (1997). Probation and cognitive skills. *Federal Probation*, *61*(2), 57–60. Washington, DC: Judiciary Branch of the United States Government.

Crawley, E., & Sparks, R. (2006). Is there life after imprisonment? How elderly men talk about imprisonment and release. *Criminology & Criminal Justice*, *6*(1), 63–82.

Dallaire, D. H., Zemen, J. L., & Thrash, T. M. (2014). Children's experiences of maternal incarceration- specific risks: Predictions to psychological maladaptation. *Journal of Clinical Child & Adolescent Psychology* (published online, May 28). doi:10.1080/15374416.2014.913248

Dye, M. H., Aday, R. H., Farney, L., & Raley, J. (2014). The rock I cling to: Religious engagement in the lives of life-sentenced women. *The Prison Journal*, *94*(3), 388–408.

Fisher, A. A., & Hatton, D. C. (2010). A study of women prisoners' use of co-payments for health care. *Women's Health Issues*, *20*(3), 185–192.

Glaze, L. E., & Maruschak, L. M. (2008). *Parents in prison and their minor children* (NCJ 222984). Washington, DC: U.S. Department of Justice.

Hahl, J. M., Alarid, L. F., Harris, R., & Firestone, J. (2016). Comparing criminal outcomes for children of fathers and mothers who are incarcerated: Dallaire revisited. *Corrections: Policy, Practice and Research* (forthcoming). doi:10.1080/23774657.2016.1183242

Hanson, R. K., Harris, A. J. R., Helmus, L., & Thornton, D. (2014). High-risk sex offenders may not be high risk forever. *Journal of Interpersonal Violence*, *29*(15), 2792–2813. doi:10.1177/0886260514526062

Harris, D. A. (2004). A typological approach to exploring pathways for rapists, child molesters, and incest offenders (Unpublished master's thesis). University of Maryland.

Haugebrook, S., Zgoba, K. M., Maschi, T., Morgen, K., & Brown, D. (2010). Trauma, stress, health and mental health among ethnically diverse older adult prisoners. *Journal of Correctional Health Care*, 16(3) 220–229.

Hellard, M. E., Aitken, C. K., & Hocking, J. S. (2007). Tattooing in prisons—Not such a pretty picture. *American Journal of Infection Control*, 35(7), 477–480.

Horowitz, M. E. (2016, February 17). Statement of Michael E. Horowitz, Inspector General, U.S. Department of Justice, before the United States Sentencing Commission hearing on *Compassionate Release and the Conditions of Supervision*. Retrieved from http://www.ussc.gov/sites/default/files/pdf/amendment-process/public-hearings-and-meetings/20160217/IG.pdf.

Horowitz, M. E. (2014, November 10). *Top management and performance challenges facing the Department of Justice-2014*. Retrieved from https://oig.justice.gov/challenges/2014.htm.

Johnson, R. (2002). *Hard time: Understanding and reforming the prison*. Belmont, CA: Wadsworth.

Kauffman, K. (2006). Prison nurseries: New beginnings and second chances. In R. Immarigeon (Ed.), *Women and girls in the criminal justice system: Policy issues and practice strategies* (pp. 1–7 in Chap. 20). Kingston, NJ: Civic Research Institute, Inc.

Landenberger, N. A., & Lipsey, M. W. (2005). The positive effects of cognitive-behavioral programs for offenders: A meta-analysis of factors associated with effective treatment. *Journal of Experimental Criminology*, 1(4), 451–476.

Lowden, K., Hetz, N., Harrison, L., Patrick, D., English, K., & Pasini-Hill, D. (2003). *Evaluation of Colorado's prison therapeutic community for sex offenders*. Denver, CO: Colorado Division of Criminal Justice, Office of Research and Statistics.

Maruschak, L. M., Berzofsky, M., & Unangst, J. (2015). *Medical problems of state and federal prisoners and jail inmates, 2011–12* (NCJ 248491). Washington, DC: U.S. Department of Justice, Office of Justice Programs.

Mears, D. P., Cochran, J. C., Siennick, S. E., & Bales, W. D. (2012). Prison visitation and recidivism. *Justice Quarterly*, 29(6), 888–918.

National Women's Law Center. (2010). *Mothers behind bars: A state-by-state report card and analysis of federal policies on conditions of confinement for pregnant and parenting women and the effect on their children*. Retrieved from http://www.nwlc.org/sites/default/files/pdfs/mothersbehindbars2010.pdf.

Noonan, M., Rohloff, H., & Ginder, S. (2015). *Mortality in local jails and state prisons, 2000–2013* (NCJ 248756). Washington, DC: U.S. Department of Justice, Office of Justice Programs.

Ollove, M. (2015, July 22). *No escaping medical co-payments, even in prison*. Pew Charitable Trust. Retrieved from http://www.pewtrusts.org/en/research-and-analysis/blogs/stateline/2015/07/22/no-escaping-medical-copayments-even-in-prison.

Parvez, F. M., Lobato, M. N., & Greifinger, R. B. (2010). Tuberculosis control: Lessons for outbreak preparedness in a correctional facility. *Journal of Correctional Health Care*, 16(3) 239–242.

Pierce, M. B. (2015). Male inmate perceptions of the visitation experience: Suggestions on how prisons can promote inmate-family relationships. *The Prison Journal*, 95(3), 370–396.

Pupovac, J. (2011, January 5). Guarding grandpa. *Chicago Reader*. Retrieved from http://www.chicagoreader.com/chicago/illinois-prisons-budget-elderly-old-inmates/Content?oid=3013140.

Reimer, G. (2008). The graying of the U.S. prisoner population. *Journal of Correctional Health Care*, 14(3) 202–208.

Sarfo, A. (2013, September 30). Deal ending Alabama HIV prisoner segregation OK'd by Judge. *Law 360*. Retrieved from www.law360.com/articles/476747/deal-ending-ala hiv-prisoner-segregation-ok-d-by-judge.

Samenow, S. E. (1984). *Inside the criminal mind*. New York, NY: Times Books.

Stevens, R. (2015). Ruling means prep school grad eyes life on sex offender list. Associated Press, October 21. Retrieved online at http://www.msn.com/en-us/news/us/ruling-means-prep-school--grad.htm.

Turanovic, J. J., Rodriguez, N., & Pratt, T. C. (2012). The collateral consequences of incarceration revisited: A qualitative analysis of the effects on caregivers of children of incarcerated parents. *Criminology*, 50(4), 913–960.

Wright, K. N., & Bronstein, L. (2007). An organizational analysis of prison hospice. *The Prison Journal*, 87(4), 391–407.

Chapter 10, Reentry Programs and Parole

Alarid, L. F., & Reichel, P. L. (2008). *Corrections: A contemporary introduction*. Boston, MA: Allyn & Bacon.

Arons, A., Culver, K., Kaufman, E., Yun, J., Metcalf, H., Quattlebaum, M., & Resnik, J. (2014). *Dislocation and relocation: Women in the federal prison system and repurposing FCI Danbury for men*. Arthur Liman Public Interest Program (September): Yale Law School. Retrieved online: https://www.law.yale.edu/sites/default/files/documents/pdf/Liman/Liman_report__Dislocation_and_Relocation_Danbury_distribution__Aug__29_2014_(1).pdf.

Batiuk, M. E., Lahm, K. F., McKeever, M., Wilcox, N., & Wilcox, P. (2005). Disentangling the effects of correctional education. *Criminal Justice*, 5(1), 55–74.

Bronson, J., Maruschak, L. M., & Berzofsky, M. (2015). *Disabilities among prison and jail inmates, 2011-12* (NCJ 249151). Washington, DC: U.S. Department of Justice, Office of Justice Programs.

Brown, J. D. (2004). Managing the transition to community: A Canadian parole officer perspective on the needs of newly released federal offenders. *Western Criminology Review*, 5(2), 97–107.

Burke, P. B. (2004). *Parole violations revisited* (NIC #019833). Washington, DC: National Institute of Corrections, and Silver Spring, MD: Center for Effective Public Policy.

Chappell, C. A. (2004). Post-secondary correctional education and recidivism: A meta-analysis of research conducted 1990–1999. *The Journal of Correctional Education, 55*(2), 148–162.

Cherney, A., & Fitzgerald, R. (2016). Finding and keeping a job: The value and meaning of employment for parolees. *International Journal of Offender Therapy and Comparative Criminology, 60*(1), 21–37.

Coulter, G., & Brookens, E. (2003). Corrective reading: A systemwide program to improve basic reading performance for adult basic education students. *Corrections Compendium, 28*(10), 1–4, 28–30.

Davis, L. M., Bozick, R., Steele, J. L., Saunders, J., & Miles, J. N. V. (2013). *Evaluating the effectiveness of correctional education: A meta-analysis of programs that provide education to incarcerated adults.* Washington, DC: Bureau of Justice Assistance. Retrieved from http://www.bja.gov/publications/rand_correctional-education-meta-analysis.pdf.

Duwe, G. (2014). A randomized experiment of a prisoner reentry program: Updated results from an evaluation of the Minnesota Comprehensive Offender Reentry Plan (MCORP). *Criminal Justice Studies, 27*(2), 172–190.

Duwe, G., & Clark, V. (2014). The effects of prison-based educational programming on recidivism and employment. *The Prison Journal, 94*(4), 454–478.

Duwe, G., & King, M. (2013). Can faith-based correctional programs work? An outcome evaluation of innerchange freedom initiative in Minnesota. *International Journal of Offender Therapy and Comparative Criminology, 57*(7), 813–841.

Garland, B. E., & Hass, A. Y. (2015). An outcome evaluation of a midwestern prisoner reentry initiative. *Criminal Justice Policy Review, 26*(3), 293–314. doi:10.1177/0887403413514438

Glaze, L. E., & Maruschak, L. M. (2008). *Parents in prison and their minor children* (NCJ 222984). Washington, DC: U.S. Department of Justice.

Harlow, C. W. (2003). *Education and correctional populations.* Washington, DC: U.S. Department of Justice, Bureau of Justice Statistics.

Hipp, J. R., & Yates, D. K. (2009). Do returning parolees affect neighborhood crime? A case study on Sacramento. *Criminology, 47*(3), 619–656.

Huebner, B. M., & Pleggenkuhle, B. (2015). Residential location, household composition, and recidivism: An analysis by gender. *Justice Quarterly, 32*(5), 818–844.

Johnson, B. R., & Larson, D. B. (2003). *The InnerChange Freedom initiative: A preliminary evaluation of faith-based prison programs.* Center for Research on Religion and Urban Civil Society, University of Pennsylvania.

Kaeble, D., Maruschak, L. M., & Bonczar, T. P. (2015). *Probation and parole in the United States, 2014* (NCJ 249057). Washington, DC: U.S. Department of Justice. Retrieved from http://www.bjs.gov/content/pub/pdf/ppus14.pdf.

Lahm, K. F. (2000). Equal or equitable: An exploration of educational and vocational program availability for male and female offenders. *Federal Probation, 64*(2), 39–46.

Lattimore, P. K., & Visher, C. A. (2009). *The multi-site evaluation of SVORI: Summary and synthesis.* Washington, DC: U.S. Department of Justice.

McKiernan, P., Shamblen, S. R., Collins, D. A., Strader, T. N., & Kokoski, C. (2013). Creating lasting family connections: Reducing recidivism with community-based family strengthening model. *Criminal Justice Policy Review, 24*(1) 94–122.

McMay, D., & Cotronea, M. (2015). Developing a leisure time management program to aid successful transition to community: A program template with recommendations for practitioners. *The Prison Journal, 95*(2), 264–284.

Meyer, S. J., Fredericks, L., Borden, C. M., & Richardson, P. L. (2010). Implementing postsecondary academic programs in state prisons: Challenges and opportunities. *Journal of Correctional Education, 61*(2), 148–183.

Miller, J., Caplan, J. M., & Ostermann, M. (2016). Home modes, criminogenic places, and parolee failure: Testing an environmental model of offender risk. *Crime and Delinquency, 62*(2), 169–199.

Morris, N. (2002). *Maconochie's gentlemen: The story of Norfolk Island and the roots of modern prison reform.* New York, NY: Oxford University Press.

National Institute of Corrections. (n.d.). *Model of Transition from Prison to the Community.* Retrieved from www.in.gov/idoc/2520.htm.

Neller, D. J., Vitacco, M. J., Magaletta, P. R., & Phillips-Boyles, A. B. (2016). Eliciting responsivity: Exploring programming interests of federal inmates as a function of security classification. *International Journal of Offender Therapy and Comparative Criminology, 60*(4), 423–434.

O'Brien, S. (2013). Former Louisiana governor Edwin Edwards, 86, hopes to run again. America Tonight, November 26. Retrieved from http://america.aljazeera.com/watch/shows/america-tonight/america-tonight-blog/2013/11/26/governor-edward-edwinspoliticsagain.html.

Paynter, B. (2004). Jesus is in the big house. *The Pitch.* Kansas City, MO: 13–21.

Petersilia, J. (2002). *Reforming probation and parole in the 21st century.* Lanham, MD: American Correctional Association.

Rydberg, J., & Grommon, E. (2016). A multimethod examination of the dynamics of recidivism following reentry. *Corrections: Policy, Practice and Research, 1*(1), 40–60.

Sabol, W. J., West, H. C., & Cooper, M. (2009). *Prisoners in 2008* (NCJ 228417). Washington, DC: U.S. Department of Justice.

Schartmueller, D. (2015). Settling down behind bars: The extensive use of life sentences in Alabama. *The Prison Journal*, 95(4), 449–471.

Scram, K. (2011, January 13). Former governor to spend three days a week at halfway house. WGMB Fox 44 News, Baton Rouge, LA. Retrieved from www.fox44.com/news/halfway-house-critical-to-edwards-success-after-prison.

Stephan, J. J. (2008). *Census of state and federal correctional facilities, 2005* (NCJ 222182). Washington, DC: U.S. Department of Justice, Bureau of Justice Statistics.

VERA Institute of Justice. (2010, October). *The continuing fiscal crisis in corrections: Setting a new course.* New York, NY. Retrieved from www.vera.org/download?file=3072/The-continuing-fiscal-crisis-in-corrections-10-2010-updated.pdf.

Veysey, B. M., Ostermann, M., & Lanterman, J. L. (2014). The effectiveness of enhanced parole supervision and community services: New Jersey's serious and violent offender reentry initiative. *The Prison Journal*, 94(4), 435–453.

Visher, C. A., Debus-Sherrill, S. A., & Yahner, J. (2011). Employment after prison: A longitudinal study of former prisoners. *Justice Quarterly*, 28(5), 698–718.

Visher, C. A., Lattimore, P. K., Barrick, K., & Tueller, S. (2016). Evaluating the long-term effects of prisoner re-entry services on recidivism: What types of services matter? *Justice Quarterly* (Published online). doi:10.1080/07418825.2015.1115539

Chapter 11, Legal Issues in Corrections

Alvarado, J. (2012). Keeping jailers from keeping the keys to the courthouse: The Prison Litigation Reform Act's exhaustion requirement and section five of the Fourteenth Amendment. *Seattle Journal for Social Justice*, 8(1), 13.

Bandy, R. (2011). Measuring the impact of sex offender notification on community adoption of protective behaviors. *Criminology & Public Policy*, 10(2), 237–263. doi:10.1111/j.1745-9133.2011.00705.x

Behrens, A., Uggen, C., & Manza, J. (2003). Ballot manipulation and the "menace of negro domination": Racial threat and felon disenfranchisement in the United States, 1850–2002. *American Journal of Sociology*, 109(3), 559–605.

Cheesman II, F. L., Ostrom, B. J., & Hanson, R. A. (2004). *A tale of two laws revisited: Investigating the impact of the Prisoner Litigation Reform Act and the antiterrorism and effective death penalty.* Retrieved from http://www.ncsconline.org/d_research/descriptions.html.

Chung, J. (2014, April). *Felony disenfranchisement: A primer.* Retrieved from http://sentencingproject.org/doc/publications/fd_Felony%20Disenfranchisement%20Primer.pdf.

del Carmen, R. V., Ritter, S. E., & Witt, B. A. (2005). *Briefs of leading cases in corrections* (4th ed.). Newark, NJ: Lexis Nexis Anderson Publishing.

Dolan, J. (2011, April 20). Lawsuit asks state to pay for inmate's sex-change operation. *Los Angeles Times.* Retrieved from http://articles.latimes.com/.

Doucette, B. (2010, August 13). Nichols' lawsuit over prison food dismissed by federal judge. Retrieved from http://www.newsok.com/.

Fellner, J., & Mauer, M. (1998, October). *Losing the vote: The impact of felony disenfranchisement laws in the United States.* Retrieved from http://www.sentencingproject.org/template/page.cfm?id=131.

Ferdico, J. N. (2005). *Criminal procedure for the criminal justice professional* (9th ed.). Belmont, CA: Thompson/Wadsworth.

Harris, A. J., & Lobanov-Rostovsky, C. (2010). Implementing the Adam Walsh Act's sex offender registration and notification provisions: A survey of the states. *Criminal Justice Policy Review*, 21(2), 202–222. doi:10.1177/0887403409346118

Jacobs, J. B. (1977). *Stateville: The penitentiary in mass society.* Chicago, IL: University of Chicago Press.

Jenness, V. (2009). *Transgender inmates in California's prisons: An empirical study of a vulnerable population.* Retrieved from http://ucicorrections.seweb.uci.edu/pubs#powerpoint.

Levenson, J. S. (2011). Sex offender policies in an era of zero tolerance. *Criminology & Public Policy*, 10(2), 229–233. doi:10.1111/j.1745-9133.2011.00704.x

Love, M. C. (2006). *Relief from the collateral consequences of a criminal conviction: A state-by-state resource guide.* Buffalo, NY: William S. Hein.

Manza, J., & Uggen, C. (2006). *Locked out: Felon disenfranchisement and American democracy.* New York, NY: Oxford University Press.

Muraskin, R. (1993). Disparate treatment in correctional facilities. In R. Muraskin & T. Alleman (Eds.), *It's a crime: Women and justice* (pp. 211–225). Englewood Cliffs, NJ: Prentice Hall.

National Association of Criminal Defense Lawyers. (2014). *Collateral damage: America's failure to forgive or forget in the war on crime – A roadmap to restore rights and status after arrest or conviction.* Retrieved from www.nacdl.org/restoration/roadmapreport.

Office of Justice Programs. (2016). *SORNA.* Retrieved from http://www.smart.gov/sorna.htm.

Ostrom, B. J., Hanson, R. A., & Cheesman II, F. L. (2003). Congress, courts and corrections: An empirical perspective on the Prison Litigation Reform Act. *Notre Dame Law Review*, 78(5), 1525–1560.

Periman, D. (2007). The hidden impact of a criminal conviction: A brief overview of collateral consequences in Alaska. *Alaska Justice Forum*, 24(3). Retrieved from http://justice.uaa.alaska.edu/forum/24/3fall2007/a_collateral.html.

Porter, N. D. (2015). *The state of sentencing 2014: Developments in policy and practice.* Retrieved from http://sentencingproject.org/doc/publications/sen_State_of_Sentencing_2014.pdf.

Porter, N. D. (2016). *The state of sentencing 2015: Developments in policy and practice.* Retrieved from http://sentencingproject.org/doc/publications/State-of-Sentencing-2015.pdf.

Prison Legal News. (2014, September 19). *Some states refuse to implement SORNA, lose federal grants.* Retrieved from https://www.prisonlegalnews.org/news/2014/sep/19/some-states-refuse-implement-sorna-lose-federal-grants/.

Prison Legal News. (2016). *Pennsylvania law requiring lifetime registration of juvenile sex offenders unconstitutional.* Retrieved from https://www.prisonlegalnews.org/news/2016/feb/3/pennsylvania-law-requiring-lifetime-registration-juvenile-sex-offenders-unconstitutional/.

ProCon.org. (2009, April 13). Opinion polls/surveys. Retrieved from http://felonvoting.procon.org/view.resource.php?resourceID=666.

ProCon.org. (2016). State felon voting laws. (February 9). Retrieved from http://felonvoting.procon.org/view.resource.php?resourceID=286.

Schlanger, M. (2003). Inmate litigation. *Harvard Law Review, 116*(6), 1555–1706.

Smith, C. E. (1993). Black Muslims and the development of prisoners' rights. *Journal of Black Studies, 24*(2), 131–146.

State of Colorado. (n.d.). Sex offender registration. Retrieved from http://sor.state.co.us/?SOR=home.sorreg.

Subramanian, R., Moreno, R., & Gebreselassie, S. (2014). *Relief in sight? States rethink the collateral consequences of criminal conviction, 2009–2014.* Retrieved from http://www.vera.org/pubs/states-rethink-collateral-consequences.

Tewksbury, R. (2011). Policy implications of sex offender residence restrictions laws. *Criminology & Public Policy, 10*(2), 345–348. doi:10.1111/j.1745-9133.2011.00712.x

Travis, J. (2002). Invisible punishment: An instrument of social exclusion. Retrieved from http://www.urban.org/url.cfm?ID=1000557.

Trice, D. T. (2010a, July 29). CPS: Good conduct certificate not good enough. *Chicago Tribune.* Retrieved from http://articles.chicagotribune.com/.

Trice, D. T. (2010b, September 26). CPS reverses itself, gives job candidate a 2nd chance. *Chicago Tribune.* Retrieved from http://articles.chicagotribune.com/.

Uggen, C., Behrens, A., & Manza, J. (2005). Criminal disenfranchisement. *Annual Review of Law and Social Science, 1*(1), 307–322. doi:10.1146/annurev.lawsocsci.1.041604.115840

Chapter 12, Capital Punishment

Aarons, D. (2013). The Marshall hypothesis and the rise of anti-death penalty judges. *Tennessee Law Review, 80*(2), 381–410.

Amnesty International. (1999, April). *Killing with prejudice: Race and the death penalty in the USA.* Retrieved from http://www.amnesty.org/en/library/info/AMR51/052/1999/en.

Bailey, W. C., & Peterson, R. D. (1994). Murder, capital punishment, and deterrence: A review of the evidence and an examination of police killings. *Journal of Social Issues, 50*(2), 53–74. doi:10.1111/j.1540-4560.1994.tb02410.x

Baldus, D. C., Pulaski, C., & Woodworth, G. (1983). Comparative review of death sentences: An empirical study of the Georgia experience. *Journal of Criminal Law and Criminology, 74*(3), 661–753.

Baldus, D. C., Woodworth, G., & Grosso, C. M. (2008). Race and proportionality since *McCleskey* v. *Kemp* (1987): Different actors with mixed strategies of denial and avoidance. *Columbia Human Rights Law Review, 39*, 143–177.

Blecker, R. (2013). *The death of punishment: Searching for justice among the worst of the worst.* New York, NY: Palgrave Macmillan.

Bohm, R. M. (1990). Death penalty opinions: A classroom experience and public commitment. *Sociological Inquiry, 60*(3), 285–297.

Bohm, R. M. (2003). *Deathquest II: An introduction to the theory and practice of capital punishment in the United States* (2nd ed.). Cincinnati, OH: Anderson Publishing.

Bohm, R. M., Clark, L. J., & Aveni, A. F. (1991). Knowledge and death penalty opinion: A test of the Marshall hypotheses. *Journal of Research in Crime and Delinquency, 28*(3), 360–387.

Bohm, R. M., Vogel, R. E., & Maisto, A. A. (1993). Knowledge and death penalty opinion: A panel study. *Journal of Criminal Justice, 21*(1), 29–45.

Burnett, C. (2002). *Justice denied: Clemency appeals in death penalty cases.* Boston, MA: Northeastern University Press.

CBS News. (2001, April 10). Justice backs death penalty freeze. Retrieved from http://www.cbsnews.com/stories/2001/04/10/deathpenalty/main284850.shtml.

Cooper, A., & Smith, E. L. (2013). *Homicide in the U.S. known to law enforcement, 2011* (NCJ 243035). Retrieved from http://www.bjs.gov/index.cfm?ty=pbdetail&iid=4863.

Daniel, S. N., & John, V. P. (Eds.). (2012). *Deterrence and the death penalty.* Washington, DC: The National Academies Press. Retrieved from http://www.nap.edu/catalog.php?record_id=13363.

Death Penalty Information Center. (2015). *Innocence and the death penalty.* Retrieved from http://www.deathpenaltyinfo.org/innocence-and-death-penalty.

Death Penalty Information Center. (2016a). *Clemency process by state.* Retrieved from http://www.deathpenaltyinfo.org/clemency.

Death Penalty Information Center. (2016b). *Description of execution methods.* Retrieved from DPIC website http://www.deathpenaltyinfo.org/descriptions-execution-methods.

Death Penalty Information Center. (2016c). *Executions in the U.S. 1608–2002: The Espy File.* Retrieved from http://www.deathpenaltyinfo.org/executions-us-1608-2002-espy-file.

Death Penalty Information Center. (2016d). *National statistics on the death penalty and race.* Retrieved from http://www.deathpenaltyinfo.org/race-death-row-inmates-executed-1976.

Death Penalty Information Center. (2016e). *Number of executions by state and region since 1976.* (February 18). Retrieved from http://www.deathpenaltyinfo.org/number-executions-state-and-region-1976.

Death Penalty Information Center. (2016f). *Part 1: Introduction to the death penalty*. Retrieved from http://www.deathpenaltyinfo.org/history-death-penalty.

Death Penalty Information Center. (2016g). *Women and the death penalty*. Retrieved from http://www.deathpenaltyinfo.org/women-and-death-penalty.

del Carmen, R. V., Vollum, S., Cheeseman, K., Frantzen, D., & San Miguel, C. (2005). *The death penalty: Constitutional issues, commentaries, and case briefs*. Cincinnati, OH: Anderson Publishing.

Dezhbakhsh, H., & Rubin, P. H. (2010). From the "econometrics of capital punishment" to the "capital punishment" of econometrics: On the use and abuse of sensitivity analysis. *Applied Economics*. doi:10.1080/00036841003670804

Dobash, R. P., Dobash, R. E., & Gutteridge, S. (1986). *The imprisonment of women*. New York, NY: Basil Blackwell.

Donohue, J. J., & Wolfers, J. (2005). Uses and abuses of empirical evidence in the death penalty debate. *Stanford Law Review*, *58*(3), 791–845. Retrieved from http://www.stanfordlawreview.org/content/article/uses-and-abuses-empirical-evidence death-penalty-debate.

Donohue, J. J., & Wolfers, J. (2006). The death penalty: No evidence for deterrence. *The Economists' Voice*, *3*(5). doi:10.2202/1553-3832.1170

Ehrlich, I. (1975). The deterrent effect of capital punishment: A question of life and death. *American Economic Review*, *65*(3), 397–417.

Equal Justice USA. (n.d.). *Executions create more victims*. Retrieved from http://ejusa.org/learn/secondary%2Btrauma.

Fagan, J. (2005, January 21). *Deterrence and the death penalty: A critical review of new evidence*. Retrieved from http://www.deathpenaltyinfo.org/FaganTestimony.pdf

Fagan, J. (2006). Death and deterrence redux: Science, law, and causal reasoning. *Ohio State Journal of Criminal Law*, *4*, 255–320.

Gallup. (2016). *Death penalty*. Retrieved from http://www.gallup.com/poll/1606/death-penalty.aspx.

Gelman, A., Liebman, J. S., West, V., & Kiss, A. (2004). A broken system: The persistent patterns of reversals of death sentences in the United States. *Journal of Empirical Legal Studies*, *1*(2), 209–261. doi:10.1111/j.1740-1461.2004.00007.x

Goertzel, T. (2004). Capital punishment and homicide: Sociological realities and econometric illusions. *Skeptical Enquirer*. Retrieved from http://www.deathpenaltyinfo.org/article.php?scid=12&did=1176.

Goldberg, S. (1991). The death penalty deters murder. In C. Wekesser (Ed.), *The death penalty: Opposing viewpoints* (pp. 113–118). San Diego, CA: Greenhaven Press.

King, R., & Bellin, J. (2004, December). The forgotten population: A look at death row in the United States through the experiences of women. Retrieved from http://www.aclu.org/files/FilesPDFs/womenondeathrow.pdf.

Kronenwetter, M. (1993). *Capital punishment: A reference handbook*. Santa Barbara, CA: ABC-CLIO.

Land, K. C., Teske, R. H. C., & Zheng, H. U. I. (2009). The short-term effects of executions on homicides: Deterrence, displacement, or both? *Criminology*, *47*(4), 1009–1043. doi:10.1111/j.1745-9125.2009.00168.x

Liebman, J., Fagan, J., & West, V. (2000). *A broken system: Error rates in capital cases, 1973–1995*. Columbia Law School, Public Law Research Paper (15). Retrived from http://ssrn.com/abstract=232712 or http://dx.doi.org/232710.232139/ssrn.232712.

Liptak, A. (2014). Court extends curbs on the death penalty in a Florida ruling. *New York Times*, May 27. Retrieved from http://www.nytimes.com/2014/05/28/us/court-rules-against-florida-iq-rule-in-death-cases.html.

NAACP Legal Defense Fund. (2016, January). *Death row USA, Winter 2016*. Retrieved from http://www.naacpldf.org/death row-usa.

National Public Radio. (2001, May 1). The last public execution in America. Retrieved from http://www.npr.org/programs/morning/features/2001/apr/010430.execution.html.

Newman, G. R. (1985). *The punishment response* (2nd ed.). Albany, NY: Harrow and Heston.

Office of Justice Programs. (1978). Capital punishment, 1977 (NCJ 49657). Retrieved from http://bjs.ojp.usdoj.gov/index.cfm?ty=pbdetail&iid=1249.

Paternoster, R. (1991). *Capital punishment in America*. New York, NY: Lexington Books.

Paternoster, R., & Brame, R. (2003). *An empirical analysis of Maryland's death sentencing system with respect to the influence of race and legal jurisdiction*. College Park: University of Maryland.

Paternoster, R., & Brame, R. (2008). Reassessing race disparities in Maryland capital cases. *Criminology*, *46*(4), 971–1008. doi:10.1111/j.1745-9125.2008.00132.x

Paternoster, R., & Deise, J. (2011). A heavy thumb on the scale: The effect of victim impact evidence on capital decision making. *Criminology*, *49*(1), 129–161. doi:10.1111/j.1745-9125.2010.00220.x

Peterson, R. D., & Bailey, W. C. (1991). Felony murder and capital punishment: An examination of the deterrence question. *Criminology*, *29*(3) 367–395.

Peterson, R. D., & Bailey, W. C. (1998). Is capital punishment an effective deterrent for murder? An examination of the social science research. In J. R. Acker, R. M. Bohm, & C. S. Lanier (Eds.), *America's experiment with capital punishment: Reflections on the past, present, and future of the ultimate sanction* (pp. 157–182). Durham, NC: Carolina Academic Press.

ProCon.org. (2013, August 13). Historical timeline: History of the death penalty. Retrieved from http://deathpenalty.procon.org/view.timeline.php?timelineID=000025.

Radelet, M. L., & Borg, M. J. (2000). The changing nature of death penalty debates. *Annual Review of Sociology*, *26*(1) 43–61.

Ruddell, R., & Urbina, M. G. (2004). Minority threat and punishment: A cross-national analysis. *Justice Quarterly*, *21*(4), 903–931.

Schottelkotte, S. (2011, February 18). Jurors cry as victim's son testifies in Leon Davis murder trial. Retrieved from http://www.theledger.com/article/20110218/NEWS/102185010&tc=ix.

Shaked-Schroer, N., Costanzo, M., & Marcus-Newhall, A. (2008). Reducing racial bias in the penalty phase of capital trials. *Behavioral Sciences & the Law, 26*(5), 603–617. doi:10.1002/bsl.829

Sharp, D. (2004). Innocence issues—The death penalty. Retrieved from http://www.prodeathpenalty.com/Innocence.htm.

Smith, R. J., Cull, S., & Robinson, Z. (2014). The failure of mitigation? *Hastings Law Journal, 65*(June), 1221–1256.

Snell, T. L. (2014). *Capital punishment, 2013—Statistical tables* (NCJ 248448). Retrieved from http://www.bjs.gov/index.cfm?ty=pbdetail&iid=5156.

Sorensen, J., Wrinkle, R., Brewer, V., & Marquart, J. W. (1999). Capital punishment and deterrence: Examining the effect of executions on murder in Texas. *Crime & Delinquency, 45*(4), 481–493.

Spohn, C. (2014). Racial disparities in prosecution, sentencing, and punishment. In S. M. Bucerius & M. H. Tonry (Eds.), *The Oxford handbook of ethnicity, crime, and immigration* (pp. 166–193). New York, NY: Oxford University Press.

Unnever, J. D., & Cullen, F. T. (2005). Executing the innocent and support for capital punishment: Implications for public policy. *Criminology & Public Policy, 4*(1), 3–38.

VanBrocklin, P. (2003). A comparison of the clemency procedures in the four census bureau regions and their effect on commutations in capital cases. *Corrections Compendium, 28*(7), 1–4, 24–26.

van den Haag, E. (1991). Guilt overrides the importance of death penalty discrimination. In C. Wekesser (Ed.), *The death penalty: Opposing viewpoints* (pp. 156–159). San Diego, CA: Greenhaven Press.

Wikberg, R. (1992). The horror show. In W. Rideau & R. Wikberg (Eds.), *Life sentences: Rage and survival behind bars* (pp. 284–303). New York, NY: Times Books.

Chapter 13, Juvenile Corrections

Arya, N. (2011). Juvenile justice. In the Smart on Crime Coalition (Ed.), *Smart on crime: Recommendations for the Administration and Congress* (Chap. 8). Retrieved from http://www.besmartoncrime.org/pdf/Complete.pdf.

Belknap, J., & Holsinger, K. (1998). An overview of delinquent girls: How theory and practice have failed and the need for innovative changes. In R. T. Zaplin (Ed.), *Female offenders: Critical perspectives and effective interventions* (pp. 31–64). Gaithersburg, MD: Aspen Publishers.

Bloom, B., Owen, B., Piper Deschenes, E., & Rosenbaum, J. (2002). Improving juvenile justice for females: A statewide assessment in California. *Crime & Delinquency, 48*(4), 526–552.

Brown, S. A. (2015). *Trends in juvenile justice state legislation 2011–2015*. Retrieved from National Conference of State Legislatures website http://www.ncsl.org/documents/cj/Juvenile_Justice_Trends_1.pdf.

Butts, J. A., & Buck, J. (2002). The sudden popularity of teen courts. *Judges Journal, 41*(1), 29–34.

Cahalan, M. W. (1986). *Historical corrections statistics in the United States, 1850–1984*. Washington, DC: Department of Justice.

Committee on Adolescence. (2011). Health care for youth in the juvenile justice system. *Pediatrics, 128*(6), 1219–1235. doi:10.1542/peds.2011-1757

Daly, R., Kapur, T., & Elliott, M. (2011). *Capital change: A process evaluation of Washington, DC's secure juvenile placement reform*. New York, NY: Vera Institute of Justice. Electronic version available at http://www.vera.org/.

Daniel, M. D. (1999). The female intervention team. *Juvenile Justice, 6*(1), 14–21. Retrieved from http://www.ncjrs.org/pdffiles1/ojjdp/178254.pdf.

Denniston, L. (2009). *Inquiring into the juvenile mind*. Retrieved from http://www.scotusblog.com/?p=12559.

Devine, P., Coolbaugh, K., & Jenkins, S. (1998). Disproportionate minority confinement: Lessons learned from five states. *Juvenile Justice Bulletin* (NCJ 173420). Retrieved from http://www.ncjrs.gov/html/ojjdp/173420/contents.html.

Equal Justice Initiative. (2011). *Death in prison for 13- and 14-year-olds*. Retrieved from www.eji.org/eji/childrenprison/deathinprison.

Equal Justice Initiative. (2012). Success stories: Kids change. Sullivan and Graham media resource kit. Retrieved from http://eji.org/childrenprison/deathinprison/graham/resourcekit.

Functional Family Therapy. (2016). *Clinical model*. Retrieved from http://www.functionalfamilytherapy.com/.

Furdella, J., & Puzzanchera, C. (2015). *Delinquency cases in juvenile court, 2013* (NCJ 248899). Retrieved from OJJDP website http://www.ojjdp.gov/pubs/248899.pdf.

Garcia, C. A., & Lane, J. (2013). What a girl wants, what a girl needs: Findings from a gender-specific focus group study. *Crime & Delinquency, 59*(4), 536–561. doi:10.1177/0011128709331790

Greenwood, P. W. (2008). Prevention and intervention programs for juvenile offenders. *Juvenile Justice, 18*(2), 185–210. Retrieved from http://www.princeton.edu/futureofchildren/publications/journals/journal_details/index.xml?journalid=31.

Griffin, P., Addie, S., Adams, B., & Firestine, K. (2011). Trying juveniles as adults: An analysis of state transfer laws and reporting. *National Report Series Bulletin*. (NCJ 232434). Retrieved from http://www.ncjrs.gov/pdffiles1/ojjdp/232434.pdf.

Hockenberry, S. (2014). Juveniles in residential facility placement, 2011. *National Report Series Bulletin*. (NCJ 246826). Retrieved from http://www.ojjdp.gov/pubs/246826.pdf.

Hockenberry, S., & Puzzanchera, C. (2014). *Delinquency cases waived to criminal court, 2011* (NCJ 248410). Retrieved from http://www.ojjdp.gov/pubs/248410.pdf.

Hockenberry, S., Sickmund, M., & Sladky, A. (2013). Juvenile residential facility census, 2010: Selected findings. *National Report Series Bulletin*. (NCJ 241134). Retrieved from http://www.ojjdp.gov/pubs/241134.pdf.

Hockenberry, S., Sickmund, M., & Sladky, A. (2015). Juvenile residential facility census, 2012: Selected findings. *National Report Series Bulletin*. (NCJ 247207). Retrieved from http://www.ojjdp.gov/pubs/247207.pdf.

Hsia, H. M., Bridges, G. S., & McHale, R. (2004). *Disproportionate minority confinement: 2002 update* (NCJ 201240). Retrieved from http://www.ojjdp.gov/publications/PubAbstract.asp?pubi=201240.

Justice Policy Institute. (2011). Factsheet: Juvenile justice. *Finding Direction: Expanding Criminal Justice Options by Considering Policies of Other Nations*. Retrieved from http://www.justicepolicy.org/research/2322.

Knoll, C., & Sickmund, M. (2012). *Delinquency cases in juvenile court, 2009* (NCJ 239081). Retrieved from http://www.ojjdp.gov/pubs/239081.pdf.

Kurlychek, M. (2014). Juvenile court. In J. Albanese (Ed.), *The encyclopedia of criminology and criminal Justice*. Blackwell Publishing Ltd. Retrieved from http://onlinelibrary.wiley.com.

Mendel, D. (2003). *Small is beautiful: The Missouri Division of Youth Services* (NCJ 202528). Retrieved from http://www.ncjrs.gov/App/publications/Abstract.aspx?id=202528.

Mendel, R. A. (2010). *The Missouri Model: Reinventing the practice of rehabilitating youthful offenders—Summary report*. Baltimore, MD: Annie E. Casey Foundation. Electronic version available at http://www.aecf.org/.

Missouri Department of Social Services. (2013). *Missouri Division of Youth Services annual report, fiscal year 2013*. Retrieved from http://www.dss.mo.gov/re/dysar.htm.

Moore, S. (2009, March 27). Missouri system treats juvenile offenders with lighter hand. *New York Times*. Retrieved from http://www.nytimes.com.

MST. (2014). MST—juvenile justice. Retrieved from http://www.mstservices.com/target-populations/juvenile-justice.

Mullins, T. G. (2003). A national overview of youth courts. *In Session, 3*(2). Retrieved from http://youthcourt.net/wp-content/uploads/2010/05/IS_2003_SpringSummer.pdf.

National Association of Youth Courts. (2015, March 21). Youth courts across the USA. Retrieved from http://www.youthcourt.net/?page_id=3.

National Juvenile Defender Center. (2014, July 17). Juvenile right to jury trial chart. Retrieved from http://njdc.info/wp-content/uploads/2014/01/Right-to-Jury-Trial-Chart-7-18-14-Final.pdf.

Norris, M., Twill, S., & Kim, C. (2011). Smells like teen spirit: Evaluating a midwestern teen court. *Crime & Delinquency, 57*(2), 199–221. doi:10.1177/0011128709354037

Office of Justice Programs. (2013a). *Functional Family Therapy*. Retrieved from http://www.crimesolutions.gov/ProgramDetails.aspx?ID=122.

Office of Justice Programs. (2013b). *Multisystemic Therapy (MST)*. Retrieved from http://www.crimesolutions.gov/ProgramDetails.aspx?ID=192.

Peters, S. R. (1998). *Guiding principles for promising female programming: An inventory of best practices*. Retrieved from http://www.ojjdp.gov/pubs/principles/contents.html.

Petteruti, A., Velazquez, T., & Walsh, N. (2009). *The costs of confinement: Why good juvenile justice policies make good fiscal sense*. Retrieved from http://www.justicepolicy.org/research/78.

Puzzanchera, C. (2013). Juvenile arrests 2010. *National Report Series Bulletin*. (NCJ 242770). Retrieved from http://www.ojjdp.gov/pubs/242770.pdf.

Puzzanchera, C. (2014). Juvenile arrests 2012. *National Report Series Bulletin*. (NCJ 248513). Retrieved from: http://www.ojjdp.gov/pubs/248513.pdf.

Puzzanchera, C., & Hockenberry, S. (2015). *National disproportionate minority contact databook*. Retrieved from: http://www.ojjdp.gov/ojstatbb/dmcdb/.

Redding, R. E. (2010). Juvenile transfer laws: An effective deterrent to delinquency? *Juvenile Justice Bulletin*. (NCJ 220595). Retrieved from OJJDP website https://www.ncjrs.gov/pdffiles1/ojjdp/220595.pdf.

Sawyer, A. M., Borduin, C. M., & Dopp, A. R. (2015). Long-term effects of prevention and treatment on youth antisocial behavior: A meta-analysis. *Clinical Psychology Review, 42*, 130–144. doi: http://dx.doi.org/10.1016/j.cpr.2015.06.009

Sedlak, A. J., & Bruce, C. (2010). Youth's characteristics and backgrounds: Findings from the survey of youth in residential placement. *Juvenile Justice Bulletin*. (NCJ 227730). Retrieved from http://www.ojjdp.gov/publications/PubAbstract.asp?pubi=249737.

Snyder, H. N., & Sickmund, M. (2006). *Juvenile offenders and victims: 2006 national report*. Retrieved from http://www.ojjdp.gov/ojstatbb/nr2006/index.html.

Substance Abuse and Mental Health Services Administration. (2013). Mendota juvenile treatment center program. Retrieved from http://nrepp.samhsa.gov/ViewIntervention.aspx?id=38.

The Oyez Project. (2011). *Graham* v. *Florida*, 560 U.S. ———— (2010). Retrieved from http://www.oyez.org/cases/2000-2009/2009/2009_08_7412.

Torbet, P. (1997, June). State responses to serious and violent juvenile offenders. *Corrections Today, 59*(3), 121–123.

Vose, B., & Vannan, K. (2013). A jury of your peers: Recidivism among teen court participants. *Journal of Juvenile Justice, 3*(1), 97–109. doi:10.11 77/0093854801028003005

Chapter 14, Revisiting Evidence-Based Practices and What Works

Association of State Correctional Administrators (2015). *Performance-based measures system counting rules: Revised counting rules for organization characteristics effective August 28, 2015*. Hagerstown, MD: Association of State Correctional Administrators. Retrieved online at http://www.asca.net/system/assets/attachments/8868/PBMS%20KeyIndicators%20%208_28_15.pdf?1440788921.

Association of State Correctional Administrators. (2016). *ASCA top four critical issues report*. Retrieved online at http://www.asca.net/articles/3628.

Bales, W., & Piquero, A. (2012). Assessing the impact of imprisonment on recidivism. *Journal of Experimental Criminology, 8*(1), 71–101.

Blumstein, A. (2016). Reflecting on the 50th Anniversary of Lyndon Johnson's President's Crime Commission. *ACJS Today, 41*(2), 1, 4–5, 7–10.

Bourgon, G., & Armstrong, B. (2006). Transferring the principles of effective treatment into a real world setting. *Criminal Justice, 32*(1), 3–25.

Byrne, J. (2013). After the fall: Assessing the impact of the great prison experiment on future crime control policy. *Federal Probation, 77*(3), 3–14.

Clear, T. R. (2011). A private-sector, incentive-based model for Justice Reinvestment. *Criminology & Public Policy, 10*(3), 585–608.

Clement, M., Schwarzfeld, M., & Thompson, M. (2011). *The national summit on justice reinvestment and public safety: Addressing recidivism, crime, and corrections.* Lexington, KY: Council of State Governments Justice Center. Available online at https://www.bja.gov/Publications/CSG_JusticeReinvestmentSummitReport.pdf.

Council of State Governments Justice Center. (2015). *Justice reinvestment in Kansas: Strengthening probation supervision and promoting successful reentry.* Lexington, KY: Council of State Governments Justice Center. Available online at https://csgjusticecenter.org/wp-content/uploads/2015/05/JusticeReinvestmentInKansas.pdf.

Davis, L. M., Bozick, R., Steele, J. L., Saunders, J., & Miles, J. N. V. (2013). *Evaluating the effectiveness of correctional education: A meta-analysis of programs that provide education to incarcerated adults.* Washington, DC: Bureau of Justice Assistance. Retrieved from http://www.bja.gov/publications/rand_correctional-education-meta-analysis.pdf.

Department of Justice. (2013). *Smart on crime: Reforming the criminal justice system for the 21st century.* Washington, DC: U.S. Department of Justice.

Drake, E. K., Aos, S., & Miller, M. G. (2009). Evidence-based public policy options to reduce crime and criminal justice costs: Implications in Washington state. *Victims and Offenders, 4*(2), 170–196.

Freiburger, T. L., & Iannacchione, B. M. (2011). An examination of the effect of imprisonment on recidivism. *Criminal Justice Studies, 24*(4), 369–379.

French, S. A., & Gendreau, P. (2006). Reducing prison misconduct: What works! *Criminal Justice and Behavior, 33*(2), 185–218.

Graves, S. M. (2015). Correctional mission statements as indicators of the criminal justice policy environment: A research note. *Criminal Justice Policy Review, 26*(5), 488–499.

Kyckelhahn, T. (2013). *Local government corrections expenditures, FY 2005-2011* (NCJ 243527). Washington, DC: Bureau of Justice Statistics.

Latessa, E. J. (2004). The challenge of change: Correctional programs and evidence-based practices. *Criminology and Public Policy, 3*(4), 547–560.

Lipsey, M. W., & Cullen, F. T. (2007). The effectiveness of correctional rehabilitation: A review of systematic reviews. *Annual Review of Law and Social Science, 3*(1), 297–320.

Lipsey, M. W., Landenberger, N. A., & Wilson, S. J. (2007). *Effects of cognitive-behavioral programs for criminal offenders.* The Campbell Collaboration. Retrieved from http://www.campbellcollaboration.org.

Lowenkamp, C. T., & Latessa, E. J. (2004). Residential community corrections and the risk principle: Lessons learned in Ohio. *Ohio Corrections Research Compendium* (Vol. II). Columbus, OH: Ohio Department of Rehabilitation and Correction. Retrieved from http://www.uc.edu/ccjr/Articles/Risk_Principle_Lessons_Learned.pdf.

Magor-Blatch, L., Bhullar, N., Thomson, B., & Thorsteinsson, E. (2014). A systematic review of studies examining effectiveness of therapeutic communities. *Therapeutic Communities: The International Journal of Therapeutic Communities, 35*(4), 168–184.

Makarios, M., Steiner, B., & Travis, L. F. (2010). Examining the predictors of recidivism of men and women released from prison in Ohio. *Criminal Justice and Behavior, 37*(12), 1377–1391.

Meade, B., Steiner, B., Makarios, M., & Travis, L. (2012). Estimating a dose-response relationship between time served in prison and recidivism. *Journal of Research in Crime and Delinquency, 50*(4), 525–550.

National Association of State Budget Officers. (2011). *The Fiscal Survey of States.* Washington, DC: National Governor's Association and National Association of State Budget Officers.

Schindler, M. (2015, December 20). Justice reform in 2015 and beyond. *Huffington Post.* Retrieved online at http://www.huffingtonpost.com.

Stephan, J. J. (2004). *State prison expenditures, 2001* (NCJ 202949). Washington, DC: Bureau of Justice Statistics.

Tonry, M. (2004). *Thinking about crime: Sense and sensibility in American penal culture.* New York, NY: Oxford University Press.

Tonry, M., & Petersilia, J. (1999). *Prisons research at the beginning of the 21st century.* Washington, DC: National Institute of Justice. Retrieved from http://www.ncjrs.org/pdffiles1/nij/184478.pdf.

Zarkin, G. A., Cowell, A. J., Hicks, K. A., Mills, M. J., Belenko, S., Dunlap, L. J., & Keyes, V. (2015). Lifetime benefits and costs of diverting substance-abusing offenders from state prison. *Crime and Delinquency, 61*(6), 829–850.

Name Index

Subject Index

Note: Page numbers in *italics* represent figures; page numbers followed by *t* represent tables.

Compassionate release, **158**

Concentration approach, **112**

Concurrent jurisdiction, 227

Concurrent sentencing, **64**

Conditional release, **93**

Congregate and silent policy, **41**

Constitution, U.S. *See* U. S. Constitution

Continuum of sanctions, **5**, 6

Contraband, **137**

Co-occurring disorders, **86**

Cooper v. *Pate*, 185, 187

Correctional Learning Network, 169

Correctional officers (COs), **118**–119

Correctional policy, mass media influence, 7–8

Corrections

    in ancient and medieval world, 34–35

    capital punishment, 35

    corporal and capital punishment, 38

    early American jails and prisons, 38*t*

    in eighteenth and nineteenth-century, 38–42, 44*t*

    future of, 244–246

    imprisonment, 36–38

    medieval period, 35

    performance measures for, **245**, 245*t*

    policy, rationality to, 244

    revisiting correctional system expectations *vs* stated mission, 239–241

    in seventeenth and eighteenth-century, 35–38

    transportation to faraway lands, **35**–36

    in twentieth century, 45–46

    in twenty-first century, 46–48

Corrections system, **2**–3

    community or institutional-based, 5–6

    cost savings best practices, 242–243, 243*t*

    postsentencing correctional sanctions, *5*

Corroborating evidence, 3

Courts, 3

Crews, **138**

Crime control policy, **8**–9, 9*t*

Crime policy in US, 6

Criminal blended sentences, **227**

Criminal justice system flowchart, *4*

Criminogenic, **117**

Critical organ surgery, 22

Cruz v. *Beto*, 184*t*

Cultivation theory, **8**

Cunningham v. *Jones*, 183

D

Day reporting center (DRC), **84**–86

Death Penalty Information Center (DPIC), 207, 213–214

Death-row prisoners, 206–207, 206*t*

Decentralization, **44**

Defendants, 3

Deferred adjudication, 3

Deferred adjudication probation, 76*t*

Deferred probation supervision, 3

Delaware

    jail systems, 95

    rewarding of meritorious good time, 64

    types of invisible punishments, 190

Deliberate indifference, **141**

Delinquency offenses, **224**

Deprivation model, *131*, **131**

Determinate sentencing, **57**–58

Deterrence philosophy of punishment, **18**–20

    death penalty, 207–209, *208*, 209*t*

    general, **18**–19

    specific, **18**–19

Detoxification, **87**

Detroit House of Correction, 42

Differential response to women offenders, **43**

Direct file procedure, **227**

Direct supervision, **101**

Disciplinary segregation, **113**

Discretionary parole, **171**, 173–174

Dismissal, **3**

Disparity sentencing, 65–67

Dispersion approach, **112**

Disproportionate Minority Contact (DMC), **232**

    issues confronting juvenile corrections, 231–233

Disproportionate prison population, **129**–130

Disturbances, **143**

Diversion, **3**, 76*t*

Domestic violence, 98–99

"Driving while black" (or "driving while brown") phenomenon, 7

Drug courts, 86

Drug education classes, 87

Drug offenders, 21, 59, 131

    correction policy, 244

    invisible punishments, 189*t*, 190

    mandatory minimum sentences, 69

    risk of felony recidivism, 240